Lecture Notes in Computer Science 8475

Commenced Publication in 1973
Founding and Former Series Editors:
Gerhard Goos, Juris Hartmanis, and Jan van Leeuwen

Michael Codish   Eijiro Sumii (Eds.)

Functional and Logic Programming

12th International Symposium, FLOPS 2014
Kanazawa, Japan, June 4-6, 2014
Proceedings

Springer

Volume Editors

Michael Codish
Ben-Gurion University of the Negev
Department of Computer Science
P.O. Box 653
84105 Beer-Sheva, Israel
E-mail: mcodish@cs.bgu.ac.il

Eijiro Sumii
Tohoku University
Graduate School of Information Sciences
Aoba-ku, Aramaki Aza-aoba 6-3-09
Sendai, 980-8579, Japan
E-mail: sumii@ecei.tohoku.ac.jp

ISSN 0302-9743 e-ISSN 1611-3349
ISBN 978-3-319-07150-3 e-ISBN 978-3-319-07151-0
DOI 10.1007/978-3-319-07151-0
Springer Cham Heidelberg New York Dordrecht London

Library of Congress Control Number: 2014938286

LNCS Sublibrary: SL 1 – Theoretical Computer Science and General Issues

Typesetting: Camera-ready by author, data conversion by Scientific Publishing Services, Chennai, India

Printed on acid-free paper

Springer is part of Springer Science+Business Media (www.springer.com)

Preface

This volume contains the proceedings of the 12th International Symposium on Functional and Logic Programming (FLOPS 2014), held in Kanazawa, Japan, during June 4–6, 2014 at the Ishikawa Prefecutural Museum of Art.

FLOPS is a forum for research on all issues concerning declarative programming, including functional programming and logic programming, and aims to promote cross-fertilization and integration between the two paradigms. The previous FLOPS meetings were held in Fuji Susono (1995), Shonan Village (1996), Kyoto (1998), Tsukuba (1999), Tokyo (2001), Aizu (2002), Nara (2004), Fuji Susono (2006), Ise (2008), Sendai (2010), and Kobe (2012). Since 1999, FLOPS proceedings have been published by Springer in its *Lecture Notes in Computer Science* series, as volumes 1722, 2024, 2441, 2998, 3945, 4989, 6009, and 7294 respectively.

In response to the call for papers, 41 papers were submitted. All papers received three reviews by members of the Program Committee assisted by expert external reviewers. A Program Committee meeting was conducted electronically, in February 2014. After careful and thorough discussion, the Program Committee selected 21 papers for presentation at the conference. In addition to the 21 contributed papers, the symposium included talks by three invited speakers: Ranjit Jhala, Shin-ya Katsumata, and Gabriele Keller.

On behalf of the Program Committee, we would like to thank the invited speakers and all those who submitted papers to FLOPS 2014. As Program Committee chairs, we would like to sincerely thank all the members of the FLOPS 2014 Program Committee for their excellent job, and all of the external reviewers for their invaluable contributions. We are also grateful to the people behind the EasyChair conference system. We are indebted to our sponsor the Japan Society for Software Science and Technology (JSSST) SIGPPL for their support and we acknowledge the cooperation with the Association for Computing Machinery (ACM) SIGPLAN, the Asian Association for Foundation of Software (AAFS), and the Association for Logic Programming (ALP). Finally, we would like to thank the members of the Local Arrangements Committee for their invaluable support throughout the preparation and organization of the symposium.

March 2014

Michael Codish
Eijiro Sumii

Organization

Program Chairs

Michael Codish	Ben-Gurion University, Israel
Eijiro Sumii	Tohoku University, Japan

General Chair

Eijiro Sumii	Tohoku University, Japan

Local Chair

Yuki Chiba	JAIST, Japan

Program Committee

Lars Birkedal	Aarhus University, Denmark
Michael Codish	Ben-Gurion University, Israel
Marina De Vos	University of Bath, UK
Moreno Falaschi	University of Siena, Italy
Carsten Fuhs	University College London, UK
John Gallagher	Roskilde University, Denmark
Samir Genaim	Universidad Complutense de Madrid, Spain
Laura Giordano	Università del Piemonte Orientale, Italy
Ichiro Hasuo	University of Tokyo, Japan
Fritz Henglein	University of Copenhagen, Denmark
Andy King	University of Kent, UK
Oleg Kiselyov	University of Tsukuba, Japan
Vitaly Lagoon	The MathWorks, USA
Shin-Cheng Mu	Academia Sinica, Taiwan
Keiko Nakata	Institute of Cybernetics, Estonia
Luke Ong	University of Oxford, UK
Peter Schachte	The University of Melbourne, Australia
Takehide Soh	Kobe University, Japan
Eijiro Sumii	Tohoku University, Japan
Tachio Terauchi	Nagoya University, Japan
Joost Vennekens	K.U. Leuven, Belgium
Janis Voigtländer	University of Bonn, Germany
Stephanie Weirich	University of Pennsylvania, USA

Additional Reviewers

Atkey, Robert
Ballis, Demis
Beckers, Sander
Ben-Amram, Amir
Bizjak, Ales
Bone, Paul
Broadbent, Christopher
Chang, Stephen
Chitil, Olaf
Christakis, Maria
Chuang, Tyng-Ruey
Comini, Marco
De Cat, Broes
Devriendt, Jo
Eisenberg, Richard
Elsman, Martin
Gange, Graeme
Goldberg, Mayer
Grathwohl, Niels Bjørn Bugge
Haemmerlé, Rémy
Hague, Matthew
Igarashi, Atsushi
Inoue, Jun
Jeltsch, Wolfgang
Joshi, Anjali
Katsumata, Shinya
Koskinen, Eric
Maher, Michael
Martelli, Alberto
Morales, Jose F.
Oliveira, Bruno C.D.S.
Pope, Bernie
Poulding, Simon
Pozzato, Gian Luca
Pu, Yewen
Rajeev, A.C.
Rasmussen, Ulrik Terp
Schmitt, Alan
Schneider-Kamp, Peter
Shashidhar, K.C.
Stampoulis, Antonis
Stroeder, Thomas
Sulzmann, Martin
Tamm, Hellis
Torella, Luca
Tsukada, Takeshi
Vidal, German
Wang, Meng
Worrell, James
Yang, Edward

Abstracts of Invited Talks

Liquid Types For Haskell

Ranjit Jhala

Department of Computer Science and Engineering
University of California, San Diego, La Jolla, CA
USA

Abstract. We present LiquidHaskell (http://goto.ucsd.edu/liquid), an automatic verifier for Haskell. LiquidHaskell uses "refinement types", a restricted form of dependent types where relationships between values are encoded by decorating types with logical predicates drawn from an efficiently SMT decidable theory (of arithmetic and uninterpreted functions). In this talk, we will describe the key ingredients of LiquidHaskell.

First, we will present a rapid overview of liquid refinement types, including SMT solver based (decidable) subtyping, and inference. Decidability is achieved by eschewing the use of arbitrary terms inside types, and the use of indices to encode rich properties of data.

Second, we will show how to recover some of the expressiveness lost by restricting the logic, with two new techniques: *measures* which encode structural properties of values and *abstract refinements* which enable generalization (i.e. quantification) over refinements.

Third, we will discuss the curious interaction of laziness and refinement typing. In a nutshell, the technique of refinement typing can be viewed as a type-based generalization of Floyd-Hoare logics. Surprisingly, we demonstrate that under non-strict evaluation, these logics (and hence, classical refinement typing) is unsound, due to the presence of potentially divergent sub-computations. Fortunately, we show how soundness can be recovered with a termination analysis, itself, circularly bootstrapped off refinement typing.

We have used LiquidHaskell to verify safety, functional correctness and termination properties of real-world Haskell libraries totalling more than 10,000 lines of code. Time permitting, we will present a demonstration of the tool and a few short case studies illustrating its use.

(Joint work with Niki Vazou and Eric Seidel and Patrick Rondon)

Relating Computational Effects by $\top\top$-Lifting

Shin-ya Katsumata

Research Institute for Mathematical Sciences, Kyoto University
Kyoto, 606-8502, Japan
sinya@kurims.kyoto-u.ac.jp

When two interpretations of a programming language are given, we are naturally interested in the problem of establishing a relationship between these interpretations. A representative case is the computational adequacy of PCF, which compares the denotational semantics and the operational semantics of PCF.

Problems of this sort are also seen in monadic representations of computational effects. They vary a lot depending on the combination of a computational effect, two monadic representations of it and a relationship between these monadic representations. For instance,

1. A simple problem is to compare two monadic representations of nondeterministic computations using the powerset monad and the list monad.
2. Filinski gave a formal relationship between the monadic representation and the CPS representation of call-by-value programs [1]. This is to compare representations of computational effects by a monad T and the continuation monad $(- \Rightarrow TR) \Rightarrow TR$.
3. Wand and Vaillancourt compared two monadic representations of backtracking computations using the stream monad and the 2-CPS monad [6].

We aim to solve these problems in a uniform manner. We give a set of conditions to show that a given relationship holds between two monadic interpretations of a call-by-value functional language. These conditions are applicable to a wide range of problems relating computational effects. The proof of this result employs the *categorical* $\top\top$*-lifting* [2], which is a semantic analogue of Lindley and Stark's leapfrog method [4, 5], and offers a flexible method to construct logical relations for monads. This talk is based on the paper [3].

References

1. Filinski, A.: Representing monads. In: Proc. POPL 1994, pp. 446–457 (1994)
2. Katsumata, S.-Y.: A semantic formulation of $\top\top$-lifting and logical predicates for computational metalanguage. In: Ong, L. (ed.) CSL 2005. LNCS, vol. 3634, pp. 87–102. Springer, Heidelberg (2005)
3. Katsumata, S.-Y.: Relating computational effects by $\top\top$-lifting. Inform. and Comput. (Special issue on ICALP 2011) 222, 228–246 (2013)
4. Lindley, S.: Normalisation by Evaluation in the Compilation of Typed Functional Programming Languages. PhD thesis, University of Edinburgh (2004)

5. Lindley, S., Stark, I.: Reducibility and ⊤⊤-lifting for computation types. In: Urzyczyn, P. (ed.) TLCA 2005. LNCS, vol. 3461, pp. 262–277. Springer, Heidelberg (2005)
6. Wand, M., Vaillancourt, D.: Relating models of backtracking. In: Proc. ICFP 2004, pp. 54–65 (2004)

Programming Language Methodologies for Systems Verification

Gabriele Keller

School of Computer Science and Engineering
The University of New South Wales
Sydney, Australia

Abstract. The need for correct and secure systems is becoming more acute as software is impacting a greater part of our daily life. Formal verification is one method to improve on the status quo. In many cases, however, the costs are still simply too high.

In this talk, I will present an outline of our approach to achieving a fully verified operating system at acceptable costs. It is based on combining insights from systems, formal methods and programming language research. I will give a brief overview of the history of the project and the goals already achieved, followed by a more detailed look at a specific subproject, namely file system verification. In particular, I will describe the role of two distinct domain-specific programming languages in this framework.

Table of Contents

PrologCheck – Property-Based Testing in Prolog

Cláudio Amaral[1,2], Mário Florido[1,2], and Vítor Santos Costa[1,3]

[1] DCC - Faculty of Sciences, University of Porto, Porto, Portugal
[2] LIACC - University of Porto, Porto, Portugal
[3] CRACS - University of Porto, Porto, Portugal
{coa,amf,vsc}@dcc.fc.up.pt

Abstract. We present PrologCheck, an automatic tool for property-based testing of programs in the logic programming language Prolog with randomised test data generation. The tool is inspired by the well known QuickCheck, originally designed for the functional programming language Haskell. It includes features that deal with specific characteristics of Prolog such as its relational nature (as opposed to Haskell) and the absence of a strong type discipline.

PrologCheck expressiveness stems from describing properties as Prolog goals. It enables the definition of custom test data generators for random testing tailored for the property to be tested. Further, it allows the use of a predicate specification language that supports types, modes and constraints on the number of successful computations. We evaluate our tool on a number of examples and apply it successfully to debug a Prolog library for AVL search trees.

1 Introduction

Software testing consists of executing a program on a pre-selected set of inputs and inspecting whether the outputs respect the expected results. Each input tested is called a *test case* and the set of inputs is a *test suite*. Testing tries to find counter-examples and choosing the test cases to this effect is often a difficult task. The approach used can be manual, with the tester designing test cases one by one, or it can be automated to some extent, in this case resorting to tools for case generation. Ideally, the best approach would be automatic testing.

In a property-based framework test cases are automatically generated and run from assertions about logical properties of the program. Feedback is given to the user about their evaluation. Property-based testing applications include black-box, white-box, unit, integration and system testing [3] [6,7].

Property-based testing naturally fits the logic programming paradigm. Assertions are first order formulas and thus easily encoded as program predicates. Therefore, a property based approach to testing is intuitive for the logic programmer.

In this paper we introduce PrologCheck[1], a property-based testing framework for Prolog. We further discuss two main contributions: a specification language for Prolog predicates and a translation procedure into testable properties.

[1] The PrologCheck tool is available at `www.dcc.fc.up.pt/~coa/PrologCheck.html`

M. Codish and E. Sumii (Eds.): FLOPS 2014, LNCS 8475, pp. 1–17, 2014.

In most programming languages interfaces to testing frameworks rely on boolean functions, such as equality, to determine primitive properties. PrologCheck states properties through a domain-specific language that naturally supports domain quantification. In this language primitive properties are Prolog goals which can be composed by PrologCheck property operators.

PrologCheck testing consists on repetitively calling the goal for a large number of test cases. Input to such goals is based on PrologCheck value abstraction, quantification over a domain represented by a randomised generator of terms. We implement randomised test case generation, which frees the user from choosing input manually. We include a number of predefined generators for relevant sets of terms, such as integers, and combinators to help define new generators. Thus other generation techniques [10] [16] [18] can be implemented to complement the power of built-in generators.

We also define a language of testable predicate specifications including types, modes and multiplicity, which the tester can use to encode interesting properties of the predicate under test. By specifying some aspects of a predicate in a proper specification language it is possible to generate a PrologCheck property and check it. This allows us to use PrologCheck and its predicate specification to test a number of non-trivial programs.

The rest of this paper is organised as follows. We proceed with motivating examples in Sec. 3. Section 2 encloses the presentation of related work. In Sec. 4 we introduce property definitions and their testing in PrologCheck and in Sec. 5 we discuss details about test case generation. Section 6 describes the predicate specification language and how to test the specifications. A case study of AVL trees is presented Sec. 7. We finalise with the conclusions in Sec. 8.

2 Related Work

There is some previous support for automated testing in the logic programming community: SWI-Prolog supports unit testing through plunit [20]; the Ciao Prolog System [13] has an assertion language integrating run-time checking and unit testing [15]. We use a property specification language but in an automatic property-based randomly generated testing context. Property specification languages for Prolog were used before [9] [15] [19] in different contexts.

Automated testing is supported in several languages and paradigms. The three most influential tools for our work were QuickCheck [5] for the functional programming language Haskell, PropEr [17] for the functional programming language Erlang and EasyCheck [4] for the functional-logic language Curry.

Easycheck is an automated tool for specification-based testing of declarative programs, which deals with logic programming features. It is written in the functional-logic programming language Curry and it is based on the view of free variables of an appropriate type as non-deterministic generators [1] and mechanisms to specify properties of non-deterministic operations by generalizing the set of combinators for non-deterministic operations of QuickCheck. In our work we focus on Prolog and, in contrast with EasyCheck, non-deterministic generators are implemented by non-deterministic Prolog programs, types are implemented by monadic logic programs [11,12], and we use a specification language for standard features of logic programming such as modes and number of answers [9].

There are several automatic testing tools for functional programming languages, namely QuickCheck, PropEr, SmallCheck [18], and G∀ST [14]. The first and most preeminent tool is QuickCheck. QuickCheck uses a domain specific language of testable specifications as does PropEr. We define a specification language in PrologCheck but with differences related to the relational nature of Prolog. As in QuickCheck, we use random testing - we choose this method compared to systematic methods due to its success in QuickCheck. QuickCheck generates test data based on Haskell types. In Erlang, types are dynamically checked and PropEr, as does as ErlangQuickCheck, guides value generation by functions, using quantified types defined by these generating functions. Prolog is an untyped language, but type information is crucial in PrologCheck test data generation as well. Similarly to the Erlang tools, we adopt the view of types defined by test case generators. Our types are intended to construct test cases that depict input instantiations. Thus we would not take advantage of the use of restricted type languages based on regular types [11,12] [21,22].

3 Motivating Examples

3.1 Append

Consider the well-known concatenation predicate.

```
app([], YS, YS).
app([X|XS], YS, [X|AS]) :- app(XS, YS, AS).
```

We specify the predicate behaviour through the predicate specification language presented in Sec. 6. The properties and predicates to be tested are in module `m`.

`app(A,B,C)` is used in a functional way in many programs, i.e., by giving it two lists as input and getting their concatenation as output. The directionality is determined by the modes of each parameter: *ground, ground, variable* to *ground, ground, ground.* The range of answers for a predicate with a (total) functional behaviour is exactly one. This behaviour is specified in PrologCheck as:

```
app of_type (A-(listOf(int)), B-(listOf(int)), C-(variable))
  where (i(g, g, v), o(g, g, g))  has_range {1,1}.
```

The property originated by this specification clause passes the tests generated by the tool.

```
   ?- prologcheck(m:prop(spec_app)).
OK: Passed 100 test(s).
```

`app/3` may be used in other situations. One can use it to create an open list bound to the third parameter by calling it with a variable in the second input parameter, which remains uninspected. The result is a list with the ground elements of the list in the first parameter and the variable in the second parameter as the tail, therefore it is neither ground nor variable. This usage also behaves as a function. We state this as specification clause `1` of predicate `app`.

```
{app, 1} of_type (A-(listOf(int)), B-(variable), C-(variable))
  where (i(g, v, v), o(g, v, ngv)) has_range {1,1}.
```

Testing reveals that the *out* part of the directionality is not satisfied.

```
 ?- prologcheck(m:prop(spec_app_1), [noshrink]).
{failed_out_modes,[[o,g,v,ngv]], [[],_10258,_10258]}
Failed: After 3 test(s).
Counterexample found: [[[],_10258,_10260]]
```

The counterexample shows that the output modes do not respect the specification when the first input parameter is the empty list. One way to solve this issue is to add the missing directionality `(i(g, v, v), o(g, v, ngv)), o(g,v,v)`. Although, the correct choice in general is to split the input types, since this is a matter between disjoint sets of terms. Multiple output directionalities are mainly intended for multiple modes of multiple answers.

```
{app, 1a} of_type (A-(listOf1(int)), B-(variable), C-(variable))
  where (i(g, v, v), o(g, v, ngv)) has_range {1,1}.

{app, 1b} of_type (A-(value([])), B-(variable), C-(variable))
  where (i(g, v, v), o(g, v, v)) has_range {1,1}.
```

3.2 List Reverse

Let us explore an example of list reversing predicates. The reversing procedure relates two lists and is polymorphic in the type of the list's elements. It is usually sufficient to check the behaviour for a single type of elements. Moreover, sometimes even a type with a finite number of values suffice, but we can safely overestimate the size of the type [2]. Therefore, we use the generator for integers, `int`, as the elements of the parametric list generator, `listOf(int)`.

```
rev([],[]).
rev([X|XS], YS) :- rev(XS,ZS), append(ZS, [X], YS).
```

We express the symmetry of the reversing relation in terms of its intended use: given a ground list in one input parameter retrieve a result in the other.

```
prop(d_rev) :- for_all(listOf(int), XS, (rev(XS, RX), rev(RX, XS)))
```

Prologchecking the property bears no surprises.

```
  ?- prologcheck(m:prop(d_rev)).
OK: Passed 100 test(s).
```

We could have mis-typed the property, making it impossible to be satisfied:

```
prop(wrong_dr) :-
  for_all(listOf(int), XS, (rev(XS,RX), rev(RX,RX))).
```

We mistakenly make the second call to `rev/2` with `RX` as the second parameter.

```
  ?- prologcheck(m:prop(wrong_dr)).
Failed: After 11 test(s).
Shrinking (6 time(s))
Counterexample found: [[0,6]]
```

A counterexample is found and shrunk to the presented counter-example [0,6].

To check that the order is being reversed we can randomly choose an element (or a set of elements) and inspect its position in the parameters. Choosing random elements prevent us from checking the whole list.

```
prop(rev_i) :- plqc:for_all(
    suchThat(structure({listOf(int), int}), m:valid_index),
    {L,I}, m:prop({double_rev_i_body , L, I}) ).
valid_index({L, I}) :- length(L,X), I<X.

prop({double_rev_i_body , L, I}) :-
  m:rev(L, LR), length(L,X), Index is I+1, RevIndex is X-I,
  lists:nth(Index, L, Val), lists:nth(RevIndex, LR, Val).
```

When performing a large number of tests this method should randomly choose enough indexes to give good element coverage.

```
  ?- prologcheck(m:prop(rev_i)).
OK: Passed 100 test(s).
```

We have another implementation of reverse, using an accumulator instead of concatenation. The previous properties can be adapted to this implementation with the same results.

```
rev_acc([], LR, LR).
rev_acc([X|XS], Acc, LR) :- rev_acc(XS, [X|Acc], LR).

rev_acc(L, LR) :- rev_acc(L, [], LR).
```

Since we have two implementations of the same concept we can explore this by stating and testing a property comparing their behaviours.

```
prop(eqv_acc_app) :-
  for_all(listOf(int), L, (rev_acc(L,LR),rev(L,LR))).
```

The comparison succeeds if both have the same behaviour.

```
  ?- prologcheck(m:prop(eqv_acc_app)).
OK: Passed 100 test(s).
```

4 Properties

Property-based testing extends program code with *property definitions*. Properties are specifications in a suitable language and are tested automatically by generating test cases.

PrologCheck is a property-based testing framework. Given a specification it randomly generates test cases for the properties to be tested, executing them to assess their validity. A *primitive property* is a Prolog goal, hence, the whole language can be used to define properties. Properties may then be composed according to composition rules described later in the paper. This enables the specification of a wide range of properties. Next, in this section we introduce PrologCheck through the append example.

We will go through the process of using the tool, beginning by turning a logical statement of a property into a PrologCheck testable property. An example of a property of `app/3` is that, assuming the first two input parameters are lists, after its execution a variable given in the third input parameter is instantiated with a list. This property can be represented by the first order formula

$$\forall\, l_1, l_2 \in \mathit{list}.\ (l_1 +\!\!+\, l_2 \in \mathit{list})$$

where l_1 and l_2 denote lists given as input and $+\!\!+$ is interpreted as list concatenation. The primitive property in the formula, $l_1 +\!\!+\, l_2 \in \mathit{list}$, can then be represented by the goal

```
app(L1, L2, L), (L = []; L = [_|_]).
```

The next step is optional. We explicitly parametrise the property into a first order object. The resulting property is written as a clause for the special predicate `prop/1` and parametrised accordingly.

```
prop({appLLL, L1, L2}) :- app(L1, L2, L), (L = []; L = [_|_]).
```

This is PrologCheck's predicate for labelling properties. The parametric label, `{appLLL, L1, L2}` in the example, uniquely identifies the property and holds the variables for all the input required. The symbol `appLLL` is the "*append of lists results in list*" property identifier and the variables `L1, L2` the input. The body of labelled properties is inspected by PrologCheck, making it possible to abstract long or frequently used properties.

A last step is needed to verify properties with PrologCheck. In order to enable random testing, we define a domain of parameter instantiations. Values from this domain are used as test cases.

```
prop(appL) :- for_all(listOf(int), L1, for_all(listOf(int), L2,
                    prop({appLLL, L1, L2}))).
```

This more precise definition states that the property `appL` is `appLLL` over two lists of integers. More accurately, we use `for_all/3` to represent PrologCheck's universal quantification. The first input parameter describes the *type* of terms we want to generate randomly, in this case lists of integers, `listOf(int)`, and the second input parameter names the variable they will bind to, in this case `L1` and `L2`. The third is the property we want to verify. To check the property we can call PrologCheck using the alias `prop(appL)`. It starts with the outer `for_all` quantifier, generates a random list of integers, unifies it with `L1` and repeats the process for the inner quantifier, unifying `L2` with the second generated list.

```
 ?- prologcheck(m:prop(appL)).
OK: Passed 100 test(s).
```

The `prologcheck/1` predicate is the simplest property tester in PrologCheck, taking a property as a parameter and checking it for a large number (100 is the default number) of generated test cases.

We could have mis-typed the property, making it impossible to be satisfied:

```
prop(wrong_appL) :- for_all(listOf(int), L1,
  for_all(listOf(int), L2, (app(L1, L2, L), (L=[], L=[_|_])))).
```

We mistakenly determine L to be both [] and [_|_].

```
?- prologcheck(m:prop(wrong_dr)).
Failed: After 1 test(s).
Shrinking (1 time(s))
Counterexample found: [[],[]]
```

A counterexample is found and showed. We observe at this point that a counterexample is immediately found. There is no possible value that can satisfy the written condition.

Often we want to find concise counterexamples. To do this we use a *shrinking* predicate that tries to reduce the counterexample found. To improve the probability of finding smaller counter-examples the tool keeps track of a growing *size parameter*. This parameter starts at an initial value and is updated with each successful test. Its purpose is to control the size of produced test cases and it is used in test case generation. The definition of the actual size of a term is flexible and definable by the generating procedure.

We can define general properties or define sub-properties individually. We can, for example, separate property appLLL into appLLE and appLLC to state the empty list and *cons* cell separately and compose them with property operators.

```
prop({appLLE, L1, L2}) :- append(L1, L2, L), L = [].
prop({appLLC, L1, L2}) :- append(L1, L2, L), L = [_|_].
```

Property operators currently include conjunction (Prop1 and Prop2), disjunction (Prop1 or Prop2), conditional execution (if Cond then Prop1 else Prop2)) and quantification (for_all(Gen, Var, Prop)). Property labelling (prop(Label)) is considered an operation. PrologCheck inspects its body for the occurrence of other tool specific operations. Using property connectives one can compose labelled properties or other PrologCheck property operations.

We now define other properties of app/3, such as the relation of lists' lengths and the left and right identity element of concatenation.

```
prop({appLLLen, L1, L2}) :- app(L1, L2, L),
  length(L1, K1), length(L2, K2), length(L, K), K is K1 + K2.
prop({appLZ,L1,L2}) :- if L1=[] then (app(L1,L2,L), L=L2).
prop({appRZ,L1,L2}) :- if L2=[] then (app(L1,L2,L), L=L1).
```

Conjunction and disjunction is used as expected. The conditional statement if A then B else C performs a conditional execution on A. If A runs successfully the tool continues by executing B and in case it fails executing C instead. A, B and C are PrologCheck properties. In the example shown the else branch is omitted. This is equivalent to having the property true in the omitted branch. The conditional statement enables conditional properties without cut.

```
prop(appAll) :- for_all(listOf(int),L1, for_all(listOf(int),L2,
  (prop({appLLLen, L1, L2}) and prop({appLZ, L1, L2})
  and prop({appRZ, L1, L2}) and prop({appLLL, L1, L2})
  and (prop({appLLE,L1,L2}) or prop({appLLC,L1,L2}))))).
```

Primitive properties are Prolog goals. In a strongly typed language (such as Haskell) only safe properties, pure functions or predicates, are allowed. In PrologCheck the user is free to use simpler or more involved properties. This provides extra flexibility but, ultimately, the user is responsible for guaranteeing the safety of impure code in a property.

5 Generators

Input for testing properties is randomly generated through explicitly defined procedures: *generators.* There are differences between PrologCheck generators and the generators in a strongly typed version of the tool. In Haskell QuickCheck, or any language with strong types, generators pick values inside a preexisting type according to some criteria. In PrologCheck generators represent procedures that randomly construct elements according to the shape of the term. In fact, the generators themselves define a set by the elements they generate, with non-zero probability. Thus, they define a set of terms, here denoted as a *type.* Note that this set of terms is not necessarily composed of only ground terms, instead it exactly represents the form of an input parameter to a property.

PrologCheck has *generators* and *generator predicates.* Generators specify the input parameters of properties. One example generator is `listOf(int)`. Generator predicates are the predicates responsible for the generation of test cases. The corresponding example of a call to a generator predicate is `listOf(Type, Output, Size)` where `Type` would be bound to `int`, `Output` would be instantiated with the produced test case and `Size` would be used to control the size of produced test cases. The value is passed to the property by the PrologCheck quantification through unification.

`choose/4` and `elements/3` are examples of generator predicates. Picking an integer in an interval is probably the most common operation in generators. The `choose/4` predicate discards the size parameter and randomly chooses an integer between the inclusive range given by the first two input parameters. `elements/3` randomly chooses an element from a non-empty list of possible elements. They are implemented as follows:

```
elements(AS, A, S) :-
  length(AS, Cap), choose(1,Cap,I,S), nth(I, AS, A).

choose(Min,Max, A, _) :- Cap is Max+1, random(Min,Cap,A).
```

Combinators. We extend generator predicates with *generator combinators* that allow us to define more complex generators. More precisely, combinators are generator predicates that are parametrised by generators. This is shown in the `app/3` example, where the generator for lists, `listOf(int)`, is parametrised by a generator for integers. Generator predicates can have several parameters, but the two last must always be, in this order, the generated value and the size. When a generator predicate uses another generator predicate to build a value, the parameter is passed in generator form.

PrologCheck combinators enable the generation of complex data and can tune the probability distribution of the generated values to better fit the needs of the tester. Next, we present some combinators distributed with the tool.

To generate lists we provide generators for arbitrary and fixed length lists. They are parametrised by a generator for the list elements. Random size lists can be generated by `listOf/3`, which randomly chooses a list length and uses `vectorOf/4`. Non-empty lists are generated by the `listOf1/3` variation. `vectorOf/4` is a fixed length generator predicate that recurs on the integer given as the first input parameter, generating each element.

```
listOf(GenA, AS, S) :- choose(0, S, K, S),vectorOf(K, GenA, AS, S).

listOf1(GenA, AS, S) :- max_list( [1,S], Cap),
  choose(1, S, K, S), vectorOf(K, GenA, AS, S).

vectorOf(0, _GenA, [], _Size) :- !.
vectorOf(K, GenA, [A|AS], Size) :-
  call(GenA, A, Size), K1 is K-1, vectorOf(K1, GenA, AS, Size).
```

Combinators can interact and, for example, create lists of random length in an interval ($[2, 5]$) and create lists whose elements are in an interval ($[0, 9]$).

```
for_all( choose(2,5),I, for_all( vectorOf(I,int),L1,
  for_all( listOf(choose(0,9)),L2, (prop({appLLC, L1, L2}))))
```

Generating specific values, ground or not, fresh variables and terms with a certain structure is possible with `value/3`, `variable/2` and `structure/3` respectively. With such generators/combinators we can describe and therefore test a different input mode.

```
for_all( structure([listOf(int), value(v), variable]),[L1,X,L],
  app(L1, X, L))
```

If the values or part of the values to be generated have to be of a certain size, we override the size parameter with the `resize/4` combinator.

```
resize(NewSize, GenA, A, _Size) :- call(GenA, A, NewSize).
```

Resizing can contribute to better chances of fulfilling a condition, e.g., a size near zero improves the chances of generating empty lists.

```
for_all(  resize(0,listOf(int)),  L1,
  for_all( listOf(int), L2, (prop({appLZ, L1, L2})) ))
```

The `suchThat/4` combinator restricts the values of a generator. If not all generated elements for a generator are useful, wrapping it with `suchThat/4` will select the elements of the generator in the first input parameter that satisfy the predicate in the second. If a generated value is valid it is returned; if not, the size parameter is slowly increased to avoid a size without valid values. This is a dangerous combinator in the sense that it can loop indefinitely if the the valid values are too sparse. We can restrict a list generator so that it only generates non-empty lists.

```
posLen([_|_]).
...
  for_all(  suchThat(listOf(int), posLen),  L1,
    for_all(listOf(int),L2, (prop({appLLC, L1, L2}))))
```

Often, it is hard to find a good generator. Choosing from a set of generators that complement each other is a good way to generate values with a desired distribution. Grouping generators can be done in several ways. We can randomly choose from a list of generators with `oneof/3`. The list of generators given in the first input parameter must be non-empty.

```
oneof(LGenA, A, S) :- length(LGenA, Cap), choose(1,Cap,I,S),
  nth(I, LGenA, GenA), call(GenA, A, S).
```

If an uniform distribution between the generators is not suitable one can specifically state the proportions of the probabilities to choose each generator. The first input parameter of `frequency/3` is a list of pairs {*weight*,*generator*} representing such proportions. The input list must be non-empty. A frequency-index list is created with the correct proportions and a generator is then randomly chosen from that list to be called.

```
frequency(FGL, A, S) :- checkFreqWeights(FGL, FIL, Cap),
  choose(1,Cap,I,S), nth(I, FIL, GenA), call(GenA, A, S).
```

We can use both combinators to randomly choose generators for each test case.

```
Gen1 = resize(0,listOf(int))
Gen2 = suchThat(listOf(int), posLen)
...
  for_all( frequency([{4,listOf(int)}, {1,Gen2}]), L1,
    for_all( oneof([Gen1,Gen2],L2, (prop({appLLC, L1, L2}))))
```

Shrinking. When a test fails the tool may try to simplify the failing input to a smaller and easier to understand counterexample. Shrinking is a process by which a *shrinker* predicate returns a possibly empty list of smaller elements than the one given as input.

Similarly to generator predicates, shrinkers are calls to the corresponding generator. To trigger shrinking a generator is called with the value to shrink, the flag `shrink` and a variable to store the list of shrunk values. An example of a shrinker behaviour for lists is to remove an element. The following auxiliary predicate builds a list of the possible shrunk lists.

```
genL(GenA, A, Size) :- listOf(GenA, A, Size).
genL(GenA, L, shrink, Shrs) :-  shrL(L, Shrs).
shrL([], []).
shrL([A], [[]]) :- !.
shrL([A|AS], [AS|Shrs]) :-
  shrL(AS, Shrs1), maplist(cons(A), Shrs1, Shrs).

cons(X, XS, [X|XS]).
```

Most combinators do not have a default shrinking procedure. Since it is hard to decide, for example, what is a proper shrink for values generated by a random choice between generators, we default the shrinking of many combinators to an empty list of shrunk values. Instead of directly using combinators in a property quantification the user can wrap them in a generator predicate with a meaningful name, implementing the shrink behaviour for this specific type. This is exemplified by the `genL` generator predicate, which is a redefinition of `listOf` and can therefore implement a different shrinking process.

6 Specification Language

In this section we describe our predicate specification language. Throughout, we follow some of the principles presented by Deville [9]. There are several ways to state a predicate's specification, we do not argue that our specification process is superior to other approaches. We do believe that this approach fits naturally our needs, namely as a form to express testable predicate features.

The general specification form of a predicate `p/n` consists, at its core, of a set of uniquely identified specification clauses about *input types* or the shape of the parameters when evoking the predicate. Various aspects of the predicate for the particular input type in question can be added to a specification clause. If there is a *parameter relation* or a relation that input parameters must fulfil one can implement it as a predicate which checks if such a relation is valid for the list of input parameters given. The *modes* of each parameter can be given for the input parameters and for output answers. The language also allows stating the number of answers of a predicate, or its *range*. Last, the user may state invariant properties that should hold both before and after the predicate is executed as *pre-* and *post-conditions*. Next, we discuss the main properties that we allow in our framework.

Types. Types are the mandatory part of the specification. They are required to guarantee that the specification may be automatically tested. We define a type as follows:

Definition 1. *A* type *is a non-empty set of terms.*
A term t belongs to a type τ ($t \in \tau$) if it belongs to the set of terms that define the type.

Types are not defined as a set of *ground* terms but rather by a set of terms. Note that types defined in this manner depict perfectly possible forms of predicate input. This approach for types already encloses, by definition, the type precondition, where the input must be compatible with the specified types.

The types mentioned in a predicate specification clause correspond to PrologCheck generators used to automatically create individual test cases. This means that the type in a specification clause is partial in the sense that it only specifies that the predicate should succeed when given elements of such types as parameters. It states nothing about parameters of other types. Other input types can be covered by other specification clauses with different generators. The behaviour of a procedure for types not covered by any of the specification clauses is considered undefined/unspecified.

We can now easily specify input types for program predicates like `app/3`. We identify the specification clauses as `{app,K}`, specification clause `K` of predicate `app`, and declare the PrologCheck types. The specifications can be tested and the predicate checked to succeed for the corresponding input types.

```
{app,1} of_type (listOf(int), value(v), variable)
{app,2} of_type (listOf(int), variable, variable)
{app,3} of_type (listOf(int), listOf(int), variable)
```

Domain. Correct typing of parameters is crucial but may be insufficient to express the allowed input. Sometimes the input parameters must obey a relation extending type information, based on the actual values of the parameters. The domain of a predicate is the set of parameters accepted by a predicate [9]. The domain precondition is a restriction over the set of parameters of a predicate. Suppose that `minimum(A,B,C)` is a predicate that succeeds when `C` is the minimum of `A` and `B`. The predicate has the type `(int, int, int)` and the domain is the restriction `(C==A; C==B),(C<=A, C<=B)`.

Definition 2. *A* domain *of a procedure p/n is a set of term n-tuples such that* $\langle t_1, ..., t_n \rangle \in (\tau_1 \times ... \times \tau_n)$
$\langle t_1, ..., t_n \rangle$ *satisfies the input parameter relation*

This definition of a domain, similarly to what happens with types, is different from the usual notion of domain. It focus on the shape of the input to a predicate and not the accepted answer set. The PrologCheck domain of a predicate is then any set of terms produced by the generator that fulfils the domain precondition. In the absence of a domain precondition relating parameters the domain is the set of terms generated. A specification clause can thus be engineered to represent a subset of a more general type. An example could be that we want to test `app` with at least one non-empty list input. This can be used, for example, to guarantee that the variable given in the third input parameter will be instantiated with a non-empty list.

```
non_empty( [[_|_],_,_] ).
non_empty( [_,[_|_],_] ).
{app,3b} of_type (listOf(int), listOf(int), variable)
   such_that m:non_empty.
```

Directionality. The directionality of a predicate describes its possible uses by specifying the possible forms of the parameters before and after execution. We follow Deville [9] where the main modes for a parameter are ground, variable and neither ground nor variable. Conjunction of modes is possible and all combinations are achieved by the notation for ground (g) and variable (v) as well as the negation ($n?$). This results in the main modes and their pairwise combinations: g, v, gv, ng, nv, ngv. A parameter that can be used in any form is denoted by the mode identifier *any*.

Definition 3. *The* modes *or* forms *a term may present are denoted by* $Modes = g, v, gv, ng, nv, ngv, any$

There are two components to a directionality: input and output. They must hold for a predicate's parameters before and after execution, respectively. This means a full directionality denotes a pre- and a post-condition to the execution of the specified predicate. In PrologCheck these properties are checked for each test case when specified before and after calling the predicate.

Input directionality acts as a sanity check for the elements of the domain, meaning that the generators must be constructed to conform to the specified input modes. Each specification clause is allowed one input directionality. If the user wishes to specify more than one input form the clause should be divided into the number of input forms and its generators adapted accordingly. This results in bigger predicate specifications with possibly duplicated code, but is a very simple way to express what happens to the parameters in finer detail.

Each input may have more than one answer and therefore more than one output form. For this reason we adopted a schema where an input directionality is paired with a list of output forms.

Definition 4. *A* directionality *of a specification clause of a predicate p/n is a sequence of* predicate modes, *with one input mode followed by one or more output modes.*
A predicate mode of p, or just mode of p, is denoted as

– $i(m_1, ..., m_n)$

– $o(M_1, ..., M_n)$

where $m_i, M_i \in Modes$ *and* i, o *respect to input and output modes respectively.*

The specification of input and output modes is important to state predicate behaviours that may be oblivious to a library user. From using the predicate app/3 with a list and two variables, for example, two distinct directionalities may arise. This is due to the fact that an empty list in the first input parameter does not contribute to instantiate any part of the third parameter.

```
{app, 4} of_type (listOf(int), variable, variable)
   where (i(g, v, v), o(g, v, ngv), o(g, v, v)).
```

PrologCheck does not check the specification for consistency. A parameter with modes such that *in* is ground and *out* is variable is caught during testing. Output modes that are redundant or invalid will not be exposed when part of a set of output directionalities since they are interpreted as a disjunction. Directionalities should be constructively defined and not over-specified. They should be separated according to disjoint input types and incremented as needed.

Multiplicity. The number of answers a predicate call has can be valuable information. Knowing a predicate has a finite search space is a termination guarantee for predicates using it. Conventionally, multiplicity information, or *range*, is given for each directionality [19]. In PrologCheck we do not require that directionality is given, in which case no tests are performed regarding parameter form and the *any* mode is assumed for all parameters. The multiplicity is tied to the domain of each specification clause where defined.

The range of answers is given with two bounds: *Min* and *Max*. These values are the lower and upper bounds to the number of answers. The lower bound should not exceed the upper bound and they both take non-negative integer values up to infinity (denoted by the atom `inf`). When no explicit multiplicity is given the default we follow is $\langle 1, inf \rangle$. When testing a specification clause, the default minimal expected behaviour is that the domain is successfully accepted by the predicate. Therefore we try to mirror this when there are other features specified but no multiplicity, expecting at least one solution. It is necessary to impose a limit when the upper bound is infinity or an excessively large number. One can state the maximum number of answers necessary to assume that the answer range is sufficiently close to the upper bound with a positive integer. We can complement the previous specification clause with a statement about the predicate behaviour regarding the number of answers. In this case we have a total function behaviour, always yielding one and only one answer.

```
{app, 4b} of_type (listOf(int), variable, variable)
   where (i(g, v, v), o(g, v, ngv), o(g, v, v))
   has_range {1,1}.
{app, 4c} of_type (variable, listOf(int), variable)
   where (i(v, g, v), o(g, g, g), o(ngv, g, ngv))
   has_range {1,inf} limit 50.
```

Pre and Post-conditions. Along with all the other features of a predicate we can have a connection between the relations represented by the predicate being specified and other predicates. These relations can be valid prior to or after execution. In the predicate specification language they are pre- and post-conditions and are expressed as PrologCheck properties.

A pre-condition is a property that only inspects its input. It does not change the generated values to be applied to the specified predicate. Post-conditions can use any of the specified parameters. Since they are no longer used, it does not matter if they are changed by the answer substitution. Now we can describe the property relating the lengths of `app/3`'s parameters in a post-condition of a specification clause of the respective type. We identify the parameters of `app` so that we can use them in the post-condition as `A`, `B` and `C`.

```
{app, 5} of_type (A-(listOf(int)), B-(listOf(int)), C-(variable))
  post_cond (length(A,K1), length(B,K2), length(C,K), K is K1+K2).
```

7 AVL Trees Case Study

We have described AVL properties and performed black-box testing of an implementation of AVL trees in a Yap [8] module, `avl.yap`, with PrologCheck[2]. Due to space restrictions we present a general description of the process and its results.

The module interface is small, with predicates to create an empty tree, insert an element and look up an element, respectively `avl_new/1`, `avl_insert/4` and `avl_lookup/3`. When performing this kind of test one does not simply test individual predicates but rather usages of the module. To do this we must be able to create sequences of interface calls and inspect intermediate results for compliance with AVL invariants. Knowledge about the shape of input/output terms can be gathered manually if it is not previously known.

[2] All the details can be found in the tool's website.

Generator. Creating a valid sequence of interface calls is not difficult, but requires attention to detail. First, we only want to generate valid sequences to save effort of checking validity and not suffer from sparse valid values. Using the `avl` module implies the existence of two sets of important terms: key terms, and value terms, which we represent as generators. In order to test the correct failure of wrong look-ups, a set of values for failed look-ups disjoint from the regular values is implemented.

The generator starts by creating the tree, independently of the size parameter, using `avl_new/1`. This implies that when size is 0 an empty AVL-tree is still created. Thus, we always append the tree creation to a sequence of calls to insert and look-up values. Each element of the sequence is obtained by randomly choosing between insert and look-ups.

When an insert command is added to the sequence, the value to be inserted is kept so that it can be used in later look-ups. Look-ups are divided between valid look-up and invalid look-up. Valid look-ups are only generated after the corresponding insert and invalid look-ups are based in a set of values that is never inserted. Valid look-ups can be further distinguished between looking up a key-value pair and looking up a key and retrieving its value. These elements are branded by a command identifier to recognise their correct behaviour during testing. The relative probabilities are such that we get a big variety of commands within relatively small sequences.

Property. The definition of the AVL property depends on several factors. It is necessary to have operations to extract information from trees, such as current node's key, key comparison, left and right sub-trees and empty tree test.

A tree may be empty, in which case it is an AVL tree of height 0. In the case of a non-empty tree we retrieve its key and sub-trees. They are used in recursive checks of the property. The recursive calls accumulate lists of keys that should be greater and less then the keys in the sub-trees. If the sub-trees are individually compliant with the property, we proceed with the last check, comparing the returned heights for balance and computing the current tree height. This is how the property is outlined in PrologCheck:

```
prop({avl, T, Gs, Ls, H}) :- if (not isNil(T)) then
 ((getKey(T, K), left(T, L),  right(T, R),
     ((forall(member(X, Ls), cmpKeys(X, K, gt))) -> error1),
     ((forall(member(X, Gs), cmpKeys(X, K, lte))) -> error2))
   and prop({avl, L, [Key|Gt], Lt, Hl})
   and prop({avl, R, Gt, [Key|Lt], Hr})
   and (( abs(Hl-Hr)>1 -> error3), H is 1+max(Hl,Hr)))
 else (H = 0).
```

We complete the property by inserting it into a loop that consumes the operations in the quantified module uses.

Table 1 summarises some relevant results of our tool applied to the AVL library. Each line corresponds to a different module version: line 1 to the original version; line 2 to a bug in the re-balancing strategy inserted by the tester; line 3 to a different bug in the re-balancing strategy inserted by someone that was not involved with the tests. The column *Tests* is the number of tests needed to achieve a particular counter-example. For the purpose of readability we will represent only the key and value input parameters of the AVL operations. Thus consider `i(N,V)` as insert an element with key `N` and value `V`, and `l(N,V)` as look up the pair `(N,V)` in the tree.

Note that the counter-example found in the original version corresponds to an unspecified behaviour in the case of two insertions with the same key. After several runs of the tool (10 for the first bug and 20 for the second) we managed to find a pattern on the counter-examples which led to the identification of the pathological behaviour caused by the bugs.

Table 1. AVL testing summary

Version	Tests	Counter-example
Original	732	`i(1,a), i(1,b), l(1,b)`
Error 1	51	`i(3,a), i(1,b), i(2,c)`
Error 2	213	`i(5,a), i(2,b), i(3,c), i(4,d), i(1,e)`

8 Conclusion

We present PrologCheck, an automatic tool for specification based testing of Prolog programs.

Compared to similar tools for functional languages, we deal with testing of non-deterministic programs in a logic programming language. We provide a language to write properties with convenient features, such as quantifiers, conditionals, directionality and multiplicity. PrologCheck also includes the notion of random test-data generation.

We show that specification based testing works extremely well for Prolog. The relational nature of the language allows to specify local properties quite well since all the dependencies between input parameters are explicit in predicate definitions.

Finally note that our tool uses Prolog to write properties, which, besides its use in the tool for test specification, increases the understanding of the program itself, without requiring extra learning for Prolog programmers.

Acknowledgements. This work is partially financed by the ERDF - European Regional Development Fund through the COMPETE Program and by National Funds through the FCT - Fundação para a Ciência e a Tecnologia (Portuguese Foundation for Science and Technology) within project ADE/PTDC/EIA-EIA/121686/2010 and by LIACC through Programa de Financiamento Pluri-anual, FCT. Cláudio Amaral is funded by FCT grant SFRH/BD/65371/2009.

References

1. Antoy, S., Hanus, M.: Overlapping rules and logic variables in functional logic programs. In: Etalle, S., Truszczyński, M. (eds.) ICLP 2006. LNCS, vol. 4079, pp. 87–101. Springer, Heidelberg (2006)

2. Bernardy, J.-P., Jansson, P., Claessen, K.: Testing polymorphic properties. In: Gordon, A.D. (ed.) ESOP 2010. LNCS, vol. 6012, pp. 125–144. Springer, Heidelberg (2010)
3. Boberg, J.: Early fault detection with model-based testing. In: Proc. of Workshop on Erlang, pp. 9–20. ACM (2008)
4. Christiansen, J., Fischer, S.: EasyCheck — test data for free. In: Garrigue, J., Hermenegildo, M.V. (eds.) FLOPS 2008. LNCS, vol. 4989, pp. 322–336. Springer, Heidelberg (2008)
5. Claessen, K., Hughes, J.: Quickcheck: a lightweight tool for random testing of haskell programs. In: Proc. of ICFP, pp. 268–279. ACM (2000)
6. Claessen, K., Hughes, J., Pałka, M., Smallbone, N., Svensson, H.: Ranking programs using black box testing. In: Proc. of AST, pp. 103–110. ACM (2010)
7. Claessen, K., Pałka, M., Smallbone, N., Hughes, J., Svensson, H., Arts, T., Wiger, U.: Finding race conditions in erlang with quickcheck and pulse. In: Proc. of ICFP, pp. 149–160. ACM (2009)
8. Costa, V.S., Rocha, R., Damas, L.: The yap prolog system. TPLP 12(1-2), 5–34 (2012)
9. Deville, Y.: Logic programming: systematic program development. Addison-Wesley Longman Publishing Co. Inc., Boston (1990)
10. Duregård, J., Jansson, P., Wang, M.: Feat: functional enumeration of algebraic types. In: Proc. of Haskell Symposium, pp. 61–72. ACM (2012)
11. Florido, M., Damas, L.: Types as theories. In: Proc. of post-conference workshop on Proofs and Types, JICSLP (1992)
12. Frühwirth, T.W., Shapiro, E.Y., Vardi, M.Y., Yardeni, E.: Logic programs as types for logic programs. In: Proc. of LICS, pp. 300–309 (1991)
13. Hermenegildo, M.V., Bueno, F., Carro, M., López-García, P., Mera, E., Morales, J.F., Puebla, G.: An overview of ciao and its design philosophy. In: TPLP, pp. 219–252 (2012)
14. Koopman, P., Alimarine, A., Tretmans, J., Plasmeijer, R.: Gast: Generic automated software testing. In: Peña, R., Arts, T. (eds.) IFL 2002. LNCS, vol. 2670, pp. 84–100. Springer, Heidelberg (2003)
15. Mera, E., Lopez-García, P., Hermenegildo, M.: Integrating software testing and run-time checking in an assertion verification framework. In: Hill, P.M., Warren, D.S. (eds.) ICLP 2009. LNCS, vol. 5649, pp. 281–295. Springer, Heidelberg (2009)
16. Naylor, M.: A logic programming library for test-data generation (2007)
17. Papadakis, M., Sagonas, K.: A proper integration of types and function specifications with property-based testing. In: Proc. of Workshop on Erlang, pp. 39–50. ACM (2011)
18. Runciman, C., Naylor, M., Lindblad, F.: Smallcheck and lazy smallcheck: automatic exhaustive testing for small values. In: Proc. of Haskell Symposium, pp. 37–48. ACM (2008)
19. Somogyi, Z., Henderson, F.J., Conway, T.C.: Mercury, an efficient purely declarative logic programming language. Australian Computer Science Communications 17, 499–512 (1995)
20. Wielemaker, J., Schrijvers, T., Triska, M., Lager, T.: Swi-prolog. TPLP 12(1-2), 67–96 (2012)
21. Yardeni, E., Shapiro, E.: A type system for logic program. J. Log. Program. 10(2), 125–153 (1991)
22. Zobel, J.: Derivation of polymorphic types for prolog programs. In: Proc. of ICLP, pp. 817–838 (1987)

Generating Constrained Random Data with Uniform Distribution

Koen Claessen, Jonas Duregård, and Michał H. Pałka

Chalmers University of Technology, Gothenburg, Sweden
{koen,jonas.duregard,michal.palka}@chalmers.se

Abstract. We present a technique for automatically deriving test data generators from a predicate expressed as a Boolean function. The distribution of these generators is uniform over values of a given size. To make the generation efficient we rely on laziness of the predicate, allowing us to prune the space of values quickly. In contrast, implementing test data generators by hand is labour intensive and error prone. Moreover, handwritten generators often have an unpredictable distribution of values, risking that some values are arbitrarily underrepresented. We also present a variation of the technique where the distribution is skewed in a limited and predictable way, potentially increasing the performance. Experimental evaluation of the techniques shows that the uniform derived generators are much easier to define than hand-written ones, and their performance, while lower, is adequate for some realistic applications.

1 Introduction

Random property-based testing has proven to be an effective method for finding bugs in programs [1, 4]. Two ingredients are required for property-based testing: a *test data generator* and a *property* (sometimes called oracle). For each test, the test data generator generates input to the program under test, and the property checks whether or not the observed behaviour is acceptable. This paper focuses on the test data generators.

The popular random testing tool QuickCheck [4] provides a library for defining random generators for data types. Typically, a generator is a recursive function that at every recursion level chooses a random constructor of the relevant data type. Relative frequencies for the constructors can be specified by the programmer to control the distribution. An extra resource argument that shrinks at each recursive call is used to control the size of the generated test data and ensures termination.

The above method for test generation works well for generating structured, well-typed data. But it becomes much harder when our objective is to generate well-typed data *that satisfies an extra condition*. A motivating example is the random generation of programs as test data for testing compilers. In order to successfully test different phases of a compiler, programs not only need to be grammatically correct, they may also need to satisfy other properties such as all variables are bound, all expressions are well-typed, certain combinations of constructs do not occur in the programs, or a combination of such properties.

In previous work by some of the authors, it was shown to be possible but very tedious to manually construct a generator that (a) could generate random well-typed programs

M. Codish and E. Sumii (Eds.): FLOPS 2014, LNCS 8475, pp. 18–34, 2014.

```
data Expr                     check :: [Type] → Expr → Type → Bool
  = Ap Expr Expr Type         check env (Vr i)      t          = env !! i == t
  | Vr Int                    check env (Ap f x tx) t          =
  | Lm Expr                      check env f (tx :→ t) && check env x tx
data Type = A | B | C         check env (Lm e)      (ta :→ tb) = check (ta : env) e tb
          | Type :→ Type      check env _           _          = False
```

Fig. 1. Data type and type checker for simply-typed lambda calculus. The *Type* in the *Ap* nodes represents the type of the argument term.

in the polymorphic lambda-calculus, and at the same time (b) maintain a reasonable distribution such that no programs were arbitrarily excluded from generation.

The problem is that generators mix concerns that we would like to separate: (1) what is the structure of the test data, (2) which properties should it obey, and (3) what distribution do we want.

In this paper, we investigate solutions to the following problem: Given a definition of the structure of test data (a data type definition), and given one or more predicates (functions computing a boolean), can we automatically generate test data that satisfies all the predicates and at the same time has a predictable, good distribution?

To be more concrete, let us take a look at Fig. 1. Here, a data type for typed lambda expressions is defined, together with a function that given an environment, an expression, and a type, checks whether or not the expression has the stated type in the environment. From this input alone, we would like to be able to generate random well-typed expressions with a good distribution.

What does a 'good' distribution mean? First, we need to have a way to restrict the size of the generated test data. In any application, we are only ever going to generate a finite number of values, so we need a decision on what test data sizes to use. An easy and common way to control test data size is to control the *depth* of a term. This is for example done in SmallCheck [10]. The problem with using depth is that the cardinality of terms of a certain depth grows extremely fast as the depth increases. Moreover, good distributions for, to give an example, the set of trees of depth d are hard to find, because there are many more almost full trees of depth d than there are sparse trees of depth d, which may lead to an overrepresentation of almost full trees in randomly generated values.

Another possibility is to work with the set of values of a given *size* n, where size is understood as the number of data constructors in the term. Previous work by one of the authors on FEAT [5] has shown that it is possible to efficiently index in, and compute cardinalities of, sets of terms of a given size n. This is the choice we make in this paper.

The simplest useful and predictable distribution that does not arbitrarily exclude values from a set is the *uniform distribution*, which is why we chose to focus on uniform distributions in this paper. We acknowledge the need for other distributions than uniform in certain applications. However, we think that a uniform distribution is at least a useful building block in the process of crafting test data generators. We anticipate methods for controlling the distribution of our generators in multiple ways, but that remains future work.

Our first main contribution in this paper is an algorithm that, given a data type definition, a predicate, and a test data size, generates random values satisfying the predicate, with a perfectly uniform distribution. It works by first computing the cardinality of the set of all values of the given size, and then randomly picking indices in this set, computing the values that correspond to those indices, until we find a value for which the predicate is true. The key feature of the algorithm is that every time a value x is found for which the predicate is false, it is removed from the set of values, together with all other values that would have lead to the predicate returning false using the same execution path as x.

Unfortunately, even with this optimisation, uniformity turns out to be a very costly property in many practical cases. We have also developed a backtracking-based generator that is more efficient, but has no guarantees on the distribution. Our second main contribution is a hybrid generator that combines the uniform algorithm and the backtracking algorithm, and is 'almost uniform' in a precise and predictable way.

2 Generating Values of Algebraic Datatypes

In this section we explain how to generate random values of an algebraic data type (ADT) uniformly. Our approach is based on a representation of sets of values that allows efficient *indexing*, inspired by FEAT [5], which is used to map random indices to random values. In the next section we modify this procedure to efficiently search for values that satisfy a predicate.

Algebraic Data Types (ADTs) are constructed using units (atomic values), disjoint unions of data types, products of data types, and may refer to their own definitions recursively. For instance, consider these definitions of Haskell data types for natural numbers and lists of natural numbers:

data *Nat* = *Z* | *Suc Nat*
data *ListNat* = *Nill* | *Cons Nat ListNat*

In general, ADTs may contain an infinite number of values, which is the case for both data types above. Our approach for generating random values of an ADT uniformly is to generate values of a specific *size*, understood as the number of constructors used in a value. For example, all of *Cons* (*Suc* (*Suc Z*)) (*Cons Z Nill*), *Cons* (*Suc Z*) (*Cons* (*Suc Z*) *Nill*) and *Cons Z* (*Cons Z* (*Cons Z Nill*)) are values of size 7. As there is only a finite number of values of each size, we can create a sampling procedure that generates a uniformly random value of *ListNat* of a given size.

2.1 Indexing

Our method for generating random values of an ADT is based on an *indexing* function, which maps integers to corresponding data type values of a given size.

$$\text{index}_{S,k} : \{i \in \mathbb{N} \mid i < |S_k|\} \rightarrow S_k$$

Here, S is the data type, and S_k is the set of k-sized values of S. The intuitive idea behind efficient indexing is to quickly calculate *cardinalities* of subsets of the indexed set. For example, when $S = T \oplus U$ is a sum type, then indexing is performed as follows:

$$\text{index}_{T\oplus U,k}(i) = \begin{cases} \text{index}_{T,k}(i) & \text{if } i < |T_k| \\ \text{index}_{U,k}(i - |T_k|) & \text{otherwise} \end{cases}$$

When $S = T \otimes U$ is a product type, we need to consider all ways size k can be divided between the components of the product. The cardinality of the product can be computed as follows:

$$|(T \otimes U)_k| = \sum_{k_1+k_2=k} |T_{k_1}||U_{k_2}|$$

When indexing $(T \otimes U)_k$ using index i, we first select the division of size $k_1 + k_2 = k$, such that:

$$0 \leq i' < |T_{k_1}||U_{k_2}| \quad \text{where} \quad i' = i - \sum_{\substack{l_1<k_1 \\ l_1+l_2=k}} |T_{l_1}||U_{l_2}|$$

Then, elements of T_{k_1} and U_{k_2} are selected using the remaining part of the index i'.

$$\text{index}_{T\otimes U,k}(i) = (\text{index}_{T,k}(i' \text{ div } |U_{k_2}|), \text{index}_{U,k}(i' \text{ mod } |U_{k_2}|))$$

In the rest of this section, we outline how to implement indexing in Haskell.

2.2 Representation of Spaces

We define a Haskell Generalized Algebraic Data Type (GADT) *Space* to represent ADTs, and allow efficient cardinality computations and indexing.

```
data Space a where
  Empty :: Space a
  Pure  :: a          → Space a
  (:+:) :: Space a → Space a → Space a
  (:∗:) :: Space a → Space b → Space (a, b)
  Pay   :: Space a → Space a
  (:$:) :: (a → b) → Space a → Space b
```

Spaces can be built using four basic operations: *Empty* for empty space, *Pure* for unit space, (:+:) for a sum of two spaces and (:∗:) for a product. Spaces also have an operator *Pay* which represents a unit cost imposed by using a constructor. The last operation (:$:), applies a function to all values in the space. We assume that spaces are constructed in such a way that all their elements are unique. If this is not the case, a 'uniform' sampling procedure would return repeated elements more often than unique ones.

A very convenient operator on spaces is the lifted application operator, that takes a space of functions and a space of parameters and produces a space of all applications of the functions to the parameters:

$$(<*>) :: Space\ (a \to b) \to Space\ a \to Space\ b$$
$$s_1 <*> s_2 = (\lambda(f,a) \to f\ a)\ :\$:\ (s_1\ :*:\ s_2)$$

With the operators defined above, the definition of spaces mirror the definitions of data types. For example, spaces for the *Nat* and *ListNat* data types can be defined as follows:

$$spaceNat :: Space\ Nat$$
$$spaceNat = Pay\ (Pure\ Z\ :+:\ (Suc\ :\$:\ spaceNat))$$
$$spaceListNat :: Space\ ListNat$$
$$spaceListNat = Pay\ (Pure\ Nill\ :+:\ (Cons\ :\$:\ spaceNat <*> spaceListNat))$$

Unit constructors are represented with *Pure*, whereas compound constructors are mapped on the subspaces of the values they contain. In this example, *Pay* is applied each time we introduce a constructor, which makes the size of values equal to number of constructors they contain, and is the usual practice. However, the user may choose to use another way of assigning costs, which would change the sizes of individual values and, as a result, the distribution of the generated values. The only rule that must be followed when assigning costs is that all recursion is guarded by at least one *Pay* operation, otherwise the sets of values of a given size might be infinite, which would lead to non-terminating cardinality computations.

2.3 Indexing on Spaces

Indexing on spaces can be reduced to two subproblems: Extracting the finite set of values of a particular set, and indexing into such finite sets. Assume we have some data type for finite sets constructed by combining the empty set ($\{\}$), singleton sets ($\{a\}$), disjoint union ($\uplus$) and Cartesian product ($\times$). From the definition of such a finite set, its cardinality can be computed as follows:

$$|\{\}| = 0 \qquad |a \times b| = |a| * |b|$$
$$|\{a\}| = 1 \qquad |a \uplus b| = |a| + |b|$$

Using this function it is possible to define an indexing function on the type:

$$indexFin\ \{a\}\quad 0 = a$$
$$indexFin\ (a \uplus b)\ i \mid i < |a| = indexFin\ a\ i$$
$$indexFin\ (a \uplus b)\ i \mid i \geqslant |a| = indexFin\ b\ (i - |a|)$$
$$indexFin\ (a \times b)\ i = (indexFin\ a\ (i \div |b|), indexFin\ b\ (i \mod |b|))$$

With these definitions at hand, all we have to do to index in spaces is to define a function *sized* which extracts the finite set of values of a given size k from a space.

$$sized\ Empty\quad k = \{\} \qquad sized\ (Pay\ a)\quad k = sized\ a\ (k-1)$$
$$sized\ (Pure\ a)\ 0 = \{a\} \qquad sized\ (a\ :+:\ b)\ k = sized\ a\ k \uplus sized\ b\ k$$
$$sized\ (Pure\ a)\ k = \{\} \qquad sized\ (f\ :\$:\ a)\ k = \{f\ x : x \in sized\ a\ k\}$$
$$sized\ (Pay\ a)\quad 0 = \{\}$$

We define *sized Pure* to be empty for all sizes except 0, since we want values of an exact size. For *Pay* we get the values of size $k-1$ in the underlying space. Union and function application translate directly to union and application on sets. Selecting k-sized values of a product space requires dividing the size between its components. Thus, we can consider the set as a disjoint union of the $k+1$ different ways of dividing size between the components:

$$\mathit{sized}\ (a :*: b)\ k = \biguplus_{k_1+k_2=k} \mathit{sized}\ a\ k_1 \times \mathit{sized}\ b\ k_2$$

Knowing how to index in finite sets, we can implement an indexing function on spaces by composing the *sized* function with the *indexFin* function.

$$\mathit{indexSized} :: \mathit{Space}\ a \to \mathit{Int} \to \mathit{Integer} \to a$$
$$\mathit{indexSized}\ s\ k\ i = \mathit{indexFin}\ (\mathit{sized}\ s\ k)\ i$$

Computing cardinalities and indexing requires arbitrarily large integers, which are provided by Haskell's *Integer* type. Calculating cardinalities can be computationally intensive, and to be practical requires memoising cardinalities of recursive data types, which is implemented using another constructor of the *Space a* data type not shown here.

3 Predicate-Guided Indexing

Having solved the problem of generating members of algebraic data types, we extend the problem with a predicate that all generated values must satisfy.

A first approach for uniform generation is to choose a size, generate values of that size, test them against the predicate and keep the ones for which the predicate is *True*. This works well for cases where the proportion of values that satisfy the predicate is large enough, for example larger than 1%, but is far too inefficient in many practical situations.

In order to speed up random generation of values satisfying a given predicate, we use the lazy behaviour of the predicate to know its result on sets of values, rather than individual values, similarly to [10]. For instance, consider a predicate that tests if a list is sorted by checking the inequality of each pair of consecutive elements in turn starting from the front. Applying the predicate to $1:2:1:3:5:[\,]$ will yield *False* after the pair $(2,1)$ is encountered, before the predicate looks at the later elements, which means that it will return *False* for all lists starting with $1,2,1$. Once we have computed a set of values for which the predicate is going to return false, we remove all of these values from our original set.

To detect this we can exploit Haskell's call-by-need semantics by applying the predicate to a partially-defined value. In this case, observing that our predicate returns *False* when applied to a partially-defined list $1:2:1:\bot$, can lead us to conclude that $\bot$ can be replaced with any value without affecting the result. Thus, we could remove all lists that start with $1,2,1$ from the space. For many realistic predicates this removes a large number of values with each failed generation attempt, improving the chances of finding a value satisfying the predicate next time.

We implement this by using the function *valid*, that determines whether a given predicate needs to investigate its argument or not in order to produce its result. The function *valid* returns *Nothing* if the predicate needed its argument, and *Just b* if the predicate returns *b* regardless of its argument.

$$valid :: (a \to Bool) \to Maybe\ Bool$$

For example $valid\ (\lambda a \to True) == Just\ True$, $valid\ (\lambda a \to False) == Just\ False$, $valid\ (\lambda x \to x+1 > x) == Nothing$. Implementing *valid* involves applying the predicate to $\bot$ and catching the resulting exception if there is one. Catching the exception is an impure operation in Haskell, so the function *valid* is also impure (specifically, it breaks monotonicity).

The function *valid* is used to implement the indexing function, which takes the predicate, the space, the size and a random index.

$$index :: (a \to Bool) \to Space\ a \to Int \to Integer \to Space\ a$$

It returns a space of values containing at least the value at the given index, and any number of values for which the predicate yields the same result. When the returned space contains values for which the predicate is false, the top level search procedure (not shown here) removes all these values from the original enumeration and retries with a new index in the now smaller enumeration.

The function *index* is implemented by recursion on its *Space a* argument, and composing the predicate with traversed constructor functions, until its result is independent of which value from the current space is chosen. In particular, *index* on a function application (:\$:) returns the current space if the predicate p' returns the same result regardless of its argument, which is determined by calling $valid\ p'$. Otherwise, it calls *index* recursively on the subspace, composing the predicate with the applied function.

```
index p (f :$: a) k i = case valid p' of
  Just _   -> f :$: a
  Nothing  -> f :$: index p' a k i
  where p' = p ∘ f
```

3.1 Predicate-Guided Refinement Order

When implementing *index* for products, it is no longer possible to choose a division of size between the components, as was the case for indexing in Section 2. Determining the size of components early causes problems when generalising to sets of partial values, as the same partial value may represent values where size is divided in different ways.

We solve this problem using the algebraic nature of our spaces to eliminate products altogether. Disregarding the order of values when indexing, spaces form an algebraic semi-ring, which means that we can use the following algebraic laws to eliminate products.

$$\begin{array}{lll} a \otimes (b \oplus c) & \equiv (a \otimes b) \oplus (a \otimes c) & [distributivity] \\ a \otimes (b \otimes c) & \equiv (a \otimes b) \otimes c & [associativity] \\ a \otimes 1 & \equiv a & [identity] \\ a \otimes 0 & \equiv 0 & [annihilation] \end{array}$$

Expressing these rules on our Haskell data type is more complicated, because we need to preserve the types of the result, i.e. we only have associativity of products if we provide a function that transforms the left associative pair back to a right associative one, etc. The four rules defined on the *Space* data type expressed as a transformation operator $(***)$ are as follows:

$$
\begin{array}{lll}
a *** (b :+: c) & = (a :*: b) :+: (a :*: c) & \textit{[distributivity]} \\
a *** (b :*: c) & = (\lambda((x,y),z) \rightarrow (x,(y,z))) :\$: ((a :*: b) :*: c) & \textit{[associativity]} \\
a *** (\mathit{Pure}\, x) & = (\lambda y \rightarrow (y,x)) :\$: a & \textit{[identity]} \\
a *** \mathit{Empty} & = \mathit{Empty} & \textit{[annihilation]}
\end{array}
$$

In addition to this, we need two laws for eliminating *Pay* and function application.

$$
\begin{array}{lll}
a *** (\mathit{Pay}\, b) & = \mathit{Pay}\, (a :*: b) & \textit{[lift-pay]} \\
a *** (f :\$: b) & = (\lambda(x,y) \rightarrow (x, f\, y)) :\$: (a :*: b) & \textit{[lift-fmap]}
\end{array}
$$

The first law states that paying for the component of a pair is the same as paying for the pair, the second that applying a function f to one component of a pair is the same as applying a modified (lifted) function on the pair. If recursion is always guarded by a *Pay*, we know that the transformation will terminate after a bounded number of steps.

Using these laws we could define *index* on products by applying the transformation, so $\mathit{index}\, p\, (a :*: b) = \mathit{index}\, p\, (a *** b)$. This is problematic, because $***$ is a right-first traversal, which means that for our generators the left component of a pair is never generated before the right one is fully defined. This is detrimental to generation, since the predicate may not require the right operand to be defined. To guide the refinement order by the evaluation order of the predicate, we need to 'ask' the predicate which component should be defined first. We define a function similar to *valid* that takes a predicate on pairs:

$$\mathit{inspectsRight} :: ((a,b) \rightarrow \mathit{Bool}) \rightarrow \mathit{Bool}$$

The expression *inspectsRight p* is *True* iff *p* evaluates the right component of the pair before the left. Just like *valid*, *inspectsRight* exposes some information of the Haskell runtime, which can not be observed directly.

To define indexing on products we combine *inspectsRight* with another algebraic law: commutativity of products. If the predicate 'pulls' at the left component, the operands of the product are swapped before applying the transformation for the recursive call.

```
index p (a :*: b) k i = if inspectsRight p
  then index p (a *** b)               k i
  else index p (swap :$: (b *** a)) k i
  where swap (a,b) = (b,a)
```

The end result is an indexing algorithm that gradually refines the value it indexes to, by expanding only the part that the predicate needs in order to progress. With every refinement, the space is narrowed down until the predicate is guaranteed to be true or false for all values in the space. In the end the algorithm removes the indexed subspace from the search space, so no specialisations of the tested value are ever generated.

Note that the generation algorithm is still uniform because we only remove values for which the predicate is false from the original set of values. The uniformity is only concerned with the set of values for which the predicate is true.

3.2 Relaxed Uniformity Constraint

When our uniform generator finds a space for which the predicate is false, the algorithm chooses a new index and retries, which is required for uniformity. We have implemented two alternative algorithms.

The first one is to backtrack and try the alternative in the most recent choice. Such generators are no longer uniform, but potentially more efficient. Even though the algorithm start searching at a uniformly chosen index, since an arbitrary number of backtracking steps is allowed the distribution of generated values may be arbitrarily skewed. In particular, values satisfying the predicate that are 'surrounded' by many values for which it does not hold may be much more likely to be generated than other values.

The second algorithm also performs backtracking, but imposes a bound b for how many values the backtracking search is allowed to skip over. When the bound b is reached, a new random index is generated and the search is restarted. The result is an algorithm which has an 'almost uniform' distribution in a precise way: the probabilities of generating any two values differ at most by a factor $b+1$. So, if we pick $b = 1000$, generating the most likely value is at most 1001 times more likely than the least likely value.

The bounded backtracking search strategy generalises both the uniform search (when the bound b is 0) and the unlimited backtracking search (when the bound b is infinite).

We expected the backtracking strategy to be more efficient in terms of time and space usage than the uniform search, and the bounded backtracking strategy to be somewhere in between, with higher bounds leading to results closer to unlimited backtracking. Our intention for developing these alternative algorithms was that trading the uniformity of the distribution for higher performance may lead to a higher rate of finding bugs. Section 4 contains experimental verification of these hypotheses.

3.3 Parallel Conjunction

It is possible to improve the generation performance by introducing the parallel conjunction operator [10], which makes pruning the search space more efficient. Suppose we have a predicate $p\,x = q\,x$ && $r\,x$. Given that && is left-biased, if *valid r* == *Just False* and *valid q* == *Nothing* then the result of *valid p* will be *Nothing*, even though we expect that refining q will make the conjunction return *False* regardless of what $q\,x$ returns.

We can define a new operator &&& for parallel conjunction with different behaviour when the first operand is undefined: $\bot$ &&& *False* == *False*. This may make the indexing algorithm terminate earlier when the second operand of a conjunction is false, without needing to perform refinements needed by the first operand at all. Similarly, we can define parallel disjunction that is *True* when either operand is *True*.

4 Experimental Evaluation

We evaluated our approach in four benchmarks. Three of them involved measuring the time and memory needed to generate 2000 random values of a given size satisfying a predicate. The fourth benchmark compared a derived simply-typed lambda term generator against a hand-written one in triggering strictness bugs in the GHC compiler. Some benchmarks were also run with a naïve generator that generates random values from a space, as in Section 2, and filters out those that do not satisfy a predicate.

4.1 Trees

Our first example is binary search trees (BSTs) with Peano-encoded natural numbers as their elements, defined as follows.

```
data Tree a = L
            | N a (Tree a) (Tree a)
isBST :: Ord a => Tree a -> Bool
data Nat = Z | Suc Nat

instance Ord Nat where
  _     < Z     = False
  Z     < Suc _ = True
  Suc x < Suc y = x < y
```

The *isBST* predicate (omitted) decides if the tree is a BST, and uses a supplied lazy comparison function for type *Nat* for increased laziness.

We measured the time and space needed to generate 2000 trees for each size from a range of sizes, allowing at most 300 s of CPU time and 4 GiB of memory to be used. Derived generators based on three different search strategies (see Section 3.2) were used: One performing uniform sampling (*uniform*), one bounded backtracking allowed to skip at most 10k values (*backtracking 10k*), and one performing unbounded backtracking (*backtracking*). A naïve generate-and-filter generator was also used for comparison.

Both *backtracking 10k* and *backtracking* generators produce non-uniform distributions of values. The skew of the *backtracking 10k* generator is limited, as the least likely values are generated at most 10k times less likely than the most common ones, as mentioned in Section 3.2.

Fig. 2 shows the time and memory consumed the runs with resource limits marked by dotted lines in the plots. Run times for all derived generators rise sharply with the increased size of generated values and seem to approach exponential growth for larger sizes. The backtracking generator performs best of all, and has a slower exponential growth rate for large sizes than the other derived generators. The *backtracking 10k* generator achieved similar performance as the *uniform* one when generating values that are about 11 size units larger. The generate-and-filter generator was not able to complete any of the runs in time, and is omitted from the graphs.

4.2 Simply-Typed Lambda Terms

Generating random simply-typed lambda terms was our motivating application. Simply-typed lambda terms can be turned into well-typed Haskell programs and used for testing compilers. Developing a hand-written recursive generator for them requires the use of

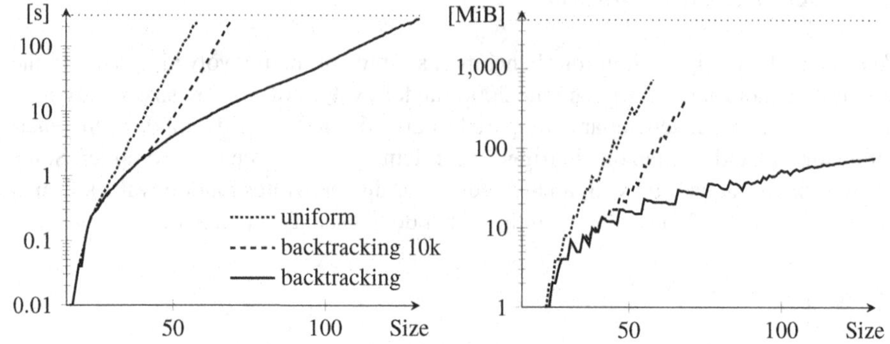

Fig. 2. Run times in (left) and memory consumption (right) of derived generators generating 2000 BSTs depending on the size of generated values

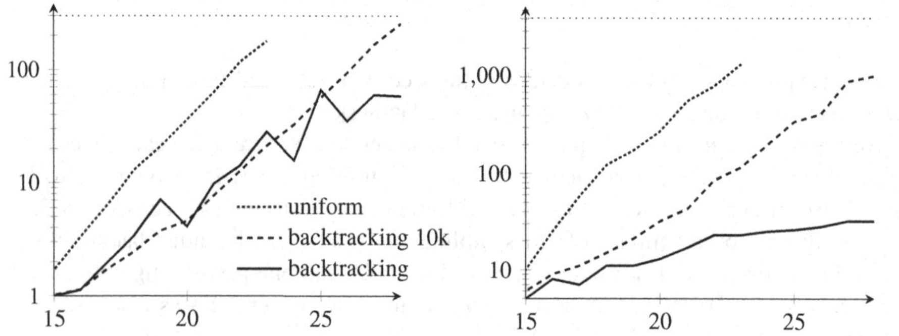

Fig. 3. Run times (left) and memory consumption (right) of derived generators generating 2000 simply-typed lambda terms depending on the size of generated terms

backtracking, because of the inability of predicting whether a given local choice can lead to a successful generation, and because typing constraints from two distant parts of a term can cause conflict. Achieving satisfactory distribution and performance requires careful tuning, and it is difficult to assess if any important values are severely underrepresented [9].

On the other hand, obtaining a generator that is based on our framework requires only the definitions from Fig. 1, and a relatively simple space definition, which we omit here. The code for the type checker is standard and uses a type stored in each application node (*tx* in *Ap f x tx*) to denote the type of the argument term for simplicity.

To evaluate the generators, we generated 2000 terms with a simple initial environment of 6 constants. The derived generator with three search strategies and one based on generate-and-filter were used. Fig. 3 shows the results. The uniform search strategy is capable of generating terms of size up to 23. For larger sizes, the generator exceeded the resource limits (300 s and 4 GiB, marked w/ dotted lines). The generator that used

Table 1. Performance of the reference hand-written term generator compared to a derived generator using backtracking with size 30. We compare the average number of terms that have to be generated before a counterexample (ctr ex.) is found, and how much CPU time the generation and testing consumes per found counterexample.

Generator	Hand-written	Derived (size 30)
Terms per ctr ex. (k)	18.6	52.5
Gen. CPU time per ctr ex. (min)	1.7	14.0
Test CPU time per ctr ex. (min)	1.8	10.4
Tot. CPU time per ctr ex. (min)	3.5	24.4

limited backtracking allowed generating terms up to size 28, using 9 times less CPU time and over 11 times less memory than the uniform one at size 23. Unlimited backtracking improved memory consumption dramatically, up to 30-fold, compared to limited backtracking. The run time is improved only slightly with unlimited backtracking. Finally, the generator based on generate-and-filter exceeded the run times for all sizes, and is not included in the plots.

4.3 Testing GHC

Discovering strictness bugs in the GHC optimising Haskell compiler was our prime reason for generating random simply-typed lambda terms. To evaluate our approach, we compared its bug finding power to a hand-written generator that had been developed before [9] using the same test property that had been used there.

Random simply-typed lambda terms were used for testing GHC by first generating type-correct Haskell modules containing the terms, and then using them as test data. In this case, we generated modules containing expressions of type $[\mathit{Int}] \rightarrow [\mathit{Int}]$ and compiled them with two different optimisation levels. Then, we tested their observable behaviour and compared them against each other, looking for discrepancies.

We implemented the generator using a similar data type as in Fig. 1 extended with polymorphic constants and type constructors. For efficiency reasons we avoided having types in term application constructors, and used a type checker based on type inference, which is more complex but still easily implementable. It allows generators to scale up to larger effective term sizes because not having types in the term representation increases the density of well-typed terms.

A generator based on this data type was capable of generating terms containing 30 term constructors, and was able to trigger GHC failures. Table 1 shows the results of testing GHC both with the hand-written simply-typed lambda term generator and our derived generator. The hand-written generator used for comparison generated terms of sizes from 0 to about 90, with most terms falling in the range of 20–50. It needed the least total CPU time to find a counterexample, and the lowest number of generated terms. The derived generator needs almost 7 times more CPU time per failure than the hand-written one.

Table 2. Maximum practical sizes of values generated by derived program generators that use unlimited backtracking and backtracking with cut-off of 10k

Predicates	Backtracking	Backtracking c/o
1, 2, 3, 4, 5	13	15
1, 3, 4, 5	13	30
1, 3, 5	31	30

The above results show that a generator derived from a predicate can be used to effectively find bugs in GHC. The derived generator is less effective than a hand-written one, but is significantly easier to develop. Developing an efficient type-checking predicate required for the derived generator took a few days, whereas the development and tuning of the hand-written generator took an order of months.

4.4 Programs

The *Program* benchmark is meant to simulate testing of a simple compiler by generating random programs, represented by the following data type.

type *Name* = *String*
data *Program* = *New Name Program* | *Name* := *Expr* | *Skip*
| *Program* :>> *Program* | *If Expr Program Program*
| *While Expr Program*
data *Expr* = *Var Name* | *Add Expr Expr*

The programs contain some common imperative constructs and declarations of new variables using *New*, which creates a new scope.

A compiler may perform a number of compilation passes, which would typically transform the program into some kind of normal form that may be required by the following pass. Our goal is to generate test data that satisfy the precondition in order to test the code of each pass separately. We considered 5 predicates on the program data type that model simple conditions that may be required by some compilation phases: (1) *boundProgram* saying that the program is well-scoped, (2) *usedProgram* saying that all bound variables are used, (3) *noLocalDecls* requiring all variables to be bound on the top level, (4) *noSkips* forbidding the redundant use of :>> and *Skip*, and (5) *noNestedIfs* forbidding nested *if* expressions.

Table 2 shows maximum value sizes that can be practically reached by the derived generators for the program data type with different combinations of predicates. All runs were generating 2000 random programs with resource limits (300 s and 4 GiB). When all predicates were used, the generators performed poorly being able to reach at most size 15. When the *usedProgram* predicate was omitted, the generator that uses limited backtracking improved considerably, whereas the one using unlimited backtracking remained at size 13. Removing the *noSkips* predicate turns the tables on the two generators improving the performance of the unlimited backtracking generator dramatically.

A generator based on generate-and-filter was also benchmarked, but did not terminate within the time limit for the sizes we tried.

4.5 Summary

All derived generators performed much better than ones based on generate-and-filter in three out of four benchmarks. In the fourth one, testing GHC, using a generator based on generate-and-filter was comparable to using our uniform or near-uniform derived generators, and slower than a derived generator using backtracking. In that benchmark the backtracking generator was the only that was able to find counterexamples, and yet it was less effective than a hand-written generator. However, as creating the derived generators was much quicker, we believe that they are still an attractive alternative to a hand-written generator.

The time and space overhead of the derived generators appeared to rise exponentially, or almost exponentially with the size of generated values in most cases we looked at, similarly to what can be seen in Figures 2 and 3.

In most cases the backtracking generator provided the best performance, which means that sometimes we may have to sacrifice our goal of having a predictable distribution. However, we found the backtracking generator to be very sensitive to the choice of the predicate. For example, some combinations of predicates in Section 4.4 destroyed its performance, while having less influence on the uniform and near-uniform generators. We hypothesise that this behaviour may be caused by regions of search space where the predicates evaluate values to a large extent before returning *False*. The backtracking search remain in such regions for a long time, in contrast to the other search that gives up and restarts after a number of values have been skipped.

Overall, the performance of the derived generators is practical for some applications, but reaching higher sizes of generated data might be needed for effective bug finding. In particular, being able to generate larger terms may improve the bug-finding performance when testing for GHC strictness bugs.

5 Related Work

Feat. Our representation of spaces and efficient indexing is based on FEAT (Functional Enumeration of Algebraic Types) [5]. The practicalities of computing cardinalities and the deterministic indexing functions are described there. The inability to deal with complex data type invariants is the major concern for FEAT, which is addressed by this paper.

Lazy SmallCheck and Korat. Lazy SmallCheck [10] uses laziness of predicates to get faster progress in an exhaustive depth-limited search. Our goal was to reach larger, potentially more useful values than Lazy SmallCheck by improving on it in two directions: using size instead of depth and allowing random search in sets that are too large to search exhaustively. Korat is a framework for testing Java programs [2]. It uses similar techniques to exhaustively generate size-bounded values that satisfy the precondition of a method, and then automatically check the result of the method for those values against a postcondition.

EasyCheck: Test Data For Free. EasyCheck is a library for generating random test data written in the Curry functional logic programming language [3]. Its generators define search spaces, which are enumerated using diagonalisation and randomising local choices. In this way values of larger sizes have a chance of appearing early in the enumeration, which is not the case when breadth-first search is used. The Curry language supports narrowing, which can be used by EasyCheck to generate values that satisfy a given predicate. The examples that are given in the paper suggest that, nonetheless, micro-management of the search space is needed to get a reasonable distribution. The authors point out that their enumeration technique has the problem of many very similar values being enumerated in the same run.

Metaheuristic Search. In the GödelTest [6] system, so-called metaheuristic search is used to find test cases that exhibit certain properties referred to as *bias objectives*. The objectives are expressed as fitness metrics for the search such as the mean height and width of trees, and requirements on several such metrics can be combined for a single search. It may be possible to write a GödelTest generator by hand for well typed lambda terms and then use bias objectives to tweak the distribution of values in a desired direction, which could then be compared to our work.

Lazy Nondeterminism. There is some recent work on embedding non-determinism in functional languages [7]. As a motivating example an *isSorted* predicate is used to derive a sorting function, a process which is quite similar to generating sorted lists from a predicate. The framework defined in [7] is very general and could potentially be used both for implementing SmallCheck style enumeration and for random generation.

Generating Lambda Terms. There are several other attempts at enumerating or generating well typed lambda terms. One such attempt uses generic programming to exhaustively enumerate lambda terms by size [11]. The description focuses mainly on the generic programming aspect, and the actual enumeration appears to be mainly proof of concept with very little discussion of the performance of the algorithm. There has been some work on counting lambda terms and generating them uniformly [8]. This includes generating well typed terms by a simple generate-and-filter approach.

6 Discussion

Performance of Limiting Backtracking. The performance of our generators depends on the strictness and evaluation order of the used predicate. The generator that performs unlimited backtracking was especially sensitive to the choice of predicate, as shown in Section 4.4. Similar effects have been observed in Korat [2], which also performs backtracking.

We found that for most predicates unbounded backtracking is the fastest. But unexpectedly, for some predicates imposing a bound on backtracking improves the run time of the generator. This also makes the distribution more predictable, at the cost of increased memory consumption. We found tweaking the degree of backtracking to be a useful tool for improving the performance of the generators, and possibly trading it for distribution guarantees.

In-place Refinement. We experimented with a more efficient mechanism for observing the evaluation order of predicates, which avoids repeated evaluation of the predicate. For that we use an indexing function that attaches a Haskell IO-action to each subcomponent of the generated value. When the predicate is applied to the value, the IO-actions will fire only for the parts that the property needs to inspect to determine the outcome. Whenever the indexing function is required to make a choice, the corresponding IO-action records the option it did not take, so after the predicate has finished executing the refined search space can be reconstructed. Guiding the evaluation order is handled automatically by the Haskell run time system, which has call-by-need built into it.

In-place refinement is somewhat more complicated than the procedure described in Section 3. Also, defining parallel conjunction for this type of refinement is difficult, because inspecting the result of a predicate irreversibly makes the choices required to compute the result. For this reason our implementation of in-place refinement remains a separate branch of development and a topic of future work.

Conclusion. Our method aims at preserving the simplicity of generate-and-filter type generators, but supporting more realistic predicates that accept only a small fraction of all values. This approach works well provided the predicates are lazy enough.

Our approach reduces the risk of having incorrect generators, as coming up with a correct predicate is usually much easier than writing a correct dedicated generator. Creating a predicate which leads to an efficient derived generator, on the other hand, is more difficult.

Even though performance remains an issue when generating large test cases, experimental results show that our approach is a viable option for generating test data in many realistic cases.

Acknowledgements. This research has been supported by the Resource-Aware Functional Programming (RAW FP) grant awarded by the Swedish Foundation for Strategic Research.

References

[1] Arts, T., et al.: Testing Telecoms Software with Quviq QuickCheck. In: Proc. 2006 Erlang Workshop, pp. 2–10. ACM (2006)

[2] Boyapati, C., Khurshid, S., Marinov, D.: Korat: Automated Testing Based on Java Predicates. In: Proc. 2002 Inl. Symp. Software Testing and Analysis (ISSTA 2002), pp. 123–133. ACM (2002)

[3] Christiansen, J., Fischer, S.: EasyCheck: test data for free. In: Garrigue, J., Hermenegildo, M.V. (eds.) FLOPS 2008. LNCS, vol. 4989, pp. 322–336. Springer, Heidelberg (2008)

[4] Claessen, K., Hughes, J.: QuickCheck: a lightweight tool for random testing of Haskell programs. In: ICFP 2000, pp. 268–279. ACM (2000)

[5] Duregard, J., Jansson, P., Wang, M.: FEAT: functional enumeration of algebraic types. In: Proc. 2012 Symp. Haskell, pp. 61–72. ACM (2012)
[6] Feldt, R., Poulding, S.: Finding Test Data with Specific Properties viaMetaheuristic Search. In: Proc. Intl. Symp. Software Reliability Engineering (ISSRE). IEEE (2013)
[7] Fischer, S., Kiselyov, O., Shan, C.C.: Purely functional lazy nondeterministic programming. J. Funct. Program. 21(4-5), 413–465 (2011)
[8] Grygiel, K., Lescanne, P.: Counting and generating lambda terms. J. Funct. Program. 23, 594–628 (2013)
[9] Palka, M.H.: Testing an Optimising Compiler by Generating Random Lambda Terms. Licentiate Thesis. Chalmers University of Technology, Gothenburg, Sweden (2012)
[10] Runciman, C., Naylor, M., Lindblad, F.: Smallcheck and lazy smallcheck: automatic exhaustive testing for small values. In: Haskell 2008, pp. 37–48. ACM (2008)
[11] Rodriguez Yakushev, A., Jeuring, J.: Enumerating Well-Typed Terms Generically. In: Schmid, U., Kitzelmann, E., Plasmeijer, R. (eds.) AAIP 2009. LNCS, vol. 5812, pp. 93–116. Springer, Heidelberg (2010)

Guided Type Debugging

Sheng Chen and Martin Erwig

Oregon State University,
Corvallis, USA
{chensh,erwig}@eecs.oregonstate.edu

Abstract. We present guided type debugging as a new approach to quickly and reliably remove type errors from functional programs. The method works by generating type-change suggestions that satisfy type specifications that are elicited from programmers during the debugging process. A key innovation is the incorporation of target types into the type error debugging process. Whereas previous approaches have aimed exclusively at the removal of type errors and disregarded the resulting types, guided type debugging exploits user feedback about result types to achieve better type-change suggestions. Our method can also identify and remove errors in type annotations, which has been a problem for previous approaches. To efficiently implement our approach, we systematically generate all potential type changes and arrange them in a lattice structure that can be efficiently traversed when guided by target types that are provided by programmers.

Keywords: Type debugging, type inference, error localization, type error messages, choice types, change suggestions.

1 Introduction

One beauty of the Hindley-Milner type system is the type inference mechanism that computes principal types for expressions without any type annotation. However, when type inference fails, it is often difficult to locate the origin of type errors and deliver precise feedback to the programmer. Despite numerous efforts devoted to improve type error diagnosis in past three decades [22,13,12,19,25], every proposed approach behaves poorly in certain situations.

A major problem for the localization and removal of type errors is the inherent ambiguity in this problem. For example, the type error in the expression `not 1` can be fixed by either replacing the function or the argument. Without any additional information it is not clear what the correct solution is. In such a situation type checkers that produce suggestions for how to fix a type error have to fall back on some form of heuristics [13,12,14,25,4] to select or rank their recommendations. These heuristics are often based on some complexity measure for suggestions (for example, prefer simple changes over complex ones), or they try to assess the likelihood of any particular suggestion. A problem with most of these approaches is that while they may work reasonably well in some cases, they can also go wrong and be misleading. This presents a problem since lack of precision in tools leads to distrust by users. Moreover, for novices it can add to confusion and frustration [12].

M. Codish and E. Sumii (Eds.): FLOPS 2014, LNCS 8475, pp. 35–51, 2014.

```
rev [] = []
rev (x:xs) = rev xs ++ x

last xs = head (rev xs)
init = rev . tail . rev

rR xs = last xs : init xs
```

```
last :: [[a]]->a
(1) Is intended type an instance? (y/n) n

... interactions (2) through (8) omitted

(++) (rev xs) :: [b]->[b]
rev :: a->[b]
xs :: a
(9) Are intended types an instance? (y/n) y
Error located. Wrong expression:
(rev xs) ++ x
```

Fig. 1. An ill-typed program (left) together with an interaction session between a user and an algorithmic debugging tool (right) [7]

As a partial solution to this problem programmers are advised to add type annotations to their program.[1] Type annotations can assist type checkers in producing better error messages, and they also enhance the readability of programs.[2]

However, type annotations are not without problems. In particular, too much trust in type annotations can have a negative impact on the precision of error localization. This happens when type annotations themselves are erroneous. A type checker that assumes that type annotations are always correct will not only miss the error in the annotation, but will also produce wrong error messages and misleading suggestions.

Incorrect type annotations are not a fringe phenomenon. Precisely because type annotations represent a useful form of redundancy in programs, they are widely used, and thus it may very well happen that, over time, they get out of sync with the rest of the program. This can happen, for example, when an annotation is not updated after its corresponding expression is changed or when another part of the program is changed so that it relies on a more generic form of an expression than expressed by the annotation. We have investigated a set of over 10,000 Haskell programs, which were written by students learning Haskell [10]. Of those, 1505 contained type errors (the remaining programs were well typed or contained parsing errors or unbound variables). We found that over 20% of the ill-typed programs contained wrong type annotations. We will discuss the impact of incorrect type annotations on type error messages in Section 5 in more depth.

We seem to face a dilemma now. To produce better feedback about type errors we have to rely on some form of user input, and information about the intended type of expressions is extremely helpful for this. At the same time, type annotations are not always reliable and sometimes even cause more problems. A solution is to elicit user input in a systematic and targeted manner. Specifically, we should ask for type information at the fewest number of possible places and where this information is most beneficial to our type debugger. This strategy ensures the availability of the latest up-to-date type information and avoids the potential problems with type annotations discussed earlier.

The idea of systematically eliciting user input for debugging (type) errors is not new [7,20]. To illustrate our approach and compare it with these previous systems we present

[1] `http://en.wikibooks.org/wiki/Haskell/Type_basics#Type_signatures_in_code`

[2] Type annotations can also improve the performance of type checkers. They also help make type inference decidable in richer type systems. A discussion of these aspects is beyond the scope of this paper.

```
What is the expected type of rR?
[a] -> [a]

Potential fixes:
1  change x from type a to type [a].
2  change ++
     from type [a] -> [a] -> [a]
     to type [a] -> a -> [a]
There are no other one-change fixes.
Show two-change fixes? (y/n)
```

```
What is the expected type of rR?
[[a]] -> [a]

Potential fixes:
1  change rev (in tail. rev)
     from type [[a]] -> [a] to type [a] -> [a]
2  change tail (in tail . rev)
     from type [a] -> [a] to type [a] -> [[a]]
Show more one-change fixes? (y/n)
```

Fig. 2. Guided Type Debugging. The target type for `rR` is `[a] -> [a]` (left) and `[[a]] -> [a]` (right). User inputs are shown in *italics*.

in Figure 1 an ill-typed program, taken from [7] (with some of the names changed). The error is attributed to the expression `rev xs ++ x`, and `x` should be replaced by `[x]`. We also show part of an interaction session between a user and the algorithmic debugger [7]. (Of the omitted seven questions, five are similar to `(1)`, asking questions about variables, whereas two are similar to `(9)`, asking questions about subexpressions and the relationships between their types.) The general strategy of this method is to systematically inquire about the correctness of each subexpression once an expression has been identified as ill typed (`rR` in the example). The first question is thus about the function `last`. If users respond "yes" to the question about a subexpression, then no more questions about that subexpression will be asked. Otherwise, the algorithmic debugger will switch the focus to that subexpression and ask questions about its subexpressions. From the debugging session, we can observe the following.

- The find the source of an error, the debugger has to work through chains of function calls and fragments of function definitions.
- The debugger interacts with users in typing jargon. Moreover, users have to track and connect information when the same type variable appears at different places (as, for example, the type variable `a` in the types for `rev` and `xs`).
- The length of a debugging trace depends on the distance between the origin of a type error and where it manifests itself. This distance can be large.
- The type debugger works in a linear fashion, and it is unclear how to support cases in which there is more than one type error.
- The final change suggestion delivered by the debugger still leaves some work for users to figure out what exactly the cause of the type error is and how to fix it.

The interactive type debugger [20] follows the same strategy and thus suffers from similar problems. We argue that even with the assistance of such debuggers, locating and removing type errors is still a nontrivial and arduous task.

In contrast, the guided type debugging (GTD) approach developed in this paper asks programmers to provide simple type signatures only. Moreover, most of the time, only one signature is needed to lead to a suggestion for how to fix the type error. More specifically, for a single expression, exactly one signature is needed. For a program with multiple function definitions and expressions containing type errors, we have to distinguish between several cases. First, if only one expression is ill typed, GTD solicits a type annotation for that expression. In case there are more expressions that are ill typed, GTD asks for a type annotation for the first ill-typed expression. In case the program still contains ill-typed expressions after the user has fixed the first one, GTD again asks for a type annotation for the next ill-typed expression. This process repeats until the whole program becomes well typed. Note that the expression for which GTD requests a type annotation is not necessarily the cause of the type error, and GTD will point to the most likely cause of the type error in the program.

Figure 2 shows two examples. Here the debugger first asks the programmer for the intended type of the ill-typed expression `rR`. If the target type is `[a] -> [a]`, the debugger infers that there are exactly two potential suggestions with only one change to the program. The first suggestions is to change `x`, whose inferred type is `a`, to something of type `[a]`. The second suggestion is to change `++` of type `[a] -> [a] -> [a]` to something of type `[a] -> a -> [a]`. There are, of course, other changes that can lead the expression `rR` to the target type, but each such suggestion requires changes in at least two places. (The right half of Figure 2 shows the suggestions in case the target type is `[[a]] -> [a]`.)

With a user interface, we can envision a more flexible way of how GTD may be used. First, GTD type checks the program and marks all expressions that are ill typed. The user can go to any expression and specify the intended result type. GTD will then suggest a most likely change that satisfies the user's intention. Note that the user may even specify an intended type for a well-typed expression. For example, if the user specifies `[[a]] -> [[a]]` as an expected type for `foldr (:) []`, which is well typed, GTD will suggest to change `(:)` of type `a -> [a] -> [a]` to something of type `[a] -> [a] -> [a]`.

In summary, GTD will ask programmers significantly fewer questions than algorithmic type debugging. GDT will then work out the details and show exact change locations and suggestions. Moreover, GTD supports changes involving multiple locations.

To work as indicated, the GTD method has to find all potential changes that can in principle fix a particular type error. Moreover, it must be able to select among all changes those that satisfy the user-provided intended types of expressions. At the same time, all these tasks have to be done efficiently.

We employ counter-factual typing [4] (CF typing for short) to realize the first task. CF typing computes all potential type changes for fixing type errors by typing expressions once. For each change, it returns the information about change locations, the expected type for each location, and the result type of applying the change. We describe the concept of variational types as the underlying representation in Section 2 and the method of CF typing in Section 3.

To implement the second task efficiently, we exploit the instance-of relationship among result types of change suggestions. Specifically, we can arrange all changes in a lattice because changes involving more locations always produce more general result types than changes involving fewer locations. Given a user-provided target type, we can search through this lattice efficiently and narrow down the set of changes to a manageable size. We describe the idea of type-change lattices and how they can help to find good type-change suggestions in Section 4.

The question of how GTD can deal with erroneous type annotations is discussed in Section 5. Section 6 discusses related work, and Section 7 concludes the paper.

2 Representing Type Errors by Variational Types

A type error results when the rules of a type system require an expression to have two conflicting (that is, non-unifiable) types. This happens, for example, when a function is applied to an argument of the wrong type or when branches of a conditional have different types. One of the simplest examples of a type error is a conflicting type annotation, as in the expression $e = $ `3::Bool`. Now the problem for a type checker is to decide whether to consider the annotation or the type of the value to be correct. Without any further information this is impossible to know. Therefore, we should defer this decision until more context information is available that indicates which one of the two is more compatible with the context.

To represent conflicting type for expressions we employ the concept of *choice types* [6]. A choice type $D\langle\phi_1,\phi_2\rangle$ has a *dimension* D and contains two alternative types ϕ_1 and ϕ_2. For example, we can express the uncertainty about the type of the expression e with the choice type $D\langle\texttt{Int},\texttt{Bool}\rangle$. Choice types may be combined with other type constructors to build *variational types*, in which choices may be nested within type expressions, as in $D\langle\texttt{Int},\texttt{Bool}\rangle \rightarrow \texttt{Int}$.

We can eliminate choices using a selection operation, which is written as $\lfloor\phi\rfloor_s$. Here ϕ is a variational type, and s is a *selector*, which is of form $D.1$ or $D.2$. Selection replaces all occurrences of $D\langle\phi_1,\phi_2\rangle$ with its ith alternative. Choice types with different dimensions are independent of one another and require separate selections to be eliminated, whereas those with the same dimension are synchronized and are eliminated by the same selection. For example, $A\langle\texttt{Int},\texttt{Bool}\rangle \rightarrow A\langle\texttt{Bool},\texttt{Int}\rangle$ encodes two function types, but $A\langle\texttt{Int},\texttt{Bool}\rangle \rightarrow B\langle\texttt{Bool},\texttt{Int}\rangle$ encodes four function types. We use δ to range over decisions, which are sets of selectors (usually represented as lists). The selection operation extends naturally to decisions through $\lfloor\phi\rfloor_{s:\delta} = \lfloor\lfloor\phi\rfloor_s\rfloor_\delta$. In this paper, when we select δ from a type ϕ, we assume that selection eliminates all choices in ϕ.

The idea of CF typing is to systematically generate all changes (for variables and constants) that could fix a type inconsistency. Each such change is represented as a choice between the current and the new type. In the example, the choice type $A\langle\texttt{Int},\alpha_1\rangle$ is created for `3`.[3] The first alternative denotes the current type of `3`, and the second alternative denotes a type that can make `3` well typed within its context. We can think of the first alternative as the type `3` should have when it is not the cause of type errors and the second alternative as the type `3` ought to have when it is. Similarly, the annotation `Bool` may also be the cause of the type error. We thus create the choice type $B\langle\texttt{Bool},\alpha_2\rangle$, which says that if the type annotation is correct, it has the type `Bool`, otherwise it has the type α_2, an arbitrary type that makes the context well typed.

But what should be the type of e? Usually, when we have two sources of type information for one expression, we unify the two types. Thus we would expect the unification result of $A\langle\texttt{Int},\alpha_1\rangle$ and $B\langle\texttt{Bool},\alpha_2\rangle$ to be the result type of e. However, the two choice types are not unifiable because `Bool` and `Int` fail to unify. (This is not surprising since the expression contains a type error.)

[3] One might wonder why a type variable is chosen and not just the type `Bool`. The reason is that when we are typing `3`, we have no knowledge about its context yet. We thus use α_1 to allow it to acquire any type that its context dictates.

We address this problem through the introduction of *error types* [5], written as $\bot$, to represent non-unifiable parts of choice types. Specifically, we have developed a unification algorithm that computes a substitution for two variational types that is (a) most general and (b) introduces as few error types as possible. Because of the possibility of error types we call such substitutions *partial unifiers*. For the two types $A\langle \texttt{Int}, \alpha_1\rangle$ and $B\langle \texttt{Bool}, \alpha_2\rangle$, the algorithm computes the following partial unifier.

$$\theta = \{\alpha_1 \mapsto A\langle \alpha_4, B\langle \texttt{Bool}, \alpha_3\rangle\rangle, \alpha_2 \mapsto B\langle \alpha_5, A\langle \texttt{Int}, \alpha_3\rangle\rangle\}$$

The algorithm also computes a *typing pattern* that captures the choice structure of the result type and represents, using error types, those variants that would lead to a type error. In our example, the typing pattern is $\pi = A\langle B\langle \bot, \top\rangle, \top\rangle$. It indicates that the types at $\lfloor A.1, B.1\rfloor$ fail to unify ($\bot$) and all other variants unify successfully ($\top$). The typing pattern is used to mask the result type that can be obtained from the partial unifier. From θ and π we obtain the type $\phi = A\langle B\langle \bot, \texttt{Int}\rangle, B\langle \texttt{Bool}, \alpha_3\rangle\rangle$ for e. Finally, from θ and ϕ we can derive following changes to potentially eliminate the type error in e.

- If we don't change e, that is, if we select $\lfloor A.1, B.1\rfloor$ from ϕ, there is a type error.
- If we change `3` but don't change the annotation `Bool`, that is, if we select $\delta = \lfloor A.2, B.1\rfloor$ from ϕ, we get the type `Bool`. Moreover, by selecting δ from $\theta(\alpha_1)$, we get `Bool`, which is the type that `3` should to be changed to.
- If we change the annotation `Bool` but don't change `3`, that is, if we select $\delta = \lfloor A.1, B.2\rfloor$ from ϕ, we get the result type `Int`. Moreover, by selecting δ from $\theta(\alpha_2)$ we get `Int` as the type the annotation `Bool` ought to be changed to.
- If we change both `3` and `Bool`, that is, if we select $\lfloor A.2, B.2\rfloor$ from ϕ, we get a more general type α_3. This means that e can be changed to some arbitrary value of any type. Note that α_3 will be very likely refined to a more concrete type if e occurs as a subexpression within some other context.

3 Counter-Factual Typing

In this section we describe the CF typing method [4], extended to handle type annotations. We work with the following syntax for expressions and types.

Expressions	e, f	::=	$c \mid x \mid \lambda x.e \mid e\ e \mid \texttt{let}\ x = e\ \texttt{in}\ e \mid e :: \tau$
Monotypes	τ	::=	$\gamma \mid \alpha \mid \tau \to \tau$
Variational types	ϕ	::=	$\tau \mid \bot \mid D\langle \phi, \phi\rangle \mid \phi \to \phi$
Type schemas	σ	::=	$\phi \mid \forall \overline{\alpha}.\phi$
Choice environments	Δ	::=	$\varnothing \mid \Delta, (l, D\langle \phi, \phi\rangle)$

We use c, γ, and α to range over value constants, type constants, and type variables, respectively. We have seen error types $\bot$ and choice types $D\langle \phi, \phi\rangle$ in Section 2. To simplify the discussion, we assume that type annotations are monotypes. However, this will not limit the expressiveness of the type system. We use η to denote substitutions mapping from type variables to variational types. We use the special symbol θ to denote substitutions that are partial unifiers. We use Γ to store the type assumptions about variables and treat Γ as a stack.

$$\textsc{Con}\ \frac{c \text{ is of type } \gamma \qquad D \text{ fresh}}{\Gamma \vdash c : D\langle \gamma, \phi \rangle | \{(\ell(c), D\langle \gamma, \phi \rangle)\}}$$

$$\textsc{Var}\ \frac{\Gamma(x) = \forall \overline{\alpha}.\phi_1 \qquad D \text{ fresh} \qquad \phi = \{\overline{\alpha \mapsto \phi'}\}(\phi_1)}{\Gamma \vdash x : D\langle \phi, \phi_2 \rangle | \{(\ell(x), D\langle \phi, \phi_2 \rangle)\}}$$

$$\textsc{Unbound}\ \frac{x \notin dom(\Gamma) \qquad D \text{ fresh}}{\Gamma \vdash x : D\langle \bot, \phi \rangle | \{(\ell(x), D\langle \bot, \phi \rangle)\}}$$

$$\textsc{Ant}\ \frac{\Gamma \vdash e : \phi_1 | \Delta \qquad D \text{ fresh} \qquad \phi_2 = D\langle \tau, \phi' \rangle \qquad \pi_1 = \phi_1 \bowtie \phi_2 \qquad \phi_3 = \pi_1 \lhd \phi_1}{\Gamma \vdash (e :: \tau) : \phi_3 | \Delta \cup \{(\ell(\tau), \phi_2)\}}$$

$$\textsc{Abs}\ \frac{\Gamma, x \mapsto \phi \vdash e : \phi' | \Delta}{\Gamma \vdash \lambda x.e : \phi \to \phi' | \Delta}$$

$$\textsc{Let}\ \frac{\Gamma, x \mapsto \phi \vdash e : \phi | \Delta \qquad \overline{\alpha} = FV(\phi) - FV(\Gamma) \qquad \Gamma, x \mapsto \forall \overline{\alpha}.\phi \vdash e' : \phi' | \Delta'}{\Gamma \vdash \mathtt{let}\ x = e\ \mathtt{in}\ e' : \phi' | \Delta \cup \Delta'}$$

$$\textsc{App}\ \frac{\Gamma \vdash e_1 : \phi_1 | \Delta_1 \qquad \Gamma \vdash e_2 : \phi_2 | \Delta_2 \qquad \phi_2' \to \phi' = \uparrow(\phi_1) \qquad \pi = \phi_2' \bowtie \phi_2 \qquad \phi = \pi \lhd \phi'}{\Gamma \vdash e_1\ e_2 : \phi | \Delta_1 \cup \Delta_2}$$

Fig. 3. Rules for counter-factual typing

We use FV to denote free type variables in types, type schemas, and typing environments. The application of a substitution to a type schema, written as $\eta(\sigma)$, replaces free type variables in σ with the bindings in η. For presentation purposes, we assume we can determine the location of any given f in e with the function $\ell_e(f)$; the exact definition doesn't matter here. We may drop the subscript e when the context is clear.

We show the typing rules in Figure 3. The typing relation $\Gamma \vdash e : \phi | \Delta$ expresses that under the assumptions in Γ the expression e has the result type ϕ. All choice types that were generated during the typing process are stored (together with their locations) in Δ. Note that, due to the presence of choice types, the result type ϕ represents a whole set of possible result types that may be obtained by changing the types of certain parts of the expression. The information about what change leads to what type can be recovered from ϕ and Δ. For example, in the case of `3::Bool` we obtain the typing

$$\varnothing \vdash (\mathtt{3::Bool}) : A\langle B\langle \bot, \mathtt{Int} \rangle, B\langle \mathtt{Bool}, \alpha_3 \rangle \rangle | \Delta$$
$$\text{where } \Delta = \{\ell(\mathtt{3}) \mapsto A\langle \mathtt{Int}, B\langle \mathtt{Bool}, \alpha_3 \rangle \rangle, \ell(\mathtt{Bool}) \mapsto B\langle \mathtt{Bool}, A\langle \mathtt{Int}, \alpha_3 \rangle \rangle\}$$

We create choices in rules Con, Var, Unbound, and Ant. The first alternative of each choice contains the type under normal typing, and the second alternative contains any type to enable a change that is as general as the context allows. In rules Abs, Let, and App, we collect generated choices from the typing of its subexpressions.

Most of the typing rules are self-explanatory. As one example let us consider the typing rule Ant for type annotations in more detail since it is new and introduces two operations that are crucial for typing applications. To type an expression $e::\tau$ we have to reconcile the inferred type ϕ_1 and the choice type ϕ_2 created for the annotation τ into one result type for e, which is achieved by using a common type ϕ_3. For the variants where ϕ_1 and ϕ_2 agree, ϕ_3 has the same type as ϕ_1. For other variants, ϕ_3 contains the error types $\perp$s. We use operations $\bowtie$ and $\lhd$ to realize this process.

The operation $\bowtie$ computes how well two types match each other. We use typing patterns introduced in Section 2 to formalize this notion.

$$\begin{aligned} \phi \bowtie \phi &= \top & D\langle\phi_1,\phi_2\rangle \bowtie D\langle\phi_3,\phi_4\rangle &= D\langle\phi_1 \bowtie \phi_3, \phi_2 \bowtie \phi_4\rangle \\ \perp \bowtie \phi &= \perp & D\langle\phi_1,\phi_2\rangle \bowtie \phi &= D\langle\phi_1 \bowtie \phi, \phi_2 \bowtie \phi\rangle \\ \phi \bowtie \perp &= \perp & \phi \bowtie D\langle\phi_1,\phi_2\rangle &= D\langle\phi_1 \bowtie \phi, \phi_2 \bowtie \phi\rangle \\ \phi \bowtie \phi' &= \perp & \phi_1 \to \phi_2 \bowtie \phi_1' \to \phi_2' &= (\phi_1 \bowtie \phi_1') \otimes (\phi_2 \bowtie \phi_2') \end{aligned}$$

Note that the definition contains overlapping cases and assumes that more specific cases are applied before more general ones. The matching of two plain types either succeeds with $\top$ or fails with $\perp$, depending on whether they have the same syntactic representation. Matching two choice types with the same choice name reduces to a matching of corresponding alternatives. Matching a type with some choice type reduces to the matching of that type with both alternatives in the choice type.

The matching of two arrow types is more involved. For a variant to be matched successfully, both the corresponding argument types and result types of that variant have to be matched successfully. The $\otimes$ operation captures this idea. The definition can be interpreted as defining a logical "and" operation by viewing $\top$ as "true" and $\perp$ as "false". For example, when computing $\texttt{Int} \to A\langle\texttt{Bool},\texttt{Int}\rangle \bowtie B\langle\texttt{Int},\perp\rangle \to \texttt{Bool}$, we first obtain $B\langle\top,\perp\rangle$ and $A\langle\top,\perp\rangle$ for matching the argument and return types, respectively. Next, we use $\otimes$ to derive the final result as $A\langle B\langle\top,\perp\rangle,\perp\rangle$. From the result, we know that only matching the first alternative of A and first alternative of B will succeed.

$$\top \otimes \pi = \pi \qquad \perp \otimes \pi = \perp \qquad D\langle\phi_1,\phi_2\rangle \otimes \pi = D\langle\phi_1 \otimes \pi, \phi_2 \otimes \pi\rangle$$

The masking operation $\pi \lhd \phi$ replaces all occurrences of $\top$ in π with ϕ and leaves all occurrences of $\perp$ unchanged. It is defined as follows [5].

$$\perp \lhd \phi = \perp \qquad \top \lhd \phi = \phi \qquad D\langle\pi_1,\pi_2\rangle \lhd \phi = D\langle\pi_1 \lhd \phi, \pi_2 \lhd \phi\rangle$$

To type function applications in App, we need a further operation $\uparrow(\phi)$ to turn ϕ into an arrow type when possible and introduce error types when necessary. We need this operation because the type of an expression may be a choice between two function types, in which case we have to factor arrows out of choices. For example, given $(\texttt{succ}, \texttt{Int} \to \texttt{Int}) \in \Gamma$, we can derive $\Gamma \vdash \texttt{succ} : \phi|\Delta$ with $\phi = D\langle\texttt{Int} \to \texttt{Int}, \texttt{Int} \to \texttt{Bool}\rangle$ and $\Delta = \{(\ell(\texttt{succ}), \phi)\}$. Thus, we have to turn ϕ into $D\langle\texttt{Int},\texttt{Int}\rangle \to D\langle\texttt{Int},\texttt{Bool}\rangle$ if we apply `succ` to some argument.

We can observe that the rules Con, Var, Unbound, and Ant introduce arbitrary types in the second alternative of result types. Thus, given e and Γ we have an infinite number of typings for e.

The following theorem expresses that there is a best typing (in the sense that it produces most general types with the fewest number of type errors) and that this is the only typing we need to care about. To compare the relation between different typings, we assume the same location at different typings generate the same fresh choice, and we write $\phi_1 \sqsubseteq \phi_2$ if there is some η such that $\eta(\phi_1) = \phi_2$.

Theorem 1 (Most general and most defined typing). *Given e and Γ, there is a unique best typing $\Gamma \vdash e : \phi_1|\Delta_1$ such that for any other typing $\Gamma \vdash e : \phi_2|\Delta_2$, $\forall\delta$: $(\lfloor\phi_1\rfloor_\delta = \bot \Rightarrow \lfloor\phi_2\rfloor_\delta = \bot) \vee \lfloor\phi_1\rfloor_\delta \sqsubseteq \lfloor\phi_2\rfloor_\delta$.*

In [4] we have presented a type inference algorithm that is sound, complete, and computes the most general result type (that is, at least as general as the result type of the best typing).

4 Climbing the Type-Change Lattice

The idea of guided type debugging is to narrow down the number of suggestions for how to remove a type error based on targeted user input. More specifically, given an ill-typed expression e for which CF typing has produced the variational type ϕ and the location information about changes Δ, we elicit from the programmer a target type τ and then want to identify the changes from ϕ and Δ that cause e to have type τ.

However, if the inference process produces a set of n choices with dimensions $\mathcal{D}$, which means that n potential changes have been identified, it seems that we have to check all 2^n combinations to find the right combination of changes that has the desired property. Fortunately, the structure of ϕ reveals some properties that we can exploit to significantly reduce the complexity of this process.

First, some of the created choices may not be needed at all. As the rules in Figure 3 show, the second alternative of created choice types can be any type. In many cases the best typing requires the second alternative to be identical to the first alternative, which means that no change is required. For example, when typing the expression `succ 1 + True`, the choice created for `1` is always $B\langle$`Int`$,$ `Int`$\rangle$. Thus, we can remove choice B.

However, even after removing such non-relevant choices, the search space can still be exponential in the number of remaining choices. We can address this problem by searching, in a systematic way, only through some of the changes. To do this, we conceptually arrange all sets of changes in a *type-change lattice* (TCL). Note that we don't ever actually construct this lattice; it is a conceptual entity that helps to explain the algorithm for identifying type-change suggestions guided by a user-provided target type.

Each node in the lattice is identified by a subset of dimensions $C \subseteq \mathcal{D}$ that indicates which changes to apply, and each C determines a decision δ_C, defined as follows.

$$\delta_C = \{D.2 \mid D \in C\} \cup \{D.1 \mid D \in \mathcal{D} - C\}$$

With δ_C we can determine the result type for e by $\lfloor\phi\rfloor_{\delta_C}$ for the case when the changes indicated by C are to be applied. Usually, we attach $\lfloor\phi\rfloor_{\delta_C}$ to the node C in TCLs.

A TCL comprises $n+1$ levels, where level k contains an entry for each combination of k individual changes. The bottom of this lattice (level 0) consists of a single node $\varnothing$, which produces the result type $\lfloor\phi\rfloor_{\delta_\varnothing} = \bot$. Level 1 consists of n entries, one for each single change $D \in \mathcal{D}$. The next level consists of all two-element subsets of $\mathcal{D}$, and so on The top-most level has one entry $\mathcal{D}$, which represents the decision to apply all changes. We show three example TCLs in Figure 4.

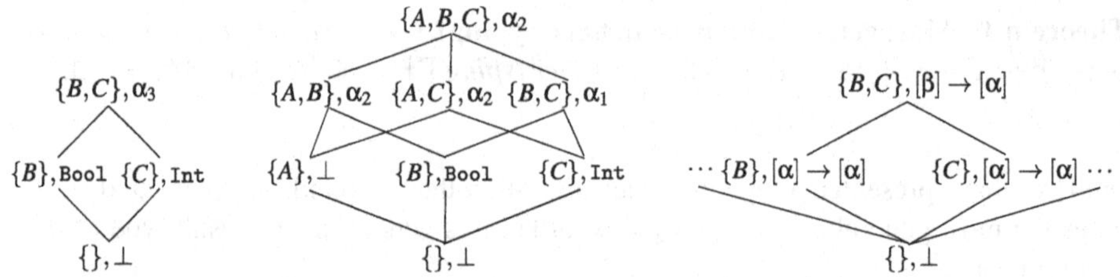

Fig. 4. Type-change lattices for the expressions `3::Bool` (left), `id (3::Bool)` (middle), and `rR` (right). The function `id` is assumed to have the type $\alpha_1 \to \alpha_1$, which could be a cause of the type error and thus a choice type is created for `id`. For the second example, the dimensions A, B, and C represent the changes for `id`, `3`, and `Bool`, respectively. For the `rR` example, B and C are created for locations `x` and `(++)`, respectively.

To find a change suggestion we traverse the TCL in a breadth-first manner from the bottom up.[4] For each entry C under consideration we check whether the type produced by it covers the target type as a generic instance, that is, $\lfloor\phi\rfloor_{\delta_C} \sqsubseteq \tau$. Once we have found such an entry, we can present the programmer with a corresponding suggestion. In case there are several suggestions with k changes that satisfy the condition, we employ the heuristics developed in CF typing [4] to order them and present them to programmers in this order. If the programmer selects a suggested change, we're done. Otherwise, we continue the search by including the next level in the lattice and offer suggestions with one more change.

We illustrate how the algorithm works with the two earlier examples e = `3::Bool` and `rR` (recall Figures 1 and 2). The TCLs are shown in Figure 4. Expression e is trivial since the algorithm will ask the user for the type of this expression and correspondingly suggest to either change the value or the annotation. To make this example more interesting, consider the slightly more general expression `id (3::Bool)`. For this expression, CF typing produces the following result, and the TCL is in the middle of Figure 4.

$$\begin{aligned}
\phi &= A\langle B\langle C\langle\bot,\texttt{Int}\rangle, C\langle\texttt{Bool},\alpha_1\rangle\rangle, B\langle C\langle\bot,\alpha_2\rangle,\alpha_2\rangle\rangle \\
\Delta &= \{(\ell(\texttt{id}), A\langle\alpha_1\to\alpha_1, B\langle\texttt{Int}\to\alpha_2, C\langle\texttt{Bool}\to\alpha_2,\alpha_3\to\alpha_2\rangle\rangle\rangle) \\
&\quad (\ell(\texttt{3}), B\langle\texttt{Int}, C\langle\texttt{Bool}, A\langle\alpha_1,\alpha_3\rangle\rangle\rangle) \\
&\quad (\ell(\texttt{Bool}), C\langle\texttt{Bool}, B\langle\texttt{Int}, A\langle\alpha_1,\alpha_3\rangle\rangle\rangle)\}
\end{aligned}$$

Suppose the user-provided target type is `Bool`. The first of the changes on level 1 ($\{A\},\bot$) will be dismissed since the application of change A cannot remove the type error. Since the result type of the next entry ($\{B\}$,`Bool`) matches exactly the target type, this change will be suggested. We will look at the third entry as well, but it is dismissed since the target type `Bool` is not an instance of the result type `Int` for that entry. Thus, we will present the suggestion of change B (that is, location ℓ(`3`)) to the programmer. From Δ we infer that the place should be changed to something of type `Bool`. Thus, the generated suggestion is to change `3` from type `Int` to type `Bool`.

[4] Again, the algorithm for finding change suggestions constructs part of this lattice on the fly as needed. The lattice is not represented explicitly.

If this suggestion is accepted, the debugger terminates. If, however, the programmer asks for more suggestions, we check change suggestions in two steps. First, we remove all the nodes in the lattice that are above the node that produced the previous suggestion. In this example, we remove all the nodes in the lattice above $\{B\}$ because the programmer doesn't want to apply any change that includes the B change, yielding a smaller lattice with only four nodes. Then we continue the search on the higher level. In this case the only node that remains on the second level is $(\{A,C\},\alpha_2)$. To get the result `Bool`, we derive the substitution $\eta = \{\alpha_2 \mapsto \texttt{Bool}\}$. By selecting $[A.2,B.1,C.2]$ from the variational type $\Delta(\ell(\texttt{id}))$, we derive that `id` should be changed from type $\alpha_1 \to \alpha_1$ to something of type $\eta(\texttt{Int} \to \alpha_2)$, which is $\texttt{Int} \to \texttt{Bool}$. By making the same selection $[A.2,B.1,C.2]$ from $\Delta(\ell(\texttt{Bool}))$, we derive that `Bool` should be changed to `Int`.

For the example `rR` we apply the same strategy. If the programmer provides the target type `[a] -> [a]`, only two of the 13 entries on level 1 qualify since their result types can be instantiated to the target type.

Despite the exponential size that TCLs can have in the worst-case and the corresponding worst-case time complexity to explore TCLs exhaustively, GTD search turns out to be very efficient in almost all cases for the following reasons.

- The change suggestions to be presented first will be encountered and found first during the search process.
- If a presented suggestion is rejected by the programmer, the lattice can be trimmed down by removing all the nodes higher in the lattice that are reachable from the node representing the rejected suggestion.
- The lattice narrows quickly toward the top since after a few layers the result types tend to become free type variables, which can be unified with the user-provided target type successfully, ending the search.

The first point is substantiated by following theorem, which states that generality of result types increases with the number of changes. We want to find suggestions that consist of as few as possible changes and whose result type is closest to the target type. This theorem ensures that when we traverse a TCL from the bottom up, we will encounter changes that have fewest locations first.

Theorem 2 (More change locations lead to more general types). *Given the best typing* $\Gamma \vdash e : \phi|\Delta$, *if* $C_1 \subseteq C_2$, *then* $\lfloor\phi\rfloor_{\delta_{C_2}} \sqsubseteq \lfloor\phi\rfloor_{\delta_{C_1}}$.

Proof. The proof is shown in Appendix A.

Guided type debugging can improve the precision of suggesting type changes for ill-typed programs at a low cost. We have tested the method and compared it with CF typing on 86 programs, which were collected from 22 publications (see [4] for details). Since many programs we collected were written in ML [9] and in OCaml [14], we have translated them into the programs written in the calculus presented in the paper plus operations stored in the initial type environment. The following table shows the percentage of the programs a correct change suggestion could be provided for after n attempts. In all cases in which GTD helped to remove the type error, only one target type had to be supplied.

Method	No. of Attempts				
	1	2	3	≥ 4	never
CF Typing	67%	80%	88%	92%	8%
GTD	83%	90%	92%	92%	8%

With GTD we can now find the correct suggestions with the first attempt in 83% of the cases. We can fix 90% of the cases with at most two attempts. At the same time GTD adds never more than 0.5 seconds to the computing time.

5 Reporting Type Errors in Type Annotations

We use following example, which was written by a student learning Haskell [10], to compare the behaviors of different tools on reporting type errors in type annotations. We copied the code literally except for removing the type definition of `Table`, which is `[[String]]` and the definition of the function `collength`, whose type is `Table->Int`. Both are irrelevant to the type error.

```
buildcol :: Table->[String]
buildcol [] = [""]
buildcol (x:xs) = [" " ++ (replicate n '-')," " ++ (spaceout n (head x))]
                  where n = collength (x:xs)

spaceout :: String->String
spaceout n str = str ++ replicate (n-(length str)) ' '
```

The type annotation of `spaceout` contains one argument, but the function definition has two arguments. Based on the same student's follow-up programs we know that the annotation is incorrect. Note that this is also the only type error in the program because removal of the type annotation of `spaceout` restores type correctness of the program.

For this program, the Glasgow Haskell Compiler (GHC) 7.6.3 reports the following four type errors. The first two point to the use of `spaceout` in `buildcol`, and the other two point to the definition of `spaceout`.

- The first blames that `spaceout` is applied to two arguments while it takes only one.
- The second complains that the first argument type of `spaceout` should be `String`, but something of `Int` is given.
- The third reports that the definition of `spaceout` has two arguments while its type has only one.
- The fourth complains that `n` is of type `String`, but it should have type `Int` because it is used as the first argument to the operation `-`.

GHC reports these errors because it always trusts type annotations, and it pushes down type information from type annotations to expressions. In the definition `spaceout`, the parameters `n` and `str` both get the type `String`. When type annotation is correct, this scheme makes type checking more efficient and helps make type inference decidable [18]. However, when type annotation is incorrect, this leads to poor error messages.

Helium[5], a research tool with high quality error messages developed to assist students in learning Haskell, reports two type errors. The first reported error is similar to GHC's first error message. Moreover, Helium suggests to remove the first argument. Helium's second error message is almost the same as GHC's third message, blaming the definition of `spaceout`, but not the annotation. Type annotations were not supported in CF typing [4].

In contrast to previous tools, our guided type debugger is the first approach that can find errors in type annotations. In this example it directly suggests to change the type annotation `String -> String` to `Int -> String -> String`, which fixes all type errors in the program.

6 Related Work

The challenge of accurately reporting type errors and producing helpful error messages has received considerable attention in the research community. Improvements for type inference algorithms have been proposed that are based on changing the order of unification, suggesting program fixes, interactive debugging, and using program slicing techniques to find all program locations involved in type errors. We will focus our discussion on debugging and change-suggesting approaches. Since this problem has been extensively studied, summaries of the work in this area are also available elsewhere [12,23,24,15,4].

The idea of debugging type errors was first proposed by Bernstein and Stark [2]. Their work was based on the observation that type inference is able to infer types for unbound variables, which allows programmers to replace suspicious program fragments with unbound variables. If a replacement leads to a type correct program, the type errors have been located. The original work requires programmers to manually locate suspicious fragments and replace them with unbound variables. Braßel [3] has later automated this process.

By employing the idea of algorithmic debugging developed in debugging Prolog errors, Chitil [7] proposed an approach for debugging type errors. Chitil developed principal typing, where type inference is fully compositional by inferring also type assumptions, for building explanation graphs. Each node is a combination of the typings of its children. The idea of algorithmic debugging is to navigate through the graphs and ask questions about the correctness of each node. Each question is of form "Is the intended type of a specific function an instance of the type inferred?", and programmers will respond "yes" or "no". In Chameleon, Stuckey at al. [20,21] presented a debugging approach that is similar to algorithmic debugging. Chameleon also allows programmers to ask why an expression has a certain type. There are other tools that don't allow user inputs but allow programmers to navigate through the programs and view their types, such as Typeview [8] and the Haskell Type Browser [17].

While previous debugging approaches are operational in the sense that programmers have to be involved in the details of the debugging process, our approach is more declarative in the sense programmers only have to specify the intended result type. Moreover, we provide more precise change suggestions, such as the change location and the types

[5] `http://www.cs.uu.nl/wiki/bin/view/Helium/WebHome`

expressions should be changed to. Moreover, in some cases we can be even more specific and suggest specific program edit actions, such as swapping function arguments (see [4] for some examples). In contrast, previous approaches can only locate a program fragment or a set of possible places as the cause of type errors, and thus often leave much work for programmers after the debugging is finished.

Researchers have paid considerable attention to the problem of making change suggestions when type inference fails. For such methods to work, however, the most likely error location has to be determined. Since there is seldom enough information to make this decision, approaches have resorted to various kinds of heuristics. For example, in the earliest work along this line, Johnson and Walz [13] used a heuristic of "usage voting", that is, when a variable has to be unified with many different types, the variable is chosen to have the type that is unified most often. Locations that require that variable to have a different type are then reported as problematic.

Seminal [14] uses the difference between the original (ill-typed) program and the changed (well-typed) programs as a heuristic. Top [12] uses more sophisticated heuristics [11], such as a participation-ratio heuristic, a trust-factor heuristic, and others. CF typing [4] uses heuristics, such as preferring expression changes to other places, favoring changes at lower places in the tree representations, and preferring simpler type changes over more complex ones. The most recent work by Zhang and Myers [25] employs Bayesian principles to locate type errors, but they don't make suggestions.

While previous approaches involve programmers only in a very limited way and allow them to accept or reject a suggestion, guided type debugging gives programmers the opportunity to provide more meaningful input and explicitly specify some of their goals. This is not complicating matters much since it requires only the formulation of type annotations. On the other hand, the input can be effectively exploited to shorten the debugging process considerably. The strategy of steering the derivation of changes by target types elicited from users is inspired by a technique to guide the debugging of spreadsheets by user-provided target values [1].

The idea of choice types seems to be similar to the concept of discriminative sum types [16,17], in which two types are combined into a sum type when an attempt to unify them fails. However, there are several important differences. Choice types are named and thus provide more fine-grained control over the grouping of types, unification, and unification failures. Sum types are *always* unified component-wise, whereas we do this only for choice types under the same dimension. For choice types with different dimensions, each alternative of a choice type is unified with all alternatives of the other choice type. Other differences between guided type debugging and the error-locating method developed in [16] are as follows. First, their method extracts all locations involved in type errors and is thus essentially a type-error slicing approach, whereas our method always blames the most likely error location. Second, guided type debugging provides change suggestions in all cases, whereas their method, like all error-slicing approaches, does not. Finally, error locations reported by their method may contain program fragments that have nothing to do with type errors. For example, a variable used for passing type information will be reported as a source of type errors only if it is unified once with some sum types during the type inference process. In our method, on the other hand, only locations that contribute to type errors are reported.

An additional contribution of guided type debugging is a better treatment of type annotations. We have investigated the reliability of type annotations and studied the problem of locating type errors in annotations, a problem that hasn't received much attention from the research community so far.

7 Conclusions

We have developed guided type debugging as an approach to produce better change suggestions faster in response to type errors in functional programs. Our approach differs from previous tools by incorporating programmer intentions more directly by asking targeted questions about types. This strategy is efficient and can effectively increase the precision of type-change suggestions. A further contribution our method is the effective identification and removal of inconsistent type annotations.

In future work, we plan to investigate the possibility of minimizing programmer input by exploiting the information about the evolution of programs. For example, the knowledge about which part of the program was changed last may in many cases allow the automatic derivation of the target types. Another question we will investigate is how to locate type errors in type annotations when omitting them will lead to undecidable type inference.

Acknowledgements. We thank Jurriaan Hage for sharing his collection of student Haskell programs with us. This work is supported by the the National Science Foundation under the grants CCF-1219165 and IIS-1314384.

References

1. Abraham, R., Erwig, M.: GoalDebug: A Spreadsheet Debugger for End Users. In: 29th IEEE Int. Conf. on Software Engineering, pp. 251–260 (2007)
2. Bernstein, K.L., Stark, E.W.: Debugging type errors. Technical report, State University of New York at Stony Brook (1995)
3. Braßel, B.: Typehope: There is hope for your type errors. In: Int. Workshop on Implementation of Functional Languages (2004)
4. Chen, S., Erwig, M.: Counter-Factual Typing for Debugging Type Errors. In: ACM Symp. on Principles of Programming Languages, pp. 583–594 (2014)
5. Chen, S., Erwig, M., Walkingshaw, E.: An Error-Tolerant Type System for Variational Lambda Calculus. In: ACM Int. Conf. on Functional Programming, pp. 29–40 (2012)
6. Chen, S., Erwig, M., Walkingshaw, E.: Extending Type Inference to Variational Programs. ACM Trans. on Programming Languages and Systems 36(1), 1–54 (2014)
7. Chitil, O.: Compositional explanation of types and algorithmic debugging of type errors. In: ACM Int. Conf. on Functional Programming, pp. 193–204 (September 2001)
8. Chitil, O., Huch, F., Simon, A.: Typeview: A tool for understanding type errors. In: International Workshop on Implementation of Functional Languages, pp. 63–69 (2000)
9. Haack, C., Wells, J.B.: Type error slicing in implicitly typed higher-order languages. In: Degano, P. (ed.) ESOP 2003. LNCS, vol. 2618, pp. 284–301. Springer, Heidelberg (2003)
10. Hage, J.: Helium benchmark programs. Private Communication (2002-2005)

11. Hage, J., Heeren, B.: Heuristics for type error discovery and recovery. In: Horváth, Z., Zsók, V., Butterfield, A. (eds.) IFL 2006. LNCS, vol. 4449, pp. 199–216. Springer, Heidelberg (2007)
12. Heeren, B.J.: Top Quality Type Error Messages. PhD thesis, Universiteit Utrecht, The Netherlands (September 2005)
13. Johnson, G.F., Walz, J.A.: A maximum-flow approach to anomaly isolation in unification-based incremental type inference. In: ACM Symp. on Principles of Programming Languages, pp. 44–57 (1986)
14. Lerner, B., Flower, M., Grossman, D., Chambers, C.: Searching for type-error messages. In: ACM Int. Conf. on Programming Language Design and Implementation, pp. 425–434 (2007)
15. McAdam, B.J.: Repairing type errors in functional programs. PhD thesis, University of Edinburgh. College of Science and Engineering. School of Informatics (2002)
16. Neubauer, M., Thiemann, P.: Discriminative sum types locate the source of type errors. In: ACM Int. Conf. on Functional Programming, pp. 15–26 (2003)
17. Neubauer, M., Thiemann, P.: Haskell type browser. In: ACM SIGPLAN Workshop on Haskell, pp. 92–93 (2004)
18. Odersky, M., Läufer, K.: Putting type annotations to work. In: ACM Symp. on Principles of Programming Languages, pp. 54–67 (1996)
19. Schilling, T.: Constraint-free type error slicing. In: Peña, R., Page, R. (eds.) TFP 2011. LNCS, vol. 7193, pp. 1–16. Springer, Heidelberg (2012)
20. Stuckey, P.J., Sulzmann, M., Wazny, J.: Interactive Type Debugging in Haskell. In: ACM SIGPLAN Workshop on Haskell, pp. 72–83 (2003)
21. Stuckey, P.J., Sulzmann, M., Wazny, J.: Improving type error diagnosis. In: ACM SIGPLAN Workshop on Haskell, pp. 80–91 (2004)
22. Wand, M.: Finding the source of type errors. In: ACM Symp. on Principles of Programming Languages, pp. 38–43 (1986)
23. Wazny, J.R.: Type inference and type error diagnosis for Hindley/Milner with extensions. PhD thesis, The University of Melbourne (January 2006)
24. Yang, J., Michaelson, G., Trinder, P., Wells, J.B.: Improved type error reporting. In: Int. Workshop on Implementation of Functional Languages, pp. 71–86 (2000)
25. Zhang, D., Myers, A.C.: Toward General Diagnosis of Static Errors. In: ACM Symp. on Principles of Programming Languages, pp. 569–581 (2014)

A Proof of Theorem 2

To prove the theorem, we need a relation between the application of a change and the corresponding result type. This idea is formally captured in the typing relation in Figure 5. Note that we omit the rules for abstractions and let expressions because they can be obtained by simply adding χ to the left of turnstile, as we did for the rule for applications.

The rule system defines the judgment $\Gamma;\chi \vdash e : \tau$, where χ is a mapping that maps the location to the type that location will be changed to. In the rules, we use the notation $\chi(e)||\tau$ to decide whether we should use the information in χ to override the type τ for the atomic expression e. More precisely, if $(\ell(e),\tau') \in \chi$, then $\chi(e)||\tau$ yields τ', and otherwise τ.

Given a decision δ and a change environment Δ, we can obtain the corresponding χ through the operation $\downarrow_\delta\Delta$, defined as follows.

$$\downarrow_\delta\Delta = \{l \mapsto \lfloor\phi_2\rfloor_\delta \mid (l, D\langle\phi_1,\phi_2\rangle) \in \Delta \wedge D.2 \in \delta\}$$

VAR-C

$$\Gamma;\chi \vdash x : \chi(x) || \{\overline{\alpha \mapsto \tau}\}(\Gamma(x))$$

ANT-C

$$\Gamma;\chi \vdash (e::\tau) : \chi(\tau) || \tau$$

CON-C

$$\frac{c \text{ is of type } \gamma}{\Gamma;\chi \vdash c : \chi(c) || \gamma}$$

APP-C

$$\frac{\Gamma;\chi \vdash e_1 : \tau_1 \to \tau \qquad \Gamma;\chi \vdash e_2 : \tau_1}{\Gamma;\chi \vdash e_1\ e_2 : \tau}$$

Fig. 5. Rules for the type-update system

We have proved that if $\Gamma \vdash e : \phi|\Delta$, then for any decision δ, we have $\Gamma;\downarrow_\delta\Delta \vdash e : \lfloor\phi\rfloor_\delta$ [4]. Thus, the proof of Theorem 2 reduces to a proof of the following lemma.

Lemma 1 (More change locations lead to more general types). *Given* $\Gamma \vdash e : \phi|\Delta$ *and two decisions* δ_1 *and* δ_2, *let* $\chi_1 = \downarrow_{\delta_1}\Delta$ *and* $\chi_2 = \downarrow_{\delta_2}\Delta$. *If* $dom(\chi_1) \subseteq dom(\chi_2)$, *then* $\Gamma;\chi_1 \vdash e : \tau_1$ *and* $\Gamma;\chi_2 \vdash e : \tau_2$ *with* $\tau_2 \sqsubseteq \tau_1$.

Proof. The proof is by induction over the typing derivations. Since $\Gamma;\chi_1 \vdash e : \tau_1$ and $\Gamma;\chi_2 \vdash e : \tau_2$ are typing the same expression e, and since we are using the same set of rules, the derivation trees for them have the same structure. We show the proof for the cases of variable reference and application. The proof for other cases is similar.

- Case VAR. There are several subcases to consider.
  (1) $\ell(x) \notin dom(\chi_1)$ and $\ell(x) \notin dom(\chi_2)$. In this case, $\chi_1(x)$ and $\chi_2(x)$ are both given by $\Gamma(x)$. Therefore, $\tau_1 = \tau_2 = \Gamma(x)$, and $\tau_2 \sqsubseteq \tau_1$ trivially holds.
  (2) $\ell(x) \notin dom(\chi_1)$ and $\ell(x) \in dom(\chi_2)$. We can formally prove that $\tau_2 \sqsubseteq \tau_1$ by an induction over the structure of expressions. An intuitive argument is that when we can change the original type (τ_1) to a new arbitrary type (τ_2) that makes its context well typed, the definition of the typing relation in Figure 3 maintains generality and doesn't make τ_2 more specific than τ_1.
  (3) $\ell(x) \in dom(\chi_1)$ but $\ell(x) \notin dom(\chi_2)$. This case is not possible.
  (4) $\ell(x) \in dom(\chi_1)$ and $\ell(x) \in dom(\chi_2)$. The proof for this case is similar to the one for case (2).
- Case APP. The induction hypotheses are $\Gamma;\chi_1 \vdash e_1 : \tau_3 \to \tau_1$, $\Gamma;\chi_1 \vdash e_2 : \tau_3$, $\Gamma;\chi_2 \vdash e_1 : \tau_4 \to \tau_2$, $\Gamma;\chi_2 \vdash e_2 : \tau_4$, with $\tau_4 \to \tau_2 \sqsubseteq \tau_3 \to \tau_1$ and $\tau_4 \sqsubseteq \tau_3$. From $\tau_4 \to \tau_2 \sqsubseteq \tau_3 \to \tau_1$, we derive $\tau_4 \sqsubseteq \tau_3$ and $\tau_2 \sqsubseteq \tau_1$, which completing the proof for this case.

Using Big-Step and Small-Step Semantics in Maude to Perform Declarative Debugging*

Adrián Riesco

Departamento de Sistemas Informáticos y Computación,
Universidad Complutense de Madrid, Madrid, Spain
ariesco@fdi.ucm.es

Abstract. Declarative debugging is a semi-automatic debugging technique that abstracts the execution details to focus on results. This technique builds a debugging tree representing an incorrect computation and traverses it by asking questions to the user until the error is found. In previous works we have presented a declarative debugger for Maude specifications. Besides a programming language, Maude is a semantic framework where several other languages can be specified. However, our declarative debugger is only able to find errors in Maude specifications, so it cannot find bugs on the programs written on the languages being specified. We study in this paper how to modify our declarative debugger to find this kind of errors when defining programming languages using big-step and small-step semantics, two generic approaches that allow to specify a wide range of languages in a natural way. We obtain our debugging trees by modifying the proof trees obtained from the semantic rules. We have extended our declarative debugger to deal with this kind of debugging, and we illustrate it with an example.

Keywords: Declarative debugging, Big-step semantics, Small-step semantics, Maude.

1 Introduction

Declarative debugging is a semi-automatic debugging technique that abstracts the execution details to focus on results. It has been widely used in logic [10,16], functional [11,12], multi-paradigm [2,8], and object-oriented [3] programming languages. The declarative debugging scheme consists of two steps: during the first one a tree representing the erroneous computation is built, while during the second one this tree is traversed by asking questions to an external oracle (usually the user) until the bug is found.

The operational semantics of a programming language can be defined in different ways [6]. One approach, called *big-step* or *evaluation semantics*, consists of defining how the final results are obtained. The complementary approach,

* Research supported by MICINN Spanish project *StrongSoft* (TIN2012-39391-C04-04) and Comunidad de Madrid program *PROMETIDOS* (S2009/TIC-1465).

M. Codish and E. Sumii (Eds.): FLOPS 2014, LNCS 8475, pp. 52–68, 2014.

small-step or *computation semantics*, defines how each step in the computation is performed.

Maude [4] is a high-level language and high-performance system supporting both equational and rewriting logic computation. Maude modules correspond to specifications in *rewriting logic* [9], a logic that allows the representation of many models of concurrent and distributed systems. This logic is an extension of *membership equational logic* [1], an equational logic that, in addition to equations, allows the statement of *membership axioms* characterizing the elements of a sort. Rewriting logic extends membership equational logic by adding rewrite rules that represent transitions in a concurrent system and can be nondeterministic.

In [18] (and in the extended version in [17]) the big-step and small-step semantics for several programming languages and its translation to Maude is presented. These papers show that big-step and small-step semantics can be easily specified in Maude by using a method called *transitions as rewrites*. This approach translates the inferences in the semantics into rewrite rules, that is, the lefthand side of the rule stands for the expression before being evaluated and the righthand side for the reached expression. The premises are specified analogously by using rewrite conditions.

Our declarative debugger for Maude specifications is presented in [14]. This debugger uses the standard calculus for rewriting logic[1] to build the debugging trees, which are used to locate bugs in equations, membership axioms, and rules. However, when a programming language is specified in Maude we cannot debug the language but only the semantics. That is, the previous version of our debugger could point out some rules as buggy (e.g. the rule in charge of executing functions) but not the specific constructs of the language being specified (e.g. the specific function going wrong in our program). We present here an improvement of this debugger to locate the user-defined functions responsible for the error when big-step or small-step semantics are used to define the programming languages. It is based on the fact these semantics contain a small number of rules that represent evaluation of functions in the specified language, so they can be isolated to extract the applied function, hence revealing an error in the program. Note that the information about the rules in charge of evaluating functions will be different in every semantics, and hence they must be provided by the user. We will see a more detailed example in the next section, showing the difference between these two kinds of debugging.

The rest of the paper is organized as follows: Section 2 describes the standard approach to big-step and small-step semantics and how to represent the semantics of programming languages in Maude following them. Section 3 develops the relation between the proof trees obtained with these approaches and the debugging trees used by our declarative debugger. Section 4 presents our declarative debugger by means of examples. Finally, Section 5 concludes and outlines some lines of future work.

---

[1] In fact, we extended the calculus to debug new kinds of errors. However, this extension of the debugger is not relevant for the present work.

Syntactic categories:

D in *Decl*	e in *Exp*	be in *BExp*	F in *FunVar*	
op in Op	bop in *BOp*	n in *Num*	x in *Var*	bx in *BVar*

Definitions:

$D ::= F(x_1, \ldots, x_k) \Longleftarrow e \mid F(x_1, \ldots, x_k) \Longleftarrow e, D, k \geq 0$
$op ::= + \mid - \mid * \mid div$
$bop ::= And \mid Or$
$e ::= n \mid x \mid e\ op\ e \mid let\ x\ =\ e\ in\ e \mid If\ be\ Then\ e\ Else\ e \mid F(e_1, \ldots, e_k), k \geq 0$
$be ::= bx \mid T \mid F \mid be\ bop\ be \mid Not\ be \mid Equal(e, e)$

Fig. 1. Syntax for Fpl

2 Preliminaries

We present in this section the basic notions used throughout the rest of the paper. First, we briefly describe a simple functional language and introduce its big-step and small-step semantics. Then, we present Maude and outline how to specify the semantics from the previous sections. The example in this section has been extracted from [6], while the translation to Maude follows [17]. Finally, we compare this approach with standard trace-debuggers.

2.1 Fpl, A Simple Functional Language

The Fpl language [6] is a simple functional language with arithmetic and Boolean expressions, let expressions, if conditions, and function definitions. The syntax for Fpl, presented in Figure 1, indicates that declarations are mappings, built with $\Longleftarrow$, between function definitions and their bodies; an expression can be either a number, a variable, two expressions combined with an arithmetic operator, a let expression, an if condition, or a function call; and a Boolean expression can be either a Boolean variable, true, false, two Boolean expressions combined with a Boolean operator, the negation of a Boolean expression, or an equality between two arithmetic expressions.

In order to execute programs, we will also need an environment ρ mapping variables to values. We will use the syntax $D, \rho \vdash e$ for our evaluations, indicating that the expression e is evaluated by using the definitions in D and the environment ρ. We explain now the different semantics to reach the final value.

Big-Step Semantics. Big-step semantics evaluates a term written in our Flp language to its final value, evaluating in the premises of each rule the auxiliary values. That is, this semantics will be used to infer judgements of the form $D, \rho \vdash e \Rightarrow_B v$, with D the function definitions, ρ an (initially empty) environment, e and expression, and v a value. For example, the rule for executing a function call is defined as follows:

$$(\mathsf{Fun_{BS}})\ \frac{D, \rho \vdash e_i \Rightarrow_B v_i \qquad D, \rho[v_i/x_i] \vdash e \Rightarrow_B v}{D, \rho \vdash F(e_1, \ldots, e_n) \Rightarrow_B v}$$

where $1 \leq i \leq n$ and $F(x_1, \ldots, x_n) \Longleftarrow e \in D$.

That is, the arguments are evaluated in the premises, and then the variables, obtained from the definition of the function on the function definitions, are bound to these values in order to evaluate the body of the function. The value thus obtained is the one returned by the rule.[2]

Small-Step Semantics. In contrast to big-step semantics, small-step semantics just try to represent each step performed by the program to reach the final value. We will use in this case judgements of the form $D, \rho \vdash e \Rightarrow_S e'$, and hence the expression may need several steps to reach its final value. For example, the rules for evaluating a function call with this semantics would be:

$$(\mathsf{Fun_{SS_1}})\ \frac{D, \rho \vdash e_i \Rightarrow_B e'_i}{D, \rho \vdash F(e_1, \ldots, e_i, \ldots, e_n) \Rightarrow_B F(e_1, \ldots, e'_i, \ldots, e_n)}$$

$$(\mathsf{Fun_{SS_2}})\ \frac{}{D, \rho \vdash F(v_1, \ldots, v_n) \Rightarrow_B e[v_1/x_1, \ldots, v_n/x_n]}$$

where $F(x_1, \ldots, x_n) \Longleftarrow e \in D$.

That is, they first evaluate all the arguments to their final values and then continue by evaluating the body of the function. Note that this semantics just shows the result of applying one step; since this is very inconvenient for execution purposes, we will define in the next section its reflexive and transitive closure.

2.2 Maude

Maude modules are executable rewriting logic specifications. Maude functional modules [4, Chap. 4], introduced with syntax `fmod ... endfm`, are executable membership equational specifications that allow the definition of sorts (by means of keyword `sort(s)`); subsort relations between sorts (`subsort`); operators (`op`) for building values of these sorts, giving the sorts of their arguments and result, and which may have attributes such as being associative (`assoc`) or commutative (`comm`), for example; memberships (`mb`) asserting that a term has a sort; and equations (`eq`) asserting that terms are equal. Both memberships and equations can be conditional (`cmb` and `ceq`). Maude system modules [4, Chap. 6], introduced with syntax `mod ... endm`, are executable rewrite theories. A system module can contain all the declarations of a functional module and, in addition, declarations for rules (`rl`) and conditional rules (`crl`).

To specify our semantics in Maude we first define its syntax in the `SYNTAX` module. This module contains the sort definitions for all the categories:

[2] Note that we are using *call-by-value* parameter passing; a modification of the rule could also define the behavior for *call-by-name*.

```
sorts Var Num Op Exp BVar Boolean BOp BExp FunVar VarList NumList
      ExpList Prog Dec .
```

Note that we need to define lists explicitly. It also defines some subsorts, e.g. the one stating that a variable or a number are specific cases of expressions:

```
subsort Var Num < Exp .
```

Then it defines the syntax for each sort. For example, variables are defined by using the operator V, which receives a Qid (a term preceded by a quote) as argument; function names, of sort FunVar, are built by the operator FV, which also receives a Qid; operators are defined as constants; and let-expressions, if-expressions, and function calls are defined by using the operators below, where underscores are placeholders, ctor indicates that the operator is a constructor, and the prec attribute indicates its precedence:

```
op V : Qid -> Var [ctor] .
op FV : Qid -> FunVar [ctor] .
ops + - * : -> Op [ctor] .
op let_=_in_ : Var Exp Exp -> Exp [ctor prec 25] .
op If_Then_Else_ : BExp Exp Exp -> Exp [ctor prec 25] .
op _(_) : FunVar ExpList -> Exp [ctor prec 15] .
```

Once this module is defined, we have others that use equations to define the behavior of the basic operators, such as addition; another to define the environment (mapping variables to values); and another one for dealing with substitutions. These modules are required by the ones in charge of defining the semantics. Following the idea of *transitions as rewrites* [17] outlined in the introduction, we can specify inference rules by using conditional rules, being the body of the rule the conclusion of the inference and the conditions, written as rewrite conditions, the premises. In this way, we can write the ($\mathsf{Fun}_{\mathsf{BS}}$) rule as:

```
crl [FunBS] : D, ro |- FV(elist) => v
 if D, ro |- elist => vlist /\
    FV(xlist) <= e & D' := D /\
    D, ro[vlist / xlist] |- e => v .
```

that is, given the set of definitions D, the environment for variables ro and a function FV applied to a list of expressions elist, the function is evaluated to the value v if (i) the expressions elist are evaluated to the list of values vlist; (ii) the body of the function FV stored in D is e and the function parameters are xlist; and (iii) the body, where the variables in xlist are substituted by the values in vlist, is evaluated to v.

We define the small-step semantics in another module. The rule FunSS1 indicates that, if the list of expressions applied to a function FV has not been evaluated to values yet, then we can take any of these expressions and replace it by a more evolved one:

```
crl [FunSS1] : D, rho |- FV(elist,e,elist') => FV(elist,e',elist')
 if D, rho |- e => e' .
```

The rule FunSS2 indicates that, once all the expressions have been evaluated into values, we can look for the definition of FV in the set of definitions D, substitute the parameters by the given values, and then reduce the function to the body:

```
crl [FunSS2] : D, rho |- FV(vlist) => e[vlist / xlist]
 if FV(xlist)<= e & D' := D .
```

Moreover, we can also define the reflexive and transitive closure, which will be required to reach final values. These rules are defined by using a different operator _|=_, which distinguishes between single steps and the closure in order to avoid infinite computations. The rule zero indicates that a value is reduced to itself:

```
rl  [zero] : D, ro |= v => v .    *** no step
```

The rule more indicates that, if the expression e has not reached a value then we can first perform a small step to reach a newer expression e', which will further evaluated using this reflexive and transitive closure until it reaches a value:

```
crl [more] : D, ro |= e => v
 if not (e :: Num) /\
    D, ro |- e => e' /\              *** one step
    D, ro |= e' => v .               *** all the rest
```

However, note that this distinction is only necessary from the executability point of view, and hence these rules can be understood as:

$$\text{(zero)}\ \frac{}{D, \rho \vdash v \Rightarrow_S v}$$

$$\text{(more)}\ \frac{D, \rho \vdash e \Rightarrow_S e' \quad D, \rho \vdash e' \Rightarrow_S v}{D, \rho \vdash e \Rightarrow_S v}$$

Using any of these semantics we can execute programs written in our Fpl language. For example, we can define in a constant exDec the Fibonacci function and use a wrong addition function, which is implemented as "times":

```
eq exDec =
  FV('Fib)(V('x)) <= If Equal(V('x), 0) Then 0
                     Else If Equal(V('x), 1) Then 1
                          Else FV('Add)(FV('Fib)(V('x) - 1),
                                        FV('Fib)(V('x) - 2)) &
  FV('Add)(V('x), V('y)) <= V('x) * V('y) .
```

and use the big-step semantics to execute Fib(2), obtaining 0 as result:

```
Maude> (rew exDec, mt |= FV('Fib)(2) .)
rewrite in BIG-STEP : exDec, mt |- FV('Fib)(2)
result Num : 0
```

$$
\text{(FunBS)}\,\dfrac{\text{(CRN)}\,\dfrac{}{D, id \vdash 2 \Rightarrow_B 2} \quad \text{(IfR2)}\,\dfrac{\text{(EqR2)}\,\dfrac{\nabla_1 \quad \nabla_2}{D, \rho \vdash \texttt{x == 0} \Rightarrow_B \texttt{F}} \quad \text{(IfR2)}\,\dfrac{\nabla_3 \quad \nabla_4}{D, \rho \vdash \texttt{If x == 1}\ldots \Rightarrow_B 0}}{D, \rho \vdash \texttt{If x == 0}\ldots \Rightarrow_B 0}}{D, id \vdash \texttt{Fib}(2) \Rightarrow_B 0}
$$

where proof tree ∇_4 is defined as:

$$
\text{(FunBS)}\,\dfrac{\text{(ExpLR)}\,\dfrac{\text{(FunBS)}\,\dfrac{\nabla \quad \nabla}{D, \rho \vdash \texttt{Fib(x} - \texttt{1)} \Rightarrow_B 1} \quad \text{(FunBS)}\,\dfrac{\nabla \quad \nabla}{D, \rho \vdash \texttt{Fib(x} - \texttt{2)} \Rightarrow_B 0}}{D, \rho \vdash \texttt{Fib(x} - \texttt{1)}, \texttt{Fib(x} - \texttt{2)} \Rightarrow_B 1, 0} \quad \nabla}{D, \rho \vdash \texttt{Add(Fib(x} - \texttt{1)}, \texttt{Fib(x} - \texttt{2))} \Rightarrow_B 0}
$$

Fig. 2. Proof tree for `Fib(2)` evaluated by using big-step semantics

This result is erroneous, and its associated proof tree, partially depicted in Figure 2, has 37 nodes. In this figure D stands for the declarations shown above, ρ for $\texttt{x} \mapsto 2$, and we have simplified the syntax to improve the readability. The labels for the rules that we have not shown are straightforward: `CRN` evaluates a value to itself, `IfR2` evaluates an if statement when the condition is false, `EqR` evaluates an equality to false, and `ExpLR` evaluates a list of expressions. The tree ∇_1 abbreviates the tree for the evaluation of `x` to 2, ∇_2 the evaluation of 0 to itself, ∇_3 evaluates `x == 1`, and the rest of ∇'s just continue with the computation following the same ideas presented above.

Similarly, the evaluation of `Fib`(2) using small-step semantics returns the following result:

```
Maude> (rew exDec2, mt |= FV('Fib)(2) .)
rewrite in COMPUTATION : exDec2, mt |= FV('Fib)(2)
result Num : 0
```

The proof tree for this case is shown in Figure 3, where D stands for the definitions, e_1 for the definition of `Fib` applied to 2, and e_2 for this definition once we have substituted the condition by `F`. We start with a transitivity step, which has a function application as left child, which replaces the call to `Fib` by the body of the function. This value is used to keep looking for the final result with another `more` rule, which evaluates the condition in this `If` expression by means of an (IfR1) inference rule. It then continues with another `more` rule, where the ∇'s stand for trees similar to the ones shown here.

If we try to use the previous version of our debugger to debug this problem it will indicate that the rule `FunBS` is buggy for the big-step semantics, while `FunSS2` will be pointed out as buggy for small-step semantics, although they are correctly defined. This happens because these rules are in charge of applying the functions (in this case `Fib` and `Add`) defined by the user, but they cannot distinguish between different calls. We will show how to improve the debugger to point out the specific user-defined function responsible for the error in the next sections.

$$
\text{(more)}\;\dfrac{\text{(FunSS}_2\text{)}\;\dfrac{}{D, id \vdash \texttt{Fib(2)} \Rightarrow_S e_1} \qquad \text{(more)}\;\dfrac{\text{(IfR1)}\;\dfrac{\text{(EqR4)}\;\dfrac{}{D, id \vdash \texttt{Equal(2,0)} \Rightarrow_S \texttt{F}}}{D, id \vdash e_1 \Rightarrow_S e_2} \qquad \text{(more)}\;\dfrac{\bigtriangledown \quad \bigtriangledown}{D, id \vdash e_2 \Rightarrow_S 0}}{D, id \vdash e_1 \Rightarrow_S 0}}{D, id \vdash \texttt{Fib(2)} \Rightarrow_S 0}
$$

Fig. 3. Proof tree for `Fib(2)` evaluated by using small-step semantics

2.3 Related Work

We compare in this section our approach with the best known debugging method for any programming language: tracing with breakpoints. Although the trace is easy to use and highly customizable, a declarative debugger provides more clarity and simplicity of usage. In a trace-debugger, programmers must set some breakpoints where they want to stop the execution. From those points they can proceed step by step, checking whether the results of the functions or the arguments and bindings are the expected ones. If they skip the evaluation of a function but they discover it returns a wrong value, they have to restart the session to enter and debug its code. The advantage of the declarative debugger is that, starting only from an expression returning a wrong value, it finds a buggy function by simply asking about the results of the functions in the computation, avoiding low-level details. It focuses on the intended meaning of functions, which is something very clear to programmers (or debuggers), and the navigation strategies saves them from choosing what functions check and in what order as with breakpoints in the trace-debugger.

Moreover, note that throughout the paper we talk about functions as potential sources of errors because they depend on the user code and have an expected result (so we can make questions about them). However, we can modify the granularity of the errors discovered by the debugger by pointing out more specific rules as potentially erroneous. For example, we could consider that a loop in an imperative language is a "computational unit" and hence it has meaning by itself (as considered when enhancing declarative debugging in [7]). In this way, the debugger would ask questions related to loops (it could also ask questions about functions, if they are included). That is, we can configure the debugger to ask questions as specific as we want, so we could also examine the code inside functions, just as a trace-debugger.

Moreover, our approach is quite useful when prototyping a new programming language, since it would not have any debugging mechanism a priori. That is, the present work provides a debugger *for free* for any programming language specified in Maude, while the trace would only provide the execution of Maude equations and rules.

3 Declarative Debugging Using the Semantics

We present in this section the relation between the proof trees obtained by using the operational semantics in the previous section and the debugging trees that should be used to debug them.

3.1 Preliminaries

Declarative debugging requires an *intended interpretation*, which corresponds to the model the user had in mind while writing the program, to locate the bug. This interpretation depends on the programming language, and hence we cannot define it a priori. For this reason, we present the assumptions that must be fulfilled by the calculus and the information provided by the user before starting the debugging process:

- There is a set S of rules whose correctness depends on the code of the program being debugged. That is, we can distinguish between the inference rules executing the user code (e.g. the rules defining function call), which will be contained in S, and the rest of rules defining the operational details (e.g. the rules defining the execution order). If the inference rules are correctly implemented, only the execution of rules in S may lead to incorrect results.
- The user must provide this set, which will fix the granularity of the debugging process. The rest of the rules will be assumed to work as indicated by the semantics (i.e. no errors can be detected through them).
- The user knows the fragment of code being executed by each rule, assuming the premises are correct.

Example 1. The obvious candidate for the set S in our functional language is $S = \{(\mathsf{FUN_{BS}})\}$ for big-step semantics (respectively, $S = \{(\mathsf{FUN_{SS_2}})\}$ for small-step semantics). This rule is in charge of evaluating a function, and thus we can indicate that, when an error is found, the responsible is F, the name given in the rule to the function being evaluated.

Corollary 1. *As a consequence of the second restriction, given a calculus with a set of inference rules R, a set of rules S fulfilling the restrictions above, a set of rules $U \subsetneq R$ such that $U \cap S = \emptyset$, a model $\mathcal{M}$ of the calculus, an intended interpretation $\mathcal{I}$, and a judgement j which is the consequence of any inference rule in U, we have $\mathcal{M} \models j \iff \mathcal{I} \models j$.*

We are interested in the judgements whose correctness may differ between the model and the intended interpretation. Given a model of the calculus, an intended interpretation $\mathcal{I}$, and a judgement j such that $\mathcal{M} \models j$ we will say that a judgement j is valid if $\mathcal{I} \models j$ and invalid otherwise. The basic declarative debugging scheme tries to locate a *buggy node*, that is, an invalid node with all its children valid. Regarding buggy nodes in the proof trees defined above, it is important to take into account the following property:

Proposition 1. *Let N be a buggy node in some proof tree in the given calculus, $\mathcal{I}$ an intended interpretation, and S the set of rules indicated by the user.*

1. *N corresponds to the consequence of an inference rule in S.*
2. *The error associated to N is the one indicated by the user to the rule in N.*

Proof. The first item is a straightforward consequence of Corollary 1. The second item is also straightforward from the third condition required on the set S.

3.2 Declarative Debugging with Big-Step Semantics

Instead of using the proof trees obtained from the calculus for declarative debugging, we will use an abbreviation to remove all the nodes that do not provide debugging information. We call this abbreviation APT_{bs}, from Abbreviated Proof Tree for big-step semantics. APT_{bs} is defined by using the set of rules S indicated by the user as follows:

$$APT_{bs}\left(\mathsf{(R)}\,\frac{T}{j}\right) = \mathsf{(R)}\,\frac{APT'_{bs}(T)}{j}$$
$$APT'_{bs}\left(\mathsf{(R)}\,\frac{T_1 \ldots T_n}{j}\right) = \left\{\mathsf{(R)}\,\frac{APT'_{bs}(T_1) \;\ldots\; APT'_{bs}(T_n)}{j}\right\},\ \mathsf{(R)} \in S$$
$$APT'_{bs}\left(\mathsf{(R)}\,\frac{T_1 \ldots T_n}{j}\right) = APT'_{bs}(T_1) \bigcup \ldots \bigcup APT'_{bs}(T_n),\ \mathsf{(R)} \notin S$$

The basic idea of the transformation is that we keep the initial evaluation and the evaluation performed by rules in S, while the rest of evaluations are removed from the tree. We show that this transformation is appropriate:

Theorem 1. *Let T be a finite proof tree representing an inference in the given calculus. Let $\mathcal{I}$ be an intended interpretation for this calculus such that the root N of T is invalid in $\mathcal{I}$. Then:*

(a) $APT_{bs}(T)$ contains at least one buggy node (completeness).
(b) Any buggy node in $APT_{bs}(T)$ has an associated error, according to the information given by the user.

Proof. We prove the items separately:

(a) By induction on the height of $APT_{bs}(T)$.
(Base case). If $height(APT_{bs}(T)) = 1$ then $APT_{bs}(T)$ only contains the root, which is invalid by hypothesis, and hence buggy.
(Inductive case). When $height(APT_{bs}(T)) = k$ then $APT_{bs}(T)$ contains a buggy node. If $height(APT_{bs}(T)) = k + 1$ we distinguish whether the root if buggy or not. If it is buggy then we have found the buggy node. Otherwise, it has at least one child node which is invalid and it contains a buggy node by hypothesis.

(b) Note first that the root is buggy iff $\mathsf{(R)} \in S$. In fact, it is easy to see that, by Proposition 2, if $\mathsf{(R)} \notin S$ then at least one of its child nodes is invalid in $\mathcal{I}$, and hence the APT'_{bs} function will contain an invalid tree, preventing the root from being buggy. Once this is stated, we realize that APT'_{bs} only keeps the inference rules in S and, since a buggy node has all its children valid and the user has assured that it can indicate the source of the error, the result holds.

where the auxiliary results are proved as follows:

Proposition 2. *Given a proof tree T, a set S of rules given by the user, an intended interpretation $\mathcal{I}$ such that the root N of T is invalid, and $\{T_1, \ldots, T_n\} = APT'_{bs}(T)$, then $\exists\ T_i$, $1 \leq i \leq n$, and N' the root of t_i such that $\mathcal{I} \not\models N'$.*

$$\dfrac{\dfrac{\dfrac{}{D,\rho \vdash \texttt{Fib(x}-1\texttt{)} \Rightarrow_B 1}\,(\mathsf{Fun_{BS}}) \quad \dfrac{}{D,\rho \vdash \texttt{Fib(x}-2\texttt{)} \Rightarrow_B 0}\,(\mathsf{Fun_{BS}})}{D,\rho \vdash \texttt{Add(Fib(x}-1\texttt{),Fib(x}-2\texttt{))} \Rightarrow_B 0}\,(\mathsf{Fun_{BS}})}{D, id \vdash \texttt{Fib(2)} \Rightarrow_B 0}\,(\mathsf{Fun_{BS}})$$

Fig. 4. Abbreviated proof tree for Fib(2)

Proof. We proceed by induction on the height of T.

Base case. If $height(T) = 1$ then, because of the restrictions on the set S, we have (R) $\in S$, with (R) the rule used to infer N, and the result holds.

Inductive case. When $height(T) = k$ we have an invalid tree w.r.t. $\mathcal{I}$ in the set $APT'_{bs}(T)$. If $height(T) = k$, then we distinguish whether the rule (R) used in the root is in S. If it is, then the result holds trivially, since the transformation will keep this tree. Otherwise, we know that there is a child node that is invalid (since we restrictions in the set S prevent this node from being buggy), and we can use the induction hypothesis to check that the result holds.

Example 2. We can apply these rules, using the set S from Example 1, to the proof tree presented in Figure 2, obtaining the tree in Figure 4. Note that the 37 nodes in the proof tree have been reduced to 4 nodes in the abbreviated one.

The major weakness of big-step semantics when used for declarative debugging resides in the fact that evaluating terms whose subterms have not been fully reduced, as shown in Figure 4. This element makes the debugging process more complicated because it forces the user to think about the expected results for the subterms before considering whether the current computation is correct or not.

To solve this problem, we propose to use the single-stepping navigation strategy [15], which starts asking from the leaves, discarding the correct ones until an invalid one (and hence buggy, since leaves have no children) is found. This strategy allows us to substitute subterms by the appropriate values when asking questions, given this property is assured by the user:

Proposition 3. *Given* $\mathcal{I} \models t \Rightarrow t'$, *we have*

$$\mathcal{I} \models f(t_1, \ldots, t, \ldots, t_n) \Rightarrow r \iff \mathcal{I} \models f(t_1, \ldots, t', \ldots, t_n) \Rightarrow r$$

That is, the user must make sure that the semantics works, for the rules he has selected, by first reducing the subterms/arguments and then applying the rules for the reduced term. Note that these reduced terms are just a specific case of the ones indicated by the user for his intended semantics, and thus are included in $\mathcal{I}$. Since the structure of the tree does not change it is easy to see that completeness holds. Regarding soundness, it only holds if we traverse the tree by checking the correctness of the inferences for the subterms before checking the correctness of the whole term (otherwise we might discard the real source

$$
\text{(Fun}_{\text{BS}}\text{)}\frac{\text{(Fun}_{\text{BS}}\text{)}\dfrac{\text{(Fun}_{\text{BS}}\text{)}\dfrac{}{(\diamondsuit)\ D,\rho \vdash \texttt{Fib}(1) \Rightarrow_B 1} \quad \text{(Fun}_{\text{BS}}\text{)}\dfrac{}{(\heartsuit)\ D,\rho \vdash \texttt{Fib}(0) \Rightarrow_B 0}}{(\clubsuit)\ D,\rho \vdash \texttt{Add}(1,0) \Rightarrow_B 0}}{D, id \vdash \texttt{Fib}(2) \Rightarrow_B 0}
$$

Fig. 5. Simplified abbreviated proof tree for Fib(2)

of the error). For this reason, we combine this transformation with the single-stepping navigation strategy [15], which performs exactly this traversal.

Using this simplification, we would obtain the tree in Figure 5, where all the subterms have been reduced. Although this change might seem trivial in this simple example, the benefits are substantial when more complex programs are debugged. Notice also that Proposition 3 may not hold in some cases, e.g. in lazy languages where the arguments are not evaluated until they are required. In this case we will follow the standard approach, asking about subterms not fully reduced and using the top-down or divide and query navigation strategies, which are more efficient in general that single-stepping.

3.3 Declarative Debugging with Small-Step Semantics

In contrast to the big-step semantics above, the small-step semantics applies a single evaluation step, making the debugging very similar to the step-by-step approach. To avoid this problem we place transitivity nodes in such a way that (i) the debugging tree becomes as balanced as possible, which improves the behavior of the navigation strategies and (ii) the questions in the debugging tree refer to final results, making the questions easier to answer. The tree transformation for this semantics, similar to the one in [14], takes advantage of transitivity rules while keeping the correctness and completeness of the technique. Thus, in this case the APT_{ss} function is defined as:

$$APT_{ss}\left(\text{(R)}\frac{T}{j}\right) = \text{(R)}\frac{APT'_{ss}(T)}{j}$$

$$APT'_{ss}\left(\text{(Tr)}\frac{\text{(R)}\dfrac{T_1 \ldots T_n}{j'} \quad T}{j}\right) = \left\{\text{(R)}\frac{APT'_{ss}(T_1)\ldots APT'_{ss}(T_n)\ APT'_{ss}(T)}{j}\right\},\ \text{(R)} \in S$$

$$APT'_{ss}\left(\text{(R)}\frac{T_1 \ldots T_n}{j}\right) = \left\{\text{(R)}\frac{APT'_{ss}(T_1)\ldots APT'_{ss}(T_n)}{j}\right\},\ \text{(R)} \in S$$

$$APT'_{ss}\left(\text{(R)}\frac{T_1 \ldots T_n}{j}\right) = APT'_{ss}(T_1) \bigcup \ldots \bigcup APT'_{ss}(T_n),\ \text{(R)} \notin S$$

That is, when we have a transitivity step whose left premise is a rule pointed out by the user, then we keep the "label" of the inference (which indicates that we will locate the error in the lefthand side of this node, which is the same as the one in the premise) in the transitivity step, that presents the final value.

Theorem 2. *Let T be a finite proof tree representing an inference in the given calculus. Let $\mathcal{I}$ be an intended interpretation for this calculus such that the root N of T is invalid in $\mathcal{I}$. Then:*

(a) $APT_{ss}(T)$ contains at least one buggy node (completeness).
(b) Any buggy node in $APT_{ss}(T)$ has an associated error, according to the information given by the user.

Proof. We prove each item separately:

(a) Analogous to the proof for Theorem 1(a).
(b) We first use Proposition 4 below to check that, if the root is buggy, then it is associated to an inference rule $(\mathsf{R}) \in S$ and the result holds by using the assumed conditions on the rules of this set. Any other buggy node must be obtained from $APT'_{ss}(T)$.
Let N be a buggy node occurring in $APT'_{ss}(T)$. Then N is the root of some tree T_N, subtree of some $T' \in APT'_{ss}(T)$. By the structure of the APT'_{ss} rules this means that there is a subtree T' of T such that $T_N \in APT'_{ss}(T')$. We prove that the inference rule used to obtain N is in the set S by induction on the number of nodes of T', $|T'|$.
If $|T'| = 1$ then T' contains only one node and $APT'_{ss}(T') = \{T'\}$, due to the restrictions in the set S. Since only the second APT'_{ss} rule can be applied in this case the rule has been kept and it is associated to the error specified by the user.
If $|T'| > 1$ we examine the APT'_{ss} rule applied at the root of T':
- In the first case, T' is of the form

$$(\mathsf{Tr})\frac{(\mathsf{R})\dfrac{T_1 \quad \dots \quad T_n}{j'} \qquad T''}{j}, \text{ with } (\mathsf{R}) \in S$$

Hence $N \equiv j$ and T_N is

$$(\mathsf{R})\frac{APT'_{ss}(T_1) \quad \dots \quad APT'_{ss}(T_n) \quad APT'_{ss}(T'')}{j}$$

Since N is buggy in T_N it is invalid w.r.t. $\mathcal{I}$. However, a transitivity step cannot be buggy in T', since it does not depend on the code written by the user. For this reason either j' or the root of T'' are invalid. But the root of T'' cannot be buggy, since Proposition 4 indicates that the APT'_{ss} applied to a tree with an invalid root produces a set where at least one tree has an invalid root, which would prevent N from being buggy. Therefore j' is invalid. Moreover, the roots of $T_1 \dots T_n$ must be valid, since otherwise N would not be buggy. Hence, j' is buggy in T' and the user is able to point out the error. Therefore, and given that in a transitivity rule the lefthand side of the root is the same as the lefthand side of the left premise, the user can identify the error in j.

- In the second case the conclusion of the inference is kept and, given that N is buggy, all the premises are valid and hence the user can identify the error.
- In the third case, $T_N \in APT'_{ss}(T_i)$ for some child subtree T_i of the root T' and the result holds by the induction hypothesis.

where the auxiliary results are proved as follows:

Proposition 4. *Given a proof tree T, a set S of rules given by the user, an intended interpretation $\mathcal{I}$ such that the root N of T is invalid, and $\{T_1, \ldots, T_n\} = APT'_{ss}(T)$, then $\exists\ T_i$, $1 \le i \le n$, and N' the root of t_i such that $\mathcal{I} \not\models N'$.*

Proof. Analogous to Proposition 2.

The tree obtained by using this abbreviation is equal to the one shown in Figure 5, although in this case the ($\mathsf{Fun}_{\mathsf{BS}}$) inferences are ($\mathsf{Fun}_{\mathsf{SS}_2}$) inferences obtained by applying the first equation for APT'_{SS}. Finally, note that, if the user does not want to use this simplification, we can still use the APT transformation for big-step and the result from Theorem 1 to perform the debugging in a "normal" tree, which will present a step-by-step-like debugging session.

4 Debugging Session

The debugger is started by loading the file `dd.maude` available at `http://maude.sip.ucm.es/debugging/`. It starts an input/output loop where commands can be introduced by enclosing them into parentheses.

Once we have introduced the modules specifying the semantics, we can introduce the set S rule by rule as follows:

```
Maude> (intended semantics FunBS culprit FV:FunVar .)
The rule FunBS has been added to the intended semantics.
If buggy, FV in the lefthand side will be pointed out as erroneous.
```

This command introduces the rule `FunBS` into the set S indicating that, when the buggy node is found, the responsible for the error will be the value matching the variable `FV`. Now we can select the single-stepping navigation strategy and start the debugging session for big-step, which reduces the subterms by default:

```
Maude> (single-stepping strategy .)
 Single-stepping strategy selected.
Maude> (debug big step semantics exDec, mt |- FV('Fib)(2) => 0 .)
Is D, V('x) = 2 |- FV('Fib)(1) evaluated to 1 ?
Maude> (yes .)
```

The first question (where we have replaced the definitions by `D` to simplify the presentation) corresponds to the node marked as ($\diamondsuit$) in Figure 5. Since we expected this result we have answered `yes`, so the subtree is removed and the next question corresponds to the node marked as ($\heartsuit$):

```
Is D, V('x) = 2 |- FV('Fib)(0) evaluated to 0 ?
Maude> (yes .)
```

This result was also expected, so we have answered yes again, and this subtree is also removed. The next question, which is related to the node marked as (♣), corresponds to an erroneous evaluation, so we answer no. Now, this node becomes an invalid node with all its children valid, and hence it reveals an error in the specification:

```
Is D, V('x) = 2 |- FV('Add)(1,0) evaluated to 1 ?
Maude> (no .)

The buggy node is:
The term D, V('x) = 2 |- FV('Add)(1, 0) has been evaluated to 0
The code responsible for the error is FV('Add)
```

That is, the debugger indicates that the function Add has been wrongly implemented in the Fpl language. We can debug the program in a similar way using the small-step semantics. In this case we have to introduce, in addition to the set of rules responsible for errors as shown above, the set of rules required for transitivity:

```
 Maude> (intended semantics FunSS2 culprit FV:FunVar .)
 The rule FunSS2 has been added to the intended semantics.
 If buggy, the FV:FunVar in the lefthand side will be pointed out
as erroneous.

 Maude> (transitivity rules more .)
 The rules more have been introduced as rules for transitivity.
```

We can now start the debugging session for small-step as follows:

```
Maude> (debug small step semantics exDec2, mt |= FV('Fib)(2) => 0 .)
Is D, mt |= FV('Add)(1, 0) evaluated to 0 ?
```

The answer is no, which allows the debugger to find the error in Add:

```
The buggy node is:
The term D, mt |= FV('Add)(1, 0) has been evaluated to 0
The code responsible for the error is FV('Add)
```

5 Concluding Remarks and Ongoing Work

We have presented in this paper a methodology to use declarative debugging on programming languages defined using big-step and small-step semantics in Maude. It uses the specific features of each semantics to improve the questions asked to the user. The big-step semantics can present terms with all the subterms in normal form, while the small-step semantics use the transitivity rule to present the final results. This approach has been implemented in a Maude prototype extending the previous declarative debugger for Maude specifications. The major drawback of this approach consists in relying on the user for most of the results, that depend on the set of rules chosen for debugging. Although this is unfortunate, we consider it is necessary to build a tool as general as the one presented here.

Thus far we have checked the adequacy of the approach for small functional and imperative languages, so we also plan to study its behavior with more complex languages. Moreover, we want to extend our declarative debugger to work with K definitions. The K framework [5] is a rewrite-based executable semantic framework where programming languages and applications can be defined. However, K performs intermediate transformations to the rules defining the semantics and thus it is difficult to reason about them.

Another interesting subject of future work would consist of studying how declarative debugging works for languages with parallelism. We could use the search engine provided by Maude to look for paths leading to errors, and then use the path leading to the errors to build the debugging tree, thus providing a simple way to combine verification and debugging. We also plan to extend the possible answers in this kind of debugging. We are specifically interested in implementing a *trust* answer that removes from the tree all the subtrees rooted by the expression being trusted. Finally, a prototype for generating test cases based on the semantics specified in Maude has been proposed in [13]. It would be interesting to connect both tools, in order to debug the failed test cases.

References

1. Bouhoula, A., Jouannaud, J.-P., Meseguer, J.: Specification and proof in membership equational logic. Theoretical Computer Science 236, 35–132 (2000)
2. Caballero, R.: A declarative debugger of incorrect answers for constraint functional-logic programs. In: Antoy, S., Hanus, M. (eds.) Proc. of the 2005 ACM SIGPLAN Workshop on Curry and Functional Logic Programming, WCFLP 2005, Tallinn, Estonia, pp. 8–13. ACM Press (2005)
3. Caballero, R., Hermanns, C., Kuchen, H.: Algorithmic debugging of Java programs. In: López-Fraguas, F. (ed.) Proc. of the 15th Workshop on Functional and (Constraint) Logic Programming, WFLP 2006, Madrid, Spain. Electronic Notes in Theoretical Computer Science, vol. 177, pp. 75–89. Elsevier (2007)
4. Clavel, M., Durán, F., Eker, S., Lincoln, P., Martí-Oliet, N., Meseguer, J., Talcott, C.: All About Maude - A High-Performance Logical Framework. LNCS, vol. 4350. Springer, Heidelberg (2007)
5. Şerbănuţă, T.F., Roşu, G.: K-Maude: A rewriting based tool for semantics of programming languages. In: Ölveczky, P.C. (ed.) WRLA 2010. LNCS, vol. 6381, pp. 104–122. Springer, Heidelberg (2010)
6. Hennessy, M.: The Semantics of Programming Languages: An Elementary Introduction Using Structural Operational Semantics. John Wiley & Sons (1990)
7. Insa, D., Silva, J., Tomás, C.: Enhancing declarative debugging with loop expansion and tree compression. In: Albert, E. (ed.) LOPSTR 2012. LNCS, vol. 7844, pp. 71–88. Springer, Heidelberg (2013)

8. MacLarty, I.: Practical declarative debugging of Mercury programs. Master's thesis, University of Melbourne (2005)
9. Meseguer, J.: Conditional rewriting logic as a unified model of concurrency. Theoretical Computer Science 96(1), 73–155 (1992)
10. Naish, L.: Declarative diagnosis of missing answers. New Generation Computing 10(3), 255–286 (1992)
11. Nilsson, H.: How to look busy while being as lazy as ever: the implementation of a lazy functional debugger. Journal of Functional Programming 11(6), 629–671 (2001)
12. Pope, B.: A Declarative Debugger for Haskell. PhD thesis, The University of Melbourne, Australia (2006)
13. Riesco, A.: Using semantics specified in Maude to generate test cases. In: Roychoudhury, A., D'Souza, M. (eds.) ICTAC 2012. LNCS, vol. 7521, pp. 90–104. Springer, Heidelberg (2012)
14. Riesco, A., Verdejo, A., Martí-Oliet, N., Caballero, R.: Declarative debugging of rewriting logic specifications. Journal of Logic and Algebraic Programming 81(7-8), 851–897 (2012)
15. Shapiro, E.Y.: Algorithmic Program Debugging. ACM Distinguished Dissertation. MIT Press (1983)
16. Tessier, A., Ferrand, G.: Declarative diagnosis in the CLP scheme. In: Deransart, P., Małuszyński, J. (eds.) DiSCiPl 1999. LNCS, vol. 1870, pp. 151–174. Springer, Heidelberg (2000)
17. Verdejo, A., Martí-Oliet, N.: Executable structural operational semantics in Maude. Technical Report 134-03, Dpto. Sistemas Informáticos y Programación, Universidad Complutense de Madrid (2003)
18. Verdejo, A., Martí-Oliet, N.: Executable structural operational semantics in Maude. Journal of Logic and Algebraic Programming 67, 226–293 (2006)

Faustine: A Vector Faust Interpreter Test Bed for Multimedia Signal Processing

System Description

Karim Barkati, Haisheng Wang, and Pierre Jouvelot

MINES ParisTech, France
name.surname@mines-paristech.fr

Abstract. Faustine is the first interpreter for the digital audio signal processing language Faust and its vector extension. This domain-specific language for sample-based audio is highly expressive and can be efficiently compiled. Faustine has been designed and implemented, in OCaml, to validate the Faust multirate vector extension proposed in the literature, without having to modify the sophisticated Faust scalar compiler. Moving to frame-based algorithms such as FFT is of paramount importance in the audio field and, more broadly, in the multimedia signal processing domain. Via the actual implementation of multidimensional FFT and morphological image processing operations, Faustine, although unable to process data in real time, illustrates the possible advantages and shortcomings of this vector extension as a language design proposal. More generally, our paper provides a new use case for the vision of interpreters as lightweight software platforms within which language design and implementation issues can be easily assessed without incurring the high costs of modifying large compiler platforms.

1 Introduction

Domain-specific languages (DSLs) are high-level, specialized, abstract programming languages that help shrink the "semantic gap" between the concepts of a particular application area and the program implementation level. These languages are, by essence, more often upgraded or extended than traditional programming languages, since the unavoidable changes to the underlying business logic often call for the introduction of new traits in the corresponding DSLs [10]. This makes the design language phase – where one looks for defining a proper balance between the choice of programming features, their practical relevance and their performance cost – an almost constant endeavor.

Finding an appropriate set of programming language features calls thus for a trial-and-error design and implementation approach, which may end up being a costly proposition when the corresponding language evaluation platform must be continuously tweaked to test new proposals. Reaching an acceptable language design is even more complicated when one deals with advanced languages that target compute-intensive applications such as signal processing. Indeed, such

M. Codish and E. Sumii (Eds.): FLOPS 2014, LNCS 8475, pp. 69–85, 2014.

performance requirements are usually only met by sophisticated compilation systems that incorporate advanced optimization phases, making such software platforms unwieldy and difficult to adapt on-the-fly to test new language ideas.

Language interpreters are often considered as simple educational tools to introduce semantic language concepts (see for instance [22]), illustrate one of the Gang-of-Four design patterns (Interpreter Pattern) [9] or motivate the introduction of compilers for performance purposes. Yet, interpreters can also be invaluable tools to assess the adequacy of various programming language traits (see for instance the seminal paper [26]), and thus help address the cost-vs-design conundrum that plagues DSLs. We illustrate this idea with Faustine, an OCaml-based interpreter for the Faust programming language. Faustine implements the core of Faust, a functional DSL dedicated to advanced audio signal processing, and is thus a useful tool in itself, for instance to debug Faust programs that use new constructs. But the development of Faustine is also motivated by the desire of testing the "interpreters as DSL design-assistant tools" idea outlined above (see also [5], an interesting blog on other positive aspects of interpreters for traditional languages).

As a case study, we augmented Faust with the vector extension proposal introduced in *Dependent vector types for data structuring in multirate Faust* [17] and tested its practical applicability using a set of typical benchmarks. As explained in Section 6, these experiments showed us that some unanticipated problems lurked within the current vector design; discovering such issues early on is what the Faustine prototype is all about. On the contrary, a positive byproduct of the introduction of vectors within the Faust programming paradigm is that such an extension not only opens the door to important audio analysis techniques such as spectral algorithms to the Faust community, but may even extend the very domain Faust has been designed for. Indeed we show how key image processing operations can be expressed in Faust, and run in Faustine.

To summarize, the major contributions introduced in this paper are:

- an illustration of the "interpreters as language design-assistant tools" idea, which, even though not new, we think could be looked at in a new light when dealing with DSLs and their unusual life cycle and performance requirements. In our case, this approach proved also quite cost-effective, since we were able to assess our design ideas after the two months it only took to implement Faustine, a short time given we were not very knowledgeable about OCaml at first;
- Faustine[1], an OCaml-based interpreter for the functional audio signal processing language Faust;
- the first implementation of the Faust vector extension proposed in [17] within Faustine, seen as a test bed for assessing the adequacy of new language constructs for Faust;
- a first look at the wider applicability of the Vector Faust programming model in the more general setting of multimedia signal processing, providing some insights to its possible use for image processing.

[1] `http://www.cri.mines-paristech.fr/~pj/faustine-1.0.zip`

After this introduction, Section 2 introduces the Faust project and its core language. Section 3 outlines the vector extension proposal, our main motivation for the development of Faustine. Section 4 describes the main features of Faustine, our Faust interpreter. Section 5 provides first experimental evidence of the practicality of its use, including running examples illustrating the applicability of the Faust vector extension to key applications such as Fast Fourier Transform (FFT) and image signal processing. Section 6 highlights some of the key preliminary results coming from the use of the Faustine system, yielding some ideas about future work. We conclude in Section 7.

2 Faust

Faust[2] (Functional Audio Stream) is a DSL originally designed to help implement real-time audio applications. Designed at Grame, a French center for music creation located in Lyon, France, the Faust project as a whole has been under development since 2002. It has been instrumental in the development of many audio applications, such as the open-source Guitarix[3] and commercial moForte[4] guitar synthesizers. It has also been an enabling technology in many of the music works and performances created at Grame. The Faust language is taught in many music-oriented institutions over the world, such as Stanford University's CCRMA and French IRCAM and Université de Saint-Etienne.

2.1 Design

DSLs derive from the knowledge of a particular application domain. This generally puts constraints upon the kind of programming constructs they provide. One popular approach is to embed such knowledge within an existing programming language [15]; this provides a general framework within which applications can be programmed. For the domain of audio processing addressed by Faust, such a generality was not deemed necessary. Deciding not to go for an embedded DSL in turn opens the door to specific optimization opportunities, which might be unreachable for more general programming languages. This is particularly true for run-time performance.

Given the high computational load required by audio signal processing programs [2], one of the requirements for Faust has indeed been, from the start, to strive to reach C++-like run-time performance, while providing high-level constructs that appeal intuitively to audio-oriented engineers and artists [20,21,3]. To reach such goals, the design of Faust adopts an unusual approach, being structured in two completely different parts:

- the Faust *core* language is a functional expression language built upon a very limited set of constructs that define an algebra over signal processors, which

[2] `http://faust.grame.fr`
[3] `http://sourceforge.net/projects/guitarix`
[4] `http://www.moforte.com`

are operators taking (theoretically infinite) streams of samples as input and yielding streams of processed samples as output;
- the Faust *macro* language is a version of the full-fledged, untyped lambda-calculus, that can be used to define parametrized functions and allows currification.

Faust expressions can mix freely constructs taken from these two language components. Full-fledged Faust programs are defined as sets of identifier definitions `i = e;` or macro definitions `f(x,y,...) = e;`. All uses of an identifier or a macro, e.g., `f(3,s,...)`, are expanded at compile time to yield only core expressions. The identifier `process` denotes the main signal processor.

2.2 Core Faust

Faust core expressions are signal processors, inputting and outputting signals. Even a constant such as `1` is seen as a signal processor that takes no input signals, and outputs one signal, all samples of which have value 1. Three main constructs, similar to the combinators used in a language such as Yampa[5], a DSL built on top of Haskell, are operators of what amounts to an algebra of signal processors.

- The "`:`" sequential combinator pipes the output of its first argument into the input of its second. Thus "`1 : sin`" is a core expression that takes no input (as does `1`) and outputs a signal of samples, all of value `0.841471`.
- The Faust parallel combinator is "`,`" and is the dual of "`:`". Here, "`1,2 : +`" takes again no inputs, but pipes two constant signals into the "`+`" signal processor, yielding a stream of samples, all of value 3.
- The Faust recursion combinator is "`~`". The output samples of its second argument are fed back, after a one sample delay, into the inputs of its first argument.

For instance, the signal that contains the infinite sequence of successive integers is defined by "`_ ~ (1,_ : +)`", where "`_`" is the identity signal processor, in Faust. Figure 1 provides a graphic explanation of the inner working of the "`~`" construct; the displayed diagram corresponds to the Faust program `process = _ ~ (1,_ : +);`. Note that the small square on the back edge denotes a 1-sample delay, and that all signals are initialized by default to 0.

The last two main constructs of the signal processor algebra are the fan-out "`<:`" and fan-in "`:>`" combinators. A fan-out duplicates the output signals of its first argument to feed the (supposedly more numerous) input signals of its second argument. A fan-in performs the dual operation, combining signals that end up mixing in the same input signal with an implicit "`+`" operation.

[5] `http://www.haskell.org/haskellwiki/Yampa`

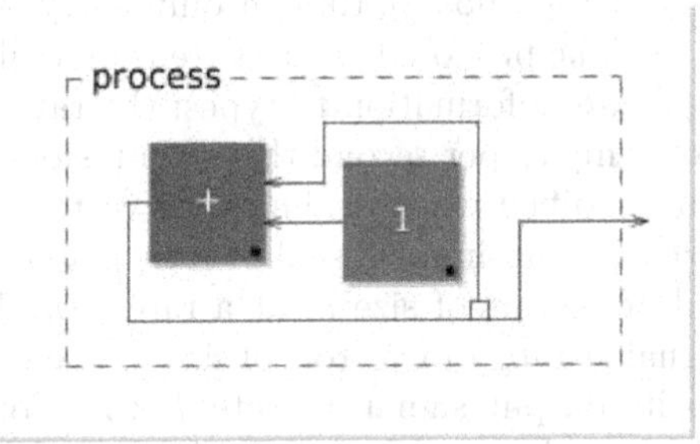

Fig. 1. The infinite stream of successive integers. The Faust platform provides a SVG block-diagram prettyprinter for Faust (text) definitions.

2.3 Implementation

Faust is a purely functional specification language, operating at the audio sample level. The Faust compiler[6] makes such specifications executable. Since all macro-level constructs are expanded-away before code generation, the compiler can devote all its attention on performing efficient code generation at the Core Faust expression level. Performance being key, this highly optimized sequential compiler uses C++ as its target language. Its more than 150,000 lines of C++ code implement a wealth of optimization techniques, needed to enable real-time processing of computing-intensive audio applications. When even more performance is needed, parallel code, using OpenMP pragmas, can be generated.

In addition to the compiler itself, the Faust software suite offers a graphical IDE (FaustWorks) and many architecture files enabling its use via standard audio interfaces or plugins such as VST, Jack, ALSA, iOS and Android. Some important computer music environments such as Max/MSP, CSound or OpenMusic embed a standalone version of the Faust compiler, opening up the way to the use of Faust within foreign systems. A SaaS-version of the Faust compiler is available on the Faust web site.

3 Faust Vector Extension

Faust current design, focused on audio signal processing, assumes that all signals carry scalar floating-point or integer values. Yet, many digital signal processing (DSP) operations such as FFT and its derivatives operate on finite arrays of values, or frames. Such a feature is lacking, and even more so if one envisions to extend Faust application domain to others, such as image processing. A proposal for a simple vector extension has been introduced [17], which we briefly summarize below.

Faust is a typed language: a signal processor is typed with the type of the scalars carried over its signal input and output arguments. To ensure efficient compilation, these types are dependent, in that each type includes an interval

[6] `http://sourceforge.net/projects/faudiostream`

of values; e.g., a signal of type float[0; 10] can only carry floating-point values within the interval [0;10]. The proposed vector extension builds upon this typing mechanism by adding a *rate* information to types; the rate or frequency f of a signal is the number of samples per second this signal is operating at. This rate information is, in turn, modified when dealing with vector operations. In short, a `vectorize` construct takes an input signal of rate f and a fixed size signal n and generates a signal of vectors of size n, at a rate f/n. The dual operation, `serialize`, takes a signal at rate f of vectors of size n, and outputs the serialized vector components in its output signal, at rate $f \times n$. Note that this scheme imposes that array sizes are known at compile time; what might appear as an unacceptable constraint is in fact quite handy within Faust, with its two-level design approach and its emphasis on efficiency for audio applications.

If `vectorize` and `serialize` are the constructor and destructor of the vector algebra, component-wise operations are still needed. The current proposal, in tune with the minimalism of Faust design, offers only two constructs, called *pick* (noted by "`[]`") and *concat* ("`#`"). To define these operations, while also providing a flavor of Faust extended typing system and how it closely constraints Faust expression construction, we give below their typing schemes:

- $\# : (\mathsf{vector}_m(\tau)^f, \mathsf{vector}_n(\tau)^f) \rightarrow (\mathsf{vector}_{m+n}(\tau)^f)$;
- $[] : (\mathsf{vector}_n(\tau)^f, \mathsf{int}[0; n-1]^f) \rightarrow (\tau^f)$.

All italic variables are supposed to be abstracted, to form type schemes. Concatenating two input signals carrying vectors of size m and n is possible only if they have the same rate, here f: the concatenated output signal operates at the same rate, but carries values that are vectors of size $m+n$, formed, at each time tick, by the concatenation of the two corresponding vectors in the input signals. Dependent typing shines in the case of pick operations: there, given vector values v carried by an input signal at rate f and a signal of scalar indexes i, which have to be integers within the bounds $[0; n-1]$ of the input vectors, pick creates an output signal, at rate f, formed with the components v_i, at each time tick.

To illustrate how the vector datatype can be used, we provide in Listing 1.1 a n-fold subsampling signal processor `subsampling(n)`. Running a subsampling-by-2 process over the list of successive integers (refer to Figure 1, if need be) yields a signal of successive odd integers.

Listing 1.1. n-fold subsampling signal processor

```
subsampling(n) = (_,n) : vectorize : [0];

integers = _ ~ (1,_ : +);
process = integers : subsampling(2);
```

4 Faustine

In this section, we motivate our decision to design and implement Faustine, while highlighting some of its salient features.

4.1 Motivation

We intend to ultimately extend the current Faust compiler with the vector API introduced above. Yet, adding this capability to the many tens of thousands of lines of C++ code of such a large program is a major undertaking. Moreover, it seems unwise to commit to a full-fledged implementation without validating our extension proposal in the first place. Thus, implementing a lightweight interpreter such as Faustine appears as a simple way, in addition to the intrinsic value of such a system for testing and debugging purposes, to provide a test bed for checking the validity and practical applicability of the proposed vector extension on actual examples.

The interpreter route is even more appealing given the nature of the Faust language we emphasized at the beginning of Section 2. Indeed, Faustine has largely benefited from its two-tiered structure, core and macro. Faust macro constructs are first processed out by the original Faust compiler, which only had to be slightly adapted, at the parser and SVG generator levels, to handle the few idiosyncratic syntactic features of the vector extension. The resulting expression is then fed to Faustine, which has been designed to only address core language expressions.

Note that an interpreter can sometimes even be converted into a full-fledged compiler using semi-automated techniques such as partial evaluation, as shown for instance in [13], which interestingly is also looking at DSLs for signal processing. Yet, in our case, we intend to eventually provide our vector extension as an upgrade to the existing Faust compiler. One reason is that we would like to leverage the wealth of optimization techniques that already exist in the current compilation infrastructure. Another one is that the modifications required to handle vectors efficiently, something our users would want, are going to be tricky. Indeed, Faust operations work at the audio sample level, and each of these samples is currently a scalar. Dealing with vector-valued samples and their corresponding more complex data structures (Reference [17] even suggests to introduce records) is going to require significant design thinking to handle memory management issues in an efficient manner.

4.2 OCaml for Executable Specifications

Faustine is an interpreter designed for testing purposes, and not for operational usage. As such, a high-level implementation language is called for, since rapid specification modification cycles can be excepted, for which a flexible and expressive programming paradigm and environment are of paramount importance [16]. Since performance is not the primary concern here, one must keep an eye on this issue when dealing with real life examples. Even though there exist frameworks such as K [7] that can be used to automatically derive interpreters, we chose OCaml for a couple of reasons.

- First, its mix of functional and object-oriented paradigms enables close-to-specification implementations. Indeed, one can even view OCaml as a language within which to express executable specifications [18,23], in particular

when using denotational-style definitions, as is the case in the vector extension paper on which Faustine is based [17].
- OCaml sports a wide variety of libraries, and in particular a binding to the `libsndfile` package[7]. This C library handles I/O operations over audio files encoded in the WAV or AIFF formats, and comes in handy when performing audio processing applications.
- In addition to the functional and OO paradigms, OCaml offers imperative constructs, which are useful, when handled with care, for performing certain optimizations such as memoization.

4.3 Implementation

Faustine is an off-line interpreter; in particular, no interactive evaluation loop is provided. Instead, Faustine takes a Faust program file (.dsp) and evaluates it, taking as input the standard input file and generating processed data on standard out. First, the original Faust compiler is called to preprocess the .dsp file, in order to eliminate all macro calls and generate a Core Faust expression. This one is passed to Faustine, which parses it and evaluates it sequentially according to the semantics defined in [17]. Input and output signal data can be encoded in two possible formats: WAV and CSV (ASCII values separated by commas), the latter being useful for spectra (see Subsection 5.1) and images.

Following Faust semantics, every expression in a program is considered as a Faust signal processor. In turn, each processor consists of subprocessors connected via Core Faust constructors by signals. In Faustine, signals are defined as OCaml functions of time to values; here "time" represents the succession of clock ticks `t`, implemented as integers. More specifically, one has:

```
class signal : rate -> (time -> value) -> signal =
  fun freq_init -> fun func_init ->
    object (self)
      method frequency = freq_init          (* signal rate *)
      method at = func_init                 (* signal initial value *)
      method add : signal -> signal
      ...
      method vectorize : signal -> signal
      method serialize : signal
```

As shown above, a signal sample rate is a key property defining a signal in our multirate context. A different sample rate is computed when a given signal is vectorized or serialized, e.g., as in the following:

```
method vectorize : signal -> signal =
  fun s_size ->
    let size = (s_size#at 0)#to_int in
    if size <= 0 then
```

[7] *Libsndfile* is a cross-platform API for reading and writing a large number of file formats containing sampled sound (`http://www.mega-nerd.com/libsndfile`)

```
    raise (Signal_operation "Vectorize: size <= 0.")
  else
    let freq = self#frequency#div size in
    let func : time -> value =
      fun t ->
        let vec = fun i -> (self#at (size * t + i))#get in
        new value (Vec (new vector size vec)) in
    new signal freq func
```

The main job of Faustine is to construct the dynamic relationship between the input and output signals of a processor. When executing a Faust program, all subprocessors are synchronized by a global clock. Every time the clock ticks, subprocessors pull the current value of their incoming processors' signals, and refresh the values of their output signals. For most non-delay processors, output signals only depend upon the current value of the input signals. Delay modules, like the primitive "mem" that uses a one-slot memory, depend on previous input frames; Faustine uses arrays to memoize signal values to avoid computing values more than once.

Faustine deals with all but GUI Faust constructs in only 2,700 lines of code, a mere 100 of which are dedicated to the vector extension design we were interested in evaluating. It took about 2 months to implement, even though we were not very knowledgeable about OCaml at the start; so, presumably, seasoned programmers could have completed this task in a shorter amount of time. Yet, this enabled us to assess in a matter of days the issues regarding the Faust vector extension and its shortcomings (see Section 6).

5 Experiments

Faustine is able to handle many Faust programs, although its off-line nature prohibits the use of GUI elements. This does not limit its usability in our case, since we are mostly interested in proof-of-design issues. To illustrate the expressive power of our Faust vector extension and the possible generalization of its application domain to non-audio multimedia systems, we provide below two significant examples. This first one is the implementation of FFT and the second, an image processing application, LicensePlate, based on mathematical morphological operators.

5.1 FFT

The Discrete Fourier Transform (DFT) of an N-element real-valued vector x_n, in our case a frame of N successive signal values, is an N-element vector X_k of complex values. This vector can informally be seen as denoting a sum of amplified sine and cosine functions. The frequency-to-amplitude mapping of these functions is called the signal *spectrum*. In practice, one has:

$$X_k = \sum_{n=0}^{N-1} x_n e^{\frac{-2\pi kni}{N}}, k = 0, ..., N-1.$$

The Fast Fourier Transform (FFT) is an efficient algorithm that uses recursion to perform a DFT in $O(N\log(N))$ steps in lieu of $O(N^2)$:

$$X_k = \sum_{m=0}^{N/2-1} x_{2m} e^{\frac{-2\pi mki}{N/2}} + e^{\frac{-2\pi ki}{N}} \sum_{m=0}^{N/2-1} x_{2m+1} e^{\frac{-2\pi mki}{N/2}}.$$

In the FFT process shown in Listing 1.2 (part of File fft.dsp), an input stream of real scalars is first vectorized in vectors of size 8. The eight elements of the vector are accessed in parallel through `picks(8)`, and then converted to 8 complex numbers in parallel by `real2pcplx(8)`. We implemented the `complex.lib` complex algebra library, a complex number being implemented, in its polar and Cartesian representations, as a 2-component vector.

Listing 1.2. Faust 8-sample length FFT (excerpts)

```
import ("complex.lib");

picks(n) = par(i, n, [i]);
fft(n) = _ <: picks(n) : real2pcplx(n) : shuffle(n) : butterflies(n);
process = vectorize(8) : fft(8) : pcplx_modules(8) : nconcat(8) : serialize;
```

The 8 complex elements are then reshuffled, and fed to a so-called butterfly processor (see Figure 2). The output of the recursively-defined butterflies (omitted here) are complex numbers. Their moduli are kept, and represent the spectrum. The eight real scalars in parallel are repacked into a vector of size 8 by `nconcat(8)`, and then serialized to produce the output stream, which represents the spectrum.

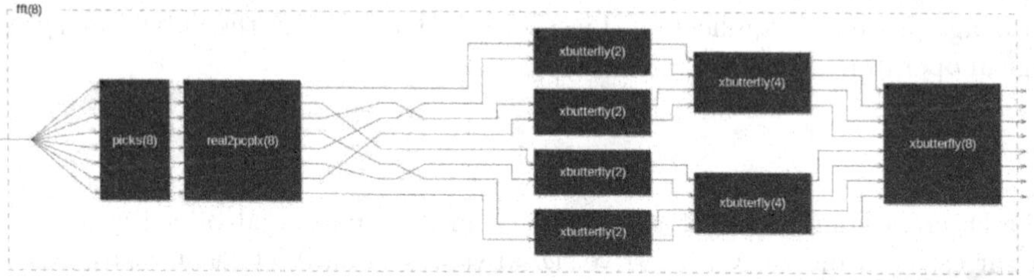

Fig. 2. FFT shuffling and butterfly

We ran a small experiment to illustrate the style of FFT outputs generated via Faustine. We fed fft.dsp the signal generated by the sum of four audio sine waves in WAV format (1.378 kHz, 2.067 kHz, 16.536 kHz and 22 kHz, sampled at 44.1 kHz) as given in Listing 1.3, where `s(f)` denotes a sine wave function at Frequency `f`, and `t` is the list of successive integers, starting at `0`. The output of `process` was encoded as a .csv file, and is here plotted in Figure 3, using Octave[8].

Listing 1.3. Sum of 4 sine waves

```
import("math.lib");
samplerate = 44100;

process = s(1378) + s(2067) , s(16536) + s(22000) : + : /(4) ;
s(f) = 2.0*PI*f*t/samplerate : sin;
t = (+(1) ~ _ ) - 1;
```

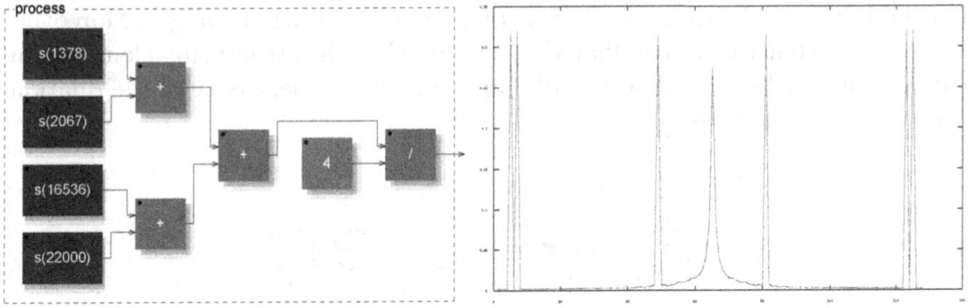

Fig. 3. FFT spectrum output of 4 sine waves: sum generation block diagram (left) and resulting analysis output (right)

5.2 Image Processing

The audio processing origins of Faust do not, a priori, preclude its usage in other domains. This should be even more the case once equipped with the vector extension described above. To test this hypothesis, we looked at how some image processing applications could be implemented in Vector Faust. As a case study, we chose LicensePlate, a car plate identification algorithm based on mathematical morphology operations.

Mathematical morphology [25] is a broad set of image processing methods based on shapes. The basic idea is to probe an image with a simple pre-defined shape, seen as a structuring element. The value of each pixel in the output image is determined by a comparison between the corresponding pixels in the

[8] Recall that, for real numbers x_n, the complex numbers X_{N-k} and X_k are conjugates, and have thus the same modulus.

input image with its neighbors, defined by the structuring element. Dilation is an important operation in mathematical morphology that uses this approach: the value of the output pixel is the maximum value of all the pixels in the input pixel's neighborhood (see Figure 4).

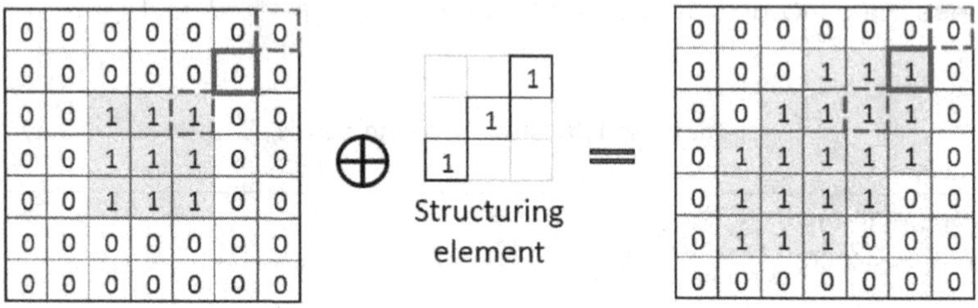

Fig. 4. Dilation $A \oplus B$ of a binary image A by a 3-point structuring element B

Implementing morphological operations in Vector Faust requires examining a 2D neighborhood of each pixel. A general solution is to examine one pixel in the neighborhood at a time, and then combine all the output images. Moreover, one can show that the image dilated by any pixel in the structuring element can be dilated firstly by line, then by column, using the associativity of the dilation operation $\oplus$ (see Figure 5).

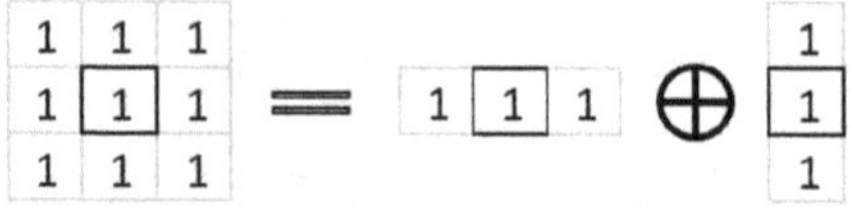

Fig. 5. Decomposition of a 3x3 square structuring element

For the example of Figure 4, one can use the code in Listing 1.4 to create `dilation_square(3)(3)`; this processor dilates each input image sample by three pixels in line, and then dilates it by three pixels in column. Each pixel in the output image is thus the maximum value of the corresponding neighborhood of 9 pixels in the input image.

Listing 1.4. Dilation by a 3x3 square structuring element in Vector Faust

```
dilating(n) = strel_shift_dilation, _, strel_shift_dilation : # , _ : # : spray_by_three(n) :
    tri_maxs(n) : nconcat(n);
dilation_line(x, y) = serialize : dilating(x) : vectorize(y);
dilation_column(x, y) = matrix_transpose(y, x) : serialize : dilating(y) : vectorize(x) :
    matrix_transpose(x, y);
dilation_square(x, y) = dilation_line(x, y) : dilation_column(x, y);
```

With the operations of dilation and erosion (the dual of dilation, which shrinks shapes), an entire morphological image processing library can be constructed. As a use case, we implemented in Vector Faust the car plate identification algorithm LicensePlate, based on mathematical morphology [14,12]; it can detect and isolate a plate in an image, as illustrated in Figure 6.

Fig. 6. LicensePlate algorithm: original image (left); detected license plate (right)

5.3 Performance

Given our goal of using Faustine as a language design test bed, no real efforts have been put into optimizing run-time efficiency. The interpreter is, in fact, unusable as is in a production setting. This is even more true when one takes into account Faust strong emphasis on very high performance, a key feature users have been counting on.

To put things in perspective and illustrate Faustine limitations, we ran both the FFT and image processing applications on an Ubuntu 12.04 LTS desktop sporting two Intel Core 2 Duo CPU E8600 64-bit processors running at 3.3 GHz each, with 3.7 GB of main memory. Dealing with a single frame of 128 64-bit floating-point numbers takes our FFT algorithm 22.4 seconds to process. A single small 195×117 image took LicensePlate 812 seconds; note that a subsequent test with a computer using a similar CPU but twice the memory size took a more reasonable 90 s to complete.

6 Future Work

The results of the previous section suggest that Vector Faust is a good candidate to express vector operations fit to perform frame-based operations, such as those present in audio spectral analysis or image processing systems. The Faustine interpreter system, as an experimental platform to run practical tests of Vector Faust programs, was instrumental in getting these results in a short period of time, proving its intrinsic value as a language design development tool. We discuss in this section some of the ideas our use of Faustine helped spur.

6.1 Vector Extension Issues

One unexpected outcome of the use of Faustine is that we found unanticipated difficulties with the current design of Faust vector extension. Since this addition to Faust is, for the time being, rather primitive, in that no higher-order constructs such as `map` or `reduce` are provided, all array operations must be specified at the element-access level, typically `a[i]`, leading to the introduction of numerous macros. For instance, Listing 1.5 implements a matrix transposition algorithm in a very straightforward manner. The block diagram resulting from the expansion of all these macros, following Faust design principle, is given in Figure 7.

Listing 1.5. Matrix transposition

```
process = matrix_transpose(3,3);
matrix_transpose(n, m) =
  _ <: par(i, n, [i]) <: par(j, m, (par(i, n, [j]) : concats(n))) : concats(m);
concats = case {
    (1) => vectorize(1);
    (n) => concats(n-1) # vectorize(1);
};
```

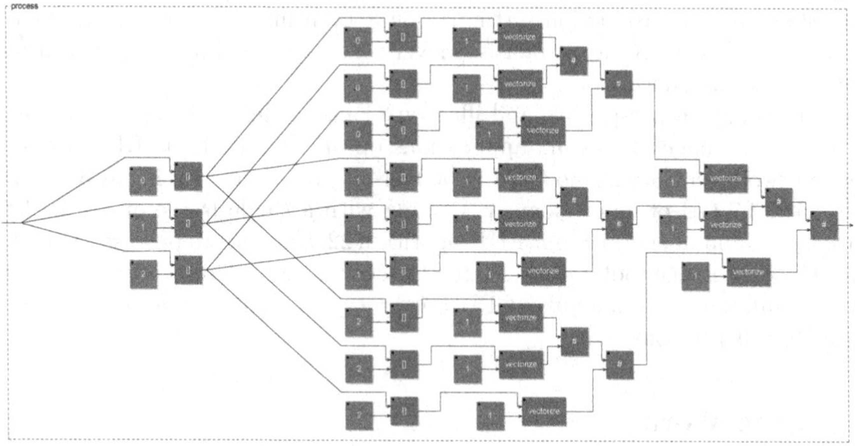

Fig. 7. Transpose diagram of a 3×3 matrix

As one can see, the `transpose` definition leads to the creation of a rather large Core Faust expression. This would have been even more patent had we used a more meaningful matrix size. In fact, when running LicensePlate, we tried to use an image of size 640×383, and the macro expansion phase of Faust original compiler (*not* Faustine per se) could not manage to complete its task, even after multiple hours. Thus addressing problems with data sets of significant size seems to make the whole "macro/core" structure of the current Faust compilation process unusable for common array operations. Discovering this problem will affect even a future Faust-with-vectors compiler, making the introduction of higher-level constructs a necessity.

One other difficult case we encountered regards the handling of "overlapping FFT", where the successive frames for which an FFT transform is required overlap. We have not yet managed to find a totally general solution, with arbitrary overlaps, to this problem. Algorithm-specific questions such as these open opportunities for possible changes to the vector extension specification, and are at the core of what DSLs are about, i.e., finding a good match between generality and domain specificity.

6.2 Static Typechecking

One of the major limitations of Faustine, beside the lack of GUI support we already alluded to, lies in the current dynamic nature of its type checking. Signal rate and type information is currently computed and checked at run time. This may lead to run-time errors when programmers plug together unmatched signals (for instance via a ":" combinator). An optimizing compiler would preferably have to sport a static checker of types and rates. This is particularly true for a language such as Faust where having a precise knowledge of some of the key parameters in a program, e.g., delays, is crucial to assuring C++-like run-time performance.

Typing Vector Faust expressions is a non-trivial problem given the sophisticated nature of their type information. In particular, the presence of dependent datatypes (e.g., intervals specify the expected range of possible values of a given numeric type) is reminiscent of refinement [11] and liquid [24] types. One standard way to approach such typing systems is to use SMT solvers such as Z3[9] to handle the value-based equalities and inequalities implied by the typing rules. In addition to such tools, we envision to look carefully at the structure of constraints induced by the specifics of Faust (which does not allow first-class function values) or to design typing assistants that may ask for inputs from programmers to ensure type-checking correctness ([1,4,8,19,6]).

7 Conclusion

Faustine is a new interpreter-based test bed implemented to assess the validity of possible language extensions, in particular regarding vector operations, for the digital audio signal processing language Faust. More specifically, this platform is the first implementation of the vector/multirate extension for Faust proposed in the literature.

We used, as test cases, multidimensional FFTs and morphological image processing algorithms. These experiments suggest that the vector extension semantics can be implemented in a compliant way regarding the Faust language design.

[9] `http://z3.codeplex.com`

Yet, these same benchmarks show that further research is needed on the optimization front, both at the implementation and language design levels. This is paramount, given that the Faust language philosophy is to prove that a high level of expressibility is compatible with ultimate efficient run-time performance.

More generally, our design and implementation of Faustine strengthen the case for the development of interpreters, seen as flexible and easy-to-modify test beds for exploring the possible evolutionary paths of compiled languages. This idea seems to be even more convincing for highly optimized languages such as DSLs, for which introducing changes and updates within their large compiler platforms is a risky and costly proposition.

Acknowledgments. We thank Yann Orlarey for his help regarding Faust, Laurent Daverio for his input on LicencePlate and Benoit Pin for his advice on the Faustine development platform. The anonymous reviewers and Oleg Kyselyov provided many suggestions that greatly improved the quality of our paper. This work is part of the FEEVER project, partially funded by the Agence nationale de la recherche, under reference ANR-13-BS02-0008-01.

References

1. Armand, M., Faure, G., Grégoire, B., Keller, C., Théry, L., Werner, B.: A modular integration of SAT/SMT solvers to Coq through proof witnesses. In: Jouannaud, J.-P., Shao, Z. (eds.) CPP 2011. LNCS, vol. 7086, pp. 135–150. Springer, Heidelberg (2011)
2. Asanovic, K., Bodik, R., Demmel, J., Keaveny, T., Keutzer, K., Kubiatowicz, J., Morgan, N., Patterson, D., Sen, K., Wawrzynek, J., Wessel, D., Yelick, K.: A view of the parallel computing landscape. Commun. ACM 52(10), 56–67 (2009)
3. Barkati, K., Jouvelot, P.: Synchronous programming in audio processing: A lookup table oscillator case study. ACM Computing Surveys 46(2) (2014)
4. Bouton, T., de Oliveira, D.C.B., Déharbe, D., Fontaine, P.: veriT: An open, trustable and efficient SMT-solver. In: Schmidt, R.A. (ed.) CADE-22. LNCS, vol. 5663, pp. 151–156. Springer, Heidelberg (2009)
5. Brunthaler, S.: Why interpreters matter (at least for high level programming languages) (2012), `http://www.ics.uci.edu/~sbruntha/why-interpreters-matter.html`
6. Cuoq, P., Signoles, J., Baudin, P., Bonichon, R., Canet, G., Correnson, L., Monate, B., Prevosto, V., Puccetti, A.: Experience report: Ocaml for an industrial-strength static analysis framework. In: Proceedings of the 14th ACM SIGPLAN International Conference on Functional Programming, ICFP 2009, pp. 281–286. ACM, New York (2009)
7. Ellison, C., Rosu, G.: An executable formal semantics of C with applications. In: Proceedings of the 39th Annual ACM SIGPLAN-SIGACT Symposium on Principles of Programming Languages, POPL 2012, pp. 533–544. ACM, New York (2012)
8. Fontaine, P., Marion, J.-Y., Merz, S., Nieto, L.P., Tiu, A.F.: Expressiveness + automation + soundness: Towards combining SMT solvers and interactive proof assistants. In: Hermanns, H., Palsberg, J. (eds.) TACAS 2006. LNCS, vol. 3920, pp. 167–181. Springer, Heidelberg (2006)

9. Gamma, E., Helm, R., Johnson, R., Vlissides, J.: Design Patterns: Elements of Reusable Object-Oriented Software. Pearson Education (1994)
10. Ghosh, D.: DSLs in Action, 1st edn. Manning Publications Co., Greenwich (2010)
11. Gordon, A.D., Fournet, C.: Principles and applications of refinement types. Logics and Languages for Reliability and Security 25, 73–104 (2010)
12. Guillou, P.: Portage et optimisation d'applications de traitement d'images sur architecture many-core. Technical report, Centre de recherche en informatique, MINES ParisTech (2013)
13. Herrmann, C.A., Langhammer, T.: Combining partial evaluation and staged interpretation in the implementation of domain-specific languages. Science of Computer Programming 62(1), 47–65 (2006), Special Issue on the First MetaOCaml Workshop 2004
14. Hsieh, J.-W., Yu, S.-H., Chen, Y.-S.: Morphology-based license plate detection from complex scenes. In: Proceedings of the 16th International Conference on Pattern Recognition, vol. 3, pp. 176–179. IEEE (2002)
15. Hudak, P.: Building domain-specific embedded languages. ACM Computing Surveys 28(4es), 196 (1996)
16. Jouvelot, P.: ML: Un langage de maquettage? In: AFCET Workshop on New Languages for Software Engineering, Evry (1985)
17. Jouvelot, P., Orlarey, Y.: Dependent vector types for data structuring in multirate Faust. Comput. Lang. Syst. Struct. 37, 113–131 (2011)
18. Leroy, X., Doligez, D., Frisch, A., Garrigue, J., Rémy, D., Vouillon, J.: The OCaml system (1998)
19. Nguyen, Q.H., Kirchner, C., Kirchner, H.: External rewriting for skeptical proof assistants. Journal of Automated Reasoning 29(3-4), 309–336 (2002)
20. Orlarey, Y., Fober, D., Letz, S.: An algebra for block diagram languages. In: Proceedings of International Computer Music Conference, pp. 542–547 (2002)
21. Orlarey, Y., Fober, D., Letz, S.: Faust: an efficient functional approach to DSP programming. In: New Computational Paradigms for Computer Music (2009)
22. Ortiz, A.: Language design and implementation using Ruby and the interpreter. In: ACM SIGCSE Bulletin, vol. 40, pp. 48–52. ACM (2008)
23. Rémy, D.: Using, understanding, and unraveling the OCaml language from practice to theory and vice versa. In: Barthe, G., Dybjer, P., Pinto, L., Saraiva, J. (eds.) APPSEM 2000. LNCS, vol. 2395, pp. 413–536. Springer, Heidelberg (2002)
24. Rondon, P.M., Kawaguci, M., Jhala, R.: Liquid types. In: Proceedings of the 2008 ACM SIGPLAN Conference on Programming Language Design and Implementation, PLDI 2008, pp. 159–169. ACM, New York (2008)
25. Serra, J., Soille, P. (eds.): Mathematical morphology and its applications to image processing. Computational Imaging and Vision. Kluwer Academic Publishers (1994)
26. Steele, G.L., Sussman, G.J.: The art of the interpreter or, the modularity complex (parts zero, one, and two). Technical report, Cambridge, MA, USA (1978)

The Design and Implementation of BER MetaOCaml*

System Description

Oleg Kiselyov

University of Tsukuba, Japan
oleg@okmij.org

Abstract. MetaOCaml is a superset of OCaml extending it with the data type for program code and operations for constructing and executing such typed code values. It has been used for compiling domain-specific languages and automating tedious and error-prone specializations of high-performance computational kernels. By statically ensuring that the generated code compiles and letting us quickly run it, MetaOCaml makes writing generators less daunting and more productive.

The current BER MetaOCaml is a complete re-implementation of the original MetaOCaml by Taha, Calcagno and collaborators. Besides the new organization, new algorithms, new code, BER MetaOCaml adds a scope extrusion check superseding environment classifiers. Attempting to build code values with unbound or mistakenly bound variables (liable to occur due to mutation or other effects) is now caught early, raising an exception with good diagnostics. The guarantee that the generated code always compiles becomes unconditional, no matter what effects were used in generating the code.

We describe BER MetaOCaml stressing the design decisions that made the new code modular and maintainable. We explain the implementation of the scope extrusion check.

1 Introduction

MetaOCaml is a conservative extension of OCaml for "writing programs that generate programs". MetaOCaml adds to OCaml the type of *code values* (denoting "program code", or future-stage computations), and two basic constructs to build them: quoting and splicing. The generated code can be printed, stored in a file – or compiled and linked-back to the running program, thus implementing run-time code optimization.

MetaOCaml has been successfully used for specializing numeric and dynamic programming algorithms; building FFT kernels, compilers for an image processing domain-specific language (DSL), OCaml server pages; and generating families of specialized basic linear algebra and Gaussian Elimination routines, and high-performance stencil computations [1–4].

M. Codish and E. Sumii (Eds.): FLOPS 2014, LNCS 8475, pp. 86–102, 2014.

MetaOCaml is distinguished from Camlp4 and other such macro-processors by: hygiene (maintaining lexical scope); generating assuredly well-typed code; and the integration with higher-order functions, modules and other abstraction facilities of ML, hence promoting modularity and reuse of code generators. A well-typed BER MetaOCaml program produces the code that shall compile without type errors. We no longer have to puzzle out a compilation error in the generated code (which is typically large, obfuscated and with unhelpful variable names). We illustrate these features in §2.

The original MetaOCaml was developed by Walid Taha, Cristiano Calcagno and collaborators [5] as a dialect of OCaml. Therefore, MetaOCaml took the full advantage of the OCaml's back-end code generation, the standard and other libraries, the top-level, etc. Alas, the divergence between the two languages has made integrating OCaml's new features and improvements progressively more and more difficult. Eventually MetaOCaml could no longer be maintained without a major investment.

BER MetaOCaml [6] is a re-design and the complete re-implementation of MetaOCaml, with different algorithms and techniques. It aims at the most harmonious integration with OCaml and lowering the barrier for contribution. The compatibility with OCaml becomes relatively easy to maintain, bringing better tools, better diagnostics, new libraries and new features to code generators. Contributors of new ways of running the generated code (e.g., translating it to C or LLVM) no longer need to be familiar with the OCaml internals and keep recompiling the system. The new goals of modularity and maintainability called for new code organization and design decisions. BER MetaOCaml also took advantage of the large experience with MetaOCaml, which prompted the drastic change of retiring environment classifiers and introducing the scope extrusion check.

Despite polar design decisions and the different implementation (BER and the old MetaOCaml share no staging-related code apart from parsing and pretty-printing), BER MetaOCaml does run the old MetaOCaml user code with little or no change. The implementation differences between the two systems are summarized in Appendix A of the full paper[1]. Here is the brief comparison from the user point of view:

- Whereas the old MetaOCaml is formalized by λ^i_{let} [7], BER MetaOCaml implements the classifier-less version of that calculus[2]. The translation from λ^i_{let} to the latter only affects types (which can be inferred); the two calculi have the same dynamic semantics.
- BER MetaOCaml requires user-defined data types be declared in a separate file, see §4.
- BER MetaOCaml accepts programs that could not be typed before, see §5.2, making it easier to use modules to structure generators.

[1] `http://okmij.org/ftp/meta-programming/ber-design.pdf`

[2] We drop single-classifier annotations of λ^i_{let} and replace a sequence of classifiers with the natural number denoting its length. Strictly speaking, we also have to replace the terms open e and close e of λ^i_{let} with just e. However, these terms never show up explicitly in the user-written code, so their disappearance is unnoticeable.

- Scope extrusion (see §2.1 for illustration) during code generation was not detected before. BER MetaOCaml detects it early and raises an exception.

All in all, a type-annotation-free old MetaOCaml program using standard data types will be accepted by BER MetaOCaml as it was. It will produce the same result (or raise the scope-extrusion exception).

Although this paper is a system description of BER MetaOCaml, it highlights the guidance from theory (§5.3 in particular), or the regrettable lack of it. Staging in the presence of user-defined data types, described in §4, is a thorny problem that seems to have not been addressed in any of the staged calculi. Implementing BER MetaOCaml thus has suggested directions for further theoretical research.

Specifically, our contributions are as follows:

- the specific approach of adding staging to OCaml that minimizes the changes to the base system (significantly, compared to the old MetaOCaml), making it easier to contribute to and maintain MetaOCaml and to keep it consistent with new revisions of OCaml (see §3 and App. A);
- constructor restriction, §4: a new trade-off in supporting values of user-defined data types within the generated code. The restriction markedly simplifies the implementation. The experience with the restriction (first introduced in the January 2013 release) showed its burden to be light, justifying the trade-off;
- scope-extrusion check, §5: detecting scope extrusion promptly at the generator run-time, aborting the code generation with an informative error message pointing to problematic locations in the generator source code. The positive experience with the check (again first introduced in the January 2013 release) led to the retirement of environment classifiers in the current version. BER MetaOCaml guarantees that the successfully generated code is well-typed and well-scoped. The guarantee is now unconditional: it holds even if the generator performed arbitrary effects, including delimited control effects.

We start with a brief introduction to MetaOCaml and finish, §6, with related work. BER MetaOCaml is available from OPAM, among other places [6].

2 The Taste of MetaOCaml

This section introduces MetaOCaml and describes its features on very simple examples. §2.1 continues with a more realistic case, also explaining the need for control effects when generating code – and the accompanying danger of producing ill-scoped code.

Our first example is very familiar and simple, letting us focus on the MetaOCaml features used in its implementation. It centers on computing the n-th element of the Fibonacci-like sequence with the user-defined first two elements:

```
let rec gib n x y = match n with
  | 0 → x | 1 → y
  | n → let z = x + y in gib (n−1) y z
```

This ordinary OCaml code can be entered into MetaOCaml as it is since MetaOCaml is source- (and binary-) compatible with OCaml. If we are to compute gib n many times for a fixed n, we want to *specialize* gib to that n, obtaining the code that will later receive x and y and efficiently compute the n-th element of the sequence. We re-write gib annotating expressions as computed 'now' (when n is given) or 'later' (when x and y are given):

```
let rec sgib n x y = match n with
  | 0 → x | 1 → y
  | n → ⟨let z = ~x + ~y in ~(sgib (n−1) y ⟨z⟩ )⟩
⇝  val sgib : int → int code → int code → int code = <fun>

let sgib4 = ⟨fun x y → ~(sgib 4 ⟨x⟩ ⟨y⟩ )⟩ ;;
⇝  val sgib4 : (int → int → int) code = ⟨fun x_1 → fun y_2 →
   let z_3 = (x_1 + y_2) in let z_4 = (y_2 + z_3) in
   let z_5 = (z_3 + z_4) in z_5⟩

(!. sgib4) 1 1;;
⇝  − : int = 5
```

The two annotations, or staging constructs, are brackets ⟨e⟩ (in code, `.<e>.`) and escape ~e (in code `.~e`). Brackets ⟨e⟩ 'quasi-quote' the expression e, annotating it as computed later, or at the *future stage*. Escape ~e, which must occur within brackets, tells that e is computed now, at the *present stage*, but produces the code for later. That code is spliced into the containing bracket. The plus + appearing in brackets is not a symbol: it is the identifier bound to the OCaml function (infix operator) (+): int →int →int. A present-stage bound identifier referred to in the future stage is called cross-stage persistent (CSP). CSP is the third, less noticeable feature of MetaOCaml.

The inferred type of sgib (printed by the MetaOCaml top-level) tells its result is not an int: rather, it is int code – the type of expressions that compute an int. Hence, sgib is a code generator. Its type spells out which argument is received now, and which are later: the future-stage arguments have the code type. The type of a future-stage code is known now – letting us type-check future stage expressions and the code that generates them, assuring that the generated code is well-typed. For example, if we replace (+) in sgib with the floating-point addition (+ .) or omit an escape, we see a type error with an informative diagnostic.

The expression sgib4 shows how to actually apply sgib to produce the specialized code and how to obtain the int code values to pass as the last two arguments of sgib. The code value ⟨x⟩ represents an open code: the free variable "x". We may store such variables in reference cells and pass them as arguments and function results. MetaOCaml hence lets us manipulate (future-stage) variables *symbolically*. We can splice variables into larger future-stage expressions but we cannot compare or substitute them, learn their name, or examine the already generated code and take it apart. This pure generativity of MetaOCaml helps maintain hygiene: open code can be manipulated but the lexical scoping is still preserved[3].

The inferred type of sgib4 shows it as a code expression that will, when compiled, be a function on integers. Code, even of functions, can be printed, which is what the MetaOCaml top-level did. The prefix operator !. lets us *run* sgib4, that is, to compile it and link back to our program. The result can be used as an ordinary int→int→int function.

Generating code and then running it is specializing a frequently used function to some data obtained at run-time, e.g., from user input. In our example, !. sgib4 is such a version of gib n x y specialized to n= 4. The sgib4 code is straight-line and can be efficiently compiled and executed. The generated code can also be saved into a file. Since the generated code is ordinary OCaml, it can be compiled with ordinary OCaml compilers, even ocamlopt, and later linked into various *ordinary* OCaml applications. Thus, MetaOCaml can be used not only for run-time specialization, but also for offline generation of specialized library code, e.g., of BLAS and Linpack libraries.

Since hygiene and lexical scoping is one of the two main topics of the paper (see §5), we illustrate it on another example – demonstrating the crucial difference between brackets and Lisp quasi-quotation. The example is a one-line generator, producing the code shown underneath:

```
   ⟨fun x → ~(let body = ⟨x⟩ in ⟨fun x → ~body⟩ )⟩
⇝ ⟨fun x_1 → fun x_2 → x_1⟩
```

Re-written in Lisp, with anti- and un-quotations, it generates the code

```
   '( lambda (x) ,( let ((body 'x)) '( lambda (x) , body)))
⇝ '( lambda (x) (lambda (x) x))
```

with two indistinguishable instances of x, which denotes a different function. MetaOCaml maintains the distinction between the variables that, although identically named, are bound at different places. A variable in MetaOCaml is not just a symbol. We return to this topic in §5.

We have thus seen the five features that MetaOCaml adds to OCaml: brackets and escapes, CSP, showing and running code values. We will now see a realistic example of their use.

2.1 Code Motion

This section gives a glimpse of a realistic application of MetaOCaml, generating high-performance numerical kernels. We demonstrate generating matrix-matrix multiplication with a loop-invariant code motion, i.e., moving the code not depending on the loop index out of the loop. We will see the need for delimited control, the actual danger of generating ill-scoped code, and how BER MetaOCaml alerts of the danger before it becomes too late. We will hence see the

[3] At first blush, the inability to examine the generated code seems to preclude any optimizations. Nevertheless, generating optimal code is possible [3, 8, 9].

scope extrusion check, explained in depth in §5. For the lack of space, the running example is presented schematically and in a less general form: see the complete code[4] and [9] for the explanation of the overall approach.

To generate a variety of specialized kernels and optimize them easily, we introduce a minimalist linear-algebra DSL (demonstrating how the abstraction facilities of OCaml such as modules benefit code generation):

```
module type LINALG = sig
  type tdom
  type tdim   type tind   type tunit
  type tmatrix
  val ( * )     : tdom →tdom →tdom
  val mat_dim  : tmatrix → tdim * tdim
  val mat_get  : tmatrix → tind → tind → tdom
  val mat_incr : tmatrix → tind → tind →  tdom →tunit
  val loop     : tdim → (tind → tunit ) → tunit
end
```

The abstract type tdom is the type of scalars, with the operation to multiply them; tdim is the type of vector dimensions (zero-based) and tind is the type of the index; tunit is the unit type in our DSL. The operation mat_get accesses an element of a matrix, and mat_incr increments it. The DSL lets us write the multiplication of matrix a by matrix b with the result in c (which is assumed zero at the beginning) in the familiar form[5]:

```
module MMUL(S: LINALG) = struct open S
  let mmul a b c = loop (fst (mat_dim a)) @@ fun i →
    loop (fst (mat_dim b)) @@ fun k →
      loop (snd (mat_dim b)) @@ fun j →
        mat_incr c i j @@ mat_get a i k * mat_get b k j
end
```

With different implementations of LINALG, we obtain either functions for matrix-matrix multiplication (in float, int or other domains), or the code for such functions. For example, the following instance of LINALG produces the familiar matrix multiplication code

```
module LAintcode = struct
  type tdom = int code   type tdim = int code ...
  type tmatrix = int array array code
  let ( * ) = fun x y → ⟨~x * ~y⟩
  let mat_get a i j = ⟨(~a).( ~i ).( ~j )⟩
  let loop n body = ⟨for i = 0 to ~n−1 do ~(body ⟨i⟩) done⟩
end
```

[4] http://okmij.org/ftp/meta-programming/tutorial/loop_motion.ml

[5] The infix operator @@ is a low-precedence application, introduced in OCaml 4.01.

We can do better: in MMUL.mmul the expression mat_get a i k does not depend on the index j of the innermost loop, and can be moved out. We extend our DSL with the operation

```
module type LINALG_GENLET = sig include LINALG
 val genlet : tind → (unit → tdom) → tdom end
```

One may think of genlet k (fun () →e) as memoizing the value of e with key k in a 1-slot memo table. We re-write mmul and manually introduce this memoization optimization:

```
module MMULopt(S: LINALG_GENLET) = struct open S
  let mmul a b c = loop (fst (mat_dim a)) @@ fun i →
    loop (fst (mat_dim b)) @@ fun k →
      loop (snd (mat_dim b)) @@ fun j →
        mat_incr c i j @@ genlet k (fun () → mat_get a i k) *
                          genlet j (fun () → mat_get b k j)
end
```

We extend LAintcode by adding genlet, the new realization of tind and the new implementation of loop. In thus extended LAintcode_opt, genlet k (fun () → ⟨e⟩) evaluates to a future-stage variable ⟨t⟩ bound by **let** t = e **in** ... inserted at the beginning of the loop with the index k. LAintcode_opt has to rely [10] on delimited control effects, provided by the library delimcc. MMULopt(LAintcode_opt).mmul then generates the following code

```
⟨fun a_7 b_8 c_9 →
   for i_10 = 0 to (Array.length a_7) − 1 do
     for i_11 = 0 to (Array.length b_8) − 1 do
       let t_14 = a_7.(i_10).(i_11) in
       for i_12 = 0 to (Array.length b_8.(0)) − 1 do
         let t_13 = b_8.(i_11).(i_12) in
         c_9.(i_10).(i_12) ← c_9.(i_10).(i_12) + t_14 * t_13
  done done done⟩
```

The expressions to access the elements of a and b are let-bound; a is accessed outside the innermost loop. The code motion is evident.

The operation genlet is powerful but dangerous. If we by mistake instead of genlet j (fun () →mat_get b k j) in MMULopt.mmul write genlet k (fun () → mat_get b k j), we pull the code generated by mat_get b k j out of the innermost loop as well. The old MetaOCaml then produces:

```
⟨fun a_7 b_8 c_9 →
   for i_10 = 0 to (Array.length a_7) − 1 do
     for i_11 = 0 to (Array.length b_8) − 1 do
       let t_13 = b_8.(i_11).(i_12) in
       let t_14 = a_7.(i_10).(i_11) in
       for i_12 = 0 to (Array.length b_8.(0)) − 1 do
         c_9.(i_10).(i_12) ← c_9.(i_10).(i_12) + t_14 * t_13
  done done done⟩
```

Although the generated code is simple, it is already hard to see what is wrong with it: as typical, variables in the generated code have unhelpful names. If we look carefully at the let-binding t_13, we see that the variable i_12, the index of the innermost loop, escaped its binding, creating the so-called scope extrusion. The escaped variable is unbound in the generated code above. More dangerously, it may be accidentally captured by another binding. The generated code will then successfully compile; the resulting bug will be very difficult to find. Since the scope extrusion has not been detected, it is hard to determine what part of the generator did it by looking only at the final result.

In contrast, BER MetaOCaml detects the scope extrusion with a good diagnostic. For example, executing the generator with the mistaken genlet aborts the execution when b_8.(i_11).(i_12) has just been moved out of the innermost loop, with the error that identifies the expression containing the escaped variable (the matrix element access), the name of the variable and where it was supposed to be bound (in the loop header). No bad code is hence generated. The exception backtrace further helps find the mistake in the generator[6].

We have seen the benefit of effects in code generation, for loop-invariant code movement. The same technique can also do loop interchange and loop tiling. We have also seen the danger of generating ill-scoped code and MetaOCaml's detecting the scope extrusion as soon as it occurs. The section hopefully has given the taste of generator abstractions; see the poster [9] for an elaborated example of using the OCaml module system to state an algorithm in a clear way and then apply various optimizations.

3 Design of BER MetaOCaml

This section briefly overviews the design of BER MetaOCaml and outlines our approach to implementing staging. The following two sections will explain in depth two particularly subtle issues, user-defined types and the scope extrusion check. Our guiding principle is to make MetaOCaml easier to maintain and use by making its changes to the OCaml code base smaller and modular.

MetaOCaml has to modify OCaml to extend its syntax with staging annotations and its type checker with the notion of the present and future stages. Unlike the original MetaOCaml, BER MetaOCaml tries to minimize the modifications and hence makes different design decisions, see below and §4. Whereas the original MetaOCaml was a fork, BER MetaOCaml is maintained as a set of patches to OCaml plus a library. Such an organization reflects the separation between the MetaOCaml 'kernel' and 'user-level'. The kernel (patched OCaml) is responsible for building and type-checking code values. The user-level processes closed code values, e.g., prints or runs them. As with the kernel/user-level separation in an OS, adding a new way to run code (e.g., to compile to Javascript) is

[6] The real linear-algebra DSL will unlikely offer genlet to the end-user. Rather, genlet will be incorporated into mat_get, where it could compare loop indices, determine which one corresponds to an innerer loop, and insert let appropriately. The scope extrusion may well happen however during the development of the DSL.

like writing a regular library, which requires no patching or recompilation of the MetaOCaml system. The separation lessens the maintenance burden and makes it easier to contribute to MetaOCaml.

Here is an example of how BER MetaOCaml minimizes changes to OCaml. For the most part, type checking is invariant of the stage (bracketing) level, with a notable exception [7]. Identifiers bound by future-stage binding forms should be annotated with their stage level. The original MetaOCaml added a field val_level to the value_description record describing an identifier in the type checker. This change has lead to the cascade of patches at every place a new identifier is added to the type environment. A new OCaml version typically modifies the type checker quite heavily. Integrating all these modifications into MetaOCaml, accounting for the new field, is a hard job. It is avoidable however: we may associate identifiers with levels differently, by adding a new map to the environment that tells the level of each future-stage identifier. Any identifier not in the domain of that map is deemed present-stage. This alternative helped BER MetaOCaml significantly reduce the amount of changes to the OCaml type checker and make MetaOCaml more maintainable[7].

BER MetaOCaml follows the general staging implementation approach by Taha et al.[5]. After type checking, the code with brackets and escapes is post-processed to translate brackets and escapes into expressions that produce code values[8]. These expressions are built from primitive code generators, which produce a representation of code values; in MetaOCaml, it is OCaml's abstract syntax tree, called Parsetree. Other possible code representations (e.g., the intermediate language or the typed AST) are more difficult to compose. The post-processing of the type-checked code by and large implements the rules in [5, Figure 3]. (The translation of binding forms is new and described in §5.) For example, <succ 1> is translated to the pure OCaml expression (slightly abbreviated) `build_apply [Pexp_ident "succ"; Pexp_constant (Const_int 1)]` which will construct, at run-time, a Pexp_apply node of the Parsetree. Here, Pexp_ident and Pexp_constant are constructors of Parsetree.

With staging annotations eliminated after the translation, the original OCaml back-end (compiling to the intermediate language, optimizing, and generating the target code) can be used as it is. To run the generated code, we follow the pattern in the OCaml top-level, which also needs to compile and execute the (user-entered) code. Having given an overview of BER MetaOCaml, we describe in depth two of its features, in which BER MetaOCaml significantly differs from the original one.

---

[7] The first version of BER MetaOCaml modified 35 files in the OCaml distributions, which is 23 fewer files compared to the original MetaOCaml. The patch to the distribution was 59KB in size, reduced to 48KB in the current version.

[8] Doing such a translation before type checking is tantalizing because it can be done as a pre-processing step and requires no changes to OCaml. Alas, we will not be able to support let-polymorphism within brackets; also, the value restriction will preclude polymorphic code values like $\langle [] \rangle$.

4 Staging User-Defined Data Types

We now illustrate the first of the two distinct features of BER MetaOCaml: the different handling of values of user-defined data types within brackets.

Algebraic data types and records are one of the salient features of OCaml, which, alas, have not been considered in staged calculi. The theory therefore gives no guidance on staging the code with constructors of user defined data types, such as the following:

```
type foo = Foo | Bar of int
⟨function Bar _ → Foo⟩
```

The generated program, which can be stored in a file, is **function** Bar _ →Foo. Compiling this file will fail since Foo and Bar are not defined. The problem is how to put a data type declaration into the generated code, which is syntactically an *expression* and hence cannot contain declarations.

The old MetaOCaml dealt with the problem by modifying the AST representing the generated code and adding a field for declarations (actually, the entire type environment) [5, §6.1]. Such a change sent ripples of modifications throughout the type checker, and was one of the main reasons for the divergence from OCaml, which contributed to MetaOCaml's demise.

We observe that there is no problem compiling the code such as **true**, raise Not_found, Some [1] and {Complex.re = 1.0; im = 2.0} – even though labels like re and data constructors like Some are likewise undefined within the compilation unit. However, the data types bool, option, list, Complex.t are either Pervasive or defined in the (separately compiled) standard library. External type declarations like those of Complex.t are found in the compiled interface complex.cmi, which can be looked up when the generated code is compiled. This observation leads to the *constructor restriction*: "all data constructors and record labels used within brackets must come from the types that are declared in separately compiled modules". The code at the beginning of the section is rejected by BER MetaOCaml. The type declaration foo must be moved into an interface file, separately compiled, and be available somewhere within the OCaml library search path – as if it were the standard library type.

Thanks to the constructor restriction, BER MetaOCaml evades the thorny problem of user-defined data types and eliminates the AST modifications by the original MetaOCaml, bringing BER MetaOCaml much closer to OCaml and making it significantly more maintainable.

We are researching the possibility to cleanly lift the constructor restriction. On the other hand, from the experience with BER MetaOCaml (for example, project [9] and the MetaOCaml tutorial at CUFP 2013) the restriction does not seem to be bothersome or hard to satisfy.

5 Detecting Scope Extrusion

MetaOCaml lets us manipulate open code. This section describes the complexities and trade-offs in making sure all free variables in such code will eventually be bound, by their intended binders. BER MetaOCaml reverses the choice of its predecessors and trades an incomplete type-level check for a comprehensive and more informative dynamic scope-extrusion check. A well-typed BER MetaOCaml program may attempt, when executed, to run an open code or construct ill-scoped code – the code with a free variable that 'escaped' its binder and hence will remain unbound or, worse, bound accidentally. BER MetaOCaml detects such attempts early, aborting the execution of the generator with an informative error message. If the code is successfully generated, it is guaranteed to be well-typed and well-scoped – no matter what effects have been used in its generation.

5.1 Scope-Extrusion Check in Action

Manipulating open code is overshadowed by two dangers. First, the operation to run the code may be applied to the code still under construction:

```
⟨fun x y → ~(let z = !. ⟨x+ 1⟩ in ⟨z⟩ ))⟩                    (1)
```

The old MetaOCaml rejects this code with the type error:[9]

```
⟨fun x y → ~(let z = .! ⟨x+ 1⟩ in ⟨z⟩ ))⟩
                        ^^^^^^^
.! error : α not generalizable in (α, int ) code
```

BER MetaOCaml type checks this generator but its evaluation aborts with the run-time exception:

```
Exception: Failure
 "The code built at Characters 29−32:
  ⟨fun x y → ~(let z = !. ⟨x+ 1⟩ in ⟨z⟩ ))⟩
                          ^^^
 is not closed: identifier x_1 bound at Characters 6−7:
  ⟨fun x y → ~(let z = !. ⟨x+ 1⟩ in ⟨z⟩ ))⟩
       ^
is free".
```

The error message is more informative, explicitly telling the name of the free variable and pointing out, in the generator source code, the binder that should have bound it.

The second, far more common danger comes from effects: a piece of code with a free variable may be stored within the scope of its future-stage binder, to be retrieved from outside:

```
let r = ref ⟨0⟩ in
let _ = ⟨fun x → ~(r := ⟨x+ 1⟩; ⟨x⟩ ))⟩ in                   (2)
⟨fun y → ~(! r)⟩ ;;
```

(A free variable can also be smuggled out of its binder by raising an exception containing open code, or through control effects, shown in §2.1). The old

[9] In the old MetaOCaml, the operation to run the code was a special form spelled .!. In BER MetaOCaml, it is the regular function and spelled !., following the OCaml lexical convention for prefix operators.

MetaOCaml accepts this generator and lets it run to completion, producing ⟨**fun** y_2 →(x_1 + 1)⟩, which can be further spliced-in. It is only when we attempt to execute the final code we get a run-time exception Unbound value x_1. If we save the code in a file for offline compilation, the error will be discovered only when we later compile this file.

Although BER MetaOCaml also accepts generator (2), it does *not* let it run to completion. The generator now produces nothing: it aborts with the informative exception:

```
Exception: Failure
 "Scope extrusion detected at Characters 96-111:
           ⟨fun y → ~(! r)⟩ ;;
           ^^^^^^^^^^^^^^^
 for code built at Characters 67-70:
           let _ = ⟨fun x → ~(r := ⟨x+ 1⟩; ⟨x⟩ )⟩ in
                                   ^^^
 for the identifier x_5 bound at Characters 52-53:
           let _ = ⟨fun x → ~(r := ⟨x+ 1⟩; ⟨x⟩ )⟩ in
                        ^".
```

5.2 The Trade-Offs of Environment Classifiers

Previous versions of MetaOCaml employed so-called environment classifiers [11] to prevent the first, quite rare, danger at compile-time: example (1) was rejected by the type checker. Environment classifiers do not help in detecting scope extrusion errors. BER MetaOCaml retired environment classifiers and introduced the dynamic scope extrusion check. The problem with example (1) now reported when running the generator rather than when type-checking it. The problem with example (2) is now reported, early and informatively.

Removing the type-level feature and introducing the dynamic check is the significant departure of BER MetaOCaml from the original system. We summarize this static-dynamic trade-off as follows.

Accepting More Good Programs. BER MetaOCaml accepts programs that did not type check previously, for example, ⟨**fun** x →!. x⟩. With environment classifiers, type-checking this code requires impredicative polymorphism. More practically relevant, the operation to run the code was a special form in the old MetaOCaml, with its special typing rules (akin to runST in Haskell). It was not first-class. In BER MetaOCaml, (!.) is the ordinary function. Removing environment classifiers simplified the type system. Previously, a code value ⟨1⟩ had the type (α,int) code where α is the classifier. When defining a new data type, we had to parameterize it by the classifier if the data type may contain code values. This extra type parameter caused not only cosmetic problems: it notably hindered the use of module system to structure generators. For example, LAintcode in §2.1 could not be an implementation of the signature LINALG. To accommodate code types and their classifiers, all abstract types in LINALG should have an extra type parameter, even though LINALG may have implementations without code values. When writing signatures we had to anticipate their implementations.

Accepting More Bad Programs. The old MetaOCaml rejected example (1) before running the generator. BER MetaOCaml detects the problem only at run-time. Extensive experience with MetaOCaml showed that the problematic code like (1) is exceedingly rare. Because of the special typing rules of .!, this operator was essentially usable only at the top level; one rarely sees it in subexpressions. Furthermore, by its very design an environment classifier represents just a staging level rather than an individual variable. Therefore, the type checker can tell that the code to run was open but it cannot tell the name of its free variable. Although BER MetaOCaml exception is raised at run-time, the error message refers to the free variable by its name, pointing out its binder.

Detecting Previously Undetected Error. Environment classifiers do not help in detecting scope extrusion. A well-typed generator could produce ill-scoped code. In contrast, in BER MetaOCaml the generator stops as soon as the ill-scoped piece of code is about to be used in any way, spliced, run, or shown. It throws an exception with a fairly detailed and helpful error message, pointing out the variable that got away and the location of the extrusion, in terms of the source code of the *generator*. Since the error is an exception, the exception stack backtrace further describes exactly which part of the generator caused that variable leak. Previously, we would discover the problem, in the best case, only when compiling the generated code. It could be quite a challenge in figuring out which part of the generator is to blame.

Implementation Complexity. On the whole, environment classifiers are easier to implement. Checking for scope extrusion is not as straightforward as it may seem, as described in the next section. It requires more code, which is however isolated in one MetaOCaml-specific module, mainly, outside the type checker.

Run-Time Cost. The scope extrusion check adds run-time overhead to code generation. As the next section mentions, micro-benchmarks and experience showed the overhead to be negligible.

The fact that the old MetaOCaml let a well-typed, effectful generator produce ill-scoped code must not be confused with an implementation bug. It was not a coding error. No practical approaches to statically prevent scope extrusion were known at the time. Even now, there are only hopeful candidates relying on fancy types. Environment classifiers are a remarkable achievement: they are relatively simple to implement, they fit within OCaml type checking and inference, and they statically preclude a class of scoping problems, illustrated by example (1). At the time of writing the original MetaOCaml, it was unclear which of the two scoping problems, example (1) or (2), turns out more common in practice. The decision to retire the classifiers was made in light of all the accumulated experience with MetaOCaml.

5.3 Implementing the Scope-Extrusion Check

Detection of scope extrusion may appear straightforward: traverse the result of a generator looking for unbound identifiers. Instead of traversing, we may annotate each code value with a list of free variables therein; code generation combinators will combine annotations as they combine code values. The code to be run must be annotated with no free variables – reflecting the requirement only closed code be run. That requirement is necessary but not sufficient however. Detecting the scope extrusion by checking the result of the entire generator is too late: it is hard to determine which part of the generator caused the extrusion. Furthermore, scope extrusion does not necessarily lead to an unbound variable: the escaped variable may be accidentally captured by a stray binder. We need early detection of scope extrusion; first we need a precise criterion for it.

The staging theory lets us define scope extrusion and identify it early. The most suitable is not the λU-staged calculus by Taha et al. [5, Fig.1] with brackets and escapes but the 'single-stage target language' of code-generation combinators [5, Fig.2], which we call λ_{AST}. The latter underlies MetaOCaml and is proven to simulate the λU [5, Corollary 1]. The insight comes from translating the characteristic example ⟨**fun** x → ~(body ⟨x⟩)⟩ (where body is a variable bound somewhere in the environment) to code combinators, and evaluating it by the rules of λ_{AST}. The result, to be called efun, is presented in a sugared form compared to [5]:

```
build_fun_simple  "x" (fun x → body (Var x))
```

where Var (and Lam below) are self-explanatory data constructors of the code representation data type, AST. Our sugared translation is a higher-order abstract syntax (HOAS) representation of the original future-stage function: the future-stage variable and the binder are translated to the present-stage variable and the binder, but of a code type. The big-step evaluation relation of λ_{AST} has the form N;e ⇝v where e is an expression, v is its value and N is a sequence of names ν (which are called symbols in [5] and denoted α). We obtain from [5, Fig.2] that N;efun ⇝Lam(ν,v) provided N,ν; (**fun** x →body (Var x)) ν ⇝v and ν is chosen to be not in N. During the evaluation of body (Var ν), Var ν is the code of the free variable, whose name however appears in the name environment N,ν. The body may store Var ν in a mutable cell. If it is retrieved after efun is evaluated, ν would no longer appear in the name environment current at that point. That is scope extrusion.

The final insight – which leads to the implementation and accommodates delimited control – is that the name environment N is the *dynamic* environment; ν created during the evaluation of build_fun_simple is in the *dynamic scope* of the latter. In other words, build_fun_simple dynamically binds the name of its free variable during the evaluation of its body.

Definition. At any point during the evaluation, an occurrence of an open-code value with a free variable whose name is not dynamically bound is called *scope extrusion.*[10]

[10] Normally, dynamic scope cannot be reentered. Therefore, a scope extrusion that occurs at one point in the evaluation will persist through the end. Delimited control however can reenter once exited dynamic scope. Therefore, our definition could potentially raise false alarm. We have not observed such cases in practice.

This definition clarifies our intuitions. It lets us detect scope extrusion without waiting for the result of the generation. It also has a straightforward implementation, without representing N explicitly. The function build_fun_simple (the actual name of the code-generating combinator) creates a fresh variable name and dynamically binds it. Each code value carries the list (heap actually, for ease of merging) of its free variables. Every code-generating combinator verifies that every free variable of the argument code value is currently dynamically bound. A scope-extrusion exception is thrown otherwise. App. B gives further details.

Microbenchmarks (generating code with up to 120 free variables) and experience shows that the scope-extrusion check imposes a linear (in the number of free variables) and negligible cost.

We have described a dynamic, generation-time test, for scope extrusion. A variable that got away is detected as soon as its code is used in any way (spliced, printed, run). The check generates very helpful error messages with precise location information. The location refers to the generator code (rather than the generated code). The test works even in presence of delimited control.

6 Related Work

Building code by quasi-quotation is the hallmark of Lisp (see [12] for overview). Any effects are permitted in code generation but the result is not even assured well-formed. Scheme macros support hygiene to some extent (see [13] for overview) but the generator is written in a restricted language of syntax transformers, which permits no effects.

Metaprogramming in Haskell is quite similar to that in Lisp. The original Template Haskell (TH) [14] provides anti- and un-quotation, generates declarations as well as expressions, and permits arbitrary IO effects in the generator. On the flip side, TH is unhygienic. The constructed code may well be ill-typed, and has to be type checked when spliced into the main program (in compile-time code generation) or run, using GHC API. Alas, type errors reported at that stage come with poor diagnostics and refer to the generated code rather than the generator. Furthermore, mistakenly bound variables escape detection. Recently, Haskell gained so-called typed template Haskell expressions TExp. Like MetaOCaml, they construct only expressions (rather than, say, declarations) and are typed checked as being constructed, hence ensuring the generated code is well-typed. TExp offer no run operation; to prevent scope extrusion, any effects during code generation are disallowed.

Code generation is part of partial evaluation (PE); hence a partial evaluator that handles effectful code and performs effects at specialization time has to contend with a possible scope extrusion. Since the user of PE has no direct control over the code generation or specialization, scope extrusion can be prevented by the careful design of PE [15]. Explicit staging annotations let the programmer directly control specialization, and take blame for scope extrusion. BER MetaOCaml places the blame early (before the code generation is finished) and precisely, within the source code of the generator.

Scala-Virtualized [16] successfully demonstrates an alternative to quasi-quotation: code-generating combinators. Normally, using them directly is inconvenient. The pervasive overloading of Scala however makes code generators look like ordinary expressions. For example, 1 + 2 may mean either the addition of two numbers or building the code for it, depending on the type of that expression. Scala-Virtualized takes the overloading to extreme: everything is an (overloaded) method call, including conditionals, loops, pattern-matching, record declarations, type annotations and other special forms. DSL expressions may look like ordinary Scala code but produce various code representations, which can then be optimized and compiled to target code. Lightweight Modular Staging (LMS) [17] further provides code representations used in the Scala compiler itself. A DSL writer then gets for free the compiler optimizations like common-subexpression elimination, loop fusion, etc. The many DSLs built with LMS proved the approach successful.

Code-generating combinators however cannot easily express polymorphic let (see §3) and often polymorphic code. LMS was not used for DSL with polymorphism. In contrast, polymorphic let is common in the generated OCaml code. With regards to hygiene and scope extrusion, LMS takes the same pragmatic approach as Lisp.

7 Conclusions and Further Plans

We have presented BER MetaOCaml, a superset of OCaml for writing, conveniently and with ease of mind, programs that generate programs. BER MetaOCaml continues the tradition of the original MetaOCaml by Taha, Calcagno and collaborators, remaining largely compatible with it. There are many design and implementation differences under the hood. They are motivated by the desire to make it easier to maintain and contribute to MetaOCaml, to make it more convenient to use and to catch more errors, and earlier. The motivations are somewhat contradictory, and we had to make choices and test them through experience. We strove to report errors as informatively as possible.

BER MetaOCaml poses questions for the staging theory, of accounting for user-defined data types, objects, modules and GADTs. On the development agenda are adding more ways to 'run' code values, by translating them to C, Fortran, LLVM, Verilog and others. MetaOCaml can then be used for generating libraries of specialized C, etc. code.

Active development, new modular structure, new features of MetaOCaml will hopefully attract more users and contributors, and incite future research into type-safe meta-programming.

Acknowledgments. I am very grateful to Walid Taha for introducing me to MetaOCaml, for his encouragement, and a great number of stimulating conversations. I thank Cristiano Calcagno, Jacques Carette, Jun Inoue, Yukiyoshi Kameyama and Chung-chieh Shan for many helpful discussions and encouragement. Many helpful comments by the anonymous reviewers are gratefully acknowledged.

References

[1] Swadi, K., Taha, W., Kiselyov, O., Pašalić, E.: A monadic approach for avoiding code duplication when staging memoized functions. In: PEPM, pp. 160–169 (2006)
[2] Carette, J., Kiselyov, O.: Multi-stage programming with functors and monads: Eliminating abstraction overhead from generic code. Science of Computer Programming 76, 349–375 (2011)
[3] Kiselyov, O., Taha, W.: Relating FFTW and split-radix. In: Wu, Z., Chen, C., Guo, M., Bu, J. (eds.) ICESS 2004. LNCS, vol. 3605, pp. 488–493. Springer, Heidelberg (2005)
[4] Lengauer, C., Taha, W. (eds.) MetaOCaml Workshop 2004, Special Issue on the 1st MetaOCaml Workshop (2004); 62(1) of Science of Computer Programming (2006)
[5] Calcagno, C., Taha, W., Huang, L., Leroy, X.: Implementing multi-stage languages using ASTs, gensym, and reflection. In: Pfenning, F., Macko, M. (eds.) GPCE 2003. LNCS, vol. 2830, pp. 57–76. Springer, Heidelberg (2003)
[6] Kiselyov, O.: BER MetaOCaml N101 (2013), `http://okmij.org/ftp/ML/MetaOCaml.html`
[7] Calcagno, C., Moggi, E., Taha, W.: ML-like inference for classifiers. In: Schmidt, D. (ed.) ESOP 2004. LNCS, vol. 2986, pp. 79–93. Springer, Heidelberg (2004)
[8] Kiselyov, O., Swadi, K.N., Taha, W.: A methodology for generating verified combinatorial circuits. In: EMSOFT, pp. 249–258 (2004)
[9] Kiselyov, O.: Modular, convenient, assured domain-specific optimizations: Can generative programming deliver? Poster at APLAS (2012), `http://okmij.org/ftp/meta-programming/Shonan1.html`
[10] Kameyama, Y., Kiselyov, O., Shan, C.-c.: Shifting the stage: Staging with delimited control. Journal of Functional Programming 21, 617–662 (2011)
[11] Taha, W., Nielsen, M.F.: Environment classifiers. In: POPL, pp. 26–37 (2003)
[12] Bawden, A.: Quasiquotation in Lisp. In: PEPM. Number NS-99-1 in Note, pp. 4–12. BRICS (1999)
[13] Herman, D.: A Theory of Typed Hygienic Macros. PhD thesis, Northeastern University, Boston, MA (2010)
[14] Sheard, T., Peyton Jones, S.L.: Template meta-programming for Haskell. In: Chakravarty, M.M.T. (ed.) Haskell Workshop, pp. 1–16 (2002)
[15] Thiemann, P., Dussart, D.: Partial evaluation for higher-order languages with state (1999), `http://www.informatik.uni-freiburg.de/~thiemann/papers/mlpe.ps.gz`
[16] Rompf, T., Amin, N., Moors, A., Haller, P., Odersky, M.: Scala-Virtualized: linguistic reuse for deep embeddings. Higher-Order and Symbolic Computation (2013)
[17] Rompf, T., Odersky, M.: Lightweight modular staging: a pragmatic approach to runtime code generation and compiled DSLs. Commun. ACM 55, 121–130 (2012)

On Cross-Stage Persistence in Multi-Stage Programming

Yuichiro Hanada and Atsushi Igarashi

Graduate School of Informatics, Kyoto University, Kyoto, Japan

Abstract. We develop yet another typed multi-stage calculus $\lambda^{\triangleright\%}$. It extends Tsukada and Igarashi's $\lambda^{\triangleright}$ with cross-stage persistence and is equipped with all the key features that MetaOCaml-style multi-stage programming supports. It has an arguably simple, substitution-based full-reduction semantics and enjoys basic properties of subject reduction, confluence, and strong normalization. Progress also holds under an alternative semantics that takes staging into account and models program execution. The type system of $\lambda^{\triangleright\%}$ gives a sufficient condition when residual programs can be safely generated, making $\lambda^{\triangleright\%}$ more suitable for writing generating extensions than previous multi-stage calculi.

1 Introduction

Multi-stage programming (MSP) is a programming paradigm in which a programmer can manipulate, generate, and execute code fragments at run time. These features enhance reusability of programs and make optimizations easier by writing program specializers [1]. A number of programming languages that support multi-stage programming have been proposed [2–7], not to mention Lisp and Scheme, and provide different sets of language constructs for MSP.

Among these MSP languages, MetaOCaml provides (hygienic) quasiquotation (called brackets and escape), eval (called run) [3]. Brackets $\langle e \rangle$ are a quotation of expression e to make a code value and escape (written $\tilde{}e$) splices the value of e, which is supposed to be a quotation, into the surrounding quotation. For example, the following MetaOCaml expression[1]

$$\textbf{let}\ a = \langle 1+2 \rangle\ \textbf{in}\ \langle \tilde{}a * \tilde{}a \rangle$$

evaluates to $\langle (1+2)*(1+2) \rangle$. Run (written **run** e here[2]) evaluates the expression inside a given code value, and so

$$\textbf{run}\ (\textbf{let}\ a = \langle 1+2 \rangle\ \textbf{in}\ \langle \tilde{}a * \tilde{}a \rangle)$$

yields 9 (without brackets).

Another interesting feature of MetaOCaml is called cross-stage persistence (CSP), which allows a computed value to be put into brackets: for example, the expression

$$\textbf{let}\ a = 1+2\ \textbf{in}\ \langle a * a \rangle$$

[1] Actually, $\langle e \rangle$ is written `.<e>.` and $\tilde{}e$ is written `.~e` in MetaOCaml.

[2] In MetaOCaml, `.!e` is used for **run** e.

M. Codish and E. Sumii (Eds.): FLOPS 2014, LNCS 8475, pp. 103–118, 2014.

(without escapes on a inside the brackets) is valid in MetaOCaml and yields $\langle 3 * 3 \rangle$. Here, a is bound to the integer value 3 and CSP (implicitly applied to variable references) allows referencing a variable declared outside of the brackets. Note that, as Taha and Sheard discuss [3], CSP is *not* lifting, which converts a value into its syntactic representation (although CSP for basic values can be implemented by lifting). In fact, CSP can be applied to a variable denoting *any value*, including functions, references, or even file descriptors, which do not always have syntactic representations. CSP is a very important feature in practice, because a programmer can freely use library functions inside brackets as in $\langle \mathit{List.map}\ (\lambda x.x + 1)\ [3; 4] \rangle$.

Most type systems for MSP languages aim at ensuring safety of the code generated by multi-stage programs, as well as that of multi-stage programs themselves. A challenging issue was how to prevent **run** from executing open code (namely, code values that contain free variables), while allowing manipulation of open code, which is necessary to generate efficient code. Taha and Nielsen [8] developed a multi-stage calculus λ^{α} with all the features above and proved that its type system guaranteed safety in the above sense. A key idea in the type system of λ^{α} is the introduction of *environment classifiers* (or simply classifiers). Roughly speaking, classifiers statically keep track of information on free variables in code values and prevents code value containing free variables from being **run**. Later, its type system was adapted to ML-style type reconstruction and has become a basis of MetaOCaml [9].

Tsukada and Igarashi [10] proposed another typed MSP calculus $\lambda^{\triangleright}$, whose type system, which uses a classifier-like mechanism, can be regarded as a certain modal logic through the Curry–Howard isomorphism. Although $\lambda^{\triangleright}$ supports only brackets, escape, and **run**, its operational semantics has a more "standard flavor" than that of λ^{α} (and MetaOCaml) in that reduction can be defined in terms of (a few kinds of) substitutions.

In this paper, we present yet another multi-stage calculus $\lambda^{\triangleright\%}$, which is an extension of $\lambda^{\triangleright}$ with CSP and study its properties. We give the semantics of $\lambda^{\triangleright\%}$ in two ways: full nondeterministic reduction, which allows any redex (even inside quotations) to be reduced, and (call-by-value) staged reduction, which is a subrelation of the full reduction and allows only a certain redex at the lowest stage to be reduced. Interestingly, the semantic "delta" over $\lambda^{\triangleright\%}$ is surprisingly small, making proofs from $\lambda^{\triangleright}$ easy to extend to $\lambda^{\triangleright\%}$. Our technical contributions are summarized as follows:

- we give the formal definition of $\lambda^{\triangleright\%}$ with its syntax, type system, full reduction, and staged reduction;
- for the full reduction, we prove subject reduction, strong normalization and confluence; and
- for the staged reduction, we prove progress and a property called Type-Safe Residualization, which means that a well-typed program of code type yields a code value whose body is also a well-typed and serializable program.

We also discuss relationship between CSP and program residualization and point out a problem that, although MetaOCaml enjoys a variant of Type-Safe Residualization, MetaOCaml is not very suitable for writing offline generators because of CSP. Our type system introduces residualizable code types to solve the problem.

1.1 Organization of the Paper

Section 2 gives an informal overview of our calculus $\lambda^{\triangleright\%}$ after a brief review of $\lambda^{\triangleright}$. Section 3 defines the syntax, type system, and full reduction of $\lambda^{\triangleright\%}$ formally and shows relevant properties. Then, Section 4 defines the staged semantics and shows Progress and Type-Safe Residualization. Finally, Section 6 discusses related work and Section 7 gives concluding remarks.

2 Informal Overview of $\lambda^{\triangleright\%}$

In this section, we give an informal overview of $\lambda^{\triangleright\%}$ after reviewing $\lambda^{\triangleright}$ [10], on which $\lambda^{\triangleright\%}$ is based.

2.1 $\lambda^{\triangleright}$

In $\lambda^{\triangleright}$, brackets and escapes are written "$\blacktriangleright_\alpha M$" and "$\blacktriangleleft_\alpha M$", respectively. For example, the first example in Section 1 can be represented as:

$$M_1 \stackrel{\text{def}}{=} (\lambda a : \tau. \blacktriangleright_\alpha(\blacktriangleleft_\alpha a * \blacktriangleleft_\alpha a))\,(\blacktriangleright_\alpha 1 + 2)$$

where τ is a suitable type for code values, which we discuss below. In addition to ordinary β-reduction, there is a reduction rule to cancel a pair of brackets under an escape:

$$\blacktriangleleft_\alpha(\blacktriangleright_\alpha M) \longrightarrow M.$$

So, M_1 reduces to $\blacktriangleright_\alpha(1 + 2) * (1 + 2)$ in three steps. The type system assigns type $\triangleright_\alpha\tau$, which means the type of code of type τ, to $\blacktriangleright_\alpha M$ when M is of type τ. The type system also enforces the argument to $\blacktriangleleft_\alpha$ to be of type $\triangleright_\alpha\tau$ to prevent values other than code from being spliced into a quotation.

The subscript α is called *transition variable*, which intuitively denotes how "thick" the bracket is. A transition variable can be abstracted by $\Lambda\alpha.M$ and instantiated by an application "$M\,A$". Here, A (called *transition*) is a (possibly empty) sequence of transition variables $\alpha_1 \cdots \alpha_n$. For example, $(\Lambda\alpha.(\blacktriangleright_\alpha(\lambda x : \mathbf{int}.x)))\,(\beta\gamma)$ reduces to $\blacktriangleright_{\beta\gamma}(\lambda x : \mathbf{int}.x)$, which is an abbreviation of $\blacktriangleright_\beta\blacktriangleright_\gamma(\lambda x : \mathbf{int}.x)$. A transition abstraction $\Lambda\alpha.M$ is given type $\forall\alpha.\tau$ if the type of M is τ and an application $M\,A$ is given type $\tau[\alpha := A]$ if the type of M is $\forall\alpha.\tau$. For example, $M_2 \stackrel{\text{def}}{=} \Lambda\alpha.(\blacktriangleright_\alpha(\lambda x : \mathbf{int}.x))$ is given type $\forall\alpha.\triangleright_\alpha(\mathbf{int} \to \mathbf{int})$ and $M_2\,(\beta\gamma)$ is $\triangleright_\beta\triangleright_\gamma(\mathbf{int} \to \mathbf{int})$. Transition variables are similar to environment classifiers in λ^α and the forms of terms also look like those in λ^α. One notable difference is that, in λ^α, a classifier abstraction can be applied only to a single classifier.

One pleasant effect of generalizing transition applications is that **run** M can be expressed as a derived form, rather than a dedicated construct. Namely, **run** M desugars into $M\,\varepsilon$, application to the *empty* sequence of transition variables. For example, the second example in Section 1 can be represented as $(\Lambda\alpha.M_1)\,\varepsilon$, which first reduces to $(\Lambda\alpha.\blacktriangleright_\alpha((1 + 2) * (1 + 2)))\,\varepsilon$ (by reducing the body of $\Lambda\alpha.$) and then to $\blacktriangleright_\varepsilon(1+2)*(1+2)$, which, as we shall see later, is identified with $(1 + 2) * (1 + 2)$. Notice that $\blacktriangleright_\alpha$ standing for quotation has disappeared by substitution of ε for α. From the typing point of view, **run** takes $\forall\alpha.\triangleright_\alpha\tau$ and returns τ, representing the behavior of **run**. It is important that **run** takes $\forall$-types, because typing rules guarantee that a term of type $\forall\alpha.\triangleright_\alpha\tau$ does not contain free variables inside $\blacktriangleright_\alpha$, making it safe to remove $\blacktriangleright_\alpha$.

2.2 Adding CSP to $\lambda^{\triangleright}$

Next, we informally explain how we extend $\lambda^{\triangleright}$ with CSP to develop $\lambda^{\triangleright\%}$. Unlike MetaOCaml, where CSP is implicit, $\lambda^{\triangleright\%}$ has a dedicated construct $\%_\alpha M$ for CSP (as in Nielsen and Taha [8] and Benaissa et al. [11]). For example, the third example in Section 1 is represented as:

$$M_3 \stackrel{\text{def}}{=} (\lambda a : \mathbf{int}.\Lambda\alpha.\blacktriangleright_\alpha(\%_\alpha a * \%_\alpha a))\ (1+2).$$

Call-by-value reduction leads to $\Lambda\alpha.\blacktriangleright_\alpha(\%_\alpha 3 * \%_\alpha 3)$, which we consider is already a value. It may appear reasonable to allow reduction to remove $\%$ and regard $\Lambda\alpha.\blacktriangleright_\alpha 3 * 3$ as a value, but such reduction means that the run-time value 3 is converted to an integer literal and lifted into a quotation. As we mentioned already, however, lifting is not always possible, so we reject this idea.

Instead, we consider the CSP operator just *a syntactic marker waiting for* **run** *to dissolve the surrounding brackets*: for example, **run** M_3 (namely $M_3\ \varepsilon$) reduces first to $(\Lambda\alpha.\blacktriangleright_\alpha(\%_\alpha 3 * \%_\alpha 3))\ \varepsilon$ and then to $\blacktriangleright_\varepsilon(\%_\varepsilon 3 * \%_\varepsilon 3)$, which will be identified with $3 * 3$. One amusing consequence of this interpretation is that we do not even have to add reduction rules for $\%$—just extending the definition of substitution of transitions suffices.

Now we consider typing. In $\lambda^{\triangleright}$, a type judgment is of the form $\Gamma \vdash^A M : \tau$, in which transition A stands for the stage of the term, or, roughly speaking, how many brackets are surrounding M. Representative typing rules are those for $\blacktriangleright$ and $\blacktriangleleft$:

$$\frac{\Gamma \vdash^{A\alpha} M : \tau}{\Gamma \vdash^{A} \blacktriangleright_\alpha M : \triangleright_\alpha \tau}\ (\blacktriangleright) \qquad \frac{\Gamma \vdash^{A} M : \triangleright_\alpha \tau}{\Gamma \vdash^{A\alpha} \blacktriangleleft_\alpha M : \tau}\ (\blacktriangleleft)$$

The rule $\blacktriangleright$ means that a quotation is given a code type at stage A if its body is well typed at the next stage $A\alpha$ and $\blacktriangleleft$ is its converse.

Then, a straightforward rule for CSP would be something like

$$\frac{\Gamma \vdash^{A} M : \tau}{\Gamma \vdash^{A\alpha} \%_\alpha M : \tau}$$

It is very similar to $\blacktriangleleft$, but M can be of an arbitrary type. Actually, this rule works as far as standard type safety is concerned: a term $\%_\alpha M$ interacts with its surrounding context only when ε is substituted for α but then, $\%_\alpha$ disappears and yields a term of type τ, which is exactly what the context expects.

However, this rule does not quite work when we consider program residualization, by which we mean that a generated code can be dumped into a file, just as partial evaluators (and generating extensions) [12] do. We expect Type-Safe Residualization, which means residual programs are type safe in the following sense:

> If $\vdash^{\varepsilon} M : \triangleright_\alpha \tau$ and $M \longrightarrow^* V$ for a value V, then $V = \blacktriangleright_\alpha N$ for some term N such that $\vdash^{\varepsilon} N : \tau$.

Notice that N has to be typed at stage ε in the conclusion. For example, if $V = \blacktriangleright_\alpha((\lambda x : \mathbf{int}.x + 4)\ 5)$, then its body is well typed at stage ε without any problem. However, if

$V = \blacktriangleright_\alpha((\%_\alpha(\lambda x : \mathbf{int}.x + 4))\ 5)$, then its body $(\%_\alpha(\lambda x : \mathbf{int}.x + 4))\ 5$ is *not* well typed because $\%_\alpha$ can appear only under $\blacktriangleright_\alpha$. One way to sidestep this anomaly is to adjust the statement to something like "N is typeable after removing occurrences of $\%_\alpha$ at stage ε" so that we can consider $\blacktriangleright_\alpha((\lambda x : \mathbf{int}.x + 4)\ 5)$ instead of $\blacktriangleright_\alpha((\%_\alpha(\lambda x : \mathbf{int}.x + 4))\ 5)$, but it would mean that residualization requires lifting of function values, which is not feasible.

We solve this problem by distinguishing two kinds of transition variables (and two kinds of code types thereby). A transition variable of one kind can be used in CSP but cannot be used to annotate residual code, whereas the other kind can be used for residual code but not for CSP. Typing rules ensure that a transition variable of the first kind is instantiated only by the empty sequence. The property above holds only when α is of the second kind.

3 $\lambda^{\triangleright\%}$

We now present $\lambda^{\triangleright\%}$ in detail. In this section, we will define syntax, (full) reduction and type system of $\lambda^{\triangleright\%}$, and prove subject reduction, strong normalization, and confluence. In the next section, we will study call-by-value staged semantics.

3.1 Syntax

Let Σ and Π be countably infinite sets of *transition variables*, ranged over by α, β, and γ, and *variables*, ranged over by x, y, and z, respectively. A *transition*, denoted by A and B, is a finite sequence of transition variables; we write ε for the empty sequence and AB for the concatenation of A and B.

The syntax of $\lambda^{\triangleright\%}$ is defined by the following grammar.

Variables	x, y, z	$\in \Pi$
Transition variables	α, β, γ	$\in \Sigma$
Transitions	A, B	$\in \Sigma^*$
Types	τ, σ, ϕ	$::= b \mid \tau \to \tau \mid \triangleright_\alpha \tau \mid \forall\alpha.\tau \mid \forall^\varepsilon\alpha.\tau$
Terms	M, N	$::= x \mid \lambda x : \tau.M \mid M\,N \mid \blacktriangleright_\alpha M \mid \blacktriangleleft_\alpha M$
		$\mid \Lambda\alpha.M \mid M\,A \mid \%_\alpha M$

A type is a base type (ranged over by b), a function type, a code type or an α-closed type (of two kinds). A code type $\triangleright_\alpha\tau$, indexed by a transition variable, denotes a code fragment of a term of type τ. Two kinds $\forall\alpha.\tau$ and $\forall^\varepsilon\alpha.\tau$ of α-closed types (where α is bound) correspond to the form of transition abstraction $\Lambda\alpha.M$. As we will see, the type system guarantees that the body M does not contain any free variable at any stage containing α. The type constructor $\triangleright_\alpha$ connects tighter than $\to$ and $\to$ tighter than the two forms of $\forall$: for example, $\triangleright_\alpha\tau \to \sigma$ means $(\triangleright_\alpha\tau) \to \sigma$ and $\forall\alpha.\tau \to \sigma$ means $\forall\alpha.(\tau \to \sigma)$.

In addition to the standard λ-terms, there are five more forms: $\blacktriangleright_\alpha M$, $\blacktriangleleft_\alpha M$, $\Lambda\alpha.M$, $M\,A$ and $\%_\alpha M$, as we discussed in the last section. A term of the form $\blacktriangleright_\alpha M$ represents a code fragment M, and $\blacktriangleleft_\alpha M$ unquote, or "escape." Terms $\Lambda\alpha.M$ and $M\,A$ are an abstraction and an instantiation of a transition variable, respectively. Finally, $\%_\alpha M$ is a primitive for cross-stage persistence.

The term constructors $\blacktriangleright_\alpha$, $\blacktriangleleft_\alpha$ and $\%_\alpha$ connects tighter than the two forms of applications and, as usual applications are left-associative and the two binders extends as far to the right as possible: for example, $\blacktriangleright_\alpha x\, y$ means $(\blacktriangleright_\alpha x)\, y$ and $\blacktriangleright_\alpha \lambda x : \tau.x\, y$ means $(\blacktriangleright_\alpha \lambda x : \tau.x\, y)$ and $\Lambda\alpha.\ \lambda x : \tau.x\, y$ means $\Lambda\alpha.\ (\lambda x : \tau.(x\, y))$.

As usual, the variable x is bound in $\lambda x : \tau.M$. The transition variable α is bound in $\Lambda\alpha.M$. We identify α-convertible terms and assume the names of bound variables are pairwise distinct. We write $\mathrm{FV}(M)$ and $\mathrm{FTV}(M)$ for the set of free transition variables and the set of free variables in M, respectively. We omit their straightforward definitions.

3.2 Reduction

Next, we define full reduction for $\lambda^{\triangleright\%}$. Before giving reduction rules, we need to define (capture-avoiding) substitutions for the two kinds of variables. We omit the straightforward definition of substitution $M[x := N]$ of a variable for a term but show the definition of substitution $[\alpha := A]$ of a transition variable for a transition in Figure 1. The definition is mostly straightforward. Note that, when a transition variable of $\blacktriangleleft$ and $\%$ is replaced, the order of transition variables is reversed because $\blacktriangleleft$ and $\%$ are kind of inverse to $\blacktriangleright$.

Definition 1 (Reduction). *The reduction relation $M \longrightarrow M'$ is the least relation closed under the three computation rules (β, $\blacktriangleleft\blacktriangleright$, and β_Λ) and (full) congruence rules, which we omit here.*

$$(\lambda x : \tau.M)\, N \longrightarrow M[x := N] \qquad (\beta)$$
$$\blacktriangleleft_\alpha \blacktriangleright_\alpha M \longrightarrow M \qquad (\blacktriangleleft\blacktriangleright)$$
$$(\Lambda\alpha.M)\, A \longrightarrow M[\alpha := A] \qquad (\beta_\Lambda)$$

In addition to ordinary β-reduction, there are two new reductions. The rule $\blacktriangleleft\blacktriangleright$ means that escape cancels a quotation. The other rule β_Λ means that a transition abstraction applied to a transition reduces to the body of the abstraction, where the argument transition is substituted for the transition variable. It is interesting to see that there is no reduction rule that explicitly concerns CSP! As we have discussed already, a CSP is just a syntactic marker waiting for the indexing transition variable to disappear by substitution of the empty sequence.

We write $\longrightarrow^*$ for the reflexive and transitive closure of $\longrightarrow$.

Using integer constants, arithmetic operations, the type of integers, and **let**, we show an example reduction sequence below (where the underlines show the redexes):

$$
\begin{array}{ll}
\textbf{let } f = \lambda x : \textbf{int}.x * 2 \textbf{ in} & \\
\quad (\Lambda\alpha.\blacktriangleright_\alpha(\%_\alpha\, \underline{(f\ 1)} + (\%_\alpha f)\,(1+2)))\,\varepsilon & (\beta)\\
\longrightarrow^* (\Lambda\alpha.\blacktriangleright_\alpha(\%_\alpha 2 + (\%_\alpha(\lambda x : \textbf{int}.x * 2))\,\underline{(1+2)}))\,\varepsilon & \\
\longrightarrow \underline{(\Lambda\alpha.\blacktriangleright_\alpha(\%_\alpha 2 + (\%_\alpha(\lambda x : \textbf{int}.x * 2))\,3))\,\varepsilon} & (\beta_\Lambda)\\
\longrightarrow 2 + ((\lambda x : \textbf{int}.x * 2)\ 3) & \\
\longrightarrow^* 6 &
\end{array}
$$

$$(A\alpha)[\alpha := B] = (A[\alpha := B])B$$
$$(A\alpha)[\beta := B] = (A[\beta := B])\alpha \quad (\text{if } \alpha \neq \beta)$$

$$b[\alpha := A] = b$$
$$(\tau \to \sigma)[\alpha := A] = (\tau[\alpha := A]) \to (\sigma[\alpha := A])$$
$$(\triangleright_\alpha \tau)[\alpha := A] = \triangleright_A(\tau[\alpha := A])$$
$$(\triangleright_\beta \tau)[\alpha := A] = \triangleright_\beta(\tau[\alpha := A]) \quad (\text{if } \alpha \neq \beta)$$
$$(\forall\alpha.\tau)[\beta := A] = \forall\alpha.(\tau[\beta := A]) \quad (\text{if } \alpha \neq \beta \text{ and } \alpha \notin A)$$
$$(\forall^\varepsilon\alpha.\tau)[\beta := A] = \forall^\varepsilon\alpha.(\tau[\beta := A]) \quad (\text{if } \alpha \neq \beta \text{ and } \alpha \notin A)$$

$$x[\alpha := A] = x$$
$$(\lambda x : \tau.M)[\alpha := A] = \lambda x : (\tau[\alpha := A]).(M[\alpha := A])$$
$$(M\,N)[\alpha := A] = (M[\alpha := A])\,(N[\alpha := A])$$
$$(\blacktriangleright_\beta M)[\alpha := A] = \blacktriangleright_{\beta[\alpha := A]}(M[\alpha := A])$$
$$(\blacktriangleleft_\beta M)[\alpha := A] = \blacktriangleleft_{\beta[\alpha := A]}(M[\alpha := A])$$
$$(\%_\beta M)[\alpha := A] = \%_{\beta[\alpha := A]}(M[\alpha := A])$$
$$(\Lambda\beta.M)[\alpha := A] = \Lambda\beta.(M[\alpha := A]) \quad (\text{if } \beta \neq \alpha \text{ and } \beta \notin A)$$
$$(M\,B)[\alpha := A] = (M[\alpha := A])\,(B[\alpha := A])$$

Here, $\triangleright_A\tau$, $\blacktriangleright_A M$, $\blacktriangleleft_A M$ and $\%_A M$ (where $A = \alpha_1\alpha_2\cdots\alpha_n$) denote:

$$\triangleright_A\tau = \triangleright_{\alpha_1}\triangleright_{\alpha_2}\cdots\triangleright_{\alpha_n}\tau$$
$$\blacktriangleright_A M = \blacktriangleright_{\alpha_1}\blacktriangleright_{\alpha_2}\cdots\blacktriangleright_{\alpha_n} M$$
$$\blacktriangleleft_A M = \blacktriangleleft_{\alpha_n}\blacktriangleleft_{\alpha_{n-1}}\cdots\blacktriangleleft_{\alpha_1} M$$
$$\%_A M = \%_{\alpha_n}\%_{\alpha_{n-1}}\cdots\%_{\alpha_1} M.$$

In particular, $\blacktriangleright_\varepsilon M = \blacktriangleleft_\varepsilon M = \%_\varepsilon M = M$.

Fig. 1. Transition Substitution

Since the reduction is full, there are other reduction sequences as well. The sequence above is not *staged* in the sense that only redexes at the lowest stage are reduced (notice that $1 + 2$ appears under a quotation). We will give staged reduction in the next section.

3.3 Type System

Next, we develop the type system of $\lambda^{\triangleright\%}$. As discussed in Section 2, we distinguish two kinds of transition variables and have two forms of types $\forall\alpha.\tau$ and $\forall^\varepsilon\alpha.\tau$ for $\Lambda\alpha.M$. The former can be applied to any transitions but M cannot contain $\%_\alpha$; the latter allows $\%_\alpha$ but can be applied only to ε. For programming convenience, we introduce subtyping between two kinds of $\forall$ types to allow promotion from the former type to the latter.

Subtyping. We first give the subtyping relation.

$$\frac{}{\forall\alpha.\tau <: \forall^{\varepsilon}\alpha.\tau} \qquad \frac{}{\tau <: \tau} \qquad \frac{\tau <: \sigma \quad \sigma <: \phi}{\tau <: \phi}$$

$$\frac{\tau_1 <: \sigma_1 \quad \sigma_2 <: \tau_2}{\sigma_1 \to \sigma_2 <: \tau_1 \to \tau_2} \qquad \frac{\tau <: \sigma}{\triangleright_\alpha\tau <: \triangleright_\alpha\sigma} \qquad \frac{\tau <: \sigma}{\forall\alpha.\tau <: \forall\alpha.\sigma} \qquad \frac{\tau <: \sigma}{\forall^{\varepsilon}\alpha.\tau <: \forall^{\varepsilon}\alpha.\sigma}$$

Fig. 2. Subtyping Rules

Definition 2 (Subtyping). *The subtyping relation* $\tau <: \sigma$ *is the least relation closed under the rules in Figure 2.*

The only interesting rule is the first one, which means that a Λ-abstraction that can be applied to any transitions can also be used in a restricted context where only applications to the empty transition are allowed. The other rules mean that subtyping is reflexive and transitive and that type constructors are covariant except for function types, which are contravariant in argument types.

Typing. A typing context in $\lambda^{\triangleright\%}$ keeps track of not only types of variables but also transitions, which represent which stage it is declared at.

Definition 3 (Typing Context). *A typing context* Γ *is a finite mapping from variables to pairs of a type and a transition.*

We often write $\Gamma, x : \tau@A$ for the typing context Γ' such that $dom(\Gamma') = dom(\Gamma) \cup \{x\}$ and $\Gamma'(x) = (\tau, A)$ and $\Gamma'(y) = \Gamma(y)$ if $x \neq y$. $\Gamma(x) = (\tau, A)$ means "the variable x at the stage A has the type τ." We write FTV(Γ) for the set of free transition variables in Γ, defined as $\bigcup_{x\in dom(\Gamma)} \{ \mathrm{FTV}(\tau) \cup \mathrm{FTV}(A) \mid (\tau, A) = \Gamma(x) \}$

A type judgment is of the form $\Gamma; \Delta \vdash^A M : \tau$, read "the term M is given type τ under the context Γ and Δ at stage A." Here, Δ is a set of transition variables and records $\forall^{\varepsilon}$-bound transition variables. Intuitively, transition variables in Δ denote the empty sequence and cross-stage persistence is allowed only for them. Conversely, a code type $\triangleright_\alpha\tau$ is residualizable if $\alpha \notin \Delta$.

Definition 4 (Typing). *The typing relation* $\Gamma; \Delta \vdash^A M : \tau$ *is the least relation closed under the rules in Figure 3.*

The rules Var, Abs and App are mostly same as those in the simply typed lambda calculus, except for stage annotations. The rule Var means that a variable can appear only at the stage in which it is declared; the rule Abs requires the parameter and the body to be at the same stage; similarly, the rule App requires M and N to be typeable at the same stage. The following four rules ▸, ◂, Gen and Ins are essentially the same as those of $\lambda^{\triangleright}$, except that Δ is added to typing judgments. The rule ▸ means that, if M is of type τ at stage $A\alpha$, $\blacktriangleright_\alpha A$ is code of type τ at stage A; the rule ◂ is its converse. The rules Gen and Ins are the introduction and elimination of $\forall$ types, respectively. The side condition of the rule (Gen) guarantees α-closedness of M, which means M has no free variable which has a transition variable α in its type or its stage.

The next two rules GenE and InsE for $\forall^{\varepsilon}$ are very similar to Gen and Ins, respectively, but there are two important differences. In GenE, the transition variable α must be in

$$\frac{}{\Gamma, x : \tau@A; \Delta \vdash^A x : \tau} \text{(VAR)} \qquad \frac{\Gamma, x : \tau@A; \Delta \vdash^A M : \sigma}{\Gamma; \Delta \vdash^A \lambda x : \tau.M : \tau \to \sigma} \text{(ABS)}$$

$$\frac{\Gamma; \Delta \vdash^A M : \tau \to \sigma \qquad \Gamma; \Delta \vdash^A N : \tau}{\Gamma; \Delta \vdash^A M\, N : \sigma} \text{(APP)}$$

$$\frac{\Gamma; \Delta \vdash^{A\alpha} M : \tau}{\Gamma; \Delta \vdash^A \blacktriangleright_\alpha M : \triangleright_\alpha \tau} (\blacktriangleright) \qquad \frac{\Gamma; \Delta \vdash^A M : \triangleright_\alpha \tau}{\Gamma; \Delta \vdash^{A\alpha} \blacktriangleleft_\alpha M : \tau} (\blacktriangleleft)$$

$$\frac{\Gamma; \Delta \vdash^A M : \tau \qquad \alpha \notin \mathrm{FTV}(\Gamma) \cup \mathrm{FTV}(A) \cup \Delta}{\Gamma; \Delta \vdash^A \Lambda\alpha.M : \forall\alpha.\tau} \text{(GEN)} \qquad \frac{\Gamma; \Delta \vdash^A M : \forall\alpha.\tau}{\Gamma; \Delta \vdash^A M\, B : \tau[\alpha := B]} \text{(INS)}$$

$$\frac{\Gamma; \Delta \cup \{\alpha\} \vdash^A M : \tau \qquad \alpha \notin \mathrm{FTV}(\Gamma) \cup \mathrm{FTV}(A) \cup \Delta}{\Gamma; \Delta \vdash^A \Lambda\alpha.M : \forall^\varepsilon\alpha.\tau} \text{(GENE)}$$

$$\frac{\Gamma;\ \Delta \vdash^A M : \forall^\varepsilon\alpha.\tau \qquad \beta \in \Delta \text{ whenever } \beta \in B}{\Gamma;\ \Delta \vdash^A M\, B : \tau[\alpha := B]} \text{(INSE)} \qquad \frac{\Gamma; \Delta \vdash^A M : \tau \qquad \alpha \in \Delta}{\Gamma; \Delta \vdash^{A\alpha} \%_\alpha M : \tau} (\%)$$

$$\frac{\Gamma; \Delta \vdash^A M : \tau \qquad \tau <: \sigma}{\Gamma; \Delta \vdash^A M : \sigma} \text{(SUB)}$$

Fig. 3. Typing Rules

the second component $\Delta \cup \{\alpha\}$ of the premise, so that CSP with α is possible. In INSE, the argument B has to consist only of transition variables from Δ—B is virtually the empty sequence. The next rule % is for CSP, which is allowed only when the indexing transition variable is in Δ.

The last rule stands for ordinary subsumption.

3.4 Properties

We show three basic properties of the calculus: subject reduction, strong normalization and confluence.

Subject Reduction. The key lemma to prove subject reduction is Substitution Lemma as usual. We show that transition substitution $[\alpha := A]$ preserves subtyping and typing; and that term substitution $[x := M]$ preserves typing. There are two separate statements for transition substitution and typing because a transition variable in Δ can be replaced only with the "virtually empty" transitions.

Lemma 1 (Substitution Lemma)

1. *If* $\tau <: \sigma$*, then* $\tau[\alpha := B] <: \sigma[\alpha := B]$
2. *If* $\Gamma, x : \tau@B; \Delta \vdash^A M : \tau$ *and* $\Gamma : \Delta \vdash^B N : \tau$*, then* $\Gamma; \Delta \vdash^A M[x := N] : \tau$
3. *If* $\alpha \notin \Delta$ *and* $\Gamma; \Delta \vdash^A M : \tau$*, then* $\Gamma[\alpha := B]; \Delta \vdash^{A[\alpha:=B]} M[\alpha := B] : \tau[\alpha := B]$
4. *If* $\alpha \in \Delta$ *and* $\Gamma; \Delta \vdash^A M : \tau$ *and* $\beta \in \Delta$ *for any* $\beta \in B$*, then* $\Gamma[\alpha := B]; (\Delta \setminus \{\alpha\} \cup \mathrm{FTV}(B)) \vdash^{A[\alpha:=B]} M[\alpha := B] : \tau[\alpha := B]$

Proof. Straightforward induction on subtyping and typing derivations.

Theorem 1 (Subject Reduction). *If* $\Gamma, \Delta \vdash^A M : \tau$ *and* $M \longrightarrow M'$ *then* $\Gamma, \Delta \vdash^A M' : \tau$.

Proof. By induction on the derivation of $M \longrightarrow M'$.

Strong Normalization. Well-typed terms are strongly normalizing:

Theorem 2 (Strong Normalization). *If a term M is typeable, there is no infinite reduction sequence* $M \longrightarrow M' \longrightarrow M'' \longrightarrow \cdots$ *starting with M.*

Proof. First we define translation from $\lambda^{\triangleright\%}$-terms to simply typed λ-terms; the translation just removes all staging annotations. Then, it is easy to show that the translation preserves typeability and one-step β reduction. It is also easy to see that an infinite reduction sequence in $\lambda^{\triangleright\%}$, which necessarily contains infinite β-reduction steps, can be translated to an infinite reduction sequence in the simply typed λ-calculus, contradicting strong normalization of the simply typed λ-calculus.

Confluence. We prove confluence by using the standard technique of parallel reduction and complete development [13]. We omit the proof since it is entirely standard.

Theorem 3 (Confluence). *For any term M, if* $M \longrightarrow^* M_1$ *and* $M \longrightarrow^* M_2$*, there exists* M_3 *that satisfies* $M_1 \longrightarrow^* M_3$ *and* $M_2 \longrightarrow^* M_3$.

4 Staged Semantics

The reduction relation given in the last section is full reduction, where an arbitrary subterm can be reduced nondeterministically, and it is not clear if computation can be properly staged in the sense that code generation can be completed without computing inside quotation.

In this section, we will define a deterministic call-by-value *staged* semantics, which can be easily seen as program execution, and show the standard progress property. We obtain the new semantics by allowing reduction at the lowest possible stages (and fixing the evaluation order). As a result, the rules β and β_Λ are allowed only at the stage ε and the rule $\blacktriangleleft\blacktriangleright$ only at a stage α. (Notice that a redex $\blacktriangleleft_\alpha \blacktriangleright_\alpha M$ is supposed to appear under a quotation in a well-typed term.)

We begin with the definitions of values and redexes.

Definition 5 (Values and Redexes). *The family* V^A *of sets of values, ranged over by* v^A *and the sets of* ε*-redexes (ranged over by* R^ε*) and* α*-redexes (ranged over by* R^α*) are defined by the following grammar. In the grammar, A is nonempty.*

$$
\begin{array}{lrl}
\textit{Values} & v^\varepsilon \in V^\varepsilon ::= & \lambda x:\tau.M \mid \blacktriangleright_\alpha v^\alpha \mid \Lambda\alpha.v^\varepsilon \\
& v^A \in V^A ::= & x \mid \lambda x:\tau.v^A \mid v^A\, v^A \mid \blacktriangleright_\alpha v^{A\alpha} \\
& & \mid \Lambda\alpha.v^A \mid v^A\, B \\
& & \mid \blacktriangleleft_\alpha v^{A'} (\textit{if } A'\alpha = A \textit{ and } A' \neq \varepsilon) \\
& & \mid \%_\alpha v^{A'} (\textit{if } A'\alpha = A) \\
\textit{Redexes} & R^\varepsilon ::= & (\lambda x:\tau.M)\, v^\varepsilon \mid (\Lambda\alpha.v^\varepsilon)\, A \\
& R^\alpha ::= & \blacktriangleleft_\alpha \blacktriangleright_\alpha M
\end{array}
$$

$$E^A_\varepsilon[(\lambda x:\tau.M)\, v^\varepsilon] \longrightarrow_s E^A_\varepsilon[M[x := v^\varepsilon]] \qquad (\beta_v)$$
$$E^A_\varepsilon[(\Lambda\alpha.v^\varepsilon)\, B] \longrightarrow_s E^A_\varepsilon[v^\varepsilon[\alpha := B]] \qquad (\beta_\Lambda)$$
$$E^A_\alpha[\blacktriangleleft_\alpha \blacktriangleright_\alpha M] \longrightarrow_s E^A_\alpha[M] \qquad (\blacktriangleleft\blacktriangleright)$$

Fig. 4. Staged Reduction

Values at stage ε consist of abstractions and quotations. The body of a λ-abstraction can be any term, whereas the body of a transition abstraction must be a value. It means that the bodies of transition abstractions are reduced before transition application is reduced. The body of a quotation is a value at a higher stage. Since evaluation at higher stages are not performed during code generation, values at higher stages contain all forms of terms.[3] Redexes are classified into two, according to the stage where they appear.

Then, we define evaluation contexts, which are indexed by two stages and written E^A_B. Intuitively, A stands for that of the whole context when the stage of the hole is B.

Definition 6 (Evaluation Contexts). *The family of sets $ECtx^A_B$ of evaluation contexts, ranged over by E^A_B, is defined by the grammar below. In the grammar, A is nonempty (whereas B, A' and B' can be empty).*

$$E^\varepsilon_B \in ECtx^\varepsilon_B ::= \square\ (\textit{if } B = \varepsilon) \mid E^\varepsilon_B\, M \mid v^\varepsilon\, E^\varepsilon_B \mid \blacktriangleright_\alpha E^\alpha_B \mid \Lambda\alpha.E^\varepsilon_B \mid E^\varepsilon_B\, A'$$
$$E^A_B \in ECtx^A_B ::= \square\ (\textit{if } A = B) \mid \lambda x:\tau.E^A_B \mid E^A_B\, M \mid v^A\, E^A_B \mid \blacktriangleright_\alpha E^{A\alpha}_B$$
$$\mid \blacktriangleleft_\alpha E^{A'}_B\ (\textit{where } A'\alpha = A) \mid \Lambda\alpha.E^A_B \mid E^A_B\, B' \mid \%_\alpha\, E^{A'}_B\ (\textit{where } A'\alpha = A)$$

We show a few examples of evaluation contexts below.

$$\square\,(\lambda x:\tau.x) \in ECtx^\varepsilon_\varepsilon$$
$$(\lambda x:\tau.x)\,(\blacktriangleright_\alpha \square) \in ECtx^\varepsilon_\alpha$$
$$\blacktriangleright_\beta \blacktriangleleft_\alpha \blacktriangleright_\alpha \blacktriangleright_\gamma \square \in ECtx^\varepsilon_{\beta\gamma}$$

We write $E^A_B[M]$ for a term obtained by filling the hole in E^A_B with M.

Definition 7 (Staged Reduction). *The staged reduction relation, written $M \longrightarrow_s M'$, is defined by the least relation closed under the rules in Figure 4.*

The rules are rather straightforward adaptations of the reduction rules for $\longrightarrow$. Note that, in the first two rules, the lower index of the evaluation context is ε, which means the redex appears at stage ε and that, in the third rule, it is α, which means the redex appears inside a (single) quotation.

[3] The only exception is that an escape cannot appear at stage α because the term of the form $\blacktriangleleft_\alpha v^\varepsilon$ is a redex (if it is well typed).)

For example, the reduction sequence for the example shown before is as follows:

$$\begin{array}{ll}
\textbf{let } f = \lambda x : \textbf{int}.x * 2 \textbf{ in} & \\
\quad (\Lambda\alpha.\blacktriangleright_\alpha(\%_\alpha \underline{(f\ 1)} + (\%_\alpha f)\ (1+2)))\ \varepsilon & (\beta) \\
\longrightarrow_s^* (\Lambda\alpha.\blacktriangleright_\alpha(\%_\alpha \underline{(1 * 2)} + (\%_\alpha(\lambda x : \textbf{int}.x * 2))\ (1+2)))\ \varepsilon & \\
\longrightarrow_s \underline{(\Lambda\alpha.\blacktriangleright_\alpha(\%_\alpha 2 + (\%_\alpha(\lambda x : \textbf{int}.x * 2))\ (1+2)))\ \varepsilon} & (\beta_\Lambda) \\
\longrightarrow_s 2 + ((\lambda x : \textbf{int}.x * 2)\ (1+2)) & \\
\longrightarrow_s^* 8. &
\end{array}$$

4.1 Properties of Staged Reduction

First, it is easy to see that $\longrightarrow_s$ is a subrelation of $\longrightarrow$. So, the relation $\longrightarrow_s$ has strong normalization and subject reduction.

Theorem 4. $\longrightarrow_s \subseteq \longrightarrow$.

Proof. By case analysis of the rules of $\longrightarrow_s$.

Every well-typed term can be either a value or decomposed into an evaluation context and a redex uniquely. Thanks to this theorem, we know that $\longrightarrow_s$ is deterministic.

Theorem 5 (Unique Decomposition). *If Γ does not have any variable declared at stage ε and $\Gamma; \Delta \vdash^A M : \tau$, then either (1) $M \in V^A$, or (2) there exists a unique pair (E_B^A, R^B) such that $M = E_B^A[R^B]$ for some B, which is either ε or a transition variable β.*

Proof. By induction on the derivation of $\Gamma; \Delta \vdash^A M : \tau$.

Unique Decomposition usually states that a term M is either a value or there is another term that it reduces to, if M is a *closed* well-typed term. In $\lambda^{\triangleright\%}$, free variables at higher-stages can be considered symbols, so we can relax the closedness condition in stating the property.

Thanks to Unique Decomposition, Progress is easy to show.

Theorem 6 (Progress). *If Γ does not have any variable declared at stage ε and $\Gamma; \Delta \vdash^A M : \tau$, then $M \in V^A$ or there exists M' such that $M \longrightarrow_s M'$.*

Proof. By induction on the derivation of $\Gamma; \Delta \vdash^A M : \tau$.

The last property we show is Type-Safe Residualization, which we have discussed in Section 2. It states that if a program of a code type is well typed under the assumption that Δ is empty, i.e., CSP (indexed by free transition variables) is not used, then the result (if any) is certainly a quotation and its body is also typeable at stage ε.

In the statement of the theorem, we use the notation $\Gamma^{-\alpha}$, defined by; $\Gamma^{-\alpha} = \{x : \tau@B \mid x : \tau@\alpha B \in \Gamma\}$.

Theorem 7 (Type-Safe Residualization). *If Γ does not have any variable declared at stage ε and $\Gamma; \emptyset \vdash^\varepsilon M : \triangleright_\alpha \tau$ is derivable then there exists $v^\varepsilon = \blacktriangleright_\alpha N \in V^\varepsilon$, $M \longrightarrow_s^* v^\varepsilon$ and $\Gamma^{-\alpha}; \emptyset \vdash^\varepsilon N : \tau$ is derivable.*

Proof. We show this theorem by two parts. First, we show the existence of $v = \blacktriangleright_\alpha N$, which is reduced from M. Next, we show that $\Gamma^{-\alpha}; \emptyset \vdash^{\varepsilon} N : \tau$ is derivable.

The first part is proved by case analysis on the form of M. By the first part and the typing rule $\blacktriangleright$, we have a derivation of $\Gamma; \emptyset \vdash^{\alpha} N : \tau$. So, all we need to show the second part is that if $\Gamma; \emptyset \vdash^{\alpha} N : \tau$ then $\Gamma^{-\alpha}; \emptyset \vdash^{\varepsilon} N : \tau$, and we can prove this by induction on the derivation of $\Gamma; \emptyset \vdash^{\alpha} N : \tau$.

5 Discussion

In this section, we investigate differences between $\lambda^{\triangleright\%}$ and BER MetaOCaml[4] in more detail. We also discuss the relationship between CSP and program residualization in $\lambda^{\triangleright\%}$.

5.1 CSP in MetaOCaml

In MetaOCaml, CSP is implicitly applied to the occurrences of value identifiers (variables and references to module members such as List.map) declared outside brackets. The behavior of CSP in MetaOCaml is, however, subtly different from that of $\lambda^{\triangleright\%}$; actually, it depends on where the identifier is declared.

First, CSP for a variable declared in the same compilation unit works (almost) the same as in $\lambda^{\triangleright\%}$. In the implementation, a code value is represented as an AST and there is a special node that contains a pointer to the value of a variable under CSP[5]. This pointer is dereferenced while the surrounding code is evaluated. In contrast to that, CSP for an identifier in another compilation unit is represented by an AST node that contains the identifier name, which is resolved while the surrounding code is evaluated. The following program (run by BER MetaOCaml version N 101) demonstrates the difference:

```
# let f = List.map in .< (f, List.map) >.;;
- : ...
= .<(((* cross-stage persistent value (id: f) *)), List.map)>.
```

The result is a quoted pair consisting of a pointer to a closure (which is the value of `List.map`) and a module member reference to be resolved later. This lazy name resolution does not affect the result of program execution, because (1) variable reference is a side-effect free operation and (2) resolving the same module name at code-generation time and at code-evaluation time results in the same module implementation.

5.2 CSP and Program Residualization

As already discussed, in $\lambda^{\triangleright\%}$, CSP with a transition variable α can be applied only if α is bound by $\Lambda\alpha$ which has a $\forall^{\varepsilon}\alpha$ type. Due to this restriction, it is impossible to use the same code value both for running and residualization if it contains a reference to a library function, (which can be considered a free variable at stage ε).

[4] A (re)implementation of the original MetaOCaml by Oleg Kiselyov.

[5] For ground values such as integers, this node is replaced with an AST node for a constant.

Consider the following term (of $\lambda^{\triangleright\%}$ extended with pairs):

$$M = \textbf{let } c = \Lambda\alpha.\blacktriangleright_\alpha(1 + 2) \textbf{ in let } d = c\,\varepsilon \textbf{ in } \blacktriangleright_\beta(\blacktriangleleft_\beta(c\,\beta), \%_\beta\, d)$$

The intention behind this term is to construct a code value representing 1 + 2, evaluate it to 3, and construct another code value representing ((1 + 2), 3) to be residualized. If + is a language primitive (just as numbers), which can be used at any stage, then this term can be given type $\triangleright_\beta(\textbf{int} \times \textbf{int})$. However, if + is a free variable at stage ε, the subterm $\Lambda\alpha.\blacktriangleright_\alpha(1 + 2)$ is ill typed. One may apply CSP to + to make this subterm well typed but the only type given to this term is $\forall^\varepsilon\alpha. \triangleright_\alpha \textbf{int}$, making another subterm $c\,\beta$ ill typed (here, β cannot be in Δ in the type derivation because the generated code is to be residualized).

Although this may sound very unfortunate because one may expect + is available everywhere, we believe that it is reasonable for the type system to reject this term, because, in general, a library function that is available during code generation may or may not be available when the generated code is executed later. In other words, using the same name at different levels may result in different values.

6 Related Work

Although many multi-stage calculi are studied in the literature, few of them are equipped with all the combination of quasiquotation, run and CSP.

Davies' λ° [14], which can model multi-level generating extensions [15], has quasiquotation but neither run nor CSP. Due to the absence of CSP, Type-Safe Residualization naturally follows.

Davies and Pfenning have proposed modal λ-calculi, whose type systems can be seen as (intuitionistic) S4 modal logic [16]. They do not model CSP but a code fragment can be embedded inside arbitrarily nested quotations. In this sense, code types can cross stages. Such a limited support of CSP is found in other calculi [17, 10].

Taha et al. [18] and Moggi et al. [19] have proposed MSP calculi with quasiquotation, run, and CSP. In these calculi, CSP is implicit as in MetaOCaml and limited to variable references. They satisfy a property similar to Type-Safe Residualization but, unfortunately, the distinction between lifting and CSP is not very clear from its semantics because a variable under implicit CSP is just replaced with a value, e.g., $(\lambda f.\langle f\ 42\rangle)(\lambda x.x{+}x)$ evaluates to $\langle(\lambda x.x{+}x)\ 42\rangle$, which looks as if the function $\lambda x.x{+}x$ were lifted.

Benaissa et al. [11] have presented λ^{BN}, which has an explicit CSP operator up that can be applied to any expressions, as well as quasiquotation and (a limited support for) **run**. Although there is a certain typing restriction on the use of up, this operator can be used for any kind of values, including functions; lifting and CSP are confused here, too.

As we already mentioned, Taha and Nielsen [8] have introduced the notion of environment classifiers to λ^α, which has quasiquotation, run, and CSP. In λ^α, CSP is explicit (in fact, we borrow the symbol % from λ^α) and can be applied to any expression and λ^α-term $\langle\%_\alpha\, 3 * \%_\alpha\, 3\rangle^\alpha$, which would correspond to $\blacktriangleright_\alpha(\%_\alpha\, 3 * \%_\alpha\, 3)$, is also considered a value. Since environment classifiers in λ^α cannot be instantiated by the empty sequence, the semantics of **run** is formalized as a reduction step which removes the outermost pair of brackets and adjusts occurrences of % by a complicated meta-level operation called demotion. For example, **run** $(\alpha)\langle(\%_\alpha 3 * \%_\alpha 3)\rangle^\alpha$ (where $(\alpha)M$ is a binder of a classifier) reduces to $(\alpha)(3 * 3)$. In the implementation (both the original one [4] and BER MetaOCaml[6] by Kiselyov), a code value is represented by an AST tree, in which CSP is a special node that points to a run-time value; when a quotation is **run** and compiled, a CSP node is compiled to an instruction to dereference the pointer to the value. This implementation scheme matches the intuition that CSP is a syntactic marker that waits for the surrounding code to start **run**ning. Lifting is not needed to implement CSP[7], as far as **run** is concerned, but dumping code values into a file is not generally possible because a CSP node might point to a nonserializable object. We think λ^α is a suitable model only of MSP languages without support of generating residual code because the type system does not distinguish code that can/cannot be residualized.

Kim et al. [5] have proposed another multi-stage calculus λ^{sim}_{open}, which is equipped with lifting of arbitrary values so that any value can be embedded into a quotation. So, it seems also difficult to support residualization.

7 Conclusions

We have given the formal definition of $\lambda^{\triangleright\%}$ with its syntax, type system, full reduction and staged reduction. A key idea here is to view CSP as a syntactic marker waiting for **run** to dissolve the surrounding brackets. For the full reduction, where an arbitrary subterm can be reduced nondeterministically, we have proven subject reduction, strong normalization and confluence. For staged reduction, which is a deterministic call-by-value operational semantics, we have proven Progress, Type-Safe Residualization and that staged reduction is a subrelation of the full reduction.

We have also discussed interactions between CSP and program residualization and pointed out a problem that residualization for a value which is put into a bracket by CSP requires lifting that is always not feasible. In this sense, MetaOCaml is not very suitable for writing offline generators. Our type system for $\lambda^{\triangleright\%}$ solves this problem by distinguishing two kinds of transition variables.

Type inference for $\lambda^{\triangleright\%}$ would not be possible as it is for the same reason as λ^α [8] and $\lambda^{\triangleright}$ [10], but we would be able to identify a subset of $\lambda^{\triangleright\%}$ in which type inference is possible by a similar approach to Calgano, Moggi and Taha [9].

Acknowledgements. We thank Kenichi Asai and Yukiyoshi Kameyama for valuable comments. We also thank three anonymous reviewers for their helpful comments (in particular, one reviewer for describing how CSP is implemented in MetaOCaml).

References

1. Taha, W.: A gentle introduction to multi-stage programming. In: Lengauer, C., Batory, D., Blum, A., Odersky, M. (eds.) Domain-Specific Program Generation. LNCS, vol. 3016, pp. 30–50. Springer, Heidelberg (2004)

---

[6] `http://okmij.org/ftp/ML/MetaOCaml.html`

[7] Basic values such as numbers or strings under CSP are converted to literals.

2. Sheard, T., Peyton Jones, S.: Template meta-programming for Haskell. In: Proceedings of Haskell Workshop (Haskell 2002), pp. 60–75 (2002)
3. Taha, W., Sheard, T.: MetaML and multi-stage programming with explicit annotations. Theoretical Computer Science 248, 211–242 (2000)
4. Calcagno, C., Taha, W., Huang, L., Leroy, X.: Implementing multi-stage languages using ASTs, gensym, and reflection. In: Pfenning, F., Macko, M. (eds.) GPCE 2003. LNCS, vol. 2830, pp. 57–76. Springer, Heidelberg (2003)
5. Kim, I.S., Yi, K., Calcagno, C.: A polymorphic modal type system for Lisp-like multi-staged languages. In: Proceedings of ACM SIGPLAN-SIGACT Symposium on Principles of Programming Languages (POPL 2006), Charleston, SC, pp. 257–268 (January 2006)
6. Chen, C., Xi, H.: Meta-programming through typeful code representation. In: Proceedings of ACM International Conference on Functional Programming (ICFP 2003), Uppsala, Sweden, pp. 275–286 (August 2003)
7. Mainland, G.: Explicitly heterogeneous metaprogramming with MetaHaskell. In: Proceedings of ACM International Conference on Functional Programming (ICFP 2012), Copenhagen, Denmark, pp. 311–322 (September 2012)
8. Taha, W., Nielsen, M.F.: Environment classifiers. In: Proceedings of the ACM SIGPLAN-SIGACT Symposium on Principles of Programming Languages (POPL 2003), pp. 26–37 (2003)
9. Calcagno, C., Moggi, E., Taha, W.: ML-like inference for classifiers. In: Schmidt, D. (ed.) ESOP 2004. LNCS, vol. 2986, pp. 79–93. Springer, Heidelberg (2004)
10. Tsukada, T., Igarashi, A.: A logical foundation for environment classifiers. Logical Methods in Computer Science 6(4:8), 1–43 (2010)
11. Benaissa, Z.E.A., Moggi, E., Taha, W., Sheard, T.: Logical modalities and multi-stage programming. In: Proceedings of Workshop on Intuitionstic Modal Logics and Applications (IMLA 1999) (1999)
12. Jones, N.D., Gomard, C.K., Sestoft, P.: Partial Evaluation and Automatic Program Generation. Prentice-Hall (1993)
13. Takahashi, M.: Parallel reductions in lambda-calculus. Inf. Comput. 118(1), 120–127 (1995)
14. Davies, R.: A temporal-logic approach to binding-time analysis. In: Proceedings of the Eleventh Annual IEEE Symposium on Logic in Computer Science (LICS 1996), pp. 184–195. IEEE Computer Society Press (July 1996)
15. Glück, R., Jørgensen, J.: Efficient multi-level generating extensions for program specialization. In: Swierstra, S.D. (ed.) PLILP 1995. LNCS, vol. 982, pp. 259–278. Springer, Heidelberg (1995)
16. Davies, R., Pfenning, F.: A modal analysis of staged computation. Journal of the ACM 48(3), 555–604 (2001)
17. Yuse, Y., Igarashi, A.: A modal type system for multi-level generating extensions with persistent code. In: Proceedings of the 8th ACM SIGPLAN Symposium on Principles and Practice of Declarative Programming (PPDP 2006), Venice, Italy, pp. 201–212 (2006)
18. Taha, W., Benaissa, Z.-E.-A., Sheard, T.: Multi-stage programming: Axiomatization and type safety. In: Larsen, K.G., Skyum, S., Winskel, G. (eds.) ICALP 1998. LNCS, vol. 1443, pp. 918–929. Springer, Heidelberg (1998)
19. Moggi, E., Taha, W., Benaissa, Z.-E.-A., Sheard, T.: An idealized MetaML: Simpler, and more expressive. In: Swierstra, S.D. (ed.) ESOP 1999. LNCS, vol. 1576, pp. 193–207. Springer, Heidelberg (1999)

Lightweight Higher-Kinded Polymorphism

Jeremy Yallop and Leo White

University of Cambridge

Abstract. Higher-kinded polymorphism —i.e. abstraction over type *constructors*— is an essential component of many functional programming techniques such as monads, folds, and embedded DSLs. ML-family languages typically support a form of abstraction over type constructors using functors, but the separation between the core language and the module language leads to awkwardness as functors proliferate.

We show how to express higher-kinded polymorphism in OCaml without functors, using an abstract type app to represent type application, and opaque brands to denote abstractable type constructors. We demonstrate the flexibility of our approach by using it to translate a variety of standard higher-kinded programs into functor-free OCaml code.

1 Introduction

Polymorphism abstracts types, just as functions abstract values. Higher-kinded polymorphism takes things a step further, abstracting both types and type constructors, just as higher-order functions abstract both first-order values and functions.

Here is a function with a higher-kinded type. The function when conditionally executes an action:

```
when b m = if b then m else return ()
```

In Haskell, when receives the following type:

```
when :: ∀ (m :: * → *). Monad m ⇒ Bool → m () → m ()
```

The kind ascription $* \rightarrow *$ makes explicit the fact that m is a *higher-kinded* type variable: it abstracts type constructors such as Maybe and [], which can be applied to types such as Int and () to build new types. The type of when says that its second argument and return value are monadic computations returning (), but the monad itself is not fixed: when can be used at any type m () where m builds a type from a type and is an instance of the Monad class.

In contrast, in OCaml, as in other ML-family languages, all type variables have kind $*$. In order to abstract a type constructor one must use a *functor*. Here is an implementation of when in OCaml:

```
module When (M : Monad) = struct
  let f b m = if b then m else M.return ()
end
```

M. Codish and E. Sumii (Eds.): FLOPS 2014, LNCS 8475, pp. 119–135, 2014.

The When functor receives the following type:

```
module When (M : Monad) :sig
  val f : bool → unit M.t → unit M.t
end
```

Defining When is more work in OCaml than in Haskell. For callers of When the difference is even more pronounced. Here is a Haskell definition of unless using when:

```
unless b m = when (not b) m
```

Defining Unless in OCaml involves binding three modules. First, we define a functor to abstract the monad once more, binding both the functor and its argument. Next, we instantiate the When functor with the monad implementation and bind the result. Finally, we can call the function:

```
module Unless(M : Monad) = struct
  module W = When(M)
  let f b m = W.f (not b) m
end
```

The situation is similar when we come to use our functions at a particular monad. We must first instantiate When or Unless with a module satisfying the Monad interface before we can use it to build computations. The following example instantiates Unless with a module implementing the state monad, then uses the result to build a computation that conditionally writes a value:

```
let module U = Unless(StateM) in
  U.unless (v < 0) (StateM.put v)
```

Why does OCaml require us to do so much work to define such simple functions? One issue is the lack of overloading: in order to use functions like when with multiple monads we must explicitly pass around dictionaries of functions. However, most of the syntactic heaviness comes from the lack of higher-kinded polymorphism: functors are the only mechanism ML provides for abstracting over type constructors. The purpose of this paper is to address this second issue, bringing higher-kinded polymorphism into the core OCaml language, and making it almost as convenient to define when and unless in OCaml as in Haskell.

1.1 The Alias Problem

At this point the reader might wonder why we do not simply adopt the Haskell approach of adding higher-kinded polymorphism directly to the core language. The answer lies in a fundamental difference between type constructors in Haskell and type constructors in OCaml.

In Haskell data and newtype definitions create fresh data types. It is possible to hide the data constructors of such types by leaving them out of the export list of the defining module, but the association between a type name and the data type it denotes cannot be abstracted. It is therefore straightforward for the type checker to determine whether two type names denote the same data type: after expanding synonyms, type names denote the same data types exactly when the names themselves are the same.

OCaml provides more flexible mechanisms for creating abstract types. An entry `type t` in a signature may hide either a fresh data type definition such as `type t = T of int` or as an alias such as `type t = int`. Abstracting types with signatures is sometimes only temporary, since instantiating a functor can replace abstract types in the argument signature with concrete representations. Checking whether two type names denote the same data type is therefore a more subtle matter in OCaml than in Haskell, since abstract types with no visible equalities may later turn out to be equal after all.

Since OCaml cannot distinguish between data types and aliases, it must support instantiating type variables with either. This works well for type variables of base kind, but breaks down with the addition of higher-kinded type variables. To see the difficulty, consider the unification of the following pair of type expressions

```
'a 'f   ~   (int * int) list
```

where `'f` is a higher-kinded type variable. If there are no other definitions in scope then there is an obvious solution, unifying `'a` with `(int * int)` and `'f` with `list`. Now suppose that we also have the following type aliases in scope:

```
type 'a plist = ('a * 'a) list
type 'a iplist = (int * int) list
```

With the addition of `plist` and `iplist` there is no longer a most general unifier. Unifying `'f` with either `plist` or `iplist` gives two new valid solutions, and none of the available solutions is more general than the others.

One possible response to the loss of most general unifiers is to give up on type inference for higher-kinded polymorphism. This is the approach taken by OCaml's functors, which avoid ambiguity by explicitly annotating every instantiation. We will now consider an alternative approach that avoids the need to annotate instantiations, bringing higher-kinded polymorphism directly into the core language.

1.2 Defunctionalization

Since we cannot use higher-kinded type variables to represent OCaml type constructors, we are faced with the problem of abstracting over type expressions of higher kind in a language where all type variables have base kind. At first sight the problem might appear intractable: how can we embed an expressive object language in a less expressive host language?

Happily, there is a well-understood variant of this problem from which we can draw inspiration. Four decades ago John Reynolds introduced *defunctionalization*, a technique for translating higher-order programs into a first-order language [Reynolds, 1972].

The following example illustrates the defunctionalization transform. Here is a higher-order ML program which computes a sum and increments a list of numbers:

```
let rec fold : type a b. (a * b → b) * b * a list → b =
 fun (f, u, l) = match l with
  | [] → u
  | x :: xs → f (x, fold (f u, xs))

let sum l = fold ((fun (x, y) → x + y), 0, l)
let add (n, l) = fold (fun (x, l') → x + n :: l') [] l
```

Defunctionalizing this program involves introducing a datatype `arrow` with two constructors, one for each of the two function terms; the arguments to each constructor represent the free variables of the corresponding function term, and the type parameters to `arrow` represent the argument and return types of the function. We follow Pottier and Gauthier [2004] in defining `arrow` as a generalised algebraic data type (GADT), which allows the instantiation of the type parameters to vary with each constructor, and so makes it possible to preserve the well-typedness of the source program.

```
type (_, _) arrow =
  Fn_plus : ((int * int), int) arrow
| Fn_plus_cons : int → ((int * int list), int list) arrow
```

The second step introduces a function, `apply`, that relates each constructor of `arrow` to the function body.

```
let apply : type a b. (a, b) arrow * a → b =
  fun (appl, v) → match appl with
   | Fn_plus → let (x, y) = v in x + y
   | Fn_plus_cons n → let (x, l') = v in x + n :: l'
```

We can now replace function terms with constructors of `arrow` and indirect calls with applications of `apply` to turn the higher-order example into a first order program:

```
let rec fold : type a b. (a * b, b) arrow * b * a list → b =
 fun (f, u, l) = match l with
  | [] → u
  | x :: xs → apply (f, (x, fold (f, u, xs)))

let sum l = fold (Fn_plus, 0, l)
let add (n, l) = fold (Fn_plus_cons n, [], l)
```

1.3 Type Defunctionalization

Defunctionalization transforms a program with higher-order values into a program where all values are first-order. Similarly, we can change a program with higher-kinded type expressions into a program where all type expressions are of kind $*$, the kind of types.

The first step is to introduce an abstract type constructor, analogous to apply, for representing type-level application:

```
type ('a, 'f) app
```

OCaml excludes higher-kinded type expressions syntactically by requiring that the type operator be a concrete name: 'a list is a valid type expression, but 'a 'f is not. The app type sidesteps the restriction, much as the apply function makes it possible to embed the application of a higher-order function in a first-order defunctionalized program. The type expression (s, t) app represents the application of the type expression t to the type expression s. We can now abstract over type constructors by using a type variable for the operator term t.

Eliminating higher-order functions associates a constructor of arrow with each function expression from the original program. In order to eliminate higher-kinded type expressions we associate each type expression with a distinct instantiation of app. More precisely, for each type constructor t which we wish to use in a polymorphic context we introduce an uninhabited opaque type T.t, called the *brand*. Brands appear as the operator argument to app; for example, we can represent the type expression 'a list as ('a, List.t) app, where List.t is the brand for list. With each brand we associate injection and projection functions for moving between the concrete type and the corresponding instantiation of app:

```
module List : sig
  type t
  val inj : 'a list → ('a, t) app
  val prj : ('a, t) app → 'a list
end
```

We now have the operations we need to build and call functions that abstract over type constructors. Here is a second OCaml implementation of the when function from the beginning of this paper:[1]

```
let when_ (d : _ #monad) b m = if b then m else d#return ()
```

The first parameter d is a dictionary of monad operations analogous to the type class dictionary passed to when in a typical implementation of Haskell [Wadler and Blott, 1989]. (We defer further discussion of dictionary representation to Section 2.3.) Our earlier implementation received the dictionary as a functor argument in order to accommodate abstraction over the type constructor, but the introduction of app makes it possible to write when entirely within the core language. This second implementation of when receives the following type:

```
val when_ : 'm #monad → bool → (unit, 'm) app → (unit, 'm) app
```

[1] We append an underscore to variable names where they clash with OCaml keywords.

```
type ('a, 'f) app

module type Newtype1 = sig
  type 'a s
  type t
  val inj : 'a s → ('a,t) app
  val prj : ('a,t) app → 'a s
end

module Newtype1(T : sig type 'a t end):
  Newtype1 with type 'a s = 'a T.t
```

Fig. 1. The *higher* interface

```
module type Newtype2 = sig
  type ('a, 'b) s
  type t
  val inj : ('a,'b) s → ('b,('a,t) app) app
  val prj : ('b,('a,t) app) app → ('a,'b) s
end

module Newtype2(T : sig type ('a,'b) t end):
  Newtype2 with type ('a,'b) s = ('a,'b) T.t
```

Fig. 2. The Newtype2 functor

The improvement becomes even clearer when we implement `unless` without a functor in sight:

```
let unless d b m = when_ d (not b) m
```

There is a similar improvement when using `when` and `unless` at particular monads. Once again we find that we no longer need to instantiate a functor, since the dictionary parameter is passed as a regular function argument. Here is our earlier example that conditionally writes a value in the state monad, adapted to our new setting:

```
unless state (v < 0) (state#put v)
```

2 The Interface

We have written a tiny library called *higher* to support programming with `app`. Figure 1 shows the interface of the *higher* library.[2] The `Newtype1` functor generates brands together with their associated injection and projection functions, preserving the underlying concrete type under the name `s` for convenience. For example, applying `Newtype1` to a structure containing the concrete `list` type gives the `List.t` brand from Section 1.3.

```
module List = Newtype1(struct type 'a t = 'a list end)
```

In fact, as the numeric suffix in the `Newtype1` name suggests, *higher* exports a family of functors for building brands. Figure 2 gives another instance, for concrete types with two parameters. However, rather than introducing a second version of `app` to accompany `Newtype2`, we use `app` in a curried style. One of the benefits of higher kinded polymorphism is the ability to partially apply multi-parameter type constructors, and the currying in `Newtype2` makes this possible in our setting.

The remainder of this section shows how various examples from the literature can be implemented using *higher*.

[2] The *higher* library is available on opam: `opam install higher`.

2.1 Example: Higher-Kinded Folds

Higher-kinded polymorphism was introduced to Haskell to support constructor classes such as `Monad` [Jones, 1995, Hudak et al., 2007]. However, not all uses of higher kinds involve constructor classes. Traversals of non-regular datatypes (whose definitions contain non-trivial instantiations of the definiendum) typically involve higher-kinded polymorphism. Here is an example: the type `perfect` describes perfectly balanced trees, with 2^n elements:

```
type 'a perfect = Zero of 'a | Succ of ('a * 'a) perfect
```

A fold over a `perfect` value is parameterised by two functions, `zero`, applied at each occurrence of `Zero`, and `succ`, applied at each occurrence of `Succ`. In diagram form the fold has the following simple shape:

```
Succ (Succ ... (Succ (Zero v))...)
  ↓     ↓        ↓     ↓
succ (succ ... (succ (zero v))...)
```

What distinguishes this fold from a similar function defined on a regular datatype is that each occurrence of `Succ` is used at a different type. If the outermost constructor builds an `int perfect` value then the next constructor builds an `(int * int) perfect`, the next an `((int * int) * (int * int)) perfect`, and so on. For maximum generality, therefore, we must allow the types of `zero` and `succ` to vary in the same way.[3] In Haskell we might define `foldp` as follows:

```
foldp :: (∀a. a → f a) → (∀a. f (a, a) → f a) → Perfect a → f a
foldp zero succ (Zero l) = zero l
foldp zero succ (Succ p) = succ (foldp zero succ p)
```

Here is a corresponding definition in OCaml, using a record type with polymorphic fields for the higher-rank types (nested quantification) and using `app` to introduce higher-kinded polymorphism:

```
type 'f perfect_folder = {
  zero: 'a. 'a → ('a, 'f) app;
  succ: 'a. ('a * 'a, 'f) app → ('a, 'f) app;
}

let rec foldp : 'f 'a. 'f perfect_folder → 'a perfect → ('a, 'f) app =
   fun { zero; succ } → function
   | Zero l → zero l
   | Succ p → succ (foldp { zero; succ } p)
```

The `foldp` function has a number of useful properties. A simple one, immediately apparent from the diagram, is that `foldp Zero Succ` is the identity. In order to instantiate the result type we need a suitable instance of `app`, which we can obtain using `Newtype1`.

[3] Hinze [2000] shows how to take generalization of folds over nested types significantly further than the implementation we present here.

```
type ('a, 'b) eq

val refl : unit → ('a, 'a) eq

module Subst (F : sig type 'a f end):
sig
 val subst : ('a, 'b) eq →
  'a F.f → 'b F.f
end
```

Fig. 3. Leibniz equality without *higher*

```
module Eq : Newtype2
type ('a, 'b) eq = ('b, ('a, Eq.t) app) app

val refl : unit → ('a, 'a) eq



val subst : ('a, 'b) eq →
  ('a, 'f) app → ('b, 'f) app
```

Fig. 4. Leibniz equality with *higher*

```
module Perfect = Newtype1(struct type 'a t = 'a perfect end)
```

Passing `Zero` and `Succ` requires a little massaging with `inj` and `prj`.

```
let idp p = Perfect.(prj (foldp { zero = (fun l → inj (Zero l));
                                  succ = (fun b → inj (Succ (prj b)))} p))
```

It is easy to verify that `idp` implements the identity function.

2.2 Example: Leibniz Equality

Our second example involves higher-kinded polymorphism in the definition of a datatype. As part of a library for dynamic typing, Baars and Swierstra [2002] introduce the following definition of type equality:

```
newtype Equal a b = Equal (∀ (f :: * → *). f a → f b)
```

The variable `f` abstracts over one-hole type contexts — type expressions which build a type from a type. The types encode Leibniz's law that `a` and `b` can be considered equal if they are interchangeable in any context `f`. A value of type `Equal a b` serves both as proof that `a` and `b` are equal and as a coercion between contexts instantiated with `a` and `b`. Ignoring $\bot$ values, there is a single inhabitant of `Equal`, the value `Equal id` of type `Equal a a`, which serves as a proof of equality between any type `a` and itself.

Yallop and Kiselyov [2010] show how first-class modules make it possible to define an OCaml type `eq` equivalent to `Equal`. A minimised version of `eq` and its core operations is given in Figure 3. There are two operations: `refl` introduces the sole inhabitant, a proof of reflexive equality, and `subst` turns an equality proof into a coercion within any context `f`.

Figure 4 gives a second definition of `eq` and its operations using *higher*. As with `unless`, using the functor version of Figure 3 is significantly heavier than the *higher* version of Figure 4. Here is a definition of the transitive property of equality using the implementation of Figure 3:

```
class virtual ['m] monad : object
  method virtual return : 'a. 'a → ('a, 'm) app
  method virtual bind : 'a 'b. ('a, 'm) app → ('a → ('b, 'm) app) → ('b, 'm) app
end
```

Fig. 5. The monad interface in OCaml

```
type ('a, 'f) free = Return of 'a | Wrap of (('a, 'f) free, 'f) app
module Free = Newtype2(struct type ('a, 'f) t = ('a, 'f) free end)
```

Fig. 6. The free monad data type in OCaml

```
let trans : type a b c. (a, b) eq → (b, c) eq → (a, c) eq =
  fun ab bc →
    let module S = Subst(struct type 'a tc = (a, 'a) eq end) in
    S.subst bc ab
```

And here is a definition using *higher*:

```
let trans ab bc = subst bc ab
```

Both implementations receive the same type:

```
val trans: ('a, 'b) eq → ('b, 'c) eq → ('a, 'c) eq
```

The contrast between the implementations of `refl` and `subst` is similarly striking. The interested reader can find the full implementations in the extended version of this paper.

2.3 Example: The Codensity Transform

Much of the appeal of higher-kinded polymorphism arises from the ability to define overloaded functions involving higher-kinded types. Constructor classes [Jones, 1995] turn monads (and other approaches to describing computation such as arrows [Hughes, 2000] and applicative functors [McBride and Paterson, 2008]) from design patterns into named program entities. The `Monad` interface requires abstraction over type constructors, and hence higher kinds, but defining it brings a slew of benefits: it becomes possible to build polymorphic functions and notation which work for any monad, and to construct a hierarchy of related interfaces such as `Functor` and `MonadPlus`.

OCaml does not currently support overloading, making many programs which find convenient expression in Haskell cumbersome to write. However, the loss of elegance does not arise from a loss of expressive power: although type classes are unavailable we can achieve similar results by programming directly in the target language of the translation which eliminates type classes in favour of dictionary passing [Wadler and Blott, 1989]. We might reasonably view these explicit dictionaries as temporary scaffolding that will vanish once the plans to introduce overloading to OCaml come to fruition [Chambart and Henry, 2012].

```
let monad_free (functor_free : 'f #functor_) = object
  inherit [('f, Free.t) app] monad
  method return v = Free.inj (Return v)
  method bind =
    let rec bind m k = match m with
      | Return a → k a
      | Wrap t → Wrap (functor_free#fmap (fun m → bind m k) t) in
    fun m k → Free.inj (bind (Free.prj m) (fun a → Free.prj (k a)))
end
```

Fig. 7. The free monad instance in OCaml

```
class virtual ['f, 'm] freelike (pf : 'f functor_) (mm : 'm monad) = object
  method pf : 'f functor_ = pf      method mm : 'm monad = mm
  method virtual wrap : 'a. (('a, 'm) app, 'f) app → ('a, 'm) app
end
```

Fig. 8. The freelike interface in OCaml

We now turn to an example of a Haskell program that makes heavy use of higher-kinded overloading. The *codensity transform* [Voigtländer, 2008] takes advantage of higher-kinded polymorphism to systematically substitute more efficient implementations of computations involving free monads, leading to asymptotic performance improvements. We will focus here on the constructs necessary to support the codensity transform rather than on the computational content of the transform itself, which is described in Voigtländer's paper. The code in this section is not complete (the definitions of `abs`, `C`, and `functor_` are missing), but we give a complete translation of the code from Voigtländer [2008, Sections 3 and 4] in the extended version of this paper.

Figure 5 shows the `monad` interface in OCaml. We represent a type class by an OCaml virtual class —i.e., a class with methods left unimplemented. The type class variable `m` of type $* \to *$ becomes a type parameter, which is used in the definition of `monad` as an argument to our type application operator `app`.

Figure 6 defines the free monad type [Voigtländer, 2008, Section 3]. The use of `app` in the definition of `free` reflects the fact that the type parameter `'f` has higher kind; without *higher* we would have to define the `free` within a functor.

Figure 7 gives the free monad instance over a functor using the `free` type. We represent type class instances in OCaml as values of object type. Instantiating and inheriting the `monad` class provides type checking for `return` and `bind`. Constraints in the instance definition in the Haskell code become arguments to the function; our definition says that `('f, Free.t) app` is an instance of `monad` if `'f` is an instance of `functor`.

Figure 8 defines the `freelike` interface. In Voigtländer's presentation `FreeLike` is a multi-parameter type class with two superclasses. In our setting the parameters become type parameters of the virtual class and the superclasses

```
type ('a, 'f) freelike_poly = {
  fl: 'm 'd. (('f, 'm) #freelike as 'd) → ('a, 'm) app
}

let improve (d : _ #functor_) { fl } =
  Free.prj (abs (monad_free d) (C.prj (fl (freelike_c d (freelike_free d)))))
```

Fig. 9. The improve function in OCaml

```
improve :: Functor f ⇒ (∀m. FreeLike f m → m a) → Free f a
improve m = abs m
```

Fig. 10. The improve function in Haskell

become class arguments which must be supplied at instantiation time. We bind the class arguments to methods so that we can easily retrieve them later.

Figure 9 shows the `improve` function, the entry point to the codensity transform. In Haskell `improve` has a concise definition (Figure 10) due to the amount of work done by the type class machinery; in OCaml we must perform the work of building and passing dictionaries ourselves. As in a previous example (Section 2.1) we use a record with a polymorphic field to introduce the necessary higher-rank polymorphism.

The extended version of this paper gives a complete implementation of the codensity transform, and a translation of Voigtländer's example which applies it to an *echo* computation.

2.4 Example: Kind Polymorphism

Standard Haskell's kind system is "simply typed": the two kind formers are the base kind $*$ and the kind arrow $\rightarrow$, and unknown types are defaulted to $*$. Recent work adds kind polymorphism, increasing the number of programs that can be expressed [Yorgey et al., 2012]. In contrast *higher* lacks a kind system altogether: the brands that represent type constructors are simply uninhabited members of the base kind $*$.

The obvious disadvantage to the lack of a kind system is that the type checker is no help in preventing the formation of ill-kinded expressions, such as `(List.t, List.t) app`. However, this drawback is not so serious as might first appear, since it does not introduce any means of forming ill-typed values, and so cannot lead to runtime errors. In fact, the absence of well-kindedness checks can be used to advantage: it allows us to write programs which require the kind polymorphism extension in Haskell.

Figure 11 defines a class `category` parameterised by a variable `'f`. In the analogous type class definition standard Haskell would give the variable corresponding to `'f` the kind $* \rightarrow * \rightarrow *$; the polymorphic kinds extension gives

```
class virtual ['f] category = object
  method virtual ident : 'a. ('a, ('a, 'f) app) app
  method virtual compose : 'a 'b 'c.
     ('b, ('a, 'f) app) app → ('c, ('b, 'f) app) app → ('c, ('a, 'f) app) app
end
```

Fig. 11. The category interface

```
module Fun = Newtype2(struct type ('a, 'b) t = 'b → 'a end)
let category_fun = object
  inherit [Fun.t] category
  method ident = Fun.inj id
  method compose f g = Fun.inj (fun x → Fun.prj g (Fun.prj f x))
end
```

Fig. 12. A category instance for →

```
type ('n, 'm) ip = { ip: 'a. ('a, 'm) app → ('a, 'n) app }
module Ip = Newtype2(struct type ('n, 'm) t = ('n, 'm) ip end)
let category_ip = object
  inherit [Ip.t] category
  method ident = Ip.inj { ip = id }
  method compose f g = Ip.inj {ip = fun x → (Ip.prj g).ip ((Ip.prj f).ip x) }
end
```

Fig. 13. A category instance for index-preserving functions

it $\forall\kappa.\ \kappa \rightarrow \kappa \rightarrow *$, allowing the arguments to be type expressions of any kind. Since there is no kind checking in *higher*, we can also instantiate the arguments of `'f` with expressions of any kind. Figure 12 gives an instance definition for →, whose arguments have kind $*$; Figure 13 adds a second instance for the category of index-preserving functions, leaving the kinds of the indexes unspecified.

The extended version of this paper continues the example, showing how *higher* supports higher-kinded non-regularity.

3 Implementations of *higher*

Up to this point we have remained entirely within the OCaml language. Both the interfaces and the examples are written using the current release of OCaml (4.01). However, running the code requires an implementation of the *higher* interface, which requires a small extension to pure OCaml. We now consider two implementations of *higher*, the first based on an unsafe cast and the second based on an extension to the OCaml language.

Let us return to the analogy of Section 1.3. The central point in an implementation of *higher* is a means of translating between values of the app family of types and values of the corresponding concrete types, much as defunctionalization involves translating between higher-order function applications and uses

```
type family Apply f p :: *
newtype App f b = Inj { prj :: Apply f b }

data List
type instance Apply List a = [a]
```

Fig. 14. Implementing *higher* with type families

```
type ('p, 'f) app

module Newtype1 (T : sig type 'a t end) = struct
  type 'a s = 'a T.t
  type t
  let inj : 'a s → ('a, t) app = Obj.magic
  let prj : ('a, t) app → 'a s = Obj.magic
end
```

Fig. 15. Implementing *higher* with an unchecked cast

of the `apply` function. However, defunctionalization is a whole program transformation: a single `apply` function handles every translated higher-order call. Since we do not wish to require that every type used with *higher* is known in advance, we need an implementation that makes it possible to extend `app` with new inhabitants as needed.

We note in passing that Haskell's type families [Schrijvers et al., 2008], which define extensible type-level functions, provide exactly the functionality we need. Figure 14 gives an implementation, with a type family `Apply` parameterised by a brand and a type and a type definition `App` with injection and projection functions `Inj` and `Prj`. The `type instance` declaration adds a case to `Apply` that matches the abstract type `List` and produces the representation type `[a]`.

3.1 First Implementation: Unchecked Cast

The first implementation is shown in Figure 15. Each instantiation of the `Newtype1` constructor generates a fresh type `t` to use as the brand. The `inj` and `prj` functions which coerce between the concrete type `'a s` and the corresponding defunctionalized type `('a, t) app` are implemented using the unchecked coercion function `Obj.magic`.

Although we are using an unchecked coercion within the implementation of `Newtype1` the module system ensures that type safety is preserved. Each module to which `Newtype1` is applied generates a fresh brand `t`. Since the only way to create a value of type `('a, t) app` is to apply `inj` to a value of the corresponding type `'a s`, it is always safe to apply `prj` to convert the value back to type `'a s`.

```
type ('p, 'f) app = ..

module Newtype1 (T : sig type 'a t end) () = struct
  type 'a s = 'a T.t
  type t
  type (_, _) app += App : 'a s → ('a, t) app
  let inj v = App v
  let prj (App v) = v
end
```

Fig. 16. Implementing *higher* using open types

3.2 Second Implementation: Open Types

We can avoid the use of an unchecked cast altogether with a small extension to the OCaml language. Löh and Hinze [2006] propose extending Haskell with *open data types*, which lift the restriction that all the constructors of a data type must be given in a single declaration. The proposal is a good fit for OCaml, which already supports a single extensible type for exceptions, and there is an implementation available.[4].

Figure 16 shows an implementation of *higher* using open data types. The ellipsis in the first line declares that `app` is an open data type; each instantiation of the `Newtype1` functor extends `app` with a fresh GADT constructor, `App` which instantiates `app` with the brand `t` and which carries a single value of the representation type `'a s`. The `inj` and `prj` functions inject and project using `App`; although the pattern in `prj` is technically inexhaustive, the fact that the functor generates a fresh `t` for each application guarantees a match in practice.

The empty parentheses in the functor definition force the functor to be generative rather than applicative[5] [Leroy, 1995], so that each application of `Newtype1` generates a fresh type `t`, even if `Newtype1` is being applied to the same argument.

This generative marker is a small deviation from the interface of Figure 1, but essential to ensure that only a single data constructor `App` is generated for each brand `t`. Without the generative marker, multiple applications of `Newtype1` to the same argument would generate modules with compatible brands but incompatible data constructors, leading to runtime pattern-matching failures in `prj`.

4 Related Work

We have shown how type defunctionalization can be used to write programs that abstract over OCaml type constructors without leaving the core language. In a

[4] Opam users can install the extended OCaml compiler with the command `opam switch 4.01.0+open-types`.

[5] Explicitly generative functors are a new feature of OCaml, scheduled for the next release: `http://caml.inria.fr/mantis/view.php?id=5905`

language with features that support case analysis on types, type defunctionalization becomes a yet more powerful tool. Kiselyov et al. [2004] use type defunctionalization together with functional dependencies to support fold operations on heterogeneous lists. Similarly, Jeltsch [2010] implements type defunctionalization using type synonym families to support folds over extensible records.

Kiselyov and Shan [2007] introduce *lightweight static capabilities*, applying phantom types and generativity to mark values as safe for use with an efficient trusted kernel, much as we use generativity in Section 3.1 to ensure the safety of an unchecked cast. Kiselyov and Shan's work is significantly more ambitious than ours; whereas we are interested in expressing programs with higher-kinded polymorphism in ML, they show how to statically ensure properties such as array lengths that were previously thought to require a dependently-typed language. The "brand" terminology is borrowed from Kiselyov and Shan, but their brands are structured type expressions, and significantly more elaborate than the simple atomic names which we use to denote type constructors.

Jones [1995] shows that standard first-order unification suffices for inferring types involving higher-kinded variables so long as the language of constructor expressions has no non-trivial equalities. This insight underlies our use of brands to embed type constructor polymorphism in OCaml.

Swamy et al. [2011] share our aim of reducing the overhead of monadic programming in ML, but take a different approach based on an elaboration of implicitly-monadic ML programs into a language with explicit monad operations. Whereas the present work aims to embed higher-kinded programs into OCaml without changing the language, their proposal calls for significant new support at the language level.

5 Limitations and Future Work

*The Newtype*N *family.* The interface presented in Section 2 consists of a type constructor `app` and a family of functors `Newtype1`, `Newtype2`, ... for extending `app` with new inhabitants. We would ideally like to replace the `Newtype` family with arity-generic operations, but it is unclear whether it is possible to do so in OCaml. For the moment the family of functors seems adequate in practice.

Variance and subtyping. Our focus so far has been on expressing higher-kinded programs from Haskell. However, we also plan to explore the interaction of higher-kinded polymorphism with features specific to OCaml. For example, we can obtain a representation of proofs of subtyping by changing the definition of Leibniz equality (Section 2.2) to quantify over positive contexts: a type `a` is a subtype of `b` if it can be coerced to `b` in a positive context (or if `b` can be coerced to `a` in a negative context.) We look forward to exploring the implications of having first-class witnesses of the subtyping relation.

Acknowledgements. We are grateful to the anonymous reviewers for their many helpful suggestions.

References

Baars, A.I., Swierstra, S.D.: Typing dynamic typing. In: ICFP 2002, pp. 157–166. ACM, New York (2002), ISBN 1-58113-487-8

Chambart, P., Henry, G.: Experiments in generic programming: runtime type representation and implicit values. In: OCaml Users and Developers Workshop (2012)

Hinze, R.: Efficient generalized folds. In: Jeuring, J. (ed.) Proceedings of the 2nd Workshop on Generic Programming, Ponte de Lima, Portugal, pp. 1–16 (July 2000)

Hudak, P., Hughes, J., Peyton Jones, S., Wadler, P.: A history of Haskell: Being lazy with class. In: Proceedings of the Third ACM SIGPLAN Conference on History of Programming Languages, HOPL III, pp. 12–1–12–55. ACM, New York (2007) ISBN 978-1-59593-766-7

Hughes, J.: Generalising monads to arrows. Science of Computer Programming 37(13), 67–111 (2000) ISSN 0167-6423

Jeltsch, W.: Generic record combinators with static type checking. In: Proceedings of the 12th International ACM SIGPLAN Symposium on Principles and Practice of Declarative Programming, pp. 143–154. ACM (2010)

Jones, M.P.: A system of constructor classes: overloading and implicit higher-order polymorphism. Journal of Functional Programming 5, 1–35 (1995) ISSN 1469-7653

Kiselyov, O., Shan, C.-C.: Lightweight static capabilities. Electron. Notes Theor. Comput. Sci. 174(7), 79–104 (2007) ISSN 1571-0661

Kiselyov, O., Lämmel, R., Schupke, K.: Strongly typed heterogeneous collections. In: Proceedings of the 2004 ACM SIGPLAN Workshop on Haskell, pp. 96–107. ACM (2004)

Leroy, X.: Applicative functors and fully transparent higher-order modules. In: Proceedings of the 22Nd ACM SIGPLAN-SIGACT Symposium on Principles of Programming Languages, POPL 1995, pp. 142–153. ACM, New York (1995) ISBN 0-89791-692-1, `http://doi.acm.org/10.1145/199448.199476`, doi:10.1145/199448.199476

Löh, A., Hinze, R.: Open data types and open functions. In: Proceedings of the 8th ACM SIGPLAN International Conference on Principles and Practice of Declarative Programming, PPDP 2006, pp. 133–144. ACM, New York (2006) ISBN 1-59593-388-3

McBride, C., Paterson, R.: Applicative programming with effects. J. Funct. Program. 18(1), 1–13 (2008) ISSN 0956-7968

Pottier, F., Gauthier, N.: Polymorphic typed defunctionalization. In: Proceedings of the 31st ACM SIGPLAN-SIGACT Symposium on Principles of Programming Languages, POPL 2004, pp. 89–98. ACM, New York (2004) ISBN 1-58113-729-X

Reynolds, J.C.: Definitional interpreters for higher-order programming languages. In: Proceedings of the ACM Annual Conference, ACM 1972, vol. 2, pp. 717–740. ACM, New York (1972)

Schrijvers, T., Peyton Jones, S., Chakravarty, M., Sulzmann, M.: Type checking with open type functions. In: Proceedings of the 13th ACM SIGPLAN International Conference on Functional Programming, ICFP 2008, pp. 51–62. ACM, New York (2008) ISBN 978-1-59593-919-7

Swamy, N., Guts, N., Leijen, D., Hicks, M.: Lightweight monadic programming in ML. In: Proceedings of the 16th ACM SIGPLAN International Conference on Functional Programming, ICFP 2011, pp. 15–27. ACM, New York (2011) ISBN 978-1-4503-0865-6

Voigtländer, J.: Asymptotic improvement of computations over free monads. In: Audebaud, P., Paulin-Mohring, C. (eds.) MPC 2008. LNCS, vol. 5133, pp. 388–403. Springer, Heidelberg (2008)
Wadler, P., Blott, S.: How to make ad-hoc polymorphism less ad hoc. In: Proceedings of the 16th ACM SIGPLAN-SIGACT Symposium on Principles of Programming Languages, POPL 1989, pp. 60–76. ACM, New York (1989) ISBN 0-89791-294-2
Yallop, J., Kiselyov, O.: First-class modules: hidden power and tantalizing promises. In: ACM SIGPLAN Workshop on ML, Baltimore, Maryland, United States (September 2010)
Yorgey, B.A., Weirich, S., Cretin, J., Peyton Jones, S., Vytiniotis, D., Magalhães, J.P.: Giving Haskell a promotion. In: Proceedings of the 8th ACM SIGPLAN Workshop on Types in Language Design and Implementation, TLDI 2012, pp. 53–66. ACM, New York (2012) ISBN 978-1-4503-1120-5

Generic Programming with Multiple Parameters

José Pedro Magalhães

Department of Computer Science, University of Oxford, Oxford, UK
jpm@cs.ox.ac.uk

Abstract. Generic programming, a form of abstraction in programming languages that serves to reduce code duplication by exploiting the regular structure of algebraic datatypes, has been present in the Haskell language in different forms for many years. Lately, a library for generic deriving has been given native support in the compiler, allowing programmers to write functions such as *fmap* that abstract over one datatype parameter generically. The power of this approach is limited to dealing with one parameter per datatype, however. In this paper, we lift this restriction by providing a generalisation of generic deriving that supports multiple parameters, making essential use of datatype promotion and kind polymorphism. We show example encodings of datatypes, and how to define a map function that operates on multiple parameters simultaneously.

1 Introduction

Haskell [12], a pure, lazy, strongly-typed functional programming language, has been a research vehicle for generic programming almost since its inception [2]. Generic programming is a form of abstraction which exploits the structure of algebraic datatypes in order to define functionality that operates on many datatypes uniformely, reducing code duplication. With generic programming, certain functions (such as data serialisation and traversals) can be written once and for all, working for existing and future types of data.

Early approaches to generic programming in Haskell were separate extensions to the compiler or preprocessors [3], but recently all approaches are bundled as libraries [13], sometimes with direct compiler support [11]. The easier availability of generic programming functionality appears to increase its usage; in particular, offering native support for an approach in the compiler confers a sense of stability to a specific approach, allowing more programmers to use and benefit from generic programming.

This switch to library approaches simplifies the task of the generic programming library developer, since it is typically easier to maintain a library than a separate extension. It also presents the library user with fewer barriers to adoption, as it requires no external tools. However, it can compromise expressivity and usability, as library approaches are limited to the capabilities of the Haskell language itself. Performance and quality of error messages are common complaints of generic programming libraries, but also reduced support for certain datatypes can be a concern. In particular, the Generic Haskell compiler [6], an early, pre-processor approach, had full support for generic functions abstracting over multiple parameters. The same goes for the generics in the Clean language [1], which were implemented in the kind-indexed style of

M. Codish and E. Sumii (Eds.): FLOPS 2014, LNCS 8475, pp. 136–151, 2014.

Generic Haskell. However, to our knowledge no library approach to generic programming in Haskell has native support for abstraction over multiple datatype parameters. Concretely, consider the following example:

$$
\begin{aligned}
&\textbf{data}\ \mathit{WTree}\ \alpha\ \omega = \mathit{Leaf}\ \alpha \\
&\qquad\qquad\qquad\quad \mid \mathit{Fork}\ (\mathit{WTree}\ \alpha\ \omega)\ (\mathit{WTree}\ \alpha\ \omega) \\
&\qquad\qquad\qquad\quad \mid \mathit{WithWeight}\ (\mathit{WTree}\ \alpha\ \omega)\ \omega \\
&\mathit{mapWTree} :: (\alpha \to \alpha') \to (\omega \to \omega') \to \mathit{WTree}\ \alpha\ \omega \to \mathit{WTree}\ \alpha'\ \omega' \\
&\mathit{mapWTree}\ f\ g\ (\mathit{Leaf}\ a) \qquad\qquad\quad = \mathit{Leaf}\ (f\ a) \\
&\mathit{mapWTree}\ f\ g\ (\mathit{Fork}\ l\ r) \qquad\qquad = \mathit{Fork}\ (\mathit{mapWTree}\ f\ g\ l)\ (\mathit{mapWTree}\ f\ g\ r) \\
&\mathit{mapWTree}\ f\ g\ (\mathit{WithWeight}\ t\ w) = \mathit{WithWeight}\ (\mathit{mapWTree}\ f\ g\ t)\ (g\ w)
\end{aligned}
$$

Clearly, functions like *mapWTree* follow the structure of the datatype, and should be defined generically, once and for all. In this paper we focus on the problem of defininig *functions* such as *mapWTree* generically; many (if not all) modern generic programming approaches support the *WTree datatype*, but not generic operations such as *mapWTree*. The only exception that we are aware of is a convoluted implementation using Scrap Your Boilerplate [5], which relies on runtime type comparison, casting, and (virtual) seralisation.[1] Our approach focuses instead on encoding the parameters adequately in the generic representation.

In this paper, we focus our attention on the `generic-deriving` approach, as implemented in the Glasgow Haskell Compiler (GHC) [8, Chapter 11]. To balance complexity and ease-of-use, `generic-deriving` was designed from the start with one compromise in mind: many generic functions (e.g. *fmap* and *traverse*) abstract over one datatype parameter (i.e. they operate on *type containers*, or types of kind $\star \to \star$), but few require abstraction over more than one parameter. As such, the design of `generic-deriving` could be kept relatively simple, at the loss of some generality. Recently, with the advent of kind polymorphism in GHC [16], many libraries are being generalised from kind-specific to kind-polymophic (e.g. *Typeable* [16]). In this paper we describe an elegant generalisation of `generic-deriving` that works with multiple parameters, lifting the one-parameter restriction without requiring the full-blown power (and complexity) of indexed functors [7]. Our solution is based on an earlier, failed attempt [9, Section 6.1], but uses new insights to overcome old challenges: we use heterogeneous collections [4] to encode a function with multiple arguments as a regular single-argument function that takes a list of arguments.

In the remainder of this paper, we first review one-parameter `generic-deriving` (Section 2). We proceed to describe our generalisation in Section 3, showing example datatype encodings (Section 3.2), and a generalised map function (Section 3.3). We list limitations and propose future work in Section 4, and conclude in Section 5.

Notation. In order to avoid syntactic clutter and to help the reader, we adopt a liberal Haskell notation in this paper. Datatype promotion makes datatype definitions *also* define a kind (with the name of the datatype being defined), while the constructors *also* become the types that inhabit that kind; we assume the existence of a **kind** keyword, which allows us to define kinds that behave as if they had arisen from datatype

[1] `http://okmij.org/ftp/Haskell/generics.html#gmap`

promotion, except that they do not define a datatype and constructors. This helps us preventing name clashes. We omit the keywords **type family** and **type instance** entirely, making type-level functions look like their value-level counterparts. Promoted lists are prefixed with a quote, to distinguish them from the list type. Additionally, we use Greek letters for type variables, apart from κ, which is reserved for kind variables. A colour version of this paper is available at `http://dreixel.net/research/pdf/gpmp_colour.pdf`. The syntactic sugar is only for presentation purposes. An executable version of the code, which compiles with GHC 7.6.2, is available at `http://dreixel.net/research/code/gpmp.zip`.

2 Generic Programming with One Parameter

In this section we review the `generic-deriving` library (in the slightly revised version of Magalhães and Löh [10]), which supports abstraction over (at most) one datatype parameter. We omit meta-information, as it is not relevant to our development.

2.1 Universe

Using datatype promotion and kind polymorphism, we can keep the "realm" of generic representations of user datatypes separate from the realm of user datatypes by defining a new kind. Like types classify values, kinds classify types. User datatypes always have kind $\star$. For the generic representation, we define a kind *Univ* that aggregates the types used to represent user datatypes in `generic-deriving`. *U* encodes constructors without arguments, *P* an occurence of the parameter, *K* a type that does not contain the parameter, *R* a type that contains the parameter, (:+:) the choice between two constructors, (:×:) is used for constructors with multiple arguments, and (:@:) encodes the application of a functor to a type. The interpretation datatype $In\ \upsilon\ \rho$ encodes the values associated with a representation type υ and parameter ρ:

```
kind Univ =                    data In (υ :: Univ) (ρ :: ⋆) :: ⋆ where
    U                              U_I   ::                        In U          ρ
  | P                              Par_I :: ρ                    → In P          ρ
  | K ⋆                            K_I   :: α                    → In (K α)      ρ
  | R (⋆ → ⋆)                      Rec_I :: φ ρ                  → In (R φ)      ρ
  | Univ :+: Univ                  L_I   :: In φ ρ               → In (φ :+: ψ)  ρ
                                   R_I   :: In ψ ρ               → In (φ :+: ψ)  ρ
  | Univ :×: Univ                  (:×:) :: In φ ρ → In ψ ρ      → In (φ :×: ψ)  ρ
  | ⋆ → ⋆ :@: Univ                 App_I :: φ (In ψ ρ)           → In (φ :@: ψ)  ρ
```

There is some redundacy in the universe codes; for example, $R\ \phi$ is essentially a shortcut for ϕ :@: *P*, but the latter has a more complicated representation ($\phi\ (In\ P\ \rho)$ instead of just $\phi\ \rho$). Our new encoding in Section 3 also solves this issue.

The *Generic* type class mediates between user datatypes and their generic representation. A *Rep* type function is used to encode the generic representation of some user datatype α, while *Par* identifies the parameter. Conversion functions *from* and *to* witness the isomorphism between α and $In\ (Rep\ \alpha)\ (Par\ \alpha)$:

$$\begin{array}{l}
\textbf{class}\ \mathit{Generic}\ (\alpha :: \star)\ \textbf{where} \\
\quad \mathit{Rep}\ \alpha :: \mathit{Univ} \\
\quad \mathit{Par}\ \alpha :: \star \\
\quad \mathit{from} :: \alpha \to \mathit{In}\ (\mathit{Rep}\ \alpha)\ (\mathit{Par}\ \alpha) \\
\quad \mathit{to}\ \ \ \ :: \mathit{In}\ (\mathit{Rep}\ \alpha)\ (\mathit{Par}\ \alpha) \to \alpha
\end{array}$$

Instances of this class are trivial, but tedious to write, and are necessary for each datatype intended to be used generically. Fortunately, these instances are automatically derivable by GHC, therefore making `generic-deriving` a "built-in" generic programming approach.

2.2 Datatype Encodings

The universe of `generic-deriving` is best understood through sample datatype instantiations, which we provide in this section. We start with the encoding of lists. A list is a choice ($(:+:)$) between an empty constructor (U) or two ($(:\times:)$) arguments—the parameter (P) and another list ($R\ [\,]$):

$$\begin{array}{l}
\textbf{instance}\ \mathit{Generic}\ [\alpha]\ \textbf{where} \\
\quad \mathit{Rep}\ [\alpha] = U :+: P :\times: R\ [\,] \\
\quad \mathit{Par}\ \ [\alpha] = \alpha \\
\quad \mathit{from}\ [\,] \qquad = L_1\ U_1 \\
\quad \mathit{from}\ (h : t) = R_1\ (\mathit{Par}_1\ h :\times: \mathit{Rec}_1\ t) \\
\quad \mathit{to}\ (L_1\ U_1) \qquad\qquad\quad = [\,] \\
\quad \mathit{to}\ (R_1\ (\mathit{Par}_1\ h :\times: \mathit{Rec}_1\ t)) = h : t
\end{array}$$

From this point forward we shall omit the *to* function, as it is always entirely symmetric to *from*.

A slightly more complicated encoding is that of rose (or multiway) trees. Since we use application of lists in the representation, the conversion functions need to be able to map over these lists. This is achieved using the *fmap* function, a generic map that can be defined for all *Generic* types (Section 2.3):

$$\begin{array}{l}
\textbf{data}\ \mathit{RTree}\ \alpha = \mathit{RTree}\ \alpha\ [\mathit{RTree}\ \alpha] \\
\textbf{instance}\ \mathit{Generic}\ (\mathit{RTree}\ \alpha)\ \textbf{where} \\
\quad \mathit{Rep}\ (\mathit{RTree}\ \alpha) = P :\times: ([\,] :@: R\ \mathit{RTree}) \\
\quad \mathit{Par}\ \ (\mathit{RTree}\ \alpha) = \alpha \\
\quad \mathit{from}\ (\mathit{RTree}\ x\ xs) = \mathit{Par}_1\ x :\times: \mathit{App}_1\ (\mathit{fmap}\ \mathit{Rec}_1\ xs)
\end{array}$$

2.3 Mapping

As `generic-deriving` supports abstraction over one parameter, we can define the standard function *fmap* generically. The user-facing class for this function abstracts over type containers ϕ of kind $\star \to \star$:

$$\begin{array}{l}
\textbf{class}\ \mathit{Functor}\ (\phi :: \star \to \star)\ \textbf{where} \\
\quad \mathit{fmap} :: (\alpha \to \beta) \to \phi\ \alpha \to \phi\ \beta
\end{array}$$

The generic version, $fmap_R$, on the other hand, operates on the generic representation. We need to give an instance of $fmap_R$ for each representation type; we use another type class for this purpose:

$$\begin{array}{l}\textbf{class}\ Functor_R\ (\upsilon :: Univ)\ \textbf{where}\\ \quad fmap_R :: (\alpha \to \beta) \to In\ \upsilon\ \alpha \to In\ \upsilon\ \beta\end{array}$$

Sums, products, units, and constants are trivial:

$$\begin{array}{l}\textbf{instance}\ Functor_R\ U\ \textbf{where}\\ \quad fmap_R\ \_\ U_I = U_I\\ \textbf{instance}\ Functor_R\ (K\ \alpha)\ \textbf{where}\\ \quad fmap_R\ \_\ (K_I\ x) = K_I\ x\\ \textbf{instance}\ (Functor_R\ \phi, Functor_R\ \psi) \Rightarrow Functor_R\ (\phi :+: \psi)\ \textbf{where}\\ \quad fmap_R\ f\ (L_I\ x) = L_I\ (fmap_R\ f\ x)\\ \quad fmap_R\ f\ (R_I\ x) = R_I\ (fmap_R\ f\ x)\\ \textbf{instance}\ (Functor_R\ \phi, Functor_R\ \psi) \Rightarrow Functor_R\ (\phi :\times: \psi)\ \textbf{where}\\ \quad fmap_R\ f\ (x :\times: y) = fmap_R\ f\ x :\times: fmap_R\ f\ y\end{array}$$

More interesting are the instances for: the parameter, where we apply the mapping function; recursion into type containers, where we recurse using *fmap*; and application of type containers, where we *fmap* on the outer container, and $fmap_R$ on the inner representation:

$$\begin{array}{l}\textbf{instance}\ Functor_R\ P\ \textbf{where}\\ \quad fmap_R\ f\ (Par_I\ x) \ = Par_I\ (f\ x)\\ \textbf{instance}\ (Functor\ \phi) \Rightarrow Functor_R\ (R\ \phi)\ \textbf{where}\\ \quad fmap_R\ f\ (Rec_I\ x) \ = Rec_I\ (fmap\ f\ x)\\ \textbf{instance}\ (Functor\ \phi, Functor_R\ \upsilon) \Rightarrow Functor_R\ (\phi :@: \upsilon)\ \textbf{where}\\ \quad fmap_R\ f\ (App_I\ x) = App_I\ (fmap\ (fmap_R\ f)\ x)\end{array}$$

Providing instances for types with a *Generic* instance, such as $[\alpha]$, requires only using $fmap_R$ and converting *from*/*to* the original datatype:

$$\begin{array}{l}\textbf{instance}\ Functor\ [\,]\ \textbf{where}\\ \quad fmap\ f = to \circ fmap_R\ f \circ from\end{array}$$

We now have an easy way to define a generic *fmap* for any user datatype with a *Generic* instance.

3 Generic Programming with Multiple Parameters

Having seen the current implementation of `generic-deriving`, we are ready to explore the changes that are necessary to make it support abstraction over multiple parameters.

3.1 Universe

The main change to the universe involves the introduction of a list of parameters, and the separation of fields into a kind of their own. A field can be one of three things.

Constant types (K) are unchanged. Parameters ($P\ \nu$) now take an argument $\nu :: \mathit{Nat}$ to indicate which of the parameters it is. The kind *Nat* encodes Peano-style natural numbers; we will write *0* for *Ze*, *1* for *Su Ze*, etc. A generalised form of application ((:@:)) replaces R and the old (:@:), encoding the application of a type of kind κ to a type-level list of fields. As we only deal with parameters of kind $\star$ (see Section 4.1), the first argument to :@: will always have a kind of the form $\star \to \ldots \to \star$, and the second argument will have as many elements as necessary to fully saturate the first argument. The interpretation now takes a list of parameters ρ instead of a single parameter. A separate *InField* $\upsilon\ \rho$ datatype interprets a field representation type υ with parameters ρ. Constants are interpreted as before. Parameters are looked-up in the parameter list with a type-level lookup operator (:!:) akin to the value-level (!) operator. An application σ :@: χ is interpreted by applying σ to each of the arguments in χ, after transforming these (with *ExpandField*) into types of kind $\star$:

```
kind Univ =                  data In (υ :: Univ) (ρ :: [⋆]) :: ⋆ where
    U                            U   ::                       In U         ρ
  | F Field                      F   :: InField υ ρ         → In (F υ)     ρ
  | Univ :+: Univ                L   :: In α ρ              → In (α :+: β) ρ
                                 R   :: In β ρ              → In (α :+: β) ρ
  | Univ :×: Univ                :×: :: In α ρ → In β ρ     → In (α :×: β) ρ
kind Field =                 data InField (υ :: Field) (ρ :: [⋆]) :: ⋆ where
    K ⋆                          K :: α                     → InField (K α)     ρ
  | P Nat                        P :: ρ :!: ν               → InField (P ν)     ρ
  | ∀κ.κ :@: [Field]             A :: AppFields σ χ ρ       → InField (σ :@: χ) ρ

kind Nat = Ze | Su Nat
(ρ :: [⋆]) :!: (ν :: Nat) :: ⋆
(α ': ρ) :!: Ze     = α
(α ': ρ) :!: (Su ν) = ρ :!: ν
AppFields σ χ ρ = σ :$: ExpandField χ ρ
(σ :: κ) :$: (ρ :: [⋆]) :: ⋆
σ :$: '[]         = σ
σ :$: (α ': β)    = (σ α) :$: β
ExpandField (χ :: [Field]) (ρ :: [⋆]) :: [⋆]
ExpandField '[]                ρ = '[]
ExpandField ((K α) ':       χ) ρ = α ':                            ExpandField χ ρ
ExpandField ((P ν) ':       χ) ρ = (ρ :!: ν) ':                    ExpandField χ ρ
ExpandField ((σ :@: ω) ': χ) ρ = (σ :$: ExpandField ω ρ) ': ExpandField χ ρ
```

The *ExpandField* type function converts a list of *Field*s into user-defined types (of kind $\star$). Constants are represented by the type in question, parameters are looked up in the parameter list, and applications are expanded into a fully applied type.

The *Generic* class to mediate between user datatypes and their representation now has a type function *Pars* which lists the parameters of the datatype:

$$\begin{array}{l}\textbf{class}\ \mathit{Generic}\ (\alpha :: \star)\ \textbf{where}\\ \quad \mathit{Rep}\ \ \alpha :: \mathit{Univ}\\ \quad \mathit{Pars}\ \alpha :: [\star]\\ \quad \mathit{from} :: \alpha \rightarrow \mathit{In}\ (\mathit{Rep}\ \alpha)\ (\mathit{Pars}\ \alpha)\\ \quad \mathit{to}\ \ \ \ :: \mathit{In}\ (\mathit{Rep}\ \alpha)\ (\mathit{Pars}\ \alpha) \rightarrow \alpha\end{array}$$

3.2 Datatype Encodings

To better understand the universe of our generalised `generic-deriving`, we show several example datatype encodings in this section. We begin with lists; their encoding is similar to that of Section 2.2, only now we use (:@:) instead of *R*:

$$\begin{array}{l}\textbf{instance}\ \mathit{Generic}\ [\alpha]\ \textbf{where}\\ \quad \mathit{Rep}\ \ [\alpha] = U :\!+\!: F\ (P\ 0) :\times: F\ ([]\ :\!@\!:\ `[P\ 0])\\ \quad \mathit{Pars}\ [\alpha] = `[\alpha]\\ \quad \mathit{from}\ []\ \ \ \ \ \ = L\ U\\ \quad \mathit{from}\ (h : t) = R\ (F\ (P\ h) :\times: F\ (A\ t))\end{array}$$

The *RTree* type of Section 2.2 can also still be encoded. In fact, since we use the type family *ExpandField* to transform fields υ of kind *Field* into $\star$, instead of using the interpretation *InField* υ recursively, we no longer need to use *fmap*; the arguments can be used directly, simplifying the implementation of *from* and *to*:

$$\begin{array}{l}\textbf{instance}\ \mathit{Generic}\ (\mathit{RTree}\ \alpha)\ \textbf{where}\\ \quad \mathit{Rep}\ \ (\mathit{RTree}\ \alpha) = F\ (P\ 0) :\times: F\ ([]\ :\!@\!:\ `[\mathit{RTree}\ :\!@\!:\ `[P\ 0]])\\ \quad \mathit{Pars}\ (\mathit{RTree}\ \alpha) = `[\alpha]\\ \quad \mathit{from}\ (\mathit{RTree}\ x\ xs) = F\ (P\ x) :\times: F\ (A\ xs)\end{array}$$

Having support for multiple parameters, we can now deal with pairs properly, for example. These are simply a product between two fields with a parameter each:

$$\begin{array}{l}\textbf{instance}\ \mathit{Generic}\ (\alpha,\beta)\ \textbf{where}\\ \quad \mathit{Rep}\ \ (\alpha,\beta) = F\ (P\ 0) :\times: F\ (P\ 1)\\ \quad \mathit{Pars}\ (\alpha,\beta) = `[\alpha,\beta]\\ \quad \mathit{from}\ (a,b) = F\ (P\ a) :\times: F\ (P\ b)\end{array}$$

A more complicated example shows how we can mix datatypes with a different number of parameters, and partially instantiated datatypes:

$$\begin{array}{l}\textbf{data}\ D\ \alpha\ \beta\ \gamma = D\ \beta\ [(\alpha,\mathit{Int})]\ (\mathit{RTree}\ [\gamma])\\ \textbf{instance}\ \mathit{Generic}\ (D\ \alpha\ \beta\ \gamma)\ \textbf{where}\\ \quad \mathit{Rep}\ \ (D\ \alpha\ \beta\ \gamma) =\\ \quad\quad F\ (P\ 1) :\times: F\ ([]\ :\!@\!:\ `[(,)\ :\!@\!:\ `[P\ 0, K\ \mathit{Int}]]) :\times: F\ (\mathit{RTree}\ :\!@\!:\ `[[]\ :\!@\!:\ `[P\ 2]])\\ \quad \mathit{Pars}\ (D\ \alpha\ \beta\ \gamma) = `[\alpha,\beta,\gamma]\\ \quad \mathit{from}\ (D\ a\ b\ c) = F\ (P\ a) :\times: F\ (A\ b) :\times: F\ (A\ c)\end{array}$$

Even nested datatypes can be encoded, as our application supports the notion of recursion with parameters instantiated to other applications:

```
data Perfect α = Perfect (Perfect (α,α)) | End α
instance Generic (Perfect α) where
  Rep  (Perfect α) = F (Perfect :@: '[(,) :@: '[P 0,P 0]]) :+: F (P 0)
  Pars (Perfect α) = '[α]
  from (Perfect x) = L (F (A x))
  from (End x)     = R (F (P x))
```

As we have seen, our generalisation of `generic-deriving` supports all the previous datatypes, plus many new ones, involving any number of parameters of kind ⋆.

3.3 Mapping

While designing a new or improved generic programming library, defining the universe and showing example datatype encodings is not enough; it is, in fact, easy to define a simple and encompassing universe that is then found not to be suitable for defining generic functions. As such, we show that our universe allows defining a generalised map function, which maps n different functions over n datatype parameters.

Preliminaries. As the generalised map takes n functions, one per datatype parameter, we need a value-level counterpart to our type-level lists of parameters. We use a strongly typed heterogenous list [4] for this purpose:

```
data HList (ρ :: [⋆]) where
  HNil  ::                    HList '[]
  HCons :: α → HList β → HList (α ': β)
```

We also need a way to pick the n-th element from such a list; we define a *Lookup* type class for this purpose, as the function is defined by induction on the type-level natural numbers. We use a *Proxy* to carry type information at the value-level (the index being looked up):

```
data Proxy (σ :: κ) = Proxy
class Lookup (ρ :: [⋆]) (ν :: Nat) where
  lookup :: Proxy ν → HList ρ → ρ :!: ν
instance Lookup ρ Ze where
  lookup _ (HCons f _) = f
instance (Lookup β ν) ⇒ Lookup (α ': β) (Su ν) where
  lookup _ (HCons _ fs) = lookup (Proxy :: Proxy ν) fs
```

User-Facing Type Class. We are now ready to see the class that generalises *Functor* of Section 2.3. This is a multi-parameter type class, taking a parameter σ for the unsaturated type we are mapping over, and a list of function types τ encoding the types of the functions we will be mapping. As σ will often be ambiguous in the code for the generic definition of map, we provide a version $gmap_P$ with an extra argument that serves to identify the σ. A version without the proxy (*gmap*) is provided with a default for convenient usage:

$$
\begin{array}{l}
\textbf{class}\ \mathit{GMap}\ (\sigma :: \kappa)\ (\tau :: [\star])\ |\ \tau \to \kappa\ \textbf{where} \\
\quad \mathit{gmap} :: \qquad\qquad\qquad \mathit{HList}\ \tau \to \sigma\ {:}\${:}\ \mathit{Doms}\ \tau \to \sigma\ {:}\${:}\ \mathit{Codoms}\ \tau \\
\quad \mathit{gmap} = \mathit{gmap}_P\ (\mathit{Proxy} :: \mathit{Proxy}\ \sigma) \\
\quad \mathit{gmap}_P :: \mathit{Proxy}\ \sigma \to \mathit{HList}\ \tau \to \sigma\ {:}\${:}\ \mathit{Doms}\ \tau \to \sigma\ {:}\${:}\ \mathit{Codoms}\ \tau
\end{array}
$$

Our generalised map, *gmap*, takes two arguments. The first is an *HList* of functions to map. The second is the type σ applied to the domains of the functions we are mapping. Its return type is again σ, but now applied to the codomains of the same functions. For example, for lists, σ is $[\,]$, and τ is $`[\alpha \to \beta]$. In this case, *gmap* gets the expected type $\mathit{HList}\ `[\alpha \to \beta] \to [\alpha] \to [\beta]$. The functional dependency $\tau \to \kappa$ is essential to prevent ambiguity when using *gmap*—and indeed the kind of σ is uniquely determined by the (length of the) list τ. The type functions *Doms* and *Codoms* compute the domains and codomains of the list of functions τ:

$$
\begin{array}{l}
\mathit{Doms}\ (\tau :: [\star]) :: [\star] \\
\mathit{Doms}\ `[\,] \qquad\qquad\quad = `[\,] \\
\mathit{Doms}\ ((\alpha \to \beta)\ `{:}\ \tau) = \alpha\ `{:}\ \mathit{Doms}\ \tau \\
\mathit{Codoms}\ (\tau :: [\star]) :: [\star] \\
\mathit{Codoms}\ `[\,] \qquad\qquad\quad = `[\,] \\
\mathit{Codoms}\ ((\alpha \to \beta)\ `{:}\ \tau) = \beta\ `{:}\ \mathit{Codoms}\ \tau
\end{array}
$$

Mapping on the Generic Representation. We have seen *GMap*, the user-facing type class for the generalised map. Its counterpart for representation types is $GMap_R$, which operates on the interpretation of a representation:

$$
\begin{array}{l}
\textbf{class}\ \mathit{GMap}_R\ (\upsilon :: \mathit{Univ})\ (\tau :: [\star])\ \textbf{where} \\
\quad \mathit{gmap}_R :: \mathit{HList}\ \tau \to \mathit{In}\ \upsilon\ (\mathit{Doms}\ \tau) \to \mathit{In}\ \upsilon\ (\mathit{Codoms}\ \tau)
\end{array}
$$

We now go through the instances of $GMap_R$ for each representation type. There is nothing to map over in units, and sums and products are simply traversed through:

$$
\begin{array}{l}
\textbf{instance}\ \mathit{GMap}_R\ U\ \tau\ \textbf{where} \\
\quad \mathit{gmap}_R\ \_\ U \qquad = U \\
\textbf{instance}\ (\mathit{GMap}_R\ \alpha\ \tau, \mathit{GMap}_R\ \beta\ \tau) \Rightarrow \mathit{GMap}_R\ (\alpha\ {:}{+}{:}\ \beta)\ \tau\ \textbf{where} \\
\quad \mathit{gmap}_R\ \mathit{fs}\ (L\ x) \quad = L\ (\mathit{gmap}_R\ \mathit{fs}\ x) \\
\quad \mathit{gmap}_R\ \mathit{fs}\ (R\ x) \quad = R\ (\mathit{gmap}_R\ \mathit{fs}\ x) \\
\textbf{instance}\ (\mathit{GMap}_R\ \alpha\ \tau, \mathit{GMap}_R\ \beta\ \tau) \Rightarrow \mathit{GMap}_R\ (\alpha\ {:}{\times}{:}\ \beta)\ \tau\ \textbf{where} \\
\quad \mathit{gmap}_R\ \mathit{fs}\ (x\ {:}{\times}{:}\ y) = \mathit{gmap}_R\ \mathit{fs}\ x\ {:}{\times}{:}\ \mathit{gmap}_R\ \mathit{fs}\ y
\end{array}
$$

Fields require more attention, so we define a separate type class $GMap_{RF}$ to handle them:

$$
\begin{array}{l}
\textbf{instance}\ (\mathit{GMap}_{RF}\ \upsilon\ \tau) \Rightarrow \mathit{GMap}_R\ (F\ \upsilon)\ \tau\ \textbf{where} \\
\quad \mathit{gmap}_R\ \mathit{fs}\ (F\ x) = F\ (\mathit{gmap}_{RF}\ \mathit{fs}\ x)
\end{array}
$$

$$\textbf{class}\ GMap_{RF}\ (\upsilon :: Field)\ (\tau :: [\star])\ \textbf{where}$$
$$\quad gmap_{RF} :: HList\ \tau \to InField\ \upsilon\ (Doms\ \tau) \to InField\ \upsilon\ (Codoms\ \tau)$$

Constants, however, just like units, are returned unchanged:

$$\textbf{instance}\ GMap_{RF}\ (K\ \alpha)\ \tau\ \textbf{where}$$
$$\quad gmap_{RF}\ \_\ (K\ x) = K\ x$$

For a parameter $P\ \nu$, we need to lookup the right function to map over. We again use a separate type class, $GMap_{RP}$, and we traverse the input list of functions until we reach the ν-th function. We thus require the list of functions τ to have its elements in the same order as the datatype parameters:

$$\textbf{instance}\ (GMap_{RP}\ \nu\ \tau) \Rightarrow GMap_{RF}\ (P\ \nu)\ \tau\ \textbf{where}$$
$$\quad gmap_{RF}\ fs\ (P\ x) = P\ (gmap_{RP}\ (Proxy :: Proxy\ \nu)\ fs\ x)$$

$$\textbf{class}\ GMap_{RP}\ (\nu :: Nat)\ (\tau :: [\star])\ \textbf{where}$$
$$\quad gmap_{RP} :: Proxy\ \nu \to HList\ \tau \to (Doms\ \tau)\ :!:\ \nu \to (Codoms\ \tau)\ :!:\ \nu$$
$$\textbf{instance}\ GMap_{RP}\ Ze\ ((\alpha \to \beta)\ `\!:\ \tau)\ \textbf{where}$$
$$\quad gmap_{RP}\ \_\ (HCons\ f\ \_)\ x = f\ x$$
$$\textbf{instance}\ (GMap_{RP}\ \nu\ \tau) \Rightarrow GMap_{RP}\ (Su\ \nu)\ ((\alpha \to \beta)\ `\!:\ \tau)\ \textbf{where}$$
$$\quad gmap_{RP}\ \_\ (HCons\ \_fs)\ p = gmap_{RP}\ (Proxy :: Proxy\ \nu)\ fs\ p$$

Handling Application. The only representation type we still have to deal with is (:@:). This is also the most challenging case. As a running example, consider the second field of the D datatype of Section 3.2. D has three parameters, α, β, and γ, and the second field of its only constructor has type $[(\alpha, Int)]$, represented as $[]$:@: `[(,) :@: `[$P\ 0, K\ Int$]]. In this situation, we intend to transform $[(\alpha, Int)]$ into $[(\alpha', Int)]$, having available a function of type $\alpha \to \alpha'$. We do this by requiring the availability of *gmap* for this particular list type; that is, we require an instance $GMap\ []\ `[(\alpha, Int) \to (\alpha', Int)]$. Having such an instance, we can simply *gmap* over the argument. However, the functions we map need to be adapted to this new argument. That is the task of *AdaptFs*, which we explain below.

A type function *MakeFs* computes the types of the functions to be mapped inside the applied type. For example, $MakeFs$ `[(,) :@: `[$P\ 0, K\ Int$]] `$[\alpha \to \alpha', \beta \to \beta', \gamma \to \gamma']$ is `$[(\alpha, Int) \to (\alpha', Int)]$. We use proxies to fix otherwise ambiguous types when invoking $gmap_P$ and *adaptFs*:

$$MakeFs\ (\rho :: [Field])\ (\tau :: [\star]) :: [\star]$$
$$MakeFs\ `[]\qquad \tau = `[]$$
$$MakeFs\ ((K\ \alpha)\ `\!:\ \rho)\qquad \tau = (\alpha \to \alpha)\ `\!:\ MakeFs\ \rho\ \tau$$
$$MakeFs\ ((P\ \nu)\ `\!:\ \rho)\qquad \tau = (\tau\ :!:\ \nu)\ `\!:\ MakeFs\ \rho\ \tau$$
$$MakeFs\ ((\sigma :@: \omega)\ `\!:\ \rho)\ \tau =$$
$$\quad (AppFields\ \sigma\ \omega\ (Doms\ \tau) \to AppFields\ \sigma\ \omega\ (Codoms\ \tau))\ `\!:\ MakeFs\ \rho\ \tau$$
$$\textbf{instance}\ (GMap\ \sigma\ (MakeFs\ \rho\ \tau)$$
$$\qquad ,AdaptFs\ \rho\ \tau$$
$$\qquad ,ExpandField\ \rho\ (Doms\quad \tau) \sim Doms\quad (MakeFs\ \rho\ \tau)$$

```
        ,ExpandField ρ (Codoms τ) ~ Codoms (MakeFs ρ τ)
        ) ⇒ GMap_RF (σ :@: ρ) τ where
  gmap_RF fs (A x) = A (gmap_P p1 (adaptFs p2 fs) x)
    where p1 = Proxy :: Proxy σ
          p2 = Proxy :: Proxy ρ
```

This instance has four constraints, two of them being equality constraints, introduced by the $\sim$ operator: a constraint of the form $\alpha \sim \beta$ indicates that the type α must be equal to the type β. The four constraints of this instance are: the ability to map over the argument type, the requirement to rearrange the functions we map over, and two coherence conditions on the behaviour of *ExpandField* and *MakeFs* over the list of functions. The latter are always true for valid ρ and τ.

We are left with the task of adapting the functions to be mapped over. In our running example, we have an *HList* '$[\alpha \to \alpha', \beta \to \beta', \gamma \to \gamma']$, and we have to produce an *HList* '$[(\alpha, Int) \to (\alpha', Int)]$. This is done by *adaptFs*, a method of the type class *AdaptFs* which is implemented by induction on the list of fields to be mapped over:

```
class AdaptFs (ρ :: [Field]) (τ :: [⋆]) where
  adaptFs :: Proxy ρ → HList τ → HList (MakeFs ρ τ)
```

For an empty list of an arguments, we return an empty list of functions. If the argument is a constant, we ignore it and proceed to the next argument. For a parameter $P\ \nu$, we use the ν-th function of the original list of functions, and proceed to the next argument:

```
instance AdaptFs '[] τ where
  adaptFs _ _ = HNil
instance (AdaptFs ρ τ) ⇒ AdaptFs ((K α) ': ρ) τ where
  adaptFs _ fs = HCons id (adaptFs (Proxy :: Proxy ρ) fs)
instance (AdaptFs ρ τ, Lookup τ ν) ⇒ AdaptFs ((P ν) ': ρ) τ where
  adaptFs _ fs = HCons (lookup p1 fs) (adaptFs p2 fs)
    where p1 = Proxy :: Proxy ν
          p2 = Proxy :: Proxy ρ
```

The most delicate case is, again, application. Back to our running example, this is where we have to produce a function of type $(\alpha, Int) \to (\alpha', Int)$. We do so by requiring an instance *GMap* (,) '$[\alpha \to \alpha', Int \to Int]$, reusing *MakeFs* and *AdaptFs* in the process. We also need to proceed recursively for the rest of the arguments. Again, we have the same two coherence conditions on the behaviour of *ExpandField* and *MakeFs* over the list of functions, and use proxies to fix ambiguous types:

```
instance (GMap σ (MakeFs ω τ)
        ,AdaptFs ω τ
        ,AdaptFs ρ τ
        ,ExpandField ω (Doms   τ) ~ Doms   (MakeFs ω τ)
        ,ExpandField ω (Codoms τ) ~ Codoms (MakeFs ω τ)
        ) ⇒ AdaptFs ((σ :@: ω) ': ρ) τ where
  adaptFs _ fs = HCons (gmap_P p1 (adaptFs p2 fs)) (adaptFs p3 fs)
    where p1 = Proxy :: Proxy σ
```

$$p_2 = Proxy :: Proxy\ \omega$$
$$p_3 = Proxy :: Proxy\ \rho$$

The generic definition of the generalised map is thus complete, and ready to be used.

3.4 Example Usage

Before we instantiate map to our example datatypes of Section 3.2, we first provide a generic default [11] to make instantiation simpler. This default, for the *GMap* class, will allow us to then give empty instances of the class, which will automatically use the generic definition for the generalised map. The default version of $gmap_P$ converts a value into its generic representation, applies $gmap_R$, and then converts back to a user datatype. This requires several constraints (which would all be inferred if the function was defined at the top level). First, we introduce α and β as synonyms for the input and output type, respectively, for mere convenience. In the case of the $GMap\ []\ `[\gamma \to \gamma']$ instance, for example, α is $[\gamma]$, and β is $[\gamma']$. We also require a $Generic\ [\gamma]$ instance (for *from*), and a $Generic\ [\gamma']$ instance (for *to*); these instances will coincide, and indeed we also require that the representation $Rep\ [\gamma]$ be the same as $Rep\ [\gamma']$ (which is the case). Furthermore, the parameters of $[\gamma]$ have to coincide with the domains of $`[\gamma \to \gamma']$, and the parameters of $[\gamma']$ have to coincide with the codomains of the same list. Finally, we require the ability to map generically over the representation of the input list:

$$
\begin{aligned}
&\textbf{default}\ gmap_P :: (\alpha \sim (\sigma :\$: Doms\ \tau)\\
&\qquad ,\beta \sim (\sigma :\$: Codoms\ \tau)\\
&\qquad ,Generic\ \alpha, Generic\ \beta\\
&\qquad ,Rep\ \alpha \sim Rep\ \beta\\
&\qquad ,Pars\ \alpha \sim Doms\ \tau\\
&\qquad ,Pars\ \beta \sim Codoms\ \tau\\
&\qquad ,GMap_R\ (Rep\ \alpha)\ \tau\\
&\qquad) \Rightarrow Proxy\ \sigma \to HList\ \tau \to \alpha \to \beta\\
&gmap_P\ \_fs = to \circ gmap_R\ fs \circ from
\end{aligned}
$$

With this default in place, we are ready to instantiate our example datatypes:

$$
\begin{aligned}
&\textbf{instance}\ GMap\ []\quad `[\alpha \to \alpha']\\
&\textbf{instance}\ GMap\ RTree\ `[\alpha \to \alpha']\\
&\textbf{instance}\ GMap\ (,)\quad `[\alpha \to \alpha', \beta \to \beta']\\
&\textbf{instance}\ GMap\ D\quad `[\alpha \to \alpha', \beta \to \beta', \gamma \to \gamma']\\
&\textbf{instance}\ GMap\ Perfect\ `[\alpha \to \alpha']
\end{aligned}
$$

Using the generic default, instantiation is kept simple and concise. We can verify that our map works as expected in an example that should cover all the representation types:

$$
\begin{aligned}
&x :: D\ Int\ Float\ Char\\
&x = D\ 0.2\ [(0,0),(1,1)]\ (RTree\ \texttt{"p"}\ [])\\
&y :: D\ Int\ String\ Char\\
&y = gmap\ (HCons\ (+1)\ (HCons\ show\ (HCons\ (const\ \texttt{'q'})\ HNil)))\ x
\end{aligned}
$$

Indeed, y evaluates to $D\ \texttt{"0.2"}\ [(1,0),(2,1)]\ (RTree\ \texttt{"q"}\ [])$ as expected.

4 Limitations and Future Work

In this section we discuss the limitations of our new `generic-deriving`, and propose future research directions.

4.1 Parameters of Higher Kinds

While our generalisation supports any number of parameters of kind $\star$, it is unable to deal with parameters of higher kinds. Consider the following two datatypes representing generalised trees:

$$\textbf{data}\ \mathit{GTree}_1\ \phi\ \alpha = \mathit{GTree}_1\ \alpha\ (\phi\ (\mathit{GTree}_1\ \phi\ \alpha))$$
$$\textbf{data}\ \mathit{GTree}_2\ \alpha\ \phi = \mathit{GTree}_2\ \alpha\ (\phi\ (\mathit{GTree}_2\ \alpha\ \phi))$$

The most general mapping function for GTree_1 has the following type:

$$(\alpha \to \beta) \to (\forall \alpha\ \beta.(\alpha \to \beta) \to \phi\ \alpha \to \psi\ \beta) \to \mathit{GTree}_1\ \phi\ \alpha \to \mathit{GTree}_1\ \psi\ \beta$$

The generalisation of this paper provides a map of type $(\alpha \to \beta) \to \mathit{GTree}_1\ \phi\ \alpha \to \mathit{GTree}_1\ \phi\ \beta$, therefore ignoring the ϕ parameter of kind $\star \to \star$. For GTree_2, however, our approach cannot even provide that simple map; we cannot give the *GMap* instance, since the parameters of kind $\star$ of interest come before a parameter of kind $\star \to \star$, and the second parameter of *GMap* is a list of kind $[\star]$ (so all arguments must have kind $\star$).

As such, we support generic abstraction only over the parameters of kind $\star$ which come after any parameters of other kinds. Lifting this restriction is not trivial. Recall that the *Pars* type family has return kind $[\star]$. To generalise to multiple parameters, we should make this return kind be a (promoted) heterogeneous list. This is currently not possible, as heterogeneous lists are implemented as GADTs, which cannot be promoted. Foregoing giving *Pars* the correct kind and working with nested tuples instead gives rise to many kind ambiguities, which are cumbersome to solve. As such, we hope that the promotion mechanism is extended to allow promotion of GADTs soon [15], and defer generalising our approach to parameters of arbitrary kinds until then.

4.2 Integration with Existing Generic Programming Libraries

The introduction of our new `generic-deriving` raises the question of how to upgrade from the old version. Our changes are not backwards compatible, but since the new version encodes strictly more information than the previous one, we can provide a conversion that automatically transforms the new representation into the old one, therefore remaining compatible with old code [10]. The core of this conversion is a type-level function $D_{n \to} D$ that converts the new representation into the old one. We show a prototype implementation here, subscripting the new `generic-deriving` codes with an n to distinguish them from the old ones. Units, sums, and products are converted trivially. Fields are handled by a separate function $D_{n \to} D_F$. Constants are converted trivially. For a parameter, we return P if it is the last parameter of the datatype (the only one supported by the old version of `generic-deriving`), or a constant otherwise. We make use of type-level if-then-else, equality on *Nat*, and length. Applications of types of kind

$\star \to \star$ are converted into compositions. For applications of types of higher arity, we first apply the type to all its arguments but the last:

$$
\begin{array}{l}
\mathit{IfThenElse}\ (\alpha :: \mathit{Bool})\ (\beta :: \kappa)\ (\gamma :: \kappa) :: \kappa \\
\mathit{IfThenElse}\ \text{`}\mathit{True}\ \ \beta\ \gamma = \beta \\
\mathit{IfThenElse}\ \text{`}\mathit{False}\ \beta\ \gamma = \gamma \\
(\alpha :: \mathit{Nat}) \equiv_{\mathit{Nat}} (\beta :: \mathit{Nat}) :: \mathit{Bool} \\
\mathit{Ze} \equiv_{\mathit{Nat}} \quad \mathit{Ze} \quad = \text{`}\mathit{True} \\
\mathit{Su}\ \upsilon \equiv_{\mathit{Nat}} \mathit{Ze} \quad = \text{`}\mathit{False} \\
\mathit{Ze} \equiv_{\mathit{Nat}} \quad \mathit{Su}\ \nu = \text{`}\mathit{False} \\
\mathit{Su}\ \upsilon \equiv_{\mathit{Nat}} \mathit{Su}\ \nu = \upsilon \equiv_{\mathit{Nat}} \nu \\
\mathit{Length}\ (\rho :: [\kappa]) :: \mathit{Nat} \\
\mathit{Length}\ \text{`}[] \qquad = \mathit{Ze} \\
\mathit{Length}\ (\alpha\ \text{`}\!:\ \rho) = \mathit{Su}\ (\mathit{Length}\ \rho) \\
D_{n \to} D\ (\upsilon :: \mathit{Univ}_n)\ (\rho :: [\star]) :: \mathit{Univ} \\
D_{n \to} D\ U_n \qquad\quad \rho = U \\
D_{n \to} D\ (\alpha :\!+_n\!: \beta)\ \rho = D_{n \to} D\ \alpha\ \rho :\!+\!: D_{n \to} D\ \beta\ \rho \\
D_{n \to} D\ (\alpha :\!\times_n\!: \beta)\ \rho = D_{n \to} D\ \alpha\ \rho :\!\times\!: D_{n \to} D\ \beta\ \rho \\
D_{n \to} D\ (F_n\ \alpha) \qquad \rho = D_{n \to} D_F\ \alpha\ \rho \\
D_{n \to} D_F\ (\upsilon :: \mathit{Field}_n)\ (\rho :: [\star]) :: \mathit{Univ} \\
D_{n \to} D_F\ (K_n\ \alpha) \qquad\qquad\qquad \rho = K\ \alpha \\
D_{n \to} D_F\ (P_n\ \nu) \qquad\qquad\qquad \rho = \mathit{IfThenElse}\ (\nu \equiv_{\mathit{Nat}} \mathit{Length}\ \rho)\ P\ (K\ (\rho :!: \nu)) \\
D_{n \to} D_F\ (\phi :\!@_n\!: \text{`}[\alpha]) \qquad\qquad \rho = \phi :\!@\!: D_{n \to} D_F\ \alpha\ \rho \\
D_{n \to} D_F\ (\phi :\!@_n\!: (\alpha\ \text{`}\!:\ \beta\ \text{`}\!:\ \gamma))\ \rho = D_{n \to} D_F\ ((\mathit{AppFields}\ \phi\ \text{`}[\alpha]\ \rho) :\!@_n\!: (\beta\ \text{`}\!:\ \gamma))\ \rho
\end{array}
$$

The introduction of yet another generic programming library underscores the need for a single mechanism for type reflection baked into the compiler, from which other mechanisms, such as our new `generic-deriving`, or *Data* and *Typeable* [5], could then be derived.

4.3 Parameter Genericity vs. Arity Genericity

The approach described in this paper allows us to define generic functions that operate over multiple datatype parameters. This is not the same as generic functions that operate at diverse arities [14]. Consider the following generic functions:

$$
\begin{array}{l}
\mathit{map}^1_n :: \mathit{HList}\ \text{`}[\alpha^1_1, \ldots, \alpha^1_n] \to \phi\ (\alpha^1_1 \ldots \alpha^1_n) \\
\mathit{map}^2_n :: \mathit{HList}\ \text{`}[\alpha^1_1 \to \alpha^2_1, \ldots, \alpha^1_n \to \alpha^2_n] \to \phi\ (\alpha^1_1 \ldots \alpha^1_n) \to \phi\ (\alpha^2_1 \ldots \alpha^2_n) \\
\mathit{map}^3_n :: \mathit{HList}\ \text{`}[\alpha^1_1 \to \alpha^2_1 \to \alpha^3_1, \ldots, \alpha^1_n \to \alpha^2_n \to \alpha^3_n] \\
\qquad \to \phi\ (\alpha^1_1 \ldots \alpha^1_n) \to \phi\ (\alpha^2_1 \ldots \alpha^2_n) \to \phi\ (\alpha^3_1 \ldots \alpha^3_n) \\
\mathit{map}^m_n :: \mathit{HList}\ \text{`}[\alpha^1_1 \to \ldots \to \alpha^m_1, \ldots, \alpha^1_n \to \ldots \to \alpha^m_n] \\
\qquad \to \phi\ (\alpha^1_1 \ldots \alpha^1_n) \to \ldots \to \phi\ (\alpha^m_1 \ldots \alpha^m_n)
\end{array}
$$

The function map^1_n, or *repeat*, creates a ϕ-structure given elements for the parameter positions. The function map^2_n, equivalent to the generic *gmap* of Section 3.3, is the function that maps over a ϕ-structure, taking one function per parameter. The function map^3_n, or *zipWith*, is the function that takes two ϕ-structures and zips them when their shapes are compatible, using the provided functions to zip the parameters. The function map_n^m is the generalisation of the previous three, in the arity-generic sense. Our approach allows defining each of map_n^1, map_n^2, map_n^3, etc., individually, as separate generic functions. It does not allow defining map_n^m; that generalisation is described by Weirich and Casinghino [14], in the dependently-typed programming language Agda. It remains to see how to transfer the concept of arity-genericity to Haskell.

5 Conclusion

In this paper we have seen how we can use the promotion mechanism together with kind polymorphism to encode a generic representation of datatypes that supports abstraction over multiple parameters (of kind $\star$). This enables a whole new class of generic functionality: we have shown a generalised map, but also folding, traversing, and zipping, for example, are now possible. We plan to implement support for the new `generic-deriving` in GHC soon, so that users can take advantage of the new functionality without needing to write their own *Generic* instances.

Acknowledgements. This work was supported by the EP/J010995/1 EPSRC grant. Jeremy Gibbons and anonymous referees provided valuable feedback on an early draft of this paper.

References

[1] Alimarine, A., Plasmeijer, R.: A generic programming extension for Clean. In: Arts, T., Mohnen, M. (eds.) IFL 2002. LNCS, vol. 2312, pp. 168–185. Springer, Heidelberg (2002)
[2] Backhouse, R., Jansson, P., Jeuring, J., Meertens, L.: Generic programming: An introduction. In: Swierstra, S.D., Oliveira, J.N. (eds.) AFP 1998. LNCS, vol. 1608, pp. 28–115. Springer, Heidelberg (1999)
[3] Hinze, R., Jeuring, J., Löh, A.: Comparing approaches to generic programming in Haskell. In: Backhouse, R., Gibbons, J., Hinze, R., Jeuring, J. (eds.) SSDGP 2006. LNCS, vol. 4719, pp. 72–149. Springer, Heidelberg (2007)
[4] Kiselyov, O., Lämmel, R., Schupke, K.: Strongly typed heterogeneous collections. In: Proceedings of the 2004 ACM SIGPLAN Workshop on Haskell, Haskell 2004, pp. 96–107. ACM (2004), doi:10.1145/1017472.1017488
[5] Lämmel, R., Peyton Jones, S.: Scrap your boilerplate: a practical design pattern for generic programming. In: Proceedings of the 2003 ACM SIGPLAN International Workshop on Types in Languages Design and Implementation, pp. 26–37. ACM (2003), doi:10.1145/604174.604179
[6] Löh, A.: Exploring Generic Haskell. PhD thesis, Universiteit Utrecht (2004), `http://igitur-archive.library.uu.nl/dissertations/2004-1130-111344`
[7] Löh, A., Magalhães, J.P.: Generic programming with indexed functors. In: Proceedings of the 7th ACM SIGPLAN Workshop on Generic Programming, pp. 1–12. ACM (2011), doi:10.1145/2036918.2036920
[8] Magalhães, J.P.: Less Is More: Generic Programming Theory and Practice. PhD thesis, Universiteit Utrecht (2012)

[9] Magalhães, J.P.: The right kind of generic programming. In: Proceedings of the 8th ACM SIGPLAN Workshop on Generic Programming, WGP 2012, pp. 13–24. ACM, New York (2012) ISBN 978-1-4503-1576-0, doi:10.1145/2364394.2364397

[10] Magalhães, J.P., Löh, A.: Generic generic programming (2014), `http://dreixel.net/research/pdf/ggp.pdf`, Accepted for publication at Practical Aspects of Declarative Languages (PADL 2014)

[11] Magalhães, J.P., Dijkstra, A., Jeuring, J., Löh, A.: A generic deriving mechanism for Haskell. In: Proceedings of the 3rd ACM Haskell Symposium on Haskell, pp. 37–48. ACM (2010), doi:10.1145/1863523.1863529

[12] Peyton Jones, S. (ed.): Haskell 98, Language and Libraries. The Revised Report. Cambridge University Press (2003), doi:10.1017/S0956796803000315, Journal of Functional Programming Special Issue 13(1)

[13] Rodriguez Yakushev, A., Jeuring, J., Jansson, P., Gerdes, A., Kiselyov, O., Oliveira, B.C.D.S.: Comparing libraries for generic programming in Haskell. In: Proceedings of the 1st ACM SIGPLAN Symposium on Haskell, pp. 111–122. ACM (2008), doi:10.1145/1411286.1411301

[14] Weirich, S., Casinghino, C.: Arity-generic datatype-generic programming. In: Proceedings of the 4th ACM SIGPLAN Workshop on Programming Languages meets Program Verification, pp. 15–26. ACM (2010), doi:10.1145/1707790.1707799

[15] Weirich, S., Hsu, J., Eisenberg, R.A.: System FC with explicit kind equality. In: Proceedings of the 18th ACM SIGPLAN International Conference on Functional Programming, ICFP 2013, pp. 275–286. ACM (2013), doi:10.1145/2500365.2500599

[16] Yorgey, B.A., Weirich, S., Cretin, J., Peyton Jones, S., Vytiniotis, D., Magalhães, J.P.: Giving Haskell a promotion. In: Proceedings of the 8th ACM SIGPLAN Workshop on Types in Language Design and Implementation, pp. 53–66. ACM (2012), doi:10.1145/2103786.2103795

Type-Based Amortized Resource Analysis with Integers and Arrays

Jan Hoffmann and Zhong Shao

Yale University

Abstract. Proving bounds on the resource consumption of a program by statically analyzing its source code is an important and well-studied problem. Automatic approaches for numeric programs with side effects usually apply abstract interpretation–based invariant generation to derive bounds on loops and recursion depths of function calls.

This paper presents an alternative approach to resource-bound analysis for numeric, heap-manipulating programs that uses type-based amortized resource analysis. As a first step towards the analysis of imperative code, the technique is developed for a first-order ML-like language with unsigned integers and arrays. The analysis automatically derives bounds that are multivariate polynomials in the numbers and the lengths of the arrays in the input. Experiments with example programs demonstrate two main advantages of amortized analysis over current abstract interpretation–based techniques. For one thing, amortized analysis can handle programs with non-linear intermediate values like $f((n+m)^2)$. For another thing, amortized analysis is compositional and works naturally for compound programs like $f(g(x))$.

Keywords: Quantitative Analysis, Resource Consumption, Amortized Analysis, Functional Programming, Static Analysis.

1 Introduction

The quantitative performance characteristics of a program are among the most important aspects that determine whether the program is useful in practice. Manually proving concrete (non-asymptotic) resource bounds with respect to a formal machine model is tedious and error-prone. This is especially true if programs evolve over time when bugs are fixed or new features are added. As a result, automatic methods for inferring resource bounds are extensively studied. The most advanced techniques for imperative programs with integers and arrays apply abstract interpretation to generate numerical invariants [1, 2, 3, 4], that is, bounds on the values of variables. These invariants form the basis of the computation of actual bounds on loop iterations and recursion depths.

For reasons of efficiency, many abstract interpretation–based resource-analysis systems rely on abstract domains such as polyhedra [5] which enable the inference of invariants through linear constraint solving. The downside of this approach is that the resulting tools only work effectively for programs in which all relevant variables are bounded by *linear invariants*. This is, for example, not the case

M. Codish and E. Sumii (Eds.): FLOPS 2014, LNCS 8475, pp. 152–168, 2014.

if programs perform non-linear arithmetic operations such as multiplication or division. A linear abstract domain can be used to derive non-linear invariants using domain lifting operations [6]. Another possibility is to use disjunctive abstract domains to generate non-linear invariants [7]. This technique has been experimentally implemented in the COSTA analysis system [8]. However, it is less mature than polyhedra-based invariant generation and it is unclear how it scales to larger examples.

In this paper, we study an alternative approach to infer resource bounds for numeric programs with side effects. Instead of abstract interpretation, it is based on type-based amortized resource analysis [9, 10]. It has been shown that this analysis technique can infer tight polynomial bounds for functional programs with nested data structures while relying on linear constraint solving only [11, 10]. A main innovation in this *polynomial amortized analysis* is the use of *multivariate resource polynomials* that have good closure properties and behave well under common size-change operations. Advantages of amortized resource analysis include precision, efficiency, and compositionality.

Our ultimate goal is to transfer the advantages of amortized resource analysis to imperative (C-like) programs. As a first important step, we develop a multivariate amortized resource analysis for numeric ML-like programs with mutable arrays in this work. We present the new technique for a simple language with unsigned integers, arrays, and pairs as the only data types in this paper. However, we implemented the analysis in Resource Aware ML (RAML) [12] which features more data types such as lists and binary trees. Our experiments (see Section 6) show that our implementation can automatically and efficiently infer complex polynomial bounds for programs that contain non-linear size changes like $f(8128 * x * x)$ and composed functions like $f(g(x))$ where the result of the function $g(x)$ is non-linear. RAML is publicly available and all of our examples as well as user-defined code can be tested in an easy-to-use online interface [12].

Technically, we treat unsigned integers like unary lists in multivariate amortized analysis [10]. However, we do not just instantiate the previous framework by providing a pattern matching for unsigned integers and implementing recursive functions. In fact, this approach would be possible but it has several shortcomings (see Section 2) that make it unsuitable in practice. The key for making amortized resource analysis work for numeric code is to give direct typing rules for the arithmetic operations *addition, subtraction, multiplication, division, and modulo.* The most interesting aspect of the rules we developed is that they can be readily represented with very succinct linear constraint systems. Moreover, the rules precisely capture the size changes in the corresponding operations in the sense that no precision (or potential) is lost in the analysis.

To deal with mutable data, the analysis ensures that the resource consumption does not depend on the size of data that has been stored in a mutable heap cell. While it would be possible to give more involved rules for array operations, all examples we considered could be analyzed with our technique. Hence we found that the additional complexity of more precise rules was not justified by the gain of expressivity in practice.

To prove the soundness of the analysis, we model the resource consumption of programs with a big-step operational semantics for terminating and non-terminating programs. This enables us to show that bounds derived within the type system hold for terminating and non-terminating programs. Refer to the literature for more detailed explanations of type-based amortized resource analysis [9, 11, 10], the soundness proof [13], and Resource Aware ML [12, 14].

The full version of this article is available online [15] and includes all technical details and additional explanations.

2 Informal Account

In this section we briefly introduce type-based amortized resource analysis. We then motivate and describe the novel developments for programs with integers and arrays.

Amortized Resource Analysis. The idea of type-based amortized resource analysis [9, 10] is to annotate each program point with a *potential function* which maps sizes of reachable data structures to non-negative numbers. The potential functions have to ensure that, for every input and every possible evaluation, the potential at a program point is sufficient to pay for the resource cost of the following transition and the potential at the next point. It then follows that the initial potential function describes an upper bound on the resource consumption of the program.

It is natural to build a practical amortized resource analysis on top of a type system because types are compositional and provide useful information about the structure of the data. In a series of papers [11, 10, 13, 14], it has been shown that *multivariate resource polynomials* are a good choice for the set of possible potential functions. Multivariate resource polynomials are a generalization of non-negative linear combinations of binomial coefficients that includes tight bounds for many typical programs [13]. At the same time, multivariate resource polynomials can be incorporated into type systems so that type inference can be efficiently reduced to LP solving [13].

The basic idea of amortized resource analysis is best explained by example. Assume we represent natural numbers as unary lists and implement addition and multiplication as follows.

```
add (n,m) = match n with | nil → m
    | _::xs → () :: (add (xs,m));

mult (n,m) = match n with | nil → nil
    | _::xs → add(m,mult(xs,m));
```

Assume furthermore that we are interested in the number of pattern matches that are performed by these functions. The evaluation of the expression $\mathsf{add}(\mathsf{n},\mathsf{m})$ performs $|n|+1$ pattern matches and evaluating $\mathsf{mult}(\mathsf{n},\mathsf{m})$ needs $|n||m|+2|n|+1$ pattern matches. To represent these bounds in an amortized resource analysis, we annotate the argument and result types of the functions with indexed families of non-negative rational coefficients of our resource polynomials. The index set depends on the type and on the maximal degree of the bounds, which has to be fixed to make the analysis feasible. For our example mult we need degree 2. The index set for the argument type $A = L(\text{unit}) * L(\text{unit})$ is then $\mathcal{I}(A) = \{(0,0),(1,0),(2,0),(1,1),(0,1),(0,2)\}$. A family $Q = (q_i)_{i\in\mathcal{I}(A)}$ denotes the resource polynomial that maps two lists n and m to the number $\sum_{(i,j)\in\mathcal{I}(A)} q_{(i,j)} \binom{|n|}{i}\binom{|m|}{j}$. Similarly, an indexed family $P = (p_i)_{i\in\{0,1,2\}}$ describes the resource polynomial $\ell \mapsto p_0 + p_1|\ell| + p_2\binom{|\ell|}{2}$ for a list $\ell : L(\text{unit})$.

A valid typing for the multiplication would be for instance mult : $(L(\text{unit}) * L(\text{unit}), Q) \to (L(\text{unit}), P)$, where $q_{(0,0)} = 1, q_{(1,0)} = 2, q_{(1,1)} = 1$, and $q_i = p_j = 0$ for all other i and all j. Another valid instantiation of P and Q, which would be needed in a larger program such as add(mult(n, m), k), is $q_{(0,0)} = q_{(1,0)} = q_{(1,1)} = 2$, $p_0 = p_1 = 1$ and $q_i = p_j = 0$ for all other i and all j.

The challenge in designing an amortized resource analysis is to develop a type rule for each syntactic construct of a program that describes how the potential before the evaluation relates to the potential after the evaluation. It has been shown [11, 13] that the structure of multivariate resource polynomials facilitates the development of relatively simple type rules. These rules enable the generation of linear constraint systems such that a solution of a constraint system corresponds to a valid instantiation of the rational coefficients q_i and p_j.

Numerical Programs and Side Effects. Previous work on polynomial amortized analysis [11, 13] (that is implemented in RAML) focused on inductive data structures such as trees and lists. In this paper, we are extending the technique to programs with unsigned integers, arrays, and the usual atomic operations such as $*$, $+$, $-$, mod, div, set, and get. Of course, it would be possible to use existing techniques and a *code transformation* that converts a program with these operations into one that uses recursive implementations such as the previously defined functions add and mult. However, this approach has multiple shortcomings.

Efficiency. In programs with many arithmetic operations, the use of recursive implementations causes the analysis to generate large constraint systems that are challenging to solve. Figure 1 shows the number of constraints that are generated by the analysis for a program with a single multiplication $a * b$ as a function of the maximal degree of the bounds. With our novel handcrafted rule for multiplication the analysis creates for example 82 constraints when searching for bounds of maximal degree 10. With the recursive implementation, 408653 constraints are generated. IBM's Cplex can still solve this constraint system in a few seconds but a precise analysis of a larger RAML program currently requires to copy the 408653 constraints for every multiplication in the program. This makes the analysis infeasible.

Effectivity. A straightforward recursive implementation of the arithmetic operations on unary lists in RAML would not allow us to analyze the same range of functions we can analyze with handcrafted typing rules for the operations. For example, the fast Euclidean algorithm cannot be analyzed with the usual, recursive definition of mod but can be analyzed with our

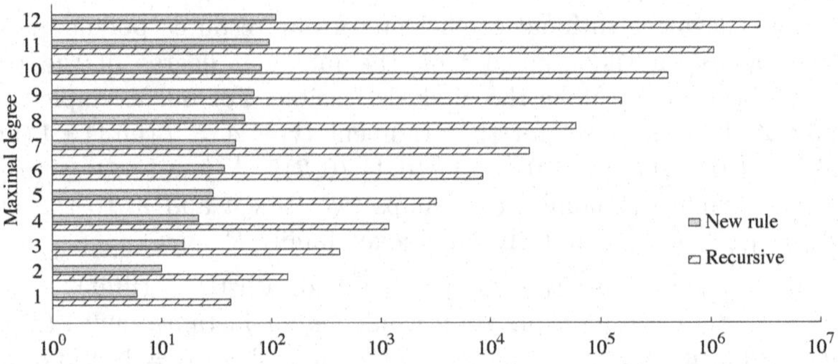

Fig. 1. Number of constraint generated by RAML for the program a ∗ b as a function of the maximal degree. The solid bars show the number of constraints generated using the novel type rule for multiplication. The striped bars show the number of constrained generated using an recursive implementation. The scale on the x-axis is logarithmic.

new rule. Similarly, we cannot define a recursive function so that the analysis is as effective as with our novel rule for minus. For example, the pattern if n > C then ... recCall(n − C) else ... for a constant $C > 0$ can be analyzed with our new rule but not with a recursive definition for minus.

Conception. A code transformation prior to the analysis complicates the soundness proof since we would have to show that the resource usage of the modified code is equivalent to the resource usage of the original code. More importantly, handling new language features merely by code transformations into well-understood constructs is conceptually less attractive since it often does not advance our understanding of the new features.

To derive a typing rule for an arithmetic operation in amortized resource analysis, we have to describe how the potential of the arguments of the operation relates to the potential of the result. For $x, y \in \mathbb{N}$ and a multiplication $x * y$ we start with a potential of the form $\sum_{(i,j)\in I} q_{(i,j)} \binom{x}{i}\binom{y}{j}$ (where $I = \{(0,0),(1,0),(2,0),(1,1),(0,1),(0,2)\}$ in the case of degree 2). We then have to ensure that this potential is always equal to the constant resource consumption M^{mult} of the multiplication and the potential $\sum_{i\in\{0,1,2\}} p_i \binom{x\cdot y}{i}$ of the result $x{\cdot}y$. This is the case if $q_{(0,0)} = M^{\mathsf{mult}} + p_0$, $q_{(1,1)} = p_1$, $q_{(1,2)} = q_{(2,1)} = p_2$, $q_{(2,2)} = 2p_2$, and $q_{(i,j)} = 0$ otherwise. We will show that such relations can be expressed for resource polynomials of arbitrary degree in a type rule for amortized resource analysis that corresponds to a succinct linear constraint system.

The challenge with arrays is to account for side effects of computations that influence the resource consumption of later computations in the presence of aliasing. We can analyze such programs but ensure that the potential of data that is stored in arrays is always 0. In this way, we prove that the influence of aliasing on the resource usage is accounted for without using the size of mutable data. As for all language features, we could achieve the same with some abstraction of the program that does not use arrays. However, this is not necessarily a simpler approach.

3 A Simple Language with Side Effects

We present our analysis for a minimal first-order functional language that only contains the features we are interested in, namely operations for integers and arrays. However, we implemented the analysis in Resource Aware ML (RAML) [14, 12] which also includes (signed) integers, lists, binary trees, Booleans, conditionals and pattern matching on lists and trees.

Syntax. The subset of RAML we use in this article includes variables x, unsigned integers n, function calls, pairs, pattern matching for unsigned integers and pairs, let bindings, an undefined expression, a sharing expression, and the built in operations for arrays and unsigned integers.

$$\begin{aligned} e ::= {} & x \mid f(x) \mid (x_1, x_2) \mid \mathsf{match}\, x\, \mathsf{with}\, (x_1, x_2) \Rightarrow e \mid \mathsf{undefined} \mid \mathsf{let}\, x = e_1\, \mathsf{in}\, e_2 \\ & \mid \mathsf{share}\, x\, \mathsf{as}\, (x_1, x_2)\, \mathsf{in}\, e \mid \mathsf{match}\, x\, \mathsf{with}\, \langle 0 \Rightarrow e_1 \mid \mathsf{S}(y) \Rightarrow e_2 \rangle \\ & \mid n \mid x_1 + x_2 \mid x_1 * x_2 \mid \mathsf{minus}(x_1, x_2) \mid \mathsf{minus}(x_1, n) \mid \mathsf{divmod}(x_1, x_2) \\ & \mid \mathsf{A.make}(x_1, x_2) \mid \mathsf{A.set}(x_1, x_2, x_3) \mid \mathsf{A.get}(x_1, x_2) \mid \mathsf{A.length}(x) \end{aligned}$$

We present the language in, what we call, share-let normal form which simplifies the type system without hampering expressivity. In the implementation, we transform input programs to share-let normal form before the analysis. Like in Haskell, the undefined expression simply aborts the program without consuming any resources. The meaning of the sharing expression $\mathsf{share}\, x\, \mathsf{as}\, (x_1, x_2)\, \mathsf{in}\, e$ is that the value of the free variable x is bound to the variables x_1 and x_2 for use in the expression e. We use it to inform the (affine) type system of multiple uses of a variable.

While all array operations as well as multiplication and addition are standard, subtraction, division, and modulo differ from the standard operations. To give stronger typing rules in our analysis system, we combine division and modulo in one operation divmod. Moreover, minus and divmod return their second argument, that is, $\mathsf{minus}(n, m) = (m, n - m)$ and $\mathsf{divmod}(n, m) = (m, n \div m, n \bmod m)$. We also distinguish two syntactic forms of minus; one in which we subtract a variable and another one in which we subtract a constant. More explanations are given in Section 5. If $m > n$ then the evaluation of $\mathsf{minus}(n, m)$ fails without consuming resources. That means that it is the responsibility of the user or other static analysis tools to show the absence of overflows.

Types and Programs. We define data types A, B and function types F.

$$A, B ::= \mathrm{nat} \mid A\ \mathrm{array} \mid A * B \qquad\qquad F ::= A \to B$$

Let $\mathcal{A}$ be the set of data types and let $\mathcal{F}$ be the set of function types. A signature $\Sigma : \mathrm{FID} \rightharpoonup \mathcal{F}$ is a partial finite mapping from function identifiers to function types. A context is a partial finite mapping $\Gamma : \mathit{Var} \rightharpoonup \mathcal{A}$ from variable identifiers to data types. A simple type judgment $\Sigma; \Gamma \vdash e : A$ states that the expression e has type A in the context Γ under the signature Σ. The definition of typing rules for this judgment is standard and we omit the rules. A *(well-typed) program* consists of a signature Σ and a family $(e_f, y_f)_{f \in \mathsf{dom}(\Sigma)}$ of expressions e_f with a distinguished variable identifier y_f such that $\Sigma; y_f{:}A \vdash e_f{:}B$ if $\Sigma(f) = A \to B$.

$$\frac{}{V, H \stackrel{M}{\vdash} e \Downarrow \circ \mid 0}\ (\text{E:Zero}) \qquad \frac{n = H(V(x_1)) \cdot H(V(x_2)) \qquad H' = H, \ell \mapsto n}{V, H \stackrel{M}{\vdash} x_1 * x_2 \Downarrow (\ell, H') \mid M^{\mathsf{mult}}}\ (\text{E:Mult})$$

$$\frac{n = H(V(x_1)) - H(V(x_2)) \qquad H' = H, \ell \mapsto (V(x_2), \ell'), \ell' \mapsto n}{V, H \stackrel{M}{\vdash} \mathsf{minus}(x_1, x_2) \Downarrow (\ell, H') \mid M^{\mathsf{sub}}}\ (\text{E:Sub})$$

$$\frac{[y_f \mapsto V(x)], H \stackrel{M}{\vdash} e_f \Downarrow \rho \mid (q, q')}{V, H \stackrel{M}{\vdash} f(x) \Downarrow \rho \mid M^{\mathsf{app}} \cdot (q, q')}\ (\text{E:App}) \qquad \frac{H(V(x_1)) = (\sigma, n) \qquad H(V(x_2)) \geqslant n}{V, H \stackrel{M}{\vdash} \mathsf{A.get}(x_1, x_2) \Downarrow \circ \mid M^{\mathsf{Afail}}}\ (\text{E:AGFail})$$

$$\frac{H(V(x_1)) = (\sigma, n) \qquad H(V(x_2)) = i \qquad 0 \leqslant i < n}{V, H \stackrel{M}{\vdash} \mathsf{A.get}(x_1, x_2) \Downarrow (\sigma(i), H) \mid M^{\mathsf{Aget}}}\ (\text{E:AGet})$$

Fig. 2. Selected rules of the operational big-step semantics

Cost Semantics. Figure 2 contains representative rules of the operational cost semantics. The full version of this article [15] contains all rules of the semantics for our subset of RAML. The semantics is standard except that it defines the cost of an evaluation. This cost depends on a resource metric $M : K \to \mathbb{Q}$ that assigns a cost to each evaluation step of the big-step semantics. Here, K is a finite set of constant symbols. We write M^k for $M(k)$.

The semantics is formulated with respect to a stack and a heap. Let *Loc* be an infinite set of *locations* modeling memory addresses on a heap. The set of RAML *values Val* is given as follows.

$$\mathit{Val} \ni v ::= n \mid (\ell_1, \ell_2) \mid (\sigma, n)$$

A value $v \in \mathit{Val}$ is either a natural number n, a pair of locations (ℓ_1, ℓ_2), or an array (σ, n). An array (σ, n) consists of a size n and a mapping $\sigma : \{0, \ldots, n-1\} \to \mathit{Loc}$ from the set $\{0, \ldots, n-1\}$ of natural numbers to locations. A *heap* is a finite partial mapping $H : \mathit{Loc} \rightharpoonup \mathit{Val}$ that maps locations to values. A *stack* is a finite partial mapping $V : \mathit{Var} \rightharpoonup \mathit{Loc}$ from variable identifiers to locations.

The big-step operational evaluation rules are defined in the full version of this article. They define an evaluation judgment of the form $V, H \stackrel{M}{\vdash} e \Downarrow (\ell, H') \mid (q, q')$. It expresses the following. Under resource metric M, if the stack V and the initial heap H are given then the expression e evaluates to the location ℓ and the new heap H'. To evaluate e one needs at least $q \in \mathbb{Q}_0^+$ resource units and after the evaluation there are $q' \in \mathbb{Q}_0^+$ resource units available. The actual resource consumption is then $\delta = q - q'$. The quantity δ is negative if resources become available during the execution of e.

In fact, the evaluation judgment is slightly more complicated because there are two other behaviors that we have to express in the semantics: failure (i.e., array access outside its bounds) and divergence. To this end, our semantics judgment does not only evaluate expressions to values but also expresses incomplete computations by using $\circ$ (pronounced *busy*). The evaluation judgment has the general form

$$V, H \stackrel{M}{\vdash} e \Downarrow \rho \mid (q, q') \qquad \text{where} \qquad \rho ::= (\ell, H) \mid \circ\,.$$

Well-Formed Environments. For each simple type A we inductively define a set $[\![A]\!]$ of values of type A.

$$[\![\text{nat}]\!] = \mathbb{N}$$
$$[\![A \text{ array}]\!] = \{(\alpha, n) \mid n \in \mathbb{N} \text{ and } \alpha : \{0, \ldots, n-1\} \to [\![A]\!]\}$$
$$[\![A * B]\!] = [\![A]\!] \times [\![B]\!]$$

If H is a heap, ℓ is a location, A is a type, and $a \in [\![A]\!]$ then we write $H \vDash \ell \mapsto a : A$ to mean that ℓ defines the semantic value $a \in [\![A]\!]$ when pointers are followed in H in the obvious way. The judgment is formally defined in the full version.

We write $H \vDash \ell : A$ to indicate that there exists a necessarily unique, semantic value $a \in [\![A]\!]$ so that $H \vDash \ell \mapsto a : A$. A stack V and a heap H are *well-formed* with respect to a context Γ if $H \vDash V(x) : \Gamma(x)$ holds for every $x \in \text{dom}(\Gamma)$. We then write $H \vDash V : \Gamma$.

4 Resource Polynomials and Annotated Types

Compared with multivariate amortized resource analysis for nested inductive data types [13], the resource polynomials that are needed for the data types in this article are relatively simple. They are multivariate, non-negative linear combinations of binomial coefficients.

Resource Polynomials. For each data type A we first define a set $P(A)$ of functions $p : [\![A]\!] \to \mathbb{N}$ that map values of type A to natural numbers. The resource polynomials for type A are then given as non-negative rational linear combinations of these *base polynomials*. We define $P(A)$ as follows.

$$P(\text{nat}) = \{\lambda n . \binom{n}{k} \mid k \in \mathbb{N}\} \qquad P(A \text{ array}) = \{\lambda(\alpha, n) . \binom{n}{k} \mid k \in \mathbb{N}\}$$

$$P(A_1 * A_2) = \{\lambda(a_1, a_2) . p_1(a_1) \cdot p_2(a_2) \mid p_1 \in P(A_1) \wedge p_2 \in P(A_2)\}$$

A *resource polynomial* $p : [\![A]\!] \to \mathbb{Q}_0^+$ for a data type A is a non-negative linear combination of base polynomials, i.e., $p = \sum_{i=1,\ldots,m} q_i \cdot p_i$ for $q_i \in \mathbb{Q}_0^+$ and $p_i \in P(A)$. We write $R(A)$ for the set of resource polynomials of data type A.

For example, $h(n, m) = 7 + 2.5 \cdot n + 5\binom{n}{3}\binom{m}{2} + 8\binom{m}{4}$ is a resource polynomial for the data type nat $*$ nat.

Names for Base Polynomials. To assign a unique name to each base polynomial, we define the *index set* $\mathcal{I}(A)$ to denote resource polynomials for a given data type A.

$$\mathcal{I}(\text{nat}) = \mathcal{I}(A \text{ array}) = \mathbb{N}$$
$$\mathcal{I}(A_1 * A_2) = \{(i_1, i_2) \mid i_1 \in \mathcal{I}(A_1) \text{ and } i_2 \in \mathcal{I}(A_2)\}$$

For each $i \in \mathcal{I}(A)$, we define a base polynomial $p_i \in P(A)$ as follows: If $A = \text{nat}$ then $p_k(n) = \binom{n}{k}$. If $A = A'$ array then $p_k(\sigma, n) = \binom{n}{k}$. If $A = (A_1 * A_2)$ is a pair type and $v = (v_1, v_2)$ then $p_{(i_1,i_2)}(v) = p_{i_1}(v_1) \cdot p_{i_2}(v_2)$. We use the notation 0_A (or just 0) for the index in $\mathcal{I}(A)$ such that $p_{0_A}(a) = 1$ for all a.

Our previous example $h : [\![\text{nat} * \text{nat}]\!] \to \mathbb{Q}_0^+$ can for instance be written as $h(n,m) = 7p_{(0,0)}(n,m) + 2.5p_{(1,0)}(n,m) + 5p_{(3,2)}(n,m) + 8p_{(0,4)}(n,m)$.

Annotated Types and Potential Functions. A *type annotation* for a data type A is defined to be a family $Q_A = (q_i)_{i \in \mathcal{I}(A)}$ with $q_i \in \mathbb{Q}_0^+$. An *annotated data type* is a pair (A, Q_A) of a data type A and a type annotation Q_A.

Let H be a heap and let ℓ be a location with $H \vDash \ell \mapsto a : A$ for a data type A. Then the type annotation Q_A defines the *potential*

$$\Phi_H(\ell{:}(A, Q_A)) = \sum_{i \in \mathcal{I}(A)} q_i \cdot p_i(a)$$

If $a \in [\![A]\!]$ then we also write $\Phi(a : (A, Q_A))$ for $\sum_i q_i{\cdot}p_i(a)$.

For example, consider the resource polynomial $h(n,m)$ again. We have $\Phi((n,m) : (\text{nat}{*}\text{nat}, Q)) = h(n,m)$ if $q_{(0,0)} = 7$, $q_{(1,0)} = 2.5$, $q_{(3,2)} = 5$, $q_{(0,4)} = 8$, and $q_{(i,j)} = 0$ for all other $(i,j) \in \mathcal{I}(\text{nat} * \text{nat})$.

The Potential of a Context. For use in the type system we need to extend the definition of resource polynomials to typing contexts. We treat a context like a tuple type. Let $\Gamma = x_1{:}A_1, \ldots, x_n{:}A_n$ be a typing context and let $k \in \mathbb{N}$. The index set $\mathcal{I}(\Gamma)$ is defined as $\mathcal{I}(\Gamma) = \{(i_1, \ldots, i_n) \mid i_j \in \mathcal{I}(A_j)\}$. A *type annotation* Q for Γ is a family $Q = (q_i)_{i \in \mathcal{I}(\Gamma)}$ with $q_i \in \mathbb{Q}_0^+$.

We denote a *resource-annotated context* with $\Gamma; Q$. Let H be a heap and V be a stack with $H \vDash V : \Gamma$ where $H \vDash V(x_j) \mapsto a_{x_j} : \Gamma(x_j)$. The potential of $\Gamma; Q$ with respect to H and V is $\Phi_{V,H}(\Gamma; Q) = \sum_{(i_1,\ldots,i_n) \in \mathcal{I}(\Gamma)} q_{\vec{\imath}} \prod_{j=1}^{n} p_{i_j}(a_{x_j})$. In particular, if $\Gamma = \varnothing$ then $\mathcal{I}(\Gamma) = \{()\}$ and $\Phi_{V,H}(\Gamma; q_{()}) = q_{()}$. We sometimes also write q_0 for $q_{()}$.

Operations on Annotations. For each arithmetic operation such as $n - 1$, $n * m$, and $n + m$, we define a corresponding operation on annotations that describes how to transfer potential from the arguments to the result.

For addition and subtraction (compare rules T:Add and T:Sub in Figure 3) we need to express the potential of a natural number n in terms of two numbers n_1 and n_2 such that $n = n_1 + n_2$. To this end, let $Q = (q_i)_{i \in \mathbb{N}}$ be an annotation for data of type nat. We define the *convolution* $\boxplus(Q)$ of the annotation Q to be the following annotation Q' for the type nat $*$ nat.

$$\boxplus(Q) = (q'_{(i,j)})_{(i,j) \in \mathcal{I}(\text{nat}*\text{nat})} \qquad \text{if} \qquad q'_{(i,j)} = q_{i+j}$$

The convolution $\boxplus(Q)$ for type annotations corresponds to Vandermonde's convolution for binomial coefficients:

$$\binom{n_1 + n_2}{k} = \sum_{i+j=k} \binom{n_1}{i}\binom{n_2}{j}$$

Using Vandermonde's convolution we derive Lemma 1.

Lemma 1. *Let Q be an annotation for type nat, $H \vDash \ell \mapsto n_1{+}n_2 : nat$, and $H' \vDash \ell' \mapsto (n_1, n_2) : nat * nat$. Then $\Phi_H(\ell{:}(nat, Q)) = \Phi_{H'}(\ell'{:}(nat * nat, \boxplus(Q)))$.*

In the type rule for subtraction of a constant K we can distribute the potential in two different ways. We can either use the convolution to distribute the potential between two numbers or we can perform K additive shifts. Of course, we can describe K shift operations directly: Let $Q = (q_i)_{i\in\mathbb{N}}$ be an annotation for data of type nat. The *K-times shift for natural numbers* $\lhd^K(Q)$ of the annotation Q is an annotation Q' for data of type nat that is defined as follows.

$$\lhd^K(Q) = (q'_i)_{i\in\mathcal{I}(\mathrm{nat})} \qquad \text{if} \qquad q'_i = \sum_{j=i+\ell} q_j \binom{K}{\ell} .$$

Recall that $\binom{n}{m} = 0$ if $m > n$. The K-times shift corresponds to the following identity (where $q_{k+1} = 0$ again) that can be derived from Vandermonde's convolution.

$$\sum_{0\leqslant i\leqslant k} q_i \binom{n+K}{i} = \sum_{0\leqslant i\leqslant k} \left(\sum_{j=i+\ell} q_j \binom{K}{\ell} \right) \binom{n}{i}$$

The K-times shift is a generalization of the additive shift (see [13]) which is equivalent to the 1-times shift. Using the previous identity we prove Lemma 2.

Lemma 2. *Let Q be an annotation for type nat, $H \models \ell \mapsto n{+}K : nat$, and $H' \models \ell' \mapsto n : nat$. Then $\Phi_H(\ell{:}(nat, Q)) = \Phi_{H'}(\ell'{:}(nat, \lhd^K Q))$.*

For multiplication and division, things are more interesting. Our goal is to define a convolution-like operation $\boxdot(Q)$ that defines an annotation for the arguments $(x_1, x_2) : \mathrm{nat} * \mathrm{nat}$ if given an annotation Q of a product $x_1 * x_2 : \mathrm{nat}$. For this purpose, we are interested in the coefficients $A(i, j, k)$ in the following identity.

$$\binom{nm}{k} = \sum_{i,j} A(i,j,k) \binom{n}{i} \binom{m}{j}$$

Fortunately, this problem has been carefully studied by Riordan and Stein [16].[1] Intuitively, the coefficient $A(i, j, k)$ is number of ways of arranging k pebbles on an $i{\times}j$ chessboard such that every row and every column has at least one pebble. Riordan and Stein obtain the following closed formulas.

$$A(i,j,k) = \sum_{r,s} (-1)^{i+j+r+s} \binom{i}{r} \binom{j}{s} \binom{rs}{k} = \sum_{n} \frac{i!j!}{k!} S(n,i)\, S(n,j)\, s(k,n)$$

Here, $S(\cdot,\cdot)$ and $s(\cdot,\cdot)$ denote the Stirling numbers of first and second kind, respectively. Furthermore they report the recurrence relation $A(i,j,k+1)(k+1) = (A(i,j,k) + A(i-1,j,k) + A(i,j-1,k) + A(i-1,j-1,k))ij - k\,A(i,j,k)$.

Equipped with a closed formula for $A(i, j, k)$, we now define the *multiplicative convolution* $\boxdot(Q)$ of an annotation Q for type nat as

$$\boxdot(Q) = (q'_{(i,j)})_{(i,j)\in\mathcal{I}(\mathrm{nat}*\mathrm{nat})} \qquad \text{if} \qquad q'_{(i,j)} = \sum_{k} A(i,j,k)\, q_k .$$

Lemma 3 is then a direct consequence of the identity of Riordan and Stein.

[1] Thanks to Mike Spivey for pointing us to that article.

Lemma 3. *Let Q be an annotation for type nat, $H \models \ell \mapsto n_1 \cdot n_2 : nat$, and $H' \models \ell' \mapsto (n_1, n_2) : nat * nat$. Then $\Phi_H(\ell{:}(nat, Q)) = \Phi_{H'}(\ell'{:}(nat * nat, \boxdot(Q)))$.*

5 Resource-Aware Type System

We now describe the type-based amortized analysis for programs with unsigned integers and arrays. We only present the novel rules for arrays and arithmetic expressions. The complete set of rules can be found in the full version of the article [15].

Type Judgments. The type rules for RAML expressions in Figure 3 define a *resource-annotated typing judgment* of the form

$$\Sigma; \Gamma; Q \vdash^{M} e : (A, Q')$$

where e is a RAML expression, M is a metric, Σ is a resource-annotated signature (see below), $\Gamma; Q$ is a resource-annotated context and (A, Q') is a resource-annotated data type. The intended meaning of this judgment is that if there are more than $\Phi(\Gamma; Q)$ resource units available then this is sufficient to cover the evaluation cost of e in metric M. In addition, there are at least $\Phi(v{:}(A, Q'))$ resource units left if e evaluates to a value v.

Programs with Annotated Types. Resource-annotated function types have the form $(A, Q) \rightarrow (B, Q')$ for annotated data types (A, Q) and (B, Q'). A *resource-annotated signature* Σ is a finite, partial mapping from function identifiers to *sets of* resource-annotated function types.

A RAML program with resource-annotated types for metric M consists of a resource-annotated signature Σ and a family of expressions with variable identifiers $(e_f, y_f)_{f \in \mathrm{dom}(\Sigma)}$ such that $\Sigma; y_f{:}A; Q \vdash^{M} e_f : (B, Q')$ for every function type $(A, Q) \rightarrow (B, Q') \in \Sigma(f)$.

Notations. If Q, P and R are annotations with the same index set I then we extend operations on $\mathbb{Q}$ pointwise to Q, P and R. For example, we write $Q \leqslant P + R$ if $q_i \leqslant p_i + r_i$ for every $i \in I$.

For $K \in \mathbb{Q}$ we write $Q = Q' + K$ to state that $q_0 = q'_0 + K \geqslant 0$ and $q_i = q'_i$ for $i \neq 0 \in I$. Let $\Gamma = \Gamma_1, \Gamma_2$ be a context, let $i = (i_1, \ldots, i_k) \in \mathcal{I}(\Gamma_1)$ and $j = (j_1, \ldots, j_l) \in \mathcal{I}(\Gamma_2)$. We write (i, j) for the index $(i_1, \ldots, i_k, j_1, \ldots, j_l) \in \mathcal{I}(\Gamma)$.

Let Q be an annotation for a context Γ_1, Γ_2. For $j \in \mathcal{I}(\Gamma_2)$ we define the *projection* $\pi_j^{\Gamma_1}(Q)$ of Q to Γ_1 to be the annotation Q' with $q'_i = q_{(i,j)}$. Sometimes we omit Γ_1 and just write $\pi_j(Q)$ if the meaning follows from the context.

Type Rules. Figure 3 contains the annotated type rules for arithmetic operations, array operations, the undefined expression, variables, and function application. The rules T:Var and T:App for variables and function application are similar to the corresponding rules in previous work [10].

In the rule T:Undef, we only require that the constant potential M^{undef} is available. In contrast to the other rules we do not relate the initial potential Q

$$\frac{Q = Q' + M^{\mathsf{var}}}{\Sigma; x{:}A; Q \overset{M}{\vdash} x : (A, Q')}\ \text{(T:VAR)} \qquad \frac{P{+}M^{\mathsf{app}} = Q \qquad (A,P) \to (A',Q') \in \Sigma(f)}{\Sigma; x{:}A; Q \overset{M}{\vdash} f(x) : (A', Q')}\ \text{(T:APP)}$$

$$\frac{Q = \boxplus(Q') + M^{\mathsf{add}}}{\Sigma; x_1{:}\mathrm{nat}, x_2{:}\mathrm{nat}; Q \overset{M}{\vdash} x_1 + x_2 : (\mathrm{nat}, Q')}\ \text{(T:ADD)}$$

$$\frac{Q' + M^{\mathsf{sub}} = \boxplus(\pi_0^{x_1:\mathrm{nat}}(Q))}{\Sigma; x_1{:}\mathrm{nat}, x_2{:}\mathrm{nat}; Q \overset{M}{\vdash} \mathsf{minus}(x_1, x_2) : (\mathrm{nat} * \mathrm{nat}, Q')}\ \text{(T:SUB)}$$

$$\frac{q_0 = M^{\mathsf{nat}} + \sum_{i \geqslant 0} q'_i \binom{n}{i}}{\Sigma; \cdot; Q \overset{M}{\vdash} n : (\mathrm{nat}, Q')}\ \text{(T:NAT)} \qquad \frac{\begin{array}{lll} Q{=}M^{\mathsf{sub}}{+}P{+}R & P'{=}\boxplus(P) & R'{=}\lhd^n(R) \\ q'_{(i,0)} = r'_i + p'_{(i,0)} & & q'_{(i,j)} = p'_{(i,j)} \text{ if } j > 0 \end{array}}{\Sigma; x{:}\mathrm{nat}; Q \overset{M}{\vdash} \mathsf{minus}(x, n) : (\mathrm{nat} * \mathrm{nat}, Q')}\ \text{(T:SUBC)}$$

$$\frac{q_0 = M^{\mathsf{undef}}}{\Sigma; \cdot; Q \overset{M}{\vdash} \mathsf{undefined} : (B, Q')}\ \text{(T:UNDEF)} \qquad \frac{Q = \boxdot(Q') + M^{\mathsf{mult}}}{\Sigma; x_1{:}\mathrm{nat}, x_2{:}\mathrm{nat}; Q \overset{M}{\vdash} x_1 {*} x_2 {:} (\mathrm{nat}, Q')}\ \text{(T:MULT)}$$

$$\frac{R + M^{\mathsf{dif}} = \boxplus(\pi_0^{x_1:\mathrm{nat}}(Q)) \qquad \forall i \in \mathbb{N} : \pi_i(R) = \boxdot(\pi_i(Q'))}{\Sigma; x_1{:}\mathrm{nat}, x_2{:}\mathrm{nat}; Q \overset{M}{\vdash} \mathsf{divmod}(x_1, x_2) : ((\mathrm{nat} * \mathrm{nat}) * \mathrm{nat}, Q')}\ \text{(T:DIV)}$$

$$\frac{\forall i{>}1 : q_{(i,0)} = q'_i \qquad q_{(0,0)} = q'_0 + M^{\mathsf{Amake}} \qquad q_{(1,0)} = q'_1 + M^{\mathsf{AmakeL}}}{\Sigma; x_1{:}\mathrm{nat}, x_2{:}A; Q \overset{M}{\vdash} \mathsf{A.make}(x_1, x_2) : (A\ \mathrm{array}, Q')}\ \text{(T:AMAKE)}$$

$$\frac{q_0 = q'_0 + M^{\mathsf{Aget}}}{\Sigma; x_1{:}A\,\mathrm{array}, x_2{:}\mathrm{nat}, x_3{:}A; Q \overset{M}{\vdash} \mathsf{A.set}(x_1, x_2, x_3) : (\mathrm{nat}, Q')}\ \text{(T:ASET)}$$

$$\frac{\forall i{\neq}0 : q'_i = 0 \qquad q_0 = q'_0 + M^{\mathsf{Aset}}}{\Sigma; x_1{:}A\,\mathrm{array}, x_2{:}\mathrm{nat}; Q \overset{M}{\vdash} \mathsf{A.get}(x_1, x_2) : (A, Q')}\ \text{(T:AGET)}$$

$$\frac{Q = Q' + M^{\mathsf{Alen}}}{\Sigma; x : A\,\mathrm{array}; Q \overset{M}{\vdash} \mathsf{A.length}(x) : (\mathrm{nat}, Q')}\ \text{(T:ALEN)}$$

Fig. 3. Annotated type rules for arithmetic and array operations

with the resulting potential Q'. Intuitively, this is sound because the program is aborted when evaluating the expression undefined. A consequence of the rule T:UNDEF is that we can type the expression let x = undefined in e with constant initial potential M^{undef} regardless of the resource cost of the expression e.

The rule T:NAT shows how to transfer constant potential to polynomial potential of a non-negative integer constant n. Since n is statically available, we simply compute the coefficients $\binom{n}{i}$ for the linear constraint system.

In the rule T:ADD, we use the convolution operation $\boxplus(\cdot)$ that we describe in Section 4. The potential defined by the annotation $\boxplus(Q')$ for the context $x_1{:}\mathrm{nat}, x_2{:}\mathrm{nat}$ is equal to the potential Q' of the result.

Subtraction is handled by the rules T:SUB and T:SUBC. To be able to conserve all the available potential, we have to ensure that subtraction is the inverse operation to addition. To this end, we abort the program if $x_2 > x_1$ and otherwise return the pair $(n, m) = (x_2, x_1 - x_2)$. This enables us to transfer the potential of x_1 to the pair (n, m) where $n + m = x_1$. This is inverse to the rule T:ADD for addition.

In the rule T:SUB, we only use the potential of x_1 by applying the projection $\pi_0^{x_1:\mathsf{nat}}(Q)$. The potential of x_2 and the mixed potential of x_1 and x_2 can be arbitrary and is wasted by the rule. This is usually not problematic since it would just be zero anyways in most useful type derivations. By using the convolution $\boxplus(\pi_0^{x_1:\mathsf{nat}}(Q))$ we then distribute the potential of x_1 to the result of $\mathsf{minus}(x_1, x_2)$.

The rule T:SUBC specializes the rule T:SUB. We can use T:SUBC to simulate T:SUB but we also have the possibility to exploit the fact that we subtract a constant. This puts us in a position to use the K-times shift that we introduced in Section 4. So we split the initial potential Q into P and R. We then assign the convolution $P' = \boxplus(P)$ to the pair of unsigned integers that is returned by minus and the n-times shift $\lhd^n(R)$ to the first component of the returned pair. In fact, it would not hamper the expressivity of our system to only use the conventional subtraction $x - n$ and the n-times shift in the case of subtraction of constants.

In practice, it would be beneficial not to expose this non-standard minus function to users and instead apply a code transformation that converts the usual subtraction $\mathsf{let}\, x = x_1 - x_2 \,\mathsf{in}\, e$ into an equivalent expression $\mathsf{let}\ (x_2, x) = \mathsf{minus}(x_1, x_2)\,\mathsf{in}\, e$ that overshadows x_2 in e. In this way, it is ensured that the potential that is returned by minus can be used within e.

The rule T:MULT is similar to T:ADD. We just use the multiplicative convolution $\boxdot(\cdot)$ (see Section 4) instead of the additive convolution $\boxplus(\cdot)$. The rule T:DIV is inverse to T:MULT in the same way that T:SUB is inverse to T:ADD. We use both, the additive and multiplicative convolution to express the fact that $n * m + r = x_1$ if $(n, m, r) = \mathsf{divmod}(x_1, x_2)$.

In the rule T:AMAKE, we transfer the potential of x_1 to the created array. We discard the potential of x_2 and the mixed potential of x_1 and x_2. At this point, it would in fact be not problematic to use mixed potential to assign it to the newly created elements of the array. We refrain from doing so solely because of the complexity that would be introduced by tracking the potential in the functions A.get and A.set. Another interesting aspect of T:AMAKE is that we have a constant cost that we deduce from the constant coefficient as usual, as well as a linear cost that we deduce from the linear coefficient. This is represented by the constraints $q_{(0,0)} = q'_0 + M^{\mathsf{Amake}}$ and $q_{(1,0)} = q'_1 + M^{\mathsf{AmakeL}}$, respectively.

For convenience, the operation A.set returns 0 in this paper. In RAML, A.set has however the return type unit. This makes no difference for the typing rule T:ASET in which we simply pay for the cost of the operation and discard the potential that is assigned to the arguments. Since the return value is 0, we do not need require that the non-constant annotations of Q' are zero.

In the rule T:AGET, we again discard the potential of the arguments and also require that the non-linear coefficients of the annotation of the result are zero. In the rule T:ALEN, we simply assign the potential of the array in the argument to the resulting integer.

Soundness. An annotated type judgment for an expression e establishes a bound on the resource cost of all evaluations of e in a well-formed environment; regardless of whether the evaluation terminates, diverges, or fails.

Additionally, the soundness theorem states a stronger property for terminating evaluations. If an expression e evaluates to a value v in a well-formed environment then the difference between initial and final potential is an upper bound on the resource usage of the evaluation.

Theorem 1 (Soundness). *Let $H \models V{:}\Gamma$ and $\Sigma; \Gamma; Q \overset{M}{\vdash} e{:}(B, Q')$.*

1. *If $V, H \overset{M}{\vdash} e \Downarrow (\ell, H') \mid (p, p')$ then we have $p \leqslant \Phi_{V,H}(\Gamma; Q)$ and $p - p' \leqslant \Phi_{V,H}(\Gamma; Q) - \Phi_{H'}(\ell{:}(B, Q'))$.*
2. *If $V, H \overset{M}{\vdash} e \Downarrow \circ \mid (p, p')$ then $p \leqslant \Phi_{V,H}(\Gamma; Q)$.*

Theorem 1 is proved by a nested induction on the derivation of the evaluation judgment and the type judgment $\Gamma; Q \vdash e{:}(B, Q')$. The inner induction on the type judgment is needed because of the structural rules. There is one proof for all possible instantiations of the resource constants.

The proof of most rules is similar to the proof of the rules for multivariate resource analysis for sequential programs [13]. The novel type rules are mainly proved by the Lemmas 1, 2, and 3. We deal with the mutable heap by requiring that array elements do not influence the potential of an array. As a result, we can prove the following lemma.

Lemma 4. *If $H \models V{:}\Gamma$, $\Sigma; \Gamma; Q \overset{M}{\vdash} e : (B, Q')$ and $V, H \overset{M}{\vdash} e \Downarrow (\ell, H') \mid (p, p')$ then $\Phi_{V,H}(\Gamma; Q) = \Phi_{V,H'}(\Gamma; Q)$.*

If the metric M is simple (all constants are 1) then it follows from Theorem 1 that the bounds on the resource usuage also prove the termination of programs.

Corollary 1. *Let M be a simple metric. If $H \models V{:}\Gamma$ and $\Sigma; \Gamma; Q \overset{M}{\vdash} e{:}(A, Q')$ then there are $w \in \mathbb{N}$ and $d \leqslant \Phi_{V,H}(\Gamma; Q)$ such that $V, H \overset{M}{\vdash} e \Downarrow (\ell, H') \mid (w, d)$ for some ℓ and H'.*

Type Inference. In principle, type inference consists of four steps. First, we perform a classic type inference for the simple types such as nat array. Second, we fix a maximal degree of the bounds and annotate all types in the derivation of the simple types with variables that correspond to type annotations for resource polynomials of that degree. Third, we generate a set of linear inequalities, which express the relationships between the added annotation variables as specified by the type rules. Forth, we solve the inequalities with an LP solver such as CLP. A solution of the linear program corresponds to a type derivation in which the variables in the type annotations are instantiated according to the solution.

In practice, the type inference is slightly more complex. Most importantly, we have to deal with resource-polymorphic recursion in many examples. This means that we need a type annotation in the recursive call that differs from the annotation in the argument and result types of the function. To infer such types we successively infer type annotations of higher and higher degree. Details can be found in previous work [17]. Moreover, we have to use algorithmic versions of the type rules in the inference in which the non-syntax-directed rules are integrated into the syntax-directed ones [13]. Finally, we use several optimizations to reduce the number of generated constraints.

An concrete example of a type derivation can be found in previous work [13].

6 Experimental Evaluation

We have implemented our analysis system in Resource Aware ML (RAML) [12, 14] and tested the new analysis on multiple classic examples algorithms. In this section we describe the results of our experiments with the evaluation-step metric that counts the number of steps of an evaluation in the operational semantics.

Table 1 contains a compilation of analyzed functions together with their simple types, the computed bounds, the run times of the analysis, and the number of generated linear constraints. We write Mat for the type (Arr(Arr(int)),nat,nat). The dimensions of the matrices are needed since array elements do not carry potential. The variables in the computed bounds correspond to the sizes of different parts of the input. The naming convention is that we use the order n, m, x, y, z, u of the variables to name the sizes in a depth-first way: n is the size of the first argument, m is the maximal size of the elements of the first argument, x is the size of the second argument, etc. The experiments were performed on an iMac with a 3.4 GHz Intel Core i7 and 8 GB memory.

All but one of the reported bounds are asymptotically tight (gcdFast is actually $O(\log m)$). We also measured the evaluation cost of the functions for several inputs in the RAML interpreter. Our experiments indicate that all constant factors in the bounds for the functions dyadAllM and mmultAll are optimal. The bounds for the other functions seem to be off by ca. 2% – 20%. However, it is sometimes not straightforward to find worst-case inputs. The full version of this article [15] contains plots for the functions dijkstra, quicksort, dyadAllM, and mmultAll that compare the measured evaluation cost for inputs of different sizes with the inferred bounds.

The function dijkstra is an implementation of Dijkstra's single-source shortest-path algorithm which uses a simple priority queue; gcdFast is an implementation of the Euclidean algorithm using modulo; pascal(n) computes the first $n{+}1$ lines of Pascal's triangle; quicksort is an implementation of Hoare's in-place quick sort for arrays; and mmultAll takes a matrix (an accumulator) and a list of matrices, and multiplies all matrices in the list with the accumulator.

The last three examples are composed functions that highlight interesting capabilities of the analysis. The function blocksort(a, n) takes an array a of length m and divides it into n/m blocks (and a last block containing the remainder) using the build-in function divmod, and sorts all blocks in-place with quicksort. The function dyadAllM(n) computes a matrix of size $(i^2{+}9i{+}28) \times (ij{+}6j)$ for every pair of numbers i, j such that $1 \leqslant j \leqslant i \leqslant n$ (the polynomials are just a random choice). Finally, the function mmultFlatSort takes two matrices and multiplies them to get a matrix of dimension $m \times u$. It then flattens the matrix into an array of length mu and sorts this array with quicksort.

Table 1. Compilation of RAML Experiments

Function / Type	Computed Bound	Time	#Constr.
dijkstra : (Arr(Arr(int)),nat) → Arr(int)	$79.5n^2 + 31.5n + 38$	0.1 s	2178
gcdFast : (nat,nat) → nat	$12m + 7$	0.1 s	105
pascal : nat → Arr(Arr(int))	$19n^2 + 95n + 30$	0.4 s	998
quicksort : (Arr(int),nat,nat) → unit	$12.25x^2 + 52.75x + 3$	0.7 s	2080
blocksort : (Arr(int),nat) → unit	$12.25n^2 + 90.25n + 18$	0.4 s	27795
mmultAll : (L(Mat),Mat) → Mat	$18nuyx + 31nuy + 38nu+ 38n + 3$	5.6 s	184270
dyadAllM : nat → unit	$1.\bar{6}n^6 + 334.8n^4 + 1485.1n^3 + 37n^5 + 2963.5n^2 + 1789.92n + 3$	3.9 s	130236
mmultFlatSort : (Mat,Mat) → Arr(int)	$12.25u^2m^2 + 18umz + 28u + 127.25um + 49m + 66$	5.9 s	167603

We did not perform an experimental comparison with abstract interpretation–based resource analysis systems. Many systems that are described in the literature are not publicly available. The COSTA system [3, 4] is an exception but it is not straightforward to translate our examples to Java code that COSTA can handle. We know that the COSTA system can compute bounds for the Euclidean algorithm (when using an extension [8]), quick sort, and Pascal's triangle. The advantages of our method are the compositionality that is needed for the analysis of compound functions such as dyadAllM and mmultFlatSort, as well as for bounds that depend on integers as well as on sizes of data structures such as dijkstra (priority queue) and mmultAll.

7 Conclusion

We have presented a novel type-based amortized resource analysis for programs with arrays and unsigned integers. We have implemented the analysis in Resource Aware ML and our experiments show that the analysis works efficiently for many example programs. Moreover, we have demonstrated that the analysis has benefits in comparison to abstract interpretation–based approaches for programs with function composition and non-linear size changes.

While the developed analysis system for RAML is useful and interesting in its own right, we view this work mainly as an important step towards the application of amortized resource analysis to C-like programs. The developed rules for arithmetic expression can be reused when moving to a different language. Our next step is to develop an analysis system that applies the ideas of this work to an imperative language with while-loops, integers, and arrays.

Acknowledgments. This research is based on work supported in part by NSF grants 1319671 and 1065451, and DARPA grants FA8750-10-2-0254 and FA8750-12-2-0293. Any opinions, findings, and conclusions contained in this document are those of the authors and do not reflect the views of these agencies.

References

1. Gulwani, S., Mehra, K.K., Chilimbi, T.M.: SPEED: Precise and Efficient Static Estimation of Program Computational Complexity. In: 36th ACM Symp. on Principles of Prog. Langs (POPL 2009), pp. 127–139 (2009)
2. Zuleger, F., Gulwani, S., Sinn, M., Veith, H.: Bound Analysis of Imperative Programs with the Size-Change Abstraction. In: Yahav, E. (ed.) Static Analysis. LNCS, vol. 6887, pp. 280–297. Springer, Heidelberg (2011)
3. Albert, E., Arenas, P., Genaim, S., Puebla, G., Zanardini, D.: Cost Analysis of Object-Oriented Bytecode Programs. Theor. Comput. Sci. 413(1), 142–159 (2012)
4. Albert, E., Arenas, P., Genaim, S., Gómez-Zamalloa, M., Puebla, G.: Automatic Inference of Resource Consumption Bounds. In: Bjørner, N., Voronkov, A. (eds.) LPAR-18 2012. LNCS, vol. 7180, pp. 1–11. Springer, Heidelberg (2012)
5. Cousot, P., Halbwachs, N.: Automatic Discovery of Linear Restraints Among Variables of a Program. In: 5th ACM Symp. on Principles Prog. Langs (POPL 1978), pp. 84–96 (1978)
6. Gulavani, B.S., Gulwani, S.: A Numerical Abstract Domain Based on *Expression Abstraction* and *Max Operator* with Application in Timing Analysis. In: Gupta, A., Malik, S. (eds.) CAV 2008. LNCS, vol. 5123, pp. 370–384. Springer, Heidelberg (2008)
7. Sankaranarayanan, S., Ivančić, F., Shlyakhter, I., Gupta, A.: Static Analysis in Disjunctive Numerical Domains. In: Yi, K. (ed.) SAS 2006. LNCS, vol. 4134, pp. 3–17. Springer, Heidelberg (2006)
8. Alonso-Blas, D.E., Arenas, P., Genaim, S.: Handling Non-linear Operations in the Value Analysis of COSTA. Electr. Notes Theor. Comput. Sci. 279(1), 3–17 (2011)
9. Hofmann, M., Jost, S.: Static Prediction of Heap Space Usage for First-Order Functional Programs. In: 30th ACM Symp. on Principles of Prog. Langs (POPL 2003), pp. 185–197 (2003)
10. Hoffmann, J., Aehlig, K., Hofmann, M.: Multivariate Amortized Resource Analysis. In: 38th ACM Symp. on Principles of Prog. Langs (POPL 2011) (2011)
11. Hoffmann, J., Hofmann, M.: Amortized Resource Analysis with Polynomial Potential. In: Gordon, A.D. (ed.) ESOP 2010. LNCS, vol. 6012, pp. 287–306. Springer, Heidelberg (2010)
12. Aehlig, K., Hofmann, M., Hoffmann, J.: RAML Web Site (2010-2013), `http://raml.tcs.ifi.lmu.de`
13. Hoffmann, J., Aehlig, K., Hofmann, M.: Multivariate Amortized Resource Analysis. ACM Trans. Program. Lang. Syst. (2012)
14. Hoffmann, J., Aehlig, K., Hofmann, M.: Resource Aware ML. In: Madhusudan, P., Seshia, S.A. (eds.) CAV 2012. LNCS, vol. 7358, pp. 781–786. Springer, Heidelberg (2012)
15. Hoffmann, J., Shao, Z.: Type-Based Amortized Resource Analysis with Integers and Arrays (2013) (full version), `http://cs.yale.edu/homes/hoffmann/papers/aa_imp2013TR.pdf`
16. Riordan, J., Stein, P.R.: Arrangements on Chessboards. Journal of Combinatorial Theory, Series A 12(1) (1972)
17. Hoffmann, J., Hofmann, M.: Amortized Resource Analysis with Polymorphic Recursion and Partial Big-Step Operational Semantics. In: Ueda, K. (ed.) APLAS 2010. LNCS, vol. 6461, pp. 172–187. Springer, Heidelberg (2010)

Linear Sized Types in the Calculus of Constructions

Jorge Luis Sacchini

Carnegie Mellon University

Abstract. Sized types provide an expressive and compositional framework for proving termination and productivity of (co-)recursive definitions. In this paper, we study sized types with linear annotations of the form $n \cdot \alpha + m$ with n and m natural numbers. Concretely, we present a type system with linear sized types for the Calculus of Constructions extended with one inductive type (natural numbers) and one coinductive type (streams). We show that this system satisfies desirable metatheoretical properties, including strong normalization, and give a sound and complete size-inference algorithm.

1 Introduction

Termination and productivity of (co-)recursive definitions are essential properties of theorem provers based on dependent type theories (such as Coq [28] and Agda [21]), as they ensure logical consistency and decidability of type checking.

Type-based systems for termination and productivity [19] provide a powerful and flexible framework for proving termination and productivity of (co-)recursive functions. The basic idea is the use of sized types (i.e. types annotated with size information) to trace the size of (co-)recursive calls. Let us illustrate the concept with a simplified typing rule for recursive functions:

$$\frac{\Gamma(f : \mathsf{nat}^{\imath} \to U) \vdash M : \mathsf{nat}^{\widehat{\imath}} \to U}{\Gamma \vdash \mathsf{fix}\, f := M : \mathsf{nat}^{\infty} \to U}$$

where $\mathsf{nat}^{\imath}$ represents the type of natural numbers smaller than $\imath$, and $\widehat{\imath}$ represents the successor of $\imath$. The above rule enforces the restriction that recursive calls must be placed on smaller arguments, as evidenced by their type. The recursive function is then defined on the whole type of natural numbers, denoted nat^{∞}.

Corecursive functions have a dual but similar rule for ensuring productivity:

$$\frac{\Gamma(f : \mathsf{stream}^{\imath}\, U) \vdash M : \mathsf{stream}^{\widehat{\imath}}\, U}{\Gamma \vdash \mathsf{cofix}\, f := M : \mathsf{stream}^{\infty}\, U}$$

where $\mathsf{stream}^{\imath}\, U$ represents the type of streams (infinite sequences) where at least $\imath$ elements can be *produced*. The above rule ensures that each iteration of the body M produces at least one more element of the stream. By repeated iterations we can produce all elements of the stream.

M. Codish and E. Sumii (Eds.): FLOPS 2014, LNCS 8475, pp. 169–185, 2014.

The algebra of size annotations determines the expressive power of the type system. Many papers on sized types [1,2,8–10,12,24] consider the simplest size algebra with sizes of the form $\imath + n$, where $\imath$ is a size variable and n is a natural number. Even with such a simple size algebra, the type systems are very expressive, allowing to type non-structural recursive programs such as quicksort. Furthermore, size annotations can be inferred [9,10].

However, using this algebra, we cannot give precise types to functions such as double, that multiplies a natural number by 2, or even, that filters the even positions of a stream (they precise types being $\mathsf{nat}^{\imath} \to \mathsf{nat}^{2\cdot\imath}$ and $\mathsf{stream}^{2\cdot\imath}\, T \to \mathsf{stream}^{\imath}\, T$, respectively). This limits the use of these functions for defining other recursive functions [15, 25]. The tradeoff between expressiveness and usability is clear: a more expressive size algebra allows to type more programs, at the expense of requiring more explicit annotations for type checking (see e.g. [22]).

In previous work [17,24,25], we showed logical consistency of an extension of the Calculus of (Co-)Inductive Constructions (CIC) with sized types introduced in [10]. In this work, we extend these results to a more expressive size algebra and a relaxed notion of types allowed for recursion. Concretely, the contributions of this paper are the following.

- We introduce $\mathrm{CI\widehat{C_\ell}}$, an extension of CIC with linear sizes of the form $n\cdot\alpha+m$, and a notion of types allowed for recursion based on the work of Abel on semi-continuity [2] (Sect. 2). We only consider natural numbers and streams, although the extension to general (co-)inductive types is straightforward.
- We show that $\mathrm{CI\widehat{C_\ell}}$ satisfies desirable metatheoretical properties, including logical consistency and strong normalization (SN) by adapting the Λ-set model [6] given in [17,24,25] (Sect. 2.3).
- We present a size-inference algorithm that requires size annotations in the types of (co-)recursive functions, based on the algorithm given in [10, 25] (Sect. 3).

2 $\mathrm{CI\widehat{C_\ell}}$

In this section we introduce the syntax and typing rules of $\mathrm{CI\widehat{C_\ell}}$ (Sect. 2.1). We show the features of this system through a series of examples (Sect. 2.2), and study its metatheory (Sect. 2.3).

2.1 Syntax and Typing Rules

Sizes. Size (or stage) expressions over a symbol set $\mathcal{X}$ are given by the following grammar:

$$\mathcal{S}(\mathcal{X}) ::= \mathcal{X} \mid \widehat{\mathcal{S}} \mid \infty \mid n \cdot \mathcal{S}$$

where $1 \leq n \in \mathbb{N}$. Let $\mathcal{V}_\mathcal{S}$ be a denumerable set of stage variables. We write $\mathcal{S}$ to denote the set of stage expressions over $\mathcal{V}_\mathcal{S}$, i.e. $\mathcal{S}(\mathcal{V}_\mathcal{S})$. We use $\imath, \jmath$ to denote stage variables, and s, r to denote stages. A size of the form $\widehat{s}$ denotes the successor of size s; we write $\widehat{s}^k$ where $k \in \mathbb{N}$ to denote k applications of the successor operator to s (by definition, $\widehat{s}^0 = s$). We write $n \cdot \imath + m$ for $\widehat{n \cdot \imath}^m$.

Sizes come equipped with a subsize relation, denoted $s \sqsubseteq r$, defined as the reflexive-transitive closure of the following rules:

$$\frac{}{s \sqsubseteq \widehat{s}} \qquad \frac{}{s \sqsubseteq \infty} \qquad \frac{n \leq m \qquad s \sqsubseteq r}{n \cdot s \sqsubseteq m \cdot r}$$

$$\frac{}{1 \cdot s = s} \qquad \frac{}{n \cdot \widehat{s} = n \cdot s + n} \qquad \frac{}{n \cdot m \cdot s = nm \cdot s}$$

where a rule with a conclusion of the form $C_1 = C_2$ is an abbreviation for two rules with conclusions $C_1 \sqsubseteq C_2$ and $C_2 \sqsubseteq C_1$. Given stages s, r, we write $s = r$ to mean that $s \sqsubseteq r$ and $r \sqsubseteq s$ are derivable. We write $\lfloor s \rfloor$, called the base of s, for the partial function defined by $\lfloor \imath \rfloor = \imath$, $\lfloor \widehat{s} \rfloor = \lfloor s \rfloor$, and $\lfloor n \cdot s \rfloor = \lfloor s \rfloor$ (it is not defined for ∞). It is easy to see that for every stage s, either there exist unique m, n such that $s = n \cdot \imath + m$ (if $\lfloor s \rfloor = \imath$), or $\infty \sqsubseteq s$ (if $\lfloor s \rfloor$ is not defined).

The introduction of linear sizes is the main difference between $\mathrm{CIC}\widehat{_\ell}$ and the system $\mathrm{CIC}\widehat{\ }$ introduced in [10].

Syntax. Similar to [9, 10, 17], we consider three classes of terms, which differ in the kind of annotations that (co-)inductive types carry: *bare terms*, where (co-)inductive types carry no annotations, *position terms*, where (co-)inductive types either carry no annotation, or use a special symbol $\aleph$, and *sized terms*, where (co-)inductive types carry a size expression.

Definition 1 (Terms). *The terms of $\mathrm{CIC}\widehat{_\ell}$ are given by the following generic grammar defined over a set a.*

$$\begin{aligned}
\mathcal{T}[a] ::= {} & \mathcal{U} \mid \Pi x{:}\mathcal{T}[a].\mathcal{T}[a] \mid \mathcal{V} \mid \lambda x{:}\mathcal{T}^\circ.\mathcal{T}[a] \mid \mathcal{T}[a]\,\mathcal{T}[a] \\
& \mid \mathsf{nat}^a \mid \mathsf{O} \mid \mathsf{S}(\mathcal{T}[a]) \mid \mathsf{stream}^a\,\mathcal{T}[a] \mid \mathsf{cons}(\mathcal{T}[a], \mathcal{T}[a]) \\
& \mid \mathsf{case}_{\mathcal{T}^\circ}\ \mathcal{V} := \mathcal{T} \text{ of } \{\mathcal{P}[a]\} \\
& \mid \mathsf{fix}\,\mathcal{V}{:}\mathcal{T}[\mathcal{S}(\{\aleph\}), \epsilon] := \mathcal{T}[a] \mid \mathsf{cofix}\,\mathcal{V}{:}\mathcal{T}[\mathcal{S}(\{\aleph\}), \epsilon] := \mathcal{T}[a] \\
\mathcal{P}[a] ::= {} & \{\mathsf{cons}(\mathcal{V}, \mathcal{V}) \Rightarrow \mathcal{T}[a]\} \mid \{\mathsf{O} \Rightarrow \mathcal{T}[a]; \mathsf{S}(\mathcal{V}) \Rightarrow \mathcal{T}[a]\}
\end{aligned}$$

where $\mathcal{V}$ is a denumerable set of term variables, and $\mathcal{U}$ is the set of sorts (universes), defined as $\mathcal{U} = \{\mathsf{Prop}\} \cup \{\mathsf{Type}_i\}_{i \in \mathbb{N}}$.

The set of bare terms, position terms, and sized terms are defined by $\mathcal{T}^\circ ::= \mathcal{T}[\epsilon]$, $\mathcal{T}[\mathcal{S}(\{\aleph\}), \epsilon]$, and $\mathcal{T} ::= \mathcal{T}[\mathcal{S}]$, respectively. We also consider the class of sized terms with no size variables: $\mathcal{T}^\infty ::= \mathcal{T}[\infty]$.

Sort Prop is impredicative, while $\{\mathsf{Type}_i\}_{i \in \mathbb{N}}$ forms a predicative hierarchy. We define a Pure Type System specification [7] for the set of sorts $\mathcal{U}$, given by the following sets:

$$\begin{aligned}
\mathsf{Axiom} &= \{(\mathsf{Prop}, \mathsf{Type}_0)\} \cup \{(\mathsf{Type}_i, \mathsf{Type}_{i+1})\}_i \\
\mathsf{Rule} &= \{(u, \mathsf{Prop}, \mathsf{Prop})\}_{u \in \mathcal{U}} \cup \{(u_1, u_2, \max(u_1, u_2))\}_{u_1, u_2 \in \mathcal{U}}
\end{aligned}$$

where Axiom is used to describe the typing rules for sorts and Rule is used to describe the typing rules for products.

A context (resp. erased context) is a finite sequence of variable declarations of the form $x{:}T$ (resp. $x{:}T^\circ$). We write $\cdot$ to denote the empty context; we use Γ, Δ to denote contexts. Given a context $\Gamma = x_1{:}T_1, \ldots, x_n{:}T_n$, we write $\Pi\Gamma.U$ for the type $\Pi x_1{:}T_1.\ldots.\Pi x_n{:}T_n.U$.

We write $|\cdot| : \mathcal{T} \to \mathcal{T}^\circ$ to denote the erasure map that erases all size annotations. Given a stage variable $\imath$, we write $|\cdot|^\imath : \mathcal{T} \to \mathcal{T}[\mathcal{S}(\{\aleph\}), \epsilon]$ for the erasure map that replaces $\imath$ with $\aleph$ and erases all stage expressions s such that $\lfloor s \rfloor \neq \imath$. We write $\mathrm{FV}(M)$ (resp. $\mathrm{SV}(M)$) for the set of free term variables (resp. the set of size variables) in term M. We omit the definition of these functions.

Let us explain briefly the constructions of the language that are related to (co-)inductive types. The type nat^s denotes the type of natural numbers of size at most s, while $\mathsf{stream}^s\, T$ denotes the type of stream, whose elements have type T, of which at least s can be produced. Constructors and case analysis are standard. As we explain below, case analysis on nat is dependent, while we only allow non-dependent case analysis on stream.

The syntax of (co-)recursive definitions needs more explanations. A recursive function has the form $\mathsf{fix}\, f : T^\aleph := M$ where T is the type (which might have occurrences of the special symbol $\aleph$) and M is the body where recursive calls to f are possible. The type $T^\aleph$ must be of the form $\Pi x{:}\mathsf{nat}^s.U^\aleph$, where $\lfloor s \rfloor = \aleph$ and $\aleph$ may occur in $U^\aleph$ (although with some restrictions). The special symbol $\aleph$ is used to type recursive arguments. For example, the function that divides a natural number by 2 can be defined with the position type $\mathsf{nat}^{2\cdot\aleph} \to \mathsf{nat}^\aleph$.

Corecursive definitions are used in a similar way, with the exception that the type must be a function that produces a stream, i.e. of the form $\Pi\Delta^\aleph.\mathsf{stream}^s\, T$, where $\lfloor s \rfloor = \aleph$. The precise form of the type of (co-)recursive functions is given by the typing rules.

In previous work [9,10,17,24,25], position types had the form $\mathcal{T}[\{\star\}, \epsilon]$, where $\star$ is used to mark recursive positions. Here we opt for a more explicit notion of position types that express the actual sizes. For example, in our case we would write $\mathsf{nat}^\aleph \to \mathsf{nat}^{\widehat{\aleph}}$, where in previous work we would simply write $\mathsf{nat}^\star \to \mathsf{nat}^\star$. This choice simplifies the size-inference algorithm.

Reduction. It is defined by β-reduction, for applications, ι-reduction, for case analysis, and μ-reduction, for unfolding of (co-)recursive definitions. β-reduction and $\imath$-reduction are standard:

$$\begin{aligned}
(\lambda x{:}T^\circ.M)\, N \;&\beta\; M\,[N/x] \\
\mathsf{case}_{P^\circ}\, \mathsf{cons}(M_1, M_2)\ \mathsf{of}\ \{\mathsf{cons}(y_1, y_2) \Rightarrow N\} \;&\iota\; N\,[M_1/y_1]\,[M_2/y_2] \\
\mathsf{case}_{P^\circ}\, \mathsf{O}\ \mathsf{of}\ \{\mathsf{O} \Rightarrow N_1; \mathsf{S}\, y \Rightarrow N_2\} \;&\iota\; N_1 \\
\mathsf{case}_{P^\circ}\, \mathsf{S}\, M\ \mathsf{of}\ \{\mathsf{O} \Rightarrow N_1; \mathsf{S}\, y \Rightarrow N_2\} \;&\iota\; N_2\,[M/y]
\end{aligned}$$

In the case of (co-)recursive definitions, unfolding must be restricted in order to obtain a strongly normalizing relation. For fixpoint definitions, unfolding occurs when it is applied to a term in constructor form:

$$\frac{T\ R\ U}{T \preceq_R U} \qquad \frac{U_1 \preceq_R T_1 \qquad T_2 \preceq_R U_2}{\Pi x{:}T_1.T_2 \preceq_R \Pi x{:}U_1.U_2} \qquad \frac{T_1 \preceq_R T_2 \qquad T_2 \preceq_R T_3}{T_1 \preceq_R T_3}$$

$$\frac{s \sqsubseteq r \qquad T \preceq_R U}{\mathsf{stream}^r\, T \preceq_R \mathsf{stream}^s\, U} \qquad \frac{s \sqsubseteq r}{\mathsf{nat}^s \preceq \mathsf{nat}^r}$$

$$\frac{\imath \notin \mathrm{SV}(T)}{\imath\ \mathsf{occ}^\xi\ T} \qquad \frac{\imath\ \mathsf{occ}^{-\xi}\ T \qquad \imath\ \mathsf{occ}^\xi\ U}{\imath\ \mathsf{occ}^\xi\ \Pi x{:}T.U}$$

$$\frac{\imath \notin s \qquad \imath\ \mathsf{pos}\ T}{\imath\ \mathsf{pos}\ (\mathsf{stream}^s\, T)} \qquad \frac{\imath\ \mathsf{neg}\ T}{\imath\ \mathsf{neg}\ (\mathsf{stream}^s\, T)} \qquad \frac{\imath \in s}{\imath\ \mathsf{pos}\ \mathsf{nat}^s}$$

Fig. 1. Subtyping and positivity rules

$$(\mathsf{fix}\ f{:}T^{\aleph} := M)C \ \ \mu\ \ M\left[\mathsf{fix}\ f{:}T^{\aleph} := M/f\right] C$$

where C is either O or of the form $\mathsf{S}\,N$. For cofixpoint definitions, we adopt a lazy strategy, where unfolding occurs only inside a case analysis.

$$\mathsf{case}_{U^\circ}\ (\mathsf{cofix}\ f{:}T^{\aleph} := M)\ \boldsymbol{N}\ \mathsf{of}\ \{P\}\ \ \mu\ \ \mathsf{case}_{U^\circ}\ M^\star\ \boldsymbol{N}\ \mathsf{of}\ \{P\}$$

where $M^\star$ is $M\left[(\mathsf{cofix}\ f{:}T^{\aleph} := M)/f\right]$. A well-known issue with this reduction strategy is that, in the presence of dependent case analysis, it does not satisfy subject reduction (SR) [16, 20, 27].

In this paper, we focus on the use of linear sizes, so we do not address the issue of subject reduction with coinductive types. We only allow non-dependent case analysis of streams.

Subtyping Rules. The typing rules depend on a notion of subtyping and positivity of stage variables (see Fig. 1). Note that size annotations are covariant in nat and contravariant in stream. The subtyping relation is parameterized by a relation R on terms: we write $T \preceq_R U$ to mean that T is a subtype of U with respect to R. In the following, R will either be the convertibility relation ($\approx$), or α-equivalence ($\equiv$). We write $\leq$ for $\preceq_{\approx}$.

We write $\imath\ \mathsf{pos}\ T$ (resp. $\imath\ \mathsf{neg}\ T$) to denote that $\imath$ occurs positively (resp. negatively) in T. To simplify the definition of positivity we introduce polarities: a polarity ξ is either $+$ or $-$. We denote with $-\xi$ for the opposite polarity of ξ. We write occ^+ (resp. occ^-) to mean pos (resp. neg).

Simple Types. As in our previous work [17, 24, 25], we restrict the occurrences of size variables in types, in order to have a set-theoretical model (or a Λ-set model to prove SN). In essence, well-typed types (i.e. terms whose type is a sort) must satisfy the simple predicate defined by the following rules:

$$\frac{\mathsf{simple}(T) \qquad \mathsf{simple}(U)}{\mathsf{simple}(\Pi x{:}T.U)} \qquad \frac{\mathrm{SV}(T) = \emptyset}{\mathsf{simple}(T)} \qquad \frac{\mathsf{simple}(T)}{\mathsf{simple}(\mathsf{stream}^s\, T)} \qquad \frac{}{\mathsf{simple}(\mathsf{nat}^s)}$$

$$\frac{}{\mathsf{WF}(\cdot)}\ (\text{wf-emp}) \qquad \frac{\mathsf{WF}(\Gamma) \qquad \Gamma \vdash T : u}{\mathsf{WF}(\Gamma(x{:}T))}\ (\text{wf-cons})$$

$$\frac{\mathsf{WF}(\Gamma)}{\Gamma \vdash x : \Gamma(x)}\ (\text{var}) \qquad \frac{\mathsf{WF}(\Gamma) \qquad (u_1, u_2) \in \mathsf{Axiom}}{\Gamma \vdash u_1 : u_2}\ (\text{sort})$$

$$\frac{\Gamma \vdash T : u_1 \qquad \Gamma(x{:}T) \vdash U : u_2 \qquad (u_1, u_2, u_3) \in \mathsf{Rule}}{\Gamma \vdash \Pi x : T.U : u_3}\ (\text{prod})$$

$$\frac{\Gamma(x{:}T) \vdash M : U \qquad \mathrm{SV}(M) = \emptyset}{\Gamma \vdash \lambda x : |T|.M : \Pi x : T.U}\ (\text{abs}) \qquad \frac{\begin{array}{c}\Gamma \vdash M : \Pi x : T.U \qquad \Gamma \vdash N : T \\ \mathrm{SV}(N) = \emptyset\end{array}}{\Gamma \vdash M\, N : U\,[N/x]}\ (\text{app})$$

$$\frac{\Gamma \vdash M : T \qquad \Gamma \vdash U : u \qquad T \leq U}{\Gamma \vdash M : U}\ (\text{conv})$$

$$\frac{\Gamma \vdash T : \mathsf{Type}_0}{\Gamma \vdash \mathsf{stream}^s\, T : \mathsf{Type}_0}\ (\text{stream}) \qquad \frac{\begin{array}{c}\Gamma \vdash M : T \qquad \Gamma \vdash N : \mathsf{stream}^s\, T \\ \mathrm{SV}(M) = \emptyset\end{array}}{\Gamma \vdash \mathsf{cons}(M, N) : \mathsf{stream}^{\widehat{s}}\, T}\ (\text{cons})$$

$$\frac{}{\Gamma \vdash \mathsf{nat}^s : \mathsf{Type}_0}\ (\text{nat}) \qquad \frac{}{\Gamma \vdash \mathsf{O} : \mathsf{nat}^{\widehat{s}}}\ (\text{zero}) \qquad \frac{\Gamma \vdash M : \mathsf{nat}^s}{\Gamma \vdash \mathsf{S}\, M : \mathsf{nat}^{\widehat{s}}}\ (\text{succ})$$

$$\frac{\begin{array}{c}\Gamma \vdash M : \mathsf{stream}^{\widehat{s}}\, T \qquad \mathrm{SV}(N) = \emptyset \\ \Gamma \vdash P : u \qquad \Gamma(y_1{:}T)(y_2{:}\mathsf{stream}^s\, T) \vdash N : P\end{array}}{\Gamma \vdash \mathsf{case}_{|P|}\ x := M\ \mathsf{of}\ \{\mathsf{cons}(y_1, y_2) \Rightarrow N\} : P}\ (\text{case-stream})$$

$$\frac{\begin{array}{c}\Gamma \vdash M : \mathsf{nat}^{\widehat{s}} \qquad \mathrm{SV}(N_1, N_2) = \emptyset \qquad \Gamma, x{:}\mathsf{nat}^{\widehat{s}} \vdash P : u \\ \Gamma \vdash N_1 : P\,[\mathsf{O}/x] \qquad \Gamma(y{:}\mathsf{nat}^s) \vdash N_2 : P\,[\mathsf{S}\, y/x]\end{array}}{\Gamma \vdash \mathsf{case}_{|P|}\ x := M\ \mathsf{of}\ \{\mathsf{O} \Rightarrow N_1; \mathsf{S}\, y \Rightarrow N_2\} : P\,[M/x]}\ (\text{case-nat})$$

$$\frac{\begin{array}{c}T \equiv \Pi \mathsf{nat}^{k \cdot \imath}.U \qquad \imath\ \mathsf{semi}^+\ T \qquad \mathrm{SV}(M) = \emptyset \\ \imath \notin \mathrm{SV}(\Gamma) \qquad \Gamma \vdash T : u \qquad \Gamma(f : T) \vdash M : T\,[\widehat{\imath}/\imath]\end{array}}{\Gamma \vdash \mathsf{fix}\ f{:}|T|^{\imath} := M : T\,[s/\imath]}\ (\text{fix})$$

$$\frac{\begin{array}{c}T \equiv \Pi \Delta.\mathsf{stream}^{k \cdot \imath}\, U \qquad \imath\ \mathsf{semi}^+\ T \qquad \mathrm{SV}(M) = \emptyset \\ \imath \notin \mathrm{SV}(\Gamma) \qquad \Gamma \vdash T : u \qquad \Gamma(f : T) \vdash M : T\,[\widehat{\imath}/\imath]\end{array}}{\Gamma \vdash \mathsf{cofix}\ f{:}|T|^{\imath} := M : T\,[s/\imath]}\ (\text{cofix})$$

Fig. 2. Typing rules of $\mathrm{CIC}\widehat{_\ell}$

We also extend the simple predicate to position types by taking $\aleph$ as a size variable.

Restricting to simple allows us to deal with features of $\mathrm{CIC}\widehat{_\ell}$ that are difficult to express in set-theoretical models—namely, erased types and contravariance. However, this restriction has no effect on practical programming [24].

Typing Rules. They are defined by the following judgments: $\mathsf{WF}(\Gamma)$, meaning that context Γ is well formed, and $\Gamma \vdash M : T$, meaning that under context Γ, term M has type T.

The typing rules are given in Fig. 2. Most of the rules are standard. In (abs) we require the body to have no size variables to ensure that we only have types satisfying the simple predicate. Similar restrictions appear in (app), (cons), and the rules for case analysis and (co-)recursive functions.

Let us explain in more detail the rules for (co-)recursive functions, (fix) and (cofix). Both rules are very similar, with only the shape of the recursion type differing. In the case of recursive functions, the type must be a function on natural numbers (in general, a function on an inductive type); we can view recursive functions as *consuming* elements of an inductive type. Dually, for corecursive functions, the type must return a stream (in general, the type must return a coinductive type); we can view corecursive functions as *producing* elements of a coinductive type.

We need to impose some restrictions on the occurrences of the recursion size variable $\aleph$ in $T^{\aleph}$; otherwise we could write non-terminating programs [2]. In previous work [17, 24, 25] we used a condition of monotonicity originated in [8]. For recursive functions, this means types of the form $\Pi x{:}\mathsf{nat}^{\imath}.U$ with $\imath$ pos U. However, this forbids valid types such as $\mathsf{nat}^{\imath} \to \mathsf{nat}^{\imath} \to \mathsf{nat}^{\imath}$.

In this work, we extend our notion of valid types for (co-)recursion by adapting the work of Abel [2] on semi-continuity. The condition $\imath\ \mathsf{semi}^{+}\ T$, read $\imath$ occurs semi-positively in T, ensures that the type is valid. The rules defining this judgment are given in Fig. 3, and are adapted to our setting from [2].

$$\frac{\imath\ \mathsf{semi}^{-}\ T \qquad \imath\ \mathsf{semi}^{+}\ U}{\imath\ \mathsf{semi}^{+}\ \Pi x{:}T.U} \qquad \frac{}{\imath\ \mathsf{semi}^{-}\ \mathsf{nat}^{n\cdot\imath}} \qquad \frac{\imath\ \mathsf{pos}\ T}{\imath\ \mathsf{semi}^{+}\ \mathsf{stream}^{n\cdot\imath}\ T} \qquad \frac{\imath\ \mathsf{occ}^{\xi}\ T}{\imath\ \mathsf{semi}^{\xi}\ T}$$

Fig. 3. Semi-continuity rules

2.2 Examples

We show some example programs in $\mathrm{CIC}\widehat{_\ell}$. The first two examples concern recursive definitions. The half function on natural numbers, that divides a number by 2, can be given the precise type $\Pi n{:}\mathsf{nat}^{2\cdot s} \to \mathsf{nat}^{s}$:

$$\begin{aligned} \mathsf{half} \stackrel{\text{def}}{=} \mathsf{fix}\ \mathsf{half} : \mathsf{nat}^{2\cdot\aleph} \to \mathsf{nat}^{\aleph} := \\ \lambda x.\ \mathsf{case}\ x\ \mathsf{of} \\ \{\mathsf{O} \Rightarrow \mathsf{O} \\ ; \mathsf{S}\, y \Rightarrow \mathsf{case}\ y\ \mathsf{of} \\ \{\mathsf{O} \Rightarrow \mathsf{O} \\ ; \mathsf{S}\, z \Rightarrow \mathsf{S}\, (\mathsf{half}\ z)\}\} \end{aligned}$$

This function is definable in Coq, however, in $\mathrm{CIC}\widehat{_\ell}$, we can give the more precise type that shows the relation between the argument and the result.

In the next example we define addition on natural numbers, plus, with the type $\mathsf{nat}^s \to \mathsf{nat}^s \to \mathsf{nat}^{2\cdot s}$:

$$\begin{aligned}\mathsf{plus} \stackrel{\mathrm{def}}{=} &\mathsf{fix}\ \mathsf{plus} : \mathsf{nat}^{\aleph} \to \mathsf{nat}^{\aleph} \to \mathsf{nat}^{2\cdot\aleph} := \\ &\lambda x.\lambda y.\ \mathsf{case}\ x\ \mathsf{of} \\ &\qquad \{\mathsf{O} \Rightarrow y \\ &\qquad ;\mathsf{S}\,x' \Rightarrow \mathsf{case}\ y\ \mathsf{of} \\ &\qquad\qquad \{\mathsf{O} \Rightarrow x \\ &\qquad\qquad ;\mathsf{S}\,y' \Rightarrow \mathsf{S}\,(\mathsf{S}\,(\mathsf{plus}\,x'\,y'))\}\}\end{aligned}$$

While the reduction behavior of the above definition is not the same as in the standard library of Coq, this example shows the extended types for recursion. In CIC$\hat{}$ [10], the type $\mathsf{nat}^{\imath} \to \mathsf{nat}^{\imath} \to \mathsf{nat}^{\infty}$ is not allowed for recursion.

The next examples concern corecursive definitions. The function odd (resp. even) on streams filters all elements in odd positions (resp. even positions). Both functions can be given type $\Pi A{:}\mathsf{Type}_0.\mathsf{stream}^{2\cdot s}\,A \to \mathsf{stream}^s\,A$. We only give the definition of odd, as even is similarly defined:

$$\begin{aligned}&\mathsf{cofix}\ \mathsf{odd} : \mathsf{stream}^{2\cdot\aleph}\,A \to \mathsf{stream}^{\aleph}\,A := \\ &\quad \lambda x.\ \mathsf{case}\ x\ \mathsf{of} \\ &\qquad \{\mathsf{cons}(y_1, y_2) \Rightarrow \mathsf{case}\ y_2\ \mathsf{of} \\ &\qquad\qquad \{\mathsf{cons}(z_1, z_2) \Rightarrow \mathsf{cons}(y_1, \mathsf{odd}\,z_2)\}\}\end{aligned}$$

The function interleave combines two streams by interleaving their elements:

$$\begin{aligned}&\mathsf{cofix}\ \mathsf{interleave} : \mathsf{stream}^{\aleph}\,A \to \mathsf{stream}^{\aleph}\,A \to \mathsf{stream}^{2\cdot\aleph}\,A := \\ &\quad \lambda x.\lambda y.\ \mathsf{case}\ x\ \mathsf{of} \\ &\qquad \{\mathsf{cons}(x_1, x_2) \Rightarrow \\ &\qquad\quad \mathsf{case}\ y\ \mathsf{of} \\ &\qquad\qquad \{\mathsf{cons}(y_1, y_2) \Rightarrow \mathsf{cons}(x_1, \mathsf{cons}(y_1, \mathsf{interleave}\,x_2\,y_2)\}\}\end{aligned}$$

While these functions are definable in Coq, the precise type given in $\mathrm{CIC}\widehat{\ell}$ allows us, for example, to define the following identity function on streams with precise type:

$$\lambda x{:}\mathsf{stream}\,A.\ \mathsf{interleave}\ (\mathsf{odd}\,A\,x)\ (\mathsf{even}\,A\,x)\ :\ \mathsf{stream}^{2\cdot s}\,A \to \mathsf{stream}^{2\cdot s}\,A$$

Consider the following Haskell definition of the Thue-Morse sequence:

```
tm = 0 : interleave (map inv (odd tm)) (tail tm)
```

where $\mathsf{inv}\,0 = 1$ and $\mathsf{inv}\,1 = 0$. Endrullis et al. [15] define a procedure for proving productivity of stream definitions that accepts the above program as productive. This definition is not typeable in $\mathrm{CIC}\widehat{\ell}$ for two reasons. First, it uses tail, which has type $\mathsf{stream}^{\hat{\imath}}\,A \to \mathsf{stream}^{\imath}\,A$, which cannot be used in a recursive definition. However, recursive functions that use tail can be represented using mutual recursion.[1] The second reason is the use of odd: we need to produce two elements

[1] We do not study mutual recursion in $\mathrm{CIC}\widehat{\ell}$, but it is relatively straightforward to add mutual recursion to a type system with sized types (see e.g. [22]).

of tm in order to apply odd. If we unfold the definition of tm above a few times (five to be precise), we arrive at the following equivalent definition:

```
tm = 0 : 1 : 1 : 0 : 1 : interleave (map inv (even tm3)) tm3
```

where $\mathtt{tm_3}$ is $\mathsf{tail}^3\,\mathtt{tm}$. We can define this version of the Thue-Morse sequence in CIC_{ℓ} as follows:

$$\begin{aligned}\mathsf{tm_0} &\stackrel{\text{def}}{=} \mathsf{cons}(0, \mathsf{cons}(1, \mathsf{cons}(1, \mathsf{tm_3})))\\ \mathsf{tm_3} &\stackrel{\text{def}}{=} \mathsf{cofix}\ \mathsf{tm_3} : \mathsf{stream}^{2\cdot\aleph}\ \mathsf{nat} :=\\ &\qquad \mathsf{cons}(1, \mathsf{cons}(0, \mathsf{interleave}\ (\mathsf{map}\,\mathsf{inv}\,(\mathsf{even}\,\mathsf{tm_3}))\,\mathsf{tm_3}))\end{aligned}$$

where $\mathsf{map} : (A \to B) \to \mathsf{stream}^s A \to \mathsf{stream}^s B$. Note that the precise type of even allows us to use it in the definition of a recursive stream. With the size algebra $\imath + n$, even can only be given the type $\mathsf{stream}^\infty A \to \mathsf{stream}^s A$, which limits its uses [15, 25].

2.3 Metatheory

CIC_{ℓ} satisfies desired metatheoretical properties including logical consistency and SN (for details of the proofs see [26]). The following lemma states several standard properties of type theories: weakening, substitution, uniqueness of types, and subject reduction. The proofs by induction on the typing judgment are standard.

Lemma 1. – *If $\Gamma \vdash M : T$, then $\Gamma\Delta \vdash M : T$.*
- *If $\Gamma_1(x : T)\Gamma_2 \vdash M : U$, $\Gamma_1 \vdash N : T$, and $\mathrm{SV}(N) = \emptyset$, then $\Gamma_1(\Gamma_2\,[N/x]) \vdash M\,[N/x] : U\,[N/x]$.*
- *If $\Gamma \vdash M : T_1$ and $\Gamma \vdash M : T_2$, then $|T_1| \approx |T_2|$.*
- *If $\Gamma \vdash M : T$ and $M \to M'$ then $\Gamma \vdash M' : T$*

Logical consistency and SN follow from the Λ-set model given in [24] for inductive types and [25] for coinductive types. To extend the model to CIC_{ℓ} we need to deal with linear sizes and semi-positive types.

Size annotations are interpreted as ordinals. In the system presented in this paper, we only need to consider ordinals up to ω—however, in the extension with full (co-)inductive types, we need to consider inaccessible cardinals. This interpretation naturally supports linear sizes and validates the subsize and subtyping relation.

For semi-positivity, consider a (co-)recursive function $\mathsf{fix}\ f{:}T^{\aleph} := M$. A sufficient condition for ensuring that this definition is valid is that $\bigcap_{i<\omega}[\![T]\!]^i \subseteq [\![T]\!]^\omega$ [1], where $[\![T]\!]^i$ is the interpretation of T at size i—more precisely, $[\![\cdot]\!]$ is the relational interpretation we defined in [24,25]. Abel [2] relaxes this condition to $\bigcap_i \bigcup_{j\geq i}[\![T]\!]^j \subseteq [\![T]\!]^\omega$ (the limit superior of $[\![T]\!]^i$, when $i \to \omega$).

The main property we need, in order to prove soundness of the Λ-set model, is the following: if $\imath\ \mathsf{semi}^+\ T$ (resp. $\imath\ \mathsf{semi}^-\ T$), then $\bigcap_i \bigcup_{j\geq i}[\![T]\!]^j \subseteq [\![T]\!]^\omega$ (resp. $[\![T]\!]^\omega \subseteq \bigcup_i \bigcap_{j\geq i}[\![T]\!]^j$. The proof proceeds by induction on the derivation of semi-continuity.

Theorem 1. *If $\Gamma \vdash M : T$, then M is strongly normalizing.*

The proof combines model construction given in [17] (for natural numbers) and [25] (for streams). The property stated above is essential to ensure soundness of rules (fix) and (cofix).

Logical consistency follows as a direct collorary of SN.

Lemma 2. *Let u be a sort. Then, there is no term M such that $\cdot \vdash M : \Pi x{:}u.x$.*

3 Size Inference

In this section we present a size-inference algorithm for $\widehat{\mathrm{CIC}_\ell}$ based on the algorithm introduced in [9, 10] (and adapted to coinductive types in [25]).

Size inference is performed on a variant of $\widehat{\mathrm{CIC}_\ell}$ where size variables are taken from a denumerable set of *inference size variables*, $\mathcal{V}_{\mathcal{S}_\mathcal{I}}$. We use α, β to denote inference size variables. We write $\mathcal{S}_\mathcal{I}$ to denote the set of stages defined over $\mathcal{V}_{\mathcal{S}_\mathcal{I}}$, i.e. $\mathcal{S}(\mathcal{V}_{\mathcal{S}_\mathcal{I}})$. A *generic term* (similarly generic context) is a term whose size variables are taken from $\mathcal{V}_{\mathcal{S}_\mathcal{I}}$. Given a generic term M, we can obtain a size term by applying a *stage substitution* ρ from inference size variables to stages.

In a nutshell, the algorithm proceeds as follows: given a context Γ and a bare term M°, the algorithm computes a generic term M (with $|M| = M^\circ$) and a generic type T, and a set of constraints C, such that, for every stage substitution ρ satisfying C, the judgment $\rho\Gamma \vdash \rho M : \rho T$ is valid. Note that bare terms contain size annotation in the types of (co-)recursive functions (in the form of position types).

A constraint set is a finite set of constraints of the form $s \sqsubseteq r$ where $s, r \in \mathcal{S}_\mathcal{I}$. A stage substitution $\rho : \mathcal{V}_{\mathcal{S}_\mathcal{I}} \to \mathcal{S}$ satisfies a constraint set C, denoted $\rho \models C$, if for every $s \sqsubseteq r \in C$, $\rho s \sqsubseteq \rho r$. Any constraint set is satisfiable by the constant substitution $\rho(\alpha) = \infty$, for all $\alpha \in \mathcal{V}_{\mathcal{S}_\mathcal{I}}$.

The size inference algorithm is defined by the following judgments:

- $V, C, \Gamma \vdash M^\circ \rightsquigarrow V', C', M' \Rightarrow T$: given a context Γ, a bare term M°, and a set of constraints C, the algorithm either computes M' satisfying $M^\circ \equiv |M'|$, a type T, and a new set of constraints C', such that for all $\rho \models C'$, $\rho\Gamma \vdash \rho M' : \rho T$; or fails if no such M', T, and C' exists.
- $V, C, \Gamma \vdash M^\circ \Leftarrow T \rightsquigarrow V', C', M'$: given a context Γ, a bare M°, a type T, and a set of constraints C, the algorithm either computes M' satisfying $M^\circ \equiv |M'|$ and a new set of constraints C', such that for all $\rho \models C'$, $\rho\Gamma \vdash \rho M' : \rho T$; or fails if no such M' and C' exists.

At the core of the type inference algorithm we have the RecCheck procedure ensuring that a constraint set can be instantiated in such a way that the conditions on size variables in rules (fix) and (cofix) are satisfied. The procedure presented here is a modification of that of [9] to deal with linear sizes.

Given a size inference variable α, a set of size inference variables $V^{\neq}$ and a constraint set C, $\mathsf{RecCheck}(\alpha, V^{\neq}, C)$ either succeeds returning a constraint set, or fails. It satisfies the following properties:

Soundness (SRC): if $\mathsf{RecCheck}(\alpha, V^{\neq}, C') = C$ then for all ρ, such that $\rho \models C$, there exists a fresh stage variable $\imath$ and ρ' such that $\rho' \models C'$, $\rho'(\alpha) = \imath$, and $\lfloor \rho'(V^{\neq}) \rfloor \neq \imath$.

Completeness (CRC): if $\rho(\alpha) = \imath$ and $\lfloor \rho(V^{\neq}) \rfloor \neq \imath$ and also $\rho \models C$ then $\mathsf{RecCheck}(\alpha, V^{\neq}, C)$ succeeds and $\rho \models \mathsf{RecCheck}(\alpha, V^{\neq}, C)$

The type inference algorithm is given in Fig. 4 and 5. We write $V, C, \Gamma \vdash M^\circ \rightsquigarrow V', C' \Rightarrow T$ for $V, C, \Gamma \vdash M^\circ \rightsquigarrow V', C', M \Rightarrow T$ when M is just $(M^\circ)^\infty$. And similarly for $V, C, \Gamma \vdash M^\circ \Leftarrow T \rightsquigarrow V', C'$. We write $V, C, \Gamma \vdash M^\circ \rightsquigarrow V', C' \Rightarrow^* W$ as a shorthand for $V, C, \Gamma \vdash M^\circ \rightsquigarrow V', C' \Rightarrow T \wedge \mathsf{whnf}(T) = W$. For checking sorts and products, we view $\mathrm{CIC}\widehat{_\ell}$ as a functional Pure Type System: we read Axiom as a function from sorts to sorts ($\mathcal{U} \to \mathcal{U}$) and Rule as a function from pair of sorts to sorts ($\mathcal{U} \times \mathcal{U} \to \mathcal{U}$).

In the type inference rules, we use the following operations:

- $T_1 \sqsubseteq T_2$ computes a constraint set C such that for all ρ, $\rho \models C$ iff $\rho T_1 \leq \rho T_2$;
- $T_1 \sqcup_{V,C} T_2 \rightsquigarrow T', V', C'$ (resp. $T_1 \sqcap_{V,C} T_2 \rightsquigarrow T', V', C'$) computes a type T' (fresh with respect to V, C), a set of variables V', and a constraint set C' such that for all $\rho \models C$ and T such that $\rho T_1, \rho T_2 \leq T$ (resp. $T \leq \rho T_1, \rho T_2$) there exists $\rho' \models C'$ such that $\rho =_V \rho'$ and $\rho' T' \leq T$ (resp. $T \leq \rho' T'$).
- $\aleph\ \mathsf{SEMI}^+\ T$, where T is a position term, checks that $\aleph$ occurs semi-positively in T. It holds iff for every stage variable $\imath$ and type T' such that $|T'|^\imath \equiv T$, $\imath\ \mathsf{semi}^+\ T'$.
- $T^\aleph =_\alpha T' \rightsquigarrow C$, where $T^\aleph$ is a position type, T' is a generic type such that $|T^\aleph| \equiv |T'|$ and $\aleph$ is an inference size variable. It replaces $\aleph$ with α in $T^\aleph$ and generates equality constraints with T' for each occurrence of α. It holds iff, for each $\rho \models C$ such that $\rho(\alpha) = \imath$, $|\rho T'|^\imath \equiv T^\aleph$. For example, $(\mathsf{nat}^{2\cdot\aleph} \to \mathsf{nat} =_\alpha \mathsf{nat}^{\beta_1} \to \mathsf{nat}^{\beta_2}) \rightsquigarrow 2 \cdot \alpha = \beta_1$.

The type-inference algorithm is sound and complete as stated in the following lemmas.

Lemma 3 (Soundness of type inference)

1. *If $V, C, \Gamma \vdash M^\circ \Leftarrow T \rightsquigarrow V', C', M'$, with $\mathrm{SV}(C) \subseteq V$, then $\mathrm{SV}(C') \subseteq V'$, $|M'| \equiv M^\circ$, and for all $\rho \models C'$, $\rho\Gamma \vdash \rho M' : \rho T$.*
2. *If $V, C, \Gamma \vdash M^\circ \rightsquigarrow V', C', M' \Rightarrow T$, with $\mathrm{SV}(C) \subseteq V$, then $\mathrm{SV}(C') \subseteq V'$, $|M'| \equiv M^\circ$, and for all $\rho \models C'$, $\rho\Gamma \vdash \rho M' : \rho T$.*

Lemma 4 (Completeness of type inference)

1. *If $\rho\Gamma \vdash M : \rho T$, $\rho \models C$, and $\mathrm{SV}(\Gamma, T) \subseteq V$, then there exist V', C', M', ρ' such that $\rho' \models C'$, $\rho =_V \rho'$, $\rho' M' \equiv M$, and $V, C, \Gamma \vdash |M| \Leftarrow T \rightsquigarrow V', C', M'$.*
2. *If $\rho\Gamma \vdash M : T$, $\rho \models C$, and $\mathrm{SV}(\Gamma) \subseteq V$, there exist V', C', M', T', ρ' such that $\rho' \models C'$, $\rho' T' \leq T$, $\rho' =_V \rho$, $\rho' M' = M$, and $V, C, \Gamma \vdash |M| \rightsquigarrow V', C', M' \Rightarrow T'$.*

RecCheck *Algorithm.* It is computed by a sequence of operations on constraint graphs. We adapt the algorithm of [9] to linear sizes and our different notion of position types.

We use the following operations on graphs: given a graph G and a set of vertex V in G, we define the upward closure of V (resp. the downward closure of V), denoted $V^{\sqsubseteq}$ (resp. $V^{\sqsupseteq}$), to the smallest set of vertex containing V that is closed by the edge relation (resp. is closed by the inverse of the edge relation).

Given an inference stage variable α (that must be mapped to a fresh stage variable $\imath$), a set of inference stage variables $V^{\neq}$ (that must be mapped to stages not containing $\imath$), and an initial set of constraints C, the computation of $\mathsf{RecCheck}(\alpha, V^{\neq}, C)$ proceeds as follows:

1. Let $S_\imath = \{\alpha\}^{\sqsupseteq}$; all variables in $S_\imath$ must be mapped to a stage with base $\imath$.
2. Let $S_{\imath\sqsubseteq} = (S_\imath)^{\sqsubseteq}$ and $S_{\neg\imath} = (V^{\neq})^{\sqsubseteq}$. Variables in $S_{\imath\sqsubseteq}$ (resp. $S_{\neg\imath}$) must be mapped to stages with base $\imath$ or to ∞ (resp. to stages with base different that $\imath$ or to ∞). Then, all variables in $S_{\imath\sqsubseteq} \cap S_{\neg\imath}$ must be set to ∞. This is done by removing all constraints with vertices in $(S_{\imath\sqsubseteq} \cap S_{\neg\imath})^{\sqsubseteq}$, and adding constraints $\infty \sqsubseteq (S_{\imath\sqsubseteq} \cap S_{\neg\imath})^{\sqsubseteq}$. Let C_1 be the constraint set obtained after this step.
3. Let $S_\infty = \{\infty\}^{\sqsubseteq}$. If $S_\imath \cap S_\infty = \emptyset$, the algorithm fails (since a variable in $S_\imath$ must be mapped to both ∞ and stage containing $\imath$).
4. *Check that constraints in* $S_\imath$ *are satisfiable.* Each variable in $S_\imath$ must be mapped to a stage of the form $x \cdot \imath + y$ for some $x \geq 1$, y; furthermore α must be mapped to $\imath$ (i.e., $1 \cdot \imath + 0$). Consider a constraint in $S_\imath$ of the form $m_1 \cdot \alpha_1 + n_1 \sqsubseteq m_2 \cdot \alpha_2 + n_2$. Assume that α_i (for $i = 1, 2$) is mapped to $x_i \cdot \imath + y_i$ (with $1 \leq x_i$). Then, $\{x_1, x_2, y_1, y_2\}$ must satisfy the following constraints:

$$m_1 x_1 \leq m_2 x_2 \qquad\qquad m_1 y_1 + n_1 \leq m_2 y_2 + n_2$$

   Let $\mathcal{C}$ be the set of (integer) constraints obtained by applying the above procedure to all constraints between variables in $S_\imath$. Then $\mathcal{C}$ is a constraint set in Presburger arithmetic—therefore, the satisfiability of $\mathcal{C}$ is decidable.
5. If $\mathcal{C}$ is satisfiable, return C_1 (computed in step 2); else, fail.

The RecCheck algorithm described above satisfies the soundness and completeness conditions needed for the size-inference algorithm.

Lemma 5. *The* RecCheck *algorithm described above satisfies (SRC) and (CRC).*

The original RecCheck [9] defined for sizes of the form $\imath + n$ has a complexity of $O(k^2)$ where k is the number of size variables. In our case, the use of linear sizes has a considerable cost, as RecCheck involves solving an integer programming problem, which makes its complexity exponential.

However, we expect that RecCheck will not have a great impact on large proofs by induction that usually use primitive recursion. For example, in a proof of the form $\mathsf{fix}\ f{:}\Pi x{:}\mathsf{nat}^{\aleph}.U := M\ldots$, where $\aleph$ does not occur in U, recursive calls to f generate constraints of the form $\beta \sqsubseteq \alpha$, where α is the size variable assigned to

$$\frac{V, C, \Gamma \vdash M^\circ \rightsquigarrow C' \Rightarrow T'}{V, C, \Gamma \vdash M^\circ \Leftarrow T \rightsquigarrow C' \cup T' \leq T} \text{ (a-check)}$$

$$\frac{}{V, C, \Gamma \vdash u \rightsquigarrow V, C \Rightarrow \mathsf{Axiom}(u)} \text{ (a-sort)} \qquad \frac{}{V, C, \Gamma \vdash x \rightsquigarrow V, C \Rightarrow \Gamma(x)} \text{ (a-var)}$$

$$\frac{\begin{array}{c} V, C, \Gamma \vdash T_1{}^\circ \rightsquigarrow V_1, C_1, T_1 \Rightarrow^* u_1 \\ V_1, C_1, \Gamma(x : T_1) \vdash M^\circ \rightsquigarrow V_2, C_2 \Rightarrow T_2 \qquad C_3 = C_2 \cup \infty \sqsubseteq \mathrm{SV}(M) \end{array}}{V, C, \Gamma \vdash \lambda x : T_1{}^\circ . M^\circ \rightsquigarrow V_2, C_3 \Rightarrow \Pi x : T_1 . T_2} \text{ (a-abs)}$$

$$\frac{\begin{array}{c} V, C, \Gamma \vdash T_1{}^\circ \rightsquigarrow V_1, C_1, T_1 \Rightarrow^* u_1 \\ V_1, C_1, \Gamma(x : T_1) \vdash T_2{}^\circ \rightsquigarrow V_2, C_2, T_2 \Rightarrow^* u_2 \end{array}}{V, C, \Gamma \vdash \Pi x : T_1{}^\circ . T_2{}^\circ \rightsquigarrow V_2, C_2, \Pi x : T_1 . T_2 \Rightarrow \mathsf{Rule}(u_1, u_2)} \text{ (a-prod)}$$

$$\frac{\begin{array}{c} V, C, \Gamma \vdash M_1{}^\circ \rightsquigarrow V_1, C_1 \Rightarrow^* \Pi x : T_2 . T \\ V_1, C_1, \Gamma \vdash M_2{}^\circ \Leftarrow T_2 \rightsquigarrow V_2, C_2 \\ C_3 = C_2 \cup \infty \sqsubseteq \mathrm{SV}(M_2) \end{array}}{V, C, \Gamma \vdash M_1{}^\circ \, M_2{}^\circ \rightsquigarrow V_2, C_3 \Rightarrow T\,[M_2/x]} \text{ (a-app)}$$

Fig. 4. Type-inference algorithm

$\aleph$ and β is the size of the argument in the recursive call. As α must be mapped to a fresh size variable, let us say $\imath$, the only possibility is that $\beta = \imath$; hence the constraint can be eliminated.

4 Related Work

Sized Types. Termination using sized types [19] has a long history (see e.g. [1, 24, 25] for more references). The system presented here is an extension of that of [17, 24], which are themselves based on CIC$\widehat{\ }$ [10]. With respect to CIC$\widehat{\ }$, we add linear sizes and a relaxed notion of allowed types for recursion, while still proving strong normalization and size inference.

We consider other works on type-based termination that use size algebras other than just $\imath + n$. Pareto [22] (see also [19]) considers an extension of Haskell with a size algebra that includes addition. The type-checking algorithm requires let-expressions annotated with types and produces a set of constraints in Presburger arithmetic (which are solved using the Omega solver [23]).

MiniAgda [3] is a prototype implementation of a dependent type theory with sized types. It features size addition and a type checking algorithm from fully annotated types for top-level functions. However, there is no metatheoretical study of the system or the type checking algorithm. Agda [21] has experimental support for sized types, but again there is no metatheoretical study.

Barthe et al. [11] consider an extension of system F with sized products and size addition. Their system is able to type quicksort with an exact measure, by giving a size zero to base constructors (like O or the empty list). However, this involves some syntactic restrictions where fixpoints and case analysis are combined in one construction. Type checking is not studied.

$$\frac{V, C, \Gamma \vdash T^{\circ} \Leftarrow \mathsf{Type}_0 \rightsquigarrow V_1, C_1, T \qquad \alpha \notin V_1}{V, C, \Gamma \vdash \mathsf{stream}\, T^{\circ} \rightsquigarrow V_1 \cup \{\alpha\}, C_1, \mathsf{stream}^{\alpha}\, T \Rightarrow \mathsf{Type}_0} \text{ (a-stream)}$$

$$\frac{\alpha \notin V}{V, C, \Gamma \vdash \mathsf{nat} \rightsquigarrow V \cup \{\alpha\}, C, \mathsf{nat}^{\alpha} \Rightarrow \mathsf{Type}_0} \text{ (a-nat)}$$

$$\frac{\begin{array}{c} V, C, \Gamma \vdash {M_1}^{\circ} \rightsquigarrow V_1, C_1 \Rightarrow T_1 \\ V_1, C, \kappa, \Gamma \vdash {M_2}^{\circ} \rightsquigarrow V_2, C_2 \Rightarrow^* \mathsf{stream}^{r}\, T_2 \\ T_1 \sqcup_{V_2, C_2} T_2 \rightsquigarrow T, V_3, C_3 \qquad C_4 = C_3 \cup \infty \sqsubseteq \mathrm{SV}(M_1) \end{array}}{V, C, \Gamma \vdash \mathsf{cons}({M_1}^{\circ}, {M_2}^{\circ}) \rightsquigarrow V_3, C_4 \Rightarrow \mathsf{stream}^{\widehat{r}}\, T} \text{ (a-cons)}$$

$$\frac{\alpha \notin V}{V, C, \Gamma \vdash \mathsf{O} \rightsquigarrow V \cup \{\alpha\}, C \Rightarrow \mathsf{nat}^{\widehat{\alpha}}} \text{ (a-zero)}$$

$$\frac{V, C, \Gamma \vdash M^{\circ} \rightsquigarrow V_1, C_1 \Rightarrow \mathsf{nat}^{r}}{V, C, \Gamma \vdash \mathsf{S}\, M^{\circ} \rightsquigarrow V \cup \{\alpha\}, C \Rightarrow \mathsf{nat}^{\widehat{r}}} \text{ (a-succ)}$$

$$\frac{\begin{array}{c} V, C, \Gamma \vdash M^{\circ} \rightsquigarrow V_1, C_1 \Rightarrow^* \mathsf{stream}^{r}\, T_1 \\ \alpha \notin V_1 \qquad V_1 \cup \{\alpha\}, (C_1 \cup \widehat{\alpha} \sqsubseteq r), \kappa, \Gamma \vdash P^{\circ} \rightsquigarrow V_2, C_2, P \Rightarrow^* u \\ V_2, C_2, \kappa, \Gamma(y_1 : T_1)(y_2 : \mathsf{stream}^{\alpha}\, T_1) \vdash N^{\circ} \Leftarrow P \rightsquigarrow V_3, C_3 \\ C_4 = C_3 \cup \infty \sqsubseteq \mathrm{SV}(N) \end{array}}{V, C, \Gamma \vdash \left(\begin{array}{l} \mathsf{case}_{P^{\circ}}\ x := M^{\circ} \\ \mathsf{of}\ \mathsf{cons}(y_1, y_2) \Rightarrow N^{\circ} \end{array} \right) \rightsquigarrow V_3, C_4 \Rightarrow P} \text{ (a-case-stream)}$$

$$\frac{\begin{array}{c} V, C, \Gamma \vdash M^{\circ} \rightsquigarrow V_1, C_1 \Rightarrow^* \mathsf{nat}^{r} \\ \alpha \notin V_1 \qquad V_1 \cup \{\alpha\}, (C_1 \cup \widehat{\alpha} \sqsubseteq r), \kappa, \Gamma(x : T) \vdash P^{\circ} \rightsquigarrow V_2, C_2, P \Rightarrow^* u \\ V_2, C_2, \kappa, \Gamma \vdash {N_1}^{\circ} \Leftarrow P\,[\mathsf{O}/x] \rightsquigarrow V_3, C_3 \\ V_3, C_3, \kappa, \Gamma(y : \mathsf{nat}^{\alpha}) \vdash {N_2}^{\circ} \Leftarrow P\,[\mathsf{S}\, y/x] \rightsquigarrow V_4, C_4 \\ C_5 = C_4 \cup \infty \sqsubseteq \mathrm{SV}(N_1, N_2) \end{array}}{V, C, \Gamma \vdash \left(\begin{array}{l} \mathsf{case}_{P^{\circ}}\ x := M^{\circ} \\ \mathsf{of}\ \mathsf{O} \Rightarrow {N_1}^{\circ}; \mathsf{S}\, y \Rightarrow {N_2}^{\circ} \end{array} \right) \rightsquigarrow V_4, C_5 \Rightarrow P\,[M/x]} \text{ (a-case-nat)}$$

$$\frac{\begin{array}{c} T^{\aleph} \equiv \Pi x{:}\mathsf{nat}^{k \cdot \alpha}.U \qquad \aleph\ \mathsf{SEMI}^{+}\ T^{\aleph} \qquad V, C, \Gamma \vdash |T^{\aleph}| \rightsquigarrow V_1, C_1, T' \Rightarrow^* u \\ \alpha \notin V_1 \qquad T^{\aleph} =_{\alpha} T' \rightsquigarrow C_{\alpha} \\ V_1 \cup \{\alpha\}, C_1 \cup C_{\alpha}, \Gamma(f : T') \vdash M^{\circ} \Leftarrow T'\,[\widehat{\alpha}/\alpha] \rightsquigarrow V_2, C_2 \\ \mathsf{RecCheck}(\alpha, V^{\neq}, C_2) = C_3 \end{array}}{V, C, \Gamma \vdash \mathsf{fix}\ f{:}T^{\aleph} := M^{\circ} \rightsquigarrow V_2, C_3 \Rightarrow T'} \text{ (a-fix)}$$

$$\frac{\begin{array}{c} T^{\aleph} \equiv \Pi \Delta.\mathsf{stream}^{\aleph}\, U \qquad \aleph\ \mathsf{SEMI}^{+}\ T^{\aleph} \\ V, C, \langle \alpha, \kappa \rangle, \Gamma \vdash |T^{\aleph}| \rightsquigarrow V_1, C_1, T' \Rightarrow^* u \\ \alpha \notin V_1 \qquad T^{\aleph} =_{\alpha} T' \rightsquigarrow C_{\alpha} \\ V_1, C_1, \kappa, \Gamma(f : T') \vdash M^{\circ} \Leftarrow T\,[\widehat{\alpha}/\alpha] \rightsquigarrow V_2, C_2 \\ \mathsf{RecCheck}(\alpha, V^{\neq}, C_2) = C_3 \end{array}}{V, C, \Gamma \vdash \mathsf{cofix}\ f{:}T^{\star} := M^{\circ} \rightsquigarrow V_2, C_3 \Rightarrow T'} \text{ (a-cofix)}$$

Fig. 5. Type-inference algorithm (continued)

Blanqui and Riba [13] consider a system with sized types and size constraints for rewrite systems with simply-typed inductive types, which can also give exact measure to quicksort. Due to the complexities of the constraint algebra, type checking is only semi-decidable.

Vasconcelos [29] uses sized types to analyze the space cost of functional programs. Using abstract interpretation techniques, his algorithm automatically infers size relations between inputs and outputs of a function, as well size constraints on stack and heap space. The resulting constraints are given in Presburger arithmetic. However, his system does not analyze the termination of functions. Nevertheless, it would be interesting to see if we could use this approach to infer the size annotations in (co-)fixpoint types (which would then be checked using the algorithm described in this paper).

Coinduction. The problems of defining coinductive types in dependent type theory were described by Giménez [16], who implemented coinduction in Coq. See also [5, 20]. While, as far as we know, the problems with coinduction in dependent type theory have not been completely solved, there are promising approaches [4, 5, 20, 27].

Endrullis et al. [14,15] describe a *data-oblivious* procedure for deciding productivity of stream definitions given as term rewriting systems. Data-oblivious refers to the fact that the procedure only looks at the number of elements consumed and produced for each rule and not the actual data—type-based termination is a form of data-oblivious analysis [15]. The analysis in [14] is able to recognize stream functions bounded by periodically-increasing (p-i) functions.

With linear sizes we can represent the type of stream functions described by p-i functions, at a loss of precision. For example, odd is described by the p-i function 1,1,2,2...; the period length is 2 and the number of elements produced in a period is 1. The type of odd, $\mathsf{stream}^{2\cdot s} \rightarrow \mathsf{stream}^{s}$, reflects this information. In general, a function with period length k, producing n elements in each period is described by the type $\mathsf{stream}^{k\cdot s} \rightarrow \mathsf{stream}^{n\cdot s}$.

Because we lose precision in the definition of p-i functions, we cannot directly type the definition of the Thue-Morse sequence given in Sect. 2.2. It would be interesting to integrate the results of [14, 15] to our setting in order to accept more definitions as productive.

5 Conclusions

We presented a type system for an extension of the Calculus of Constructions with two (co-)inductive types and linear sized types. We have proved that this system is logically consistent and strongly normalizing. We also presented a sound and complete size-inference algorithm that requires size annotations in (co-)recursive definitions. This work is part of a larger project whose objective is to integrate sized types in the Coq kernel.

There are still several issues to resolve in order to incorporate sized types in Coq. In this work we focused on aspects that pertain the Coq kernel. However,

Coq is large system and many of its components will be affected by the addition of sized types in the kernel. In particular, we need to understand how to handle incomplete proof terms and how to present size constraints to the user.

Acknowledgments. The author would like to thank the anonymous reviewers for their valuable comments and suggestions that helped to considerably improve this paper.

This publication was made possible by a JSREP grant (JSREP 4-004-1-001) from the Qatar National Research Fund (a member of The Qatar Foundation). The statements made herein are solely the responsibility of the author.

References

1. Abel, A.: A Polymorphic Lambda-Calculus with Sized Higher-Order Types. PhD thesis, Ludwig-Maximilians-Universität München (2006)
2. Abel, A.: Semi-continuous sized types and termination. Logical Methods in Computer Science 4(2) (2008)
3. Abel, A.: MiniAgda: Integrating sized and dependent types. In: Bove, A., Komendantskaya, E., Niqui, M. (eds.) PAR (2010)
4. Abel, A., Pientka, B.: Wellfounded recursion with copatterns: a unified approach to termination and productivity. In: Morrisett, G., Uustalu, T. (eds.) ICFP, pp. 185–196. ACM (2013)
5. Abel, A., Pientka, B., Thibodeau, D., Setzer, A.: Copatterns: programming infinite structures by observations. In: Giacobazzi, R., Cousot, R. (eds.) POPL, pp. 27–38. ACM (2013)
6. Altenkirch, T.: Constructions, Inductive Types and Strong Normalization. PhD thesis, University of Edinburgh (November 1993)
7. Barendregt, H.: Lambda calculi with types. In: Abramsky, S., Gabbay, D., Maibaum, T. (eds.) Handbook of Logic in Computer Science, pp. 117–309. Oxford Science Publications (1992)
8. Barthe, G., Frade, M.J., Giménez, E., Pinto, L., Uustalu, T.: Type-based termination of recursive definitions. Mathematical Structures in Computer Science 14(1), 97–141 (2004)
9. Barthe, G., Grégoire, B., Pastawski, F.: Practical inference for type-based termination in a polymorphic setting. In: Urzyczyn, P. (ed.) TLCA 2005. LNCS, vol. 3461, pp. 71–85. Springer, Heidelberg (2005)
10. Barthe, G., Grégoire, B., Pastawski, F.: $\mathrm{CIC}\widehat{}$: Type-based termination of recursive definitions in the Calculus of Inductive Constructions. In: Hermann, M., Voronkov, A. (eds.) LPAR 2006. LNCS (LNAI), vol. 4246, pp. 257–271. Springer, Heidelberg (2006)
11. Barthe, G., Grégoire, B., Riba, C.: Type-based termination with sized products. In: Kaminski, M., Martini, S. (eds.) CSL 2008. LNCS, vol. 5213, pp. 493–507. Springer, Heidelberg (2008)
12. Blanqui, F.: A type-based termination criterion for dependently-typed higher-order rewrite systems. In: van Oostrom, V. (ed.) RTA 2004. LNCS, vol. 3091, pp. 24–39. Springer, Heidelberg (2004)

13. Blanqui, F., Riba, C.: Combining typing and size constraints for checking the termination of higher-order conditional rewrite systems. In: Hermann, M., Voronkov, A. (eds.) LPAR 2006. LNCS (LNAI), vol. 4246, pp. 105–119. Springer, Heidelberg (2006)
14. Endrullis, J., Grabmayer, C., Hendriks, D.: Data-oblivious stream productivity. In: Cervesato, I., Veith, H., Voronkov, A. (eds.) LPAR 2008. LNCS (LNAI), vol. 5330, pp. 79–96. Springer, Heidelberg (2008)
15. Endrullis, J., Grabmayer, C., Hendriks, D., Isihara, A., Klop, J.W.: Productivity of stream definitions. Theor. Comput. Sci. 411(4-5), 765–782 (2010)
16. Giménez, E.: A Calculus of Infinite Constructions and its application to the verification of communicating systems. PhD thesis, Ecole Normale Supérieure de Lyon (1996)
17. Grégoire, B., Sacchini, J.L.: On strong normalization of the calculus of constructions with type-based termination. In: Fermüller, C.G., Voronkov, A. (eds.) LPAR-17. LNCS, vol. 6397, pp. 333–347. Springer, Heidelberg (2010)
18. Hermann, M., Voronkov, A. (eds.): LPAR 2006. LNCS (LNAI), vol. 4246. Springer, Heidelberg (2006)
19. Hughes, J., Pareto, L., Sabry, A.: Proving the correctness of reactive systems using sized types. In: POPL, pp. 410–423 (1996)
20. McBride, C.: Let's see how things unfold: Reconciling the infinite with the intensional (extended abstract). In: Kurz, A., Lenisa, M., Tarlecki, A. (eds.) CALCO 2009. LNCS, vol. 5728, pp. 113–126. Springer, Heidelberg (2009)
21. Norell, U.: Towards a practical programming language based on dependent type theory. PhD thesis, Chalmers University of Technology (2007)
22. Pareto, L.: Types for Crash Prevention. PhD thesis, Chalmers University of Technology (2000)
23. Pugh, W.: The omega test: a fast and practical integer programming algorithm for dependence analysis. In: Martin, J.L. (ed.) SC, pp. 4–13. IEEE Computer Society/ACM (1991)
24. Sacchini, J.L.: On Type-Based Termination and Dependent Pattern Matching in the Calculus of Inductive Constructions. PhD thesis, École Nationale Supérieure des Mines de Paris (2011)
25. Sacchini, J.L.: Type-based productivity of stream definitions in the calculus of constructions. In: LICS, pp. 233–242. IEEE Computer Society (2013)
26. Sacchini, J.L.: Linear sized types in the calculus of constructions. Technical Report CMU-CS-14-104, Carnegie Mellon University (2014)
27. Setzer, A.: Coalgebras as types determined by their elimination rules. In: Dybjer, P., Lindström, S., Palmgren, E., Sundholm, G. (eds.) Epistemology versus Ontology. Logic, Epistemology, and the Unity of Science, vol. 27, pp. 351–369. Springer (2012)
28. The Coq Development Team. The Coq Reference Manual, version 8.4 (2012)
29. Pedro, B.: Vasconcelos. Space cost analysis using sized types. PhD thesis, University of St. Andrews (2008)

Dynamic Programming via Thinning and Incrementalization

Akimasa Morihata[1], Masato Koishi[2], and Atsushi Ohori[1]

[1] Research Institute of Electrical Communication, Tohoku University, Sendai, Japan
[2] Toshiba Solutions Corporation, Kawasaki, Japan

Abstract. We demonstrate that it is useful to combine two independently studied methods, thinning and incrementalization, to develop programs that use dynamic programming. While dynamic programming is a fundamental algorithmic pattern, its development is often difficult for average programmers. There are several methods for systematically developing dynamic programming from plain problem descriptions by program transformations. We show that by combining two known methods, thinning and incrementalization, we can systematically derive efficient dynamic-programming implementations from high-level descriptions. The derivations cannot be achieved by using only one of them. We illustrate our approach with the 0-1 knapsack problem, the longest common subsequence problem, and association rule mining from numeric data.

1 Introduction

Dynamic programming is a fundamental algorithmic pattern. It avoids unnecessary recomputations by using tables that store calculated values and filling the tables in a certain order. A standard approach to designing the tables is to reveal the *principle of optimality*, namely, how the optimal solution can be composed from the optimal solutions of subproblems. However, this standard approach is often too difficult for average programmers. It is desirable that plain programs written with little care about the principle of optimality be systematically transformed to programs that use dynamic programming. Many methods [1–14] have been proposed to achieve this goal.

This paper is also about systematic developments of dynamic programming. We do not introduce any new methods but rather propose combining two independently studied methods: *thinning* and *incrementalization*. Thinning, proposed by Bird and de Moor [2], transforms a problem description specified by a generator, which enumerates all solution candidates, and a criterion of the best one, to a program that does not consider most candidates. It can mechanically derive dynamic programming for a large class of problems [6, 3, 12]. Incrementalization [15–18, 7, 9] improves efficiency by caching and reusing values calculated in the previous iterations. Liu and Stoller [7, 9] demonstrated that it is useful for developing efficient table-filling computation patterns for dynamic programming. To the best of the authors' knowledge, there was no study on their cooperation.

M. Codish and E. Sumii (Eds.): FLOPS 2014, LNCS 8475, pp. 186–202, 2014.

Our major contribution is to point out that thinning and incrementalization complement each other for developing dynamic programming. On one hand, thinning is useful for revealing the principle of optimality from trivial problem descriptions; however, its outputs are rather high-level and do not immediately lead to efficient implementation. On the other hand, incrementalization helps us to design the tables for dynamic programming if the principle of optimality is exposed in the input program. Therefore, applying incrementalization after thinning brings efficient dynamic programming from high-level descriptions.

We demonstrate the effectiveness of our approach through the rest of this paper. After outlining our approach in Section 3, we illustrate, in Section 4, our approach with the 0-1 knapsack problem [19]. Our approach leads to a sophisticated algorithm by de Moor [4]. In Section 5, we apply our approach to the longest common subsequence problem [19] and derive an $O(n^2)$-time implementation. We deal with a more complex problem, association-rule mining from two-dimensional numeric data [22], in Section 6. For some instances, our approach results in $O(n^3)$-time algorithms, which are as fast as those developed by Fukuda et al. [22]. In Section 7, we compare ours to thinning and incrementalization and discuss the possibility of mechanizing our approach. In Section 8, we discuss related work.

2 Preliminary

We use Haskell [23] with apparent syntactic sugars for describing programs. We overload *map* and *filter* to manipulate sets. We use $a \mathbin{\ddot{:}} x$ as a shorthand for *map* $(a\ :)\ x$. For an associative and commutative operator $(\oplus) :: A \to A \to A$ and a set $x :: 2^A$, we abbreviate $\bigoplus_{a \in x} a$ to $\bigoplus x$. We regard $\bigoplus \emptyset$ as the unit of $\oplus$.

A binary relation $\preceq$ is a *preorder* if it is transitive, $(a \preceq b \wedge b \preceq c) \Rightarrow a \preceq c$, and reflective, $a \preceq a$. A preorder $\preceq$ on a set A is total if either $a \preceq b$ or $b \preceq a$ holds for any $a, b \in A$. On a preorder $\preceq$, $(:)$ is said to be *monotone* if $x \preceq y \Rightarrow (a : x) \preceq (a : y)$ and *increasing* if $x \preceq a : x$. For a preorder $\preceq$ on A and a function $f :: B \to A$, $\preceq_f$ is a preorder on B such that $a \preceq_f b \iff f\ a \preceq f\ b$. For preorders $\preceq$ and $\ll$, a preorder $\preceq \cap \ll$ is defined as $a\ (\preceq \cap \ll)\ b \iff (a \preceq b \wedge a \ll b)$. We may write the converses of $\preceq$ and $\ll$ as $\succeq$ and $\gg$, respectively.

We use $max_{\preceq} :: 2^A \to 2^A$ to extract all *maximal* solution candidates on the preorder $\preceq$. For simplicity, we assume that no two have the same priority, i.e., $\forall a, b.\ a \neq b \Rightarrow \neg(a \preceq b \wedge b \preceq a)$. This assumption is not crucial because for all examples in this paper arbitrarily choosing one among equivalent solution candidates leads to one of the optimal solutions. Under the assumption, $max_{\preceq}$ is defined by $max_{\preceq}\ x = \{a \mid a \in x \wedge (\forall b \in (x \setminus \{a\}).\ \neg(a \preceq b))\}$.

2.1 Thinning

Thinning replaces an enumeration of all solution candidates with a more efficient one that touches only useful ones. We use the following variant, which slightly generalizes the one formalized by Morihata [12]. It squeezes the pruning operations, *max* and *filter*, into the candidate enumeration step; then, *gen* retains only those that are feasible and maximal on $\preceq \cap \gg_h$.

Theorem 1. *For* $gen :: \forall\beta.\ (\beta \to \beta \to \beta) \to (A \to \beta \to \beta) \to \beta$,

$$\begin{aligned}&max_{\preceq}\ (filter\ p\ (gen\ (\cup)\ (\tilde{:})\ \{[]\})) =\\ &\quad max_{\preceq}\ (gen\ (\lambda x\ y \to max_{\preceq\cap\gg_h}\ (x \cup y))\\ &\qquad\qquad (\lambda a\ x \to max_{\preceq\cap\gg_h}\ (filter\ p\ (a\,\tilde{:}\,x)))\ (filter\ p\ \{[]\})),\end{aligned}$$

provided that $\preceq$ *and* $\ll$ *are preorders,* $(:)$ *is monotone on* $\preceq$ *and moreover monotone and increasing on* $\ll_h$*, and* p *satisfies either* $p\ x = h\ x \ll c$ *or* $p\ x = \neg(c \ll h\ x)$. □

Theorem 1 requires two conditions. First, the candidate enumeration should be specified by a function of a certain polymorphic type. This requirement guarantees that *gen* appropriately captures the value flow for the candidate enumeration. The second requirement is that the criterion of the best candidate is characterized by preorders satisfying certain properties. It guarantees that discarded candidates will not lead to better ones.

2.2 Incrementalization

Incrementalization improves efficiency by reusing values that have been calculated in the previous iterations. For example, from a quadratic-time suffix sum program, $ssum\ (a : x) = sum\ (a : x) : ssum\ x$, incrementalization derives a liner-time equivalent, $ssum\ (a : x) = \mathbf{let}\ r = ssum\ x\ \mathbf{in}\ (a + head\ r) : r$; here $head\ (ssum\ x)$ is reused so as to calculate $sum\ (a : x)$. We will use the following incrementalization rule, which is an instance of known methods [15, 17, 18, 7, 9].

Theorem 2. *For an associative and commutative operator* $\oplus$ *and a series of sets* $s_1 \subseteq \cdots \subseteq s_n$*, the following equation holds.*

$$\begin{aligned}[\textstyle\bigoplus s_n, \bigoplus s_{n-1}, \ldots, \bigoplus s_1] &= foldr\ f\ [\textstyle\bigoplus s_1]\ [s_n \setminus s_{n-1}, \ldots, s_3 \setminus s_2, s_2 \setminus s_1]\\ &\quad \mathbf{where}\ f\ s\ (r : rs) = ((\textstyle\bigoplus s) \oplus r) : r : rs\end{aligned}$$ □

Theorem 2 states that if we calculate $\bigoplus s_1, \ldots, \bigoplus s_n$ in this order, it is sufficient to deal with $s_i \setminus s_{i-1}$ to calculate each $\bigoplus s_i$ $(i \geq 2)$.

3 Combining Thinning and Incrementalization

Figure 1 outlines our approach, which consists of two major steps.

1. Given a naive enumerate-and-choose-style implementation, we apply thinning to it. The resulted program calculates optimal solutions of subproblems only.

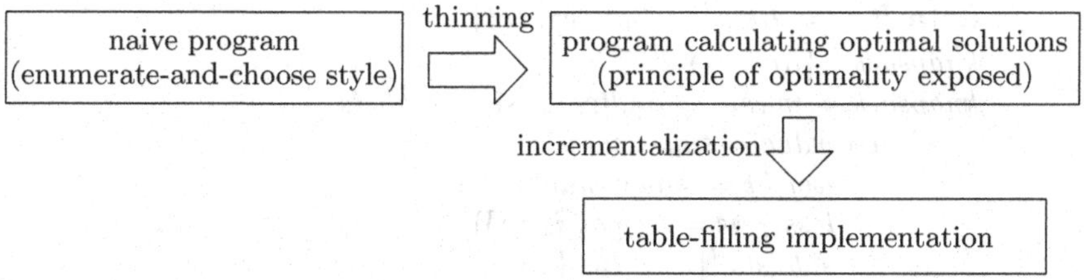

Fig. 1. Outline of our approach

2. Then, we apply incrementalization so as to derive efficient implementation for calculating the optimal solutions of the subproblems. The order of iterations is important for incrementalization. An appropriate order is often implied by the preorder that characterizes the feasibility.

To understand the effect of our approach, it would be helpful to compare it with the standard, textbook approach to dynamic programming. For example, [20] addresses the following three as the keys to dynamic programming:

1. *There are only a polynomial number of subproblems.*
2. *The solution to the original problem can be easily computed from solutions to the subproblems. ([...])*
3. *There is a natural ordering on subproblems from "smallest" to "largest," together with an easy-to-compute recurrence ([...]) that allows one to determine the solutions to a subproblem from the solution to some number of smaller subproblems.*

The first one is concerned with efficiency. We neglect it here. The second is often called the "principle of optimality". The third requires an ordering for efficiently calculating the optimal solutions of the subproblems; the order is often realized as the order to fill the table entries used to implement dynamic programming.

In our approach, thinning and incrementalization respectively help us to deal with the second and the third points. Thinning enables us to expose the principle of optimality. Then, incrementalization helps us to find an appropriate order.

4 0-1 Knapsack Problem

In the following three sections, we illustrate our approach. The first example is the 0-1 knapsack problem [19]: find the most valuable set of items among those whose weights are no more than a limit, say W.

Developing a Naive Program: The first step is to provide an enumerate-and-choose-style implementation to the problem. The following *knapsack* enumerates all possible item sets, filters those heavier than the limit, and then extracts the most valuable one.

$$
\begin{array}{l}
\textbf{data}\ \mathit{Item} = \mathit{Item}\{v :: \mathit{Int}, w :: \mathit{Int}\} \\
\mathit{knapsack} :: [\mathit{Item}] \to 2^{[\mathit{Item}]} \\
\mathit{knapsack} = \mathit{max}_{\leq_{\mathit{value}}} \circ \mathit{filter}\ \mathit{less}_W \circ \mathit{sublists} \\
\quad \textbf{where}\ \mathit{value} = \mathit{sum} \circ \mathit{map}\ v \\
\qquad\qquad \mathit{weight} = \mathit{sum} \circ \mathit{map}\ w \\
\qquad\qquad \mathit{less}_W\ \mathit{is} = \mathit{weight}\ \mathit{is} \leq W \\
\qquad\qquad \mathit{sublists}\ [\,] \qquad\quad = \{[\,]\} \\
\qquad\qquad \mathit{sublists}\ (a : x) = \textbf{let}\ r = \mathit{sublists}\ x\ \textbf{in}\ r \cup (a \mathbin{\tilde{:}} r)
\end{array}
$$

Thinning: We replace *sublists* with a more efficient one by using Theorem 1. The theorem requires two premises. First, the candidate enumeration should be specified by a function of a certain polymorphic type. For all examples in this paper, we obtain such polymorphic implementations by just abstracting all set/list constructing operators by using the corresponding parameters. For instance, consider *genSublists* defined below.

$$
\begin{array}{l}
\mathit{genSublists}\ [\,]\ u\ s\ e \qquad\ = e \\
\mathit{genSublists}\ (a : x)\ u\ s\ e = \textbf{let}\ r = \mathit{genSublists}\ x\ u\ s\ e\ \textbf{in}\ r\ `u`\ (a\ `s`\ r)
\end{array}
$$

Apparently $\mathit{sublists}\ x = \mathit{genSublists}\ x\ (\cup)\ (\tilde{:})\ \{[\,]\}$; moreover, $\mathit{genSublists}\ x$ has the polymorphic type. The second requirement is that the criterion of the best candidate is characterized by preorders satisfying certain properties. It is not difficult to see that $\leq_{value}$ and $\leq_{weight}$ satisfy the required properties. Thus, we can apply Theorem 1 to *knapsack*.

$$
\begin{array}{ll}
 & \mathit{knapsack} \\
= & \{\ \text{definition of } \mathit{knapsack}\ \} \\
 & \mathit{max}_{\leq_{\mathit{value}}} \circ \mathit{filter}\ \mathit{less}_W \circ \mathit{sublists} \\
= & \{\ \text{Theorem 1, where } \preceq\ =\ \leq_{\mathit{value}} \cap \geq_{\mathit{weight}}\ \} \\
 & \mathit{max}_{\leq_{\mathit{value}}} \circ \mathit{candidates} \\
 & \quad \textbf{where}\ \mathit{candidates}\ [\,] \qquad\ = \{[\,]\} \\
 & \qquad\qquad \mathit{candidates}\ (a : x) = \textbf{let}\ r = \mathit{candidates}\ x \\
 & \qquad\qquad\qquad\qquad\qquad\qquad \textbf{in}\ \mathit{max}_{\preceq}\ (r \cup \mathit{max}_{\preceq}\ (\mathit{filter}\ \mathit{less}_W\ (a \mathbin{\tilde{:}} r)))
\end{array}
$$

A Digression: Exposed Principle of Optimality: It is worth noting that Theorem 1 reveals the principle of optimality: each result of $\mathit{max}_{\preceq}$ is the most valuable among those that are composed from optimal solutions of subproblems and are not heavier than a certain threshold. More formally, we can regard the derived program as essentially denoting the following recurrence equation that exposes the principle of optimality, where $\mathit{opt}_{k,x}$ denotes the most valuable subset of x whose weight is no more than k and $a \oplus b = \textbf{if}\ a \leq_{value}\ b\ \textbf{then}\ b\ \textbf{else}\ a$.

$$
\mathit{opt}_{k,a:x} = \bigoplus(\{\mathit{opt}_{k',x} \mid k' \leq k\} \cup \{a : \mathit{opt}_{k',x} \mid w\ a + k' \leq w\})
$$

It is nontrivial to formally extract the above recurrence equation from the program; yet, this view is helpful to understand the effect of our approach.

Incrementalization: Although the derived program is much better than the original, it is not satisfactory. First, *candidates* repeatedly invokes auxiliary functions, *weight* and *value*, for each candidate. We do not tackle this issue because the standard and simple solutions, such as caching calculated *value* and *weight* values, are sufficient. It is worth nothing that incrementalization can be used for streamlining this. In the rest of this paper, we regard such auxiliary functions as being constant time.

Second, it is nontrivial to efficiently implement $max_{\preceq}$. The direct implementation of the definition of *max* takes time quadratic to its input size. The following reasoning shows that $max_{\preceq}$ is in the domain of Theorem 2.

$$\begin{aligned}
& max_{\preceq}\ iss \\
= & \ \{ \text{ definitions of } max \text{ and } \preceq \} \\
& \{is \mid is \in iss, (\forall is' \in (iss \setminus \{is\}).\ (is' \leq_{weight} is) \Rightarrow \neg(is \leq_{value} is'))\} \\
= & \ \{ \text{ assumption: no two item sets are equally valuable } \} \\
& \{\bigoplus\{is' \mid is' \in iss, is' \leq_{weight} is\} \mid is \in iss\}
\end{aligned}$$

The preorder that characterizes the feasibility, $\leq_{weight}$, leads to a chain of subset relations that Theorem 2 requires. For $iss = \{is_1, \ldots, is_k\}$, where $is_1 \leq_{weight} \cdots \leq_{weight} is_k$, let $s_j = \{is \mid is \in iss, is \leq_{weight} is_j\}$. Then, $s_j = \{is_1, \ldots, is_j\}$ and, thus, $s_1 \subseteq \cdots \subseteq s_k$. Therefore, Theorem 2 brings the following implementation, which calculates the optimal candidates from lighter ones.

$$\begin{aligned}
max_{\preceq}\ iss &= Data.Set.fromList\ (foldr\ f\ [is_1]\ [is_k, \ldots, is_2]) \\
\textbf{where}\ & f\ is\ (r : rs) = (is \oplus r) : r : rs
\end{aligned}$$

Implementing Candidate Sets: The derived implementation of $max_{\preceq}$ is linear time if the input is sorted by weights. Although it is possible to achieve this by, as the usual dynamic programming, implementing the candidate set with a table from weights to candidates, it is more natural to use an ordered list. For this implementation, it is sufficient to use, instead of $(\cup)$, the *merge* operation used in the merge sort; we do not need to modify *filter* and $(\widehat{:})$ because they preserve the order.

The obtained implementation is essentially the one introduced by de Moor [4].

Computational Complexity: Our implementation is an $O(nW)$-time algorithm, where n is the number of given items, because each recursive step of *candidates* takes time proportional to the number of candidates, which is $O(W)$. The space complexity is also $O(nW)$. While the asymptotic complexities are the same as those of the standard table-filling dynamic programming, it is faster if the number of candidates is actually much less than W.

5 Longest Common Subsequence Problem

We derived an efficient implementation for the 0-1 knapsack problem. Keen readers may have noticed that the derivation uses few properties specific to the problem, and thus, other problems can be similarly dealt with. One such instance is the longest common subsequence problem [19]. The problem is to find the longest (possibly non-consecutive) common sublists of given two lists. For example, the longest common subsequence of $[a, a, b, c, b]$ and $[a, c, c, b, a]$ is $[a, c, b]$. In this example, we assume that the inputs are in fact arrays, and therefore, even the last elements can be accessed in O(1) time.

Developing a Naive Program: The following enumerate-and-choose-style function, *lcs*, expresses the problem.

$$\begin{array}{l} \mathit{lcs}\ x\ y = \mathit{max}_{\leq_{\mathit{length}}}\ (\mathit{filter}\ (\mathit{isSub}\ x)\ (\mathit{sublists}\ y)) \\ \quad \textbf{where}\ \mathit{isSub}\ x\ r = \mathit{elim}\ x\ r \neq \mathit{Nothing} \\ \qquad\quad \mathit{elim}\ x\ r = \mathit{foldr}\ \mathit{step}\ (\mathit{Just}\ x)\ r \\ \qquad\quad \mathit{step}\ a\ (\mathit{Just}\ (z +\!\!+ [b])) = \textbf{if}\ a \equiv b\ \textbf{then}\ \mathit{Just}\ z\ \textbf{else}\ \mathit{step}\ a\ (\mathit{Just}\ z) \\ \qquad\quad \mathit{step}\ \_\ \_ \qquad\qquad\qquad\ = \mathit{Nothing} \end{array}$$

Thinning: Theorem 1 requires us to express *isSub* by a preorder, say $\ll$. Note that (:) should be increasing on $\ll_{\mathit{elim}\,x}$, namely, $\mathit{elim}\ x$ should yield larger results for longer lists. Therefore, it is natural to let $\mathit{Just}\ (x +\!\!+ z) \ll \mathit{Just}\ x \ll \mathit{Nothing}$; then, $\mathit{isSub}\ x\ r = r \ll_{\mathit{elim}\,x} \mathit{Just}\ []$. It is not difficult to see that (:) is monotone and increasing on $\ll_{\mathit{elim}\,x}$. Writing *elim* by *foldr* helps us to confirm these properties; see [12] for more discussions. Now, we can use Theorem 1.

$$\begin{array}{ll} & \mathit{lcs}\ x \\ = & \{\ \text{definition of } \mathit{lcs}\text{; note that } \mathit{isSub}\ x\ r = r \ll_{\mathit{elim}\,x} \mathit{Just}\ []\ \} \\ & \mathit{max}_{\leq_{\mathit{length}}} \circ \mathit{filter}\ (\lambda r \to r \ll_{\mathit{elim}\,x} \mathit{Just}\ []) \circ \mathit{sublists} \\ = & \{\ \text{Theorem 1, where } \preceq\ =\ \leq_{\mathit{length}} \cap \gg_{\mathit{elim}\,x}\ \} \\ & \mathit{max}_{\leq_{\mathit{length}}} \circ \mathit{candidates} \\ & \quad \textbf{where}\ \mathit{candidates}\ [] \qquad\ = \{[]\} \\ & \qquad\quad\ \ \mathit{candidates}\ (a : y) = \textbf{let}\ r = \mathit{candidates}\ y \\ & \qquad\qquad\qquad\qquad\qquad\quad\ \ \textbf{in}\ \mathit{max}_{\preceq}\ (r \cup \mathit{max}_{\preceq}\ (\mathit{filter}\ (\mathit{isSub}\ x)\ (a \tilde{:} r))) \end{array}$$

Incrementalize $max_{\preceq}$: We incrementalize $\mathit{max}_{\preceq}$ by using the same approach as that for the 0-1 knapsack problem. Let $rs = \{r_1, \ldots, r_k\}$, where $r_1 \ll_{\mathit{elim}\,x} \cdots \ll_{\mathit{elim}\,x} r_k$.

$$\begin{array}{ll} & \mathit{max}_{\preceq}\ rs \\ = & \{\ \text{definition of } \mathit{max}_{\preceq}\text{, where } a \oplus b = \textbf{if}\ a \leq_{\mathit{length}} b\ \textbf{then}\ b\ \textbf{else}\ a\ \} \\ & \{\bigoplus\{r' \mid r' \in rs, r' \ll_{\mathit{elim}\,x} r\} \mid r \in rs\} \\ = & \{\ \text{Theorem 2}\ \} \\ & \mathit{Data.Set.fromList}\ (\mathit{foldr}\ f\ [r_1]\ [r_k, r_{k-1}, \ldots, r_2]) \\ & \qquad \textbf{where}\ f\ r'\ (r : rs) = (r' \oplus r) : r : rs \end{array}$$

Further Incrementalization: The derived program is not efficient enough. For each recursive call of *candidate*, we need to calculate $\{\mathit{elim}\ x\ (a : r) \mid r \in rs\}$

where *rs* is the current candidate set. Even if we memorize *elim* x r, each *step* (and thereby *elim*) may take time proportional to the length of x. We would like to perform *step* in O(1) time.

Further incrementalization removes this inefficiency. Observe that what we need to calculate is $\{step\ a\ (Just\ x_k) \mid 0 \leq k \leq n\}$ where $x = [b_0, \ldots, b_{n-1}]$ and $x_k = [b_0, \ldots, b_{k-1}]$. A rule similar to Theorem 2 enables us to incrementalize this computation as follows. The rule, Theorem 3, is shown in Appendix.

$$\begin{array}{l}[step\ a\ (Just\ x_k) \mid n \geq k \geq 0] = foldr\ f_a\ [Nothing]\ [n-1, \ldots, 0] \\ \quad \textbf{where}\ f_a\ i\ (r : rs) = (\textbf{if}\ a \equiv b_i\ \textbf{then}\ Just\ x_{i-1}\ \textbf{else}\ r) : r : rs\end{array}$$

Caching this result enables us to calculate $\{elim\ x\ (a : r) \mid r \in rs\}$ in time proportional to the size of *rs*. We omit the details due to space limitations.

Implementing Candidate Sets: This step is exactly the same as the previous. It is appropriate to implement the candidate set by using a list whose elements are sorted in accordance with $\ll_{elim\ x}$.

Computational Complexity: Let n and m be the lengths of x and y, respectively. Since $\ll_{elim\ x}$ categorizes the candidates into $n + 1$ equivalence classes, it is sufficient to consider O(n) candidates in the computation of *candidates*. Function *candidates* consists of O(m) recursions. In total, the algorithm runs in time O(nm). The space complexity is also O(nm). These are the same as those of the textbook algorithm [19].

6 Association-Rule Mining from Numeric Data

Given a collection of elements, which are characterized by a set of attributes, association rule mining [24] finds correlations between attribute values. For example, it may reveal that most customers who buy diapers buy beer as well. If some attributes have numeric values, it is reasonable to consider ranges. For example, it would be useful to know ranges of the ages and/or salaries that most customers fall in. Fukuda et al. [21, 22] formalized such cases as problems of locating the most interesting subregion of the solution space and proposed efficient algorithms for several instances. We try to deal with them in our approach.

6.1 Formalizing Problems

We consider the following situation. We have a two-dimensional rectangular solution space divided into a grid consisting of $m \times n$ blocks. We capture the structure by using a list of m lists (rows) of length n. Our objective is to locate its most interesting subregion. Although several criteria can be thought of, here we consider finding the maximum-sum connected subregion whose lower parts are wider, as shown in Figure 2. This problem is intended as a simpler variant of the

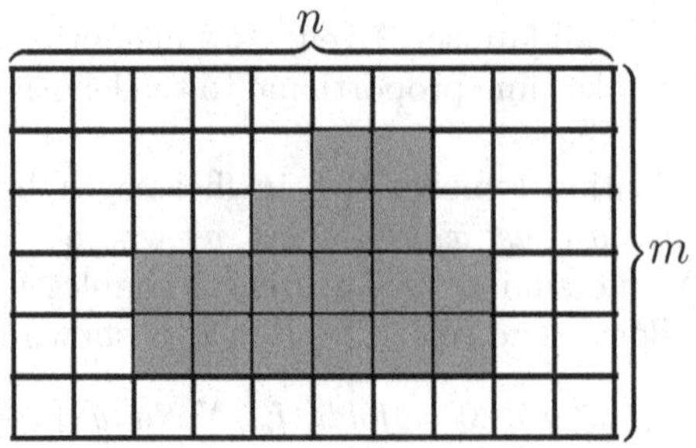

Fig. 2. Connected subregion whose lower parts are wider; grey grids are selected, whereas white ones not

problem of finding the maximum-sum rectilinear convex subregion studied by Fukuda et al. [22]. We will discuss the capability of other criteria in Section 6.7.

We express a subregion by using a list each of whose elements is a consecutive sublist of a row. A sublist of a row is a triple of the following type.

$$\textbf{type } \mathit{Sublist} = ([\mathit{Int}], \mathit{Int}, \mathit{Int})$$

Given a row x, we denote by x_{i-j} a sublist $(\tilde{x}, i, j)$ such that $\tilde{x}$ consists of elements come from the i-th to the j-th positions in x. For example, for $x = [a_0, a_1, a_2, a_3, a_4]$, $x_{2-3} = ([a_2, a_3], 2, 3)$. Since each sublist consists of essentially two pointers, we assume that x_{i-j} is constant space and obtained from x in O(1) time.

The following program formulates the problem. Function *subregions* enumerates all candidates by selecting a sublist for each row of each consecutive subset of rows; *filter feasible* eliminates those that violate the requirement, and then, $max_{\leq_{score}}$ extracts the maximum-sum subregion.

$$
\begin{array}{l}
\mathit{locate} :: [[\mathit{Int}]] \to [\mathit{Sublist}] \\
\mathit{locate} = \mathit{max}_{\leq_{score}} \circ \mathit{filter\ feasible} \circ \mathit{subregions} \\
\quad \textbf{where } \mathit{subregions\ xs} = \textbf{let } (r_1, r_2) = \mathit{rows\ xs} \textbf{ in } r_1 \cup r_2 \\
\qquad\quad \mathit{rows}\ [] \qquad\quad = (\emptyset, \{[]\}) \\
\qquad\quad \mathit{rows}\ (x : xs) = \textbf{let } (r_1, r_2) = \mathit{rows\ xs} \\
\qquad\qquad\qquad\qquad\quad \textbf{in } (r_1 \cup r_2, \{[]\} \cup \bigcup \{c \,\tilde{:}\, r_2 \mid c \in \mathit{cols}\ x\}) \\
\qquad\quad \mathit{cols}\ x = \{x_{i-j} \mid 0 \leq i \leq j \leq n-1\} \\
\qquad\quad \mathit{score} = \mathit{sum} \circ \mathit{map}\ (\lambda(x, i, j) \to \mathit{sum}\ x) \\
\qquad\quad \mathit{feasible\ xs} = \mathit{check\ xs} \neq \mathit{Bad} \\
\qquad\quad \mathit{check} = \mathit{foldr\ step\ None} \\
\qquad\quad \mathit{step}\ (\_, i, j)\ (W(i', j')) \mid \neg(i \leq i' \leq j' \leq j) = \mathit{Bad} \\
\qquad\quad \mathit{step}\ (\_, i, j)\ \_ \qquad\qquad\qquad\qquad\quad\ = W(i, j)
\end{array}
$$

6.2 Thinning

The first step of our derivation is to apply Theorem 1. As in the case of the longest common subsequence problem, we characterize *feasible* by using a preorder $\ll$

so that *check* yields larger results for longer lists: $None \ll b$, $a \ll Bad$, and $W(i', j') \ll W(i, j) \iff i \leq i' \leq j' \leq j$. The monotonicity and the increasing properties are not difficult to check. Now, we apply Theorem 1.

$$\begin{array}{ll}
& locate \\
= & \{\text{ definitions }\} \\
& max_{\leq_{score}} \circ filter\ (\lambda xs \rightarrow \neg(Bad \ll check\ xs)) \circ subregions \\
= & \{\text{ Theorem 1; let } \preceq\, = \,\leq_{score} \cap \gg_{check} \text{ and } x \sqcup y = max_{\preceq}\ (x \cup y)\ \} \\
& max_{\leq_{score}} \circ candidates \\
& \quad \textbf{where} \\
& \quad\ candidates\ xs = \textbf{let}\ (r_1, r_2) = crows\ xs\ \textbf{in}\ r_1 \sqcup r_2 \\
& \quad\ crows\ [\,] \qquad\quad = (\emptyset, \{[\,]\}) \\
& \quad\ crows\ (x : xs)\ = \textbf{let}\ (r_1, r_2) = crows\ xs \\
& \qquad\qquad\qquad\qquad\ \textbf{in}\ (r_1 \sqcup r_2, \\
& \qquad\qquad\qquad\qquad\qquad \{[\,]\} \sqcup (\bigsqcup\{max_{\preceq}\ (filter\ feasible\ (c\,\tilde{:}\,r_2)) \mid c \in cols\ x\}))
\end{array}$$

Since $\ll$ categorizes solution candidates into $O(n^2)$ equivalence classes, only $O(n^2)$ candidates are considered in *candidates*.

6.3 Elaboration before Incrementalization

Before deriving an implementation of $max_{\preceq}$, we discuss another source of inefficiency. In $\bigsqcup\{max_{\preceq}\ (filter\ feasible\ (c\,\tilde{:}\,r_2)) \mid c \in cols\ x\}$, $O(n^4)$ candidates are considered if the size of r_2 is $O(n^2)$. However, because $check\ (x_{i-j} : r) \neq Bad$ if and only if $check\ r \ll W(i, j)$, it is unnecessary to consider every combination of x_{i-j} and r.

The reasoning below formalizes this observation. We use the following notations. For a set of candidates, rs, let $rs|_v = \{r \mid r \in rs, check\ r = v\}$ and $rs|_v^{\ll} = \{r \mid r \in rs, check\ r \ll v\}$. Let $a \oplus b = \textbf{if}\ a \leq_{score} b\ \textbf{then}\ b\ \textbf{else}\ a$.

$$\begin{array}{ll}
& \bigsqcup\{max_{\preceq}\ (filter\ feasible\ (c\,\tilde{:}\,r_2)) \mid c \in cols\ x\} \\
= & \{\text{ unfolding } feasible \text{ and } cols\ \} \\
& \bigsqcup\{max_{\preceq}\{x_{i-j} : r \mid r \in r_2, \neg(Bad \ll check\ (x_{i-j} : r))\} \mid 0 \leq i \leq j \leq n-1\} \\
= & \{\ check\ (x_{i-j} : r) \text{ results in either } Bad \text{ or } W(i,j)\ \} \\
& \{\bigoplus\{x_{i-j} : r \mid r \in r_2, check\ (x_{i-j} : r) = W(i,j)\} \mid 0 \leq i \leq j \leq n-1\} \\
= & \{\ check\ (x_{i-j} : r) = W(i,j) \text{ iff } check\ r \ll W(i,j)\ \} \\
& \{\bigoplus\{x_{i-j} : r \mid r \in r_2|_{W(i,j)}^{\ll}\} \mid 0 \leq i \leq j \leq n-1\} \\
= & \{\text{ monotonicity }\} \\
& \{x_{i-j} : (\bigoplus r_2|_{W(i,j)}^{\ll}) \mid 0 \leq i \leq j \leq n-1\}
\end{array}$$

Therefore, we would like to develop efficient implementation of $\{\bigoplus r_2|_{W(i,j)}^{\ll} \mid 0 \leq i \leq j \leq n-1\}$. Note that this computation also appears in $max_{\preceq}$, since $max_{\preceq}\ rs = \{\bigoplus rs|_{W(i,j)}^{\ll} \mid 0 \leq i \leq j \leq n-1\} \cup \{\bigoplus rs, \bigoplus rs|_{None}\}$.

6.4 Incrementalization

Let us incrementalize $\{\bigoplus rs|_{W(i,j)}^{\ll} \mid 0 \leq i \leq j \leq n-1\}$. Unfortunately, we cannot immediately use Theorem 2 because $rs|_{W(i,j)}^{\ll}$ is incomparable to $rs|_{W(i',j')}^{\ll}$ if

$i < i' < j < j'$. Therefore, we look for a subset of $\{rs|^{\ll}_{W(i,j)} \mid 0 \le i \le j \le n-1\}$ for which Theorem 2 is applicable. In fact, $rs|^{\ll}_{W(i,i)} \subseteq \cdots \subseteq rs|^{\ll}_{W(i,n-1)}$ holds.

$$\begin{aligned}
& rs|^{\ll}_{W(i,j+1)} \setminus rs|^{\ll}_{W(i,j)} \\
= & \ \{ \text{ definition of } \ll\text{; note that both include } rs|_{None}. \ \} \\
& (\bigcup\{rs|_{W(i',j')} \mid i \le i' \le j' \le j+1\}) \setminus (\bigcup\{rs|_{W(i',j')} \mid i \le i' \le j' \le j\}) \\
= & \ \{ \text{ simplify } \} \\
& \bigcup\{rs|_{W(i',j+1)} \mid i \le i' \le j+1\}
\end{aligned}$$

We apply Theorem 2 for this kind of series of sets. In the following, a set $arr = \{v_1 \mapsto w_1, \ldots, v_k \mapsto w_k\}$ denotes an association array, i.e., map, such that $arr\ v_i = w_i$. The range of *arr* is denoted by *range arr*.

$$\begin{aligned}
& \{\textstyle\bigoplus rs|^{\ll}_{W(i,j)} \mid 0 \le i \le j \le n-1\} \\
= & \ \{ \text{ case analysis on } i \ \} \\
& \bigcup\{\{\textstyle\bigoplus rs|^{\ll}_{W(i,j)} \mid i \le j \le n-1\} \mid 0 \le i \le n-1\} \\
= & \ \{ \text{ Theorem 2; we abbreviate } \mathit{Data.Set.fromList} \text{ to } \mathit{toSet} \ \} \\
& \bigcup \left\{ \begin{array}{l} \mathit{toSet}\ (\mathit{foldr}\ f\ [e]\ [s_{n-1}, s_{n-2}, \ldots, s_{i+1}]) \\ \quad \textbf{where } e = \textstyle\bigoplus(rs|_{W(i,i)} \cup rs|_{None}) \\ \qquad\quad f\ s\ (r : rs') = ((\textstyle\bigoplus s) \oplus r) : r : rs' \\ \qquad\quad s_k = \bigcup\{rs|_{W(i',k)} \mid i \le i' \le k\} \end{array} \middle| \ 0 \le i \le n-1 \right\} \\
= & \ \{ \text{ hoisting (explained below) } \} \\
& \textbf{let } rsv = \{(i,j) \mapsto \textstyle\bigoplus\{rs|_{W(i',j)} \mid i \le i' \le j\} \mid 0 \le i \le j \le n-1\} \\
& \textbf{in } \bigcup \left\{ \begin{array}{l} \mathit{toSet}\ (\mathit{foldr}\ f'\ [e]\ [(i,j) \mid n-1 \ge j \ge i+1]) \\ \quad \textbf{where } e = rsv\ (i,i) \oplus (\textstyle\bigoplus rs|_{None}) \\ \qquad\quad f'\ k\ (r : rs') = (rsv\ k \oplus r) : r : rs' \end{array} \middle| \ 0 \le i \le n-1 \right\}
\end{aligned}$$

At the last step, we hoist computation shared among iterations by introducing an association array *rsv*. It is worth noting that hoisting is a standard technique for effective incrementalization; see [9] for instance. The hoisting reveals that Theorem 2 is applicable once again because $\{rs|_{W(k,j)} \mid i \le k \le j\} \subseteq \{rs|_{W(k,j)} \mid i-1 \le k \le j\}$.

$$\begin{aligned}
& rsv = \{(i,j) \mapsto \textstyle\bigoplus\{rs|_{W(i',j)} \mid i \le i' \le j\} \mid 0 \le i \le j \le n-1\} \\
= & \ \{ \text{ introducing a nested loop } \} \\
& rsv = \bigcup\{\{(i,j) \mapsto \textstyle\bigoplus\{rs|_{W(i',j)} \mid i \le i' \le j\} \mid 0 \le i \le j\} \mid 0 \le j \le n-1\} \\
= & \ \{ \text{ Theorem 2 (with apparent extensions to association arrays) } \} \\
& rsv = \bigcup\{\mathit{Data.Map.fromList}\ (\mathit{foldr}\ g_j\ [(j,j) \mapsto v_j]\ rsl_j) \mid 0 \le j \le n-1\} \\
& \quad \textbf{where } rsl_j = [((i,j), rs|_{W(i,j)}) \mid 0 \le i \le j-1] \\
& \qquad\qquad v_j = \textstyle\bigoplus rs|_{W(j,j)} \\
& \qquad\qquad g_j\ (k', s)\ ((k \mapsto r) : rs') = (k' \mapsto ((\textstyle\bigoplus s) \oplus r)) : (k \mapsto r) : rs'
\end{aligned}$$

We summarize the outcome of our derivation in Figure 3. *maxCore* performs the incrementalized computation and results in an association array so as to efficiently use its result.

$$
\begin{array}{l}
locate\ xs = max_{\leq_{score}}\ (candidates\ xs)\\
candidates\ xs = \mathbf{let}\ (r_1, r_2) = crows\ xs\ \mathbf{in}\ r_1 \sqcup r_2\\
crows\ []\ \ = (\emptyset, \{[]\})\\
crows\ (x : xs) = \mathbf{let}\ (r_1, r_2) = crows\ xs\\
\qquad\qquad\qquad\qquad \hat{r_2} = maxCore\ r_2\\
\qquad\qquad\quad\ \ \mathbf{in}\ (r_1 \sqcup r_2, \{[]\} \sqcup \{x_{i-j} : \hat{r_2}\ (i,j) \mid 0 \leq i \leq j \leq n-1\})\\
rs_1 \sqcup rs_2 = \mathbf{let}\ rs = rs_1 \cup rs_2\ \mathbf{in}\ range\ (maxCore\ rs) \cup \{\bigoplus rs|_{None}\}\\
maxCore\ rs =\\
\qquad \bigcup\{toMap\ (foldr\ f'\ [(i,i) \mapsto e]\ [(i,j) \mid n-1 \geq j \geq i+1]) \mid 0 \leq i \leq n-1\}\\
\quad \mathbf{where}\ rsl_j = [((i,j), rs|_{W(i,j)}) \mid 0 \leq i \leq j-1]\\
\qquad\qquad g_j\ (k', s)\ ((k \mapsto r) : rs') = (k' \mapsto ((\bigoplus s) \oplus r)) : (k \mapsto r) : rs'\\
\qquad\qquad rsv = \bigcup\{toMap\ (foldr\ g_j\ [(j,j) \mapsto (\bigoplus rs|_{W(j,j)})]\ rsl_j) \mid 0 \leq j \leq n-1\}\\
\qquad\qquad e = rsv\ (i,i) \oplus (\bigoplus rs|_{None})\\
\qquad\qquad f'\ k'\ ((k \mapsto r) : rs') = (k' \mapsto (rsv\ k' \oplus r)) : (k \mapsto r) : rs'
\end{array}
$$

Fig. 3. Derived implementation of *locate*; *Data.Map.fromList* is abbreviated to *toMap*

6.5 Implementing Candidate Sets

Since we would like to immediately extract $rs|_v$ from rs, we implement the candidate set by using an association array from v to $rs|_v$. It is easy to implement the $\cup$ operator accordingly.

6.6 Computational Complexity

Observe that for any candidate set rs and any value v, $rs|_v$ contains O(1) elements, and hence, a candidate set consists of $O(n^2)$ elements. Thus, *maxCore* necessitates $O(n^2)$ time. Since *maxCore* is the major component of a recursive call of *crows* and *crows* causes $O(m)$ recursive calls, the time complexity of our algorithm is $O(mn^2)$. The space complexity is the same, $O(mn^2)$.

6.7 Capability of Other Problem Variants

While we have discussed a simple problem, Fukuda et al. [21, 22] discussed several others. The authors [25] have observed that, in addition to the problem we have discussed, our approach can uniformly deal with two cases considered by Fukuda et al.: finding the maximum-sum rectangular subregion, and finding the maximum-sum rectilinear convex region. The derived algorithms are asymptotically as fast as those proposed by Fukuda et al. These results show the usefulness of our approach.

Nevertheless, there are several examples for which our approach is not satisfactory. One such example is the problem of finding the maximum-sum admissible region, which is a connected subregion obtained from *subregions*. While our approach yields an $O(mn^2)$-time algorithm, theirs is $O(mn)$ time. It is not usual dynamic programming in the sense that it fills only a part of the entries of the table, and hence, a more sophisticated incrementalization rule seems necessary for deriving it. Other instances include problems of finding the maximum density regions. Mu [26] studied, from the perspective of thinning, the problem of finding the maximum density consecutive sublist of a list, and pointed out that thinning is not applicable because the monotonicity condition does not hold. Thus, it seems hopeless for our approach to deal with them.

7 Discussion

7.1 Textbook Approach vs. Thinning vs. Incrementalization vs. Thinning + Incrementalization

As discussed in Section 3, our approach can be regarded as formalizing the standard, textbook approach to dynamic programming by program transformations[1]. Hence our approach is not quite different from the standard one; moreover, as discussed in Section 6, it cannot deal with all the problems that the standard one can. Nevertheless, it has two advantages.

- Ours is more formal and thus better suitable to proving the correctness of developed algorithms. The algorithms we have developed are *correct by construction*, namely the developments guarantee their correctness.
- Ours is based on program transformations and thus better suitable for mechanization, though there are still several issues for it.

This view, namely, understanding ours as a systematization of the standard approach, is also helpful for comparing ours with others, in particular thinning and incrementalization. Thinning can expose the principle of optimality, but is not helpful for giving efficient table-filling implementations. In particular, it is known that implementing *max* needs further elaborations [2, 26]. Incrementalization is useful for developing table-filling computations but is less useful for revealing the principle of optimality. In fact, Liu and Stoller [7] takes recurrence equations for dynamic programming as the inputs of their method. From this viewpoint, one can understand that thinning, incrementalization, and thinning + incrementalization are all different in the sense that their inputs and/or outputs differ. Moreover, only thinning + incrementalization has the same functionality as the textbook approach.

7.2 Toward Mechanization of Developments

We have carried out derivations by hand. Derivations are often complex. It is desirable to use methods of mechanizing thinning and incrementalization.

For mechanizing thinning, combinator-based approaches were studied [4, 6, 10, 12]. Programmers specify their problems by using given sets of combinators so that a system can automatically apply thinning laws. Liu et al. [17, 7, 9] studied automatic incrementalization with the help of constraint solvers. In particular,

[1] Indeed, Takeshi Tokuyama said "these two steps are exactly what we did for developing algorithms in [21, 22]" (personal communication).

their incrementalization algorithms can deal with programs whose conditionals are expressed by linear inequalities, as the case of association rule mining studied in Section 6. Another important step is to choose the appropriate implementation of candidate sets depending on the costs of operations performed. There are studies on automatic data structure selection [27–29]. These existing methods may be useful for our approach, in particular for mechanizing applications of Theorems 1 and 2. Nevertheless, there are issues to fully mechanizing our approach.

First, it is often nontrivial to describe the result of thinning in the form for which incrementalization works well. For effective automatic incrementalization, the result of thinning should do iterations in such an order that efficient programs will be derived by reusing the results of the previous iterations. However, it is nontrivial to mechanically find such an iteration order. A possible strategy is to exhaustively try to incrementalize programs of different iteration orders. This strategy was used to deal with association rule mining problems in our approach [25].

Second, as we encountered in Sections 5 and 6.3, problem-specific developments are sometimes necessary for obtaining efficient programs. It is worth noting that similar developments are often applicable to similar problems. For instance, the improvement in Section 6.3 is useful for many association rule mining problems [25]. This observation suggests considering problems in a certain domain. For a restricted class of problems, we may be able to prepare a sufficient amount of improvement strategies.

8 Related Work

8.1 Thinning

Our method is based on thinning [1–3]. The essence of thinning is to improve a naive enumerate-and-choose-style program by identifying that each candidate generation step is monotone on the order that specifies the best solution.

The most related study in this context is one by de Moor [4]. He developed a program transformation rule that can derive efficient programs for a class of problems called *sequential decision processes*. When the feasibility of candidates is characterized by a total preorder, his method is similar to ours in the sense that, for example, it derives the same algorithm for the 0-1 knapsack problem. From this perspective, our approach can be regarded as a refinement on his method. We modularlize his rule into two independent components, thinning and incrementalization, and generalized both parts. Theorem 1 can deal with problems other than sequential decision processes. As seen in Section 6, incrementalization is potentially applicable even if the preorder is not total.

Mu [26] studied some optimal list problems from the perspective of thinning. He pointed out that it is often nontrivial to provide efficient implementation to the *max* operator as well as the candidate set. For instance, in order to efficiently solve the length-constrained maximum-sum sublist problem, he implemented candidate sets by using a sophisticated priority queue. Our study is motivated by his observation. Our approach slightly streamlines his development; yet, problem-specific developments are necessary for deriving his algorithm.

8.2 Incrementalization Based on Fixed-Point Transformation

Our incrementalization is based on fixed point calculations by Cai and Paige [16]. The approach identifies a problem as a fixed point of a set-calculating function and then derives an efficient implementation by incrementalization and selecting data structures for implementing the set.

Liu and Stoller [7] applied the approach to derive efficient programs that use dynamic programming from recursive programs. There is a subtle issue. Since incrementalization relies on reusing the results of the previous iterations, the efficiency of obtained implementation does depend on the order of iteration. This issue is crucial for deriving dynamic programming; the order of iteration corresponds to the order to fill the table. Liu and Stoller proposed a method of finding an appropriate iteration order from computations on recursion parameters.

Unfortunately, max, which is the major subject of incrementalization in our approach, is not such the recursive function that the method by Liu and Stoller expects. Instead, we extracted an appropriate iteration order from the preorder that specifies the feasibility. This approach seems natural because the thinning law, Theorem 1, indicates that the principle of optimality can be read from that preorder. Our approach is effective if the preorder is total; however, it is nontrivial to specify an appropriate iteration order otherwise.

8.3 Other Approaches to Systematic Dynamic Programming

There are several other approaches for systematically or automatically developing efficient dynamic programming from relatively high-level problem specifications, including [5, 8, 11, 13, 14]. Each method has its own strength and weakness. For example, the algebraic dynamic programming framework [8, 14] automatically compiles high-level specifications of the problems in an enumerate-and-choose manner to efficient programs that use dynamic programming. The framework is useful especially for solving problems on sequences such as DNA analyses; however, it cannot solve the association-rule mining problem discussed in Section 6 in $O(n^3)$ time.

We do not intend to argue that our approach is more powerful. Our message is that it is worthwhile to combine them. As thinning and incrementalization, existing approaches often fail to bring the same algorithm as the textbook approach from high-level problem descriptions. We expect that such missing links can be completed by combining other methods.

9 Conclusion and Future Work

We demonstrated that it is useful to combine thinning and incrementalization for developing efficient programs that use dynamic programming from plain problem descriptions. We discussed the 0-1 knapsack problem, the longest common subsequence problem, and association rule mining from numeric data. It is future work to mechanize our approach and to find a class of problems for which efficient algorithms can be automatically obtained. It seems also interesting to study other combinations of existing methods.

Acknowledgements. The authors are grateful to Takeshi Tokuyama for our discussion with him and his suggestion of applying our approach to the longest common subsequence problem. The authors are also grateful to anonymous reviewers for comments useful for improving presentations.

References

1. de Moor, O.: Categories, Relations and Dynamic Programming. PhD thesis, Oxford University Computing Laboratory, Technical Monograph PRG-98 (1992)
2. Bird, R.S., de Moor, O.: Algebra of Programming. Prentice Hall (1997)
3. Bird, R.S.: Maximum marking problems. J. Funct. Program. 11(4), 411–424 (2001)
4. de Moor, O.: A generic program for sequential decision processes. In: Swierstra, S.D. (ed.) PLILP 1995. LNCS, vol. 982, pp. 1–23. Springer, Heidelberg (1995)
5. Pettorossi, A., Proietti, M.: Rules and strategies for transforming functional and logic programs. ACM Computing Surveys 28(2), 360–414 (1996)
6. Sasano, I., Hu, Z., Takeichi, M., Ogawa, M.: Make it practical: a generic linear-time algorithm for solving maximum-weightsum problems. In: Proceedings of the 5th ACM SIGPLAN International Conference on Functional Programming, ICFP 2000, pp. 137–149. ACM Press (2000)
7. Liu, Y.A., Stoller, S.D.: Dynamic programming via static incrementalization. Higher-Order and Symbolic Computation 16(1-2), 37–62 (2003)
8. Giegerich, R., Meyer, C., Steffen, P.: A discipline of dynamic programming over sequence data. Sci. Comput. Program. 51(3), 215–263 (2004)
9. Liu, Y.A., Stoller, S.D., Li, N., Rothamel, T.: Optimizing aggregate array computations in loops. ACM Trans. Program. Lang. Syst. 27(1), 91–125 (2005)
10. Sasano, I., Ogawa, M., Hu, Z.: Maximum marking problems with accumulative weight functions. In: Van Hung, D., Wirsing, M. (eds.) ICTAC 2005. LNCS, vol. 3722, pp. 562–578. Springer, Heidelberg (2005)
11. Puchinger, J., Stuckey, P.J.: Automating branch-and-bound for dynamic programs. In: Proceedings of the 2008 ACM SIGPLAN Symposium on Partial Evaluation and Semantics-based Program Manipulation, PEPM 2008, pp. 81–89. ACM Press (2008)
12. Morihata, A.: A short cut to optimal sequences. New Generation Comput. 29(1), 31–59 (2011)
13. Pu, Y., Bodík, R., Srivastava, S.: Synthesis of first-order dynamic programming algorithms. In: Lopes, C.V., Fisher, K. (eds.) Proceedings of the 26th Annual ACM SIGPLAN Conference on Object-Oriented Programming, Systems, Languages, and Applications, OOPSLA 2011, pp. 83–98. ACM Press (2011)
14. Sauthoff, G., Janssen, S., Giegerich, R.: Bellman's gap: a declarative language for dynamic programming. In: Proceedings of the 13th International ACM SIGPLAN Conference on Principles and Practice of Declarative Programming, pp. 29–40. ACM Press (2011)

15. Paige, R., Koenig, S.: Finite differencing of computable expressions. ACM Trans. Program. Lang. Syst. 4(3), 402–454 (1982)
16. Cai, J., Paige, R.: Program derivation by fixed point computation. Sci. Comput. Program. 11(3), 197–261 (1989)
17. Liu, Y.A., Teitelbaum, T.: Systematic derivation of incremental programs. Sci. Comput. Program. 24(1), 1–39 (1995)
18. Liu, Y.A., Stoller, S.D., Teitelbaum, T.: Static caching for incremental computation. ACM Trans. Program. Lang. Syst. 20(3), 546–585 (1998)
19. Cormen, T.H., Stein, C., Rivest, R.L., Leiserson, C.E.: Introduction to algorithms. MIT Press, Cambridge (2001)
20. Kleinberg, J., Tardos, É.: Algorithm Design Pearson Education Inc. (2006)
21. Fukuda, T., Morimoto, Y., Morishita, S., Tokuyama, T.: Mining optimized association rules for numeric attributes. J. Comput. Syst. Sci. 58(1), 1–12 (1999)
22. Fukuda, T., Morimoto, Y., Morishita, S., Tokuyama, T.: Data mining with optimized two-dimensional association rules. ACM Trans. Database Syst. 26(2), 179–213 (2001)
23. Peyton Jones, S. (ed.): Haskell 98 Language and Libraries: The Revised Report. Cambridge University Press, Cambridge (2003)
24. Agrawal, R., Imielinski, T., Swami, A.N.: Mining association rules between sets of items in large databases. In: Proceedings of the 1993 ACM SIGMOD International Conference on Management of Data, pp. 207–216. ACM Press (1993)
25. Koishi, M.: Derivation of two-dimensional maximum weighted sum problems using program transformations. Master's thesis, Graduate School of Information Science, Tohoku University (2013) (in Japanese)
26. Mu, S.C.: Maximum segment sum is back: deriving algorithms for two segment problems with bounded lengths. In: Proceedings of the 2008 ACM SIGPLAN Symposium on Partial Evaluation and Semantics-based Program Manipulation, PEPM 2008, pp. 31–39. ACM Press (2008)
27. Schwartz, J.T.: Automatic data structure choice in a language of very high level. Commun. ACM 18(12), 722–728 (1975)
28. Schonberg, E., Schwartz, J.T., Sharir, M.: An automatic technique for selection of data structures in SETL programs. ACM Trans. Program. Lang. Syst. 3(2), 126–143 (1981)
29. Paige, R., Henglein, F.: Mechanical translation of set theoretic problem specifications into efficient ram code—a case study. J. Symb. Comput. 4(2), 207–232 (1987)

Appendix

Theorem 3. *For lists s and t, let $s \subseteq t$ if s is a suffix of t, and let $t \setminus s$ be the prefix of t obtained by eliminating the suffix s. For a series of lists $s_1 \subseteq \cdots \subseteq s_n$, the following equation holds.*

$$\begin{aligned}&[\mathit{foldr}\ g\ e\ s_n, \mathit{foldr}\ g\ e\ s_{n-1}, \ldots, \mathit{foldr}\ g\ e\ s_1]\\ &\quad = \mathit{foldr}\ f\ [\mathit{foldr}\ g\ e\ s_1]\ [s_n \setminus s_{n-1}, \ldots, s_3 \setminus s_2, s_2 \setminus s_1]\\ &\qquad \mathbf{where}\ f\ s\ (r : rs) = \mathit{foldr}\ g\ r\ s : r : rs\end{aligned}$$

□

POSIX Regular Expression Parsing with Derivatives

Martin Sulzmann[1] and Kenny Zhuo Ming Lu[2]

[1] Hochschule Karlsruhe - Technik und Wirtschaft, 76133 Karlsruhe, Germany
martin.sulzmann@hs-karlsruhe.de
[2] School of Information Technology, Nanyang Polytechnic,
180 Ang Mo Kio Avenue 8, Singapore 569830, Singapore
luzhuomi@gmail.com

Abstract. We adapt the POSIX policy to the setting of regular expression parsing. POSIX favors longest left-most parse trees. Compared to other policies such as greedy left-most, the POSIX policy is more intuitive but much harder to implement. Almost all POSIX implementations are buggy as observed by Kuklewicz. We show how to obtain a POSIX algorithm for the general parsing problem based on Brzozowski's regular expression derivatives. Correctness is fairly straightforward to establish and our benchmark results show that our approach is promising.

1 Introduction

We consider the parsing problem for regular expressions. Parsing produces a parse tree which provides a detailed explanation of which subexpressions match which substrings. The outcome of parsing is possibly ambiguous because there may be two distinct parse trees for the same input. For example, for input string ab and regular expression $(a + b + ab)^*$, there are two possible ways to break apart input ab: (1) a, b and (2) ab. Either in the first iteration subpattern a matches substring a, and in the second iteration subpattern b matches substring b, or subpattern ab immediately matches the input string.

There are two popular disambiguation strategies for regular expressions: POSIX [10] and greedy [21]. In the above, case (1) is the greedy result and case (2) is the POSIX result. For the variation $(ab + a + b)^*$, case (2) is still the POSIX result whereas now the greedy result equals case (2) as well.

We find that greedy parsing is directly tied to the structure and the order of alternatives matters. In contrast, POSIX is less sensitive to the order of alternatives because longest matches are favored. Only in case of equal matches preference is given to the left-most match. This is a useful property for applications where we build an expression as the composition of several alternatives, e.g. consider lexical analysis.

As it turns out, POSIX appears to be much harder to implement than greedy. Kuklewicz [11] observes that almost all POSIX implementations are buggy

M. Codish and E. Sumii (Eds.): FLOPS 2014, LNCS 8475, pp. 203–220, 2014.

which is confirmed by our own experiments. These implementations are also restricted in that they do not produce full parse trees and only provide submatch information. For example, in case of Kleene star only the last match is recorded instead of the matches for each iteration.

In this work, we propose a novel method to compute POSIX parse trees based on Brzozowski's regular expression derivatives [1]. A sketch of how derivatives could be applied to compute POSIX submatches is given in our own prior work [24]. The present work includes some significant improvements such as a rigorous correctness result, dealing with the more general parsing problem and numerous optimizations.

Specifically, we make the following contributions:

- We formally define POSIX parsing by viewing regular expressions as types and parse trees as values (Section 2). We also relate parsing to the more specific submatching problem.
- We present a method for computation of POSIX parse trees based on Brzozowski's regular expression derivatives [1] and verify its correctness (Section 3).
- We have built optimized versions for parsing as well as for the special case of submatching where we only keep the last match in case of a Kleene star. We conduct experiments to measure the effectiveness of our method (Section 4).

Section 5 discusses related work and concludes.

2 Regular Expressions and Parse Trees

We follow [8] and phrase parsing as a type inhabitation relation. Regular expressions are interpreted as types and parse trees as values of some regular expression type. Figure 1 contains the details which will be explained in the following.

The syntax of regular expressions r is standard. As it is common, concatenation and alternation is assumed to be right associative. The example $(a+b+ab)^*$ from the introduction stands for $(a+(b+ab))^*$. Words w are formed using literals l taken from a finite alphabet Σ. Parse trees v are represented via some standard data constructors such as lists, pairs, left/right injection into a disjoint sum etc. We write $[v_1, ..., v_n]$ as a short-hand for $v_1 : ... : v_n : []$.

Parse trees v and regular expressions r are related via a natural deduction style proof system where inference rules make use of judgments $\vdash v : r$. For example, rule (Left+) covers the case that the left alternative r_1 has been matched. We will shortly see some examples making use of the other rules.

For each derivable statement $\vdash v : r$, the parse tree v provides a proof that the word underlying v is contained in the language described by r. That is, $L(r) = \{|v| \mid \vdash v : r\}$ where the flattening function $|\cdot|$ extracts the underlying word. In general, proofs are not unique because there may be two distinct parse trees for the same input.

Recall the example from the introduction. For expression $(a + (b + ab))^*$ and input ab we find parse trees $[\mathit{Left}\ a, \mathit{Right}\ \mathit{Left}\ b]$ and $[\mathit{Right}\ \mathit{Right}\ (a, b)]$. For

Words:

$$\begin{array}{lll} w ::= & \epsilon & \text{Empty word} \\ \mid & l \in \Sigma & \text{Literal} \\ \mid & ww & \text{Concatenation} \end{array}$$

Regular expressions:

$$\begin{array}{lll} r ::= & l & \\ \mid & r^* & \text{Kleene star} \\ \mid & rr & \text{Concatenation} \\ \mid & r + r & \text{Choice} \\ \mid & \epsilon & \text{Empty word} \\ \mid & \phi & \text{Empty language} \end{array}$$

Parse trees:

$$v ::= () \mid l \mid (v, v) \mid \mathit{Left}\ v \mid \mathit{Right}\ v \mid vs$$
$$vs ::= [] \mid v : vs$$

$\boxed{\vdash v : r}$

$$(\text{None}^*)\quad \vdash [] : r^*$$

$$(\text{Once}^*)\quad \frac{\vdash v : r \qquad \vdash vs : r^*}{\vdash (v : vs) : r^*}$$

$$(\text{Pair})\quad \frac{\vdash v_1 : r_1 \qquad \vdash v_2 : r_2}{\vdash (v_1, v_2) : r_1 r_2}$$

$$(\text{Left+})\quad \frac{\vdash v_1 : r_1}{\vdash \mathit{Left}\ v_1 : r_1 + r_2}$$

$$(\text{Right+})\quad \frac{\vdash v_2 : r_2}{\vdash \mathit{Right}\ v_2 : r_1 + r_2}$$

$$(\text{Empty})\quad \vdash () : \epsilon \qquad (\text{Lit})\quad \frac{l \in \Sigma}{\vdash l : l}$$

Flattening:

$$\begin{array}{llll} |()| = \epsilon & |l| = l & |\mathit{Left}\ v| = |v| & |v : vs| = |v||vs| \\ |[]| = \epsilon & |(v_1, v_2)| = |v_1||v_2| & |\mathit{Right}\ v| = |v| & \end{array}$$

Fig. 1. Regular Expressions and Parse Trees

brevity, some parentheses are omitted, e.g. we write *Right Left b* as a short-hand for *Right* (*Left b*). The derivation trees are shown below:

$$\dfrac{\dfrac{\dfrac{\dfrac{\vdash a : a \qquad \vdash b : b}{\vdash (a, b) : ab}}{\vdash \mathit{Right}\ (a, b) : b + ab}}{\vdash \mathit{Right}\ \mathit{Right}\ (a, b) : a + (b + ab)} \qquad \vdash [] : (a + (b + ab))^*}{\vdash [\mathit{Right}\ \mathit{Right}\ (a, b)] : (a + (b + ab))^*}$$

$$\dfrac{\dfrac{\vdash a : a}{\vdash \mathit{Left}\ a : (a + (b + ab))^*} \qquad \dfrac{\dfrac{\dfrac{\vdash b : b}{\vdash \mathit{Left}\ b : b + ab}}{\vdash \mathit{Right}\ \mathit{Left}\ b : a + (b + ab)} \qquad \vdash [] : (a + (b + ab))^*}{\vdash [\mathit{Right}\ \mathit{Left}\ b] : (a + (b + ab))^*}}{\vdash [\mathit{Left}\ a, \mathit{Right}\ \mathit{Left}\ b] : (a + (b + ab))^*}$$

To avoid such ambiguities, the common approach is to impose a disambiguation strategy which guarantees that for each regular expression r matching a word w there exists a unique parse tree v such that $|v| = w$. Our interest is in the computation of POSIX parse trees. Below we give a formal specification of POSIX parsing by imposing an order among parse trees.

Definition 1 (POSIX Parse Tree Ordering). *We define a POSIX ordering $v_1 >_r v_2$ among parse trees v_1 and v_2 where r is the underlying regular expression. The ordering rules are as follows*

$$(C1)\ \frac{v_1 = v_1' \quad v_2 >_{r_2} v_2'}{(v_1, v_2) >_{r_1 r_2} (v_1', v_2')} \qquad (C2)\ \frac{v_1 >_{r_1} v_1'}{(v_1, v_2) >_{r_1 r_2} (v_1', v_2')}$$

$$(A1)\ \frac{len\ |v_2| > len\ |v_1|}{Right\ v_2 >_{r_1+r_2} Left\ v_1} \qquad (A2)\ \frac{len\ |v_1| \geq len\ |v_2|}{Left\ v_1 >_{r_1+r_2} Right\ v_2}$$

$$(A3)\ \frac{v_2 >_{r_2} v_2'}{Right\ v_2 >_{r_1+r_2} Right\ v_2'} \qquad (A4)\ \frac{v_1 >_{r_1} v_1'}{Left\ v_1 >_{r_1+r_2} Left\ v_1'}$$

$$(K1)\ \frac{|v : vs| = \epsilon}{[] >_{r^*} v : vs} \qquad (K2)\ \frac{|v : vs| \neq \epsilon}{v : vs >_{r^*} []}$$

$$(K3)\ \frac{v_1 >_r v_2}{v_1 : vs_1 >_{r^*} v_2 : vs_2} \qquad (K4)\ \frac{v_1 = v_2 \quad vs_1 >_{r^*} vs_2}{v_1 : vs_1 >_{r^*} v_2 : vs_2}$$

where helper function len computes the number of letters in a word.

Let r be a regular expression and v_1 and v_2 parse trees such that $\vdash v_1 : r$ and $\vdash v_2 : r$. We define $v_1 \geq_r v_2$ iff either v_1 and v_2 are equal or $v_1 >_r v_2$ where $|v_1| = |v_2|$. We say that v_1 is the POSIX *parse tree w.r.t. r iff $\vdash v_1 : r$ and $v_1 \geq_r v_2$ for any parse tree v_2 where $\vdash v_2 : r$ and $|v_1| = |v_2|$.*

The above ordering relation is an adaptation of the *Greedy* parse tree order defined in [8]. The (Greedy) rule $Left\ v >_{r_1+r_2} Right\ v'$ is replaced by rules (A1) and (A2). All other rules remain unchanged compared to [8].

Rules (A1) and (A2) guarantee that preference is given to *longest* left-most parse trees as stipulated by the POSIX submatching policy [10]:

> "Subpatterns should match the longest possible substrings, where sub- patterns that start earlier (to the left) in the regular expression take priority over ones starting later. Hence, higher-level subpatterns take priority over their lower-level component subpatterns. Matching an empty string is considered longer than no match at all."

For example, consider again our running example. For expression $(a+(b+ab))^*$ and word ab we find parse trees $[Right\ Right\ (a,b)]$ and $[Left\ a, Right\ Left\ b]$. Due to rule (A1), we have that $Right\ Right\ (a,b)$ is greater than $Left\ a$ because $Right\ Right\ (a,b)$ contains a longer match than $Left\ a$. Hence,

$$[Right\ Right\ (a,b)] \geq_{(a+(b+ab))^*} [Left\ a, Right\ Left\ b]$$

In contrast, under the Greedy order we would find that [*Left* a, *Right Left* b] is greater than [*Right Right* (a, b)].

POSIX is Non-Problematic. In case of the Greedy parse tree order, it is well-observed [8] that special care must be given to problematic expressions/parse trees. Roughly, an expression induces problematic parse trees if we find empty matches under a Kleene star. The potential danger of problematic expressions is that we might end up with an infinite chain of larger parse trees. This causes possible complications for a Greedy parsing algorithm, as the algorithm attempts to compute the "largest" parse tree. Fortunately, none of this is an issue for POSIX.

For example, consider the problematic expression ϵ^*. For the empty input we find the following infinite chain of parse trees

$$v_0 = [], \, v_1 = [()], \, v_2 = [(), ()] \; ...$$

Parse tree v_0 is the largest according to our ordering relation. See rule (K1).

Let's consider another more devious, problematic expression $(\epsilon + a)^*$ where for input a we find

$$v_0 = [\mathit{Right}\ a], \, v_1 = [\mathit{Left}\ (), \mathit{Right}\ a], \, v_2 = [\mathit{Left}\ (), \mathit{Left}\ (), \mathit{Right}\ a] \; ...$$

Due to rule (A1), v_0 is the largest parse tree according to our POSIX ordering relation. In contrast, under the Greedy order each v_{i+1} is larger than v_i. Hence, the Greedy order does not enjoy maximal elements unless we take special care of problematic expressions. For details see [8].

To summarize, expressions which are problematic under the Greedy order are "not problematic" under the POSIX order. For *any* expression, the POSIX order defined in Definition 1 is well-defined in the sense that the order is total and enjoys maximal elements.

Proposition 1 (Maximum and Totality of POSIX Order). *For any expression r, the ordering relation $\geq_r$ is total and has a maximal element.*

Parsing versus Submatching. For space reasons, practical implementations only care about certain subparts and generally only record the last match in case of a Kleene star iteration. For example, consider expression $((x : a^*) + (b + c)^*)^*$ where via an annotation we have marked the subparts we are interested in. Matching the above against word *abaacc* yields the submatch binding $x \mapsto aa$. For comparison, here is the parse tree resulting from the match against the input word *abaacc*

$$[\mathit{Left}\ [a], \mathit{Right}\ \mathit{Left}\ [b], \mathit{Left}\ [a, a], \mathit{Right}\ \mathit{Right}\ [c, c]]$$

Instead of providing a stand-alone definition of POSIX submatching, we show how to derive submatchings from parse trees. In Figure 2, we extend the syntax of regular expressions with submatch annotations $(x : r)$ where variables x

Annotated regular expressions: $r ::= (x : r) \mid l \mid r^* \mid rr \mid r + r \mid \epsilon \mid \phi$
Submatch binding environment: $\Gamma ::= \{\} \mid \{x \mapsto w\} \mid \Gamma \cup \Gamma$

$$\boxed{v \vdash r \leadsto \Gamma}$$

$$\frac{v \vdash r \leadsto \Gamma}{v \vdash (x : r) \leadsto \{x \mapsto |v|\} \cup \Gamma} \quad () \vdash \epsilon \leadsto \{\} \quad l \vdash l \leadsto \{\}$$

$$[] \vdash r^* \leadsto \{\} \quad \frac{v \vdash r \leadsto \Gamma}{[v] \vdash r^* \leadsto \Gamma} \quad \frac{v \vdash r \leadsto \Gamma_1 \; vs \vdash r^* \leadsto \Gamma_2}{v : vs \vdash r^* \leadsto \Gamma_1 \cup \Gamma_2}$$

$$\frac{\begin{array}{c} v_1 \vdash r_1 \leadsto \Gamma_1 \\ v_2 \vdash r_2 \leadsto \Gamma_2 \end{array}}{(v_1, v_2) \vdash r_1 r_2 \leadsto \Gamma_1 \cup \Gamma_2} \quad \frac{v_1 \vdash r_1 \leadsto \Gamma_1}{\mathit{Left}\ v_1 \vdash r_1 + r_2 \leadsto \Gamma_1} \quad \frac{v_2 \vdash r_2 \leadsto \Gamma_2}{\mathit{Right}\ v_2 \vdash r_1 + r_2 \leadsto \Gamma_2}$$

Fig. 2. From Parsing to Submatching

are always distinct. For parsing purposes, submatch annotations will be ignored. Given a parse tree v of a regular expression r, we obtain the submatch environment Γ via judgments $v \vdash r \leadsto \Gamma$. We simply traverse the structure of v and r and collect the submatch binding Γ.

For our above example, we obtain the binding $\{x \mapsto a, x \mapsto aa\}$. Repeated bindings resulting from Kleene star are removed by only keeping the last submatch. Technically, we achieve this by exhaustive application of the following rule on submatch bindings (from left to right):

$$\Gamma_1 \cup \{x \mapsto w_1\} \cup \Gamma_2 \cup \{x \mapsto w_2\} \cup \Gamma_3 = \Gamma_1 \cup \Gamma_2 \cup \{x \mapsto w_2\} \cup \Gamma_3$$

Hence, we find the final submatch binding $\{x \mapsto aa\}$. As another example, consider expression $(x : a^*)^*$ and the empty input string. The POSIX parse tree for $(x : a^*)^*$ is $[]$ which implies the POSIX submatching $\{x \mapsto \epsilon\}$.

We believe that the submatchings resulting from POSIX parse trees correspond to the POSIX submatchings described in [25]. The formal details need yet to be worked out.

Construction of a full parse tree is of course wasteful, if we are only interested in certain submatchings. However, both constructions are equally challenging in case we wish to obtain the proper POSIX candidate. That is, even if we only keep the last match in case of a Kleene star iteration, we must compare the set of accumulated submatches to select the appropriate POSIX, i.e. longest left-most, match.

A naive method to obtain the POSIX parse tree is to perform an exhaustive search. Such a method is obviously correct but potentially has an exponential run time due to backtracking. Next, we develop a systematic method to compute the POSIX parse trees.

3 Parse Tree Construction via Derivatives

Our idea is to apply Brzozowski's regular expression derivatives [1] for parsing. The derivative operation $r\backslash l$ performs a symbolic transformation of regular expression r and extracts (takes away) the leading letter l. In formal language terms, we find

$$lw \in L(r) \text{ iff } w \in L(r\backslash l)$$

Thus, it is straightforward to obtain a regular expression matcher. To check if regular expression r matches word $l_1...l_n$, we simply build a sequence of derivatives and test if the final regular expression is nullable, i.e. accepts the empty string:

$$\text{Matching by extraction:} \qquad r_0 \xrightarrow{l_1} r_1 \xrightarrow{l_2} ... \xrightarrow{l_n} r_n$$

Regular expression derivatives:

$$\begin{array}{ll}
\phi\backslash l & = \phi \\
\epsilon\backslash l & = \phi \\
l_1\backslash l_2 & = \begin{cases} \epsilon \text{ if } l_1 == l_2 \\ \phi \text{ otherwise} \end{cases} \\
(r_1 + r_2)\backslash l & = r_1\backslash l + r_2\backslash l \\
(r_1 r_2)\backslash l & = \begin{cases} (r_1\backslash l)r_2 + r_2\backslash l & \text{if } \epsilon \in L(r_1) \\ (r_1\backslash l)r_2 & \text{otherwise} \end{cases} \\
r^*\backslash l & = (r\backslash l)r^*
\end{array}$$

Empty parse tree construction and parse tree transformation:

$$\begin{array}{l}
mkEps_{r^*} = [] \\
mkEps_{r_1 r_2} = (mkEps_{r_1}, mkEps_{r_2}) \\
mkEps_{r_1+r_2} \\
\quad |\epsilon \in L(r_1) = Left\ mkEps_{r_1} \\
\quad |\epsilon \in L(r_2) = Right\ mkEps_{r_2} \\
mkEps_{\epsilon} = ()
\end{array}$$

$$\begin{array}{l}
inj_{r^*\backslash l}(v, vs) = (inj_{r\backslash l}\ v) : vs \\
inj_{(r_1 r_2)\backslash l} = \\
\quad \lambda v.\text{case } v \text{ of} \\
\qquad (v_1, v_2) \rightarrow (inj_{r_1\backslash l}\ v_1, v_2) \\
\qquad Left\ (v_1, v_2) \rightarrow (inj_{r_1\backslash l}\ v_1, v_2) \\
\qquad Right\ v_2 \rightarrow (mkEps_{r_1}, inj_{r_2\backslash l}\ v_2) \\
inj_{(r_1+r_2)\backslash l} = \\
\quad \lambda v.\text{case } v \text{ of} \\
\qquad Left\ v_1 \rightarrow Left\ (inj_{r_1\backslash l}\ v_1) \\
\qquad Right\ v_2 \rightarrow Right\ (inj_{r_2\backslash l}\ v_2) \\
inj_{l\backslash l}() = l
\end{array}$$

Parsing with derivatives:

$$\begin{array}{l}
parse\ r\ \epsilon \\
\quad |\epsilon \in L(r) = mkEps_r \\
parse\ r\ lw = inj_{r\backslash l}(parse\ r\backslash l\ w)
\end{array}$$

Fig. 3. Parsing Tree Construction with Derivatives

In the above, we write $r \xrightarrow{l} r'$ for applying the derivative operation on r where r' equals $r\backslash l$. In essence, derivatives represent DFA states and $\xrightarrow{l}$ represents the DFA transition relation.

Our insight is that based on the first *matching* pass we can build the POSIX parse tree via a second *injection* pass:

$$\text{Parse trees by injection} \qquad v_0 \xleftarrow{l_1} v_1 \xleftarrow{l_2} \ldots \xleftarrow{l_n} v_n$$

The basic idea is as follows. After the final matching step, we compute the parse tree v_n for a nullable expression r_n. Then, we apply a sequence of parse tree transformations. In each transformation step, we build the parse tree v_i for expression r_i given the tree v_{i+1} for r_{i+1} where $r_i \xrightarrow{l} r_{i+1}$ This step is denoted by $v_i \xleftarrow{l} v_{i+1}$. In essence, the derivative operation removes leading letters from an expression whereas the transformation via injection step simply reverses this effect at the level of parse trees. In the above, we *inject* the *removed* letter l into the parse tree v_{i+1} of the derived expression r_{i+1} which results in a parse tree v_i of expression r_i. Thus, we incrementally build the parse tree v_0 for the initial expression r_0. Importantly, our method yields POSIX parse tree because (a) we build the POSIX parse tree v_n for the nullable expression r_n and (b) each parse tree transformation step $v_i \xleftarrow{l} v_{i+1}$ maintains the POSIX property.

Next, we introduce the details of the above sketched POSIX parsing method followed by a worked out example. Finally, we present an improvement parsing algorithm which performs the 'backward' construction of POSIX parse trees during the 'forward' matching pass.

POSIX Parse Tree Construction via Injection. Figure 3 summarizes our method for construction of POSIX parse trees based on the above idea. We first repeat the standard derivative operation $r\backslash l$. Next, we find function $mkEps_r$ to compute an empty parse tree assuming that r is nullable. The function is defined by structural induction over r where as a notational convention the cases are written as subscripts. Similarly, we find function $inj_{r\backslash l}$ which takes as an input a parse tree of the derivative $r\backslash l$ and yields a parse of r by (re)injecting the removed letter l. Thus, we can define the transformation step $v_i \xleftarrow{l} v_{i+1}$ by $v_i = inj_{r_i\backslash l}\ v_{i+1}$. Function *parse* computes a parse tree by first applying the derivative operation until we obtain a parse tree for the empty tree via *mkEps*. Starting with this parse tree, we then repeatedly apply *inj*.

Let us take a closer look at $mkEps_r$. We recurse over the structure of r. There is no case for letter l and empty language ϕ as we assume that r must be nullable. The cases for Kleene star r^* and empty word ϵ are straightforward and yield [], respectively, (). For concatenation $r_1 + r_2$, we build the pair consisting of the empty parse trees for r_1 and r_2. The most interesting case is choice $r_1 + r_2$ where we are careful to first check if r_1 is nullable. Otherwise, we consider r_2. Thus, we can guarantee that the resulting parse tree is the largest according to our POSIX order in Definition 1.

Lemma 1 (Empty POSIX Parse Tree). *Let r be a regular expression such that $\epsilon \in L(r)$. Then, $\vdash mkEps_r : r$ and $mkEps_r$ is the POSIX parse tree of r for the empty word.*

Next, we take a closer look at the definition inj. For example, the most simple (last) case is $inj_{l\backslash l}() = l$ where we transform the empty parse tree $()$ into l. Recall that $l\backslash l$ equals ϵ. The definition for choice is also simple. We check if either a parse for the left or right component exists. Then, we apply inj on the respective component.

Let's consider the first case dealing with Kleene star. By definition $r^*\backslash l = (r\backslash l)r^*$. Hence, the input consists of a pair (v, vs). Function $inj_{r\backslash l}$ is applied recursively on v to yield a parse tree for r.

Concatenation r_1r_2 is the most involved case. There are three possible subcases. The first subcase covers the case that r_1 is not nullable. The other two cases deal with the nullable case.

In case r_1 is not nullable, we must find a pair (v_1, v_2). Recall that for this case $(r_1r_2)\backslash l = (r_1\backslash l)r_2$. Hence, the derivative operation has been applied on r_1 which implies that inj will also be applied on v_1.

Let's consider the two subcases dealing with nullable expressions r_1. Recall that in such a situation we have that $(r_1r_2)\backslash l = (r_1\backslash l)r_2 + r_2\backslash l$. Hence, we need to check if either a parse tree for the left or right expression exists. In case of a left parse tree, we apply inj on the leading component (like for non-nullable r_1). In case of a right parse tree, none of the letters have been extracted from r_1. Hence, we build a pair consisting of an 'empty' parse tree $mkEps_{r_1}$ for r_1 and r_2's parse tree by injecting l back into v_2 via $inj_{r_2\backslash l}$.

It is not difficult to see that $inj_{r\backslash l}$ applied on a parse tree of $r\backslash l$ yields a parse tree of r. The important property for us is that injection also maintains POSIX parse trees.

Lemma 2 (POSIX Preservation under Injection). *Let r be a regular expression, l a letter, v a parse tree such that $\vdash v : r\backslash l$ and v is POSIX parse tree of $r\backslash l$ and $|v|$. Then, $\vdash (inj_{r\backslash l}\ v) : r$ and $(inj_{r\backslash l}\ v)$ is POSIX parse tree of r and $l|v|$ where $|(inj_{r\backslash l}\ v)| = l|v|$.*

We have a rigorous proof for this statement. The proof is rather involved and requires a careful analysis of the various (sub)cases. Briefly, *inj* strictly injects letters at the *left-most* position. Recall that derived expressions are obtained by greedily removing leading letters from the left. Injection also preserves the *longest* left-most property because the derivative operation favors subexpressions that start earlier. Recall the case for choice

$$(r_1r_2)\backslash l = \begin{cases} (r_1\backslash l)r_2 + r_2\backslash l \text{ if } \epsilon \in L(r_1) \\ (r_1\backslash l)r_2 \qquad\qquad \text{otherwise} \end{cases}$$

where we favor subexpression r_1. Thus, injection can guarantee that longest left-most parse trees are preserved.

Based on the above lemmas we reach the following result.

Theorem 1 (POSIX Parsing). *Function parse computes POSIX parse trees.*

POSIX Parsing Example. To illustrate our method, we consider expression $(a+ab)(b+\epsilon)$ and word ab for which we find parse trees $(\mathit{Right}\ (a,b), \mathit{Right}\ ())$ and $(\mathit{Left}\ a, \mathit{Left}\ b)$. The former is the POSIX parse tree whereas the latter is the Greedy parse tree.

We first build the derivative w.r.t. a and then w.r.t. b. For convenience, we use notation $\xrightarrow{l}$ to denote derivative steps. For our example, we find:

$$\begin{array}{l} (a+ab)(b+\epsilon) \\ \xrightarrow{a} (\epsilon+\epsilon b)(b+\epsilon) \\ \xrightarrow{b} (\phi+(\phi b+\epsilon))(b+\epsilon)+(\epsilon+\phi) \end{array}$$

where the last step $\xrightarrow{b}$ in more detail is as follows:

$$\begin{array}{l} \quad ((\epsilon+\epsilon b)(b+\epsilon))\backslash b \\ = ((\epsilon+\epsilon b)\backslash b)(b+\epsilon)+(b+\epsilon)\backslash b \\ = (\epsilon\backslash b+(\epsilon b)\backslash b)(b+\epsilon)+(b\backslash b+\epsilon\backslash b) \\ = (\phi+((\epsilon\backslash b)b+b\backslash b))(b+\epsilon)+(\epsilon+\phi) \\ = (\phi+(\phi b+\epsilon))(b+\epsilon)+(\epsilon+\phi) \end{array}$$

Next, we check that the final expression $(\phi+(\phi b+\epsilon))(b+\epsilon)+(\epsilon+\phi)$ is nullable which is the case here. Hence, we can compute the empty POSIX parse tree via

$$\mathit{mkEps}_{(\phi+(\phi b+\epsilon))(b+\epsilon)+(\epsilon+\phi)} = \mathit{Left}\ (\mathit{Right}\ (\mathit{Right}\ ()), \mathit{Right}\ ())$$

What remains is to apply the 'backward' injection pass where the POSIX parse tree v' of $r\backslash l$ is transformed into a POSIX parse tree v of r by injecting the letter l appropriately into v'.

We find

$$\begin{array}{l} \quad \mathit{inj}_{((\epsilon+\epsilon b)(b+\epsilon))\backslash b}\ (\mathit{Left}\ (\mathit{Right}\ (\mathit{Right}\ ()), \mathit{Right}\ ())) \\ = (\mathit{inj}_{(\epsilon+\epsilon b)\backslash b}\mathit{Right}\ (\mathit{Right}\ ()), \mathit{Right}\ ()) \\ = (\mathit{Right}\ (\mathit{inj}_{(\epsilon b)\backslash b}\ (\mathit{Right}\ ())), \mathit{Right}\ ()) \\ = (\mathit{Right}\ (\mathit{mkEps}_\epsilon, \mathit{inj}_{b\backslash b}()), \mathit{Right}\ ()) \\ = (\mathit{Right}\ ((), b), \mathit{Right}\ ()) \end{array}$$

where $(\mathit{Right}\ ((), b), \mathit{Right}\ ())$ is the POSIX parse tree of $(\epsilon+\epsilon b)(b+\epsilon)$ and word b.

Another injection step yields

$$\mathit{inj}_{((a+ab)(b+\epsilon))\backslash a}\ (\mathit{Right}\ ((), b), \mathit{Right}\ ()) \ = \ (\mathit{Right}\ (a,b), \mathit{Right}\ ())$$

As we know the above is the POSIX parse tree for expression $(a+ab)(b+\epsilon)$ and word ab.

Incremental Bit-Coded Forward Parse Tree Construction. Next, we show how to perform parsing more efficiently by incrementally building up parse trees during matching. That is, the 'second' injection step is immediately applied during matching. Thus, we avoid to record the entire path of derived expressions. In addition, we use bit-codes to represent parse trees more compactly.

Our bit-code representation of parse trees follows the description in [17]. See Figure 4. Bit-code sequences are represented as lists where we use Haskell notation. The symbol [] denotes the empty list and $b : bs$ denotes a list with head b and tail bs. We write ++ to concatenate two lists. Function $encode_r$ computes a bit-code representation of parse tree v where $\vdash v : r$. Function $decode_r$ turns a bit-code representation back into a parse tree.

The main challenge is the incremental construction of parse trees during matching. The idea is to incrementally annotate regular expressions with partial parse tree information during the derivative step.

Annotated regular expressions ri are defined in Figure 5. Each annotation bs represents some partial parse tree information in terms of bit-code sequences. There is no annotation for ϕ as there is no parse tree for the empty language.

Function *internalize* transforms a standard regular expressions r into an annotated regular expressions ri by inserting empty annotations []. In addition,

$$\text{Bit-codes}\quad b ::= 0 \mid 1 \qquad bs ::= [\,] \mid b : bs$$

$$\begin{array}{l}
encode_\epsilon\ () = [\,] \\
encode_l\ l = [\,] \\
encode_{r_1+r_2}\ (Left\ v) = 0 : encode_{r_1}\ v \\
encode_{r_1+r_2}\ (Right\ v) = 1 : encode_{r_2}\ v \\
encode_{r_1 r_2}\ (v_1, v_2) = encode_{r_1}\ v_1 \ \text{++}\ encode_{r_2}\ v_2 \\
encode_{r^*}\ [\,] = [1] \\
encode_{r^*}\ (v : vs) = (0 : encode_r\ v)\ \text{++}\ encode_{r^*}\ vs
\end{array}$$

$$\begin{array}{l}
decode_r\, bs = \mathsf{let}\ (v, p) = decode'_r\, bs \\
\qquad\qquad\quad \mathsf{in\ case}\ p\ \mathsf{of} \\
\qquad\qquad\qquad [\,] \to v \\
decode'_\epsilon\ bs = ((), bs) \\
decode'_l\ bs = (l, bs) \\
decode'_{r_1+r_2}\ (0 : bs) = \mathsf{let}\ (v, p) = decode'_{r_1}\ bs \\
\qquad\qquad\qquad\qquad\quad \mathsf{in}\ (Left\ v, p) \\
decode'_{r_1+r_2}\ (1 : bs) = \mathsf{let}\ (v, p) = decode'_{r_2}\ bs \\
\qquad\qquad\qquad\qquad\quad \mathsf{in}\ (Right\ v, p) \\
decode'_{r_1 r_2}\ bs = \mathsf{let}\ (v_1, p_1) = decode'_{r_1}\ bs \\
\qquad\qquad\qquad\quad\ \ (v_2, p_2) = decode'_{r_2}\ p_1 \\
\qquad\qquad\quad \mathsf{in}\ ((v_1, v_2), p_2) \\
decode'_{r^*}\ (0 : bs) = \mathsf{let}\ (v, p_1) = decode'_r\ bs \\
\qquad\qquad\qquad\qquad\ \ (vs, p_2) = decode'_{r^*}\ p_1 \\
\qquad\qquad\qquad \mathsf{in}\ ((v : vs), p_2) \\
decode'_{r^*}\ (1 : bs) = ([\,], bs)
\end{array}$$

Fig. 4. Bit-Code Representation of Parse Trees

choice + is transformed into $\oplus$. The purpose of this transformation is that all parse tree information can be derived from the operands of $\oplus$ without having to inspect the surrounding structure. For example, we attach 0 ("left position") to the internalized expression resulting from left alternative r_1 of $r_1 + r_2$ where helper function *fuse* attaches a bit-code sequence to the top-most position of an annotated regular expression.

As an example, consider application of function *internalize* to the expression $(a + ab)(b + \epsilon)$ which yields the annotated expression

$$[]@(([0]@a) \oplus ([1]@([]@a)([]@b)))(([0]@b) \oplus ([1]@\epsilon)) \quad (1)$$

The derivative operation now operates on annotated regular expressions. See Figure 5. To avoid confusion, we denote the refined derivative operation by $ri\backslash_b l$. As can be seen, the definition of $ri\backslash_b l$ follows closely the definition of the standard derivative operation $r\backslash l$. The difference is that $ri\backslash_b l$ propagates and inserts parse tree information in terms of annotations. In essence, $ri\backslash_b l$ is an amalgamation of $r\backslash l$ and $inj_{r\backslash l}$.

For example, consider $ri_1\ ri_2$ where $\epsilon \in L(ri_1)$. Like in the standard case, the letter l could either be extracted from ri_1 or ri_2. We keep track of both alternatives by combining them via $\oplus$. The interesting case is if l is extracted from ri_2 which implies that the parse tree of ri_1 must be empty. We record this information via *fuse* $mkEpsBC_{ri_1}\ (ri_2\backslash_b l)$. Helper function $mkEpsBC_{ri_1}$ computes an empty parse tree of ri_1 in terms of the bit-code representation. This information is then attached to the top-most annotation in $ri_2\backslash_b l$ via the helper function *fuse*.

Similarly, the annotations resulting from Kleene star must record the number of iterations we have performed. For example, *fuse* $[0]\ ri\backslash_b l$ records that the Kleene star has been unrolled once. The existing annotation bs is moved to the resulting concatenation whereas we attach $[]$ to ri^* to indicate the start of a new Kleene star iteration.

For example, $\backslash_b a$ applied on the above annotated expression (1) yields

$$[]@(([0]@\epsilon) \oplus ([1]@([]@\epsilon)([]@b)))(([0]@b) \oplus ([1]@\epsilon))$$

Let us take a closer look at $mkEpsBC_{ri}$ which follows the definition of *mkEps* in Figure 3. Like in case of *mkEps*, we first check the left and then the right alternative in $ri_1 \oplus ri_2$. One difference is that operands themselves record the information which alternative (left or right) they originated. Recall the definition of *internalize*. Hence, it suffices to collect the annotations in either ri_1 or ri_2.

Thus, incremental parsing via function *parseBC* is performed by (1) internalizing the regular expression, (2) repeated application of the refined derivative operation, (3) extraction of the accumulated annotations of the final 'empty' regular expression, and (4) turning the bit-code representation into parse tree from.

Simplifications. A well-known issue is that the size and number of derivatives may explode. For example, consider the following derivative steps.

Bit-code annotated regular expressions:

$$ri ::= \phi \mid (bs@\epsilon) \mid (bs@l) \mid (bs@ri \oplus ri) \mid (bs@ri\ ri) \mid (bs@ri^*)$$

$$\begin{array}{l}
internalize\ \phi = \phi \\
internalize\ \epsilon = ([]@\epsilon) \\
internalize\ l = ([]@l) \\
internalize\ (r_1 + r_2) = ([]@(fuse\ [0]\ (internalize\ r_1)) \oplus (fuse\ [1]\ (internalize\ r_2))) \\
internalize\ (r_1\ r_2) = ([]@(internalize\ r_1)\ (internalize\ r_2)) \\
internalize\ r^* = ([]@(internalize\ r)^*)
\end{array}$$

$$\begin{array}{l}
fuse\ bs\ \phi = \phi \\
fuse\ bs\ (p@\epsilon) = (bs{+}{+}p@\epsilon) \\
fuse\ bs\ (p@l) = (bs{+}{+}p@l) \\
fuse\ bs\ (p@ri_1 \oplus ri_2) = (bs{+}{+}p@ri_1 \oplus ri_2) \\
fuse\ bs\ (p@ri_1\ ri_2) = (bs{+}{+}p@ri_1\ ri_2) \\
fuse\ bs\ (p@ri^*) = (bs{+}{+}p@ri^*)
\end{array}$$

Incremental POSIX parsing:

$$\begin{array}{ll}
\phi\backslash_b l & = \phi \\
(bs@\epsilon)\backslash_b l & = \phi \\
(bs@l_1)\backslash_b l_2 & = \begin{cases} (bs@\epsilon) \text{ if } l_1 == l_2 \\ \phi \quad\quad \text{otherwise} \end{cases} \\
(bs@ri_1 \oplus ri_2)\backslash_b l & = (bs@ri_1\backslash_b l \oplus ri_2\backslash_b l) \\
(bs@ri_1\ ri_2)\backslash_b l & = \begin{cases} (bs@(ri_1\backslash_b l)\ ri_2) \oplus\ (fuse\ mkEpsBC_{ri_1}\ (ri_2\backslash_b l)) \text{ if } \epsilon \in L(ri_1) \\ (bs@(ri_1\backslash_b l))\ ri_2 \quad\quad\quad\quad\quad\quad\quad\quad\quad\quad \text{otherwise} \end{cases} \\
(bs@ri^*)\backslash_b l & = (bs@(fuse\ [0]\ ri\backslash_b l)\ ([]@ri^*))
\end{array}$$

$$\begin{array}{l}
mkEpsBC_{(bs@\epsilon)} = bs \\
mkEpsBC_{(bs@ri_1 \oplus ri_2)} \\
\quad\quad |\epsilon \in L(ri_1) = bs{+}{+}mkEpsBC_{ri_1} \\
\quad\quad |\epsilon \in L(ri_2) = bs{+}{+}mkEpsBC_{ri_2} \\
mkEpsBC_{(bs@ri_1\ ri_2)} = bs{+}{+}mkEpsBC_{ri_1}{+}{+}mkEpsBC_{ri_2} \\
mkEpsBC_{(bs@ri^*)} = bs{+}{+}[1]
\end{array}$$

$$\begin{array}{l}
parseBC'\,ri\ \epsilon \\
\quad\quad |\epsilon \in L(r) = mkEpsBC_{ri} \\
parseBC'\,ri\ lw = parseBC'\ ri\backslash_b l\ w \\
parseBCrw = decode_r(parseBC'(internalize\ r)w)
\end{array}$$

Fig. 5. Incremental Bit-Coded Forward POSIX Parse Tree Construction

$$a^* \xrightarrow{a} \epsilon a^* \xrightarrow{a} \phi a^* + \epsilon a^* \xrightarrow{a} (\phi a^* + \epsilon a^*) + (\phi a^* + \epsilon a^*) \xrightarrow{a} ...$$

As can easily be seen, subsequent derivatives are all equivalent to ϵa^*.

To ensure that that the size and number of derivatives remains finite, we simplify regular expressions. Each simplification step must maintain the parse tree information represented by the involved regular expression. Figure 6 performs

$$
\begin{aligned}
&isPhi\ (bs@ri^*) = False\\
&isPhi\ (bs@ri_1\ ri_2) = isPhi\ ri_1 \vee isPhi\ ri_2\\
&isPhi\ (bs@ri_1 \oplus ri_2) = isPhi\ ri_1 \wedge isPhi\ ri_2\\
&isPhi\ (bs@l) = False\\
&isPhi\ (bs@\epsilon) = False\\
&isPhi\ \phi = True
\end{aligned}
$$

We assume that $\oplus$ takes a list of operands, written $(bs@ \oplus [ri_1, ..., ri_n])$.

$$
\begin{aligned}
&simp\ (bs@(bs'@\epsilon)\ ri)\\
&\quad |isPhi\ r = \phi\\
&\quad |\mathsf{otherwise} = fuse\ (bs{+}{+}bs')ri\\
&simp\ (bs@ri_1\ ri_2)\\
&\quad |isPhi\ ri_1 \vee isPhi\ ri_2 = \phi\\
&\quad |\mathsf{otherwise} = bs@(simp\ ri_1)\ (simp\ ri_2)\\
&simp\ (bs@ \oplus\ []) = \phi\\
&simp\ (bs@ \oplus\ ((bs'@ \oplus rsi_1) : rsi_2)) = bs@ \oplus\ ((map\ (fuse\ bs')\ rsi_1){+}{+}rsi_2)\\
&simp\ (bs@ \oplus [ri]) = fuse\ bs(simp\ ri)\\
&simp\ (bs@ \oplus (ri : rsi)) = bs@ \oplus\ (nub\ (filter\ (not.isPhi\ )\ ((simp\ ri) : map\ simp\ rsi)))
\end{aligned}
$$

Fig. 6. Simplifications

simplification of annotated expressions in terms of function *simp*. We assume that *simp* is applied repeatedly until a fixpoint is reached.

For convenience, we assume that $\oplus$ takes a list of operands, instead of just two, and therefore write $(bs@ \oplus [ri_1, ..., ri_n])$. This notational convention makes it easier to put alternatives into right-associative normal form and apply simplification steps to remove duplicates and expressions equivalent to the empty language. Helper *isPhi* indicates if an expression equals the empty language. We can safely remove such cases via *filter*. In case of duplicates in a list of alternatives, we only keep the first occurrence via *nub*.

Linear-Time Complexity Claim. It is easy to see that each call of one of the functions/operations $\backslash_b$, *simp*, *fuse*, *mkEpsBC* and *isPhi* leads to subcalls whose number is bound by the size of the regular expression involved. We claim that thanks to aggressively applying *simp* this size remains finite. Hence, we can argue that the above mentioned functions/operations have constant time complexity which implies that we can incrementally compute bit-coded parse trees in linear time in the size of the input. We yet need to work out detailed estimates regarding the space complexity of our algorithm.

Correctness Claim. We further claim that the incremental parsing method in Figure 5 in combination with the simplification steps in Figure 6 yields POSIX parse trees. We have tested this claim extensively by using the method in Figure 3 as a reference but yet have to work out all proof details.

For example, we claim that $r\backslash_b l$ is related to $inj_{r\backslash l}$ as follows. Let r be a regular expression, l be a letter and v' a parse tree such that $\vdash v' : r\backslash l$. Then, we claim that $inj_{r\backslash l}\ v' = decode_r\ (retrieve_{(internalize\ r)\backslash_b l}\ v')$ where

$$
\begin{array}{l}
retrieve_{(bs\ @\ \epsilon)}\ () = bs \\
retrieve_{(bs\ @\ l)}\ l = bs \\
retrieve_{(bs\ @\ ri_1 \oplus ri_2)}\ (Left\ v) = bs\ {+}{+}\ retrieve_{ri_1}\ v \\
retrieve_{(bs\ @\ ri_1 \oplus ri_2)}\ (Right\ v) = bs\ {+}{+}\ retrieve_{ri_2}\ v \\
retrieve_{(bs\ @\ ri_1\ \ ri_2)}\ (v_1, v_2) = bs\ {+}{+}\ retrieve_{ri_1}\ v_1\ {+}{+}\ retrieve_{ri_2}\ v_2 \\
retrieve_{(bs\ @\ ri^*)}\ [] = bs\ {+}{+}\ [1] \\
retrieve_{(bs\ @\ ri^*)}\ (v : vs) = bs\ {+}{+}\ [0]\ {+}{+}\ retrieve_{ri}\ v\ {+}{+}\ retrieve_{([]\ @\ ri^*)}\ vs
\end{array}
$$

Function *retrieve* assembles a complete parse tree in bit-code representation based on the annotations in $(internalize\ r)\backslash_b l$ with respect to a given parse tree v'.

A similar claim applies to *simp*. We plan to work out the formal proof details in future work.

4 Experiments

We have implemented the incremental bit-coded POSIX parsing approach in Haskell. An explicit DFA is built where each transition has its associated parse tree transformer attached. Thus, we avoid repeated computations of the same calls to $\backslash_b$ and *simp*. Bit codes are built lazily using a purely functional data structure [18,6].

Experiments show that our implementation is competitive for inputs up to the size of about 10 Mb compared to highly-tuned C-based tools such as [2]. For larger inputs, our implementation is significantly slower (between 10-50 times) due to what seems to be high memory consumption. A possible solution is to use our method to compute the proper POSIX 'path' and then use this information to guide a space-efficient parsing algorithm such as [9] to build the POSIX parse tree. This is something we are currently working on.

For the specialized submatching case we have built another Haskell implementation referred to as **DERIV**. In DERIV, we only record the last match in case of Kleene star which is easily achieved in our implementation by 'overwriting' earlier with later matches.

We have benchmarked DERIV against three contenders which also claim to implement POSIX submatching: **TDFA**, a Haskell-based implementation [23] of an adapted Laurikari-style tagged NFA. The original implementation [14] does not always produce the proper POSIX submatch and requires the adaptations described in [13]. **RE2**, the google C++ re2 library [2] where for benchmarking the option `RE2::POSIX` is turned on. **C-POSIX**, the Haskell wrapper of the default C POSIX regular expression implementation [22].

To our surprise, RE2 and C-POSIX report incorrect results, i.e. non-POSIX matches, for some examples. For RE2 there exists a prototype version [3] which appears to compute the correct POSIX match. We have checked the behavior

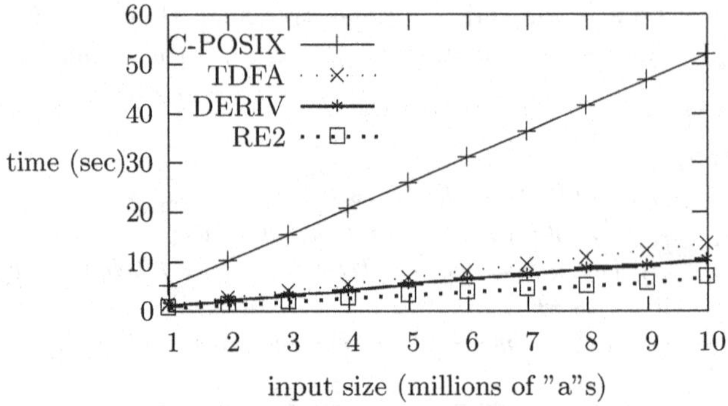

(a) Matching $(a + b + ab)^*$ with sequences of as

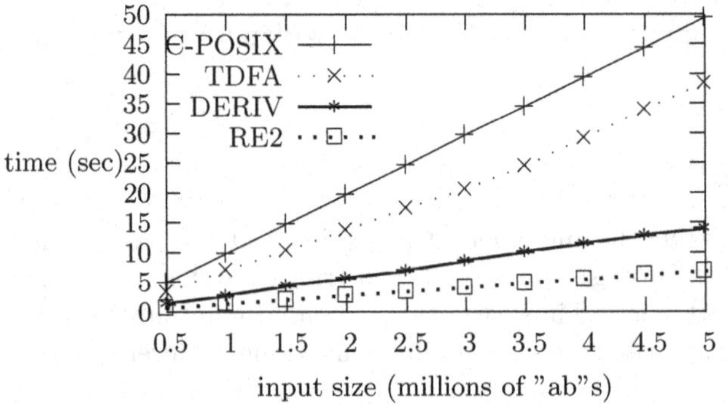

(b) Matching $(a + b + ab)^*$ with sequences of abs

Fig. 7. Ambiguous Pattern Benchmark

for a few selected cases. Regardless, we include RE2 and C-POSIX in our experiments.

We have carried out an extensive set of benchmarks consisting of contrived as well as real-world examples which we collected from various sources, e.g. see [12,17,5]. The benchmarks were executed under Mac OS X 10.7.2 with 2.4GHz Core 2 Duo and 8GB RAM where results were collected based on the median over several test runs. The complete set of results as well as the implementation can be retrieved via [15]. A brief summary of our experimental results follows.

Overall our DERIV performs well and for most cases we beat TDFA and C-POSIX. RE2 is generally faster but then we are comparing a Haskell-based implementation against a highly-tuned C-based implementation.

Our approach suffers for cases where the size of a DFA is exponentially larger compared to the equivalent NFA. Most of the time is spent on building the DFA. The actual time spent on building the match is negligible. A surprisingly simple and efficient method to improve the performance of our approach is to apply some form of abstraction. Instead of trying to find matches for all subpattern locations, we may only be interested in certain locations. That is, we use the POSIX DFA only for subparts we are interested in. For subparts we don't care about, rely on an NFA.

For us the most important conclusion is that DERIV particularly performs well for cases where computation of the POSIX result is non-trivial. See Figure 7 which shows the benchmarks results for our example from the introduction. We see this as an indication that our approach is promising to compute POSIX results correctly *and* efficiently.

5 Related Work and Conclusion

The work in [7] studies like us the efficient construction of regular expression parse trees. However, the algorithm in [7] neither respects the Greedy nor the POSIX disambiguation strategy.

Most prior works on parsing and submatching focus on Greedy instead of POSIX. The greedy result is closely tied to the structure of the regular expression where priority is given to left-most expressions. Efficient methods for obtaining the greedy result transform the regular expression into an NFA. A 'greedy' NFA traversal then yields the proper result. For example, consider [14] for the case of submatching and [9,8] for the general parsing case.

Adopting greedy algorithms to the POSIX setting requires some subtle adjustments to compute the POSIX, i.e. longest left-most, result. For example, see [4,13,19]. Our experiments confirm that our method particularly performs well for cases where there is a difference between the POSIX and Greedy result. By construction our method yields the POSIX result whereas the works in [4,13,19] require some additional bookkeeping (which causes overhead) to select the proper POSIX result.

The novelty of our approach lies in the use of derivatives. Regular expression derivatives [1] are an old idea and recently attracted again some interest in the context of lexing/parsing [20,16]. We recently became aware of [26] which like us applies the idea of derivatives but only considers submatching.

To the best of our knowledge, we are the first to give an efficient algorithm for constructing POSIX parse trees including a formal correctness result. Our experiments show good results for the specialized submatching case. We are currently working on improving the performance for the full parsing case.

Acknowledgments. We thank referees for LATA'14 and FLOPS'14 for their helpful comments on earlier versions of this paper. We thank Christian Urban and Mark Sangster for their comments.

References

1. Brzozowski, J.A.: Derivatives of regular expressions. J. ACM 11(4), 481–494 (1964)
2. Cox, R.: re2 – an efficient, principled regular expression library, `http://code.google.com/p/re2/+`

3. Cox, R.: NFA POSIX (2007), http://swtch.com/~rsc/regexp/nfa-posix.y.txt
4. Cox, R.: Regular expression matching: the virtual machine approach - digression: Posix submatching (2009), http://swtch.com/~rsc/regexp/regexp2.html
5. Cox, R.: Regular expression matching in the wild (2010), http://swtch.com/~rsc/regexp/regexp3.html
6. http://hackage.haskell.org/package/dequeue-0.1.5/docs/Data-Dequeue.html
7. Dubé, D., Feeley, M.: Efficiently building a parse tree from a regular expression. Acta Inf. 37(2), 121–144 (2000)
8. Frisch, A., Cardelli, L.: Greedy regular expression matching. In: Díaz, J., Karhumäki, J., Lepistö, A., Sannella, D. (eds.) ICALP 2004. LNCS, vol. 3142, pp. 618–629. Springer, Heidelberg (2004)
9. Grathwohl, N.B.B., Henglein, F., Nielsen, L., Rasmussen, U.T.: Two-pass greedy regular expression parsing. In: Konstantinidis, S. (ed.) CIAA 2013. LNCS, vol. 7982, pp. 60–71. Springer, Heidelberg (2013)
10. Institute of Electrical and Electronics Engineers (IEEE): Standard for information technology – Portable Operating System Interface (POSIX) – Part 2 (Shell and utilities), Section 2.8 (Regular expression notation). IEEE Standard 1003.2, New York (1992)
11. Kuklewicz, C.: Regex POSIX, http://www.haskell.org/haskellwiki/Regex_Posix
12. Kuklewicz, C.: The regex-posix-unittest package, http://hackage.haskell.org/package/regex-posix-unittest
13. Kuklewicz, C.: Forward regular expression matching with bounded space (2007), http://haskell.org/haskellwiki/RegexpDesign
14. Laurikari, V.: NFAs with tagged transitions, their conversion to deterministic automata and application to regular expressions. In: SPIRE, pp. 181–187 (2000)
15. Lu, K.Z.M., Sulzmann, M.: POSIX Submatching with Regular Expression Derivatives, http://code.google.com/p/xhaskell-regex-deriv
16. Might, M., Darais, D., Spiewak, D.: Parsing with derivatives: a functional pearl. In: Proc. of ICFP 2011, pp. 189–195. ACM (2011)
17. Nielsen, L., Henglein, F.: Bit-coded regular expression parsing. In: Dediu, A.-H., Inenaga, S., Martín-Vide, C. (eds.) LATA 2011. LNCS, vol. 6638, pp. 402–413. Springer, Heidelberg (2011)
18. Okasaki, C.: Purely functional data structures. Cambridge University Press (1999)
19. Okui, S., Suzuki, T.: Disambiguation in regular expression matching via position automata with augmented transitions. In: Domaratzki, M., Salomaa, K. (eds.) CIAA 2010. LNCS, vol. 6482, pp. 231–240. Springer, Heidelberg (2011)
20. Owens, S., Reppy, J., Turon, A.: Regular-expression derivatives reexamined. Journal of Functional Programming 19(2), 173–190 (2009)
21. PCRE - Perl Compatible Regular Expressions, http://www.pcre.org/
22. regex-posix: The posix regex backend for regex-base, http://hackage.haskell.org/package/regex-posix
23. regex-tdfa: A new all haskell tagged dfa regex engine, inspired by libtre, http://hackage.haskell.org/package/regex-tdfa
24. Sulzmann, M., Lu, K.Z.M.: Regular expression sub-matching using partial derivatives. In: Proc. of PPDP 2012, pp. 79–90. ACM (2012)
25. Vansummeren, S.: Type inference for unique pattern matching. ACM TOPLAS 28(3), 389–428 (2006)
26. Vouillon, J.: ocaml-re - Pure OCaml regular expressions, with support for Perl and POSIX-style strings, https://github.com/avsm/ocaml-re

Proving Correctness of Compilers Using Structured Graphs

Patrick Bahr

Department of Computer Science, University of Copenhagen, Denmark
paba@di.ku.dk

Abstract. We present an approach to compiler implementation using Oliveira and Cook's structured graphs that avoids the use of explicit jumps in the generated code. The advantage of our method is that it takes the implementation of a compiler using a tree type along with its correctness proof and turns it into a compiler implementation using a graph type along with a correctness proof. The implementation and correctness proof of a compiler using a tree type without explicit jumps is simple, but yields code duplication. Our method provides a convenient way of improving such a compiler without giving up the benefits of simple reasoning.

1 Introduction

Verification of compilers – like other software – is difficult [13]. In such an endeavour one typically has to balance the "cleverness" of the implementation with the simplicity of reasoning about it. A concrete example of this fact is given by Hutton and Wright [10] who present correctness proofs of compilers for a simple language with exceptions. The authors first present a naïve compiler implementation that produces a tree representing the possible control flow of the input program. The code that it produces is essentially the right code, but the compiler *loses information* since it duplicates code instead of sharing it. However, the simplicity of the implementation is matched with a clean and simple proof by equational reasoning. Hutton and Wright also present a more realistic compiler, which uses labels and explicit jumps, resulting in a target code in linear form and without code duplication. However, the cleverer implementation also requires a more complicated proof, in which one has to reason about the freshness and scope of labels.

In this paper we present an intermediate approach, which is still simple, both in its implementation and in its correctness proof, but which avoids the loss of information of the simple approach described by Hutton and Wright [10]. The remedy for the information loss of the simple approach is obvious: we use a graph instead of a tree structure to represent the target code. The linear representation with labels and jumps is essentially a graph as well – it is just a very inconvenient one for reasoning. Instead of using unique names to represent sharing, we use the *structured graphs* representation of Oliveira and Cook [18]. This representation

M. Codish and E. Sumii (Eds.): FLOPS 2014, LNCS 8475, pp. 221–237, 2014.

of graphs uses parametric higher-order abstract syntax [5] to represent binders, which in turn are used to represent sharing. This structure allows us to take the simple compiler implementation using trees, make a slight adjustment to it, and obtain a compiler implementation using graphs that preserves the sharing information.

In essence our approach teases apart two aspects that are typically combined in code generation: (1) the translation into the target language, and (2) generating fresh (label) names for representing jumps in the target language. By keeping the two aspects separate, we can implement further transformations, e.g. code optimisations, without having to deal with explicit jumps and names. Only in the final step, when the code is linearised, names have to be generated in order to produce explicit jump instructions. Consequently, the issues that ensue in this setting can be dealt with in isolation – separately from the actual translation and subsequent transformation steps.

Our main goal is to retain the simplicity of the correctness proof of the tree-based compiler. The key observation making this possible is that the semantics of the tree-based and the graph-based target language, i.e. their respective *virtual machines*, are equivalent after *unravelling* of the graph structure. More precisely, given the semantics of the tree-based and the graph-based target language as $exec_{\mathsf{T}}$ and $exec_{\mathsf{G}}$, respectively, we have the following equation:

$$exec_{\mathsf{G}} = exec_{\mathsf{T}} \circ unravel$$

We show that this correspondence is an inherent consequence of the recursion schemes that are used to define these semantics. In fact, this correspondence follows from the correctness of *short cut fusion* [8, 12]. That is, the above property is independent of the target language of the compiler. As a consequence, the correctness proof of the improved, graph-based compiler is reduced to a proof that its implementation is equivalent to the tree-based implementation modulo unravelling. More precisely, it then suffices to show that

$$comp_{\mathsf{T}} = unravel \circ comp_{\mathsf{G}}$$

which is achieved by a straightforward induction proof.

In sum, the technique that we propose here improves existing simple compiler implementations to more realistic ones using a graph representation for the target code. This improvement requires minimal effort – both in terms of the implementation and the correctness proof. The fact that we consider both the implementation and its correctness proof makes our technique the ideal companion to improve a compiler that has been obtained by calculation [16]. Such calculations derive a compiler from a specification, and produce not only an implementation of the compiler but also a proof of its correctness. The example compiler that we use in this paper has in fact been calculated in this way by Bahr and Hutton [3], and we have successfully applied our technique to other compilers derived by Bahr and Hutton [3], which includes compilers for languages with features such as (synchronous and asynchronous) exceptions, (global and local) state and non-determinism. Thus, despite its simplicity, our technique is quite powerful, especially when combined with other techniques such as the abovementioned calculation techniques.

In short, the contributions of this paper are the following:

- From a compiler with code duplication we derive a compiler that avoids duplication using a graph representation.
- Using short cut fusion, we prove that folds over graphs are equal to corresponding folds over the unravelling of the input graphs.
- Using the above result, we derive the correctness of the graph-based compiler implementation from the correctness of the tree-based compiler.
- We further simplify the proof by using free monads to represent tree types together with a corresponding monadic graph type.

Throughout this paper we use Haskell [14] as the implementation language.

2 A Simple Compiler

The example language that we use throughout the paper is a simple expression language with integers, addition and exceptions:

```
data Expr = Val Int | Add   Expr Expr
          | Throw   | Catch Expr Expr
```

The semantics of this language is defined using an evaluation function that evaluates a given expression to an integer value or returns *Nothing* in case of an uncaught exception:

```
eval :: Expr → Maybe Int
eval (Val n)     = Just n
eval (Add x y)   = case eval x of
                     Nothing → Nothing
                     Just n  → case eval y of
                                 Nothing → Nothing
                                 Just m  → Just (n + m)
eval  Throw      = Nothing
eval (Catch x h) = case eval x of
                     Nothing → eval h
                     Just n  → Just n
```

This is the same language and semantics used by Hutton and Wright [10]. Like Hutton and Wright, we chose a simple language in order to focus on the essence of the problem, which in our case is control flow in the target language and the use of duplication or sharing to represent it. Moreover, this choice allows us to compare our method to the original work of Hutton and Wright whose focus was on the simplicity of reasoning.

The target for the compiler is a simple stack machine with the following instruction set:

$$\textbf{data}\ \mathit{Code} = \mathit{PUSH}\ \mathit{Int}\ \mathit{Code} \mid \mathit{ADD}\ \mathit{Code} \mid \mathit{HALT} \mid \mathit{UNMARK}\ \mathit{Code} \mid \mathit{MARK}\ \mathit{Code}\ \mathit{Code} \mid \mathit{THROW}$$

The intended semantics (which is made precise later) for the instructions is:

- *PUSH* n pushes the integer value n on the stack,
- *ADD* expects two integers on the stack and replaces them with their sum,
- *MARK* c pushes the exception handler code c on the stack,
- *UNMARK* removes such a handler code from the stack,
- *THROW* unwinds the stack until an exception handler code is found, which is then executed, and
- *HALT* stops the execution.

For the implementation of the compiler we deviate slightly from the presentation of Hutton and Wright [10] and instead write the compiler in a style that uses an additional accumulation parameter c, which simplifies the proofs [9]:

$$\begin{aligned}
&\mathit{comp}^{\mathsf{A}} :: \mathit{Expr} \to \mathit{Code} \to \mathit{Code}\\
&\mathit{comp}^{\mathsf{A}}\ (\mathit{Val}\ n)\quad c = \mathit{PUSH}\ n\ c\\
&\mathit{comp}^{\mathsf{A}}\ (\mathit{Add}\ x\ y)\quad c = \mathit{comp}^{\mathsf{A}}\ x\ (\mathit{comp}^{\mathsf{A}}\ y\ (\mathit{ADD}\ c))\\
&\mathit{comp}^{\mathsf{A}}\ \mathit{Throw}\quad c = \mathit{THROW}\\
&\mathit{comp}^{\mathsf{A}}\ (\mathit{Catch}\ x\ h)\ c = \mathit{MARK}\ (\mathit{comp}^{\mathsf{A}}\ h\ c)\ (\mathit{comp}^{\mathsf{A}}\ x\ (\mathit{UNMARK}\ c))
\end{aligned}$$

Since the code generator is implemented in this code continuation passing style, function application corresponds to concatenation of code fragments. To stress this reading, we shall use the operator $\triangleright$, which is simply defined as function application and is declared to associate to the right with minimal precedence:

$$\begin{aligned}
&(\triangleright) :: (a \to b) \to a \to b\\
&f \triangleright x = f\ x
\end{aligned}$$

For instance, the equation for the *Add* case of the definition of $\mathit{comp}^{\mathsf{A}}$ then reads:

$$\mathit{comp}^{\mathsf{A}}\ (\mathit{Add}\ x\ y)\ c = \mathit{comp}^{\mathsf{A}}\ x \triangleright \mathit{comp}^{\mathsf{A}}\ y \triangleright \mathit{ADD} \triangleright c$$

To obtain the final code for an expression, we supply *HALT* as the initial value of the accumulator of $\mathit{comp}^{\mathsf{A}}$. The use of the $\triangleright$ operator to supply the argument indicates the intuition that *HALT* is placed at the end of the code produced by $\mathit{comp}^{\mathsf{A}}$:

$$\begin{aligned}
&\mathit{comp} :: \mathit{Expr} \to \mathit{Code}\\
&\mathit{comp}\ e = \mathit{comp}^{\mathsf{A}}\ e \triangleright \mathit{HALT}
\end{aligned}$$

The following examples illustrate the workings of the compiler *comp*:

$$\begin{aligned}
&\mathit{comp}\ (\mathit{Add}\ (\mathit{Val}\ 2)\ (\mathit{Val}\ 3)) \rightsquigarrow \mathit{PUSH}\ 2 \triangleright \mathit{PUSH}\ 3 \triangleright \mathit{ADD} \triangleright \mathit{HALT}\\
&\mathit{comp}\ (\mathit{Catch}\ (\mathit{Val}\ 2)\ (\mathit{Val}\ 3)) \rightsquigarrow \mathit{MARK}\ (\mathit{PUSH}\ 3 \triangleright \mathit{HALT})\\
&\qquad\qquad \triangleright \mathit{PUSH}\ 2 \triangleright \mathit{UNMARK} \triangleright \mathit{HALT}\\
&\mathit{comp}\ (\mathit{Catch}\ \mathit{Throw}\ (\mathit{Val}\ 3)) \rightsquigarrow \mathit{MARK}\ (\mathit{PUSH}\ 3 \triangleright \mathit{HALT}) \triangleright \mathit{THROW}
\end{aligned}$$

For the virtual machine that executes the code produced by the above compiler, we use the following type for the stack:

$$\begin{array}{l} \textbf{type}\ Stack = [Item] \\ \textbf{data}\ Item\ \ = VAL\ Int \mid HAN\ (Stack \rightarrow Stack) \end{array}$$

This type deviates slightly from the one for the virtual machine defined by Hutton and Wright [10]. Instead of having the code of an exception handler on the stack (constructor *HAN*), we have the continuation of the virtual machine on the stack. This will simplify the proof as we shall see later on. However, this type and the accompanying definition of the virtual machine that is given below is exactly the result of the calculation given by Bahr and Hutton [3] just before the last calculation step (which then yields the virtual machine of Hutton and Wright [10]). The virtual machine that works on this stack is defined as follows:

$$\begin{array}{lll} \multicolumn{3}{l}{exec :: Code \rightarrow Stack \rightarrow Stack} \\ exec\ (PUSH\ n\ c) & s = & exec\ c\ (VAL\ n : s) \\ exec\ (ADD\ c) & s = & \textbf{case}\ s\ \textbf{of} \\ & & \quad (VAL\ m : VAL\ n : t) \rightarrow exec\ c\ (VAL\ (n+m) : t) \\ exec\ THROW & s = & unwind\ s \\ exec\ (MARK\ h\ c) & s = & exec\ c\ (HAN\ (exec\ h) : s) \\ exec\ (UNMARK\ c) & s = & \textbf{case}\ s\ \textbf{of}\ (x : HAN\ \_ : t) \rightarrow exec\ c\ (x : t) \\ exec\ HALT & s = & s \\ \multicolumn{3}{l}{unwind :: Stack \rightarrow Stack} \\ unwind\ [\,] & = & [\,] \\ unwind\ (VAL\ \_ : s) & = & unwind\ s \\ unwind\ (HAN\ h : s) & = & h\ s \end{array}$$

The virtual machine does what is expected from the informal semantics that we have given above. The semantics of *MARK*, however, may seem counterintuitive at first: as mentioned above, *MARK* does not put the handler code on the stack but rather the continuation that is obtained by executing it. Consequently, when the unwinding of the stack reaches a handler h on the stack, this handler h is directly applied to the remainder of the stack. This slight deviation from the semantics of Hutton and Wright [10] makes sure that *exec* is in fact a fold.

We will not go into the details of the correctness proof for the compiler *comp*. One can show that it satisfies the following correctness property [3]:

Theorem 1 (compiler correctness)

$$exec\ (comp\ e)\ [\,] = conv\ (eval\ e) \qquad \textit{for all } e :: Expr$$

where
$$\begin{array}{l} conv\ (Just\ n) = [\,Val\ n] \\ conv\ Nothing = [\,] \end{array}$$

That is, in particular, we have that

$$exec\ (comp\ e)\ [\,] = [\,Val\ n] \quad \Longleftrightarrow \quad eval\ e = Just\ n$$

While the compiler has the nice property that it can be derived from the language semantics, the code that it produces is quite unrealistic. Note the duplication that occurs for generating the code for *Catch*: the continuation code c is inserted both after the handler code (in $comp^{A}\ h\ c$) and after the *UNMARK* instruction. This is necessary since the code c may have to be executed regardless whether an exception is thrown in the scope x of the *Catch* or not.

This duplication can be avoided by using explicit jumps in the code. Instead of duplicating code, jumps to a single copy of the code are inserted. However, this complicates both the implementation of the compiler and its correctness proof [10]. Also the derivation of such a compiler by calculation is equally cumbersome.

The approach that we suggest in this paper takes the above compiler and derives a slightly different variant that instead of a tree structure produces a graph structure. Along with the compiler we derive a virtual machine that also works on the graph structure. The two variants of the compiler and its companion virtual machine only differ in the sharing that the graph variant provides. This fact allows us to derive the correctness of the graph-based compiler very easily from the correctness of the original tree-based compiler.

3 From Trees to Graphs

Before we derive the graph-based compiler and the corresponding virtual machine, we restructure the definition of the original compiler and the corresponding virtual machine. This will smoothen the process and simplify the presentation.

3.1 Preparations

Instead of defining the type *Code* directly, we represent it as the initial algebra of a functor. To distinguish this representation from the graph representation we introduce later, we use the name *Tree* for the initial algebra construction.

$$\mathbf{data}\ \mathit{Tree}\ f = \mathit{In}\ (f\ (\mathit{Tree}\ f))$$

The functor that induces the initial algebra that we shall use for representing the target language is easily obtained from the original *Code* data type:

$$\begin{aligned}\mathbf{data}\ \mathit{Code}_{\mathsf{F}}\ a = {} & \mathit{PUSH}_{\mathsf{F}}\ \mathit{Int}\ a \mid \mathit{ADD}_{\mathsf{F}}\ a \mid \mathit{HALT}_{\mathsf{F}} \\ \mid {} & \mathit{MARK}_{\mathsf{F}}\ a\ a \mid \mathit{UNMARK}_{\mathsf{F}}\ a \mid \mathit{THROW}_{\mathsf{F}}\end{aligned}$$

The type representing the target code is thus $\mathit{Tree}\ \mathit{Code}_{\mathsf{F}}$, which is isomorphic to *Code* modulo non-strictness. We proceed by reformulating the definition of *comp* to work on the type $\mathit{Tree}\ \mathit{Code}_{\mathsf{F}}$ instead of *Code*:

$$\begin{aligned}&\mathit{comp}^{\mathsf{A}}_{\mathsf{T}} :: \mathit{Expr} \to \mathit{Tree}\ \mathit{Code}_{\mathsf{F}} \to \mathit{Tree}\ \mathit{Code}_{\mathsf{F}}\\ &\mathit{comp}^{\mathsf{A}}_{\mathsf{T}}\ (\mathit{Val}\ n)\quad\ \ c = \mathit{PUSH}_{\mathsf{T}}\ n \rhd c\\ &\mathit{comp}^{\mathsf{A}}_{\mathsf{T}}\ (\mathit{Add}\ x\ y)\ \ c = \mathit{comp}^{\mathsf{A}}_{\mathsf{T}}\ x \rhd \mathit{comp}^{\mathsf{A}}_{\mathsf{T}}\ y \rhd \mathit{ADD}_{\mathsf{T}} \rhd c\end{aligned}$$

$$\begin{aligned}
&comp^{\mathsf{A}}_{\mathsf{T}}\ Throw\quad\ \ c = THROW_{\mathsf{T}}\\
&comp^{\mathsf{A}}_{\mathsf{T}}\ (Catch\ x\ h)\ c = MARK_{\mathsf{T}}\ (comp^{\mathsf{A}}_{\mathsf{T}}\ h \rhd c) \rhd comp^{\mathsf{A}}_{\mathsf{T}}\ x \rhd UNMARK_{\mathsf{T}} \rhd c\\
&comp_{\mathsf{T}} :: Expr \to Tree\ Code_{\mathsf{F}}\\
&comp_{\mathsf{T}}\ e = comp^{\mathsf{A}}_{\mathsf{T}}\ e \rhd HALT_{\mathsf{T}}
\end{aligned}$$

Note that we do not use the constructors of $Code_{\mathsf{F}}$ directly, but instead we use *smart constructors* that also apply the constructor *In* of the type constructor *Tree*. These smart constructors serve as drop-in replacements for the constructors of the original *Code* data type. For example, $PUSH_{\mathsf{T}}$ is defined as follows:

$$\begin{aligned}
&PUSH_{\mathsf{T}} :: Int \to Tree\ Code_{\mathsf{F}} \to Tree\ Code_{\mathsf{F}}\\
&PUSH_{\mathsf{T}}\ i\ c = In\ (PUSH_{\mathsf{F}}\ i\ c)
\end{aligned}$$

Lastly, we also reformulate the semantics of the target language, i.e. we define the function *exec* on the type *Tree* $Code_{\mathsf{F}}$. To do this, we use the following definition of a fold on an initial algebra:

$$\begin{aligned}
&fold :: Functor\ f \Rightarrow (f\ r \to r) \to Tree\ f \to r\\
&fold\ alg\ (In\ t) = alg\ (fmap\ (fold\ alg)\ t)
\end{aligned}$$

The definition of the semantics is a straightforward transcription of the definition of *exec* into an algebra:

$$\begin{aligned}
&execAlg :: Code_{\mathsf{F}}\ (Stack \to Stack) \to Stack \to Stack\\
&execAlg\ (PUSH_{\mathsf{F}}\ n\ c)\quad s = c\ (VAL\ n : s)\\
&execAlg\ (ADD_{\mathsf{F}}\ c)\qquad s = \mathbf{case}\ s\ \mathbf{of}\\
&\qquad\qquad\qquad\qquad\qquad (VAL\ m : VAL\ n : t) \to c\ (VAL\ (n+m) : t)\\
&execAlg\ THROW_{\mathsf{F}}\qquad s = unwind\ s\\
&execAlg\ (MARK_{\mathsf{F}}\ h\ c)\quad s = c\ (HAN\ h : s)\\
&execAlg\ (UNMARK_{\mathsf{F}}\ c)\ s = \mathbf{case}\ s\ \mathbf{of}\ (x : HAN\ _ : t) \to c\ (x : t)\\
&execAlg\ HALT_{\mathsf{F}}\qquad\ \ s = s\\
&exec_{\mathsf{T}} :: Tree\ Code_{\mathsf{F}} \to Stack \to Stack\\
&exec_{\mathsf{T}} = fold\ execAlg
\end{aligned}$$

From the correctness of the original compiler from Section 2, as expressed in Theorem 1, we obtain the correctness of our reformulation of the implementation:

Corollary 1 (correctness of $comp_{\mathsf{T}}$)

$$exec_{\mathsf{T}}\ (comp_{\mathsf{T}}\ e)\ [\,] = conv\ (eval\ e) \qquad for\ all\ e :: Expr$$

Proof. Let $\phi :: Code \to Tree\ Code_{\mathsf{F}}$ be the function that recursively maps each constructor of *Code* to the corresponding smart constructor of *Tree* $Code_{\mathsf{F}}$. We can easily check that $comp_{\mathsf{T}}$ and $exec_{\mathsf{T}}$ are equivalent to the original functions *comp* respectively *exec* via ϕ, i.e.

$$comp_{\mathsf{T}} = \phi \circ comp \quad \text{and} \quad exec_{\mathsf{T}} \circ \phi = exec$$

Consequently, we have that $exec_{\mathsf{T}} \circ comp_{\mathsf{T}} = exec \circ comp$, and thus the corollary follows from Theorem 1. □

3.2 Deriving a Graph-Based Compiler

Finally, we turn to the graph-based implementation of the compiler. Essentially, this implementation is obtained from $comp_{\mathsf{T}}$ by replacing the type $Tree\ Code_{\mathsf{F}}$ with a type $Graph\ Code_{\mathsf{F}}$, which instead of a tree structure has a graph structure, and using explicit sharing instead of duplication.

In order to define graphs over a functor, we use the representation of Oliveira and Cook [18] called *structured graphs*. Put simply, a structured graph is a tree with added sharing facilitated by let bindings. In turn, let bindings are represented using parametric higher-order abstract syntax [5].

$$
\begin{aligned}
\textbf{data}\ Graph'\ f\ v = {} & GIn\ (f\ (Graph'\ f\ v)) \\
\mid\ & Let\ (Graph'\ f\ v)\ (v \to Graph'\ f\ v) \\
\mid\ & Var\ v
\end{aligned}
$$

The first constructor has the same structure as the constructor of the *Tree* type constructor. The other two constructors will allow us to express let bindings: $Let\ g\ (\lambda x \to h)$ binds g to the metavariable x in h. Metavariables bound in a let binding have type v; the only way to use them is with the constructor *Var*. To enforce this invariant, the type variable v is made polymorphic:

$$\textbf{newtype}\ Graph\ f = MkGraph\ (\forall\ v\ .\ Graph'\ f\ v)$$

We shall use the type constructor *Graph* (and *Graph'*) as a replacement for *Tree*. For the purposes of our compiler we only need acyclic graphs. That is why we only consider non-recursive let bindings as opposed to the more general structured graphs of Oliveira and Cook [18]. This restriction to non-recursive let bindings is crucial for the reasoning principle that we use to prove correctness.

We can use the graph type almost as a drop-in replacement for the tree type. The only thing that we need to do is to use smart constructors that use the constructor *GIn* instead of *In*, e.g.

$$
\begin{aligned}
& PUSH_{\mathsf{G}} :: Int \to Graph'\ Code_{\mathsf{F}}\ v \to Graph'\ Code_{\mathsf{F}}\ v \\
& PUSH_{\mathsf{G}}\ i\ c = GIn\ (PUSH_{\mathsf{F}}\ i\ c)
\end{aligned}
$$

From the type of the smart constructors we can observe that graphs are constructed using the type constructor *Graph'*, not *Graph*. Only after the construction of the graph is completed, the constructor *MkGraph* is applied in order to obtain a graph of type $Graph\ Code_{\mathsf{F}}$.

The definition of $comp^{\mathsf{A}}_{\mathsf{T}}$ can be transcribed into graph style by simply using the abovementioned smart constructors instead:

$$
\begin{aligned}
& comp^{\mathsf{A}}_{\mathsf{G}} :: Expr \to Graph'\ Code_{\mathsf{F}}\ a \to Graph'\ Code_{\mathsf{F}}\ a \\
& comp^{\mathsf{A}}_{\mathsf{G}}\ (Val\ n) \qquad\ \ c = PUSH_{\mathsf{G}}\ n \rhd c \\
& comp^{\mathsf{A}}_{\mathsf{G}}\ (Add\ x\ y) \quad c = comp^{\mathsf{A}}_{\mathsf{G}}\ x \rhd comp^{\mathsf{A}}_{\mathsf{G}}\ y \rhd ADD_{\mathsf{G}} \rhd c \\
& comp^{\mathsf{A}}_{\mathsf{G}}\ (Throw) \qquad c = THROW_{\mathsf{G}} \\
& comp^{\mathsf{A}}_{\mathsf{G}}\ (Catch\ x\ h)\ c = MARK_{\mathsf{G}}\ (comp^{\mathsf{A}}_{\mathsf{G}}\ h \rhd c) \rhd comp^{\mathsf{A}}_{\mathsf{G}}\ x \rhd UNMARK_{\mathsf{G}} \rhd c
\end{aligned}
$$

The above is a one-to-one transcription of $comp_{\mathsf{T}}^{\mathsf{A}}$. But this is not what we want. We want to make use of the fact that the target language allows sharing. In particular, we want to get rid of the duplication in the code generated for *Catch*.

We can avoid this duplication by simply using a let binding to replace the two occurrences of c with a metavariable c' that is then bound to c. The last equation for $comp_{\mathsf{G}}^{\mathsf{A}}$ is thus rewritten as follows:

$$\begin{aligned} comp_{\mathsf{G}}^{\mathsf{A}}\ (Catch\ x\ h)\ c = Let\ c\ (\lambda c' \to\ & MARK_{\mathsf{G}}\ (comp_{\mathsf{G}}^{\mathsf{A}}\ h \rhd Var\ c') \\ & \rhd comp_{\mathsf{G}}^{\mathsf{A}}\ x \rhd UNMARK_{\mathsf{G}} \rhd Var\ c') \end{aligned}$$

The right-hand side for the case *Catch* x h has now only one occurrence of c.

The final code generator function $comp_{\mathsf{G}}^{\mathsf{A}}$ is then obtained by supplying $HALT_{\mathsf{G}}$ as the initial value of the code continuation and wrapping the result with the *MkGraph* constructor so as to return a result of type *Graph* $Code_{\mathsf{F}}$:

$$\begin{aligned} & comp_{\mathsf{G}} :: Expr \to Graph\ Code_{\mathsf{F}} \\ & comp_{\mathsf{G}}\ e = MkGraph\ (comp_{\mathsf{G}}^{\mathsf{A}}\ e \rhd HALT_{\mathsf{G}}) \end{aligned}$$

To illustrate the difference between $comp_{\mathsf{G}}$ and $comp_{\mathsf{T}}$, we apply both of them to an example expression $e = Add\ (Catch\ (Val\ 1)\ (Val\ 2))\ (Val\ 3)$:

$$\begin{aligned} comp_{\mathsf{T}}\ e \leadsto\ & MARK_{\mathsf{T}}\ (PUSH_{\mathsf{T}}\ 2 \rhd PUSH_{\mathsf{T}}\ 3 \rhd ADD_{\mathsf{T}} \rhd HALT_{\mathsf{T}}) \\ & \rhd PUSH_{\mathsf{T}}\ 1 \rhd UNMARK_{\mathsf{T}} \rhd PUSH_{\mathsf{T}}\ 3 \rhd ADD_{\mathsf{T}} \rhd HALT_{\mathsf{T}} \\ comp_{\mathsf{G}}\ e \leadsto\ & MkGraph\ (Let\ (PUSH_{\mathsf{G}}\ 3 \rhd ADD_{\mathsf{G}} \rhd HALT_{\mathsf{G}})\ (\lambda v \to \\ & MARK_{\mathsf{G}}\ (PUSH_{\mathsf{G}}\ 2 \rhd Var\ v) \rhd PUSH_{\mathsf{G}}\ 1 \rhd UNMARK_{\mathsf{G}} \rhd Var\ v)) \end{aligned}$$

Note that $comp_{\mathsf{T}}$ duplicates the code fragment $PUSH_{\mathsf{T}}\ 3 \rhd ADD_{\mathsf{T}} \rhd HALT_{\mathsf{T}}$, which is supposed to be executed after the catch expression, whereas $comp_{\mathsf{G}}$ binds this code fragment to a metavariable v, which is then used as a substitute.

The recursion schemes on structured graphs make use of the parametricity in the metavariable type as well. The general fold over graphs as given by Oliveira and Cook [18] is defined as follows:[1]

$$\begin{aligned} & gfold :: Functor\ f \Rightarrow (v \to r) \to (r \to (v \to r) \to r) \to (f\ r \to r) \to \\ & \qquad\qquad Graph\ f \to r \\ & gfold\ v\ l\ i\ (MkGraph\ g) = trans\ g \\ & \quad \textbf{where}\ trans\ (Var\ x) \quad = v\ x \\ & \qquad\quad trans\ (Let\ e\ f) = l\ (trans\ e)\ (trans \circ f) \\ & \qquad\quad trans\ (GIn\ t) \quad = i\ (fmap\ trans\ t) \end{aligned}$$

The combinator takes three functions, which are used to interpret the three constructors of *Graph'*. This general form is needed for example if we want to transform the graph representation into a linearised form [2], but for our purposes we only need a simple special case of it:

[1] Oliveira and Cook [18] considered the more general case of cyclic graphs, the definition of *gfold* given here is specialised to the case of acyclic graphs.

$$
\begin{aligned}
&\mathit{ufold} :: \mathit{Functor}\ f \Rightarrow (f\ r \to r) \to \mathit{Graph}\ f \to r \\
&\mathit{ufold} = \mathit{gfold}\ \mathit{id}\ (\lambda e\ f \to f\ e)
\end{aligned}
$$

Note that the type signature is identical to the one for *fold* except for the use of *Graph* instead of *Tree*. Thus, we can reuse the algebra *execAlg* from Section 3.1, which defines the semantics of $\mathit{Tree}\ \mathit{Code}_\mathsf{F}$, in order to define the semantics of $\mathit{Graph}\ \mathit{Code}_\mathsf{F}$:

$$
\begin{aligned}
&\mathit{exec}_\mathsf{G} :: \mathit{Graph}\ \mathit{Code}_\mathsf{F} \to \mathit{Stack} \to \mathit{Stack} \\
&\mathit{exec}_\mathsf{G} = \mathit{ufold}\ \mathit{execAlg}
\end{aligned}
$$

4 Correctness Proof

In this section we shall prove that the graph-based compiler that we defined in Section 3.2 is indeed correct. This turns out to be rather simple: we derive the correctness property for comp_G from the correctness property for comp_T. The simplicity of the argument is rooted in the fact that comp_T is the same as comp_G followed by unravelling. In other words, comp_G only differs from comp_T in that it adds sharing – as expected.

4.1 Compiler Correctness by Unravelling

Before we prove this relation between comp_T and comp_G, we need to specify what unravelling means:

$$
\begin{aligned}
&\mathit{unravel} :: \mathit{Functor}\ f \Rightarrow \mathit{Graph}\ f \to \mathit{Tree}\ f \\
&\mathit{unravel} = \mathit{ufold}\ \mathit{In}
\end{aligned}
$$

While this definition is nice and compact, we gain more insight into what it actually does by unfolding it:

$$
\begin{aligned}
&\mathit{unravel} :: \mathit{Functor}\ f \Rightarrow \mathit{Graph}\ f \to \mathit{Tree}\ f \\
&\mathit{unravel}\ (\mathit{MkGraph}\ g) = \mathit{unravel}'\ g \\
&\mathit{unravel}' :: \mathit{Functor}\ f \Rightarrow \mathit{Graph}'\ f\ (\mathit{Tree}\ f) \to \mathit{Tree}\ f \\
&\mathit{unravel}'\ (\mathit{Var}\ x) \quad\ = x \\
&\mathit{unravel}'\ (\mathit{Let}\ e\ f) = \mathit{unravel}'\ (f\ (\mathit{unravel}'\ e)) \\
&\mathit{unravel}'\ (\mathit{GIn}\ t) \quad = \mathit{In}\ (\mathit{fmap}\ \mathit{unravel}'\ t)
\end{aligned}
$$

We can see that *unravel* simply replaces *GIn* with *In*, and applies the function argument f of a let binding to the bound value e. For example, we have that

$$
\begin{aligned}
&\mathit{MkGraph}\ (\mathit{Let}\ (\mathit{PUSH}_\mathsf{G}\ 2 \rhd \mathit{HALT}_\mathsf{G})\ (\lambda v \to \mathit{MARK}_\mathsf{G}\ (\mathit{Var}\ v) \rhd \mathit{Var}\ v)) \\
&\overset{\mathit{unravel}}{\rightsquigarrow}\ \mathit{MARK}_\mathsf{T}\ (\mathit{PUSH}_\mathsf{T}\ 2 \rhd \mathit{HALT}_\mathsf{T}) \rhd \mathit{PUSH}_\mathsf{T}\ 2 \rhd \mathit{HALT}_\mathsf{T}
\end{aligned}
$$

We can now formulate the relation between comp_T and comp_G:

Lemma 1 $comp_{\mathsf{T}} = unravel \circ comp_{\mathsf{G}}$

This lemma, which we shall prove at the end of this section, is one half of the argument for deriving the correctness property for $comp_{\mathsf{G}}$. The other half is the property that $exec_{\mathsf{T}}$ and $exec_{\mathsf{G}}$ have the converse relationship, viz.

$$exec_{\mathsf{G}} = exec_{\mathsf{T}} \circ unravel$$

Proving this property is much simpler, though, because it follows from a more general property of *fold*.

Theorem 2. *Given a strictly positive functor f, a type c, and $alg :: f\ c \to c$, we have the following:*

$$ufold\ alg = fold\ alg \circ unravel$$

The equality $exec_{\mathsf{G}} = exec_{\mathsf{T}} \circ unravel$ is an instance of Theorem 2 where $alg = execAlg$. We defer discussion of the proof of this theorem until Section 4.2.

We derive the correctness of $comp_{\mathsf{G}}$ by combining Lemma 1 and Theorem 2:

Theorem 3 (correctness of $comp_{\mathsf{G}}$)

$$exec_{\mathsf{G}}\ (comp_{\mathsf{G}}\ e)\ [\,] = conv\ (eval\ e) \qquad \textit{for all } e :: Expr$$

Proof.
$$\begin{aligned} exec_{\mathsf{G}}\ (comp_{\mathsf{G}}\ e)\ [\,] &= exec_{\mathsf{T}}\ (unravel\ (comp_{\mathsf{G}}\ e)\ [\,] && \text{(Theorem 2)} \\ &= exec_{\mathsf{T}}\ (comp_{\mathsf{T}}\ e)\ [\,] && \text{(Lemma 1)} \\ &= conv\ (eval\ e) && \text{(Corollary 1)} \end{aligned}$$
□

We conclude this section by giving the proof of Lemma 1.

Proof (of Lemma 1). Instead of proving the equation directly, we prove the following equation for all $e :: Expr$ and $c :: Graph'\ Code_{\mathsf{F}}\ (Tree\ Code_{\mathsf{F}})$:

$$comp^{\mathsf{A}}_{\mathsf{T}}\ e \triangleright unravel'\ c = unravel'\ (comp^{\mathsf{A}}_{\mathsf{G}}\ e \triangleright c) \qquad (1)$$

In particular, the above equation holds for all $c :: \forall\ v\ .\ Graph'\ Code_{\mathsf{F}}\ v$. Thus, the lemma follows from the above equation as follows:

$$\begin{aligned} & comp_{\mathsf{T}}\ e \\ = &\quad \{ \text{ definition of } comp_{\mathsf{T}} \} \\ & comp^{\mathsf{A}}_{\mathsf{T}}\ e \triangleright HALT_{\mathsf{T}} \\ = &\quad \{ \text{ definition of } unravel' \} \\ & comp^{\mathsf{A}}_{\mathsf{T}}\ e \triangleright unravel'\ HALT_{\mathsf{G}} \\ = &\quad \{ \text{ Equation (1) } \} \\ & unravel'\ (comp^{\mathsf{A}}_{\mathsf{G}}\ e \triangleright HALT_{\mathsf{G}}) \\ = &\quad \{ \text{ definition of } unravel \} \\ & unravel\ (MkGraph\ (comp^{\mathsf{A}}_{\mathsf{G}}\ e \triangleright HALT_{\mathsf{G}})) \\ = &\quad \{ \text{ definition of } comp_{\mathsf{G}} \} \\ & unravel\ (comp_{\mathsf{G}}\ e) \end{aligned}$$

We prove (1) by induction on e:

- Case $e = Val\ n$:

$$\begin{aligned}
& unravel'\,(comp^{\mathsf{A}}_{\mathsf{G}}\,(Val\ n) \triangleright c) \\
= & \quad \{\ \text{definition of } comp^{\mathsf{A}}_{\mathsf{G}}\ \} \\
& unravel'\,(PUSH_{\mathsf{G}}\ n \triangleright c) \\
= & \quad \{\ \text{definition of } unravel'\ \} \\
& PUSH_{\mathsf{T}}\ n \triangleright unravel'\ c \\
= & \quad \{\ \text{definition of } comp^{\mathsf{A}}_{\mathsf{T}}\ \} \\
& comp^{\mathsf{A}}_{\mathsf{T}}\,(Val\ n) \triangleright unravel'\ c
\end{aligned}$$

- Case $e = Throw$:

$$\begin{aligned}
& unravel'\,(comp^{\mathsf{A}}_{\mathsf{G}}\ Throw \triangleright c) \\
= & \quad \{\ \text{definition of } comp^{\mathsf{A}}_{\mathsf{G}}\ \} \\
& unravel'\ THROW_{\mathsf{G}} \\
= & \quad \{\ \text{definition of } unravel'\ \} \\
& THROW_{\mathsf{T}} \\
= & \quad \{\ \text{definition of } comp^{\mathsf{A}}_{\mathsf{T}}\ \} \\
& comp^{\mathsf{A}}_{\mathsf{T}}\ Throw \triangleright unravel'\ c
\end{aligned}$$

- Case $e = Add\ x\ y$:

$$\begin{aligned}
& unravel'\,(comp^{\mathsf{A}}_{\mathsf{G}}\,(Add\ x\ y) \triangleright c) \\
= & \quad \{\ \text{definition of } comp^{\mathsf{A}}_{\mathsf{G}}\ \} \\
& unravel'\,(comp^{\mathsf{A}}_{\mathsf{G}}\ x \triangleright comp^{\mathsf{A}}_{\mathsf{G}}\ y \triangleright ADD_{\mathsf{G}} \triangleright c) \\
= & \quad \{\ \text{induction hypothesis}\ \} \\
& comp^{\mathsf{A}}_{\mathsf{T}}\ x \triangleright unravel'\,(comp^{\mathsf{A}}_{\mathsf{G}}\ y \triangleright ADD_{\mathsf{G}} \triangleright c) \\
= & \quad \{\ \text{induction hypothesis}\ \} \\
& comp^{\mathsf{A}}_{\mathsf{T}}\ x \triangleright comp^{\mathsf{A}}_{\mathsf{T}}\ y \triangleright unravel'\,(ADD_{\mathsf{G}} \triangleright c) \\
= & \quad \{\ \text{definition of } unravel'\ \} \\
& comp^{\mathsf{A}}_{\mathsf{T}}\ x \triangleright comp^{\mathsf{A}}_{\mathsf{T}}\ y \triangleright ADD_{\mathsf{T}} \triangleright unravel'\ c \\
= & \quad \{\ \text{definition of } comp^{\mathsf{A}}_{\mathsf{T}}\ \} \\
& comp^{\mathsf{A}}_{\mathsf{T}}\,(Add\ x\ y) \triangleright unravel'\ c
\end{aligned}$$

- Case $e = Catch\ x\ h$:

$$\begin{aligned}
& unravel'\,(comp^{\mathsf{A}}_{\mathsf{G}}\,(Catch\ x\ h) \triangleright c) \\
= & \quad \{\ \text{definition of } comp^{\mathsf{A}}_{\mathsf{G}}\ \} \\
& unravel'\,(Let\ c\ (\lambda c' \to MARK_{\mathsf{G}}\,(comp^{\mathsf{A}}_{\mathsf{G}}\ h \triangleright Var\ c') \\
& \qquad \triangleright comp^{\mathsf{A}}_{\mathsf{G}}\ x \triangleright UNMARK_{\mathsf{G}} \triangleright Var\ c')) \\
= & \quad \{\ \text{definition of } unravel' \text{ and } \beta\text{-reduction}\ \} \\
& unravel'\,(MARK_{\mathsf{G}}\,(comp^{\mathsf{A}}_{\mathsf{G}}\ h \triangleright Var\,(unravel'\ c)) \\
& \qquad \triangleright comp^{\mathsf{A}}_{\mathsf{G}}\ x \triangleright UNMARK_{\mathsf{G}} \triangleright Var\,(unravel'\ c)) \\
= & \quad \{\ \text{definition of } unravel'\ \} \\
& MARK_{\mathsf{T}}\,(unravel'\,(comp^{\mathsf{A}}_{\mathsf{G}}\ h \triangleright Var\,(unravel'\ c))) \\
& \quad \triangleright unravel'\,(comp^{\mathsf{A}}_{\mathsf{G}}\ x \triangleright UNMARK_{\mathsf{G}} \triangleright Var\,(unravel'\ c)) \\
= & \quad \{\ \text{induction hypothesis}\ \} \\
& MARK_{\mathsf{T}}\,(comp^{\mathsf{A}}_{\mathsf{T}}\ h \triangleright unravel'\,(Var\,(unravel'\ c))) \\
& \quad \triangleright comp^{\mathsf{A}}_{\mathsf{T}}\ x \triangleright unravel'\,(UNMARK_{\mathsf{G}} \triangleright Var\,(unravel'\ c)) \\
= & \quad \{\ \text{definition of } unravel'\ \} \\
& MARK_{\mathsf{T}}\,(comp^{\mathsf{A}}_{\mathsf{T}}\ h \triangleright unravel'\ c) \triangleright comp^{\mathsf{A}}_{\mathsf{T}}\ x \triangleright UNMARK_{\mathsf{T}} \triangleright unravel'\ c \\
= & \quad \{\ \text{definition of } comp^{\mathsf{A}}_{\mathsf{T}}\ \} \\
& comp^{\mathsf{A}}_{\mathsf{T}}\,(Catch\ x\ h) \triangleright unravel'\ c
\end{aligned}$$

□

4.2 Proof of Theorem 2

Theorem 2 states that folding a structured graph $g :: Graph\ f$ over a strictly positive functor f with an algebra alg yields the same result as first unravelling g and then folding the resulting tree with alg, i.e.

$$ufold\ alg = fold\ alg \circ unravel$$

Since *unravel* is defined as *ufold In*, the above equality follows from a more general law of folds over algebraic data types, known as *short cut fusion* [8]:

$$b\ alg = fold\ alg\ (b\ In) \quad \text{for all } b :: \forall\, c\,.\,(f\ c \rightarrow c) \rightarrow c$$

This law holds for all strictly positive functors f as proved by Johann [12]. Essential for its correctness is the polymorphic type of b.

For any given graph $g :: Graph\ f$, we can instantiate b with the function $\lambda a \rightarrow ufold\ a\ g$, which yields that

$$(\lambda a \rightarrow ufold\ a\ g)\ alg = fold\ alg\ ((\lambda a \rightarrow ufold\ a\ g)\ In)$$

Note that $\lambda a \rightarrow ufold\ a\ g$ has indeed the required polymorphic type. After applying beta-reduction, we obtain the equation

$$ufold\ alg\ g = fold\ alg\ (ufold\ In\ g)$$

Since g was chosen arbitrarily, and *unravel* is defined as *ufold In*, we thus obtain the equation as stated in Theorem 2:

$$ufold\ alg = fold\ alg \circ unravel$$

5 Other Approaches

5.1 Other Graph Representations

The technique presented here is not necessarily dependent on the particular representation of graphs that we chose. However, while other representations are conceivable, structured graphs have two properties that make them a suitable choice for this application: (1) they have a simple representation in Haskell and (2) they provide a convenient interface for introducing sharing, viz. variable binding in the host language.

Nevertheless, in other circumstances a different representation may be advantageous. For example the use of higher-order abstract syntax may have a negative impact on performance in practical applications. Moreover, the necessity of reasoning over parametricity may be inconvenient for a formalisation of the proofs in a proof assistant.

Therefore, we also studied an alternative representation of graphs that uses de Bruijn indices for encoding binders instead of parametric higher-order abstract syntax (PHOAS). To this end, we have used the technique proposed by

Bernardy and Pouillard [4] to provide a PHOAS interface to this graph representation. This allows us to use essentially the same simple definition of the graph-based compiler as presented in Section 3.2. Using this representation of graphs – PHOAS interface on the outside, de Bruijn indices under the hood – we formalised the proofs presented here in the Coq theorem prover[2].

5.2 A Monadic Approach

We briefly describe a variant of our technique that is based on free monads and a corresponding monadic graph structure. The general approach of this variant is similar to what we have seen thus far; however, the monadic structure simplifies some of the proofs. The details can be found in the companion report [2].

The underlying idea, originally developed by Matsuda et al. [15], is to replace a function f with accumulation parameters by a function f' that produces a *context* with the property that

$$f\ x\ a_1 \ldots a_n = (f'\ x)\langle a_1, \ldots, a_n \rangle$$

That is, we obtain the result of the original function f by plugging in the accumulation arguments $a_1, \ldots, a_n$ in to the context that f' produces.

In order to represent contexts, we use a free monad type $\mathit{Tree}_{\mathsf{M}}$ instead of a tree type Tree, where $\mathit{Tree}_{\mathsf{M}}$ is obtained from Tree by adding a constructor of type $a \to \mathit{Tree}_{\mathsf{M}}\ f\ a$. A context with n holes is represented by a type $\mathit{Tree}_{\mathsf{M}}\ f\ (\mathit{Fin}\ n)$ – where $\mathit{Fin}\ n$ is a type with exactly n distinct inhabitants – and context application is represented by the monadic bind operator $\gg\!=$. The compiler is then reformulated as follows – using the shorthand $\mathit{hole} = \mathit{return}\ ()$:

$$\begin{aligned}
&\mathit{comp}^{\mathsf{C}}_{\mathsf{M}} :: \mathit{Expr} \to \mathit{Tree}_{\mathsf{M}}\ \mathit{Code}_{\mathsf{F}}\ () \\
&\mathit{comp}^{\mathsf{C}}_{\mathsf{M}}\ (\mathit{Val}\ n) &&= \mathit{PUSH}_{\mathsf{M}}\ n\ \mathit{hole} \\
&\mathit{comp}^{\mathsf{C}}_{\mathsf{M}}\ (\mathit{Add}\ x\ y) &&= \mathit{comp}^{\mathsf{C}}_{\mathsf{M}}\ x \gg \mathit{comp}^{\mathsf{C}}_{\mathsf{M}}\ y \gg \mathit{ADD}_{\mathsf{M}}\ \mathit{hole} \\
&\mathit{comp}^{\mathsf{C}}_{\mathsf{M}}\ (\mathit{Throw}) &&= \mathit{THROW}_{\mathsf{M}} \\
&\mathit{comp}^{\mathsf{C}}_{\mathsf{M}}\ (\mathit{Catch}\ x\ h) &&= \mathit{MARK}_{\mathsf{M}}\ (\mathit{comp}^{\mathsf{C}}_{\mathsf{M}}\ h)\ (\mathit{comp}^{\mathsf{C}}_{\mathsf{M}}\ x \gg \mathit{UNMARK}_{\mathsf{M}}\ \mathit{hole})
\end{aligned}$$

As we only have a single accumulator for the compiler, we use the type $() \simeq \mathit{Fin}\ 1$ to express that there is exactly one type of hole.

Also graphs can be given monadic structure by adding a constructor of type $a \to \mathit{Graph}'_{\mathsf{M}}\ f\ v\ a$ to the data type Graph'. And the compiler $\mathit{comp}^{\mathsf{A}}_{\mathsf{G}}$ can be reformulated in terms of this type accordingly.

We can define fold combinators for the monadic structures as well. The virtual machines are thus easily adapted to this monadic style by simply reusing the same algebra *execAlg*. Again, one half of the correctness proof follows from a generic theorem about folds corresponding to Theorem 2. The other half of the proof can be simplified. In the corresponding proof of Lemma 1 it suffices to show the following simpler equation, in which *unravel′* only appears once:

$$\mathit{comp}^{\mathsf{A}}_{\mathsf{T}} = \mathit{unravel}' \circ \mathit{comp}^{\mathsf{A}}_{\mathsf{G}}$$

[2] Available from the author's web site.

This simplifies the induction proof. While this proof requires an additional lemma, viz. that unravelling distributes over $\gg$, this lemma can be proved (once and for all) for any strictly positive functor f:

$$unravel'\ (g_1 \gg g_2) = unravel'\ g_1 \gg unravel'\ g_2$$

Unfortunately, we cannot exploit short cut fusion to prove this lemma because it involves a genuine graph transformation, viz. $\gg$ on graphs . However, with the representation mentioned in Section 5.1, we can prove it by induction.

Note that the full monadic structure of $Tree_{\mathsf{M}}$ and $Graph_{\mathsf{M}}$ is not needed for our example compiler since we only use the simple bind operator $\gg$, not $\gg=$. However, a different compiler implementation may use more than one accumulation parameter (for example an additional code continuation that contains the current exception handler), for which we need the more general bind operator.

6 Concluding Remarks

6.1 Related Work

Compiler verification is still a hard problem and in this paper we only cover one – but arguably the central – part of a compiler, viz. the translation of a high-level language to a low-level language. The literature on the topic of compiler verification is vast (e.g. see the survey of Dave [7]). More recent work has shown impressive results in verification of a realistic compiler for the C language [13]. But there are also efforts in verifying compilers for higher-level languages (e.g. by Chlipala [6]).

This paper, however, focuses on identifying simple but powerful techniques for reasoning about compilers rather than engineering massive proofs for full-scale compilers. Our contributions thus follow the work on calculating compilers [21, 16, 1] as well as Hutton and Wright's work on equational reasoning about compilers [10, 11].

Structured graphs have been used in the setting of programming language implementation before: Oliveira and Löh [17] used structured graphs to represent embedded domain-specific languages. That is, graphs are used for the representation of the source language. Graph structures used for representing intermediate languages in a compiler typically employ pointers (e.g. Ramsey and Dias [20]) or labels (e.g. Ramsey et al. [19]). We are not aware of any work that makes use of higher-order abstract syntax or de Bruijn indices in the representation of graph structures in this setting.

6.2 Discussion and Future Work

The underlying goal of our method is to separate the transformation to the target language from the need to generate fresh names for representing jumps. For a full compiler, we still have to deal with explicit jumps eventually, but we can do so in isolation. That is, (1) we have to define a function

$$linearise :: Graph\ Code_{\mathsf{F}} \rightarrow Code_{\mathsf{L}}$$

that transforms the graph-based representation into a linear representation of the target language, and (2) we have to prove that it preserves the semantics. The proof can focus solely on the aspect of fresh names and explicit jumps. Since *linearise* is trivial for all cases except for the let bindings of the graph representation, we expect that the proof can be made independently of the actual language under consideration.

While our method reduces the proof obligations for the graph-based compiler considerably, there is still room for improvement. Indeed, we only require a simple induction proof showing the equality $comp_{\mathsf{T}} = unravel \circ comp_{\mathsf{G}}$. But since the two compiler variants differ only in the sharing they produce, one would hope the proof obligation could be further reduced to the only interesting case, i.e. the case for *Catch* in our example. In a proof assistant such as Coq, we can indeed take care of all the other cases with a single tactic and focus on the interesting case. However, it would be desirable to have a more systematic approach that captures this intuitive understanding.

A shortcoming of our method is its limitation to acyclic graphs. Nevertheless, the implementation part of our method easily generalises to cyclic structures, which permits compilation of cyclic control structures like loops. Corresponding correctness proofs, however, need a different reasoning principle.

Acknowledgements. The author is indebted to Janis Voigtländer for his many helpful suggestions to improve both the substance and the presentation of this paper. In particular, the idea to use short cut fusion to prove Theorem 2 was his. The author would like to thank Nicolas Pouillard and Daniel Gustafsson for their assistance in the accompanying Coq development.

This work was supported by the Danish Council for Independent Research, Grant 12-132365, "Efficient Programming Language Development and Evolution through Modularity".

References

[1] Ager, M.S., Biernacki, D., Danvy, O., Midtgaard, J.: From interpreter to compiler and virtual machine: A functional derivation. Tech. Rep. RS-03-14, BRICS, Department of Computer Science, University of Aarhus (2003)

[2] Bahr, P.: Proving correctness of compilers using structured graphs (extended version). Tech. rep., University of Copenhagen (2014)

[3] Bahr, P., Hutton, G.: Calculating correct compilers (2014) (unpublished manuscript)

[4] Bernardy, J.P., Pouillard, N.: Names for free: polymorphic views of names and binders. In: Proceedings of the 2013 ACM SIGPLAN Symposium on Haskell, pp. 13–24. ACM (2013)

[5] Chlipala, A.: Parametric higher-order abstract syntax for mechanized semantics. In: Proceeding of the 13th ACM SIGPLAN International Conference on Functional Programming, pp. 143–156. ACM (2008)

[6] Chlipala, A.: A verified compiler for an impure functional language. In: Proceedings of the 37th Annual ACM SIGPLAN-SIGACT Symposium on Principles of Programming Languages, pp. 93–106. ACM (2010)
[7] Dave, M.A.: Compiler verification: a bibliography. SIGSOFT Softw. Eng. Notes 28(6), 2 (2003)
[8] Gill, A., Launchbury, J., Peyton Jones, S.L.: A short cut to deforestation. In: Proceedings of the Conference on Functional Programming Languages and Computer Architecture, pp. 223–232. ACM (1993)
[9] Hutton, G.: Programming in Haskell, vol. 2. Cambridge University Press, Cambridge (2007)
[10] Hutton, G., Wright, J.: Compiling exceptions correctly. In: Kozen, D. (ed.) MPC 2004. LNCS, vol. 3125, pp. 211–227. Springer, Heidelberg (2004)
[11] Hutton, G., Wright, J.: What is the meaning of these constant interruptions? J. Funct. Program. 17(6), 777–792 (2007)
[12] Johann, P.: A generalization of short-cut fusion and its correctness proof. Higher Order Symbol. Comput. 15(4), 273–300 (2002)
[13] Leroy, X.: Formal certification of a compiler back-end or: programming a compiler with a proof assistant. In: Conference record of the 33rd ACM SIGPLAN-SIGACT Symposium on Principles of Programming Languages, pp. 42–54. ACM (2006)
[14] Marlow, S.: Haskell 2010 language report (2010)
[15] Matsuda, K., Inaba, K., Nakano, K.: Polynomial-time inverse computation for accumulative functions with multiple data traversals. In: Proceedings of the ACM SIGPLAN 2012 Workshop on Partial Evaluation and Program Manipulation, pp. 5–14. ACM (2012)
[16] Meijer, E.: Calculating Compilers. Ph.D. thesis, Katholieke Universiteit Nijmegen (1992)
[17] Oliveira, B.C.D.S., Löh, A.: Abstract syntax graphs for domain specific languages. In: Proceedings of the ACM SIGPLAN 2013 Workshop on Partial Evaluation and Program Manipulation, pp. 87–96. ACM (2013)
[18] Oliveira, B.C., Cook, W.R.: Functional programming with structured graphs. In: Proceedings of the 17th ACM SIGPLAN International Conference on Functional Programming, pp. 77–88. ACM (2012)
[19] Ramsey, N., Dias, J.A., Peyton Jones, S.: Hoopl: a modular, reusable library for dataflow analysis and transformation. In: Proceedings of the Third ACM Haskell Symposium on Haskell, pp. 121–134. ACM (2010)
[20] Ramsey, N., Dias, J.: An applicative control-flow graph based on huet's zipper. In: Proceedings of the ACM-SIGPLAN Workshop on ML, pp. 105–126 (2006)
[21] Wand, M.: Deriving target code as a representation of continuation semantics. ACM Trans. Program. Lang. Syst. 4(3), 496–517 (1982)

A New Formalization of Subtyping to Match Subclasses to Subtypes

Hyunik Na[1] and Sukyoung Ryu[2]

[1] S-Core., Ltd., Seongnam, Korea
hina@kaist.ac.kr
[2] Department of Computer Science, KAIST, Daejeon, Korea
sryu.cs@kaist.ac.kr

Abstract. Most object-oriented languages do not support explicit recursive types, which are useful to define binary methods and some kinds of factory methods, because explicit recursive types lead to a mismatch between subclassing and subtyping. This mismatch means that an expression of a subclass may not always be usable in a context where an expression of a superclass is expected, which is not intuitive in an object-oriented setting.

In this paper, we present a new subtyping formalization, which allows subclassing to match subtyping even in the presence of recursive types in an object-oriented language. The formalization comes from a new perspective on object types and subtyping, which clearly distinguishes object types and *some-object types* and defines a new subtype relation on some-object types. We formally prove that the new subtype relation can successfully replace the traditional one and that subclassing always matches subtyping even in the presence of recursive types in a language. We believe that our formalization makes it easier to understand objects than the traditional formalization because of a simple encoding of objects in a typed lambda calculus.

1 Introduction

When defining an object in an object-oriented language, programmers often need to declare that the object has a method which takes or returns an object of the same type with the object. A recursive type is natural and effective in expressing this type constraint. For example, one might want to declare a point object in a one-dimensional space to have the following recursively defined record type (under the conventional interpretation of objects as records [8,26,16]):

$$\mathtt{P} = \{\mathtt{x} : \mathtt{int},\ \mathtt{equals} : \mathtt{P} \rightarrow \mathtt{bool},\ \mathtt{move} : \mathtt{int} \rightarrow \mathtt{P}\}$$

This object type specifies that the method `equals` takes a point object of the same type as the current point object, and that the method `move` returns a point object of the same type as the current point object.

However, researchers reported that recursive types break a valuable property *subtyping-by-subclassing* (or *subtyping-by-inheritance*) of object-oriented languages

M. Codish and E. Sumii (Eds.): FLOPS 2014, LNCS 8475, pp. 238–252, 2014.

[10,11]: if an object type T has a negative[1] type recursion (as is the case in P), then any extension T′ of T is not a subtype of T. For example, the following object type P′ which extends P is not a subtype of P:

$$\mathtt{P}' = \{\mathtt{x} : \mathtt{int},\ \mathtt{y} : \mathtt{int}, \mathtt{equals} : \mathtt{P}' \to \mathtt{bool},\ \mathtt{move} : \mathtt{int} \to \mathtt{P}'\ \}$$

Note that similar type extensions frequently occur in object-oriented programs to add fields or methods while subclassing. This mismatch between subclassing and subtyping means that programmers may not be able to use an expression of a subclass in a context where an expression of a superclass is expected, which is not intuitive in object-oriented languages. This is why most object-oriented languages do not support (explicit) recursive types.

The lack of recursive types, however, results in insufficient expressiveness of the languages. When programmers want to describe "the same type relation" on class members, instead of using recursive types, they often have to use dynamic typechecking and casting, which lead to a nontrivial amount of routine code (for example, see [23, Chapter 28]). One example of class members with the same type relation is *binary methods* [3].

While an extension of Java [14], LOOJ [4], addresses the mismatch between subclassing and subtyping, the main obstacle for an object-oriented language to adopt recursive types, it does not describe the theoretical reason behind it compared to the traditional formalization of subtyping [8]. In LOOJ, programmers can use an expression of a subclass in any context where an expression of a superclass is expected even when the superclass has a negative occurrence of a This type, which designates type recursion, in its definition.

In this paper, we present a new formalization of subtyping to explain the coexistence of recursive types and the subtyping-by-subclassing. We suppress subtyping between object types by dropping the traditional subtyping on record types and recursive types [8,9]. Instead, we define a new subtype relation on existential types of a special form which we call *some-object types*. In the new subtype relation, unlike in the traditional one, negative type recursions do not limit subtyping. Some-object types correspond to class types (class names used as types) in nominal type systems of object-oriented languages, and hence the new subtype relation explains the coexistence of recursive types and subtyping-by-subclassing seamlessly.

In addition, we explain that the new subtype relation supports the *self-application interpretation* [16]. Although the self-application interpretation is the most realistic (in that most object-oriented language implementations are based on it) and simplest interpretation of objects, researchers considered it unsatisfactory because it cannot explain subtyping between object types due to the negative type recursion inherent in the interpretation (see [2, Section 6.7.1]). However, we believe that the problem is not in the interpretation but in the traditional formalization of subtyping which defines subtyping on object types. With the new formalization of subtyping, which distinguishes between

[1] Roughly, a position in a type expression is positive (or covariant) if it is on the left side of an even number of function types, and is negative (or contravariant) if it is on the left of an odd number of function types. In particular, the position of the return type of a function is positive and the position of a parameter type of a function is negative.

object types and some-object types and defines subtyping on some-object types as mentioned before, the self-application interpretation becomes satisfactory.

The remainder of this paper is as follows. In Section 2, we discuss some historical background and motivation of this work. After summarizing the traditional formalization of subtyping in Section 3, we present the new formalization and compare it with the traditional one in Section 4. We also prove that the new formalization can successfully replace the traditional one. In Section 5, we discuss the self-application interpretation and explain that the interpretation is satisfactory and acceptable under the new formalization of subtyping. In Section 6, we show that the newly defined relation is indeed a subtype relation by proving that it conforms to the substitutability notion of subtyping in a simple core language. We conclude in Section 7.

2 Motivation and Related Work

Many researchers have proposed various names such as *MyType* [7,6], *Self* type [2], *ThisType* [5,4,27], and *like Current* [10] to designate type recursion in object types. They all denote the type of the current object `this` or `self` in a class definition. We henceforth use a single type name `This` to collectively refer to the various type names listed above. One can extend any class-based object-oriented language with `This` types to express that, in any invocation of a method, an argument or the result of the method invocation should have the same type as the method's receiver. For example, in a Java-like language equipped with `This` types, one can define point classes having `equals` methods as follows:

```
class Point {
  int x;
  Point(int i) { this.x = i; }
  boolean equals(This other) {
      return this.x == other.x;
  }
}

class ColorPoint extends Point {
  int color;
  ColorPoint(int i, int c) {
      super(i); this.color = c;
  }
  boolean equals(This other) {
      return this.x == other.x &&
             this.color == other.color;
  }
}
```

In these class definitions, the formal parameter type `This` of each `equals` method puts a type constraint which specifies that the argument and the receiver in any invocation of the method should have the same type. This *the-same-type* constraint is often desirable or required for implementations of binary operations such as numeric operations, set operations, equality checks and comparisons ($<$, $\leq$, etc). Implementations of binary operations in object-oriented languages are usually called *binary methods* [3] and a negative occurrence of a `This` type is their distinctive characteristic.

Traditionally, the-same-type constraint expressed by a `This` type means matching of object type,. which results in a breach in the soundness of a type system equipped with `This` types and leads to the conclusion that inheritance is not subtyping [10,11]. For example, the following method definition is well-typed under the traditional notion of the-same-type constraint (or of `This` types) because, in the invocation of `equals`, the argument `q` has the same type `Point` as the receiver `p`:

```
boolean testEQ(Point p, Point q) {
    return p.equals(q);
}
```

More specifically, the formal parameter type `This` of the `equals` method is substituted with the type `Point` of the receiver `p` while typechecking. Though the method definition is well-typed, the following invocation of `testEQ` will cause a run-time type error when executed because it will try to access the `color` field from an object of the `Point` class:

```
testEQ(new ColorPoint(1,2), new Point(1));
```

Therefore, any sound type system should reject this example.

To recover type soundness, researchers have proposed the perspective that inheritance is not (always) subtyping [10,11], which points out that if a traditional object type R has a negative type recursion, any extension R' of R is not a subtype of R. For example, the type μ`t.{x:int, color:int, eq:t`$\rightarrow$`bool}` of objects that the class `ColorPoint` generates is not a subtype of the type μ`t.{x:int, eq:t`$\rightarrow$`bool}` of objects that the class `Point` generates, and hence `ColorPoint` is not a subtype of `Point`. This approach rejects the above invocation of `testEQ` because it passes an incompatible `ColorPoint` object as an argument bound to a `Point` variable `p`. This approach, however, does not fully localize the cause of the breach in type soundness. A more direct cause of the breach is the binary method invocation rather than the argument passing; the argument passing would not cause a run-time type error if it was not followed by the binary method invocation `p.equals(q)`. Most of all, the perspective of *inheritance-is-not-subtyping* is the biggest obstacle for a language to adopt recursive types to increase its expressiveness.

On the other hand, the possibility that inheritance may be subtyping originates from LOOM [6]. LOOM clearly distinguishes *hash types* and *non-hash types*, and it allows binary method invocations on expressions of non-hash types, but *not* on expressions of hash types (see the typing rules *Msg* and *Msg#* of [6]). A successor of LOOM, LOOJ [4], inherits this compatibility with a similar strategy for typing binary methods in the sense that it "allows binary method invocations *only* on expressions whose exact run-time classes are known at compile-time." In LOOJ and subsequent work [27,22,21], a class is always compatible with its superclasses; if a class `D` is a subclass of another class `C`, then one can use an expression of type `D` in any context where an expression of type `C` is expected even when `C` has a negative occurrence of a `This` type in its definition. This manifests more clearly the possibility that inheritance is subtyping. While the compatibility well matches the general idea of subtyping discussed in Section 3, the traditional formalization of subtyping does not explain the relationship. LOOJ accepts the above invocation of `testEQ` because it considers `ColorPoint` as a subtype of

`Point`, but it rejects the definition of `testEQ` because it cannot know run-time classes of the receiver `p` in the invocation of `equals` at compile-time. Though LOOJ effectively achieves subtyping-by-subclassing with recursive types, its strategy for typing binary methods has some limitations: programmers should maintain exact type information using type annotations and they cannot use dynamic dispatch of binary methods (and hence their generic uses).

We address the limitations of LOOJ by proposing two static typing techniques, *exact type capture* and *named wildcards*, in our earlier work [22,21]. With those techniques, it becomes possible in some cases to dynamically dispatch a binary method without limiting the type of the method's receiver to a single exact type.

3 Traditional Formalization of Subtyping

Subtyping or subtype polymorphism relates two types by the following notion of substitutability [8,18,24]:

> If T is a subtype of U (or equivalently U is a supertype of T), then any expression of type T can be safely used in any context where an expression of type U is expected.

where the safety here usually means that any well typed program does not cause a run-time type error.

In his seminal work [8], Cardelli formalized this notion of subtyping with a relation $\leq$ on type expressions consisting of primitive types (of basic values such as unity, booleans, and integers), record types, variant types, and function types. Soon afterwards, in the presentation of the Amber language [9], he extended the relation to recursive types. The subtyping rules of [8,9] are listed in Figure 1. In the figure, we omit the subtyping rule for variant types presented in [8] because variant types are less significant in most object-oriented languages and they are beyond the scope of this paper. For the same reason, we limit type recursions to record types; we syntactically preclude type expressions of the forms $\mu t.u$, $\mu t.T \rightarrow U$ and $\mu u.\mu t.T$.

In Figure 1, the metavariable R actually ranges over two syntactic forms of type expressions $\mu t.\{l_i : T_i \ ^{i \in 1..n}\}$ and $\{l_i : T_i \ ^{i \in 1..n}\}$ because we identify these two (that is, they are freely interchangeable in any context) when the type recursion variable t does not occur free in each T_i. We also identify $\mu t.\{l_i : T_i \ ^{i \in 1..n}\}$ and $\mu u.\{l_i : T_i[u/t] \ ^{i \in 1..n}\}$ where $[u/t]$ denotes a capture-avoiding substitution of t with u. The metavariable ρ ranges over a finite number of primitive types. For convenience, we take $\rho_1 = \texttt{unit}$, $\rho_2 = \texttt{bool}$, $\rho_3 = \texttt{int}$ in this paper.

As Cook *et al.* pointed out [11], if a record type R has a negative occurrence of a type recursion variable, then for any record type R' that extends R, the relation $\leq$ does not relate R' and R due to the interaction between the negative occurrence of the type recursion variable and the subtyping rule for function types. For example, one cannot derive the following judgement:

$$\vdash \mu t.\{\texttt{x}:\texttt{int}, \texttt{y}:\texttt{int}, \texttt{eq}:\texttt{t} \rightarrow \texttt{bool}\} \leq \mu t.\{\texttt{x}:\texttt{int}, \texttt{eq}:\texttt{t} \rightarrow \texttt{bool}\}$$

This limitation has led most language designers to the conclusion that they should abandon recursive types in favor of arguably more valuable subtyping-by-subclassing. The

Metavariables:

t, u	type variable
ρ	primitive type
l	label

$T, U ::= t \mid \rho \mid R \mid T \to T$	type
$R ::= \mu t.\{l_i : T_i \ ^{i \in 1..n}\}$	record type

Type variables: $\boxed{vars(\{t_i \leq u_i \ ^{i \in 1..n}\})}$ $vars(\{t_i \leq u_i \ ^{i \in 1..n}\}) = \{t_i, u_i \ ^{i \in 1..n}\}$

Traditional subtyping: $\boxed{\Delta \vdash T \leq U \text{ where } \Delta ::= \{t_i \leq u_i \ ^{i \in 1..n}\}}$

[TS-PRIM]
$$\frac{}{\Delta \vdash \rho \leq \rho}$$

[TS-FUNC]
$$\frac{\Delta \vdash U \leq T \qquad \Delta \vdash T' \leq U'}{\Delta \vdash T \to T' \ \leq \ U \to U'}$$

[TS-RECORD]
$$\frac{\forall i \in 1..n\colon \Delta \vdash T_i \leq U_i \quad n \geq 0, m \geq 0}{\Delta \vdash \{l_i : T_i \ ^{i \in 1..n+m}\} \ \leq \ \{l_i : U_i \ ^{i \in 1..n}\}}$$

[TS-AMBER1]
$$\frac{t \leq u \in \Delta}{\Delta \vdash t \leq u}$$

[TS-AMBER2]
$$\frac{t \neq u \qquad t, u \notin vars(\Delta) \qquad \Delta \cup \{t \leq u\} \vdash T \leq U}{\Delta \vdash \mu t.T \ \leq \ \mu u.U}$$

Fig. 1. Traditional subtyping

lack of recursive types, however, results in the lack of simple static typing for binary methods [3].

4 Revised Formalization of Subtyping

In this section, we discuss our new formalization of subtyping. Figure 2 presents a relation $<_{\mathsf{I}}$ on record types called *specializing* and another relation $<:$ on types called *revised subtyping*. The specializing is very similar to *matching* [7], but unlike matching, it is defined together with subtyping in a mutually dependent manner. Specializing relates two record types even in the presence of a negative occurrence of a type recursion variable. Therefore, it relates more pairs of record types than the traditional subtyping does. Straightforward inductions on derivations prove reflexivity and transitivity of the relations $<_{\mathsf{I}}$ and $<:$.

As briefly discussed in Section 1, the revised subtyping $<:$ does not relate two different record types because it does not have the record subtyping and Amber rules. The rationale of dropping the rules is that the traditional subtyping based on them is not fully satisfactory (it sometimes fails to produce a desirable subtyping result as discussed in the previous section) and we can establish an alternative subtyping which does not have such drawback.

Two rules [RS-RTOS] and [RS-STOS] in Figure 2 suggest the main idea of the alternative subtyping. In the rules, the type $\exists s <_{\mathsf{I}} \beta.s$, which we call a *some-record type*, denotes the set of records whose types specialize the record type β. When a record type α specializes another record type β ($\emptyset \vdash \alpha <_{\mathsf{I}} \beta$), one can safely use a record of type α in any context where an expression of type $\exists s <_{\mathsf{I}} \beta.s$ is expected ([RS-RTOS]), and

Metavariables:

$$\begin{array}{rll} \tau, \upsilon ::= & t \mid \rho \mid \alpha \mid \gamma \mid \tau \to \tau & \text{type (revised)} \\ \alpha, \beta ::= & \mu t.\{l_i : \tau_i \ ^{i \in 1..n}\} & \text{record type (revised)} \\ \gamma ::= & \exists s <_! \alpha.s & \text{some-record type} \end{array}$$

Specializing: $\boxed{\Delta \vdash \alpha <_! \beta \text{ where } \Delta ::= \{t_i \ ^{i \in 1..n}\}}$

[SPECIALIZING]

$$\frac{n \geq 0,\ m \geq 0 \qquad t \notin \Delta \qquad \forall i \in 1..n\colon\ \Delta \cup \{t\} \vdash \tau_i <: \upsilon_i}{\Delta \vdash \mu t.\{l_i : \tau_i \ ^{i \in 1..n+m}\} <_! \mu t.\{l_i : \upsilon_i \ ^{i \in 1..n}\}}$$

Revised subtyping: $\boxed{\Delta \vdash \tau <: \upsilon \text{ where } \Delta ::= \{t_i \ ^{i \in 1..n}\}}$

[RS-PRIM]
$$\frac{}{\Delta \vdash \rho <: \rho}$$

[RS-FUNC]
$$\frac{\Delta \vdash \upsilon <: \tau \qquad \Delta \vdash \tau' <: \upsilon'}{\Delta \vdash \tau \to \tau' \ <: \ \upsilon \to \upsilon'}$$

[RS-TVAR]
$$\frac{t \in \Delta}{\Delta \vdash t <: t}$$

[RS-RTOR]
$$\frac{}{\Delta \vdash \alpha <: \alpha}$$

[RS-RTOS]
$$\frac{\Delta \vdash \alpha <_! \beta}{\Delta \vdash \alpha \ <: \ \exists s <_! \beta.s}$$

[RS-STOS]
$$\frac{\Delta \vdash \alpha <_! \beta}{\Delta \vdash \exists s <_! \alpha.s \ <: \ \exists s <_! \beta.s}$$

Fig. 2. Revised subtyping

one can safely use an expression of type $\exists s <_! \alpha.s$ in any context where an expression of type $\exists s <_! \beta.s$ is expected ([RS-STOS]). We prove this substitutability in Theorem 1 in Section 6.

Note, however, that $<:$ does not directly relate α and β (α is not a subtype of β in our type system). Allowing a record of type α in a context where a record of type β is expected may lead to a situation at run-time where a binary method with a receiver object of type α takes an object of type β as its argument, which may result in a run-time type error. In our type system, some-record types take the traditional role of record types as discussed further below. Two advantages of this replacement are as follows:

- The revised subtyping $<:$ always relates a some-record type and each of its extensions even in the presence of a negative occurrence of a type recursion variable. For example, unlike the last example in Section 3, the following judgement is derivable:

$$\begin{array}{l} \emptyset \vdash \exists s <_! \mu t.\{x : \mathit{int}, y : \mathit{int}, eq : t \to \mathit{bool}\}.s \ <: \\ \qquad \exists \mathtt{s} <_! \mu \mathtt{t}.\{\mathtt{x} : \mathtt{int}, \mathtt{eq} : \mathtt{t} \to \mathtt{bool}\}.\mathtt{s} \end{array}$$

- It provides a theoretical base of the *exact type capture* presented in [22,21]. Class types (class names used as types) in a nominal type system correspond to some-record types in our type system, and the exact type capture correspond to implicit unpacking of some-record types (which are existential types).

The syntactic form of a record type R in Figure 1 is similar to that of a record type α in Figure 2. However, the behavior of R with respect to subtyping is closer to that of a some-record type γ in Figure 2 rather than to that of α. Each of R and γ can be a supertype of another extended type whereas it is not the case for α; α can be a supertype of *only* itself by [RS-RTOR].

The following function $[\![\text{-}]\!]$, which maps a T to a τ, formalizes the intuitive correspondence between T and τ. Note that there is no T which corresponds to an α. That is, $[\![\text{-}]\!]$ is not a surjective function:

$$\begin{aligned}
[\![\mu t.\{l_i : T_i\ ^{i\in 1..n}\}]\!] &= \exists s <_{\mathsf{I}} \mu t.\{l_i : [\![T_i]\!]\ ^{i\in 1..n}\}.s \\
[\![T \rightarrow U]\!] &= [\![T]\!] \rightarrow [\![U]\!] \\
[\![\rho]\!] &= \rho \\
[\![t]\!] &= t
\end{aligned}$$

We define the function FTV, which maps a type to a set of free type variables in it:

$$\begin{array}{ll}
FTV(\mu t.\{l_i : \tau_i\ ^{i\in 1..n}\}) & = \bigcup_{i\in 1..n} FTV(\tau_i) - \{t\} \\
FTV(\exists s <_{\mathsf{I}} \alpha.s) & = FTV(\alpha) \\
FTV(\rho) & = \emptyset \\
FTV(t) & = \{t\} \\
FTV(\tau \rightarrow \upsilon) & = FTV(\tau) \cup FTV(\upsilon)
\end{array}$$

Note that an existentially quantified type variable s of $\exists s <_{\mathsf{I}} \alpha.s$ does not occur free in α by construction (using a different symbol s other than t and u). Thus, $FTV(\exists s <_{\mathsf{I}} \alpha.s)$ does not need to be $FTV(\alpha) - \{s\}$.

A type τ is well formed under a type variable environment Δ:

$$\Delta \vdash \tau \ \mathsf{ok} \quad \text{if} \quad FTV(\tau) \subseteq \Delta.$$

We define $FTV(T)$ and $\Delta \vdash T$ ok similarly, and we say "τ (T) is well-formed" instead of "τ (T) is well-formed under $\emptyset$." With the well-formedness of types, we state the reflexivity and transitivity of the two relations $<:$ and $<_{\mathsf{I}}$ and omit their proofs due to the space limitation:

Proposition 1 (Reflexivity)

1. *If* $\Delta \vdash \tau$ ok, *then* $\Delta \vdash \tau <: \tau$.
2. *If* $\Delta \vdash \alpha$ ok, *then* $\Delta \vdash \alpha <_{\mathsf{I}} \alpha$.

Proposition 2 (Transitivity)

1. *If* $\Delta \vdash \tau_1 <: \tau_2$ *and* $\Delta \vdash \tau_2 <: \tau_3$, *then* $\Delta \vdash \tau_1 <: \tau_3$.
2. *If* $\Delta \vdash \alpha_1 <_{\mathsf{I}} \alpha_2$ *and* $\Delta \vdash \alpha_2 <_{\mathsf{I}} \alpha_3$, *then* $\Delta \vdash \alpha_1 <_{\mathsf{I}} \alpha_3$.

Now, the following proposition states that $<:$ is more general than $\leq$:

Proposition 3. *For well-formed types T and U, $\emptyset \vdash T \leq U$ implies $\emptyset \vdash [\![T]\!] <: [\![U]\!]$.*

The converse of the implication does not hold in general: for a counter example, take $T = \mu t.\{\mathtt{x}:\mathtt{int},\ \mathtt{y}:\mathtt{int},\ \mathtt{eq}:\mathtt{t} \rightarrow \mathtt{bool}\}$ and $U = \mu t.\{\mathtt{x}:\mathtt{int},\ \mathtt{eq}:\mathtt{t} \rightarrow \mathtt{bool}\}$. However, negative occurrences of type recursion variables are the only reason that invalidates the converse as shown by the following proposition:

Proposition 4. *For well-formed types T and U which are free of negative occurrences of type recursion variables, $\emptyset \vdash T \leq U$ if and only if $\emptyset \vdash [\![T]\!] <: [\![U]\!]$.*

This proposition suggests that replacing the traditional subtyping with the revised one does not change subtyping results in legacy programs written in a recursive-type-free object-oriented language. Of course, if an object-oriented language is to adopt recursive types, then the revised formalization is more adequate than the traditional one because an extended some-record type is always a subtype of its original type under the revised formalization even when the original has a negative occurrence of a type recursion variable.

We consider that a record type $\mu t.\{l_i : \tau_i \ ^{i \in 1..n}\}$ is the type of a *run-time object* that has exactly those members $l_1, l_2, ..., l_n$ and a some-record type $\exists s <_{\mathsf{I}} \mu t.\{l_i : \tau_i \ ^{i \in 1..n}\}.s$ is the type of a *compile-time expression* that may be evaluated at run-time to objects of various record types each of which specializes $\mu t.\{l_i : \tau_i \ ^{i \in 1..n}\}$. From this perspective, record types well amount to *exact types*[2] of LOOJ [4] and some-record types well amount to class types of any class-based object-oriented language.

5 Subtyping in Self-application Interpretation

In the course of understanding core features of object-oriented languages such as objects, object types, classes, subtyping, inheritance and object member access via the special variable `this` (or `self`), researchers have developed several interpretations (or encodings) of those features into typed lambda calculi [2,13,8,26,16,20,17,25,12,15].

Self-application [16,17] is the simplest one of those interpretations. In the interpretation, every object is a record of self-applying functions: for an object member access, it first passes the whole object to the member. This interpretation provides a simple explanation about what objects and object types are and about object-related features such as late-binding of the special variable `this`, object member lookup and update, and object cloning. In comparison, the other interpretations have limitations and complications such as limited update and cloning, different encodings for internal and external operations, and inefficient implementations (see [2, Chapter. 18] for detailed comparisons). Therefore, it is no surprise that most implementations of object-oriented languages are based on the self-application interpretation: in most object-oriented languages, every non-static method takes the current object as the argument to its hidden formal parameter `this` (for example, see the specification of the *invokevirtual* instruction of the Java Virtual Machine [19]).

Even with all its advantages, the researchers have considered the self-application interpretation unsatisfactory because the interpretation could not explain subtyping between object types clearly. In the interpretation, object types generally have the form $\mu t.\{l_i : t \rightarrow \tau_i \ ^{i \in 1..n}\}$ (note the negative occurrence of the type recursion variable t),

---

[2] For a class `C`, LOOJ [4] uses `@C` to denote a type which has the following properties: (1) an object generation expression `new C(...)` has the type `@C`, and (2) `@C` is a subtype of `C`, but *not* vice versa. The types of the form `@C` are called *exact types*. LOOJ suppresses proper subtyping between exact types: when `D` is a subclass of `C`, LOOJ does not consider `@D` to be a subtype of `@C` while it considers `D` to be a subtype of `C`.

and the traditional subtyping cannot relate an object type and each of its extensions due to the negative type recursion in the object type [2, Section 6.7.1]. However, we believe that this problem is due to the weakness of the traditional formalization of subtyping rather than to the weakness of the self-application interpretation.

Under the revised formalization of subtyping presented in the previous section, the negative type recursion in object types is not a problem in subtyping because:

- the formalization distinguishes object types (record types) and some-object types (some-record types), and
- it relates some-object types instead of object types.

With the revised formalization of subtyping, the simple and elegant self-application interpretation becomes satisfactory and acceptable because object types do not need to be related by subtyping. To highlight this point, we use the self-application interpretation while we prove in the next section that the relation $<:$ conforms to the substitutability notion of subtyping.

6 Substitutability of $<:$

In this section, we define a simple language to show that the relation $<:$ is indeed a subtype relation. Figure 3 presents the syntax and typing rules of the language and Figure 4 the dynamic semantics of the language.

The language is a typed lambda calculus extended with primitive values and records of self-applying functions of the form $\{l_i = \lambda z : \omega.\, e_i \;^{i \in 1..n}\}$. As we take $\rho_1 = \mathtt{unit}$, $\rho_2 = \mathtt{bool}$, and $\rho_3 = \mathtt{int}$ in Section 3, we accordingly let p_1, p_2 and p_3 range over $\{\mathtt{unity}\}$, $\{\mathtt{true}, \mathtt{false}\}$ and $\{\ldots, -1, 0, 1, \ldots\}$, respectively. According to the self-application interpretation discussed in the previous section, we refer to the records of self-applying functions as objects. Note, however, that general record member retrieval is not allowed for objects (an object member expression is denoted by $e_\diamond l$, not by $e.l$). When an object member expression is evaluated, the self-variable of the member is first bound to the whole object and then the body of the member is evaluated (self-application, see [R-MEM] in Figure 4). In this sense, an object is not a normal record. If a member's self-variable is not used in its body (such a member is sometimes called a field [2]), then the self-application is actually not necessary for the member. However, we do not distinguish such cases for presentation brevity.

Due to the self-application, object types ranged over by a metavariable ω has the form $\mu t.\{l_i : t \to \tau_i \;^{i \in 1..n}\}$. That is, a type recursion variable always occurs negatively in each member's type. In the above form, we call τ_i the *body type* of member l_i for each $i \in 1..n$. For an object type ω, a some-object type $\exists s <_{\mathsf{I}} \omega.s$ is a supertype of every object type that specializes ω. A metavariable σ ranges over the some-object types. Note that the term "object type" means a rather different thing in this paper; object types in the literature are closer to some-object types in this paper.

Typing rules for variables, functions, function applications and primitive values are standard and straightforward. An object is well typed to an object type ω annotated to the self-variable of its members if ω is well-formed and each member's body is well typed to a subtype of the corresponding body type declared in ω. Note that we use

Syntax:

$e ::=$	expression
$\mid x$	variable
$\mid \lambda x : \epsilon.\, e$	function expression
$\mid e\; e$	function application
$\mid p$	primitive values
$\mid \{l_i = \lambda z : \omega.\, e_i\ ^{i \in 1..n}\}$	object
$\mid e_\diamond l$	object member
$\epsilon, \delta ::= \rho \mid \omega \mid \sigma \mid \epsilon \to \epsilon$	expression type
$\omega ::= \mu t.\{l_i : t \to \tau_i\ ^{i \in 1..n}\}$	object type
$\sigma ::= \exists s <\!\!\cdot\, \omega.s$	some-object type

Typing: $\boxed{\Gamma \vdash e : \epsilon \text{ where } \Gamma ::= \{x_i : \epsilon_i\ ^{i \in 1..n}\}}$

$$\text{[T-VAR]}\ \frac{\Gamma(var) = \epsilon}{\Gamma \vdash var : \epsilon} \qquad \text{[T-FUNC]}\ \frac{\emptyset \vdash \epsilon\ \mathsf{ok}' \qquad \Gamma\, x{:}\epsilon \vdash e : \epsilon'}{\Gamma \vdash \lambda x : \epsilon.\, e : \epsilon \to \epsilon'} \qquad \text{[T-APP]}\ \frac{\Gamma \vdash e : \epsilon \to \epsilon' \qquad \Gamma \vdash e' : \delta \qquad \emptyset \vdash \delta <: \epsilon}{\Gamma \vdash e\, e' : \epsilon'}$$

$$\text{[T-PRIM]}\ \frac{i = 1, 2, 3, \ldots}{\Gamma \vdash p_i : \rho_i} \qquad \text{[T-OBJ]}\ \frac{\emptyset \vdash \omega\ \mathsf{ok}' \qquad \omega = \mu t.\{l_i : t \to \tau_i\ ^{i \in 1..n}\} \qquad \forall i \in 1..n : (\Gamma\, z{:}\omega \vdash e_i : \epsilon_i' \quad \emptyset \vdash \epsilon_i' <: \tau_i[\omega/t])}{\Gamma \vdash \{l_i = \lambda z : \omega.\, e_i\ ^{i \in 1..n}\} : \omega}$$

$$\text{[T-MEM1]}\ \frac{\Gamma \vdash e : \omega \qquad \omega = \mu t.\{l : t \to \tau, \ldots\}}{\Gamma \vdash e_\diamond l : \tau[\omega/t]} \qquad \text{[T-MEM2]}\ \frac{\Gamma \vdash e : \sigma \qquad \sigma = \exists s <\!\!\cdot\, \mu t.\{l : t \to \tau, \ldots\}.s \qquad \text{no free } t \text{ occurs negatively in } \tau}{\Gamma \vdash e_\diamond l : \tau[\sigma/t]}$$

Fig. 3. Syntax and static semantics

Value:
$v ::= p \mid \lambda x : \epsilon.\, e \mid \{l_i = \lambda z : \omega.\, e_i\ ^{i \in 1..n}\}$

Evaluation context:
$E ::= \square \mid E\, e \mid v\, E \mid E_\diamond l$

Reduction and evaluation: $\boxed{e \Rightarrow e', e \longmapsto e'}$

$$\text{[R-MEM]}\ \frac{j \in 1..n}{\{l_i = \lambda z : \omega.\, e_i\ ^{i \in 1..n}\}_\diamond l_j \Rightarrow e_j[\{l_i = \lambda z : \omega.\, e_i\ ^{i \in 1..n}\}/z]}$$

$$\text{[R-APP]}\ \frac{}{\lambda x : \epsilon.\, e\ v \Rightarrow e[v/x]} \qquad \text{[EVAL]}\ \frac{e \Rightarrow e'}{E[e] \longmapsto E[e']}$$

Fig. 4. Dynamic semantics

another definition of well-formed types which is stronger (more restrictive) than that presented in Section 4:

$$\emptyset \vdash \tau\ \mathsf{ok}' \quad \text{if} \quad \emptyset \vdash \tau\ \mathsf{ok} \text{ and } \emptyset \vdash \alpha\ \mathsf{ok} \text{ for every subexpression } \alpha \text{ of } \tau.$$

We use this stronger definition of type well-formedness in the typing rules [T-FUNC] and [T-OBJ] in Figure 3 to prevent using a type recursion variable in a nested scope. For example, the following type is well-formed under the stronger definition:

$$\mu\texttt{t}.\{\texttt{a:t, b:}\mu\texttt{u}.\{\texttt{c:int, d:int}\rightarrow\texttt{u}\}\}$$

but, the following is not though it is well-formed under the definition given in Section 4:

$$\mu\texttt{t}.\{\texttt{a:t, b:}\mu\texttt{u}.\{\texttt{c:int, d:t}\rightarrow\texttt{u}\}\}.$$

An object member $e_\diamond l$ is well typed in two cases: firstly, when e is well typed to an object type ω, and secondly, when e is well typed to a some-object type σ and l's body type declared in σ does not have a negative occurrence of the outermost type recursion variable appearing in σ.

With this language, we show that the relation <: conforms to the substitutability notion of subtyping discussed at the beginning of Section 3 by proving the following theorem.

Theorem 1 (Substitutability). *If* $\vdash e_1 : \epsilon_1$, $\vdash E[e_1] : \epsilon$ *and* $\vdash e_2 : \epsilon_2$ *for some* ϵ_2 *with* $\emptyset \vdash \epsilon_2 <: \epsilon_1$, *then*

1. $E[e_2]$ *is a value or there exists an* e' *such that* $E[e_2] \longmapsto e'$, *and*
2. *if there exists an* e'' *such that* $E[e_2] \longmapsto e''$, *then there exists an* ϵ' *such that* $\vdash e'' : \epsilon'$ *and* $\emptyset \vdash \epsilon' <: \epsilon$.

This theorem says that using an expression e_2 of a type ϵ_2 in place of another expression e_1 of another type ϵ_1 with $\emptyset \vdash \epsilon_2 <: \epsilon_1$ results in a value or a reducible expression, and in case of a reducible expression, it produces an expression of a type ϵ' which relates to the type ϵ of the original whole expression $E[e_1]$ by $\emptyset \vdash \epsilon' <: \epsilon$. In short, substituting e_1 with e_2 does not make the computation of the whole expression stuck. Note that this theorem also states the *progress* and *subject reduction* properties of the type system, and hence proves its *type soundness* with respect to the dynamic semantics in the standard manner [28].

6.1 An Interpretation of Classes

In this subsection, we present an interpretation of classes in a typed lambda calculus which is very similar to that of [1,2] except that it uses the *specializing* relation instead of subtyping or matching in the bounded type abstraction.

As discussed in [1,2], one can consider a class as an object-generating object which consists of a special member `new` and other members called *pre-methods*. The `new` member of a class takes the class itself for self-application and zero or more additional values for object fields initialization, and it generates an object with the pre-methods obtained from the given class together with the given initial values for fields. A pre-method is a function which is embedded into each generated object to be its member. The object type is abstracted in a pre-method definition so that the pre-method can be inherited and reused in other classes. For example, the following object (class) $\mathtt{c}_1$ generates objects of type $\mathtt{P}_1$:

$$\begin{aligned}\mathtt{c}_1 = \{&\mathtt{new}{=}\lambda \mathtt{z}'{:}\mathtt{C}_1.\, \lambda \mathtt{i}{:}\mathtt{int}.\, \{\mathtt{x}{=}\lambda \mathtt{z}{:}\mathtt{P}_1.\,\mathtt{i},\ \mathtt{eq}{=}\lambda \mathtt{z}{:}\mathtt{P}_1.\,(\mathtt{z}'_\diamond \mathtt{pre\text{-}eq}\,\mathtt{P}_1\,\mathtt{z})\},\\ &\mathtt{pre\text{-}eq}{=}\lambda \mathtt{z}'{:}\mathtt{C}_1.\,\lambda \mathtt{Z} <_{\mathsf{I}} \mathtt{P}_1.\,\lambda \mathtt{z}{:}\mathtt{Z}.\,\lambda \mathtt{o}{:}\mathtt{Z}.(\mathtt{z}_\diamond \mathtt{x} == \mathtt{o}_\diamond \mathtt{x})\}\end{aligned}$$

where:

$$\begin{aligned}\mathtt{P}_1 &= \mu \mathtt{t}.\{\mathtt{x}{:}\mathtt{t}\to\mathtt{int},\ \mathtt{eq}{:}\mathtt{t}\to\mathtt{t}\to\mathtt{bool}\}\\ \mathtt{C}_1 &= \mu \mathtt{t}.\{\mathtt{new}{:}\mathtt{t}\to\mathtt{int}\to\mathtt{P}_1,\\ &\qquad \mathtt{pre\text{-}eq}{:}\mathtt{t}\to(\forall \mathtt{Z} <_{\mathsf{I}} \mathtt{P}_1.\mathtt{Z}\to\mathtt{Z}\to\mathtt{bool})\}.\end{aligned}$$

With these definitions, $\mathtt{c}_{1\diamond}\mathtt{new}\ 1$, $\mathtt{c}_{1\diamond}\mathtt{new}\ 2$, $\mathtt{c}_{1\diamond}\mathtt{new}\ 3$, and so forth respectively evaluate to:

$$\begin{aligned}&\{\mathtt{x}{=}\lambda \mathtt{z}{:}\mathtt{P}_1.\,1,\ \mathtt{eq}{=}\lambda \mathtt{z}{:}\mathtt{P}_1.\,\lambda \mathtt{o}{:}\mathtt{P}_1.\,(\mathtt{z}_\diamond \mathtt{x} == \mathtt{o}_\diamond \mathtt{x})\},\\ &\{\mathtt{x}{=}\lambda \mathtt{z}{:}\mathtt{P}_1.\,2,\ \mathtt{eq}{=}\lambda \mathtt{z}{:}\mathtt{P}_1.\,\lambda \mathtt{o}{:}\mathtt{P}_1.\,(\mathtt{z}_\diamond \mathtt{x} == \mathtt{o}_\diamond \mathtt{x})\},\\ &\{\mathtt{x}{=}\lambda \mathtt{z}{:}\mathtt{P}_1.\,3,\ \mathtt{eq}{=}\lambda \mathtt{z}{:}\mathtt{P}_1.\,\lambda \mathtt{o}{:}\mathtt{P}_1.\,(\mathtt{z}_\diamond \mathtt{x} == \mathtt{o}_\diamond \mathtt{x})\},\\ &\ldots\end{aligned}$$

A class can reuse pre-methods of another class when the type of objects that it generates specializes the type of objects that the latter class generates. Consider the following example:

$$\begin{aligned}\mathtt{P}_{1x} &= \mu \mathtt{t}.\{\mathtt{x}{:}\mathtt{t}\to\mathtt{int},\ \mathtt{eq}{:}\mathtt{t}\to\mathtt{t}\to\mathtt{bool}, \mathtt{dist}{:}\mathtt{t}\to\mathtt{int}\}\\ \mathtt{C}_{1x} &= \mu \mathtt{t}.\{\mathtt{new}{:}\mathtt{t}\to\mathtt{int}\to\mathtt{P}_{1x},\\ &\qquad \mathtt{pre\text{-}eq}{:}\mathtt{t}\to(\forall \mathtt{Z} <_{\mathsf{I}} \mathtt{P}_{1x}.\mathtt{Z}\to\mathtt{Z}\to\mathtt{bool}),\\ &\qquad \mathtt{pre\text{-}dist}{:}\mathtt{t}\to(\forall \mathtt{Z} <_{\mathsf{I}} \mathtt{P}_{1x}.\mathtt{Z}\to\mathtt{int})\}\\ \mathtt{c}_{1x} &= \{\mathtt{new}{=}\lambda \mathtt{z}'{:}\mathtt{C}_{1x}.\,\lambda \mathtt{i}{:}\mathtt{int}.\,\{\mathtt{x}{=}\lambda \mathtt{z}{:}\mathtt{P}_{1x}.\,\mathtt{i},\\ &\qquad\qquad \mathtt{eq}{=}\lambda \mathtt{z}{:}\mathtt{P}_{1x}.\,(\mathtt{z}'_\diamond \mathtt{pre\text{-}eq}\,\mathtt{P}_{1x}\,\mathtt{z}),\\ &\qquad\qquad \mathtt{dist}{=}\lambda \mathtt{z}{:}\mathtt{P}_{1x}.\,(\mathtt{z}'_\diamond \mathtt{pre\text{-}dist}\,\mathtt{P}_{1x}\,\mathtt{z})\},\\ &\qquad \mathtt{pre\text{-}eq}{=}\lambda \mathtt{z}'{:}\mathtt{C}_{1x}.\ \mathtt{c}_{1\diamond}\mathtt{pre\text{-}eq},\\ &\qquad \mathtt{pre\text{-}dist}{=}\lambda \mathtt{z}'{:}\mathtt{C}_{1x}.\,\lambda \mathtt{Z} <_{\mathsf{I}} \mathtt{P}_{1x}.\,\lambda \mathtt{z}{:}\mathtt{Z}.\ |\mathtt{z}_\diamond \mathtt{x}|\}\end{aligned}$$

In this example, the object type $\mathtt{P}_{1x}$ specializes $\mathtt{P}_1$ only with a single additional member `dist` (distance to the origin). Therefore, $\mathtt{c}_{1x}$ can reuse the pre-method `pre-eq` of $\mathtt{c}_1$ (see the definition of `pre-eq` in $\mathtt{c}_{1x}$). For such kind of pre-method reuse, it is essential to abstract the object type with an appropriate bound in the definition of each pre-method, as done in the above example: in the definition of `pre-eq` of $\mathtt{c}_1$, the type of the self-variable is abstracted with the bound $\mathtt{P}_1$ ($\ldots \lambda \mathtt{Z} <_{\mathsf{I}} \mathtt{P}_1.\,\lambda \mathtt{z}{:}\mathtt{Z}.\ldots$) and in the definition of `pre-dist` of $\mathtt{c}_{1x}$, the type of the self-variable is abstracted with the bound

$\mathtt{P_{1x}}$ $(\ldots \lambda\mathtt{Z} <_{\mathsf{I}} \mathtt{P_{1x}}.\ \lambda\mathtt{z}:\mathtt{Z}.\ldots)$. Note that the above examples use specialization-bounded type abstraction rather than subtype-bounded type abstraction. This example cannot use subtype-bounded type abstraction because the revised subtyping cannot relate object types over which the type variable Z ranges, and the traditional subtyping cannot relate object types when the types have a negative type recursion [1,2].

7 Conclusion

We present a new formalization of subtyping to explain the subtyping-by-subclassing observed in recent developments of object-oriented languages [4,27,22,21]. In the formalization, we drop the traditional subtype relation on recursive record types and define a new one on the specialization-bounded existential types which we call some-object types. Negative type recursions do not limit subtyping in the new formalization, and some-object types well correspond to class types in ordinary object-oriented languages. This explains the coexistence of subtyping-by-subclassing and recursive types. Negative type recursions always arise in typing binary methods, and moreover, they are already inherent in real implementations of object-oriented languages. Therefore, our formalization of subtyping is helpful to better understand objects.

Though we limit type recursions to record types in this paper to focus on object-oriented languages which are our main concern, our approach—dropping the Amber rules and establishing subtyping via specializing and existential types—may be applicable to other kinds of recursive types such as recursive function types and recursive variant types, because the interaction between the subtyping rule for function types and the negative type recursion limits subtyping between those recursive types too. We hope that this work will serve as a new direction for a desirable formalization of subtyping in the programming language research community.

Acknowledgments. This work is supported in part by Korea Ministry of Education, Science and Technology(MEST) / National Research Foundation of Korea(NRF) (Grants NRF-2011-0016139 and NRF-2008-0062609), Microsoft Research Asia, Samsung Electronics, and S-Core., Ltd.

References

1. Abadi, M., Cardelli, L.: On subtyping and matching. ACM Trans. Program. Lang. Syst. 18(4), 401–423 (1996)
2. Abadi, M., Cardelli, L.: A Theory of Objects. Springer-Verlag New York, Inc., Secaucus (1996)
3. Bruce, K., Cardelli, L., Castagna, G., Leavens, G.T., Pierce, B.: On binary methods. Theory and Practice of Object Systems 1, 221–242 (1995)
4. Oulmakhzoune, S., Foster, J.N.: LOOJ: Weaving LOOM into Java. In: Odersky, M. (ed.) ECOOP 2004. LNCS, vol. 3086, pp. 390–414. Springer, Heidelberg (2004)
5. Bruce, K., Odersky, M., Wadler, P.: A statically safe alternative to virtual types. In: Jul, E. (ed.) ECOOP 1998. LNCS, vol. 1445, Springer, Heidelberg (1998)

6. Bruce, K., Petersen, L., Fiech, A.: Subtyping is not a good "match" for object-oriented languages. In: Akşit, M., Matsuoka, S. (eds.) ECOOP 1997. LNCS, vol. 1241, Springer, Heidelberg (1997)
7. Bruce, K., Schuett, A., van Gent, R., Fiech, A.: PolyTOIL: A type-safe polymorphic object-oriented language. ACM TOPLAS 25, 225–290 (2003)
8. Cardelli, L.: A semantics of multiple inheritance. In: Kahn, G., MacQueen, D.B., Plotkin, G. (eds.) Semantics of Data Types. LNCS, vol. 173, pp. 51–67. Springer, Heidelberg (1984)
9. Cardelli, L.: Amber. In: Cousineau, G., Curien, P.-L., Robinet, B. (eds.) LITP 1985. LNCS, vol. 242, pp. 21–47. Springer, Heidelberg (1986)
10. Cook, W.: A proposal for making Eiffel type-safe. The Computer Journal, 57–70 (1989)
11. Cook, W.R., Hill, W., Canning, P.S.: Inheritance is not subtyping. In: Proceedings of the 17th ACM SIGPLAN-SIGACT Symposium on Principles of Programming Languages, pp. 125–135. ACM, New York (1990)
12. Eifrig, J., Smith, S., Trifonov, V., Zwarico, A.: An interpretation of typed oop in a language with state. LISP and Symbolic Computation 8, 357–397 (1995)
13. Fisher, K., Mitchell, J.C.: The development of type systems for object-oriented languages. Technical report, Stanford, CA, USA (1996)
14. Gosling, J., Joy, B., Steele, G., Bracha, G., Buckley, A.: The Java™ Language Specification, Java SE 7 Edition. Oracle America, Inc. (February 2012)
15. Hofmann, M., Pierce, B.: A unifying type-theoretic framework for objects. Journal of Functional Programming 5(04), 593–635 (1995)
16. Kamin, S.: Inheritance in Smalltalk-80: a denotational definition. In: Proceedings of the 15th ACM SIGPLAN-SIGACT Symposium on Principles of Programming Languages (1988)
17. Kamin, S.N., Reddy, U.S.: Two semantic models of object-oriented languages. In: Gunter, C.A., Mitchell, J.C. (eds.) Theoretical Aspects of Object-Oriented Programming, pp. 463–495. MIT Press (1994)
18. LaLonde, W., Pugh, J.: Subclassing $\neq$ subtyping $\neq$ is-a. J. Object Oriented Program. 3(5), 57–62 (1991)
19. Lindholm, T., Yellin, F., Bracha, G., Buckley, A.: The Java™ Virtual Machine Specification, Java SE 7 Edition. Oracle America, Inc. (February 2012)
20. Mitchell, J.C.: Toward a typed foundation for method specialization and inheritance. In: POPL 1990 (1990)
21. Na, H., Ryu, S.: ThisJava: An extension of Java with exact types. In: Shan, C.-c. (ed.) APLAS 2013. LNCS, vol. 8301, pp. 233–240. Springer, Heidelberg (2013)
22. Hyunik, N., Sukyoung, R., Kwangmoo, C.: Exact type parameterization and ThisType support. In: TLDI 2012 (2012)
23. Odersky, M., Spoon, L., Venners, B.: Programming in Scala. Artima Inc. (2008)
24. Pierce, B.C.: Types and Programming Languages. The MIT Press (2002)
25. Pierce, B.C., Turner, D.N.: Simple type-theoretic foundations for object-oriented programming. Journal of Functional Programming 4(02), 207–247 (1994)
26. Reddy, U.: Objects as closures: abstract semantics of object-oriented languages. In: Proceedings of the 1988 ACM Conference on LISP and Functional Programming (1988)
27. Saito, C., Igarashi, A.: Matching ThisType to subtyping. In: Proceedings of the 2009 ACM Symposium on Applied Computing, SAC 2009, pp. 1851–1858. ACM, New York (2009)
28. Wright, A.K., Felleisen, M.: A syntactic approach to type soundness. Information and Computation 115, 38–94 (1992)

Type Soundness and Race Freedom for Mezzo

Thibaut Balabonski, François Pottier, and Jonathan Protzenko

INRIA Paris-Rocquencourt, France

Abstract. The programming language Mezzo is equipped with a rich type system that controls aliasing and access to mutable memory. We incorporate shared-memory concurrency into Mezzo and present a modular formalization of its core type system, in the form of a concurrent λ-calculus, which we extend with references and locks. We prove that well-typed programs do not go wrong and are data-race free. Our definitions and proofs are machine-checked.

1 Introduction

Strongly-typed programming languages rule out some programming mistakes by ensuring at compile-time that every operation is applied to arguments of suitable nature. As per Milner's slogan, "well-typed programs do not go wrong". If one wishes to obtain stronger static guarantees, one must usually turn to static analysis or program verification techniques. For instance, separation logic [13] can prove that private state is properly encapsulated; concurrent separation logic [10] can prove the absence of interference between threads; and, in general, program logics can prove that a program meets its specification.

The programming language Mezzo [12] is equipped with a static discipline that goes beyond traditional type systems and incorporates some of the ideas of separation logic. The Mezzo type-checker reasons about aliasing and ownership. This increases expressiveness, for instance by allowing gradual initialization, and rules out more errors, such as representation exposure or data races. Mezzo is descended from ML: its core features are immutable local variables, possibly-mutable heap-allocated data, and first-class functions. In this paper, we incorporate shared-memory concurrency into Mezzo and present its meta-theory.

A Race. In order to illustrate Mezzo, let us consider the tiny program in Fig. 1. This code exhibits a data race, hence is incorrect, and is rejected by the type system. Let us explain how it is type-checked. At line 1, we allocate a reference

```
1 val r = newref 0
2 val f (| r @ ref int)
3     : (| r @ ref int) =
4   r := !r + 1
5 val () =
6   spawn f; spawn f
```

Fig. 1. Ill-typed code. The function `f` increments the global reference `r`. The main program spawns two threads that call `f`. There is a data race: both threads may attempt to modify `r` at the same time.

M. Codish and E. Sumii (Eds.): FLOPS 2014, LNCS 8475, pp. 253–269, 2014.

(i.e., a memory cell), and store its address in the global variable `r`. In the eyes of the type-checker, this gives rise to a *permission*, written `r @ ref int`. This permission has a double reading: it describes the layout of memory (i.e., "the variable `r` denotes the address of a cell that stores an integer") and grants *exclusive* read-write access to this cell. That is, the type constructor `ref` denotes a uniquely-owned reference, and the permission `r @ ref int` is a unique token that one must possess in order to dereference `r`. This token exists at type-checking time only.

A permission `r @ ref int` looks like a traditional assumption `r : ref int`. However, a type assumption would be valid everywhere in the scope of `r`, whereas a permission is a token: it can be passed from caller to callee, returned from callee to caller, passed from one thread to another, etc. If one gives away this token, then, even though `r` is still in scope, one can no longer read or write it.

Although `r @ ref int` is an affine permission (i.e., it cannot be copied), some permissions are duplicable. For instance, `x @ int` is a duplicable permission. If one can get ahold of such a permission, then one can keep it forever (i.e., as long as `x` is in scope) *and* pass copies of it to other threads, if desired. Such a permission behaves like a traditional type assumption `x : int`.

The function `f` in Fig. 1 takes no argument and returns no result. Its type is not just `() -> ()`, though. Because `f` needs access to `r`, it must explicitly request the permission `r @ ref int` and return it. (The fact that this permission is available at the definition site of `f` is not good enough: a closure cannot capture an affine permission.) This is declared by the type annotation[1] at lines 2 and 3. Thus, at line 5, in conjunction with `r @ ref int`, we get a new permission, `f @ (| r @ ref int) -> (| r @ ref int)`. This means that `f` is a function with zero (runtime) argument and result, which (at type-checking time) requires and returns the permission `r @ ref int`. The type `T | P` denotes a package of a value of type `T` and the permission `P`. We write `(| P)` for `(() | P)`, where `()` is the unit type.

At line 6, the type-checker analyzes the sequencing construct in a manner analogous to separation logic: the second `spawn` instruction is checked using the permissions that are left over by the first `spawn`. An instruction `spawn f` requires two permissions: a permission to invoke the function `f`, and `r @ ref int`, which `f` itself requires. It does *not* return these permissions: they are transferred to the spawned thread. Thus, in line 6, between the two `spawn`s, we no longer have a permission for `r`. (We still have `f @ (|...) -> (|...)`, because it is duplicable.) Therefore, the second `spawn` is ill-typed. The racy program of Fig. 1 is rejected.

A Fix. In order to fix this program, one must introduce enough synchronization so as to eliminate the race. A common way of doing so is to introduce a lock and place all accesses to `r` within critical sections. In Mezzo, this can be done, and causes the type-checker to recognize that the code is now data-race free.

[1] In the surface syntax of Mezzo, in the absence of a `consumes` keyword, a permission that is taken by a function is considered also returned, so one need not repeat `r @ ref int` in the header or in the type of `f`. In this paper, we do not use this convention. We work in a simpler, lower-level syntax where functions consume their arguments.

```
1 val hide [a, b, s : perm]
2   (f : (a | s) -> (b | s) | s)
3 : (a -> b) =
4   let l : lock s = newlock() in
5   release l;
6   fun (x : a) : b =
7     acquire l;
8     let y = f x in
9     release l;
10    y
```

Fig. 2. The polymorphic, higher-order function **hide** takes a function `f` of type `(a | s) -> (b | s)`, which means that `f` needs access to some state represented by the permission `s`. The function **hide** requires `s`, and consumes it. It returns a function of type `a -> b`, which does not require `s`, hence can be invoked by multiple threads concurrently.

In fact, this common pattern can be implemented abstractly as a polymorphic, higher-order function, `hide` (Fig. 2).

In Fig. 2, `f` is a parameter of `hide`. It has a visible side effect: it requires and returns a permission `s`. When `hide` is invoked, it creates a new lock `l`, whose role is to guard the use of the possibly affine permission `s`. This is materialized by a duplicable permission `l @ lock s`, which is produced by the `newlock` instruction, and added to the two permissions `s` and `f @ (a | s) -> (b | s)` already present at the beginning of line 4. The fact that `l @ lock s` is duplicable is a key point: this enables multiple threads to compete for the lock even if the guarded permission is affine. The lock is created in the "locked" state, and released at line 5. This consumes `s`: when one releases a lock, one must give up and give back the permission that it controls. The permissions for `f` and `l` remain, and, because they are duplicable, they are also available within the anonymous function defined at line 6. (A closure *can* capture a duplicable permission.)

The anonymous function at line 6 does not require or return `s`. Yet, it needs `s` in order to invoke `f`. It obtains `s` by acquiring the lock, and gives it up by releasing the lock. Thus, `s` is available only to a thread that has entered the critical section. The side effect is now hidden, in the sense that the anonymous function has type `a -> b`, which does not mention `s`.

It is easy to fix the code in Fig. 1 by inserting the redefinition `val f = hide f` before line 5. This call consumes `r @ ref int` and produces `f @ () -> ()`, so the two `spawn` instructions are now type-checked without difficulty.

Channels. Acquiring or releasing a lock produces or consumes a permission: a transfer of ownership takes place between the lock and the active thread. This can be used to encode other patterns of ownership transfer. For example, a (multiple-writer, multiple-reader) communication channel, which allows exchanging messages and permissions between threads, is easily implemented as a FIFO queue, protected by a lock. Let us briefly describe the interface and implementation of this user-defined abstraction.

Channels are described by the interface in Fig. 3. Line 1 advertises the existence of an abstract type `channel a` of channels along which values of type `a` may be transferred. Line 2 advertises the fact that this type is duplicable. (We explain below why the definition of `channel` satisfies this claim.) This means that the permission to use a channel (for sending or receiving) can be shared

```
abstract channel a
fact duplicable (channel a)
val new:     [a] ()              -> channel a
val send:    [a] (channel a, a) -> ()
val receive: [a] (channel a)    -> a
```

Fig. 3. An interface for communication channels

```
1  alias channel a =
2    (q: unknown, lock (q @ fifo a))
3  val new [a] () : channel a =
4    let q = queue::create () in
5    let l : lock (q @ fifo a) = newlock() in
6    release l;
7    (q, l)
8  val send [a] (c: channel a, x: a) : () =
9    let (q, l) = c in
10   acquire l;
11   queue::insert (x, q);
12   release l
13 val receive [a] (c : channel a) : a =
14   let (q, l) = c in
15   acquire l;
16   let rec loop (| q @ fifo a * l @ locked) : a =
17     match queue::retrieve q with
18     | None ->                     loop()
19     | Some { contents = x } -> release l; x
20     end
21   in loop()
```

Fig. 4. A simple implementation of channels using a queue and a lock

between several threads. The type of `send` means that sending a value `x` along a channel `c` of type `channel a` consumes the permission `x @ a`. Symmetrically, the type of `receive` means that receiving a value `x` along such a channel produces the permission `x @ a`. It is important to note that the type `a` of messages is not necessarily duplicable. If it is not, then a transfer of ownership, from the sender thread to the receiver thread, is taking place.

Fig. 4 implements channels using a FIFO queue and a lock. The lock guards the exclusive permission to access the queue. In lines 1–2, the type `channel a` is defined as an abbreviation for a pair[2] of a value `q` of *a priori* unknown type (i.e., no permission is available for it) and a lock of type `lock (q @ fifo a)`. Acquiring the lock produces the permission `q @ fifo a`, so that, within a critical section, `q` is recognized by the type-checker as a queue, which can be accessed and updated.

[2] The dependent pair notation used in this definition is desugared into existential types and singleton types, which are part of Mezzo's core type discipline (§2).

The type-checker accepts the claim that the type `channel a` is duplicable because it is defined as a pair of two duplicable types, namely `unknown` and `lock (...)`.

Contributions. Mezzo appeared in a previous paper by Pottier and Protzenko [12]. That paper does not cover concurrency. It presents Mezzo's type discipline in a monolithic manner, and does not contain any details about the proof of type soundness. In the present paper, Mezzo includes shared-memory concurrency, and its presentation is modularly organized in several layers. We identify a kernel layer: a concurrent, call-by-value λ-calculus extended with a construct for dynamic thread creation (§2). In its typed version, it is a polymorphic, value-dependent system, which enjoys type erasure: values exist at runtime, whereas types and permissions do not. The system provides a framework for handling duplicable as well as affine permissions, and is equipped with a rich set of subsumption rules that are analogous to separation logic entailment. Although this calculus does not have explicit side effects, we endow it with an abstract notion of machine state, and we organize the proof of type soundness in such a way that the statements of the main lemmas need not be altered as we introduce new forms of side effects. The next two layers, which are independent of one another, are heap-allocated references (§3) and locks (§4). Our definitions and proofs are machine-checked [2].

2 Kernel

2.1 Machine States and Resources

The kernel calculus does not include any explicit effectful operations. Yet, in order to later add such operations without altering the statements of the main lemmas that lead to the type soundness result, we build into the kernel calculus the idea of a *machine state* s. At this stage, the nature of machine states is unspecified. Later on, we make it partially concrete, by specifying that a machine state is a tuple of a heap (§3), a lock heap (§4), and possibly more: the type of machine states is informally considered open-ended. The execution of a program begins in a distinguished machine state *initial*.

A program under execution is composed of multiple threads, each of which has partial knowledge of the current machine state and partial rights to alter this state. In the proof of type soundness, we account for this by working with a notion of *resource*, of which one can think as the "view" of a thread [7]. At this stage, again, the nature of resources is unspecified. One should think of a resource as a partial, instrumented machine state: a resource may contain additional information that does not exist at runtime, such as an access right for a memory location (§3), or the invariant associated with a lock (§4).

We require resources to form a *monotonic separation algebra* [11, §10]. That is, we assume the following:

- A composition operator $\star$ allows two resources (i.e., the views of two threads) to be combined. It is total, commutative, and associative.
- A predicate, R *ok*, identifies the well-formed resources. It is preserved by splitting, i.e., $R_1 \star R_2$ *ok* implies R_1 *ok*.

- A total function $\widehat{\cdot}$ maps every resource R to its *core* $\widehat{R}$, which represents the duplicable (shareable) information contained in R.
  - This element is a unit for R, i.e., $R \star \widehat{R} = R$.
  - Two compatible elements have a common core, i.e., $R_1 \star R_2 = R$ and R *ok* imply $\widehat{R_1} = \widehat{R}$.
  - A duplicable resource is its own core, i.e., $R \star R = R$ implies $R = \widehat{R}$.
  - Every core is duplicable, i.e., $\widehat{R} \star \widehat{R} = \widehat{R}$.
- A relation $R_1 \lhd R_2$, the *rely*, represents the interference that "other" threads are allowed to inflict on "this" thread. For instance, the allocation of new memory blocks, or of new locks, is typically permitted by this relation.
  - This relation is reflexive.
  - It preserves consistency, i.e., R_1 *ok* and $R_1 \lhd R_2$ imply R_2 *ok*.
  - It is preserved by core, i.e., $R_1 \lhd R_2$ implies $\widehat{R_1} \lhd \widehat{R_2}$.
  - Finally, it is compatible with $\star$, in the following sense:

$$\frac{R_1 \star R_2 \lhd R' \qquad R_1 \star R_2 \; ok}{\exists R'_1 R'_2,\; R'_1 \star R'_2 = R' \wedge R_1 \lhd R'_1 \wedge R_2 \lhd R'_2}$$

We assume that a connection between machine states and resources is given by a relation $s \sim R$. In the case of heaps, for instance, this would mean that the heap s and the instrumented heap R have a common domain and that, by erasing the extra information in R, one finds s. We assume that the initial machine state corresponds to a distinguished void resource, i.e., *initial* $\sim$ *void*. We assume that $s \sim R$ implies R *ok*. No other assumptions are required at this abstract stage.

2.2 Syntax

Values, terms, types, and permissions form a single syntactic category. There is a single name space of variables. Within this universe, defined in Fig. 5, we impose a kind discipline, so as to distinguish the following sub-categories[3].

The values v have kind value. They are the variables of kind value (the λ binder introduces such a variable) and the λ-abstractions.

The terms t have kind term. They encompass values. Function application $v\ t$ and thread creation spawn $v_1\ v_2$ are also terms (the latter is meant to execute the function call $v_1\ v_2$ in a new thread). The sequencing construct let $x = t_1$ in t_2 is encoded as $(\lambda x.t_2)\ t_1$. We reduce the number of evaluation contexts by requiring the left-hand side of an application to be a value. This does not reduce expressiveness: $t_1\ t_2$ can be encoded as let $x = t_1$ in $x\ t_2$.

The soups, also written t, have kind soup. They are parallel compositions of threads. A thread takes the form thread (t), where t has kind term.

The types T, U have kind type; the permissions P, Q have kind perm. We write θ for a syntactic element of kind type or perm.

[3] For the sake of conciseness, we omit the definition of the well-kindedness judgement, and omit the well-kindedness premises in the definition of the typing judgement. Instead, we use conventional metavariables (v, t, etc.) to indicate the intended kind of each syntactic element.

$$\begin{array}{rcll}
\kappa & ::= & \textsf{value} \mid \textsf{term} \mid \textsf{soup} \mid \textsf{type} \mid \textsf{perm} & \text{(Kinds)} \\
v, t, T, U, P, Q, \theta & ::= & x & \text{(Everything)} \\
& \mid & \lambda x.t & \text{(Values: } v\text{)} \\
& \mid & v\ t \mid \textsf{spawn}\ v\ v & \text{(Terms: } t\text{)} \\
& \mid & \textsf{thread}\ (t) \mid t \parallel t & \text{(Soups: } t\text{)} \\
& \mid & =v \mid T \rightarrow T \mid (T \mid P) & \text{(Types: } T,\ U\text{)} \\
& \mid & v \mathbin{@} T \mid \textsf{empty} \mid P * P \mid \textsf{duplicable}\ \theta & \text{(Permissions: } P,\ Q\text{)} \\
& \mid & \forall x : \kappa.\theta \mid \exists x : \kappa.\theta & \text{(Types or permissions: } \theta\text{)} \\
E & ::= & v\ [] & \text{(Shallow evaluation contexts)} \\
D & ::= & [] \mid E[D] & \text{(Deep evaluation contexts)}
\end{array}$$

Fig. 5. Kernel: syntax of programs, types, and permissions

initial configuration		*new configuration*	*side condition*
$s\ /\ (\lambda x.t)\ v$	$\longrightarrow$	$s\ /\ [v/x]t$	
$s\ /\ E[t]$	$\longrightarrow$	$s'\ /\ E[t']$	$s\ /\ t \longrightarrow s'\ /\ t'$
$s\ /\ \textsf{thread}\ (t)$	$\longrightarrow$	$s'\ /\ \textsf{thread}\ (t')$	$s\ /\ t \longrightarrow s'\ /\ t'$
$s\ /\ t_1 \parallel t_2$	$\longrightarrow$	$s'\ /\ t_1' \parallel t_2$	$s\ /\ t_1 \longrightarrow s'\ /\ t_1'$
$s\ /\ t_1 \parallel t_2$	$\longrightarrow$	$s'\ /\ t_1 \parallel t_2'$	$s\ /\ t_2 \longrightarrow s'\ /\ t_2'$
$s\ /\ \textsf{thread}\ (D[\textsf{spawn}\ v_1\ v_2])$	$\longrightarrow$	$s\ /\ \textsf{thread}\ (D[()]) \parallel \textsf{thread}\ (v_1\ v_2)$	

Fig. 6. Kernel: operational semantics

The types T include the singleton type $=v$, inhabited by the value v only; the function type $T \rightarrow U$; and the conjunction $T \mid P$ of a type and a permission.

The permissions P include the atomic form $v \mathbin{@} T$, which can be viewed as an assertion that the value v currently has type T, or can be used at type T; the trivial permission empty; the conjunction of two permissions, $P * Q$; and the permission duplicable θ, which asserts that the type or permission θ is duplicable. A permission of the form duplicable θ is typically used as part of a constrained quantified type. For instance, $\forall x : \textsf{type}.(x \mid (\textsf{duplicable}\ x)) \rightarrow \ldots$ describes a polymorphic function which, for every duplicable type x, is able to take an argument of type x.

Universal and existential quantification is available in the syntax of both types and permissions. The bound variable x has kind κ, which is restricted to be one of value, type, or perm: that is, we never quantify over terms or soups.

2.3 Operational Semantics

The calculus is equipped with a small-step operational semantics (Fig. 6). The reduction relation acts on configurations c, which are pairs of a machine state s and a closed term or soup t. In the kernel rules, the machine state is carried around, but never consulted or modified.

2.4 Typing Judgement and Interpretation of Permissions

The main two judgements, which depend on each other, are the *typing judgement* $R; K; P \vdash t : T$ and the *permission interpretation judgement* $R; K \Vdash P$. The kind environment K is a finite map of variables to kinds. It introduces the

$$\textsc{Singleton}\quad R; K; P \vdash v : {=}v$$

$$\textsc{Frame}\quad \frac{R; K; P \vdash t : T}{R; K; P \ast Q \vdash t : T \mid Q}$$

$$\textsc{Function}\quad \frac{\widehat{R}; K, x : \mathsf{value}; P \ast x @ T \vdash t : U}{R; K; (\mathsf{duplicable}\ P) \ast P \vdash \lambda x.t : T \rightarrow U}$$

$$\textsc{ForallIntro}\quad \frac{t \textit{ is harmless} \qquad R; K, x : \kappa; P \vdash t : T}{R; K; \forall x : \kappa.P \vdash t : \forall x : \kappa.T}$$

$$\textsc{ExistsIntro}\quad \frac{R; K; P \vdash v : [U/x]T}{R; K; P \vdash v : \exists x : \kappa.T}$$

$$\textsc{Cut}\quad \frac{R_2; K; P_1 \ast P_2 \vdash t : T \qquad R_1; K \Vdash P_1}{R_1 \star R_2; K; P_2 \vdash t : T}$$

$$\textsc{ExistsElim}\quad \frac{R; K, x : \kappa; P \vdash t : T}{R; K; \exists x : \kappa.P \vdash t : T}$$

$$\textsc{SubLeft}\quad \frac{K \vdash P_1 \leq P_2 \qquad R; K; P_2 \vdash t : T}{R; K; P_1 \vdash t : T}$$

$$\textsc{SubRight}\quad \frac{R; K; P \vdash t : T_1 \qquad K \vdash T_1 \leq T_2}{R; K; P \vdash t : T_2}$$

$$\textsc{Application}\quad \frac{R; K; Q \vdash t : T}{R; K; (v @ T \rightarrow U) \ast Q \vdash v\ t : U}$$

$$\textsc{Spawn}\quad R; K; (v_1 @ T \rightarrow U) \ast (v_2 @ T) \vdash \mathsf{spawn}\ v_1\ v_2 : \top$$

Fig. 7. Kernel: typing rules

variables that may occur free in P, t, and T[4]. The kind environment K contains information that does not evolve with time (i.e., the kind of every variable) whereas the precondition P contains information that evolves with time (i.e., the available permissions).

The typing judgement $R; K; P \vdash t : T$ states that, under the assumptions represented by the resource R and by the permission P, the term t has type T. One can view the typing judgement as a Hoare triple, where R and P form the precondition and T is the postcondition. The resource R plays a role only when reasoning about programs under execution: it is the "view" that each thread has of the machine state. When type-checking source programs, R is *void*.

The permission interpretation judgement $R; K \Vdash P$ means that R justifies, or satisfies, the permission P. If one thinks of R as an (instrumented) heap fragment and of P as a separation logic assertion, one finds that this judgement is analogous to the interpretation of assertions in separation logic. It gives meaning, in terms of resources, to the syntax of permissions.

The typing judgement is defined in Fig. 7. The first five rules are introduction rules: they define the meaning of the type constructors. Singleton states that v is one (and the only) inhabitant of the singleton type $=v$. Frame can be applied to a value v or to a term t. In the latter case, it is a frame rule in the sense of separation logic. Because every function type is considered duplicable, a function body must be type-checked under duplicable assumptions. For this reason, in Function, P is required to be duplicable and R is replaced in the premise with its core $\widehat{R}$. ForallIntro can be applied to a value or to a term: there is no value restriction. Once hidden state is introduced (§4), polymorphism must be restricted to a syntactic category of *harmless* terms. For now, every term is harmless. ExistsIntro is standard.

[4] The parameter K is used only in the well-kindedness premises, all of which we have elided in this paper. Nevertheless, we mention K as part of the typing judgement.

$$\textsc{Atomic}\ \frac{R_1; K; P \vdash v : T \qquad R_2; K \Vdash P}{R_1 \star R_2; K \Vdash v \mathbin{@} T} \qquad \textsc{Empty}\ R; K \Vdash \textsf{empty} \qquad \textsc{Star}\ \frac{R_1; K \Vdash P_1 \qquad R_2; K \Vdash P_2}{R_1 \star R_2; K \Vdash P_1 * P_2}$$

$$\textsc{Duplicable}\ \frac{\theta \textit{ is duplicable}}{R; K \Vdash \textsf{duplicable}\ \theta} \qquad \textsc{Forall}\ \frac{R; K, x : \kappa \Vdash P}{R; K \Vdash \forall x : \kappa.P} \qquad \textsc{Exists}\ \frac{R; K \Vdash [U/x]P}{R; K \Vdash \exists x : \kappa.P}$$

Fig. 8. Kernel: the interpretation of permissions

$$\textsc{MixStarIntroElim}\ (v \mathbin{@} T) * P \equiv v \mathbin{@} T \mid P \qquad \textsc{Frame}\ v \mathbin{@} T_1 \rightarrow T_2 \leq v \mathbin{@} (T_1 \mid P) \rightarrow (T_2 \mid P)$$

$$\textsc{Duplicate}\ (\textsf{duplicable}\ P) * P \leq P * P \qquad \textsc{DupSingleton}\ \textsf{empty} \leq \textsf{duplicable} =\!v \qquad \textsc{DupArrow}\ \textsf{empty} \leq \textsf{duplicable}\ (T \rightarrow U)$$

Fig. 9. Kernel: permission subsumption (a few rules only; $K \vdash$ omitted)

Cut moves information between the parameters P and R of a judgement. In short, it says, if t is well-typed under the assumption P_1, then it is well-typed under R_1, provided the resource R_1 satisfies the permission P_1.

Next, we find three non-syntax-directed rules, namely ExistsElim, SubLeft, SubRight. An important part of the type soundness proof consists in proving that every well-typed, closed value can be type-checked without using these rules.

Application is standard. Spawn states that spawn $v_1\ v_2$ is type-checked just like a function application $v_1\ v_2$, except a unit value is returned in the original thread. We write $\top$ for the type $\exists x : \textsf{value}.{=}x$.

We now review the interpretation of permissions (Fig. 8). These rules play a role in the proof of type soundness, where they establish a connection between the syntax of permissions and their intended meaning in terms of resources. Empty, Star, Forall, Exists correspond to the interpretation of assertions in separation logic. Atomic states, roughly, that the resource R satisfies the permission $v \mathbin{@} T$ if the value v has type T under R. Duplicable defines the meaning of the permission duplicable θ in terms of a meta-level predicate, θ *is duplicable.* The latter is defined by cases over the syntax of θ, as follows: a variable x is not duplicable; a singleton type $=v$ is duplicable; a function type $T \rightarrow U$ is duplicable; a conjunction $T \mid P$ is duplicable if T and P are duplicable; and so on. We omit the full definition.

2.5 Subsumption

The permission subsumption judgement takes the form $K \vdash P \leq Q$. It is inductively defined by many rules, of which, by lack of space, we show very few (Fig. 9). MixStarIntroElim is a compact way of summing up the relationship between the two forms of conjunction. Frame is analogous to the typing rule by the same name (Fig. 7), and means that a function that performs fewer side effects can be passed where a function that performs more side effects is allowed.

$$\frac{R; \varnothing; \mathsf{empty} \vdash t : T}{R \vdash \mathsf{thread}\ (t)}\ \text{Thread} \qquad \frac{R_1 \vdash t_1 \qquad R_2 \vdash t_2}{R_1 \star R_2 \vdash t_1 \parallel t_2}\ \text{Par} \qquad \frac{s \sim R \qquad R \vdash t}{\vdash s \,/\, t}\ \text{JConf}$$

Fig. 10. Kernel: typing rules for soups and configurations

Duplicate states that if P is provably duplicable, then P can be turned into $P * P$. DupSingleton, DupArrow, and a family of similar rules (not shown) allow constructing permissions of the form $\mathsf{duplicable}\ \theta$.

The subtyping judgement used in SubRight is defined in terms of permission subsumption: we write $K \vdash T \leq U$ when $K, x : \mathsf{value} \vdash x @ T \leq x @ U$ holds.

2.6 Typing Judgements for Soups and Configurations

The typing judgement for soups $R \vdash t$ (Fig. 10, first two rules) ensures that every thread is well-typed (the type of its eventual result does not matter) and constructs the composition of the resources owned by the individual threads. It means that, under the precondition R, the thread soup t is safe to execute.

The typing judgement for configurations $\vdash s \,/\, t$ (Fig. 10, last rule) ensures that the thread soup t is well-typed under some resource R that corresponds to the machine state s. This judgement means that $s \,/\, t$ is safe to execute.

2.7 Type Soundness

The kernel calculus is quite minimal: in its untyped form, it is a pure λ-calculus. As a result, there is no way that a program can "go wrong". Nevertheless, it is useful to prove that (the typed version of) the kernel calculus enjoys subject reduction and progress properties. Because abstract notions of machine state s, resource R, and correspondence $s \sim R$ have been built in, our proofs are parametric in these notions. Instantiating these parameters with concrete definitions (as we do when we introduce references, §3, and locks, §4) does not require any alteration to the statements or proofs of the main lemmas. Introducing new primitive operations (such as the operations that manipulate references and locks) does not require altering the statements either; naturally, it does create new proof cases.

For the sake of brevity, we state only the main two lemmas.

Theorem 1 (Subject reduction). *If $c_1 \longrightarrow c_2$, then $\vdash c_1$ implies $\vdash c_2$.*

Theorem 2 (Progress). *$\vdash c$ implies that c is acceptable.*

At this stage, a configuration is deemed acceptable if every thread either has reached a value or is able to take a step. This definition is later extended (§4) to allow for the possibility for a thread to be blocked (i.e., waiting for a lock).

v, t, T, P	$::=$	$\ldots$	(Everything)
		$\mid \ell$	(Values: v)
		$\mid \mathsf{newref}\ v \mid\ !v \mid v := v$	(Programs: t)
		$\mid \mathsf{ref}_m\ T$	(Types: T)
m	$::=$	$D \mid X$	(Modes)

Fig. 11. References: syntax

initial config.		*new configuration*	*side condition*
h / $\mathsf{newref}\ v$	$\longrightarrow$	$h +\!\!+ v$ / *limit* h	
h / $!\ell$	$\longrightarrow$	h / v	$h(\ell) = v$
h / $\ell := v'$	$\longrightarrow$	$h[\ell \mapsto v']$ / $()$	$h(\ell) = v$

Fig. 12. References: operational semantics

3 References

We extend the kernel calculus with heap-allocated references. We show how the type system is extended and prove that it ensures data-race freedom.

Syntax. We extend the syntax as per Fig. 11. Values now include the memory locations ℓ, which are natural numbers. Terms now include the three standard primitive operations on references, namely allocating, reading, and writing. Types now include the type $\mathsf{ref}_m\ T$ of references whose current content is a value of type T. The mode m indicates whether the reference is shareable (*duplicable*, D) or uniquely-owned (*exclusive*, X). Only the latter mode allows writing: this is key to enforcing data-race freedom. The type $\mathsf{ref}\ T$ (§1) is short for $\mathsf{ref}_X\ T$.

Operational Semantics. A *heap* h is a function of an initial segment of the natural numbers to values. We write *limit* h for the first unallocated address in the heap h. We write $h +\!\!+ v$ for the heap that extends h with a mapping of *limit* h to the value v. If the memory location ℓ is in the domain of h, then $h[\ell \mapsto v]$ is the heap that maps ℓ to v and agrees with h elsewhere.

We specify that a machine state s is a tuple, one of whose components is a heap h. In Fig. 12, we abuse notation and pretend that a machine state *is* a heap; thus, the reduction rules for references are written in a standard way. In Coq, we use overloaded "get" and "set" functions to mediate between the two levels.

Assigning Types to Terms. The typing rules for the operations on references appear in Fig. 13. A memory allocation expression $\mathsf{newref}\ v$ consumes the permission $v @ T$ and produces a new memory location of type $\mathsf{ref}_m\ T$ with mode m. Reading or writing a reference x requires a permission $x @ \mathsf{ref}_m\ T$, which guarantees that x is a valid memory location, and holds a value of type T. Because reading a reference creates a new copy of its content without consuming $x @ \mathsf{ref}_m\ T$, Read requires T to be duplicable. Write requires the exclusive mode X, in which the permission $x @ \mathsf{ref}_X\ T$ ensures that "nobody else" has any knowledge of (or access to) x. The rule allows strong update: the type of x changes to

NewRef
$R; K; v @ T \vdash \mathsf{newref}\ v : \mathsf{ref}_m\ T$

Read
$R; K; (\mathsf{duplicable}\ T) * (v @ \mathsf{ref}_m\ T) \vdash !v : T \mid (v @ \mathsf{ref}_m\ T)$

Write
$R; K; (v @ \mathsf{ref}_X\ T) * (v' @ T') \vdash v := v' : \top \mid (v @ \mathsf{ref}_X\ T')$

Loc
$$\frac{R_1; K \Vdash v @ T \qquad R_2(\ell) = m\,v}{R_1 \star R_2; K; P \vdash \ell : \mathsf{ref}_m\ T}$$

Fig. 13. References: typing rules for terms and values

DecomposeRef
$$v @ \mathsf{ref}_m\ T \equiv \exists x : \mathsf{value}.((v @ \mathsf{ref}_m = x) * (x @ T))$$

CoRef
$$\frac{T \leq U}{v @ \mathsf{ref}_m\ T \leq v @ \mathsf{ref}_m\ U}$$

Fig. 14. References: subsumption rules

$\mathsf{ref}_X\ T'$, where T' is the type of v'. All three operations are harmless: there is no adverse interaction between polymorphism and uniquely-owned references [4,11].

Subsumption. Subsumption is extended with new rules for reasoning about references (Fig. 14). DecomposeRef introduces a fresh name x for the content of the reference v. This allows separate reasoning about the ownership of the reference cell and about the ownership of its content. This step is reversible. CoRef states that ref is covariant. For uniquely-owned references, this is standard [4,11].

Resources. An *instrumented value* is $\lightning$, N, Dv, or Xv, where v is a value. N represents no information and no access right about a memory location, whereas for any $m \in \{D, X\}$, $m\ v$ represents full information (one knows that the value stored there is v). Dv (resp. Xv) moreover indicates a shared read-only access right (resp. an exclusive read/write access right). The type of instrumented values forms a monotonic separation algebra, where $Dv \star Dv$ is Dv, $N \star Xv$ and $Xv \star N$ are Xv; $N \star N$ is N; and every other combination yields $\lightning$.

A *heap resource* is either $\lightning$ or an instrumented value heap. Heap resources form a monotonic separation algebra, whose $\star$ operation requires agreement of the allocation limits (i.e., the next unallocated location is shared knowledge) and is defined pointwise. A heap resource is essentially a heap fragment in the sense of separation logic [13] and $\star$ is a union operation that requires disjointness at mutable locations and agreement at immutable locations. We specify that a *resource* R is a tuple of several components, one of which is a heap resource.

A notion of agreement between a value and an instrumented value is defined by "*v and $m\ v$ agree*". This is lifted to agreement between a heap and a heap resource, and is taken as the definition of correspondence between a machine state and a resource, $s \sim R$.

Assigning Types to Values. Loc (Fig. 13) is the introduction rule for the type constructor ref. It splits R: intuitively, the type $\mathsf{ref}_m\ T$ represents the separate ownership of the memory cell at address ℓ *and* of the value v that is currently stored there, to the extent dictated by the type T.

$v, t, T, P ::= \ldots$		(Everything)
	$\mid k$	(Values: v)
	$\mid$ newlock $\mid$ acquire v $\mid$ release v	(Programs: t)
	$\mid$ lock P $\mid$ locked	(Types: T)

Fig. 15. Locks: syntax

initial config.		*new configuration*	*side condition*
kh / newlock	$\longrightarrow$	$kh +\!\!+ L$ / *limit* kh	
kh / acquire k	$\longrightarrow$	$kh[k \mapsto L]$ / ()	$kh(k) = U$
kh / release k	$\longrightarrow$	$kh[k \mapsto U]$ / ()	$kh(k) = L$

Fig. 16. Locks: operational semantics

Data-Race Freedom. The auxiliary jugdement t accesses ℓ for am (whose definition is omitted) means that the term t (which represents either a single thread or a thread soup) is ready to access the memory location ℓ for reading or writing, as indicated by the access mode am, which is R or W. A *racy* thread soup t is one where two distinct threads are ready to access a single memory location ℓ and at least one of these accesses is a write.

The key reason why racy programs are ill-typed is the following lemma. If a thread soup t is well-typed with respect to R and is about to access ℓ, then the instrumented heap R must contain a right to access ℓ; moreover, in the case of a write access, this access right must be exclusive.

Lemma 3 (Typed access). *Every memory access is justified by a suitable access right.*

$$\frac{R \vdash t \qquad t \text{ accesses } \ell \text{ for } am \qquad R \text{ ok}}{\exists m, \exists v, (R(\ell) = m\, v) \wedge (am = W \Rightarrow m = X)}$$

Theorem 4 (Data-race freedom). *A well-typed configuration is not racy.*

4 Locks

We extend the kernel calculus with dynamically-allocated locks. This extension is independent of the previous one (§3), although references and locks are of course intended to be used in concert.

Syntax. We extend the syntax as per Fig. 15. Values now include lock addresses k, which are implemented as natural numbers. (We allocate references and locks in two separate heaps, with independent address spaces.) Terms now include the three standard primitive operations on locks, namely allocating, acquiring, and releasing. Types now include the type lock P of a lock whose invariant is the permission P. The type lock P is duplicable, regardless of P. Types now also include the type locked. This type is not duplicable. It serves as a proof that a lock is held and (hence) as a permission to release the lock.

Operational Semantics. We specify that a machine state s comprises a lock heap kh. A lock heap maps a valid lock address to a lock status: either U (unlocked) or L (locked). The reduction rules for locks appear in Fig. 16.

$$\textsc{NewLock}\quad R; K; Q \vdash \mathsf{newlock} : \exists x : \mathsf{value}.(=x \mid (x \,@\, \mathsf{lock}\ P) * (x \,@\, \mathsf{locked}))$$

$$\textsc{Acquire}\quad R; K; v \,@\, \mathsf{lock}\ P \vdash \mathsf{acquire}\ v : \top \mid P * (v \,@\, \mathsf{locked})$$

$$\textsc{Release}\quad R; K; P * (v \,@\, \mathsf{locked}) * (v \,@\, \mathsf{lock}\ P) \vdash \mathsf{release}\ v : \top$$

Fig. 17. Locks: typing rules for terms

$$\textsc{Lock}\quad \frac{R(k) = (P, \_)}{R; K; Q \vdash k : \mathsf{lock}\ P} \qquad \textsc{Locked}\quad \frac{R(k) = (\_, X)}{R; K; Q \vdash k : \mathsf{locked}}$$

Fig. 18. Locks: typing rules for values

Assigning Types to Terms. We create new locks in the locked state, because this is more flexible: a lock of type lock P can be created before the invariant P is established. The expression newlock creates a new lock, say x, and produces the permissions $x \,@\, \mathsf{lock}\ P$ and $x \,@\, \mathsf{locked}$[5] (Fig. 17). The former guarantees that x is a lock and records its invariant, whereas the latter guarantees that x is held and represents a permission to release it. The expressions acquire x and release x have the precondition $x \,@\, \mathsf{lock}\ P$, which guarantees that x is a valid lock with invariant P. acquire x produces the permissions P and $x \,@\, \mathsf{locked}$, whereas, symmetrically, release x requires (and consumes) these permissions.

The interaction between polymorphism and hidden state is unsound. When a new lock is allocated by newlock, its invariant (a permission P) becomes hidden, and it is necessary, at this point, to ensure that P is closed: newlock must not be allowed to execute under ForallIntro. This is why this rule is restricted to a class of *harmless* terms. This class does not contain any term of the form $D[\mathsf{newlock}]$; encompasses the values; and is stable by substitution and reduction. It is nevertheless possible to use the typing rule NewLock with a permission P that is not closed, as illustrated by `hide` (§1).

Resources. An *instrumented lock status* is a pair of a closed permission P and an access right, one of $\lightning$, N, and X. (These are the same as the instrumented values of §3, except this time X does not carry an argument and D does not appear.) The permission P is the lock invariant. The access right indicates whether releasing the lock is permitted: N represents no right, whereas X means that the lock is held and represents an exclusive right to release the lock. Instrumented lock statuses form a monotonic separation algebra, where, e.g., $(P, X) \star (P, N)$ is (P, X). That is, the lock invariant is shared (and immutable) information, whereas the ownership of a held lock is exclusive.

A *lock resource* is $\lightning$ or an instrumented lock status heap. Lock resources form a monotonic separation algebra. Agreement between a lock status and an instrumented lock status is defined by "*U and (P, N) agree*" and "*L and (P, X) agree*". This is lifted to agreement between a lock heap and a lock resource.

[5] In surface Mezzo, the type of newlock is written `(x: lock p | x @ locked)`.

To summarize, if we extend the kernel with both references (§3) and locks, then a machine state s is a pair of a value heap and a lock heap; a resource R is a pair of an instrumented value heap and an instrumented lock heap. The agreement relation s *and* R *agree* requires agreement between each heap and the corresponding instrumented heap.

Hidden State. One might expect the correspondence relation $s \sim R$ to be just agreement, i.e., s *and* R *agree*, as in the previous section (§3). However, there is something more subtle to locks. Locks introduce a form of hidden state: when a lock is released, its invariant P disappears; when the lock is acquired again (possibly by some other thread), P reappears, seemingly out of thin air. While the lock is unlocked, the resource that justifies P is not available to any thread.

This leads us to refine our understanding of the correspondence $s \sim R$. The assertion should no longer mean that R is the entire instrumented (value/lock) heap; instead, it should mean that R is the fragment of the instrumented heap that is visible to the program, while the rest is hidden.

To account for this, we define the relation $s \sim R$ as follows.

$$\frac{s \textit{ and } R \star R' \textit{ agree} \qquad R'; \varnothing \Vdash \textsf{hidden invariants of } (R \star R')}{s \sim R}$$

The machine state s represents the entire (value/lock) heap. Thus, the agreement assertion s *and* $R \star R'$ *agree* implies that $R \star R'$ represents the entire instrumented (value/lock) heap. We split this resource between a visible part R, which appears in the conclusion, and a hidden part R', which must justify the conjunction of the invariants of all currently unlocked locks. This conjunction is constructed by inspection of $R \star R'$. We omit its definition, and denote it $\textsf{hidden invariants of } (R \star R')$.

Assigning Types to Values. The typing rules Lock and Locked (Fig. 18) assign types to lock addresses, thus giving meaning to the types $\textsf{locked}\, P$ and $\textsf{locked}$. Their premises look up the (lock) resource R. A lock address k whose invariant (as recorded in R) is P receives the type $\textsf{lock}\ P$. A lock address k whose access right (as recorded in R) is X receives the type $\textsf{locked}$.

Soundness. A configuration is now deemed acceptable if every thread either (i) has reached a value; or (ii) is waiting on a lock that is currently held; or (iii) is able to take a step. The statements of type soundness are unchanged. Well-typed programs remain acceptable (§2.7) and are data-race free (§3).

5 Related Work

Mezzo has close ties with L^3 [1]. Both are affine λ-calculi with strong references. They distinguish between a pointer and a capability to dereference it; the former is duplicable, the latter affine. Both record must-alias information via singleton types. However, Mezzo is meant to be a surface language, as opposed to a low-level calculus, and this leads to different designs. For instance, L^3 has type-level names ϱ for values, whereas, for greater conciseness and simplicity, Mezzo allows types to depend directly on values. Also, L^3 views capabilities as unit values, which one hopes can be erased by the compiler, whereas Mezzo views permissions as purely static entities, and has no syntax for manipulating them.

Mezzo is strongly inspired by separation logic [13] in its treatment of heap-allocated data and by concurrent separation logic [10] and its successors [8,3] in its treatment of locks. Like second-order separation logic, as found at the core of CaReSL [14], Mezzo supports higher-order functions and quantification over permissions (assertions) and types (predicates). Our duplicable permissions are analogous to Turon *et al.*'s necessary assertions, and our function `hide` (§1) is essentially identical to their `mkSync` [14, §3.2].

Although the formalization of Mezzo was carried out independently, and in part grew out of earlier work by the second author [11], it is in several ways closely related to the Views framework [7]. In both cases, an abstract calculus is equipped with a notion of machine state; a commutative semigroup of views, or *resources*; and a projection, or *correspondence*, between the two levels. This abstract system is proven sound, and is later instantiated and extended to accommodate features such as references, locks, and more.

We have emphasized the modular organization of the meta-theory of Mezzo. When one extends the kernel in a new direction (references; locks), one must of course extend existing inductive definitions with new cases and extend the state with new components. However, one does not need to alter existing rules, or to alter the statements of the main type soundness lemmas. Of course, one sometimes must add new cases to existing proofs—only sometimes, though, as it is often possible to express an Ltac "recipe" that magically takes care of the new cases [5, chapter 16].

The manner in which this modularity is reflected in our Coq formalization reveals pragmatic compromises. We use monolithic inductive types. Delaware *et al.* [6] have shown how to break inductive definitions into fragments that can be modularly combined. This involves a certain notational and conceptual overhead, as well as a possible loss of flexibility, so we have not followed this route. A moderate use of type classes allows us to access or update one component of the state without knowing what other components might exist. A similar feature is one of the key strengths of the MSOS notation [9]. As often as possible, we write statements that concern just one component of the state, and in the few occasions where it seems necessary to explicitly work with all of them at once, we strive to write Ltac code in a style that is insensitive to the number and nature of these components. It has been our experience that each extension (references; locks) required very few undesirable amendments to the existing code base.

6 Conclusion

We have presented a formalisation of three basic layers of Mezzo, namely:

- a concurrent call-by-value λ-calculus, equipped with an affine, polymorphic, value-dependent type-and-permission system;

- an extension with strong (i.e., affine, uniquely-owned) mutable references;
- an extension with dynamically-allocated, shareable locks.

This paper is accompanied with a Coq proof [2], which covers just these three layers. It is about ten thousand (non-blank, non-comment) lines of code. Out of this, a de Bruijn index library and a monotonic separation algebra library, both of which are reusable, occupy about 2Kloc each. The remaining 6Kloc are split between the kernel (4Kloc), references (1Kloc), and locks (1Kloc).

The full Mezzo language offers more features, including richer memory blocks, carrying a tag and multiple fields; the possibility of turning a mutable block into an immutable one; iso-recursive types; and adoption and abandon [12], a mechanism that allows the unique-owner policy to be relaxed and enforced in part at runtime. All of these features are covered by an older Coq proof. In the future, we plan to port these features into the new proof without compromising its modularity. In particular, we wish to revisit the treatment of adoption and abandon so as to better isolate it from the treatment of memory blocks.

References

1. Ahmed, A., Fluet, M., Morrisett, G.: L^3: A linear language with locations. Fundamenta Informaticæ 77(4), 397–449 (2007)
2. Balabonski, T., Pottier, F.: A Coq formalization of Mezzo (December 2013), `http://gallium.inria.fr/~fpottier/mezzo/mezzo-coq.tar.gz`
3. Buisse, A., Birkedal, L., Støvring, K.: A step-indexed Kripke model of separation logic for storable locks. Electronic Notes in Theoretical Computer Science 276, 121–143 (2011)
4. Charguéraud, A., Pottier, F.: Functional translation of a calculus of capabilities. In: International Conference on Functional Programming (ICFP), pp. 213–224 (2008)
5. Chlipala, A.: Certified Programming and Dependent Types. MIT Press (2013)
6. Delaware, B., Oliveira, B.C.D.S., Schrijvers, T.: Meta-theory à La Carte. In: Principles of Programming Languages (POPL), pp. 207–218 (2013)
7. Dinsdale-Young, T., Birkedal, L., Gardner, P., Parkinson, M.J., Yang, H.: Views: compositional reasoning for concurrent programs. In: Principles of Programming Languages (POPL), pp. 287–300 (2013)
8. Gotsman, A., Berdine, J., Cook, B., Rinetzky, N., Sagiv, M.: Local reasoning for storable locks and threads. Tech. Rep. MSR-TR-2007-39, Microsoft Research (2007)
9. Mosses, P.D.: Modular structural operational semantics. Journal of Logic and Algebraic Programming 60, 195–228 (2004)
10. O'Hearn, P.W.: Resources, concurrency and local reasoning. Theoretical Computer Science 375(1-3), 271–307 (2007)
11. Pottier, F.: Syntactic soundness proof of a type-and-capability system with hidden state. Journal of Functional Programming 23(1), 38–144 (2013)
12. Pottier, F., Protzenko, J.: Programming with permissions in Mezzo. In: International Conference on Functional Programming (ICFP), pp. 173–184 (2013)
13. Reynolds, J.C.: Separation logic: A logic for shared mutable data structures. In: Logic in Computer Science (LICS), pp. 55–74 (2002)
14. Turon, A., Dreyer, D., Birkedal, L.: Unifying refinement and Hoare-style reasoning in a logic for higher-order concurrency. In: International Conference on Functional Programming (ICFP), pp. 377–390 (2013)

Semantics for Prolog with Cut – Revisited

Jael Kriener[1] and Andy King[2]

[1] Centre de Recherche Commun INRIA-Microsoft Research, 91120 Palaiseau, France
[2] School of Computing, University of Kent, UK

Abstract. This paper revisits the semantics for Prolog with cut from the perspective of formulating a semantic base that is amenable to abstract interpretation. It argues that such a semantics should separate the question of divergence from questions pertaining to the number of answers and determinacy. It also shows how to replace prefix ordering, that is classically used in these semantics, with a domain that is set up for abstraction, whilst simultaneously retaining a fixpoint construction, albeit one in a stratified form.

1 Introduction

The cut is arguably the most widely used non-logical feature of Prolog; by giving the programmer control over the search it is crucially important for making Prolog programs efficient. Prolog programmers use the cut operator to literally cut off all choice points that may lead to additional answers, once a goal has succeeded. A cut that is used to (brutely) enforce determinacy in this way is classified as red [14]. Cuts that are coloured green and blue are used, respectively, to avoid repeating tests in clause selection and exploring clauses which would ultimately fail. Such classifications have been introduced to aid manual reasoning about the effects of cut in different contexts. Arguably, though, a more principled approach would to be define a semantics that encapsulated the effect of cut in a given context. Then, in principle, abstract interpretation [3] could be applied to systematically derive from the semantics an abstract interpreter (a tool) for program comprehension that could automatically classify different applications of cut, and thereby support program development.

This is an attractive idea since the programmer would be insulated from the conceptual complexity of the semantics, yet would benefit from its rigour. One might expect that there is nothing left to be said on this subject: denotational semantics for cut can be traced back at least twenty years [2,6,7], and analyses for reasoning about determinacy and cut also have a long and distinguished history [4,11,12,13,16].

Yet reasoning about cut does not sit comfortably with abstract interpretation; something that has been exposed in our attempt to certify our own determinacy inference tool [10] in Coq. First, semantically justifying a determinacy analysis that is faithful in its handling of cut requires a computational (concrete) domain that is amenable to abstraction, and that can express the existence of several alternative possibilities and the order in which they occur. Second, a semantics

M. Codish and E. Sumii (Eds.): FLOPS 2014, LNCS 8475, pp. 270–284, 2014.

should ideally separate the question of divergence from questions pertaining to the number of answers and determinacy. Third, cut is not monotonic; in fact, it can be used to define "not" as negation-by-failure. This means that defining a fixpoint semantics is non-trivial, to say the least. The first and second of these issues are subtle and therefore we amplify these points by way of an extended introduction that motivates the design choices taken in the rest of paper.

1.1 Contributions and Outline

The paper makes the following contributions:

1. We discuss the state-of-the-art in denotational semantics for Prolog with cut, addressing in particular their amenability to abstract interpretation.
2. We identify and correct mistakes in previously published work on this topic [10], which were discovered by means of interactive theorem proving.
3. We present the first well-defined denotational semantics for cut designed to serve as a basis for abstract interpretation.
4. Our definitions are accompanied by a collection of Coq-scripts, available at

   `http://www.cs.kent.ac.uk/people/rpg/jek26/thesis/`

   thus presenting the first formalisation of a semantics for Prolog with cut; the work presented here forms part of a larger project of formalising abstract-interpretation-based analyses for Prolog [8].

The paper is structured as follows: the remainder of Section 1 discusses the state-of-the-art; Section 2 presents the domains underlying our constructions, and in that context discusses mistakes and deficiencies in previously published work; Section 3 briefly presents the required syntactic definitions and fixpoint theory; Section 4 presents the semantics; and finally Section 5 concludes.

1.2 Domains for Abstraction

Existing semantics [2,6,7] are defined over computational domains of sequences of substitutions or states, ordered by a prefix order (sequence a is less than sequence b iff a is a (strict) prefix of b). These domains are not amenable to abstraction. This is because off-the-shelf domains from logic programming typically represent sets of substitutions or, equivalently, sets of constraints. A sequence of substitutions is therefore naturally abstracted by a sequence of sets of substitutions; cruder abstractions can be derived from sequences of sets by applying a further layer of abstraction. (The alternative of using domains where the elements are sets of sequences of single substitutions, appears to be less straightforward to compactly represent, though a regular grammar might provide a natural representation for sequences of substitutions). However, working with sets of substitutions, rather than sequences of single substitutions, engenders a loss of precision which means that a goal can possibly generate additional answers, hence a sequence of n sets of substitutions actually represents a sequence of m substitutions, where $m \leq n$. This requires an order on sequences based on set containment and sub-sequencing that is strictly more general than the prefix order on sequences of individual substitutions.

1.3 Monotonicity and Divergence

These semantics achieve monotonicity in the presence of cut by establishing a subtle connection between cut and divergence. To explain, consider the non-monotone predicate `liar :- (liar, !, fail) ; true.` which is a Prolog version of the liar paradox: it succeeds if it fails, and it fails if it succeeds. The predicate `liar` exemplifies the non-monotonicity of cut. However, `liar` also diverges. In the discussed semantics, the fact that `liar` diverges gives it a stable value, namely $\perp$. This way the problem that `liar` poses for the monotonicity of a semantic operator is avoided. Divergence trumps non-monotonicity, so to speak, and these semantics for cut are well-defined only because they propagate divergence over any other semantic value, which allows them to avoid handling the non-monotonicity of cut.

These semantics model both, divergence and the application of cut, by sequence truncation; when either occurs, all possible later alternatives are cut off from a sequence of alternative answers. Truncation as a basic operation naturally goes with the prefix order on sequences. Therefore, treating the cut in this style requires one to work with the prefix order, which is an obstacle to abstraction, as explained above.

Furthermore, divergence and determinacy are two independent properties of programs which should be orthogonal in the semantics. Termination analysis for Prolog with [17] and without [5] cut is an independent, well-developed field of analysis within itself. In programming practice divergence comes first; there is little correctness and no efficiency gained in knowing that a goal can succeed only once, when it diverges. An analysis that reasons about cut is therefore only really useful for goals which do not diverge. This suggests that an analysis for cut may plausibly avoid the complexity connected with modelling divergence; this follows the principle that an analysis should be based on a semantics that expresses the property of interest, and ideally nothing else. Obviously, since divergence is a complex issue, the conceptual simplicity gained by disentangling determinacy from divergence is considerable. The classical semantics of [2,6,7] are not suited for our task, since they do not allow the reasoning about cut to be separated from reasoning about divergence.

We therefore choose to limit ourselves to non-divergent goals, and construct a semantics for Prolog with cut with a similarly limited scope. The semantics defined in Section 4 is defined for a subset of legal Prolog programs, namely the terminating, cut-stratified ones (where cut-stratification is defined below in Section 3). While this avoids much complication in the correctness argument, the construction of the semantics itself is not trivial: without being able to resort to divergence, non-monotone uses of cut have to be handled in some other way. The remainder of this paper explains this construction and the novel structure of our computational domain. In all, the work can be considered to be a revisit of our own denotational semantics for Prolog with cut [10]; a report on the subtleties that were exposed in a Coq formulation.

2 Domains

In this section we incrementally construct the domain by a series of lifts. The base domain of constraints, defined in Section 2.1, is lifted to downward closed sets of ideals in Section 2.3. A generic sequence domain is defined in Section 2.4 which is then instantiated with ideals in Section 2.5. Over and above this, a domain of parameteric constraints is introduced in Section 2.2 that is used, in conjunction with a higher-order abstract syntax [15], to formalise the semantics.

2.1 Constraint Domain

Our domain of sequences is built on a domain of constraints *con* over a set of variables $\mathbb{V}$; *con* is partially ordered by entailment $\models$, and contains a least and a greatest element *false* and *true*. This structure can be instantiated to the domain of Herbrand constraints, or some enriched set of Herbrand constraints, e.g. their extension by linear arithmetic, and hence can serve as a basis for expressing Prolog states. Note that any set of constraints is implicitly sorted into subsets, based on the number of variables mentioned in a constraint: there are two constraints over zero variables, ${}_0con = \{true, false\}$, ${}_1con$ are unary constraints over a single variable, ${}_2con$ are dyadic constraints over pairs of variables, and so on.

2.2 Parameterised Constraint Domain

We will refer to the set of variables mentioned in a constraint as the vector of variables that are constrained by the constraint. The Coq development that underlies this study, uses a dependently typed representation of vectors and, as a consequence, the representation of the type of constraints is also as a dependent type. In fact, this dependency is propagated from here on all the way through to the type of a program (see Section 3); everything is really a family of things dependent on an arity. Hence we assume a family of partially ordered constraints, depending on the number of constrained variables.

To formulate our semantics in a parametric (higher-order) setting (see Section 4), we require a parametric notion of constraint. The idea is simply to bind the free variables in a constraint with a λ, that is to say, to turn the constraint into a function of its free variables; e.g. $x = [], y = z$ becomes $\lambda xyz, x = [], y = z$. We call the family of types constructed in this fashion *pcon*. Like *con*, *pcon* is implicitly sorted into subsets, with each ${}_n\underline{\phi} \in {}_npcon$ expecting a vector of n variables, and returning a constraint over them. Note that each ${}_n\underline{\phi}$ has infinitely many semantically equivalent siblings of higher arity: $\lambda x, x = [] \in {}_1pcon$ is equivalent to $\lambda xy, x = [] \in {}_2pcon$ and $\lambda xyz, x = [] \in {}_3pcon$ and so forth.

In the following, we denote elements of *con* by small Greek letters θ, ϕ, ψ; we denote the results of closing them, i.e. elements of *pcon*, by the same small Greek letters with an underline to indicate that they are closed terms $\underline{\theta}, \underline{\phi}, \underline{\psi}$; we denote sets of (open) constraints by capital Greek letters Θ, Φ, Ψ.

2.3 Ideal Domain

Next we define the domain $\mathcal{C}$ as the *non-empty* ideals, i.e. downward closed sets, of constraints; the elements of $\mathcal{C}$ represent program states by capturing all possible bindings to the complete set of program variables consistent with a specific set of constraints; formally ${}_n\mathcal{C} := \{\Theta \subseteq {}_ncon \mid \Theta \neq \emptyset \wedge \Downarrow\Theta = \Theta\}$ where $\Downarrow\Theta = \{\psi \in {}_ncon \mid \exists\theta \in \Theta.\psi \models \theta\}$. Note that in the sequel $\downarrow$ will denote downward closure, and it will be used as a device for constructing ideals over different partial orders. We exclude the empty set, because we would like $\{false\}$ to be the bottom element of the set, representing a failed state. The empty set is not required at this level and excluding it will simplify the reasoning slightly. In this representation of states, unification, and more generally constraint solving, is straightforwardly modelled by set intersection, that is to say the result of unifying variable x with Herbrand term t at state Θ is simply $\Downarrow\{x{=}t\} \cap \Theta$.

2.4 Generic Sequence Domain

We now show how to construct a complete lattice for sequences over a generic partially ordered set by constructing an order that combines the notion of a sub-sequence with point-wise comparison of the elements of two sequences. In what follows, sequences are written as lists of elements, e.g. '$[a, b, c]$'; the result of *cons*tructing a sequence from an element a and a sequence s is written as '$a :: s$'; the result of concatenating two sequences s_1 and s_2 is written as '$s_1 + +s_2$'; the result of mapping a function $f : A \rightarrow B$ onto a sequence s of elements drawn from A is written as '$\mathsf{map}\, f\, s$' ; the result of removing all occurrences of an element a from a sequence s is written as '$\mathsf{remove}\, a\, s$'; finally, the empty sequence is denoted by 'ϵ'.

Our sub-sequence order is defined as follows:

Definition 1 (combined subsequence order). *Given a partial order $\sqsubseteq_A$ on $\mathcal{A}$, the set $Seq(\mathcal{A})$ of sequences over $\mathcal{A}$ is partially ordered by the relation:*

$$\forall\, s_1\, s_2 \,.\, s_1 \sqsubseteq s_2 \qquad \textit{iff} \qquad \exists\, s_3 \,.\, s_3 \trianglelefteq s_2 \wedge |s_3| = |s_1| \,\wedge\, s_1 \sqsubseteq_{pw} s_3$$

where $\sqsubseteq_{pw}$ is the point-wise lifting $\sqsubseteq_A$ sequences of equal length, and $t \trianglelefteq s$ means that t is a (possibly non-contiguous) sub-sequence of s, defined as follows:

$$\begin{array}{ll} \forall s. & \epsilon \trianglelefteq s \\ \forall s\, s'\, a. & s \trianglelefteq s' \Rightarrow a :: s \trianglelefteq a :: s' \\ \forall s\, s'\, a. & s \trianglelefteq s' \Rightarrow s \trianglelefteq a :: s' \end{array}$$

Whilst attempting to formalise in Coq the definitions and proofs published in [9,10], we found the set of sequences of downward closed sets of partially ordered constraints, as defined there is not a complete lattice. The mistake is in the definition of a join over sequences of partially ordered elements. The paper attempts to define a join in terms of a meet by means of a standard construction. The meet is defined by first defining a binary operator $\otimes$ and then lifting it to potentially infinite subsets. The operator $\otimes$ is defined as follows:

Definition 2 (candidate meet over sequences [10, Section 2.1.2])

$$s_1 \otimes s_2 = \begin{cases} s_2 \otimes s_1 & \textit{if } |s_2| < |s_1| \\ \mathsf{remove}\{\,\textit{false}\,\}\,(\bigsqcup_{pw}\{s_1 \sqcap_{pw} s_3 \mid s_3 \trianglelefteq s_2 \wedge |s_3| = |s_1|\}) & \textit{otherwise} \end{cases}$$

where $\bigsqcup_{pw}$ *and* $\sqcap_{pw}$ *are point-wise join and point-wise binary meet, which require all elements in the joined set, resp. both operands of the binary meet, to have the same length.*

As defined above, $s_1 \otimes s_2$ is not a greatest lower bound of s_1 and s_2. The attempted proof that $s_1 \otimes s_2$ is the greatest lower bound of s_1 and s_2 relies on the unproven assertion that $\otimes$ is monotone. In fact, the following counter-example shows it is not:

Example 1 ($\otimes$ is not *monotone).* To construct a counter-example to the monotonicity of $\otimes$, it is sufficient to provide three sequences s_1, s_2, and s_3, such that $s_1 \sqsubseteq s_2$ and $s_1 \otimes s_3 \not\sqsubseteq s_2 \otimes s_3$. Take any partial order $\sqsubseteq_A$ on $\mathcal{A}$, and any two elements a and $b \in \mathcal{A}$, such that $a \sqsubseteq_A b$. Consider the two sequences $[b, b]$ and $[b, b, a]$ and note that clearly $[b, b] \sqsubseteq [b, b, a]$. Combining each of these with the third sequence $[a, b, b]$ by $\otimes$ gives: $[a, b, b] \otimes [b, b] = \bigsqcup_{pw}\{\, [a, b] \sqcap_{pw} [b, b], [b, b] \sqcap_{pw} [b, b], [a, b] \sqcap_{pw} [b, b] \,\} = \bigsqcup_{pw}\{\, [a, b], [b, b], [a, b] \,\} = [b, b]$, and $[a, b, b] \otimes [b, b, a] = [a, b, a]$. Clearly $[b, b] \not\sqsubseteq [a, b, a]$.

The problem lies in the fact that comparison between lists of different lengths depends on shorter, but point-wise 'maximal' sub-sequences of lists, which may get destroyed when point-wise combining lists of equal lengths by $\otimes$. To obtain a complete lattice, in this paper we move instead to the domain of ideals of sequences closed under our order:

Definition 3 ($\mathcal{S}eq^{\downarrow}(\mathcal{A})$). *Given any partial order $\mathcal{A}$, the domain of ideals of sequences of $\mathcal{A}$ is defined as:*

$$\mathcal{S}eq^{\downarrow}(\mathcal{A}) := \{\, S \mid S \subseteq \mathcal{S}eq(\mathcal{A}) \wedge S = {\downarrow}S \,\}.$$

It follows that $\mathcal{S}eq^{\downarrow}(\mathcal{A})$ is a complete lattice if $\mathcal{A}$ is a partial order.

The definition of our semantics will require a notion of concatenation:

Definition 4 (concatenation over $\mathcal{S}eq^{\downarrow}(\mathcal{A})$). *Given a partial order $\mathcal{A}$ and to downward closed sets of sequences over $\mathcal{A}$, S_1 and S_2, we define the binary operator $+\!\!\!+\!\!\!+$ over $\mathcal{S}eq^{\downarrow}(\mathcal{A})$ as:*

$$S_1 +\!\!\!+\!\!\!+ S_2 := \{\, s_1 +\!\!+ s_2 \mid s_1 \in S_1 \wedge s_2 \in S_2 \,\}$$

Note that $\mathcal{S}eq^{\downarrow}(\mathcal{A})$ as defined on the basis of our combined sub-sequence order is closed under $+\!\!\!+\!\!\!+$, i.e. $S_1 +\!\!\!+\!\!\!+ S_2 = {\Downarrow}(S_1 +\!\!\!+\!\!\!+ S_2)$, which is why the above definition need not explicitly close the constructed set. Note further that $S_1 +\!\!\!+\!\!\!+ S_2 = \emptyset$ if either $S_1 = \emptyset$ or $S_2 = \emptyset$. The following lemma states that the lifted concatenation operators as defined above does not undermine the continuity of a semantic operators defined in terms of it.

Lemma 1 (concatenation over $\mathcal{S}eq^{\downarrow}(\mathcal{A})$ is monotone and continuous)

- $\forall\, S_1\ S_2\ T_1\ T_2\ \in \mathcal{S}eq^{\downarrow}(\mathcal{A}).S_1 \subseteq S_2\ \Rightarrow\ T_1 \subseteq T_2\ \Rightarrow\ S_1 +\!\!\!+\!\!\!+ T_1 \subseteq S_2 +\!\!\!+\!\!\!+ T_2$
- $\forall\, \mathcal{S}_1\ \mathcal{S}_2 \in \mathcal{P}(\mathcal{S}eq^{\downarrow}(\mathcal{A})).(\bigcup \mathcal{S}_1) +\!\!\!+\!\!\!+ (\bigcup \mathcal{S}_2) = \{\, S_1 +\!\!\!+\!\!\!+ S_2 \mid S_1 \in \mathcal{S}_1 \wedge S_2 \in \mathcal{S}_2 \,\}$

2.5 Ideal Sequence Domain

Finally, we are in a position to define the domain underlying our denotational semantics for Prolog with cut, as that of ideals of sequences of states: $\mathcal{S}eq^{\downarrow}(\mathcal{C})$. We denote elements of $\mathcal{S}eq(\mathcal{C})$, i.e. individual sequences of states, by $\boldsymbol{\Theta}, \boldsymbol{\Phi}, \boldsymbol{\Psi}$; we denote elements of $\mathcal{S}eq^{\downarrow}(\mathcal{C})$ by small Greek letters σ, τ. Note that $\mathcal{S}eq^{\downarrow}(\mathcal{C})$ has two elements which are less than all its other elements: $\bot = \emptyset$ and $\{\epsilon\}$ $(= \downarrow\!\{\epsilon\})$, which is greater only than $\bot$. Each has an intuitive interpretation: $\{\epsilon\}$ represents failure and $\bot$ represents divergence.

3 Syntax

As observed above, the cut is essentially a contextual construct: its effect, be it to remove open possibilities (red), or just to improve efficiency by failing quicker (blue, green), depends on its context. Rather than giving a meaning to cut itself, therefore, we chose to treat it contextually. That is to say, the semantics we are constructing will not have a rule for $[\![!]\!]$ like those in [2,6,7]. Rather, we construct a semantics in which cut influences the evaluation of the goals in its context. In order to do so in a uniform way, and avoid enumerating cases upon cases of different uses, we normalise the use of cut syntactically.

3.1 Cut-Normal Form

This is achieved by normalising the format for predicate definitions: we assume each predicate in the analysed program to be defined in a single clause of the form $p(\boldsymbol{x}) \leftarrow G_1; G_2, !, G_3; G_4$, where each G_i is a conjunctive goal (see Definition 5 below). We say a program in which each predicate is defined in this way is in cut-normal form.

Example 2. For example consider the following pair of predicates:

```
memberchk(X,L) :- member(X,L), !.
member(X,[X|_]).
member(X,[_|L]) :- member(X,L).
```

The cut-normal program containing definitions of the predicates `memberchk` and `member` looks like this:

```
memberchk(X, L) :- false;
                   (member(X, L), !, true);
                   false.
member(X, L) :- L = [X| _];
                (false, !, true);
                (L = [_| R], member(X, R)).
```

Working with programs in cut-normal form does not introduce a loss of generality, since all Prolog programs can be transformed into cut-normal form by applying simple transformations which we do not elaborate on here (see [10] for a more detailed discussion).

3.2 Higher Order Abstract Syntax

The logic programming semantics community usually deals with the issue of free variables by applying renaming operators, that are constructed from projections, which are approximating in the abstract context. The functional community has a similar, if somewhat harder, problem with name capturing; and has developed an elegant non-approximating solution - higher order abstract syntax (HOAS) [15]. Applying this approach in the logical context relieves us of the need to apply renamings, and thus renders the corresponding requirements on the domains superfluous and the definitions and proofs less complex. In particular: the case of a predicate call becomes trivial throughout. Though not conceptually easier then renaming, the HOAS-approach is much more natural when working within the functional setting of Coq, because it is based on function abstraction and application, native concepts in the Coq proof assistant, the tool we have adopted to certify our proofs. Adopting this approach, the syntax of Prolog programs with cut is defined in the HOAS-style as follows:

Definition 5 (cut-normal form Prolog syntax). *Goals (of arity n) are constructed from parametric goals (pGoal) defined as follows:*

$$\begin{aligned} pGoal &:: \mathbb{V}^n \to Goal \\ &:= \text{TELL } \underline{\theta} \mid \text{HEAD } p \mid \text{CONJ } pGoal\ pGoal \end{aligned}$$

where $\mathbb{V}$ *is the set of program variables,* $\mathbb{P}$ *is a set of predicate identifiers,* $p \in \mathbb{P}$*, and* $\underline{\theta} \in pcon$*. Predicates are defined from parametric goals in cut-normal form, and programs are simply lists of predicates:*

$$\begin{aligned} Predicate &:= p \leftarrow pGoal\ ; pGoal\ , !\ , pGoal\ ;\ pGoal\,. \\ Program &:= \epsilon \mid Predicate.Program. \end{aligned}$$

where again $p \in \mathbb{P}$.

Notice that parametric goals are themselves functions. When applied to a vector $\boldsymbol{x}$, CONJ passes $\boldsymbol{x}$ down to its component parametric goals. In this way $\boldsymbol{x}$ is propagated down to the atomic goals, where it is either used as an argument for a parametric constraint under a TELL, or is passed on to the body of the predicate called by HEAD. This propagation is realised by the semantic operators described in Section 4.

3.3 Cut-Stratification

Before we define our semantics, there is the issue of non-monotonicity to be addressed. As discussed previously, a motivation for defining a new semantics for cut is to keep it conceptually separate from divergence. This means we cannot resort to divergence in order to assign a stable meaning to predicates such as the `liar` predicate, but rather have to address the non-monotonic aspect of it directly.

The influential work [1] addresses the parallel problem in the context of negation by banning the use of such viciously circular definitions. To this end, they introduce the notion of stratification with respect to negation. In their view, negation is used 'safely', if all predicates falling under the scope of a negation are defined independently of the predicate in which that negation occurs. Given the connection between cut and negation, it is natural to adopt a similar approach towards our analogous problem. We define stratification with respect to cut as follows: cut is used safely, if the decision whether a cut is reached or not depends only on predicates that are defined independently of the context of that cut:

Definition 6 (cut-stratification). *A program P is cut-stratified, if P can be partitioned into n separate strata, such that $P = \bigcup_0^n S_i$, S_0 is cut-free, and the following two conditions are met for all $1 \leq i \leq n$:*

1. *For all $p \leftarrow G_1; G_2, !, G_3; G4$ in S_i, all calls in G_2 are to predicates in $\bigcup_{k<i} S_k$.*
2. *For all $p \leftarrow G_1; G_2, !, G_3; G4$ in S_i, all calls in G_1, G_3 and G_4 are to predicates in $\bigcup_{k\leq i} S_k$.*

A stratified program can be represented as a list of strata, each of which is itself a program, i.e. a list of predicates in cut-normal form.

Notice that this restriction is, as far as we can see, purely theoretical. In the worst case, a cut after a recursive call produces a situation like or similar to that of the `liar`-predicate above, which has no stable semantics *and* diverges. In the best case, such a cut is simply redundant. Either way, we have not been able to come up with an example in which such a cut is put to good use; nor have we been able to find such a cut in an actual Prolog program, which suggests that treating cut in this way – separate from divergence and stratified – is an appropriate mathematical way to capture programming practice.

3.4 Environments

The driving intuition behind the semantics described in Section 4 is to simulate the effect that execution of a goal will have on a current state of computation. To evaluate predicate calls, semantic summaries of their definitions are looked up in an environment, a mapping from predicate identifiers and vectors of variables (to construct goals from the parametric goals in a predicate definition) to continuous functions from a current state to a new state; formally we define:

Definition 7 (poly-environment). *The type of a (n-ary) poly-environment is defined as follows (where '$\mathfrak{E}$' stands for 'environment'):*

$$\mathfrak{E} := \mathbb{P} \to \mathbb{V}^n \to \mathcal{S}eq^{\downarrow}(\mathcal{C}) \xrightarrow{c} \mathcal{S}eq^{\downarrow}(\mathcal{C}).$$

We use small German letters $\mathfrak{e}$ and $\mathfrak{f}$ as variables for poly-environments. We write the result of updating $\mathfrak{f}$ with a mapping from p to $\lambda \boldsymbol{x}\ \sigma.\sigma'$, which overwrites any previous mapping $\mathfrak{f}$ may contain for p, as: $\mathfrak{f}[p \mapsto \lambda \boldsymbol{x}\ \sigma.\sigma']$.

Observe that environments model programs by mapping each predicate identifier to a function simulating the result of executing its (syntactic) definition. Note too that the 'inner' functions from $\mathcal{S}eq^{\downarrow}(\mathcal{C})$ to $\mathcal{S}eq^{\downarrow}(\mathcal{C})$ are annotated with c indicating that they are continuous. The reason is that the semantic operator $\mathcal{F}_G$ defined below (see Definition 8) is defined in terms of looking up predicate summaries in environments. To guarantee continuity of $\mathcal{F}_G$, the results of these look-ups need to be continuous.

The bottom poly-environment $\mathfrak{e}_\perp$ maps predicate identifiers to a default value. Following [2,6,7], we initialise $\mathfrak{e}_\perp$ to map those predicate identifiers which have definitions in the evaluated program to $\perp$, and those which do not to $\{\,\epsilon\,\}$, reflecting the fact that Prolog implementations generally fail with an error when encountering a call to an undefined predicate; formally:

$$\mathfrak{e}_\perp := \mathsf{if}\ p \in \mathbb{P}\ \mathsf{then}\ \lambda\, \boldsymbol{x}\, \sigma.\, \perp\ \mathsf{else}\ \lambda\, \boldsymbol{x}\, \sigma.\, \{\,\epsilon\,\}$$

This case distinction is not reflected in the Coq scripts used to check the results. We have the necessary structure in place and could easily reflect it; however, experience has shown that it introduces considerable complexity, without much gain: the interesting part of any fixpoint construction is that dealing with $p \in \mathbb{P}$; and since $\{\,\epsilon\,\}$ is well-behaved as a value, the additional case-split would have amounted to little more than code duplication. (The situation would be different, if, e.g. concatenation over $\mathcal{S}eq^{\downarrow}(\mathcal{C})$ contained a check that neither argument is $\{\,\epsilon\,\}$.)

3.5 Fixpoint Semantics of Stratified Programs

Given a stratified program represented as a list of strata $P = P_1, \ldots, P_n$, the semantic operator $\mathcal{F}_P$ at the heart of the denotational semantics will map each stratum P_i to a growing function of type $\mathfrak{E} \to \mathfrak{E}$. A growing function [1] of type $f : \mathfrak{E} \to \mathfrak{E}$ satisfies a relaxed monotonicity property of the form $\forall \mathfrak{f}\mathfrak{g}\mathfrak{h} \in \mathfrak{E}.\mathfrak{f} \sqsubseteq \mathfrak{g} \sqsubseteq \mathfrak{h} \sqsubseteq f \uparrow \omega(\mathfrak{f}) \Rightarrow f(\mathfrak{g}) \sqsubseteq f(\mathfrak{h})$ where $\sqsubseteq$ is the natural pointwise ordering on $\mathfrak{E}$. Applying $\mathcal{F}_P$ to each P_i constructs a sequence of growing functions $\mathcal{F}_{P_1}, \ldots, \mathcal{F}_{P_n}$ which can be combined thus

$$\mathfrak{f}_1 = \mathcal{F}_{P_1} \uparrow \omega(\perp), \mathfrak{f}_2 = \mathcal{F}_{P_2} \uparrow \omega(\mathfrak{f}_1), \ldots, \mathfrak{f}_n = \mathcal{F}_{P_n} \uparrow \omega(\mathfrak{f}_{n-1})$$

Following [1], we then define $\mathsf{iter}(\mathcal{F}_{P_1}, \ldots, \mathcal{F}_{P_n}, (\perp)) = \mathfrak{f}_n$. This poly-environment is the join of all $\mathfrak{f}_i$ and therefore a good candidate for a well-defined fixpoint semantics of stratified programs. Complete details for a formulation of this construction can be found in [8].

There is, however, one potential worry to be discussed: given a stratified program P, there are several representations of it as lists of strata, that is to say, there are several ways of stratifying a stratified program. Since the construction of $\mathsf{iter}(\mathcal{F}_{P_1}, \ldots, \mathcal{F}_{P_n}, (\perp))$ syntactically depends on the particular stratification, this could mean that it is not uniquely defined. In response, [1] show that the fixpoint construction is independent of these stratifications, i.e. that for two different stratifications $P_1, \ldots, P_n$ and $P'_1, \ldots, P'_n$ of P, $\mathsf{iter}(\mathcal{F}_{P_1}, \ldots, \mathcal{F}_{P_n}, (\bot)) = \mathsf{iter}(\mathcal{F}_{P'_1}, \ldots, \mathcal{F}_{P'_n}, (\bot))$ (see [1, Theorem 11, p.116]). Their proof is rather complex, however, the result is not surprising: though there are several possible stratifications, it seems plausible that there is a canonical stratification for each program, which could serve as the basis for a canonical, thus unique, fixpoint.

4 Denotational Semantics for Prolog with *cut*

Now we are in a position to define the semantics of a cut-stratified Prolog programs as the stratified fixpoint of the sequence of growing functions induced by the operator $\mathcal{F}_P$ below. Note that due to its contextual treatment, the cut only appears at the level of predicate definitions ($\mathcal{F}_H$). This means that goals can be treated in the standard way; $\mathcal{F}_G$ is monotone and continuous.

Definition 8. *For a given stratified program $P = P_1, \ldots, P_n$, its semantics is defined as a least fixpoint, namely $\mathit{iter}(\mathcal{F}_{P_1}, \ldots, \mathcal{F}_{P_n}, (\bot))$, where each $\mathcal{F}_{P_i} = \mathcal{F}_P [\![P_i]\!]$, and $\mathcal{F}_P$ is defined as follows:*

$$
\begin{array}{lcl}
\mathcal{F}_P & : & \mathit{Program} \to \mathfrak{E} \xrightarrow{g} \mathfrak{E} \\
\mathcal{F}_P [\![\epsilon]\!] \mathfrak{f} & = & \mathfrak{f} \\
\mathcal{F}_P [\![p \leftarrow B : P]\!] \mathfrak{f} & = & (\mathcal{F}_P [\![P]\!] \mathfrak{f})[p \mapsto \mathcal{F}_H [\![p \leftarrow B]\!] \mathfrak{f}] \\
 & & \quad \mathit{where}\ B = G_1; G_2, !, G_3; G_4.
\end{array}
$$

$$
\begin{array}{lcl}
\mathcal{F}_H & : & \mathit{Predicate} \to \mathfrak{E} \to \mathbb{V}^n \to \mathit{Seq}^{\downarrow}(\mathcal{C}) \xrightarrow{c} \mathit{Seq}^{\downarrow}(\mathcal{C}) \\
\mathcal{F}_H [\![p \leftarrow B]\!] \mathfrak{f} & = & \lambda\, \boldsymbol{x}\, \sigma. \bigsqcup \{ \mathsf{if}\ \{\epsilon\} \subset \tau_2\ \mathsf{then}\ \tau_1 +\!\!\!+\!\!\!+ \tau_3\ \mathsf{else}\ \tau_1 +\!\!\!+\!\!\!+ \tau_4 \mid \Theta \in \sigma \} \\
 & & \mathit{where}\ B = G_1; G_2, !, G_3; G_4. \\
 & & \quad \mathit{and}\ \ \tau_1 = \mathcal{F}_G\ [\![G_1\, \boldsymbol{x}]\!]\ \mathfrak{f} \Downarrow\{\Theta\} \\
 & & \quad \mathit{and}\ \ \tau_2 = \mathcal{F}_G\ [\![G_2\, \boldsymbol{x}]\!]\ \mathfrak{f} \Downarrow\{\Theta\} \\
 & & \quad \mathit{and}\ \ \tau_3 = \mathcal{F}_G\ [\![G_3\, \boldsymbol{x}]\!]\ \mathfrak{f} \Downarrow\{[\Psi] \mid (\Psi : \_) \in \tau_2\} \\
 & & \quad \mathit{and}\ \ \tau_4 = \mathcal{F}_G\ [\![G_4\, \boldsymbol{x}]\!]\ \mathfrak{f} \Downarrow\{\Theta\}
\end{array}
$$

$$
\begin{array}{ll}
\mathcal{F}_G & : \mathit{Goal} \to \mathfrak{E} \to \mathit{Seq}^{\downarrow}(\mathcal{C}) \xrightarrow{c} \mathit{Seq}^{\downarrow}(\mathcal{C}) \\
\mathcal{F}_G [\![\text{TELL}\ \underline{\phi}\ \boldsymbol{x}]\!]\ \mathfrak{f} \sigma & = \Downarrow\{ \mathsf{remove}\, \{\mathit{false}\}\, (\mathsf{map}\, (\lambda\Theta.\ \Theta \sqcap \Downarrow\{\underline{\phi}(\boldsymbol{x})\})\, \Theta) \mid \Theta \in \sigma \} \\
\mathcal{F}_G [\![\text{HEAD}\ \underline{p}\ \boldsymbol{x}]\!]\ \mathfrak{f} \sigma & = \mathfrak{f}\ p\ \boldsymbol{x}\ \sigma \\
\mathcal{F}_G [\![\text{CONJ}\ G_1\, G_2\, \boldsymbol{x}]\!]\ \mathfrak{f}\ \sigma & = \mathcal{F}_G [\![G_2\, \boldsymbol{x}]\!]\ \mathfrak{f}\ (\mathcal{F}_G [\![G_1\, \boldsymbol{x}]\!]\ \mathfrak{f}\ \sigma)
\end{array}
$$

Note that '$\subset$' denotes strict subset; the predicate $\{\epsilon\} \subset \tau_2$ checks whether τ_2 contains a non-empty sequence. Before explaining in detail, let us attempt to give an intuition by considering again the `member`- and `memberchk`- predicates:

Example 3. To illustrate, consider again the `member(A,S)` and `memberchk(A,S)` (see Example 2 for their definitions in cut-normal form); suppose each is called at a point in a program where there is only one possible set of bindings, namely

$A = 3$ and $S = [3, 2, 3]$, represented by a state $\sigma = \Downarrow\!\{[\Theta]\}$ where $\Theta = \downarrow\!\{A = 3 \wedge S = [3, 2, 3]\}$. Below $\mathfrak{f}_P = \mathsf{iter}(\mathcal{F}_{P_1}, \mathcal{F}_{P_2}, (\bot))$, i.e. the semantics of the program containing only these two predicates in two separate strata.

$\mathcal{F}_G\,[\![\text{HEAD}\, member\,\langle A, S\rangle]\!]\,\mathfrak{f}_P\,\sigma \supseteq$

$\Downarrow\!\{[\Theta \sqcap \downarrow\!\{S = [A|\_]\}]\}$ +++ $\Downarrow\!\{\mathcal{F}_G\,[\![\text{HEAD}\, member\,\langle A, S_1\rangle]\!]\,\mathfrak{f}_P \Downarrow\!\{[\Theta \sqcap \downarrow\!\{S = [\_|S_1]\}]\}\}$

$= \Downarrow\!\{\,[\Theta \sqcap \downarrow\!\{S = [A|\_]\},\ \Downarrow\!\{\mathcal{F}_G\,[\![\text{HEAD}\, member\,\langle A, S_1\rangle]\!]\,\mathfrak{f}_P \Downarrow\!\{[\Theta \sqcap \downarrow\!\{S = [\_|S_1]\}]\}\}]\,\}$

$\mathcal{F}_G\,[\![\text{HEAD}\, memberchk\,\langle A, S\rangle]\!]\,\mathfrak{f}_P\,\sigma = \bigsqcup\{\emptyset +\!\!+\!\!+ \Downarrow\!\{[\Psi \sqcap \downarrow\!\{true\}]\}\}$
where $\Psi : \_ = \mathcal{F}_G\,[\![\text{HEAD}\, member\,\langle A, S\rangle]\!]\,\mathfrak{f}_P\,\sigma$

There are rather a lot of different brackets involved here. The important thing to notice is that the longest sequence in the denotation of `memberchk` has exactly one element, while the longest sequence in the denotation of `member` has more than one element. Thus, the fact that the former is deterministic, while the latter is not, is reflected in their denotations.

Now let us explain in more detail by examining each operator in turn:

4.1 Evaluation of Single Goals ($\mathcal{F}_G$)

$\mathcal{F}_G\,[\![G]\!]\,\mathfrak{f}\,\sigma$ evaluates the single goal G in the context of an environment $\mathfrak{f}$; it simulates the effect that execution of G would have in the context of a program summarised by $\mathfrak{f}$ on the 'current state' σ. Note that $\mathcal{F}_G$ propagates both failure ($\{false\}$), and divergence ($\bot$), as long as $\mathfrak{f}$ does.

The clauses for HEAD and CONJ should seem unsurprising; the former is a straightforward look up of a predicate summary in the context; the latter models consecutive execution of two goals by executing the left-most goal first, and channelling the result as the new 'current state' into the execution of the other.

The clause for TELL simulates the effect of adding a conditional constraint $\underline{\phi}(\boldsymbol{x})$ to the current store, by adding it in all alternatives, i.e. mapping the operation of intersection with $\downarrow\!\{\underline{\phi}(\boldsymbol{x})\}$ onto a sequence. Some of these alternatives may fail when the additional constraint is posted, i.e. $\Theta \sqcap \downarrow\!\{\underline{\phi}(\boldsymbol{x})\}$ may reduce to $\{false\}$. Rather than carrying these failures around, we remove them from the sequence, making sure that only *open* branches are retained in the defining sequence of the ideal.

4.2 Evaluation of Cut in Context ($\mathcal{F}_H$)

As stated above, $\mathcal{F}_H$ does not evaluate cut by itself; rather, it reflects the effect that it has on the execution of the goals around it. Cut is used in the context of choice, i.e. disjunction. When encountering a disjunction in cut normal form, the pre-cut disjunct G_1 is not affected by the cut. However, depending on the success of G_2, the result of executing G_1, τ_1, is concatenated with one of two possible second disjuncts: If G_2 fails, i.e. all possibilities open in σ are closed after its execution and σ is reduced to $\{\epsilon\}$, τ_1 is concatenated with the result of executing G_4 in the initial state σ.

If G_2 does not fail, i.e. the state after its execution has some open branches left and is thus strictly larger than $\{\epsilon\}$, only the first of these possibilities are used for a basis of evaluating G_3, and the result of that evaluation is appended to τ_1 . This implements the effect of the 'red cut' to remove open possibilities for backtracking when it is reached.

Note that this treatment of cut is direct; that is to say, it does not require additional technical machinery such as cut-flags [7,2] or cut-markers [6] which propagate the effect of cut implicitly by means of a special concatenation operation. The price we pay for this is a rather coarse over-approximation of divergence: if any of the two open branches of a predicate diverges, the entire predicate is taken to diverge.

4.3 Evaluation of Programs ($\mathcal{F}_P$)

Finally, $\mathcal{F}_P \llbracket Prog \rrbracket$ does the obvious thing: it evaluates each predicate P defined in $Prog$ in turn, and updates the constructed environment with a mapping from the name of P to its evaluation under $\mathcal{F}_H$.

4.4 Note on Monotonicity

The reader may be wondering about the use of set comprehension and join in the definition of $\mathcal{F}_H$. Prima facie, the definition should look as follows:

$$\begin{aligned}\mathcal{F}_H \llbracket p \leftarrow G_1; G_2, !, G_3; G_4 . \rrbracket \mathfrak{f} \quad &= \quad \lambda \boldsymbol{x}\, \sigma . \,\mathsf{if}\ \{\epsilon\} \subset \tau_2\ \mathsf{then}\ \tau_1 +\!\!+\!\!+ \tau_3\ \mathsf{else}\ \tau_1 +\!\!+\!\!+ \tau_4 \\ &\quad\ where\ \tau_1 = \mathcal{F}_G \llbracket G_1\, \boldsymbol{x} \rrbracket\, \mathfrak{f}\, \sigma \\ &\quad\ and\ \ \tau_2 = \mathcal{F}_G \llbracket G_2\, \boldsymbol{x} \rrbracket\, \mathfrak{f}\, \sigma \\ &\quad\ and\ \ \tau_3 = \mathcal{F}_G \llbracket G_3\, \boldsymbol{x} \rrbracket\, \mathfrak{f} \Downarrow \{[\Theta] \mid (\Theta : \_) \in \tau_2\} \\ &\quad\ and\ \ \tau_4 = \mathcal{F}_G \llbracket G_4\, \boldsymbol{x} \rrbracket\, \mathfrak{f}\, \sigma\end{aligned}$$

The reason why $\mathcal{F}_H$ is not defined like this, is that it needs to construct a *continuous*, hence *monotone* function from $\mathcal{S}eq^{\downarrow}(\mathcal{C})$ to $\mathcal{S}eq^{\downarrow}(\mathcal{C})$. The if-then-else construct above is not monotone, since $\sigma_1 \subseteq \sigma_2$ does not in general guarantee that $\{\epsilon\} \subset \mathcal{F}_G \llbracket G_2\, \boldsymbol{x} \rrbracket\, \mathfrak{f}\, \sigma_1$ iff $\{\epsilon\} \subset \mathcal{F}_G \llbracket G_2\, \boldsymbol{x} \rrbracket\, \mathfrak{f}\, \sigma_2$; it is possible for the left hand side of this if-and-only-if to be false, and the right hand side true. The only solution we see is to 'push' the if-then-else 'down a level' inside the set comprehension. By considering each element of a set of sequences individually, and then working with the join of the outcomes, monotonicity is recovered. Note that it is the same problem, on the level of the environment parameter, that stratification solves: $\mathfrak{f}_1 \sqsubseteq \mathfrak{f}_2$ is not sufficient to guarantee that $\{\epsilon\} \subset \mathcal{F}_G \llbracket G_2\, \boldsymbol{x} \rrbracket\, \mathfrak{f}_1\, \sigma$ iff $\{\epsilon\} \subset \mathcal{F}_G \llbracket G_2\, \boldsymbol{x} \rrbracket\, \mathfrak{f}_2\, \sigma$. This problem is solved by partitioning the input environment into a stable part $\mathfrak{f}$ and a current part $\mathfrak{f}$. The stability of $\mathfrak{f}$ means it can be used to branch on in an if-then-else statement without compromising monotonicity.

The reader will also have observed that the set comprehension in the definition of $\mathcal{F}_H$ has an unintuitive consequence: all non-empty σ contain sequences $\boldsymbol{\Theta}$ for which $\{\epsilon\} \not\subseteq \mathcal{F}_G [\![G_2\, \boldsymbol{x}]\!] \mathsf{f} \Downarrow\!\{\boldsymbol{\Theta}\}$ (at the very least ϵ is such a sequence); some σ also contain some sequences $\boldsymbol{\Psi}$ for which this is not the case, i.e. $G_2\, \boldsymbol{x}$ succeeds. The fact that a σ which contains some such sequence $\boldsymbol{\Psi}$ will always contain smaller $\boldsymbol{\Theta}$s is a consequence of the move from sequences to ideals of sequences, necessitated by the need for a complete lattice. It is a bad consequence, because as a result the choice between τ_3 and τ_4 is not uniform for some σ.

Example 4 ($\mathcal{F}_H$ is a strict over-approximation). To appreciate the effect consider the conjunctive goal $G =$ `q(X, Y), X = 2.`, which calls the following predicate:

```
q(X, Y) :- false ; (X = 0, !, Y = 0) ; Y = 1.
```

The goal G will fail when neither `X` nor `Y` are bound; the cut will prevent the third disjunct of `q` from ever being explored. However, in the domain of ideals of sequences such a completely unconstrained state is represented by the ideals $\Downarrow\!\{[\Downarrow\!\{true\}]\}$. This contains the sequence $[\Downarrow\!\{\mathtt{X} = 2\}]$ for which the third branch of `q` is reachable so G will succeed with some σ, such that $\Downarrow\!\{[\Downarrow\!\{\mathtt{X} = 2, \mathtt{Y} = 1\}]\} \subseteq \sigma$.

This is not desirable, however, it is not fatal in the context of an analysis that over-approximates the number of solutions to a predicate, as in determinacy analysis. $\mathcal{F}_H$ does not adequately capture the behaviour of cut, but rather over-approximates success coarsely. That is to say, it under-estimates the extent of determinacy gained by a cut: in reality `q` is more deterministic than $\mathcal{F}_H$ makes it out to be. Such an over-approximation is safe in the context of determinacy analysis; any analysis which is correct wrt $\mathcal{F}_H$ will certainly be correct in practice. If anything, the conditions it derives will be overly strong.

5 Concluding Discussion

There is no doubt that formalisation in Coq has proved to be useful, albeit in uncovering holes in a denotational semantics that we previously thought to be well-defined (and which, incidentally, had undergone careful reviewing [10]). The impetus for the work was initially to repair the join operator of sequences of ideals, though this had far reaching implications for the whole semantics.

Formalisation, and specifically the act of trying to prove the monotonicity of $\mathcal{F}_H$, also exposed a deficiency in the semantics: that $\mathcal{F}_H$ is a coarse over-approximation of the solution set. This seems to be an inevitable consequence of working with a domain of downward closed sequences of downward closed ideals. This is clear in hindsight, and suggests that the architect of a semantics is not always the best person to prove their correctness of their semantics since they can come with the baggage of their own false suppositions; at this stage proof assistants have an important role to play.

We suspect that the problem of over-approximation can be solved by migrating to a domain of downward closed sequences of pairs of ideals where one ideal is upward closed and the other ideal is downward closed which, in tandem, describe a range of possible constraints, akin to an interval. This will be one direction for future work. Another will be to investigate conditions under which it is possible to push if-then-else up one level in $\mathcal{F}_H$. Yet another direction will be to synthesise a determinacy analysis from the semantics and certify its correctness relative to the semantics presented in this paper using a proof assistant, which is the overarching goal of this work.

Acknowledgements. The authors would like to thank the reviewers for their insightful comments.

References

1. Apt, K.R., Blair, H.A., Walker, A.: Towards a Theory of Declarative Knowledge. In: Foundations of Deductive Databases and Logic Programming, pp. 89–148. Morgan Kaufmann (1988)
2. Billaud, M.: Simple Operational and Denotational Semantics for Prolog with Cut. Theoretical Computer Science 71(2), 193–208 (1990)
3. Cousot, P., Cousot, R.: Abstract interpretation and application to logic programs. Journal of Logic Programming 13(2&3), 103–179 (1992)
4. Dawson, S., Ramakrishnan, C.R., Ramakrishnan, I.V., Sekar, R.C.: Extracting Determinacy in Logic Programs. In: International Conference on Logic Programming, pp. 424–438. MIT Press (1993)
5. De Schreye, D., Decorte, S.: Termination of logic programs: The never-ending story. Joural of Logic Programming 19(20), 199–260 (1994)
6. de Vink, E.P.: Comparative Semantics for Prolog with Cut. Science of Computer Programming 13(1), 237–264 (1989)
7. Debray, S.K., Mishra, P.: Denotational and Operational Semantics for Prolog. Journal of Logic Programming 5(1), 81–91 (1988)
8. Kriener, J.: Towards A Verified Determinacy Analysis for Prolog with cut. PhD thesis, School of Computing, University of Kent (December 2013)
9. Kriener, J., King, A.: Appendix for RedAlert: Determinacy Inference for Prolog. Technical Report 1-11, School of Computing, University of Kent, CT2 7NF, UK (2011), http://arxiv.org/corr/home
10. Kriener, J., King, A.: RedAlert: Determinacy inference for Prolog. TPLP 11(4-5), 537–553 (2011)
11. Le Charlier, B., Rossi, S., Van Hentenryck, P.: An Abstract Interpretation Framework which Accurately Handles Prolog Search-Rule and the Cut. In: Symposium on Logic Programming, pp. 157–171. MIT Press (1994)
12. López-García, P., Bueno, F., Hermenegildo, M.V.: Automatic Inference of Determinacy and Mutual Exclusion for Logic Programs Using Mode and Type Analyses. New Generation Computing 28(2), 177–206 (2010)
13. Mogensen, T.Æ.: A Semantics-Based Determinacy Analysis for Prolog with Cut. In: Bjorner, D., Broy, M., Pottosin, I.V. (eds.) PSI 1996. LNCS, vol. 1181, pp. 374–385. Springer, Heidelberg (1996)
14. O'Keefe, R.A.: The Craft of Prolog. MIT Press, Cambridge (1990)
15. Pfenning, F., Elliott, C.: Higher-Order Abstract Syntax. In: Wexelblat, R.L. (ed.) PLDI, pp. 199–208. ACM (1988)
16. Sahlin, D.: Determinacy Analysis for Full Prolog. In: Symposium on Partial Evaluation and Semantics-Based Program Manipulation, pp. 23–30. ACM (1991)
17. Schneider-Kamp, P., Giesl, J., Ströder, T., Serebrenik, A., Thiemann, R.: Automated termination analysis for logic programs with cut. TPLP 10(4-6), 365–381 (2010)

Constraint Logic Programming for Hedges: A Semantic Reconstruction

Besik Dundua[1,3], Mário Florido[1], Temur Kutsia[2], and Mircea Marin[4]

[1] DCC-FC & LIACC, University of Porto, Portugal
[2] RISC, Johannes Kepler University, Linz, Austria
[3] VIAM, Ivane Javakhishvili Tbilisi State University, Georgia
[4] West University of Timişoara, Romania

Abstract. We describe the semantics of CLP(H): constraint logic programming over hedges. Hedges are finite sequences of unranked terms, built over variadic function symbols and three kinds of variables: for terms, for hedges, and for function symbols. Constraints involve equations between unranked terms and atoms for regular hedge language membership. We give algebraic semantics of CLP(H) programs, define a sound, terminating, and incomplete constraint solver, and describe some fragments of constraints for which the solver returns a complete set of solutions.

1 Introduction

Hedges are finite sequences of unranked terms. These are terms in which function symbols do not have a fixed arity: The same symbol may have a different number of arguments in different places. Manipulation of such expressions has been intensively studied in recent years in the context of XML processing, rewriting, automated reasoning, knowledge representation, just to name a few.

When working with unranked terms, variables that can be instantiated with hedges (hedge variables) are a pragmatic necessity. In (pattern-based) programming, hedge variables help to write neat, compact code. Using them, for instance, one can extract duplicates from a list with just one line of a program. Several languages and formalisms operate on unranked terms and hedges. The programming language of Mathematica [21] is based on hedge pattern matching. Languages such as Tom [1], Maude [2], ASF+SDF [19] provide capabilities similar to hedge matching (via associative functions). ρLog [17] extends logic programming with hedge transformation rules. XDuce [13] enriches untyped hedge matching with regular expression types. The Constraint Logic Programming schema has been extended to work with hedges in CLP(Flex) [3], which is a basis for the XML processing language XCentric [5] and a Web site verification language VeriFLog [4].

The goal of this paper is to describe a precise semantics of constraint logic programs over hedges. We consider positive CLP programs with two kinds of primitive constraints: equations between hedges, and membership in a hedge regular language. Function symbols are unranked. Predicate symbols have a

M. Codish and E. Sumii (Eds.): FLOPS 2014, LNCS 8475, pp. 285–301, 2014.

fixed arity. Terms may contain three kinds of variables: for terms (term variables), for hedges (hedge variables), and for function symbols (function symbol variables). Moreover, we may have function symbols whose argument order does not matter (unordered symbols): a kind of generalization of the commutativity property to unranked terms. As it turns out, such a language is very flexible and permits to write short, yet quite clear and intuitive code: One can see examples in Sect. 2. We call this language CLP(H), for CLP over hedges. It generalizes CLP(Flex) with function variables, unordered functions, and membership constraints. Hence, as a special case, our paper describes the semantics of CLP(Flex). Moreover, as hedges generalize strings, CLP(H) can be seen also as a generalization of CLP over strings CLP($\mathcal{S}$) [18], string processing features of Prolog III [6], and CLP over regular sets of strings CLP(Σ^*) [20].

Note that some of these languages allow an explicit size factor for string variables, restricting the length of strings they can be instantiated with. We do not have size factors, but can express this information easily with constraints. For instance, to indicate the fact that a hedge variable $\overline{x}$ can be instantiated with a hedge of minimal length 1 and maximal length 3, we can write a disjunction $\overline{x} \doteq x \vee \overline{x} \doteq (x_1, x_2) \vee \overline{x} \doteq (x_1, x_2, x_3)$, where the lower case x's are term variables.

Flexibility and the expressive power of CLP(H) has its price: Equational constraints with hedge variables, in general, may have infinitely many solutions [15]. Therefore, any complete equational constraint solving procedure with hedge variables is nonterminating. The solver we describe in this paper is sound and terminating, hence incomplete for arbitrary constraints. However, there are fragments of constraints for which it is complete, i.e., computes all solutions. One such fragment is so called well-moded fragment, where variables in one side of equations (or in the left hand side of the membership atom) are guaranteed to be instantiated with ground expressions at some point. This effectively reduces constraint solving to hedge matching (which is known to be NP-complete [16]), plus some early failure detection rules. Another fragment for which the solver is complete is named after the Knowledge Interchange Format, KIF [12], where hedge variables are permitted only in the last argument positions. We identify forms of CLP(H) programs which give rise to well-moded or KIF constraints.

We can easily model lists with ordered function symbols and multisets with the help of unordered ones. In fact, since we may have several such symbols, we can directly model colored multisets. Constraint solving over lists, sets, and multisets has been intensively studied, see, e.g., [10] and references there, and the CLP schema can be extended to accommodate them. In our case, an advantage of using hedge variables in such terms is that hedge variables can give immediate access to collections of subterms via unification. It is very handy in programming.

The paper is organized as follows: We start with motivating examples in Sect. 2. In Sect. 3 we describe the syntax of CLP(H). Sect. 4 is about semantics. The constraint solver is introduced in Sect. 5. The operational semantics of CLP(H) is described in Sect. 6. In Sect. 7, we introduce well-moded and KIF fragments of CLP(H) programs, for which the constraint solver is complete. Due to space restrictions, proofs of technical lemmas are put in the report [11].

2 Motivating Examples

In this section we show how to write programs in CLP(H). For illustration, we chose two examples: the rewriting of terms from some regular hedge language and an implementation of the recursive path ordering with status.

Example 1. The general rewriting mechanism can be implemented with two CLP(H) clauses: The base case $rewrite(x, y) \leftarrow rule(x, y)$ and the recursive case $rewrite(X(\overline{x}, x, \overline{y}), X(\overline{x}, y, \overline{y})) \leftarrow rewrite(x, y)$, where x, y are term variables, $\overline{x}, \overline{y}$ are hedge variables, and X is a function symbol variable. It is assumed that there are clauses which define the *rule* predicate. The base case says that a term x can be rewritten to y if there is a rule which does it. The recursive case rewrites a nondeterministically selected subterm x of the input term to y, leaving the context around it unchanged. Applying the base case before the recursive case gives the outermost strategy of rewriting, while the other way around implements the innermost one.

An example of the definition of the *rule* predicate is

$$rule(X(\overline{x}_1, \overline{x}_2), X(\overline{y})) \leftarrow \overline{x}_1 \text{ in } f(a^*) \cdot b^*,\ \overline{x}_1 \doteq (x, \overline{z}),\ \overline{y} \doteq (x, f(\overline{z})),$$

where the constraint[1] $\overline{x}_1$ in $f(a^*) {\cdot} b^*$ requires $\overline{x}_1$ to be instantiated by hedges from the language generated by the regular hedge expression $f(a^*) \cdot b^*$ (that is, from the language $\{f, f(a), f(a, a), \dots, (f, b), (f(a), b), \dots, (f(a, \dots, a), b, \dots, b), \dots\}$).

With this program, the goal $\leftarrow rewrite(f(f(f(a, a), b)), x)$ has two answers: $\{x \mapsto f(f(f(a, a), f))\}$ and $\{x \mapsto f(f(f(a, a), f(b)))\}$.

Example 2. The recursive path ordering (rpo) $>_{\text{rpo}}$ is a well-known term ordering [8] used to prove termination of rewriting systems. Its definition is based on a precedence order $\succ$ on function symbols, and on extensions of $>_{\text{rpo}}$ from terms to tuples of terms. There are two kinds of extensions: lexicographic $>^{lex}_{\text{rpo}}$, when terms in tuples are compared from left to right, and multiset $>^{mul}_{\text{rpo}}$, when terms in tuples are compared disregarding the order. The status function τ assigns to each function symbol either *lex* or *mul* status. Then for all (ranked) terms s, t, we define $s >_{\text{rpo}} t$, if $s = f(s_1, \dots, s_m)$ and

1. either $s_i = t$ or $s_i >_{\text{rpo}} t$ for some s_i, $1 \le i \le m$, or
2. $t = g(t_1, \dots, t_n)$, $s >_{\text{rpo}} t_i$ for all $i, 1 \le i \le n$, and either (a) $f \succ g$, or (b) $f = g$ and $(s_1, \dots, s_n) >^{\tau(f)}_{\text{rpo}} (t_1, \dots, t_n)$.

To implement this definition in CLP(H), we use the predicate *rpo* for $>_{\text{rpo}}$ between two terms, and four helper predicates: *rpo_all* to implement the comparison $s >_{\text{rpo}} t_i$ for all i; *prec* to implement the comparison depending on the precedence; *ext* to implement the comparison with respect to an extension

[1] In the notation defined later, strictly speaking, we need to write this constraint as $f(a(\mathbf{eps})^*) \cdot b(\mathbf{eps})^*$, where **eps** is the regular expression for the empty hedge. However, for brevity and clarity of the presentation we omit **eps** here.

of $>_{\mathrm{rpo}}$; and *status* to give the status of a function symbol. The predicate *lex* implements $>^{lex}_{\mathrm{rpo}}$ and *mul* implements $>^{mul}_{\mathrm{rpo}}$. The symbol $\langle\rangle$ is an unranked function symbol, and $\{\}$ is an unordered unranked function symbol. As one can see, the implementation is rather straightforward and closely follows the definition. $>_{\mathrm{rpo}}$ requires four clauses, since there are four alternatives in the definition:

1. $rpo(X(\overline{x}, x, \overline{y}), x). \qquad rpo(X(\overline{x}, x, \overline{y}), y) \leftarrow rpo(x, y).$

2a. $rpo(X(\overline{x}), Y(\overline{y})) \leftarrow rpo\_all(X(\overline{x}), \langle\overline{y}\rangle), prec(X, Y).$

2b. $rpo(X(\overline{x}), X(\overline{y})) \leftarrow rpo\_all(X(\overline{x}), \langle\overline{y}\rangle), ext(X(\overline{x}), X(\overline{y})).$

rpo_all is implemented with recursion:

$$rpo\_all(x, \langle\,\rangle). \qquad rpo\_all(x, \langle y, \overline{y}\rangle) \leftarrow rpo(x, y), rpo\_all(x, \langle\overline{y}\rangle).$$

The definition of *prec* as an ordering on finitely many function symbols is straightforward. More interesting is the definition of *ext*:

$$ext(X(\overline{x}), X(\overline{y})) \leftarrow status(X, lex), lex(\langle\overline{x}\rangle, \langle\overline{y}\rangle).$$
$$ext(X(\overline{x}), X(\overline{y})) \leftarrow status(X, mul), mul(\{\overline{x}\}, \{\overline{y}\}).$$

status can be given as a set of facts, *lex* needs one clause, and *mul* requires three:

$$lex(\langle\overline{x}, x, \overline{y}\rangle, \langle\overline{x}, y, \overline{z}\rangle) \leftarrow rpo(x, y).$$
$$mul(\{x, \overline{x}\}, \{\}). \qquad mul(\{x, \overline{x}\}, \{x, \overline{y}\}) \leftarrow mul(\{\overline{x}\}, \{\overline{y}\}).$$
$$mul(\{x, \overline{x}\}, \{y, \overline{y}\}) \leftarrow rpo(x, y), \; mul(\{x, \overline{x}\}, \{\overline{y}\}).$$

That's all. This example illustrates the benefits of all three kinds of variables we have and unordered function symbols.

3 Preliminaries

For common notation and definitions, we mostly follow [14]. The alphabet $\mathcal{A}$ consists of the following pairwise disjoint sets of symbols:

- $\mathcal{V}_{\mathsf{T}}$: term variables, denoted by $x, y, z, \ldots$,
- $\mathcal{V}_{\mathsf{H}}$: hedge variables, denoted by $\overline{x}, \overline{y}, \overline{z}, \ldots$,
- $\mathcal{V}_{\mathsf{F}}$: function variables, denoted by $X, Y, Z, \ldots$,
- $\mathcal{F}_{\mathsf{u}}$: unranked unordered function symbols, denoted by $f_{\mathsf{u}}, g_{\mathsf{u}}, h_{\mathsf{u}}, \ldots$,
- $\mathcal{F}_{\mathsf{o}}$: unranked ordered function symbols, denoted by $f_{\mathsf{o}}, g_{\mathsf{o}}, h_{\mathsf{o}}, \ldots$,
- $\mathcal{P}$: ranked predicate symbols, denoted by $p, q, \ldots$.

The sets of variables are countable, while the sets of function and predicate symbols are finite. In addition, $\mathcal{A}$ also contains

- The propositional constants true and false, the binary equality predicate $\doteq$, and the unranked membership predicate in.
- Regular operators: eps, $\cdot, +, *$.

– Logical connectives and quantifiers: $\neg$, $\vee$, $\wedge$, $\rightarrow$, $\leftrightarrow$, $\exists$, $\forall$.
– Auxiliary symbols: parentheses and the comma.

Function symbols, denoted by $f, g, h, \ldots$, are elements of the set $\mathcal{F} = \mathcal{F}_{\mathsf{u}} \cup \mathcal{F}_{\mathsf{o}}$. A *variable* is an element of the set $\mathcal{V} = \mathcal{V}_{\mathsf{T}} \cup \mathcal{V}_{\mathsf{H}} \cup \mathcal{V}_{\mathsf{F}}$. A *functor,* denoted by F, is a common name for a function symbol or a function variable.

We define *terms, hedges,* and other syntactic categories over $\mathcal{A}$ as follows:

$t ::= x \mid f(H) \mid X(H)$	Term
$T ::= t_1, \ldots, t_n \quad (n \geq 0)$	Term sequence
$h ::= t \mid \overline{x}$	Hedge element
$H ::= h_1, \ldots, h_n \quad (n \geq 0)$	Hedge

We denote the set of terms by $\mathcal{T}(\mathcal{F}, \mathcal{V})$ and the set of ground (variable-free) terms by $\mathcal{T}(\mathcal{F})$. For readability, we put parentheses around hedges, writing, e.g., $(f(a), \overline{x}, b)$ instead of $f(a), \overline{x}, b$. The empty hedge is written as ϵ. Besides the letter t, we use also r and s to denote terms. Two hedges are *disjoint* if they do not share a common element. For instance, $(f(a), x, b)$ and $(f(x), f(b, f(a)))$ are disjoint, whereas $(f(a), x, b)$ and $(f(b), f(a))$ are not.

An *atom* is a formula of the form $p(t_1, \ldots, t_n)$, where $p \in \mathcal{P}$ is an n-ary predicate symbol. Atoms are denoted by A.

Regular hedge expressions R are defined inductively:

$$\mathsf{R} ::= \mathsf{eps} \mid (\mathsf{R} \cdot \mathsf{R}) \mid \mathsf{R} + \mathsf{R} \mid \mathsf{R}^* \mid f(\mathsf{R})$$

where the dot $\cdot$ stands for concatenation, $+$ for choice, and $*$ for repetition. *Primitive constraints* are either term equalities $\doteq (t_1, t_2)$ or membership for hedges $\mathsf{in}(H, \mathsf{R})$. They are written in infix notation, such as $t_1 \doteq t_2$, and H in R. Instead of $F_1() \doteq F_2()$ and $f_{\mathsf{o}}(H_1) \doteq f_{\mathsf{o}}(H_2)$ we write $F_1 \doteq F_2$ and $H_1 \doteq H_2$ respectively. We denote the symmetric closure of the relation $\doteq$ by $\simeq$.

A *literal* L is an atom or a primitive constraint. *Formulas* are defined as usual. A *constraint* is an arbitrary first-order formula built over true, false, and primitive constraints. The set of free variables of a syntactic object O is denoted by $var(O)$. We let $\exists_V N$ denote the formula $\exists v_1 \cdots \exists v_n N$, where $V = \{v_1, \ldots, v_n\} \subset \mathcal{V}$. $\overline{\exists}_V N$ denotes $\exists_{var(N) \setminus V} N$. We write $\exists N$ (resp. $\forall N$) for the existential (resp. universal) closure of N. We refer to a language over the alphabet $\mathcal{A}$ as $\mathcal{L}(\mathcal{A})$.

A *substitution* is a mapping from term variables to terms, from hedge variables to hedges, and from function variables to functors, such that all but finitely many term, hedge, and function variables are mapped to themselves. Substitutions extend to terms, hedges, literals, conjunction of literals.

A *(constraint logic) program* is a finite set of *rules* of the form $\forall(L_1 \wedge \cdots \wedge L_n \rightarrow A)$, usually written as $A \leftarrow L_1, \ldots, L_n$, where A is an atom and $L_1, \ldots, L_n$ are literals ($n \geq 0$). A *goal* is a formula of the form $\exists(L_1 \wedge \cdots \wedge L_n)$, $n \geq 0$, usually written as $L_1, \ldots, L_n$.

We say a variable is *solved* in a conjunction of primitive constraints $\mathcal{K} = \mathbf{c}_1 \wedge \cdots \wedge \mathbf{c}_n$, if there is a $\mathbf{c}_i$, $1 \leq i \leq n$, such that

- the variable is x, $\mathbf{c}_i = x \doteq t$, and x occurs neither in t nor elsewhere in $\mathcal{K}$, or
- the variable is $\overline{x}$, $\mathbf{c}_i = \overline{x} \doteq H$, and $\overline{x}$ occurs neither in H nor elsewhere in $\mathcal{K}$, or
- the variable is F, $\mathbf{c}_i = X \doteq F$ and X occurs neither in F nor elsewhere in $\mathcal{K}$, or
- the variable is x, $\mathbf{c}_i = x \mathsf{\ in\ } f(\mathsf{R})$ and x does not occur in membership constraints elsewhere in $\mathcal{K}$, or
- the variable is $\overline{x}$, $\mathbf{c}_i = \overline{x} \mathsf{\ in\ } \mathsf{R}$, $\overline{x}$ does not occur in membership constraints elsewhere in $\mathcal{K}$, and R has the form $\mathsf{R}_1 \cdot \mathsf{R}_2$ or R_1^*.

In this case we also say that $\mathbf{c}_i$ is *solved in* $\mathcal{K}$. Moreover, $\mathcal{K}$ is called *solved* if for any $1 \leq i \leq n$, $\mathbf{c}_i$ is solved in it. $\mathcal{K}$ is *partially solved*, if for any $1 \leq i \leq n$, $\mathbf{c}_i$ is solved in $\mathcal{K}$, or has one of the following forms:

- Membership atom:
  - $f_{\mathsf{u}}(H_1, \overline{x}, H_2) \mathsf{\ in\ } f_{\mathsf{u}}(\mathsf{R})$.
  - $(\overline{x}, H) \mathsf{\ in\ } \mathsf{R}$ where R has a form $\mathsf{R}_1 \cdot \mathsf{R}_2$ or R_1^*.
- Equation:
  - $(\overline{x}, H_1) \doteq (\overline{y}, H_2)$ where $\overline{x} \neq \overline{y}$, $H_1 \neq \epsilon$ and $H_2 \neq \epsilon$.
  - $(\overline{x}, H_1) \doteq (T, \overline{y}, H_2)$, where $\overline{x} \notin var(T)$, $H_1 \neq \epsilon$, and $T \neq \epsilon$. The variables $\overline{x}$ and $\overline{y}$ are not necessarily distinct.
  - $f_{\mathsf{u}}(H_1, \overline{x}, H_2) \doteq f_{\mathsf{u}}(H_3, \overline{y}, H_4)$ where $(H_1, \overline{x}, H_2)$ and $(H_3, \overline{y}, H_4)$ are disjoint.

A constraint is *solved*, if it is either true or a non-empty quantifier-free disjunction of solved conjunctions. A constraint is *partially solved*, if it is either true or a non-empty quantifier-free disjunction of partially solved conjunctions.

4 Semantics

For a given set S, we denote by S^* the set of finite, possibly empty, sequences of elements of S, and by S^n the set of sequences of length n of elements of S. The empty sequence of symbols from any set S is denoted by ϵ. Given a sequence $s = (s_1, s_2, \ldots, s_n) \in S^n$, we denote by $perm(s)$ the set of sequences $\{(s_{\pi(1)}, s_{\pi(2)}, \ldots, s_{\pi(n)}) \mid \pi \text{ is a permutation of } \{1, 2, \ldots, n\}\}$.

A *structure* $\mathfrak{S}$ for a language $\mathcal{L}(\mathcal{A})$ is a tuple $\langle D, I \rangle$ made of a non-empty carrier set of *individuals* and an interpretation function I that maps each function symbol $f \in \mathcal{F}$ to a function $I(f) : D^* \to D$, and each n-ary predicate symbol $p \in \mathcal{P}$ to an n-ary relation $I(p) \subseteq D^n$. Moreover, if $f \in \mathcal{F}_{\mathsf{u}}$ then $I(f)(s) = I(f)(s')$ for all $s \in D^*$ and $s' \in perm(s)$. A *variable assignment* for such a structure is a function with domain $\mathcal{V}$ that maps term variables to elements of D, hedge variable to elements of D^*, and function variables to functions from D^* to D.

The interpretations of our syntactic categories w.r.t. a structure $\mathfrak{S} = \langle D, I \rangle$ and variable assignment σ is shown below. The interpretations $[\![H]\!]_{\mathfrak{S},\sigma}$ of hedges (including terms) is defined as follows ($v \in \mathcal{V}_{\mathsf{T}} \cup \mathcal{V}_{\mathsf{H}}$):

$$[\![(H_1, \ldots, H_n)]\!]_{\mathfrak{S},\sigma} := ([\![H_1]\!]_{\mathfrak{S},\sigma}, \ldots, [\![H_n]\!]_{\mathfrak{S},\sigma}), \qquad [\![v]\!]_{\mathfrak{S},\sigma} := \sigma(v),$$

$$[\![f(H)]\!]_{\mathfrak{S},\sigma} := I(f)([\![H]\!]_{\mathfrak{S},\sigma}), \qquad [\![X(H)]\!]_{\mathfrak{S},\sigma} := \sigma(X)([\![H]\!]_{\mathfrak{S},\sigma}).$$

Note that terms are interpreted as elements of D and hedges as elements of D^*. We may omit σ and write simply $[\![E]\!]_{\mathfrak{S}}$ for the interpretation of a ground expression E. The interpretation of regular expressions is defined as follows:

$$[\![\mathsf{eps}]\!]_{\mathfrak{S}} := \{\epsilon\}, \qquad [\![f(\mathsf{R})]\!]_{\mathfrak{S}} := \{I(f)(H) \mid H \in [\![\mathsf{R}]\!]_{\mathfrak{S}}\},$$
$$[\![\mathsf{R}_1 + \mathsf{R}_2]\!]_{\mathfrak{S}} := [\![\mathsf{R}_1]\!]_{\mathfrak{S}} \cup [\![\mathsf{R}_2]\!]_{\mathfrak{S}}, \quad [\![\mathsf{R}_1 \cdot \mathsf{R}_2]\!]_{\mathfrak{S}} := \{(H_1, H_2) \mid H_1 \in [\![\mathsf{R}_1]\!]_{\mathfrak{S}}, H_2 \in [\![\mathsf{R}_2]\!]_{\mathfrak{S}}\},$$
$$[\![\mathsf{R}^*]\!]_{\mathfrak{S}} := [\![\mathsf{R}]\!]_{\mathfrak{S}}^*.$$

Primitive constraints are interpreted w.r.t. a structure $\mathfrak{S}$ and variable assignment σ as follows: $\mathfrak{S} \models_\sigma t_1 \doteq t_2$ iff $[\![t_1]\!]_{\mathfrak{S},\sigma} = [\![t_2]\!]_{\mathfrak{S},\sigma}$; $\mathfrak{S} \models_\sigma H \text{ in } \mathsf{R}$ iff $[\![H]\!]_{\mathfrak{S},\sigma} \in [\![\mathsf{R}]\!]_{\mathfrak{S}}$; and $\mathfrak{S} \models_\sigma p(t_1, \dots, t_n)$ iff $I(p)([\![t_1]\!]_{\mathfrak{S},\sigma}, \dots, [\![t_n]\!]_{\mathfrak{S},\sigma})$ holds. The notions $\mathfrak{S} \models N$ for validity of an arbitrary formula N in $\mathfrak{S}$, and $\models N$ for validity of N in any structure are defined in the standard way.

An *intended structure* is a structure $\mathfrak{I}$ with the carrier set $\mathcal{T}(\mathcal{F})$ and interpretations I defined for every $f \in \mathcal{F}$ by $I(f)(H) := f(H)$. Thus, intended structures identify terms and hedges by themselves. Also, if R is any regular hedge expression then $[\![\mathsf{R}]\!]_{\mathfrak{I}}$ is the same in all intended structures, and will be denoted by $[\![\mathsf{R}]\!]$. Other remarkable properties of intended structures $\mathfrak{I}$ are: Variable assignments are substitutions, $\mathfrak{I} \models_\vartheta t_1 \doteq t_2$ iff $t_1\vartheta = t_2\vartheta$, and $\mathfrak{I} \models_\vartheta H \text{ in } \mathsf{R}$ iff $H\vartheta \in [\![\mathsf{R}]\!]$.

Given a program P, its Herbrand base $\mathcal{B}_P$ is, naturally, the set of all atoms $p(t_1, \dots, t_n)$, where p is an n-ary user-defined predicate in P and $(t_1, \dots, t_n) \in \mathcal{T}(\mathcal{F})^n$. Then an intended interpretation of P corresponds uniquely to a subset of $\mathcal{B}_P$. An *intended model* of P is an intended interpretation of P that is its model. We will write shortly $\mathcal{H}$-structure, $\mathcal{H}$-interpretation, $\mathcal{H}$-model for intended structures, interpretations, and models, respectively.

As usual, we will write $P \models G$ if G is a goal which holds in every model of P. Since our programs consist of positive clauses, the following facts hold:

1. Every program P has a least $\mathcal{H}$-model, which we denote by $lm(P, \mathcal{H})$.
2. If G is a goal then $P \models G$ iff $lm(P, \mathcal{H})$ is a model of G.

A *partially solved form of a constraint* $\mathcal{C}_1$ is a constraint $\mathcal{C}_2$ such that $\mathcal{C}_2$ is partially solved and $\mathfrak{I} \models \forall\left(\mathcal{C}_1 \leftrightarrow \overline{\exists}_{var(\mathcal{C}_1)}\mathcal{C}_2\right)$ for any $\mathcal{H}$-structure $\mathfrak{I}$.

A ground substitution ϑ is a $\mathcal{H}$-*solution* (or simply *solution*) of a constraint $\mathcal{C}$ if $\mathfrak{I} \models \mathcal{C}\vartheta$ for all $\mathcal{H}$-structures $\mathfrak{I}$. The notation $\models_{\mathcal{H}} \mathcal{C}$ stands for $\mathfrak{I} \models \mathcal{C}$ for all $\mathcal{H}$-structures $\mathfrak{I}$.

Theorem 1. *If the constraint $\mathcal{D}$ is solved, then $\mathfrak{I} \models \exists \mathcal{D}$ holds.*

Proof. Since $\mathcal{D}$ is solved, each disjunct $\mathcal{K}$ in it has a form $v_1 \doteq e_1 \wedge \cdots \wedge v_n \doteq e_n \wedge v_1' \text{ in } \mathsf{R}_1 \wedge \cdots \wedge v_m' \text{ in } \mathsf{R}_m$ where $m, n \geq 0$, $v_i, v_j' \in \mathcal{V}$ and e_i is an expression corresponding to v_i. Moreover, $v_1, \dots, v_n, v_1', \dots, v_m'$ are distinct and $[\![\mathsf{R}_j]\!] \neq \emptyset$ for all $1 \leq j \leq m$. Assume σ_i' is a grounding substitution for e_i for all $1 \leq i \leq n$, and let e_j' be an element of $[\![\mathsf{R}_j]\!]$ for all $1 \leq j \leq m$. Then $\sigma = \{v_1 \mapsto e_1\sigma_1', \dots, v_n \mapsto e_n\sigma_n', v_1' \mapsto e_1', \dots, v_m' \mapsto e_m'\}$ solves $\mathcal{K}$. Therefore, $\mathfrak{I} \models \exists \mathcal{D}$ holds.

5 Solver

We consider constraints in DNF: $\mathcal{K}_1 \vee \cdots \vee \mathcal{K}_n$, where $\mathcal{K}$'s are conjunctions of of true, false, and primitive constraints. The solver defined below transforms a constraint into a partially solved form. The solver is formulated in a rule-based way. The number of rules is not small (as it is usual for such kind of solvers, cf., e.g., [9,7]). To make their comprehension easier, we group them so that similar ones are collected together in subsections. Within each subsection, for better readability, they are put in frames. In the rules, $\mathcal{K}$ stands for a maximal conjunction of primitive constraints. The rules are applied in any context.

5.1 Rules

Logical Rules. There are eight logical rules which are applied at any depth in constraints, modulo associativity and commutativity of disjunction and conjunction. N stands for any formula. We denote the whole set of rules by Log.

$N \wedge N \rightsquigarrow N$	$N \vee N \rightsquigarrow N$	$H \doteq H \rightsquigarrow \mathsf{true}$	$\mathsf{true} \wedge N \rightsquigarrow N$
$\mathsf{false} \wedge N \rightsquigarrow \mathsf{false}$	$\mathsf{false} \vee N \rightsquigarrow N$	$\epsilon\ \mathsf{in}\ \mathsf{R} \rightsquigarrow \mathsf{true}$, if $\epsilon \in [\![\mathsf{R}]\!]$	$\mathsf{true} \vee N \rightsquigarrow \mathsf{true}$

Failure Rules. The first two rules perform occurrence check, rules (F3) and (F5) detect function symbol clash, and rules (F4), (F6), (F7) detect inconsistent primitive constraints. We denote the set of rules (F1)–(F7) by Fail.

(F1) $x \simeq (H_1, F(H), H_2) \rightsquigarrow \mathsf{false}$, if $x \in var(H)$.
(F2) $\overline{x} \simeq (H_1, t, H_2) \rightsquigarrow \mathsf{false}$, if $\overline{x} \in var(H_1, t, H_2)$.
(F3) $f_1(H_1) \simeq f_2(H_2) \rightsquigarrow \mathsf{false}$, if $f_1 \neq f_2$.
(F4) $\epsilon \simeq (H_1, t, H_2) \rightsquigarrow \mathsf{false}$.
(F5) $f_1(H)\ \mathsf{in}\ f_2(\mathsf{R}) \rightsquigarrow \mathsf{false}$, if $f_1 \neq f_2$.
(F6) $\epsilon\ \mathsf{in}\ \mathsf{R} \rightsquigarrow \mathsf{false}$, if $\epsilon \notin [\![\mathsf{R}]\!]$,
(F7) $(H_1, t, H_2)\ \mathsf{in}\ \mathsf{eps} \rightsquigarrow \mathsf{false}$.

Decomposition Rules. Each of the decomposition rules operates on a conjunction of constraint literals and gives back either a conjunction of constraint literals again, or constraints in DNF. We denote the set of rules (D1) and (D2) by Dec.

(D1) $f_{\mathsf{u}}(H) \simeq f_{\mathsf{u}}(T) \wedge \mathcal{K} \rightsquigarrow \bigvee_{T' \in perm(T)} (H \doteq T' \wedge \mathcal{K})$,

where H and T are disjoint.

(D2) $(t_1, H_1) \simeq (t_2, H_2) \rightsquigarrow t_1 \doteq t_2 \wedge H_1 \doteq H_2$, where $H_1 \neq \epsilon$ or $H_2 \neq \epsilon$.

Deletion Rules. These rules delete identical terms or hedge variables from both sides of an equation. We denote this set of rules by Del.

(Del1) $(\overline{x}, H_1) \simeq (\overline{x}, H_2) \rightsquigarrow H_1 \doteq H_2$.
(Del2) $f_{\mathsf{u}}(H_1, h, H_2) \simeq f_{\mathsf{u}}(H_3, h, H_4) \rightsquigarrow f_{\mathsf{u}}(H_1, H_2) \doteq f_{\mathsf{u}}(H_3, H_4)$.
(Del3) $\overline{x} \simeq H_1, \overline{x}, H_2 \rightsquigarrow H_1 \doteq \epsilon \wedge H_2 \doteq \epsilon$, if $H_1 \neq \epsilon$.

Variable Elimination Rules. These rules eliminate variables from the given constraint keeping only a solved equation for them. They apply to disjuncts. The first two rules replace a variable with the corresponding expression, provided that the occurrence check fails:

(E1) $x \simeq t \wedge \mathcal{K} \rightsquigarrow x \doteq t \wedge \mathcal{K}\vartheta$,
where $x \notin var(t)$, $x \in var(\mathcal{K})$ and $\vartheta = \{x \mapsto t\}$. If t is a variable then in addition it is required that $t \in var(\mathcal{K})$.
(E2) $\overline{x} \simeq H \wedge \mathcal{K} \rightsquigarrow \overline{x} \doteq H \wedge \mathcal{K}\vartheta$,
where $\overline{x} \notin var(H)$, $\overline{x} \in var(\mathcal{K})$, and $\vartheta = \{\overline{x} \mapsto H\}$. If $H = \overline{y}$ for some $\overline{y}$, then in addition it is required that $\overline{y} \in var(\mathcal{K})$.

The next two rules (E3) and (E4) assign to a variable an initial part of the hedge in the other side of the selected equation. The hedge has to be a sequence of terms T in the first rule. The disjunction in the rule is over all possible splits of T. In the second rule, only a split of the prefix T of the hedge is relevant and the disjunction is over all such possible splits of T. The rest is blocked by the term t due to occurrence check: No instantiation of $\overline{x}$ can contain it.

(E3) $(\overline{x}, H) \simeq T \wedge \mathcal{K} \rightsquigarrow \bigvee_{T=(T_1,T_2)} \left(\overline{x} \doteq T_1 \wedge H\vartheta \doteq T_2 \wedge \mathcal{K}\vartheta\right)$,
where $\overline{x} \notin var(T)$, $\vartheta = \{\overline{x} \mapsto T_1\}$, and $H \neq \epsilon$.
(E4) $(\overline{x}, H_1) \simeq (T, t, H_2) \wedge \mathcal{K} \rightsquigarrow \bigvee_{T=(T_1,T_2)} \left(\overline{x} \doteq T_1 \wedge H_1\vartheta \doteq (T_2, t, H_2)\vartheta \wedge \mathcal{K}\vartheta\right)$
where $\overline{x} \notin var(T)$, $\overline{x} \in var(t)$, $\vartheta = \{\overline{x} \mapsto T_1\}$, and $H_1 \neq \epsilon$.

Finally, there are three rules for function variable elimination. Their behavior is standard:

(E5) $X \simeq F \wedge \mathcal{K} \rightsquigarrow X \doteq F \wedge \mathcal{K}\vartheta$,
where $X \neq F$, $X \in var(\mathcal{K})$, and $\vartheta = \{X \mapsto F\}$. If F is a function variable, then in addition it is required that $F \in var(\mathcal{K})$.
(E6) $X(H_1) \simeq F(H_2) \wedge \mathcal{K} \rightsquigarrow X \doteq F \wedge F(H_1)\vartheta \doteq F(H_2)\vartheta \wedge \mathcal{K}\vartheta$.
where $X \neq F$, $\vartheta = \{X \mapsto F\}$, and $H_1 \neq \epsilon$ or $H_2 \neq \epsilon$.
(E7) $X(H_1) \simeq X(H_2) \wedge \mathcal{K} \rightsquigarrow \bigvee_{f \in \mathcal{F}} \left(X \doteq f \wedge f(H_1)\vartheta \doteq f(H_2)\vartheta \wedge \mathcal{K}\vartheta\right)$,
where $\vartheta = \{X \mapsto f\}$, and $H_1 \neq H_2$.

We denote the set of rules (E1)–(E7) by Elim.

Membership Rules. The membership rules apply to disjuncts of constraints in DNF, to preserve the DNF structure. They provide the membership check, if the hedge H in the membership atom H in R is ground. Nonground hedges require more special treatment as one can see.

To solve membership constraints for term sequences of the form (t, H) with t a term, we rely on the possibility to compute the linear form of a regular expression, that is, to express it as a finite sum of concatenations of regular hedge expressions that identify all plausible membership constraints for t and H. Formally, the *linear form* of a regular expression R, denoted $\mathit{lf}(\mathsf{R})$, is a finite set of pairs $(f(\mathsf{R}_1), \mathsf{R}_2)$ called *monomials*, which is defined recursively as follows:

$$\mathit{lf}(\mathsf{eps}) = \emptyset. \qquad \mathit{lf}(\mathsf{R}^*) = \mathit{lf}(\mathsf{R}) \odot \mathsf{R}^*. \qquad \mathit{lf}(f(\mathsf{R})) = \{(f(\mathsf{R}), \mathsf{eps})\}.$$
$$\mathit{lf}(\mathsf{R}_1 + \mathsf{R}_2) = \mathit{lf}(\mathsf{R}_1) \cup \mathit{lf}(\mathsf{R}_2).$$
$$\mathit{lf}(\mathsf{R}_1 \cdot \mathsf{R}_2) = \mathit{lf}(\mathsf{R}_1) \odot \mathsf{R}_2, \text{ if } \epsilon \notin [\![\mathsf{R}_1]\!].$$
$$\mathit{lf}(\mathsf{R}_1 \cdot \mathsf{R}_2) = \mathit{lf}(\mathsf{R}_1) \odot \mathsf{R}_2 \cup \mathit{lf}(\mathsf{R}_2), \text{ if } \epsilon \in [\![\mathsf{R}_1]\!].$$

These equations involve an extension of concatenation $\odot$ that acts on a linear form and a regular expression and returns a linear form. It is defined as $l \odot \mathsf{eps} = l$, and $l \odot \mathsf{R} = \{(f(\mathsf{R}_1), \mathsf{R}_2 \cdot \mathsf{R}) \mid (f(\mathsf{R}_1), \mathsf{R}_2) \in l, \mathsf{R}_2 \neq \mathsf{eps}\} \cup \{(f(\mathsf{R}_1), \mathsf{R}) \mid (f(\mathsf{R}_1), \mathsf{eps}) \in l\}$, if $\mathsf{R} \neq \mathsf{eps}$.

The rules are as follows:

(M1) $(\overline{x}_1, \ldots, \overline{x}_n)$ in $\mathsf{eps} \wedge \mathcal{K} \rightsquigarrow \wedge_{i=1}^{n} \overline{x}_i \doteq \epsilon \wedge \mathcal{K}\vartheta$,
where $\vartheta = \{\overline{x}_1 \mapsto \epsilon, \ldots, \overline{x}_n \mapsto \epsilon\}, n > 0$.

(M2) (t, H) in $\mathsf{R} \wedge \mathcal{K} \rightsquigarrow \bigvee_{(f(\mathsf{R}_1),\mathsf{R}_2) \in \mathit{lf}(\mathsf{R})} \Big(t \text{ in } f(\mathsf{R}_1) \wedge H \text{ in } \mathsf{R}_2 \wedge \mathcal{K}\Big)$,
where $H \neq \epsilon$ and $\mathsf{R} \neq \mathsf{eps}$.

(M3) $(\overline{x}, H)$ in $f(\mathsf{R}) \wedge \mathcal{K} \rightsquigarrow$
$\Big(\overline{x} \text{ in } f(\mathsf{R}) \wedge H \doteq \epsilon \wedge \mathcal{K}\Big) \vee \Big(\overline{x} \doteq \epsilon \wedge H \text{ in } f(\mathsf{R}) \wedge \mathcal{K}\Big)$,
where $H \neq \epsilon$.

(M4) t in $\mathsf{R}^* \rightsquigarrow t$ in R.

(M5) t in $\mathsf{R}_1 \cdot \mathsf{R}_2 \wedge \mathcal{K} \rightsquigarrow \Big(t \text{ in } \mathsf{R}_1 \wedge \epsilon \text{ in } \mathsf{R}_2 \wedge \mathcal{K}\Big) \vee \Big(\epsilon \text{ in } \mathsf{R}_1 \wedge t \text{ in } \mathsf{R}_2 \wedge \mathcal{K}\Big)$.

(M6) t in $\mathsf{R}_1 + \mathsf{R}_2 \wedge \mathcal{K} \rightsquigarrow \Big(t \text{ in } \mathsf{R}_1 \wedge \mathcal{K}\Big) \vee \Big(t \text{ in } \mathsf{R}_2 \wedge \mathcal{K}\Big)$.

(M7) $(\overline{x}, H)$ in $\mathsf{R}_1 + \mathsf{R}_2 \wedge \mathcal{K} \rightsquigarrow \Big((\overline{x}, H) \text{ in } \mathsf{R}_1 \wedge \mathcal{K}\Big) \vee \Big((\overline{x}, H) \text{ in } \mathsf{R}_2 \wedge \mathcal{K}\Big)$.

(M8) v in $\mathsf{R}_1 \wedge v$ in $\mathsf{R}_2 \rightsquigarrow v$ in R, where $v \in \mathcal{V}_\mathsf{T} \cup \mathcal{V}_\mathsf{H}, [\![\mathsf{R}]\!] = [\![\mathsf{R}_1]\!] \cap [\![\mathsf{R}_2]\!]$.

Next, we have rules which constrain singleton hedges to be in a term language. They proceed by the straightforward matching or decomposition of the structure. Note that in (M12), we require the arguments of the unordered function symbol to be terms. (M10) and (M9) do not distinguish whether f is ordered or unordered:

(M9)	$\overline{x}$ in $f(\mathsf{R}) \wedge \mathcal{K} \rightsquigarrow \overline{x} \doteq x \wedge x$ in $f(\mathsf{R}) \wedge \mathcal{K}\{\overline{x} \mapsto x\}$, where x is fresh.
(M10)	$X(H)$ in $f(\mathsf{R}) \wedge \mathcal{K} \rightsquigarrow X \doteq f \wedge f(H)\{X \mapsto f\}$ in $f(\mathsf{R}) \wedge \mathcal{K}\{X \mapsto f\}$.
(M11)	$f_{\mathsf{o}}(H)$ in $f_{\mathsf{o}}(\mathsf{R}) \rightsquigarrow H$ in R.
(M12)	$f_{\mathsf{u}}(T)$ in $f_{\mathsf{u}}(\mathsf{R}) \wedge \mathcal{K} \rightsquigarrow \bigvee_{T' \in perm(T)} \Big(T'$ in $\mathsf{R} \wedge \mathcal{K}\Big)$.

We denote the set of rules (M1)–(M12) by Memb.

5.2 The Constraint Solving Algorithm

In this section, unless otherwise stated, by a constraint we mean a formula $\mathcal{K}_1 \vee \cdots \vee \mathcal{K}_n$, where $\mathcal{K}$'s are conjunctions of true, false, and primitive constraints. First, we define the rewrite step

step := first(Log, Fail, Del, Dec, Elim, Memb).

When applied to a constraint, step transforms it by the *first* applicable rule of the solver, looking successively into the sets Log, Fail, Del, Dec, Elim, and Memb.

The constraint solving algorithm implements the strategy solve defined as a computation of a normal form with respect to step:

solve := NF(step).

That means, step is applied to a constraint repeatedly as long as possible. It remains to show that this definition yields an algorithm, which amounts to proving that a constraint to which none of the rules Log, Fail, Del, Dec, Elim, and Memb applies, is produced by NF(step) for any constraint $\mathcal{C}$.

Theorem 2 (Termination of solve). solve *terminates on any input constraint.*

Proof (Sketch). We define a complexity measure $cm(\mathcal{C})$ for quantifier-free constraints in DNF, and show that $cm(\mathcal{C}') < cm(\mathcal{C})$ holds whenever $\mathcal{C}' = \mathsf{step}(\mathcal{C})$.

For a hedge H (resp. regular expression R), we denote by $size(H)$ (resp. by $size(\mathsf{R})$) its denotational length, e.g., $size(\mathsf{eps}) = 1$, $size(f(f(a)), \overline{x}) = 4$, and $size(f(f(a \cdot b^*))) = 6$. The complexity measure $cm(\mathcal{K})$ of a conjunction of primitive constraints $\mathcal{K}$ is the tuple $\langle N_1, M_1, N_2, M_2, M_3 \rangle$ defined as follows ($\{\!|\,|\!\}$ stands for a multiset):

- N_1 is the number of unsolved variables in $\mathcal{K}$.
- $M_1 := \{\!| size(H) \mid H \text{ in } \mathsf{R} \in \mathcal{K}, H \neq \epsilon |\!\}$.
- N_2 is the number of primitive constraints in the form v in R where $v \in \mathcal{V}$ plus the number of primitive constraints in the form $\overline{x}$ in R in $\mathcal{K}$.
- $M_2 := \{\!| size(\mathsf{R}) \mid H \text{ in } \mathsf{R} \in \mathcal{K} |\!\}$.
- $M_3 := \{\!| size(t_1) + size(t_2) \mid t_1 \doteq t_2 \in \mathcal{K} |\!\}$.

The complexity measure $cm(\mathcal{C})$ of a constraint $\mathcal{C} = \mathcal{K}_1 \vee \cdots \vee \mathcal{K}_n$ is defined as $\{\!| cm(\mathcal{K}_1), \ldots, cm(\mathcal{K}_n) |\!\}$. Measures are compared by the multiset extension of the lexicographic ordering on tuples. The Log rules strictly reduce the measure. For the other rules, the table below shows which rule reduces which component of the measure, which implies termination of the algorithm solve.

Rule	N_1	M_1	N_2	M_2	M_3
(M1),(M10),(E1)–(E7)	$>$				
(F5),(F7),(M2),(M3), (M11), (M12)	$\geq$	$>$			
(M8), (M9)	$\geq$	$\geq$	$>$		
(F6),(M4)–(M7)	$\geq$	$\geq$	$\geq$	$>$	
(D1), (D2), (F1)–(F4), (Del1)–(Del3)	$\geq$	$\geq$	$\geq$	$\geq$	$>$

The next lemma is needed to prove that the solver reduces a constraint to its equivalent constraint:

Lemma 1. *If* $\mathsf{step}(\mathcal{C}) = \mathcal{D}$, *then* $\models_{\mathcal{H}} \forall\Big(\mathcal{C} \leftrightarrow \overline{\exists}_{var(\mathcal{C})}\mathcal{D}\Big)$.

Theorem 3. *If* $\mathsf{solve}(\mathcal{C}) = \mathcal{D}$, *then* $\models_{\mathcal{H}} \forall\Big(\mathcal{C} \leftrightarrow \overline{\exists}_{var(\mathcal{C})}\mathcal{D}\Big)$ *and* $\mathcal{D}$ *is a partially solved form of* $\mathcal{C}$.

Proof. $\models_{\mathcal{H}} \forall(\mathcal{C} \leftrightarrow \overline{\exists}_{var(\mathcal{C})}\mathcal{D})$ follows from Lemma 1 and the following property: If $\models_{\mathcal{H}} \forall(\mathcal{C}_1 \leftrightarrow \overline{\exists}_{var(\mathcal{C}_1)}\mathcal{C}_2)$ and $\models_{\mathcal{H}} \forall(\mathcal{C}_2 \leftrightarrow \overline{\exists}_{var(\mathcal{C}_2)}\mathcal{C}_3)$, then $\models_{\mathcal{H}} \forall(\mathcal{C}_1 \leftrightarrow \overline{\exists}_{var(\mathcal{C}_1)}\mathcal{C}_3)$. The property itself relies on the fact that $\models_{\mathcal{H}} \forall(\overline{\exists}_{var(\mathcal{C}_1)}\overline{\exists}_{var(\mathcal{C}_2)}\mathcal{C}_3 \leftrightarrow \overline{\exists}_{var(\mathcal{C}_1)}\mathcal{C}_3)$, which holds because all variables introduced by the rules of the solver in $\mathcal{C}_3$ are fresh not only for $\mathcal{C}_2$, but also for $\mathcal{C}_1$.

As for the partially solved form, by the definition of solve and Theorem 2, $\mathcal{D}$ is in a normal form. Assume by contradiction that it is not partially solved. By inspection of the solver rules, based on the definition of partially solved constraints, we can see that there is a rule that applies to $\mathcal{D}$. But this contradicts the fact that $\mathcal{D}$ is in a normal form. Hence, $\mathcal{D}$ is partially solved. By Lemma 1, we conclude that $\mathcal{D}$ is a partially solved form of $\mathcal{C}$.

6 Operational Semantics of CLP(H)

In this section we describe the operational semantics of CLP(H), following the approach for the CLP schema given in [14]. A *state* is a pair $\langle G \parallel \mathcal{C}\rangle$, where G is the sequence of literals and $\mathcal{C} = \mathcal{K}_1 \vee \cdots \vee \mathcal{K}_n$, where $\mathcal{K}$'s are conjunctions of true, false, and primitive constraints. The *definition of an atom* $p(t_1, \ldots, t_m)$ *in program* P, $defn_P(p(t_1, \ldots, t_m))$, is the set of rules in P such that the head of each rule has a form $p(r_1, \ldots, r_m)$. We assume that $defn_P$ each time returns fresh variants.

A state $\langle L_1, \ldots, L_n \parallel \mathcal{C}\rangle$ can be *reduced with respect to* P as follows: Select a literal L_i. Then:

- If L_i is a primitive constraint literal and $\mathsf{solve}(\mathcal{C} \wedge L_i) \neq \mathsf{false}$, then it is reduced to $\langle L_1, \ldots, L_{i-1}, L_{i+1}, \ldots, L_n \parallel \mathsf{solve}(\mathcal{C} \wedge L_i)\rangle$.
- If L_i is a primitive constraint literal and $\mathsf{solve}(\mathcal{C} \wedge L_i) = \mathsf{false}$, then it is reduced to $\langle \square \parallel \mathsf{false}\rangle$.
- If L_i is an atom $p(t_1, \ldots, t_m)$, then it is reduced to

$$\langle L_1, \ldots, L_{i-1}, t_1 \doteq r_1, \ldots, t_m \doteq r_m, B, L_{i+1}, \ldots, L_n \parallel \mathcal{C}\rangle$$

  for some $(p(r_1, \ldots, r_m) \leftarrow B) \in \mathit{defn}_P(L_i)$.
- If L_i is a atom and $\mathit{defn}_P(L_i) = \emptyset$, then it is reduced to $\langle \square \parallel \mathsf{false}\rangle$.

A *derivation from a state* S in a program P is a finite or infinite sequence of states $S_0 \rightarrowtail S_1 \rightarrowtail \cdots \rightarrowtail S_n \rightarrowtail \cdots$ where S_0 is S and there is a reduction from each S_{i-1} to S_i, using rules in P. A *derivation from a goal* G in a program P is a derivation from $\langle G \parallel \mathsf{true}\rangle$. The *length* of a (finite) derivation of the form $S_0 \rightarrowtail S_1 \rightarrowtail \cdots \rightarrowtail S_n$ is n. A derivation is *finished* if the last goal cannot be reduced, that is, if its last state is of the form $\langle \square \parallel \mathcal{C}\rangle$ where $\mathcal{C}$ is partially solved or false. If $\mathcal{C}$ is false, the derivation is said to be *failed.*

7 Well-Moded and KIF Programs

In this section we consider syntactic restrictions that lead to well-moded and KIF style CLP(H) programs. They are interesting, because the constraints that appear in derivations for such programs can be completely solved by solve.

7.1 Well-Moded Programs

A mode for an n-ary predicate symbol p is a function $m_p : \{1, \ldots, n\} \longrightarrow \{\mathsf{i}, \mathsf{o}\}$. If $m_p(i) = \mathsf{i}$ (resp. $m_p(i) = \mathsf{o}$) then the position i is called an *input* (resp. *output*) *position* of p. The predicates in and $\doteq$ have only output positions. For a literal $L = p(t_1, \ldots, t_n)$ (where p can be also in or $\doteq$), we denote by $\mathit{invar}(L)$ and $\mathit{outvar}(L)$ the sets of variables occurring in terms in the input and output positions of p.

A sequence of literals $L_1, \ldots, L_n$ is *well-moded* if the following hold:

1. For all $1 \leq i \leq n$, $\mathit{invar}(L_i) \subseteq \bigcup_{j=1}^{i-1} \mathit{outvar}(L_j)$.
2. If for some $1 \leq i \leq n$, L_i is $t_1 \doteq t_2$, then $\mathit{var}(t_1) \subseteq \bigcup_{j=1}^{i-1} \mathit{outvar}(L_j)$ or $\mathit{var}(t_2) \subseteq \bigcup_{j=1}^{i-1} \mathit{outvar}(L_j)$.
3. If for some $1 \leq i \leq n$, L_i is a membership atom, then the inclusion $\mathit{var}(L_i) \subseteq \bigcup_{j=1}^{i-1} \mathit{outvar}(L_j)$ holds.

A conjunction of literals G is *well-moded* if there exists a well-moded sequence of literals $L_1, \ldots, L_n$ such that $G = \bigwedge_{i=1}^{n} L_i$ modulo associativity and commutativity. A *formula in DNF is well-moded* if each of its disjuncts is. A *state* $\langle L_1, \ldots, L_n \parallel \mathcal{K}_1 \vee \cdots \vee \mathcal{K}_n\rangle$ *is well-moded*, where $\mathcal{K}$'s are conjunctions of true, false, and primitive constraints, if the formula $(L_1 \wedge \cdots \wedge L_n \wedge \mathcal{K}_1) \vee \cdots \vee (L_1 \wedge \cdots \wedge L_n \wedge \mathcal{K}_n)$ is well-moded. A *clause* $A \leftarrow L_1, \ldots, L_n$ *is well-moded* if the following hold:

1. For all $1 \le i \le n$, $invar(L_i) \subseteq \bigcup_{j=1}^{i-1} outvar(L_j) \cup invar(A)$.
2. $outvar(A) \subseteq \bigcup_{j=1}^{n} outvar(L_j) \cup invar(A)$.
3. If for some $1 \le i \le n$, L_i is $H_1 \doteq H_2$, then $var(H_1) \subseteq \bigcup_{j=1}^{i-1} outvar(L_j) \cup invar(A)$ or $var(H_2) \subseteq \bigcup_{j=1}^{i-1} outvar(L_j) \cup invar(A)$.
4. If for some $1 \le i \le n$, L_i is a membership atom, then $outvar(L_i) \subseteq \bigcup_{j=1}^{i-1} outvar(L_j) \cup invar(A)$.

A *program is well-moded* if all its clauses are well-moded.

Example 3. In Example 1, if the first argument is the input position and the second argument is the output position in the user-defined predicates, it is easy to see that the program is well-moded. In Example 2, for well-modedness we need to define both positions in the user-defined predicates to be the input ones.

Well-modedness is preserved by program derivation steps:

Lemma 2. *Let P be a well-moded* CLP(H) *program and $\langle G \parallel \mathcal{C}\rangle$ be a well-moded state. If $\langle G \parallel \mathcal{C}\rangle \rightarrowtail \langle G' \parallel \mathcal{C}'\rangle$ is a reduction using clauses in P, then $\langle G' \parallel \mathcal{C}'\rangle$ is also a well-moded state.*

The solver reduces well-moded constrains either to a solved form of to false:

Lemma 3. *Let $\mathcal{C}$ be a well-moded constraint and $\mathsf{solve}(\mathcal{C}) = \mathcal{C}'$, where $\mathcal{C}' \neq \mathsf{false}$. Then $\mathcal{C}'$ is solved.*

The theorem below is the main theorem for well-moded CLP(H) programs. It states that any finished derivation from a well-moded goal leads to a solved constraint or to a failure:

Theorem 4. *Let $\langle G \parallel \mathsf{true}\rangle \rightarrowtail \cdots \rightarrowtail \langle \Box \parallel \mathcal{C}'\rangle$ be a finished derivation with respect to a well-moded* CLP(H) *program, starting from a well-moded goal G. If $\mathcal{C}' \neq \mathsf{false}$, then $\mathcal{C}'$ is solved.*

Proof. We prove a more general statement: Let $\langle G \parallel \mathsf{true}\rangle \rightarrowtail \cdots \rightarrowtail \langle G' \parallel \mathcal{C}'\rangle$ be a derivation with respect to a well-moded program, starting from a well-moded goal G and ending with G' that is either $\Box$ or consists only of atomic formulas without arguments (propositional constants). If $\mathcal{C}' \neq \mathsf{false}$, then $\mathcal{C}'$ is solved.

To prove this statement, we use induction on the length n of the derivation. When $n = 0$, then $\mathcal{C}' = \mathsf{true}$ and it is solved. Assume the statement holds when the derivation length is n, and prove it for the derivation with the length $n+1$. Let such a derivation be $\langle G \parallel \mathsf{true}\rangle \rightarrowtail \cdots \rightarrowtail \langle G_n \parallel \mathcal{C}_n\rangle \rightarrowtail \langle G_{n+1} \parallel \mathcal{C}_{n+1}\rangle$. There are two possibilities to make the last step:

1. G_n has a form (modulo permutation) $L, p_1, \ldots, p_n$, where L is primitive constraint, the p's are propositional constants, $G_{n+1} = p_1, \ldots, p_n$, and $\mathcal{C}_{n+1} = \mathsf{solve}(\mathcal{C}_n \wedge L)$.
2. G_n has a form (modulo permutation) $q, p_1, \ldots, p_n$, where q and p's are propositional constants, $G_{n+1} = p_1, \ldots, p_n$, and $\mathcal{C}_{n+1} = \mathcal{C}_n$.

In the first case, note that by Lemma 2, $\langle G_n \parallel C_n \rangle$ is well-moded. Since the p's have no influence on well-modedness (they are just propositional constants), $C_n \wedge L$ is well-moded. By Lemma 3 we get that if $C_{n+1} = \mathsf{solve}(C_n \wedge L) \neq \mathsf{false}$ then C_{n+1} is solved.

In the second case, since G_n consists of propositional constants only, by the induction hypothesis we have that if C_n is not false, then it is solved. But $C_n = C_{n+1}$. It finishes the proof.

7.2 Programs in the KIF Form

A term is in the *KIF form* (*KIF-term*) if hedge variables occur only below ordered function symbols,[2] and they occupy only the last argument position in each subterm where they appear. For example, the term $f_{\mathsf{o}}(x, f_{\mathsf{o}}(a, \overline{x}), f_{\mathsf{u}}(x, b), \overline{x})$ is in the KIF form, while $f_{\mathsf{o}}(\overline{x}, a, \overline{x})$, $f_{\mathsf{u}}(x, f_{\mathsf{o}}(a, \overline{x}), f_{\mathsf{u}}(x, b), \overline{x})$ are not. A hedge (T, h) is in the KIF form, if T is a sequence of KIF-terms and h is either a KIF-term or a hedge variable.

An atom $p(t_1, \ldots, t_n)$ (including $t_1 \doteq t_2$) is in the KIF form, if each t_i, $1 \leq i \leq n$, is a KIF-term. A membership atom H in R is in the KIF-form, if H is a KIF-hedge. A CLP(H) program is in the KIF form, if it is constructed from literals in the KIF form. Note that the programs in examples 1 and 2 are not KIF programs. One could rewrite them in this form, but the code size would become a bit larger.

The notion of KIF form extends naturally to constraints and states, requiring that all their literals should be in the KIF form. KIF-programs, like well-moded ones discussed above, also show a good behavior. As the lemmas below state, reductions preserve the KIF form and the solver is complete:

Lemma 4. *Let P be a* CLP(H) *program in the KIF form and $\langle G \parallel C \rangle$ be a KIF-state. If $\langle G \parallel C \rangle \rightarrowtail \langle G' \parallel C' \rangle$ is a reduction using clauses in P, then $\langle G' \parallel C' \rangle$ is also a KIF-state.*

Lemma 5. *Let C be a KIF-constraint and* $\mathsf{solve}(C) = C'$, *where* $C' \neq \mathsf{false}$. *Then C' is solved.*

We illustrate how to solve a simple KIF constraint:

Example 4. Let $C = f(x, \overline{x}) \doteq f(g(\overline{y}), a, \overline{y}) \wedge \overline{x}$ in $a(\mathsf{eps})^* \wedge \overline{y}$ in $a(\mathsf{eps}) \cdot a(b(\mathsf{eps})^*)^*$. Then solve performs the following derivation:

$$
\begin{aligned}
C \rightsquigarrow^2 & \; x \doteq g(\overline{y}) \wedge \overline{x} \doteq (a, \overline{y}) \wedge (a, \overline{y}) \text{ in } a(\mathsf{eps})^* \wedge \overline{y} \text{ in } a(\mathsf{eps}) \cdot a(b(\mathsf{eps})^*)^* \\
\rightsquigarrow & \; x \doteq g(\overline{y}) \wedge \overline{x} \doteq (a, \overline{y}) \wedge \overline{y} \text{ in } a(\mathsf{eps})^* \wedge \overline{y} \text{ in } a(\mathsf{eps}) \cdot a(b(\mathsf{eps})^*)^* \\
\rightsquigarrow & \; x \doteq g(\overline{y}) \wedge \overline{x} \doteq (a, \overline{y}) \wedge \overline{y} \text{ in } a(\mathsf{eps}) \cdot a(\mathsf{eps})^*
\end{aligned}
$$

The obtained constraint is solved.

[2] If the language does not contain unordered function symbols, then hedge variables are permitted under function symbols as well.

The theorem below is the main theorem for KIF programs and can be proved similarly to the analogous theorem for well-moded programs (Theorem 4). It states that any finished derivation from a KIF-goal with respect to a KIF-program leads to a solved constraint or to a failure:

Theorem 5. *Let* $\langle G \parallel \mathsf{true}\rangle \rightarrowtail \cdots \rightarrowtail \langle \square \parallel C'\rangle$ *be a finished derivation with respect to a* CLP(H) *program in the KIF form, starting from a KIF-goal G. If* $C' \neq \mathsf{false}$, *then* C' *is solved.*

8 Conclusion

We defined a semantics for CLP(H) programs and introduced a solver for positive equational and membership constraints over hedges. The solver, in general, is incomplete. It is natural, since hedge unification is infinitary. We identified two special cases of CLP(H) programs which lead to constraints, for which the solver computes a complete set of solutions.

Acknowledgments. This research has been partially supported by LIACC through Programa de Financiamento Plurianual of the Fundação para a Ciência e Tecnologia (FCT), by the FCT fellowship (ref. SFRH/BD/62058/2009), by the Austrian Science Fund (FWF) under the project SToUT (P 24087-N18), and the Rustaveli Science Foundation under the grants DI/16/4-120/11 and FR/611/4-102/12.

References

1. Balland, E., Brauner, P., Kopetz, R., Moreau, P.-E., Reilles, A.: Tom: Piggybacking rewriting on Java. In: Baader, F. (ed.) RTA 2007. LNCS, vol. 4533, pp. 36–47. Springer, Heidelberg (2007)
2. Clavel, M., Durán, F., Eker, S., Lincoln, P., Martí-Oliet, N., Meseguer, J., Talcott, C.: All About Maude - A High-Performance Logical Framework. LNCS, vol. 4350. Springer, Heidelberg (2007)
3. Coelho, J., Florido, M.: CLP (Flex): constraint logic programming applied to XML processing. In: Meersman, R. (ed.) CoopIS/DOA/ODBASE 2004. LNCS, vol. 3291, pp. 1098–1112. Springer, Heidelberg (2004)
4. Coelho, J., Florido, M.: VeriFLog: a constraint logic programming approach to verification of website content. In: Shen, H.T., Li, J., Li, M., Ni, J., Wang, W. (eds.) APWeb Workshops 2006. LNCS, vol. 3842, pp. 148–156. Springer, Heidelberg (2006)
5. Coelho, J., Florido, M.: XCentric: logic programming for XML processing. In: Fundulaki, I., Polyzotis, N. (eds.) WIDM, pp. 1–8. ACM (2007)
6. Colmerauer, A.: An introduction to Prolog III. Commun. ACM 33(7), 69–90 (1990)
7. Comon, H.: Completion of rewrite systems with membership constraints. Part II: constraint solving. J. Symb. Comput. 25(4), 421–453 (1998)
8. Dershowitz, N.: Orderings for term-rewriting systems. Theor. Comput. Sci. 17, 279–301 (1982)

9. Dovier, A., Piazza, C., Pontelli, E., Rossi, G.: Sets and constraint logic programming. ACM Trans. Program. Lang. Syst. 22(5), 861–931 (2000)
10. Dovier, A., Piazza, C., Rossi, G.: A uniform approach to constraint-solving for lists, multisets, compact lists, and sets. ACM Trans. Comput. Log. 9(3) (2008)
11. Dundua, B., Florido, M., Kutsia, T., Marin, M.: Constraint logic programming for hedges: A semantic reconstruction. RISC Report Series 14-02, RISC, University of Linz, Austria (2014)
12. Genesereth, M.R., Fikes, R.E.: Knowledge Interchange Format, Version 3.0 Reference Manual. Technical Report Logic-92-1, Stanford University, Stanford, CA, USA (1992)
13. Hosoya, H., Pierce, B.C.: Regular expression pattern matching for XML. J. Funct. Program. 13(6), 961–1004 (2003)
14. Jaffar, J., Maher, M.J., Marriott, K., Stuckey, P.J.: The semantics of constraint logic programs. J. Log. Program. 37(1-3), 1–46 (1998)
15. Kutsia, T.: Solving equations with sequence variables and sequence functions. J. Symb. Comput. 42(3), 352–388 (2007)
16. Kutsia, T., Marin, M.: Solving, reasoning, and programming in Common Logic. In: SYNASC, pp. 119–126. IEEE Computer Society (2012)
17. Marin, M., Kutsia, T.: Foundations of the rule-based system ρlog. Journal of Applied Non-Classical Logics 16(1-2), 151–168 (2006)
18. Rajasekar, A.: Constraint logic programming on strings: Theory and applications. In: SLP, p. 681 (1994)
19. van den Brand, M.G.J., et al.: The ASF+SDF meta-environment: A component-based language development environment. In: Wilhelm, R. (ed.) CC 2001. LNCS, vol. 2027, pp. 365–370. Springer, Heidelberg (2001)
20. Walinsky, C.: CLP(Σ^*): constraint logic programming with regular sets. In: Levi, G., Martelli, M. (eds.) ICLP, pp. 181–196. MIT Press (1989)
21. Wolfram, S.: The Mathematica book, 5th edn. Wolfram-Media (2003)

How Many Numbers Can a Lambda-Term Contain?

Paweł Parys*

University of Warsaw, Warsaw, Poland
parys@mimuw.edu.pl

Abstract. It is well known, that simply-typed λ-terms can be used to represent numbers, as well as some other data types. We prove, however, that in a λ-term of a fixed type we can store only a fixed number of natural numbers, in such a way that they can be extracted using λ-terms. More precisely, while representing k numbers in a closed λ-term of some type we only require that there are k closed λ-terms $M_1, \ldots, M_k$ such that M_i takes as argument the λ-term representing the k-tuple, and returns the i-th number in the tuple (we do not require that, using λ-calculus, one can construct the representation of the k-tuple out of the k numbers in the tuple). Moreover, the same result holds when we allow that the numbers can be extracted approximately, up to some error (even when we only want to know whether a set is bounded or not).

1 Introduction

It is well known, that simply-typed λ-terms can be used to represent numbers, as well as some other data types (for an introduction see e.g. [1]). In particular we can represent pairs or tuples of representable data types. Notice however that the sort[1] of terms representing pairs is more complex than the sort of terms representing the elements of pairs. We prove that, indeed, for representing k-tuples of natural numbers for big k, we need terms of complex sort. For this reason, for each sort α we define a number $dim(\alpha)$, the *dimension* of sort α. It gives an upper bound on how large tuples of natural numbers can be represented by a term of sort α.

To represent a natural number in a λ-term we use two constants: $\mathbf{0}$ of sort o, and $\mathbf{1+}$ of sort $o \to o$. We define the *value* of a closed term M of sort o as the natural number saying how many times the constant $\mathbf{1+}$ appears in the β-normal form of M. Notice that each β-normalized closed term of sort o is of the form $\mathbf{1+}\ (\mathbf{1+}\ (\ldots(\mathbf{1+}\ \mathbf{0})\ldots))$. Of course the number of constants $\mathbf{1+}$ used in a term may change during β-reduction; we count it in the β-normal form of a term.

* The author holds a post-doctoral position supported by Warsaw Center of Mathematics and Computer Science. Work supported by the National Science Center (decision DEC-2012/07/D/ST6/02443).

[1] We use the name "sort" instead of "type" (except of the abstract) to avoid confusion with the types introduced later, used for describing terms more precisely.

M. Codish and E. Sumii (Eds.): FLOPS 2014, LNCS 8475, pp. 302–318, 2014.

It is not a problem to pack arbitrarily many natural numbers into a term, so that for each list (arbitrarily long tuple) of natural numbers we obtain a different term, even of a very simple sort. We however consider the opposite direction, that is extracting numbers from terms. We do not require anything about how a representation of a tuple can be created out of the numbers in the tuple. But what we require is that using λ-terms we can extract the numbers from the representation of the tuple. That is, while representing k-tuples in terms of sort α, we want to have closed terms $M_1, \dots, M_k$, all of the same sort $\alpha \to o$. Then the k-tuple *extracted* by $M_1, \dots, M_k$ from a closed term N (representing a k-tuple) of sort α is defined as the k-tuple of values of $M_1\ N, \dots, M_k\ N$. Our main result is described by the following theorem.

Theorem 1. *Let $M_1, \dots, M_k$ be closed terms of sort $\alpha \to o$, for $k > dim(\alpha)$. Let X be the set of all k-tuples which are extracted by $M_1, \dots, M_k$ from any closed term of sort α. Then $X \neq \mathbb{N}^k$. Moreover, there exist at most $dim(\alpha)$ indices $i \in \{1, \dots, k\}$ for which there exists a subset $X_i \subseteq X$ containing tuples with arbitrarily big numbers on the i-th coordinate, but such that all numbers on all other coordinates are bounded.*

In the last sentence of the theorem we say that the set X is, in some sense, really at most $dim(\alpha)$-dimensional. It follows that it is impossible to represent k-tuples in terms of sort α with $k > dim(\alpha)$ even when we allow some approximation of the numbers in tuples. The next theorem states a similar property.

Theorem 2. *Fix a sort α. We define an equivalence relation over closed terms of sort $\alpha \to o$: we have $M \sim M'$ when for each sequence $N_1, N_2, \dots$ of closed terms of sort α, the sequences of values of the terms $M\ N_1, M\ N_2, \dots$ and $M'\ N_1, M'\ N_2, \dots$ are either both bounded or both unbounded. Then this relation has at most $dim(\alpha)$ equivalence classes.*

Beside of the final result, we believe that the techniques used in the proofs are interesting on their own. First, we introduce a type system which describes, intuitively, whether a subterm adds something to the value of a term, or not. Second, we describe a closed term of any sort α by a tuple (of arity depending only on α) of natural numbers, which approximate all possible values which can be extracted from the term. This description is compositional: the tuple for MN depends only on the tuples for M and for N.

Related Work. Results in the spirit of this paper (but with significant differences) were an important part of the proof [2] that Collapsible Higher-Order Pushdown Systems generate more trees than Higher-Order Pushdown Systems without the collapse operation. However the appropriate lemmas of [2] were almost completely hidden in the appendix, and stated in the world of stacks of higher-order pushdown systems. Because we think that these results are of independent interest, we present them here, in a more natural variant.

The types defined in our paper resemble the intersection types used in [3]. However, comparing to [3], we additionally have a productive/nonproductive flag in our types.

One may wonder why we represent natural numbers using constants **1+** and **0**, instead of using the standard representation as terms of sort $(o \to o) \to o \to o$, where the representation $[k]$ of a number k is defined by $[0] = \lambda f.\lambda x.x$ and $[k+1] = \lambda f.\lambda x.f\ ([k]\ f\ x)$. Observe, however, that a number in the "standard" representation can be easily converted to a number in our representation: the term $[k]$ **1+** **0** has value k. Since in this paper we only talk about extracting numbers from terms (we never start from representations of numbers), all our results also hold for the standard representation. We believe that thanks to distinguishing the constants **0** and **1+** from other variables, the argumentation in the paper becomes more clear.

Schwichtenberg [4] and Statman [5] show that the functions over natural numbers representable in the simply-typed λ-calculus are precisely the "extended polynomials". Notice that our results does not follow from this characterization, since they describe only first-order functions (functions $\mathbb{N}^k \to \mathbb{N}$). Similarly, Zaionc [6] characterizes the class of functions over words which are represented by closed λ-terms (for appropriate representation of words in λ-calculus).

Structure of the Paper. In Section 2 we define some basic notions. In Section 3 we introduce a type system which has two roles. First, it allows us to determine which arguments of a term will be used (i.e. will not be ignored, as in $\lambda x.\mathbf{0}$). Second, the type of a subterm says whether this subterm is productive, that is whether it adds something to the value of the whole term. In Section 4 we introduce the Krivine machine, and we define its variant which beside of terms stores type judgements, and even derivation trees for them. This machine allows us to trace how a derivation tree changes during β-reductions. Next, in Section 5, to configurations of the Krivine machine we assign some numbers, which give a lower and an upper bound on the value of the term. To obtain them, we basically count in how many places in derivation trees for type judgements something "productive" happens. Finally, in Section 6 we conclude the proof of our main theorems, and in Section 7 we give some further remarks.

2 Preliminaries

The set of *sorts* is constructed from a unique basic sort o using a binary operation $\to$. Thus o is a sort and if α, β are sorts, so is $(\alpha \to \beta)$. The order of a sort is defined by: $ord(o) = 0$, and $ord(\alpha \to \beta) = \max(1 + ord(\alpha), ord(\beta))$.

A *signature* is a set of typed constants, that is symbols with associated sorts. In our paper we use a signature consisting of two constants: **0** of sort o, and **1+** of sort $o \to o$.

The set of *simply-typed λ-terms* is defined inductively as follows. A constant of sort α is a term of sort α. For each sort α there is a countable set of variables $x^\alpha, y^\alpha, \dots$ that are also terms of sort α. If M is a term of sort β and x^α a variable of sort α then $\lambda x^\alpha.M$ is a term of sort $\alpha \to \beta$. Finally, if M is of sort $\alpha \to \beta$ and N is of sort α then MN is a term of sort β. As usual, we identify λ-terms up to α-conversion. We often omit the sort annotation of variables, but please keep in mind that every variable is implicitly sorted. A term is called *closed* when it does not have free variables. For a term M of sort α we write $ord(M)$ for $ord(\alpha)$.

3 Type System

In this section we define types which will be used to describe our terms. These types differ from sorts in that on the left-hand side of $\to$, instead of a single type, we have a set of pairs (f, τ), where τ is a type, and f is a flag from $\{\mathsf{pr}, \mathsf{np}\}$ (where pr stands for productive, and np for nonproductive). The unique atomic type is denoted $\mathbf{r}$. More precisely, for each sort α we define the set $\mathcal{T}^\alpha$ of types of sort α as follows:

$$\mathcal{T}^o = \{\mathbf{r}\}, \qquad \mathcal{T}^{\alpha\to\beta} = \mathcal{P}(\{\mathsf{pr}, \mathsf{np}\} \times \mathcal{T}^\alpha) \times \mathcal{T}^\beta,$$

where $\mathcal{P}$ denotes the powerset. A type $(T, \tau) \in \mathcal{T}^{\alpha\to\beta}$ is denoted as $\bigwedge T \to \tau$, or $\bigwedge_{i\in I}(f_i, \tau_i) \to \tau$ when $T = \{(f_i, \tau_i) \mid i \in I\}$. Moreover, to our terms we will not only assign a type τ, but also a flag $f \in \{\mathsf{pr}, \mathsf{np}\}$ (which together form a pair (f, τ)).

Intuitively, a term has type $\bigwedge T \to \tau$ when it can return τ, while taking an argument for which we can derive all pairs (of a flag and a type) from T. And, we assign the flag pr (productive), when this term (while being a subterm of a term of sort o) increases the value. To be more precise, a term is productive in two cases. First, when it uses the constant $\mathbf{1+}$. Notice however that this $\mathbf{1+}$ has to be really used: there exist terms which syntactically contain $\mathbf{1+}$, but the result of this $\mathbf{1+}$ is then ignored, like in $(\lambda x.\mathbf{0})\mathbf{1+}$. Second, a term which takes a productive argument and uses it at least twice is also productive.

A *type judgement* is of the form $\Gamma \vdash M : (f, \tau)$, where we require that the type τ and the term M are of the same sort. The *type environment* Γ is a set of bindings of variables of the form $x^\alpha : (f, \tau)$, where $\tau \in \mathcal{T}^\alpha$. In Γ we may have multiple bindings for the same variable. By $dom(\Gamma)$ we denote the set of variables x which are binded by Γ, and by $\Gamma{\restriction_{\mathsf{pr}}}$ we denote the set of those binding from Γ which use flag pr.

The type system consists of the following rules:

$$\emptyset \vdash \mathbf{0} : (\mathsf{np}, \mathbf{r}) \qquad \emptyset \vdash \mathbf{1+} : (\mathsf{pr}, (f, \mathbf{r}) \to \mathbf{r}) \qquad x : (f, \tau) \vdash x : (\mathsf{np}, \tau)$$

$$\frac{\Gamma \cup \{x : (f_i, \tau_i) \mid i \in I\} \vdash M : (f, \tau) \qquad x \notin dom(\Gamma)}{\Gamma \vdash \lambda x.M : (f, \bigwedge_{i\in I}(f_i, \tau_i) \to \tau)}\ (\lambda)$$

$$\frac{\Gamma \vdash M : (f', \bigwedge_{i\in I}(f_i^\bullet, \tau_i) \to \tau) \qquad \Gamma_i \vdash N : (f_i^\circ, \tau_i) \text{ for each } i \in I}{\Gamma \cup \bigcup_{i\in I}\Gamma_i \vdash MN : (f, \tau)}\ (@)$$

where in the (@) rule we assume that

- each pair $(f_i^\bullet, \tau_i)$ is different (where $i \in I$), and
- for each $i \in I$, $f_i^\bullet = \mathsf{pr}$ if and only if $f_i^\circ = \mathsf{pr}$ or $\Gamma_i\restriction_{\mathsf{pr}} \neq \emptyset$, and
- $f = \mathsf{pr}$ if and only if $f' = \mathsf{pr}$, or $f_i^\circ = \mathsf{pr}$ for some $i \in I$, or $|\Gamma\restriction_{\mathsf{pr}}| + \sum_{i\in I} |\Gamma_i\restriction_{\mathsf{pr}}| > |(\Gamma \cup \bigcup_{i\in I} \Gamma_i)\restriction_{\mathsf{pr}}|$.

Let us explain the conditions of the (@) rule. The second condition says that when M requires a "productive" argument, either we can apply an N which is itself productive, or we can apply a nonproductive N which uses a productive variable; after substituting something for the variable N will become productive. The third condition says that MN is productive if M is productive, or if N is productive, or if some productive free variable is duplicated.

Notice that strengthening of type environment is disallowed (i.e., $\Gamma \vdash M : (f,\tau)$ does not necessarily imply $\Gamma, x : (g,\sigma) \vdash M : (f,\tau)$), but contraction is allowed (i.e., $\Gamma, x : (g,\sigma), x : (g,\sigma) \vdash M : (f,\tau)$ implies $\Gamma, x : (g,\sigma) \vdash M : (f,\tau)$, since a type environment is a set of type bindings); such contractions will be counted by *duplication factors* defined below.

A *derivation tree* is defined as usual: it is a tree labeled by type judgements, such that each node together with its children fit to one of the rules of the type system. Consider a node of a derivation tree in which the (@) rule is used, with type environments Γ and Γ_i for $i \in I$. For $a \in \mathbb{N}$, the *order-a duplication factor* in such a node is defined as

$$|\{(x : (\mathsf{pr},\sigma)) \in \Gamma \mid ord(x) = a\}| + \sum_{i\in I} |\{(x : (\mathsf{pr},\sigma)) \in \Gamma_i \mid ord(x) = a\}| - \\ - |\{(x : (\mathsf{pr},\sigma)) \in \Gamma \cup \bigcup_{i\in I} \Gamma_i \mid ord(x) = a\}|.$$

In other words, this is equal to the number of productive type bindings for variables of order a together in all the type environments Γ, $(\Gamma_i)_{i\in I}$, minus the number of such type bindings in their union.

Example 3. Below we give two example derivation trees. In the first tree, we denote by b_y the binding $y : (\mathsf{pr}, (\mathsf{pr}, \mathbf{r}) \to \mathbf{r})$, and by b_z the binding $z : (\mathsf{pr}, \mathbf{r})$.

$$\dfrac{b_y \vdash y : (\mathsf{np}, (\mathsf{pr},\mathbf{r}) \to \mathbf{r}) \qquad \dfrac{b_y \vdash y : (\mathsf{np}, (\mathsf{pr},\mathbf{r}) \to \mathbf{r}) \qquad b_z \vdash z : (\mathsf{np}, \mathbf{r})}{b_z,\ b_y \vdash y\ z : (\mathsf{np}, \mathbf{r})}\ (@)}{b_z,\ b_y \vdash y\ (y\ z) : (\mathsf{pr}, \mathbf{r})}\ (@)$$

$$\dfrac{\dfrac{\vdash 1{+} : (\mathsf{pr}, (\mathsf{pr},\mathbf{r}) \to \mathbf{r}) \qquad \dfrac{\vdash 1{+} : (\mathsf{pr}, (\mathsf{pr},\mathbf{r}) \to \mathbf{r}) \qquad x : (\mathsf{pr},\mathbf{r}) \vdash x : (\mathsf{np}, \mathbf{r})}{x : (\mathsf{pr},\mathbf{r}) \vdash 1{+}\ x : (\mathsf{pr}, \mathbf{r})}\ (@)}{x : (\mathsf{pr},\mathbf{r}) \vdash 1{+}\ (1{+}\ x) : (\mathsf{pr}, \mathbf{r})}\ (@)}{\vdash \lambda x.1{+}\ (1{+}\ x) : (\mathsf{pr}, (\mathsf{pr},\mathbf{r}) \to \mathbf{r})}\ (\lambda)$$

The order-1 duplication factor of the root node of the first tree is 1, because the binding for y is used in both subtrees (and y is of order 1); the other nodes have duplication factors 0.

It is possible to derive six other type judgements containing the term $y\ (y\ z)$:

$$y : (\mathsf{np}, (\mathsf{pr}, \mathbf{r}) \to \mathbf{r}),\ z : (\mathsf{pr}, \mathbf{r}) \vdash y\ (y\ z) : (\mathsf{np}, \mathbf{r}),$$
$$y : (\mathsf{pr}, (\mathsf{pr}, \mathbf{r}) \to \mathbf{r}),\ y : (\mathsf{np}, (\mathsf{pr}, \mathbf{r}) \to \mathbf{r}),\ z : (\mathsf{pr}, \mathbf{r}) \vdash y\ (y\ z) : (\mathsf{np}, \mathbf{r}),$$
$$y : (\mathsf{pr}, (\mathsf{pr}, \mathbf{r}) \to \mathbf{r}),\ y : (\mathsf{pr}, (\mathsf{np}, \mathbf{r}) \to \mathbf{r}),\ z : (\mathsf{np}, \mathbf{r}) \vdash y\ (y\ z) : (\mathsf{np}, \mathbf{r}),$$
$$y : (\mathsf{pr}, (\mathsf{np}, \mathbf{r}) \to \mathbf{r}),\ y : (\mathsf{np}, (\mathsf{np}, \mathbf{r}) \to \mathbf{r}),\ z : (\mathsf{np}, \mathbf{r}) \vdash y\ (y\ z) : (\mathsf{np}, \mathbf{r}),$$
$$y : (\mathsf{np}, (\mathsf{pr}, \mathbf{r}) \to \mathbf{r}),\ y : (\mathsf{pr}, (\mathsf{np}, \mathbf{r}) \to \mathbf{r}),\ z : (\mathsf{np}, \mathbf{r}) \vdash y\ (y\ z) : (\mathsf{np}, \mathbf{r}),$$
$$y : (\mathsf{np}, (\mathsf{np}, \mathbf{r}) \to \mathbf{r}),\ z : (\mathsf{np}, \mathbf{r}) \vdash y\ (y\ z) : (\mathsf{np}, \mathbf{r}).$$

4 Krivine Machine

The Krivine machine [7] is an abstract machine that computes the weak head normal form of a λ-term, using explicit substitutions, called environments. Two properties of the Krivine machine are important for us. First, the Krivine machine performs β-reductions starting from the head redex; this redex is always a closed term. Second, the Krivine machine isolates closed subterms of a term using closures; we will be deriving types for each closure separately. We could perform β-reductions in this order and identify closed subterms also without the Krivine machine, but we believe that using it simplifies the presentation.

An *environment* is a function mapping some variables into closures. A *closure* is a pair $C = (M, \rho)$, where M is a term and ρ is an environment. We use the notation $\mathit{term}(C) := M$ and $\mathit{env}(C) := \rho$. A *configuration* of the Krivine machine is a pair (C, S), where C is a closure and S is a *stack*, which is a sequence of closures (with the topmost element on the left).

We require that in a closure (M, ρ), the environment is defined for every free variable of M; moreover $\mathit{term}(\rho(x))$ has to be of the same sort as x. We also require that in a configuration (C, S), when $\mathit{term}(C)$ is of sort $\alpha_1 \to \cdots \to \alpha_k \to o$, then the stack S has k elements $C_1, \dots, C_k$, where $\mathit{term}(C_i)$ is of sort α_i, for each i. Let us also emphasize that we only consider "finite" closures, environments, configurations: an environment binds only finitely many variables, and after going repeatedly to a closure in the environment of a closure we will find an empty environment after finitely many steps.

The rules of the Krivine machine are as follows:

$$((\lambda x.M, \rho), CS) \xrightarrow{\lambda} ((M, \rho[x \mapsto C]), S),$$
$$((MN, \rho), S) \xrightarrow{@} ((M, \rho), (N, \rho)S),$$
$$((x, \rho), S) \xrightarrow{Var} (\rho(x), S),$$
$$((\mathbf{1+}, \rho), C) \xrightarrow{\mathbf{1+}} (C, \varepsilon).$$

Intuitively, a closure $C = (M, \rho)$ denotes the closed λ-term $[\![C]\!]$ which is obtained from M by substituting for every its free variable x the λ-term $[\![\rho(x)]\!]$. Also a configuration (C, S) denotes a closed λ-term $[\![C, S]\!]$ of sort o; this is the application $[\![C]\!][\![C_1]\!] \dots [\![C_k]\!]$, where $S = C_1 \dots C_k$. It is not difficult to see that

- when $(C,S) \xrightarrow{@} (C',S')$ or $(C,S) \xrightarrow{Var} (C',S')$, then $[\![C,S]\!] = [\![C',S']\!]$;
- when $(C,S) \xrightarrow{\lambda} (C',S')$, then $[\![C,S]\!]$ β-reduces to $[\![C',S']\!]$ (the head redex is eliminated);
- when $(C,S) \xrightarrow{1+} (C',S')$, then $[\![C,S]\!] = (\mathbf{1+}\ [\![C',S']\!])$ (in particular the value of the new term is smaller by one than that of the old term).

From each configuration (C,S), as long as $term(C) \neq \mathbf{0}$, a (unique) step can be performed. Next, observe that each computation terminates after finite time. Indeed, the **1+** rule changes the denoted term into one with smaller value (and the value is not changed by the other rules). The λ rule performs β-reduction (and the term is not changed by the @ and *Var* rules), so as well it can be applied only finitely many times. The *Var* rule removes one closure from the configuration; the total number of closures (computed recursively) in the configuration decreases. The @ rule does not change this number, but increases the size of the stack, which is necessarily bounded by the number of closures. It follows that to compute the value of the term $[\![C,S]\!]$, it is enough to start the Krivine Machine from (C,S), and count how many times the **1+** rule was used.

In this paper we use an extension of the Krivine Machine, which also stores derivation trees. An *extended closure* is a triple (M, D, ρ), where M is a term of some sort α, and ρ is an environment (mapping variables to extended closures), and D is a partial function from $\{\mathsf{pr}, \mathsf{np}\} \times \mathcal{T}^\alpha$ to derivation trees. Beside of $term(C)$ and $env(C)$ we use the notation $der(C) := D$, as well as $tp(C) := dom(D)$. The root of the tree assigned by D to a pair $(f^\bullet, \tau)$ has to be labeled by $\Gamma \vdash M : (f^\circ, \tau)$ such that $f^\bullet = \mathsf{pr}$ if and only if $f^\circ = \mathsf{pr}$ or $\Gamma\restriction_{\mathsf{pr}} \neq \emptyset$. Moreover, for each binding $(x : (g,\sigma)) \in \Gamma$ we require that $(g,\sigma) \in tp(\rho(x))$; denote this condition by $(\star)$. The partial function D can be also seen as a set of derivation trees: the pair (f,τ) to which a tree is assigned is determined by its root (however this is not an arbitrary set: to each pair we assign at most one tree).

A *configuration* of the extended Krivine machine is a pair (C,S), where C is an extended closure such that $|tp(C)| = 1$, and $S = C_1 \dots C_k$ is a *stack* of extended closures. We require that, when $tp(C) = \{(f, \bigwedge T_1 \to \dots \to \bigwedge T_k \to \mathbf{r})\}$, it holds $T_i \subseteq tp(C_i)$ for each i; denote this condition by $(\star\star)$.

The rules of the extended Krivine machine are as follows:

- $((\lambda x.M, D, \rho), CS) \xrightarrow{\lambda} ((M, D', \rho[x \mapsto C]), S)$, where the only tree in D' is obtained from the only tree in D by cutting off the root;
- $((MN, D, \rho), S) \xrightarrow{@} ((M, D_M, \rho), (N, D_N, \rho)S)$, where D_M contains the subtree of the tree in D which derives a type for M, and D_N contains all other subtrees (rooted in children of the root) of the tree in D;
- $((x, D, \rho), S) \xrightarrow{Var} ((term(\rho(x)), der(\rho(x))\restriction_{dom(D)}, env(\rho(x))), S)$;
- $((\mathbf{1+}, D, \rho), (M, D', \rho')) \xrightarrow{1+} ((M, D'\restriction_{\{(f,\mathbf{r})\}}, \rho'), \varepsilon)$, when the only element of $dom(D)$ is $(\mathsf{pr}, (f,\mathbf{r}) \to \mathbf{r})$.

Let π be the projection from configurations of the extended machine to configurations of the standard one, which just drops the "*der*" component of every extended closure. Notice that when $(C, S) \to (C', S')$ in the extended machine, then $\pi(C, S) \to \pi(C', S')$ in the standard machine. Next, we observe that from each configuration, as long as the term in its main closure is not $\mathbf{0}$, we can perform a step (in particular, the result of the step satisfies all conditions of a configuration).

- In the case of $\lambda x.M$, the root of the derivation tree in D is labeled by $\Gamma \vdash \lambda x.M : (f, \bigwedge_{i \in I}(f_i, \tau_i) \to \tau)$. This tree begins by the (λ) rule, so $x \notin dom(\Gamma)$, and the only child of the root (which becomes the root of the new tree) is labeled by $\Gamma \cup \{x : (f_i, \tau_i) \mid i \in I\} \vdash M : (f, \tau)$. Notice that (due to conditions ($\star$) and ($\star\star$)) for each binding $(y : (g, \sigma)) \in \Gamma$ we have $(g, \sigma) \in tp(\rho(y)) = tp(\rho[x \mapsto C](y))$, and for each $i \in I$ we have $(f_i, \tau_i) \in tp(C) = tp(\rho[x \mapsto C](x))$, which gives condition ($\star$) for the new closure.
- In the application case, the derivation tree in D uses the (@) rule in the root. Thus one child of the root is labeled by $\Gamma \vdash M : (f', \bigwedge_{i \in I}(f_i^\bullet, \tau_i) \to \tau)$, and the other children by $\Gamma_i \vdash N : (f_i^\circ, \tau_i)$ for each $i \in I$, where $f_i^\bullet = \mathsf{pr}$ if and only if $f_i^\circ = \mathsf{pr}$ or $\Gamma_i{\restriction_{\mathsf{pr}}} \neq \emptyset$. It follows that $dom(D_N) = \{(f_i^\bullet, \tau_i) \mid i \in I\}$. Simultaneously $dom(D_M) = \{(f'^\bullet, \bigwedge_{i \in I}(f_i^\bullet, \tau_i) \to \tau)\}$ for some $f'^\bullet$, so condition ($\star\star$) holds for the new configuration. The definition of the (@) rule ensures that each pair $(f_i^\bullet, \tau_i)$ is different, so D_N is really a (partial) function. Condition ($\star$) for both the new closures is ensured by condition ($\star$) for the original closure, since the type environment in the root of the derivation tree in D is a superset of Γ and of each Γ_i.
- In the *Var* case, the root of the tree in D is labeled by $x : (f, \tau) \vdash x : (\mathsf{np}, \tau)$, where $dom(D) = \{(f, \tau)\}$. Thus condition ($\star$) for (x, D, ρ) ensures that $dom(D) \subseteq tp(\rho(x))$.
- In the **1+** case, the root of the tree in D is labeled by $\emptyset \vdash \mathbf{1+} : (\mathsf{pr}, (f, \mathbf{r}) \to \mathbf{r})$, so $dom(D)$ is as in the rule, and condition ($\star\star$) ensures that $(f, \mathbf{r}) \in dom(D')$.

Example 4. We give an example computation of the extended Krivine machine. In our closures we use fragments of the derivation trees given in Example 3. By $T_1, T_2, T_3, U_1, U_2, U_3, U_4$ we denote the subtrees of these trees, where:

- T_1 derives $y : (\mathsf{pr}, (\mathsf{pr}, \mathbf{r}) \to \mathbf{r}),\ z : (\mathsf{pr}, \mathbf{r}) \vdash y\ (y\ z) : (\mathsf{pr}, \mathbf{r})$,
- T_2 derives $y : (\mathsf{pr}, (\mathsf{pr}, \mathbf{r}) \to \mathbf{r}) \vdash y : (\mathsf{np}, (\mathsf{pr}, \mathbf{r}) \to \mathbf{r})$,
- T_3 derives $y : (\mathsf{pr}, (\mathsf{pr}, \mathbf{r}) \to \mathbf{r}),\ z : (\mathsf{pr}, \mathbf{r}) \vdash y\ z : (\mathsf{np}, \mathbf{r})$,
- U_1 derives $\vdash \lambda x.\mathbf{1+}\ (\mathbf{1+}\ x) : (\mathsf{pr}, (\mathsf{pr}, \mathbf{r}) \to \mathbf{r})$,
- U_2 derives $x : (\mathsf{pr}, \mathbf{r}) \vdash \mathbf{1+}\ (\mathbf{1+}\ x) : (\mathsf{pr}, \mathbf{r})$,
- U_3 derives $\vdash \mathbf{1+} : (\mathsf{pr}, (\mathsf{pr}, \mathbf{r}) \to \mathbf{r})$,
- U_4 derives $x : (\mathsf{pr}, \mathbf{r}) \vdash \mathbf{1+}\ x : (\mathsf{pr}, \mathbf{r})$.

Additionally, we use the following derivation tree, which we denote V_1.

$$\frac{\vdash \mathbf{1+} : (\mathsf{pr}, (\mathsf{np}, \mathbf{r}) \to \mathbf{r}) \qquad \vdash \mathbf{0} : (\mathsf{np}, \mathbf{r})}{\vdash \mathbf{1+}\ \mathbf{0} : (\mathsf{pr}, \mathbf{r})}\ (@)$$

To shorten the notation, we denote:

$$\rho := [y \mapsto (\lambda x.\mathbf{1+}\ (\mathbf{1+}\ x), \{U_1\}, \emptyset),\ z \mapsto (\mathbf{1+}\ \mathbf{0}, \{V_1\}, \emptyset)],$$
$$\eta := [x \mapsto (y\ z, \{T_3\}, \rho)].$$

The extended Krivine machine can transition as follows:

$$((y\ (y\ z), \{T_1\}, \rho), \varepsilon) \xrightarrow{@} ((y, \{T_2\}, \rho), (y\ z, \{T_3\}, \rho)) \xrightarrow{Var}$$
$$\xrightarrow{Var} ((\lambda x.\mathbf{1+}\ (\mathbf{1+}\ x), \{U_1\}, \emptyset), (y\ z, \{T_3\}, \rho)) \xrightarrow{\lambda} ((\mathbf{1+}\ (\mathbf{1+}\ x), \{U_2\}, \eta), \varepsilon) \xrightarrow{@}$$
$$\xrightarrow{@} ((\mathbf{1+}, \{U_3\}, \eta), (\mathbf{1+}\ x, \{U_4\}, \eta)) \xrightarrow{\mathbf{1+}} ((\mathbf{1+}\ x, \{U_4\}, \eta), \varepsilon) \xrightarrow{@} \dots$$

Next, we observe that we can really add some derivation trees to a configuration.

Lemma 5. *For each configuration (C, S) of the standard Krivine machine there exists a configuration (C', S') of the extended machine such that $\pi(C', S') = (C, S)$.*

Proof. We use induction on the length of the longest computation starting from the configuration (C, S) (this computation is unique and has finite length). We have five cases depending on the form of the term in the main closure. Before starting the case analysis, we observe that for each closure B there exists an extended closure B' such that $\pi(B') = B$. To construct such B' we can add the partial function with empty domain everywhere inside B. (This cannot be applied for a configuration: the *tp* of the main closure of a configuration is required to have size 1).

Consider first a configuration of the form $((\mathbf{0}, \rho_s), \varepsilon)$. Then to the main closure we can add the derivation tree using the rule $\emptyset \vdash \mathbf{0} : (\mathsf{np}, \mathbf{r})$, and everywhere inside ρ_s we can add the partial function with empty domain.

Next, consider a configuration of the form $((\lambda x.M, \rho_s), C_s S_s)$. Its successor is $((M, \rho_s[x \mapsto C_s]), S_s)$, which by the induction assumption can be extended to a configuration $((M, D', \rho[x \mapsto C]), S)$ of the extended machine. Potentially $\rho_s(x)$ can be defined. In such situation we can assume that $\rho(x)$ is defined and $\pi(\rho(x)) = \rho_s(x)$; otherwise we assume that $\rho(x)$ is undefined. Notice that these assumptions do not change $\rho[x \mapsto C]$, where $\rho(x)$ is overwritten. The label of the root of the tree in D' can be denoted as $\Gamma \cup \{x : (f_i, \tau_i) \mid i \in I\} \vdash M : (f, \tau)$, where $x \notin dom(\Gamma)$. We can apply the (λ) rule, and obtain a tree rooted by $\Gamma \vdash \lambda x.M : (f, \bigwedge_{i \in I}(f_i, \tau_i) \to \tau)$. The thesis is satisfied by the configuration $((\lambda x.M, D, \rho), CS)$, where D contains this new tree. Notice that conditions $(\star)$ and $(\star\star)$ are satisfied for this configuration, since they were satisfied for $((M, D', \rho[x \mapsto C]), S)$.

Before considering the next case, notice that any two extended closures C_1, C_2 such that $\pi(C_1) = \pi(C_2)$ can be merged into one extended closure C such that $\pi(C) = \pi(C_1)$ and $tp(C) = tp(C_1) \cup tp(C_2)$. To do that, by induction we create an environment ρ, which maps each variable $x \in dom(env(C_1))$ into the extended closure obtained by merging $env(C_1)(x)$ and $env(C_2)(x)$. We also create D which is equal to $der(C_1)$ on $tp(C_1)$, and is equal to $der(C_2)$ on $tp(C_2) \setminus tp(C_1)$. As C we take $(term(C_1), D, \rho)$; notice that condition $(\star)$ remains satisfied.

Next, consider a configuration of the form $((MN, \rho_s), S_s)$. Its successor is $((M, \rho_s), (N, \rho_s)S_s)$, which by the induction assumption can be extended to a configuration $((M, D_M, \rho_M), (N, D_N, \rho_N)S)$ of the extended machine. Let ρ be obtained by merging ρ_M and ρ_N, as described in the previous paragraph. Denote $dom(D_M)$ as $\{(f'^\bullet, \bigwedge_{i\in I}(f_i^\bullet, \tau_i) \to \tau)\}$, where each pair $(f_i^\bullet, \tau_i)$ is different. Then $(f_i^\bullet, \tau_i) \in dom(D_N)$ for each $i \in I$, by condition $(\star\star)$. Let $\Gamma \vdash M : (f', \bigwedge_{i\in I}(f_i^\bullet, \tau_i) \to \tau)$ be the label of the root of the tree in D_M, and let $\Gamma_i \vdash N : (f_i^\circ, \tau_i)$ be the label of the root of $D_N(f_i^\bullet, \tau_i)$ for each i; recall that $f_i^\bullet = \mathsf{pr}$ if and only if $f_i^\circ = \mathsf{pr}$ or $\Gamma_i\restriction_{\mathsf{pr}} \neq \emptyset$. We can apply the (@) rule to these roots, and obtain a derivation tree with root labeled by $\Gamma \cup \bigcup_{i\in I}\Gamma_i \vdash MN : (f, \tau)$ (for some f). Then $((MN, D, \rho), S)$, where D contains this new tree, is a correct configuration and satisfies the thesis.

Next, consider a configuration $((x, \rho_s), S_s)$. Its successor is $(\rho_s(x), S_s)$, which by the induction assumption can be extended to a configuration (C, S) of the extended machine. Let $\{(f, \tau)\} := tp(C)$. We take D containing the derivation $x : (f, \tau) \vdash x : (\mathsf{np}, \tau)$, and we take ρ mapping x to C, and each other variable $y \in dom(\rho_s)$ into any extended closure E_y such that $\pi(E_y) = \rho_s(y)$. Then $((x, D, \rho), S)$ is a configuration and satisfies the thesis.

Finally, consider a configuration of the form $((\mathbf{1+}, \rho_s), C_s)$. Its successor is (C_s, ε), which by the induction assumption can be extended to a configuration (C, ε) of the extended machine. Let $\{(f, \mathbf{r})\} := tp(C)$. We take D containing the derivation $\emptyset \vdash \mathbf{1+} : (\mathsf{pr}, (f, \mathbf{r}) \to \mathbf{r})$, and we take ρ mapping each variable $x \in dom(\rho_s)$ into any extended closure E_x such that $\pi(E_x) = \rho_s(x)$. Then $((\mathbf{1+}, D, \rho), C)$ is a configuration and satisfies the thesis. □

5 Assigning Values to Configurations

To a configuration of a Krivine machine we assign two numbers, *low* and *high*, which estimate (from below and from above, respectively) the value of the term represented by the configuration.

Let C be an extended closure, and let $(f, \tau) \in tp(C)$. By $inc_0(C, f, \tau)$ we denote the number of leaves of $der(C)(f, \tau)$ using the $\mathbf{1+}$ rule, and by $inc_a(C, f, \tau)$ for $a > 0$ we denote the sum of order-$(a-1)$ duplication factors of all (@) nodes of $der(C)(f, \tau)$.

We define $low(C, f, \tau)$, and $high_a(C, f, \tau)$, and $rec_a(C, f, \tau)$, and $ext_a(C, f, \tau)$ for each $a \in \mathbb{N}$ by induction on the structure of C (where *rec* stands for "recursive" and *ext* for "external"). Let Γ be the type environment used in the root of $der(C)(f, \tau)$. We take

$$low(C, f, \tau) := \sum_{a\in\mathbb{N}} inc_a(C, f, \tau) + \sum_{(x:(g,\sigma))\in\Gamma} low(env(C)(x), g, \sigma),$$

$$rec_a(C, f, \tau) := inc_a(C, f, \tau) + \sum_{(x:(g,\sigma))\in\Gamma} ext_a(env(C)(x), g, \sigma),$$

$$high_a(C, f, \tau) := (rec_a(C, f, \tau) + 1) \cdot 2^{high_{a+1}(C,f,\tau)} - 1,$$
$$high_a(C, f, \tau) := 0 \qquad \text{if } rec_b(C, f, \tau) = 0 \text{ for all } b \geq a,$$
$$ext_a(C, f, \tau) := \begin{cases} 0 & \text{if } a > ord(term(C)), \\ high_a(C, f, \tau) & \text{if } a = ord(term(C)), \\ rec_a(C, f, \tau) & \text{if } a < ord(term(C)). \end{cases}$$

For a configuration (C_0, S) with $S = C_1 \dots C_k$ and $tp(C_0) = \{(f, \bigwedge T_1 \to \dots \to \bigwedge T_k \to \mathbf{r})\}$ we define, denoting $T_0 := tp(C_0)$:

$$low(C_0, S) := \sum_{i=0}^{k} \sum_{(g,\sigma) \in T_i} low(C_i, g, \sigma),$$

$$rec_a(C_0, S) := \sum_{i=0}^{k} \sum_{(g,\sigma) \in T_i} ext_a(C_i, g, \sigma),$$

$$high_a(C_0, S) := (rec_a(C_0, S) + 1) \cdot 2^{high_{a+1}(C_0,S)} - 1,$$
$$high_a(C_0, S) := 0 \qquad \text{if } rec_b(C_0, S) = 0 \text{ for all } b \geq a,$$
$$high(C_0, S) := high_0(C_0, S).$$

Example 6. We will compute these numbers for the first configuration from Example 4. Denoting

$$C_2 = (\lambda x.\mathbf{1+}\ (\mathbf{1+}\ x), \{U_1\}, \emptyset), \qquad C_3 = (\mathbf{1+}\ \mathbf{0}, \{V_1\}, \emptyset),$$

$$C_1 = (y\ (y\ z), \{T_1\}, [y \mapsto C_2,\ z \mapsto C_3]),$$

this configuration is (C_1, ε). It denotes the term

$$(\lambda x.\mathbf{1+}\ (\mathbf{1+}\ x))\ ((\lambda x.\mathbf{1+}\ (\mathbf{1+}\ x))\ (\mathbf{1+}\ \mathbf{0})),$$

which has value 5. It holds $tp(C_1) = tp(C_3) = \{(\mathsf{pr}, \mathbf{r})\}$ and $tp(C_2) = \{(\mathsf{pr}, \tau)\}$, where $\tau = ((\mathsf{pr}, \mathbf{r}) \to \mathbf{r})$. Because we have two **1+** nodes in U_1, and one in V_1, it holds $inc_0(C_2, \mathsf{pr}, \tau) = 2$ and $inc_0(C_3, \mathsf{pr}, \mathbf{r}) = 1$. The order-1 duplication factor in the root of T_1 causes that $inc_2(C_1, \mathsf{pr}, \mathbf{r}) = 1$. All other $inc_i(\cdot, \cdot, \cdot)$ equal 0. It follows that

$$low(C_2, \mathsf{pr}, \tau) = ext_0(C_2, \mathsf{pr}, \tau) = high_0(C_2, \mathsf{pr}, \tau) = rec_0(C_2, \mathsf{pr}, \tau) = 2,$$
$$low(C_3, \mathsf{pr}, \mathbf{r}) = ext_0(C_3, \mathsf{pr}, \mathbf{r}) = high_0(C_3, \mathsf{pr}, \mathbf{r}) = rec_0(C_3, \mathsf{pr}, \mathbf{r}) = 1,$$
$$low(C_1, \mathsf{pr}, \mathbf{r}) = low(C_2, \mathsf{pr}, \tau) + low(C_3, \mathsf{pr}, \mathbf{r}) + inc_2(C_1, \mathsf{pr}, \mathbf{r}) = 4,$$
$$rec_0(C_1, \mathsf{pr}, \mathbf{r}) = 3, \qquad high_2(C_1, \mathsf{pr}, \mathbf{r}) = rec_2(C_1, \mathsf{pr}, \mathbf{r}) = 1,$$
$$high_1(C_1, \mathsf{pr}, \mathbf{r}) = (0 + 1) \cdot 2^1 - 1 = 1,$$
$$ext_0(C_1, \mathsf{pr}, \mathbf{r}) = high_0(C_1, \mathsf{pr}, \mathbf{r}) = (3 + 1) \cdot 2^1 - 1 = 7,$$
$$low(C, \varepsilon) = 4, \qquad high(C, \varepsilon) = 7.$$

In the second configuration of the computation we do not have any duplication factor, and we count five **1+** nodes. Notice that both C_2 and C_3 appear in two environments, but C_3 is not used in the first of them (more precisely, no binding for z is appears in the type environment of T_2), so the **1+** node in C_3 is counted only once. Thus both *low* and *high* of this configuration are 5, which is equal to its value.

Let us explain the intuitions behind the definitions of *low* and *high*. First, concentrate on *low*. It counts the number of **1+** leaves of our derivation trees. Our type system ensures that each such **1+** will be used (and thus it will add 1 to the value of the term). It also counts duplication factors of (@) nodes of derivation trees. When a duplication factor in some node is 1 (and similarly for any positive number), some "productive" subtree of the (@) node will be used twice. And such a subtree increases the value of the term at least by one—it either contains some **1+**, or some other duplication, which will be now performed twice instead of once.

In the formula for *high*, which is going to be an upper bound for the value, we have to overapproximate. For that reason, it is not enough to look on the sum of duplication factors; the orders on which they appear start to play a role. Consider the highest k for which the order-k duplication factor is positive in some (@) node, and consider an innermost node such that it is positive; say, it is equal to 1. Inside, we only have duplication factors of smaller order, and some **1+** nodes. When the application described by the (@) node is performed, they will be replicated twice. Similarly, the next (@) node also can multiply their number by two, and so on. Next, analogous analysis for order-$(k-1)$ duplication factors (whose number is already increased by order-k duplication factors) shows that each of them can multiply by two the number of duplication factors of order smaller than $k-1$ (and of **1+** nodes), and so on. This justifies on the intuitive level the exponential character of the formula[2] for *high*, but in fact this analysis cannot be formalized (in some sense it is incorrect). The problem is that the innermost node with positive duplication factor for the highest order does not necessarily denote a closed term. So a positive duplication factor not only implies that the subterms will be replicated, but also the free variables will be used more times (and we do not know how "big" terms will be substituted there). Thus it is important in our correctness proof that we reduce only such redexes $(\lambda x.M)N$ in which N is closed; this is always the case for the head redex, which is reduced by the Krivine machine.

However in the formula we do not make just one tower of exponentials at the end, but we compute some exponentials already for some inner closures. This is essential for the proof of correctness, since otherwise Lemma 9 would be false (although this modification makes the *high* value even smaller). The idea behind that is as follows. When we have a closed term M, its subterm of order $a \geq ord(M)$ cannot be duplicated by anything outside M; only the whole M can be duplicated (or subterms of M which are of order smaller order than M). Oppositely, a subterm of order $a < ord(M)$ can be duplicated by things from

[2] One can observe that the order-0 duplication factor always equals 0 (an order-0 term can be used only once). Thus in $high_0$ we could multiply rec_0 directly by 2^{high_2}. However this observation would only complicate the proof.

outside of M, because we can pass this subterm as an argument to an argument of M. Thus basically inc_a is cumulated recursively along closures; however for a closure of some order k we can forget about its duplication factors in inc_a for $a > k$—they will only be applied to inc_k contained inside this closure, so we can predict their result in $high_k$.

The next two propositions state that *low* and *high* extend quantitatively the information in the pr/np flag: 0 corresponds to np, and positive numbers to pr.

Proposition 7. *Let C be a closure, and let $(\mathsf{np}, \tau) \in tp(C)$. Then it holds $rec_a(C, \mathsf{np}, \tau) = 0$ for each $a \in \mathbb{N}$.*

Proof. The root of $der(C)(\mathsf{np}, \tau)$ is labeled by a type judgement $\Gamma \vdash term(C) : (\mathsf{np}, \tau)$, where $\Gamma\restriction_{\mathsf{pr}} = \emptyset$. It is easy to see by induction on the tree structure, that a derivation tree ending with the np flag has duplication factors of each (@) node (and each order) equal to zero, as well as it does not contain **1+** leaves. It follows that $inc_a(C, \mathsf{np}, \tau) = 0$. Because $\Gamma\restriction_{\mathsf{pr}} = \emptyset$, the added rec_a components are also equal to 0, by induction on the structure of the closure. □

Proposition 8. *Let C be a closure, and let $(\mathsf{pr}, \tau) \in tp(C)$. Then it holds $low(C, \mathsf{pr}, \tau) > 0$.*

Proof. When $der(C)(\mathsf{pr}, \tau)$ is labeled by a type judgement $\Gamma \vdash term(C) : (f, \tau)$, we have one of two cases. One possibility is that $f = \mathsf{pr}$. Then it is easy to see by induction on the tree structure, that a derivation tree ending with the pr flag either has a **1+** leaf, or an (@) node with a positive duplication factor for some order. Otherwise we have $\Gamma\restriction_{\mathsf{pr}} \neq \emptyset$. Then by induction on the structure of the closure we obtain that some of the added *low* components (for closures in the environment) is positive. □

Below we have the key lemma about the *low* and *high* numbers.

Lemma 9. *Let (C, S) be a configuration of the extended Krivine machine, which evolves to (C', S') in one step. If this was the* **1+** *step, we have $low(C, S) \leq 1 + low(C', S')$ and $high(C, S) \geq 1 + high(C', S')$; otherwise we have $low(C, S) \leq low(C', S')$ and $high(C, S) \geq high(C', S')$.*

Proof (sketch). The proof consists of tedious but straightforward calculations. We have four rules of the Krivine machine, which we have to analyze. We will see that only in the application rule we can have inequalities; for the other rules we have equalities. In all cases only the "front" of the configuration changes. In *low* and *high* for the old configuration we include some *low* and *high* of closures in the environment or on the stack, for some pairs (g, σ). We see that for the new configuration we include exactly the same closures with the same (g, σ) pairs. Thus we have to locally analyze what changes only near the "front" of the configuration.

For the **1+** rule this is immediate. We remove a closure $(\mathbf{1+}, D, \rho)$, where the only tree in D uses the rule $\emptyset \vdash \mathbf{1+} : (\mathsf{pr}, (f, \mathbf{r}) \to \mathbf{r})$. Since inc_0 for this closure is 1, and inc_a for $a > 0$ is 0, during the step we subtract 1 from *low* and *high*.

Also the case of the *Var* rule is very easy. This time we remove a closure (x, D, ρ), where the only tree in D uses the rule $x : (f, \tau) \vdash x : (\mathsf{np}, \tau)$. This closure has inc_a equal to 0 for each a, so *low* and *high* do not change.

In the λ rule we only move one closure from the stack to the environment, so *low* and *high* do not change as well. It can happen that the order of $\lambda x.M$ and of M is different, and the definition of ext_a is sensitive for that. But, since all other terms in the stack are of order smaller than the order of M (and the order of $\lambda x.M$), this change of order does not influence the result: some exponents which were computed outside of the closure with $\lambda x.M$ will be now computed inside the closure with M.

Finally, consider the case $((MN, D, \rho), S) \xrightarrow{@} ((M, D_M, \rho), (N, D_N, \rho)S)$. For *low* the analysis is quite simple. The root of the tree in D had some duplication factor, which were added to *low* in the old configuration, but is not in the new one. But such duplication factor counts how many times a productive binding of a variable in the type environment in D is replicated in the type environments of the trees in D_M and D_N. In the new configuration, the *low* for these bindings will be added for each copy. Since by Proposition 8 these *low* are positive, they will compensate the duplication factor of the root, which is subtracted.

For *high* we have two phenomena. The first concerns the replication of variable bindings in the type environments. We do not have to care about nonproductive bindings, since by Proposition 7 their rec_a is 0. Let dp_a be the order-a duplication factor at the root of the tree in D. A productive binding for a variable of order a is replicated at most dp_a times (instead of once in D it appears at most $dp_a + 1$ times in D_M and D_N). Notice the shift of orders: in the old configuration we were adding dp_a to inc_{a+1}. Thus without it, $high_a$ decreases 2^{dp_a} times. On the other hand, a closure (from ρ) of order a adds something to rec_b only for $b \leq a$ (otherwise its ext_b is 0), and now this rec_b will be multiplied by (at most) $dp_a + 1$. Due to the inequality $2^{dp_a} \geq dp_a + 1$, we see that $high_a$ will not increase. In fact it decreases by at least dp_a, thanks to the $+1$ in the formula for $high_a$. Thus we can repeat the same argument for $a - 1$, and continue by induction for all $b \leq a$. The second phenomenon is that $ord(N)$ is smaller than $ord(M)$. This implies that previously we were first adding together some ext_a for elements of ρ, and then making a tower of exponents in the closure (MN, D, ρ), while now we are making the tower of exponents inside (N, D_N, ρ), separately for each pair $(g, \sigma) \in dom(D_N)$, and then we are summing the results. But this can only decrease the result, as described by the inequality

$$(a + b + 1) \cdot 2^{c+d} - 1 \geq (a + 1) \cdot 2^c - 1 + (b + 1) \cdot 2^d - 1.$$

We also notice that $ord(MN)$ can be smaller than $ord(M)$, but this does not influence the result, since all other elements on the stack are of smaller order (similarly to the λ case). □

Corollary 10. *Let (C, S) be a configuration of the extended Krivine machine. Then the value of the term $[\![C, S]\!]$ is not smaller than $low(C, S)$, and not greater than $high(C, S)$.*

Proof. Induction on the length of the maximal computation from (C, S). If this length is 0, we have $term(C) = \mathbf{0}$, and $tp(C) = \{(\mathsf{np}, \mathbf{r})\}$, and $der(C)(\mathsf{np}, \mathbf{r})$ consists of the rule $\emptyset \vdash \mathbf{0} : (\mathsf{np}, \mathbf{r})$, so $low(C, S) = 0 = high(C, S)$, and $[\![C, S]\!] = \mathbf{0}$ has value 0. Otherwise we use the induction assumption and Lemma 9.

Next, we state that if $low(C, S)$ is small, then also $high(C, S)$ is small, so $low(C, S)$ (and $high(C, S)$ as well) really approximates the value of $[\![C, S]\!]$.

Lemma 11. *For all $k, L \in \mathbb{N}$ there exists a number $H_{k,L}$ such that for each configuration (C, S) such that $low(C, S) \leq L$ and such that each variable appearing anywhere inside (C, S) (inside a term or an environment) is of order at most k, it holds $high(C, S) \leq H_{k,L}$.*

Proof. We define

$$H_{0,L} := (L + 1) \cdot 2^L - 1,$$
$$H_{a+1,L} := (L + 1) \cdot 2^{H_{a,L}} - 1 \qquad \text{for each } a \in \mathbb{N}.$$

Let $\#_{cl}(C, S)$ denote the number of closures everywhere (recursively) inside (C, S), and let $|S|$ denote the length of the stack. We prove the inequality by induction on $2 \cdot \#_{cl}(C, S) - |S|$.

Assume first that S and $env(C)$ are empty. Let $tp(C) = \{(f, \tau)\}$. Then $low(C, S) = low(C, f, \tau) = \sum_{a\in\mathbb{N}} inc_a(C, f, \tau)$, and $high(C, S) = high_0(C, f, \tau)$ with $rec_a(C, f, \tau) = inc_a(C, f, \tau) \leq low(C, S)$ for each $a \in \mathbb{N}$. Since each variable in $term(C)$ is of order at most k, for $a > k + 1$ (which gives $a - 1 > k$) the order-$(a-1)$ duplication factor of any (@) node in $der(C)(f, \tau)$ is zero, thus also $inc_a(C, f, \tau) = 0$. We see for $a \in \{0, 1, \dots, k\}$ that $high_a(C, f, \tau) \leq H_{k-a,L}$.

Next, assume that S is nonempty. Denote $((M, D_M, \rho_M), (N, D_N, \rho_N)S') := (C, S)$. W.l.o.g. we can assume that $dom(\rho_M) \cap dom(\rho_N) = \emptyset$; otherwise we can rename the variables in M, D_M, ρ_M so that they are different from the variables in $dom(\rho_N)$, and such renaming does not change the *low* and *high* values. Denote $\rho := \rho_M \cup \rho_N$. Notice that $((M, D_M, \rho), (N, D_N, \rho)S')$ is a configuration with the same *low* and *high* as (C, S). The tree in D_M has root's label of the form $\Gamma \vdash M : (f', \bigwedge_{i\in I}(f_i^\bullet, \tau_i) \to \tau)$, where each pair $(f_i^\bullet, \tau_i)$ is different. Moreover, for each $i \in I$, we have a derivation tree $D_N(f_i^\bullet, \tau_i)$ rooted by some $\Gamma_i \vdash N : (f_i^\circ, \tau_i)$ such that $f_i^\bullet = \mathsf{pr}$ if and only if $f_i^\circ = \mathsf{pr}$ or $\Gamma_i{\restriction_{\mathsf{pr}}} \neq \emptyset$. Thus we can apply the (@) rule to these trees, and obtain a tree rooted by $\Gamma \cup \bigcup_{i\in I} \Gamma_i \vdash MN : (f, \tau)$ for some f. Let $C' := (MN, D, \rho)$, where D contains this new tree. We notice that (C', S') is a configuration (satisfies conditions $(\star)$ and $(\star\star)$), and the machine can make a step from it to $((M, D_M, \rho), (N, D_N, \rho)S')$. Lemma 9 implies that $low(C', S') \leq low(C, S) \leq L$ and $high(C, S) \leq high(C', S')$. It holds $\#_{cl}(C', S') = \#_{cl}(C, S) - 1$, and $|S'| = |S| - 1$, and the maximal order of a variable in these two configurations is the same. The induction assumption for (C', S') tells us that $high(C', S') \leq H_{k,L}$.

Finally, assume that S is empty, but $env(C)$ is nonempty. Fix some variable $x \in dom(env(C))$, and denote $(M, D, \rho[x \to C_x]) := C$, where $x \notin dom(\rho)$. Let $\Gamma \cup \{x : (f_i, \tau_i) \mid i \in I\} \vdash M : (f, \tau)$ with $x \notin dom(\Gamma)$ be the label of the root of the tree in D. We can append the (λ) rule to this tree, and obtain a tree with root labeled by $\Gamma \vdash \lambda x.M : (f, \bigwedge_{i\in I}(f_i, \tau_i) \to \tau)$. Let $C' := (\lambda x.M, D', \rho)$, where D' contains this new tree. We notice that $(C', C_x S')$ is a configuration (satisfies ($\star$) and ($\star\star$)), and the machine can make a step from it to (C, S). Lemma 9 implies that $low(C', C_x S') \le low(C, S) \le L$ and $high(C, S) \le high(C', C_x S')$. Notice that $\#_{cl}(C', C_x S') = \#_{cl}(C, S)$, and $|S'| = |S| + 1$, and the maximal order of a variable in these two configurations is the same. The induction assumption for $(C', C_x S')$ tells us that $high(C', C_x S') \le H_{k,L}$. □

6 Representing Tuples

In this section conclude the proof of Theorems 1 and 2.

Proof (Theorem 2). We define $dim(\alpha) = |\mathcal{P}(\{\mathsf{pr}, \mathsf{np}\} \times \mathcal{T}^{\alpha\to o})|$. For a closed term M of sort $\alpha \to o$, let $types(M)$ be the set of pairs $(f, \bigwedge T \to \mathbf{r})$ such that we can derive $\emptyset \vdash nf(M) : (f, \bigwedge T \to \tau)$, where $nf(M)$ is the β-normal form of M. We will show that when $types(M) = types(M')$ then also $M \sim M'$; the thesis of the theorem will follow, since we have at most $dim(\alpha)$ possible sets $types(M)$.

Thus suppose $types(M) = types(M')$, and consider a sequence $N_1, N_2, \dots$ of terms of sort α, such that the sequence of values of $M\ N_1, M\ N_2, \dots$ is bounded. W.l.o.g. we can assume that M, M', and all N_i are in β-normal form (since the value of $M\ N_i$ and of $nf(M)\ nf(N_i)$ is exactly the same). For each $i \in \mathbb{N}$, there exists a correct configuration of the form $((M, D_i^M, \emptyset), (N_i, D_i^N, \emptyset))$, denote it (C_i, E_i) (we use Lemma 5 for $((M, \emptyset), (N_i, \emptyset))$). Let $\{(f_i, \bigwedge T_i \to \mathbf{r})\} := dom(D_i^M)$, and let $D_i^{M'}$ contain a derivation tree rooted by $\emptyset \vdash M' : (f_i, \bigwedge T_i \to \mathbf{r})$, which exists thanks to equality of $types$. Let $C_i' := (M', D_i^{M'}, \emptyset)$. Then (C_i', E_i) is a correct configuration as well. Since $low(C_i, E_i)$ is not greater than the value of $M\ N_i$ (Corollary 10), also $low(C_i, E_i)$ is bounded (when ranging over $i = 1, 2, \dots$). Next, we see that

$$
\begin{aligned}
&low(C_i', E_i) + low(C_i, f_i, \bigwedge T_i \to \mathbf{r}) = \\
&= low(C_i', f_i, \bigwedge T_i \to \mathbf{r}) + \sum_{(g,\sigma)\in T_i} low(E_i, g, \sigma) + low(C_i, f_i, \bigwedge T_i \to \mathbf{r}) = \\
&= low(C_i, E_i) + low(C_i', f_i, \bigwedge T_i \to \mathbf{r}).
\end{aligned}
$$

Since C_i, f_i, T_i, C_i' come from a finite set, we obtain that $low(C_i', E_i)$ is bounded as well (by some L). Notice that the maximal order of a variable appearing anywhere inside M' or some N_i is $ord(\alpha)$, because these terms are in β-normal form. Thus $high(C_i', E_i)$ is bounded by $H_{ord(\alpha),L}$ (Lemma 11). It follows that the sequence of values of $M'\ N_1, M'\ N_2, \dots$ is bounded by $H_{ord(\alpha),L}$ as well (Corollary 10). The opposite implication (from M' to M) is completely symmetric. □

Proof (Theorem 1). This is an immediate consequence of Theorem 2. Assume that for some i there exists a set X_i as in the statement of the theorem. This means that there is a sequence of terms $N_1, N_2, \dots$, such that the values of

$M_i\ N_1, M_i\ N_2, \ldots$ are unbounded, but the values of $M_j\ N_1, M_j\ N_2, \ldots$ are bounded for each $j \neq i$. Then, by definition $M_i \not\sim M_j$ for each $j \neq i$. Since we only have $dim(\alpha)$ equivalence classes of $\sim$, we can have at most $dim(\alpha)$ such indices i. In particular it holds $X \neq \mathbb{N}^k$. □

7 Future Work

One can consider λ-calculus enriched by the Y combinator, describing recursion. Then, instead of a finite β-normal form of a term, we may obtain an infinite limit tree, called the Böhm tree. An algorithmic question arises: given a λY-term, how to calculate its "value", that is the "value" of its Böhm tree. In particular, can we decide whether this value is finite? (It turns out that when the value is finite, one can compute it precisely, using standard techniques.) The question starts to become interesting when we can have arbitrary constants of order 0 and 1, instead of just **0** and **1**+, and the value (of a Böhm tree) is defined by a finite tree automaton with counters (e.g. a parity B-automaton), given as a part of the input. (Notice that the value can be finite even when the tree is infinite.) This question (in several variants) were approached only for order 1 (all subterms of the input term are of order 1), that is for pushdown systems [8,9]; in general it remains open.

Acknowledgement. We thank Igor Walukiewicz and Sylvain Salvati for a discussion on this topic.

References

1. Barendregt, H., Dekkers, W., Statman, R.: Lambda calculus with types. In: Perspectives in Logic. Cambridge University Press (2013)
2. Parys, P.: On the significance of the collapse operation. In: LICS, pp. 521–530. IEEE (2012)
3. Kobayashi, N.: Pumping by typing. In: LICS, pp. 398–407. IEEE Computer Society (2013)
4. Schwichtenberg, H.: Definierbare funktionen im lambda-kalkl mit typen. Archiv Logic Grundlagenforsch 17, 113–114 (1976)
5. Statman, R.: The typed lambda-calculus is not elementary recursive. Theor. Comput. Sci. 9, 73–81 (1979)
6. Zaionc, M.: Word operation definable in the typed lambda-calculus. Theor. Comput. Sci. 52, 1–14 (1987)
7. Krivine, J.L.: A call-by-name lambda-calculus machine. Higher-Order and Symbolic Computation 20(3), 199–207 (2007)
8. Lang, M.: Resource-bounded reachability on pushdown systems. Master's thesis, RWTH Aachen (2011)
9. Chatterjee, K., Fijalkow, N.: Infinite-state games with finitary conditions. In: Rocca, S.R.D. (ed.) CSL. LIPIcs, vol. 23, pp. 181–196. Schloss Dagstuhl - Leibniz-Zentrum fuer Informatik (2013)

AC-KBO Revisited*

Akihisa Yamada[1], Sarah Winkler[2], Nao Hirokawa[3], and Aart Middeldorp[2]

[1] Graduate School of Information Science, Nagoya University, Japan
[2] Institute of Computer Science, University of Innsbruck, Austria
[3] School of Information Science, JAIST, Japan

Abstract. We consider various definitions of AC-compatible Knuth-Bendix orders. The orders of Steinbach and of Korovin and Voronkov are revisited. The former is enhanced to a more powerful AC-compatible order and we modify the latter to amend its lack of monotonicity on non-ground terms. We further present new complexity results. An extension reflecting the recent proposal of subterm coefficients in standard Knuth-Bendix orders is also given. The various orders are compared on problems in termination and completion.

1 Introduction

Associative and commutative (AC) operators appear in many applications, e.g. in automated reasoning with respect to algebraic structures such as commutative groups or rings. We are interested in proving termination of term rewrite systems with AC symbols. AC termination is important when deciding validity in equational theories with AC operators by means of completion.

Several termination methods for plain rewriting have been extended to deal with AC symbols. Ben Cherifa and Lescanne [4] presented a characterization of polynomial interpretations that ensures compatibility with the AC axioms. There have been numerous papers on extending the recursive path order (RPO) of Dershowitz [6] to deal with AC symbols, starting with the associative path order of Bachmair and Plaisted [3] and culminating in the fully syntactic AC-RPO of Rubio [16]. Several authors [1, 7, 12, 15] adapted the influential dependency pair method of Arts and Giesl [2] to AC rewriting.

We are aware of only two papers on AC extensions of the order of Knuth and Bendix (KBO) [8]. In this paper we revisit these orders and present yet another AC-compatible KBO. Steinbach [17] presented a first version, which comes with the restriction that AC symbols are minimal in the precedence. By incorporating ideas of [16], Korovin and Voronkov [9] presented a version without this restriction. Actually, they present two versions. One is defined on ground terms and another one on arbitrary terms. For (automatically) proving AC termination of

* The research described in this paper is supported by the Austrian Science Fund (FWF) international project I963, the bilateral programs of the Japan Society for the Promotion of Science and the KAKENHI Grant No. 25730004.

M. Codish and E. Sumii (Eds.): FLOPS 2014, LNCS 8475, pp. 319–335, 2014.

rewrite systems, an AC-compatible order on arbitrary terms is required.[1] We show that the second order of [9] lacks the monotonicity property which is required by the definition of simplification orders. Nevertheless we prove that the order is sound for proving termination by extending it to an AC-compatible simplification order. We furthermore present a simpler variant of this latter order which properly extends the order of [17]. In particular, Steinbach's order is a correct AC-compatible simplification order, contrary to what is claimed in [9]. We also present new complexity results which confirm that AC rewriting is much more involved than plain rewriting. Apart from these theoretical contributions, we implemented the various AC-compatible KBOs to compare them also experimentally.

The remainder of this paper is organized as follows. After recalling basic concepts of rewriting modulo AC and orders, we revisit Steinbach's order in Section 3. Section 4 is devoted to the two orders of Korovin and Voronkov. We present a first version of our AC-compatible KBO in Section 5, where we also give the non-trivial proof that it has the required properties. (The proofs in [9] are limited to the order on ground terms.) Then we prove in Section 6 that the problem of orienting a ground rewrite system with the order of Korovin and Voronkov as well as our new order is NP-hard. In Section 7 our order is strengthened with subterm coefficients. In order to show effectiveness of these orders experimental data is provided in Section 8. The paper is concluded in Section 9. Due to lack of space, some of the proofs can be found in the full version of this paper [21].

2 Preliminaries

We assume familiarity with rewriting and termination. Throughout this paper we deal with rewrite systems over a set $\mathcal{V}$ of variables and a *finite* signature $\mathcal{F}$ together with a designated subset $\mathcal{F}_{\mathsf{AC}}$ of binary AC symbols. The congruence relation induced by the equations $f(x,y) \approx f(y,x)$ and $f(f(x,y),z) \approx f(x,f(y,z))$ for all $f \in \mathcal{F}_{\mathsf{AC}}$ is denoted by $=_{\mathsf{AC}}$. A term rewrite system (TRS for short) $\mathcal{R}$ is AC terminating if the relation $=_{\mathsf{AC}} \cdot \rightarrow_{\mathcal{R}} \cdot =_{\mathsf{AC}}$ is well-founded. In this paper AC termination is established by *AC-compatible simplification orders* $\succ$, which are strict orders (i.e., irreflexive and transitive relations) closed under contexts and substitutions that have the subterm property $f(t_1,\ldots,t_n) \succ t_i$ for all $1 \leqslant i \leqslant n$ and satisfy $=_{\mathsf{AC}} \cdot \succ \cdot =_{\mathsf{AC}} \subseteq \succ$. A strict order $\succ$ is *AC-total* if $s \succ t$, $t \succ s$ or $s =_{\mathsf{AC}} t$, for all ground terms s and t. A pair $(\succsim, \succ)$ consisting of a preorder $\succsim$ and a strict order $\succ$ is said to be an *order pair* if the *compatibility* condition $\succsim \cdot \succ \cdot \succsim \subseteq \succ$ holds.

Definition 1. *Let $\succ$ be a strict order and $\succsim$ be a preorder on a set A. The* lexicographic extensions *$\succ^{\mathsf{lex}}$ and $\succsim^{\mathsf{lex}}$ are defined as follows:*

[1] Any AC-compatible reduction order $\succ_{\mathrm{g}}$ on ground terms can trivially be extended to arbitrary terms by defining $s \succ t$ if and only if $s\sigma \succ_{\mathrm{g}} t\sigma$ for all grounding substitutions σ. This is, however, only of (mild) theoretical interest.

- $\boldsymbol{x} \succsim^{\mathsf{lex}} \boldsymbol{y}$ *if* $\boldsymbol{x} \sqsupset_k^{\mathsf{lex}} \boldsymbol{y}$ *for some* $1 \leqslant k \leqslant n$,
- $\boldsymbol{x} \succ^{\mathsf{lex}} \boldsymbol{y}$ *if* $\boldsymbol{x} \sqsupset_k^{\mathsf{lex}} \boldsymbol{y}$ *for some* $1 \leqslant k < n$.

Here $\boldsymbol{x} = (x_1, \ldots, x_n)$, $\boldsymbol{y} = (y_1, \ldots, y_n)$, *and* $\boldsymbol{x} \sqsupset_k^{\mathsf{lex}} \boldsymbol{y}$ *denotes the following condition:* $x_i \succsim y_i$ *for all* $i \leqslant k$ *and either* $k < n$ *and* $x_{k+1} \succ y_{k+1}$ *or* $k = n$. *The* multiset extensions $\succ^{\mathsf{mul}}$ *and* $\succsim^{\mathsf{mul}}$ *are defined as follows:*

- $M \succsim^{\mathsf{mul}} N$ *if* $M \sqsupset_k^{\mathsf{mul}} N$ *for some* $0 \leqslant k \leqslant \min(m, n)$,
- $M \succ^{\mathsf{mul}} N$ *if* $M \sqsupset_k^{\mathsf{mul}} N$ *for some* $0 \leqslant k \leqslant \min(m-1, n)$.

Here $M \sqsupset_k^{\mathsf{mul}} N$ *if* M *and* N *consist of* $x_1, \ldots, x_m$ *and* $y_1, \ldots, y_n$ *respectively such that* $x_j \succsim y_j$ *for all* $j \leqslant k$, *and for every* $k < j \leqslant n$ *there is some* $k < i \leqslant m$ *with* $x_i \succ y_j$.

Note that these extended relations depend on both $\succsim$ and $\succ$. The following result is folklore; a recent formalization of multiset extensions in Isabelle/HOL is presented in [18].

Theorem 2. *If* $(\succsim, \succ)$ *is an order pair then* $(\succsim^{\mathsf{lex}}, \succ^{\mathsf{lex}})$ *and* $(\succsim^{\mathsf{mul}}, \succ^{\mathsf{mul}})$ *are order pairs.* □

3 Steinbach's Order

In this section we recall the AC-compatible KBO $>_{\mathsf{S}}$ of Steinbach [17], which reduces to the standard KBO if AC symbols are absent.[2] The order $>_{\mathsf{S}}$ depends on a precedence and an admissible weight function. A *precedence* $>$ is a strict order on $\mathcal{F}$. A *weight function* (w, w_0) for a signature $\mathcal{F}$ consists of a mapping $w\colon \mathcal{F} \to \mathbb{N}$ and a constant $w_0 > 0$ such that $w(c) \geqslant w_0$ for every constant $c \in \mathcal{F}$. The *weight* of a term t is recursively computed as follows: $w(t) = w_0$ if $t \in \mathcal{V}$ and $w(f(t_1, \ldots, t_n)) = w(f) + w(t_1) + \cdots + w(t_n)$. A weight function (w, w_0) is *admissible* for $>$ if every unary f with $w(f) = 0$ satisfies $f > g$ for all function symbols g different from f. Throughout this paper we assume admissibility.

The *top-flattening* [16] of a term t with respect to an AC symbol f is the multiset $\triangledown_f(t)$ defined inductively as follows: $\triangledown_f(t) = \{t\}$ if $\mathsf{root}(t) \neq f$ and $\triangledown_f(f(t_1, t_2)) = \triangledown_f(t_1) \uplus \triangledown_f(t_2)$.

Definition 3. *Let* $>$ *be a precedence and* (w, w_0) *a weight function. The order* $>_{\mathsf{S}}$ *is inductively defined as follows:* $s >_{\mathsf{S}} t$ *if* $|s|_x \geqslant |t|_x$ *for all* $x \in \mathcal{V}$ *and either* $w(s) > w(t)$, *or* $w(s) = w(t)$ *and one of the following alternatives holds:*

(0) $s = f^k(t)$ *and* $t \in \mathcal{V}$ *for some* $k > 0$,
(1) $s = f(s_1, \ldots, s_n)$, $t = g(t_1, \ldots, t_m)$, *and* $f > g$,
(2) $s = f(s_1, \ldots, s_n)$, $t = f(t_1, \ldots, t_n)$, $f \notin \mathcal{F}_{\mathsf{AC}}$, $(s_1, \ldots, s_n) >_{\mathsf{S}}^{\mathsf{lex}} (t_1, \ldots, t_n)$,
(3) $s = f(s_1, s_2)$, $t = f(t_1, t_2)$, $f \in \mathcal{F}_{\mathsf{AC}}$, *and* $\triangledown_f(s) >_{\mathsf{S}}^{\mathsf{mul}} \triangledown_f(t)$.

[2] The version in [17] is slightly more general, since non-AC function symbols can have arbitrary status. To simplify the discussion, we do not consider status in this paper.

The relation $=_{\mathsf{AC}}$ *is used as preorder in* $>^{\mathsf{lex}}_{\mathsf{S}}$ *and* $>^{\mathsf{mul}}_{\mathsf{S}}$.

Cases (0)–(2) are the same as in the classical Knuth-Bendix order. In case (3) terms rooted by the same AC symbol f are treated by comparing their top-flattenings in the multiset extension of $>_{\mathsf{S}}$.

Example 4. Consider the signature $\mathcal{F} = \{\mathsf{a}, \mathsf{f}, \mathsf{g}\}$ with $\mathsf{f} \in \mathcal{F}_{\mathsf{AC}}$, precedence $\mathsf{g} > \mathsf{a} > \mathsf{f}$ and admissible weight function (w, w_0) with $w(\mathsf{f}) = w(\mathsf{g}) = 0$ and $w_0 = w(\mathsf{a}) = 1$. Let $\mathcal{R}_1$ be the following ground TRS:

$$\mathsf{g}(\mathsf{f}(\mathsf{a},\mathsf{a})) \to \mathsf{f}(\mathsf{g}(\mathsf{a}),\mathsf{g}(\mathsf{a})) \qquad (1) \qquad\qquad \mathsf{f}(\mathsf{a},\mathsf{g}(\mathsf{g}(\mathsf{a}))) \to \mathsf{f}(\mathsf{g}(\mathsf{a}),\mathsf{g}(\mathsf{a})) \qquad (2)$$

For $1 \leqslant i \leqslant 2$, let ℓ_i and r_i be the left- and right-hand side of rule (i), $S_i = \nabla_{\mathsf{f}}(\ell_i)$ and $T_i = \nabla_{\mathsf{f}}(r_i)$. Both rules vacuously satisfy the variable condition. We have $w(\ell_1) = 2 = w(r_1)$ and $\mathsf{g} > \mathsf{f}$, so $\ell_1 >_{\mathsf{S}} r_1$ holds by case (1). We have $w(\ell_2) = 2 = w(r_2)$, $S_2 = \{\mathsf{a}, \mathsf{g}(\mathsf{g}(\mathsf{a}))\}$, and $T_2 = \{\mathsf{g}(\mathsf{a}), \mathsf{g}(\mathsf{a})\}$. Since $\mathsf{g}(\mathsf{a}) >_{\mathsf{S}} \mathsf{a}$ holds by case (1), $\mathsf{g}(\mathsf{g}(\mathsf{a})) >_{\mathsf{S}} \mathsf{g}(\mathsf{a})$ holds by case (2), and therefore $\ell_2 >_{\mathsf{S}} r_2$ by case (3).

Theorem 5 ([17])**.** *If every symbol in* $\mathcal{F}_{\mathsf{AC}}$ *is minimal with respect to* $>$ *then* $>_{\mathsf{S}}$ *is an AC-compatible simplification order.*[3] □

In Section 5 we reprove[4] Theorem 5 by showing that $>_{\mathsf{S}}$ is a special case of our new AC-compatible Knuth-Bendix order.

4 Korovin and Voronkov's Orders

In this section we recall the orders of [9]. The first one is defined on ground terms. The difference with $>_{\mathsf{S}}$ is that in case (3) of the definition a further case analysis is performed based on terms in S and T whose root symbols are not smaller than f in the precedence. Rather than recursively comparing these terms with the order being defined, a lighter non-recursive version is used in which the weights and root symbols are considered. This is formally defined below.

Given a multiset T of terms, a function symbol f, and a binary relation R on function symbols, we define the following submultisets of T:

$$T{\restriction_{\mathcal{V}}} = \{x \in T \mid x \in \mathcal{V}\} \qquad\qquad T{\restriction^{R}_{f}} = \{t \in T \setminus \mathcal{V} \mid \mathsf{root}(t)\ R\ f\}$$

Definition 6. *Let* $>$ *be a precedence and* (w, w_0) *a weight function.*[5] *First we define the auxiliary relations* $=_{\mathsf{kv}}$ *and* $>_{\mathsf{kv}}$ *as follows:*

- $s =_{\mathsf{kv}} t$ *if* $w(s) = w(t)$ *and* $\mathsf{root}(s) = \mathsf{root}(t)$,
- $s >_{\mathsf{kv}} t$ *if either* $w(s) > w(t)$ *or both* $w(s) = w(t)$ *and* $\mathsf{root}(s) > \mathsf{root}(t)$.

[3] In [17] AC symbols are further required to have weight 0 because terms are flattened. Our version of $>_{\mathsf{S}}$ does not impose this restriction due to the use of top-flattening.

[4] The counterexample in [9] against the monotonicity of $>_{\mathsf{S}}$ is invalid as the condition that AC symbols are *minimal* in the precedence is not satisfied.

[5] Here we do not impose totality on precedences, cf. [9]. See also Example 25.

The order $>_{\mathsf{KV}}$ is inductively defined on ground terms as follows: $s >_{\mathsf{KV}} t$ if either $w(s) > w(t)$, or $w(s) = w(t)$ and one of the following alternatives holds:

(1) $s = f(s_1, \ldots, s_n)$, $t = g(t_1, \ldots, t_m)$, and $f > g$,
(2) $s = f(s_1, \ldots, s_n)$, $t = f(t_1, \ldots, t_n)$, $f \notin \mathcal{F}_{\mathsf{AC}}$, $(s_1, \ldots, s_n) >_{\mathsf{KV}}^{\mathsf{lex}} (t_1, \ldots, t_n)$,
(3) $s = f(s_1, s_2)$, $t = f(t_1, t_2)$, $f \in \mathcal{F}_{\mathsf{AC}}$, and for $S = \nabla_f(s)$ and $T = \nabla_f(t)$
  (a) $S{\restriction}_f^{\not<} >_{\mathsf{kv}}^{\mathsf{mul}} T{\restriction}_f^{\not<}$, or
  (b) $S{\restriction}_f^{\not<} =_{\mathsf{kv}}^{\mathsf{mul}} T{\restriction}_f^{\not<}$ and $|S| > |T|$, or
  (c) $S{\restriction}_f^{\not<} =_{\mathsf{kv}}^{\mathsf{mul}} T{\restriction}_f^{\not<}$, $|S| = |T|$, and $S >_{\mathsf{KV}}^{\mathsf{mul}} T$.

Here $=_{\mathsf{AC}}$ is used as preorder in $>_{\mathsf{KV}}^{\mathsf{lex}}$ and $>_{\mathsf{KV}}^{\mathsf{mul}}$ whereas $=_{\mathsf{kv}}$ is used in $>_{\mathsf{kv}}^{\mathsf{mul}}$.

Only in cases (2) and (3c) the order $>_{\mathsf{KV}}$ is used recursively. In case (3) terms rooted by the same AC symbol f are compared by extracting from the top-flattenings S and T the multisets $S{\restriction}_f^{\not<}$ and $T{\restriction}_f^{\not<}$ consisting of all terms rooted by a function symbol not smaller than f in the precedence. If $S{\restriction}_f^{\not<}$ is larger than $T{\restriction}_f^{\not<}$ in the multiset extension of $>_{\mathsf{kv}}$, we conclude in case (3a). Otherwise the multisets must be equal (with respect to $=_{\mathsf{kv}}^{\mathsf{mul}}$). If S has more terms than T, we conclude in case (3b). In the final case (3c) S and T have the same number of terms and we compare S and T in the multiset extension of $>_{\mathsf{KV}}$.

Theorem 7 ([9]). *The order $>_{\mathsf{KV}}$ is an AC-compatible simplification order on ground terms. If $>$ is total then $>_{\mathsf{KV}}$ is AC-total on ground terms.* □

The two orders $>_{\mathsf{KV}}$ and $>_{\mathsf{S}}$ are incomparable on ground TRSs.

Example 8. Consider again the ground TRS $\mathcal{R}_1$ of Example 4. To orient rule (1) with $>_{\mathsf{KV}}$, the weight of the unary function symbol g must be 0 and admissibility demands $\mathsf{g} > \mathsf{a}$ and $\mathsf{g} > \mathsf{f}$. Hence rule (1) is handled by case (1) of the definition. For rule (2), the multisets $S = \{\mathsf{a}, \mathsf{g}(\mathsf{g}(\mathsf{a}))\}$ and $T = \{\mathsf{g}(\mathsf{a}), \mathsf{g}(\mathsf{a})\}$ are compared in case (3). We have $S{\restriction}_f^{\not<} = \{\mathsf{g}(\mathsf{g}(\mathsf{a}))\}$ if $\mathsf{f} > \mathsf{a}$ and $S{\restriction}_f^{\not<} = S$ otherwise. In both cases we have $T{\restriction}_f^{\not<} = T$. Note that neither $\mathsf{a} >_{\mathsf{kv}} \mathsf{g}(\mathsf{a})$ nor $\mathsf{g}(\mathsf{g}(\mathsf{a})) >_{\mathsf{kv}} \mathsf{g}(\mathsf{a})$ holds. Hence case (3a) does not apply. But also cases (3b) and (3c) are not applicable as $\mathsf{g}(\mathsf{g}(\mathsf{a})) =_{\mathsf{kv}} \mathsf{g}(\mathsf{a})$ and $\mathsf{a} \neq_{\mathsf{kv}} \mathsf{g}(\mathsf{a})$. Hence, independent of the choice of $>$, $\mathcal{R}_1$ cannot be proved terminating by $>_{\mathsf{KV}}$. Conversely, the TRS $\mathcal{R}_2$ resulting from reversing rule (2) in $\mathcal{R}_1$ can be proved terminating by $>_{\mathsf{KV}}$ but not by $>_{\mathsf{S}}$.

Next we present the second order of [9], the extension of $>_{\mathsf{KV}}$ to non-ground terms. Since it coincides with $>_{\mathsf{KV}}$ on ground terms, we use the same notation for the order.

In case (3) of the following definition, also variables appearing in the top-flattenings S and T are taken into account in the first multiset comparison. Given a relation $\sqsupset$ on terms, we write $S \sqsupset^f T$ for $S{\restriction}_f^{\not<} \sqsupset^{\mathsf{mul}} T{\restriction}_f^{\not<} \uplus T{\restriction}_{\mathcal{V}} - S{\restriction}_{\mathcal{V}}$. Note that $\sqsupset^f$ depends on a precedence $>$. Whenever we use $\sqsupset^f$, $>$ is defined.

Definition 9. *Let $>$ be a precedence and (w, w_0) a weight function. First we extend the orders $=_{\mathsf{kv}}$ and $>_{\mathsf{kv}}$ as follows:*

- $s =_{\mathsf{kv}} t$ *if* $|s|_x = |t|_x$ *for all* $x \in \mathcal{V}$, $w(s) = w(t)$ *and* $\mathsf{root}(s) = \mathsf{root}(t)$,
- $s >_{\mathsf{kv}} t$ *if* $|s|_x \geqslant |t|_x$ *for all* $x \in \mathcal{V}$ *and either* $w(s) > w(t)$ *or both* $w(s) = w(t)$ *and* $\mathsf{root}(s) > \mathsf{root}(t)$.

The order $>_{\mathsf{KV}}$ *is now inductively defined as follows:* $s >_{\mathsf{KV}} t$ *if* $|s|_x \geqslant |t|_x$ *for all* $x \in \mathcal{V}$ *and either* $w(s) > w(t)$, *or* $w(s) = w(t)$ *and one of the following alternatives holds:*

(0) $s = f^k(t)$ *and* $t \in \mathcal{V}$ *for some* $k > 0$,
(1) $s = f(s_1, \ldots, s_n)$, $t = g(t_1, \ldots, t_m)$, *and* $f > g$,
(2) $s = f(s_1, \ldots, s_n)$, $t = f(t_1, \ldots, t_n)$, $f \notin \mathcal{F}_{\mathsf{AC}}$, $(s_1, \ldots, s_n) >^{\mathsf{lex}}_{\mathsf{KV}} (t_1, \ldots, t_n)$,
(3) $s = f(s_1, s_2)$, $t = f(t_1, t_2)$, $f \in \mathcal{F}_{\mathsf{AC}}$, *and for* $S = \nabla_f(s)$ *and* $T = \nabla_f(t)$
   (a) $S >^f_{\mathsf{kv}} T$, *or*
   (b) $S =^f_{\mathsf{kv}} T$ *and* $|S| > |T|$, *or*
   (c) $S =^f_{\mathsf{kv}} T$, $|S| = |T|$, *and* $S >^{\mathsf{mul}}_{\mathsf{KV}} T$.

Here $=_{\mathsf{AC}}$ *is used as preorder in* $>^{\mathsf{lex}}_{\mathsf{KV}}$ *and* $>^{\mathsf{mul}}_{\mathsf{KV}}$ *whereas* $=_{\mathsf{kv}}$ *is used in* $>^{\mathsf{mul}}_{\mathsf{kv}}$.

Contrary to what is claimed in [9], the order $>_{\mathsf{KV}}$ of Definition 9 is not a simplification order because it lacks the monotonicity property (i.e., $>_{\mathsf{KV}}$ is not closed under contexts), as shown in the following example.

Example 10. Let f be an AC symbol and g a unary function symbol with $w(\mathsf{g}) = 0$ and $\mathsf{g} > \mathsf{f}$.[6] We obviously have $\mathsf{g}(x) >_{\mathsf{KV}} x$. However, $\mathsf{f}(\mathsf{g}(x), y) >_{\mathsf{KV}} \mathsf{f}(x, y)$ does not hold. Let $S = \nabla_{\mathsf{f}}(s) = \{\mathsf{g}(x), y\}$ and $T = \nabla_{\mathsf{f}}(t) = \{x, y\}$. We have $S{\restriction}_{\mathsf{f}}^{\not<} = \{\mathsf{g}(x)\}$, $S{\restriction}_{\mathcal{V}} = \{y\}$, $T{\restriction}_{\mathsf{f}}^{\not<} = \varnothing$, and $T{\restriction}_{\mathcal{V}} = \{x, y\}$. Note that $\mathsf{g}(x) >_{\mathsf{kv}} x$ does not hold since $\mathsf{g} \not> x$. Hence case (3a) in Definition 9 does not apply. But also $\mathsf{g}(x) =_{\mathsf{kv}} x$ does not hold, excluding cases (3b) and (3c).

The example does not refute the soundness of $>_{\mathsf{KV}}$ for proving AC termination; note that also $\mathsf{f}(x, y) >_{\mathsf{KV}} \mathsf{f}(\mathsf{g}(x), y)$ does not hold. We prove soundness by extending $>_{\mathsf{KV}}$ to $>_{\mathsf{KV}'}$ which has all desired properties.

Definition 11. *The order* $>_{\mathsf{KV}'}$ *is obtained as in Definition 9 after replacing* $=^f_{\mathsf{kv}}$ *by* $\geqslant^f_{\mathsf{kv}'}$ *in cases (3b) and (3c), and using* $\geqslant_{\mathsf{kv}'}$ *as preorder in* $>^{\mathsf{mul}}_{\mathsf{kv}}$ *in case (3a). Here the relation* $\geqslant_{\mathsf{kv}'}$ *is defined as follows:*

- $s \geqslant_{\mathsf{kv}'} t$ *if* $|s|_x \geqslant |t|_x$ *for all* $x \in \mathcal{V}$ *and either* $w(s) > w(t)$, *or* $w(s) = w(t)$ *and either* $\mathsf{root}(s) \geqslant \mathsf{root}(t)$ *or* $t \in \mathcal{V}$.

Note that $\geqslant_{\mathsf{kv}'}$ is a preorder that contains $=_{\mathsf{AC}}$.

Example 12. Consider again Example 10. We have $\mathsf{f}(\mathsf{g}(x), y) >_{\mathsf{KV}'} \mathsf{f}(x, y)$ because now case (3c) applies: $S{\restriction}_{\mathsf{f}}^{\not<} = \{\mathsf{g}(x)\} \geqslant^{\mathsf{mul}}_{\mathsf{kv}'} \{x\} = T{\restriction}_{\mathsf{f}}^{\not<} \uplus T{\restriction}_{\mathcal{V}} - S{\restriction}_{\mathcal{V}}$, $|S| = 2 = |T|$, and $S = \{\mathsf{g}(x), y\} >^{\mathsf{mul}}_{\mathsf{KV}'} \{x, y\} = T$ because $\mathsf{g}(x) >_{\mathsf{KV}'} x$.

[6] The use of a unary function of weight 0 is not crucial, see [21].

The order $>_{\mathsf{KV}'}$ is an AC-compatible simplification order. Since the inclusion $>_{\mathsf{KV}} \subsetneq >_{\mathsf{KV}'}$ obviously holds, it follows that $>_{\mathsf{KV}}$ is a sound method for establishing AC termination, despite the lack of monotonicity.

Theorem 13. *The order $>_{\mathsf{KV}'}$ is an AC-compatible simplification order.*

Proof. See [21]. □

The order $>_{\mathsf{KV}'}$ lacks one important feature: a polynomial-time algorithm to decide $s >_{\mathsf{KV}'} t$ when the precedence and weight function are given. By using the reduction technique of [18, Theorem 4.2], NP-hardness of this problem can be shown. Note that for KBO the problem is known to be linear [13].

Theorem 14. *The decision problem for $>_{\mathsf{KV}'}$ is NP-hard.*

Proof. See [21]. □

5 AC-KBO

In this section we present another AC-compatible simplification order. In contrast to $>_{\mathsf{KV}'}$, our new order $>_{\mathsf{ACKBO}}$ contains $>_{\mathsf{S}}$. Moreover, its definition is simpler than $>_{\mathsf{KV}'}$ since we avoid the use of an auxiliary order in case (3). Finally, $>_{\mathsf{ACKBO}}$ is decidable in polynomial-time. Hence it will be used as the basis for the extension discussed in Section 7.

Definition 15. *Let $>$ be a precedence and (w, w_0) a weight function. We define $>_{\mathsf{ACKBO}}$ inductively as follows: $s >_{\mathsf{ACKBO}} t$ if $|s|_x \geqslant |t|_x$ for all $x \in \mathcal{V}$ and either $w(s) > w(t)$, or $w(s) = w(t)$ and one of the following alternatives holds:*

(0) $s = f^k(t)$ and $t \in \mathcal{V}$ for some $k > 0$,

(1) $s = f(s_1, \ldots, s_n)$, $t = g(t_1, \ldots, t_m)$, and $f > g$,

(2) $s = f(s_1, \ldots, s_n)$, $t = f(t_1, \ldots, t_n)$, $f \notin \mathcal{F}_{\mathsf{AC}}$, $(s_1, \ldots, s_n) >^{\mathsf{lex}}_{\mathsf{ACKBO}} (t_1, \ldots, t_n)$,

(3) $s = f(s_1, s_2)$, $t = f(t_1, t_2)$, $f \in \mathcal{F}_{\mathsf{AC}}$, and for $S = \nabla_f(s)$ and $T = \nabla_f(t)$

(a) $S >^f_{\mathsf{ACKBO}} T$, or

(b) $S =^f_{\mathsf{AC}} T$, and $|S| > |T|$, or

(c) $S =^f_{\mathsf{AC}} T$, $|S| = |T|$, and $S{\restriction}^{<}_{f} >^{\mathsf{mul}}_{\mathsf{ACKBO}} T{\restriction}^{<}_{f}$.

The relation $=_{\mathsf{AC}}$ is used as preorder in $>^{\mathsf{lex}}_{\mathsf{ACKBO}}$ and $>^{\mathsf{mul}}_{\mathsf{ACKBO}}$.

Note that in case (3c) we compare the multisets $S{\restriction}^{<}_{f}$ and $T{\restriction}^{<}_{f}$ rather than S and T in the multiset extension of $>_{\mathsf{ACKBO}}$.

Steinbach's order is a special case of the order defined above.

Theorem 16. *If every AC symbol has minimal precedence then $>_{\mathsf{S}} = >_{\mathsf{ACKBO}}$.*

Proof. Suppose that every function symbol in $\mathcal{F}_{\mathsf{AC}}$ is minimal with respect to $>$. We show that $s >_{\mathsf{S}} t$ if and only if $s >_{\mathsf{ACKBO}} t$ by induction on s. It is clearly sufficient to consider case (3) in Definition 3 and cases (3a)–(3c) in Definition 15. So let $s = f(s_1, s_2)$ and $t = f(t_1, t_2)$ such that $w(s) = w(t)$ and $f \in \mathcal{F}_{\mathsf{AC}}$. Let $S = \nabla_f(s)$ and $T = \nabla_f(t)$.

- Let $s >_{\mathsf{S}} t$ by case (3). We have $S >_{\mathsf{S}}^{\mathsf{mul}} T$. Since $S >_{\mathsf{S}}^{\mathsf{mul}} T$ involves only comparisons $s' >_{\mathsf{S}} t'$ for subterms s' of s, the induction hypothesis yields $S >_{\mathsf{ACKBO}}^{\mathsf{mul}} T$. Because f is minimal in $>$, $S = S{\restriction}_f^{\not<} \uplus S{\restriction}_{\mathcal{V}}$ and $T = T{\restriction}_f^{\not<} \uplus T{\restriction}_{\mathcal{V}}$. For no elements $u \in S{\restriction}_{\mathcal{V}}$ and $v \in T{\restriction}_f^{\not<}$, $u >_{\mathsf{ACKBO}} v$ or $u =_{\mathsf{AC}} v$ holds. Hence $S >_{\mathsf{ACKBO}}^{\mathsf{mul}} T$ implies $S >_{\mathsf{ACKBO}}^{f} T$ or both $S =_{\mathsf{AC}}^{f} T$ and $S{\restriction}_{\mathcal{V}} \supsetneq T{\restriction}_{\mathcal{V}}$. In the former case $s >_{\mathsf{ACKBO}} t$ is due to case (3a) in Definition 15. In the latter case we have $|S| > |T|$ and $s >_{\mathsf{ACKBO}} t$ follows by case (3b).
- Let $s >_{\mathsf{ACKBO}} t$ by applying one of the cases (3a)–(3c) in Definition 15.
  - Suppose (3a) applies. Then we have $S >_{\mathsf{ACKBO}}^{f} T$. Since f is minimal in $>$, $S{\restriction}_f^{\not<} = S - S{\restriction}_{\mathcal{V}}$ and $T{\restriction}_f^{\not<} \uplus T{\restriction}_{\mathcal{V}} = T$. Hence $S >_{\mathsf{ACKBO}}^{\mathsf{mul}} (T - S{\restriction}_{\mathcal{V}}) \uplus S{\restriction}_{\mathcal{V}} \supseteq T$. We obtain $S >_{\mathsf{S}}^{\mathsf{mul}} T$ from the induction hypothesis and thus case (3) in Definition 3 applies.
  - Suppose (3b) applies. Analogous to the previous case, the inclusion $S =_{\mathsf{AC}}^{\mathsf{mul}} (T - S{\restriction}_{\mathcal{V}}) \uplus S{\restriction}_{\mathcal{V}} \supseteq T$ holds. Since $|S| > |T|$, $S =_{\mathsf{AC}}^{\mathsf{mul}} T$ is not possible. Thus $(T - S{\restriction}_{\mathcal{V}}) \uplus S{\restriction}_{\mathcal{V}} \supsetneq T$ and hence $S >_{\mathsf{S}}^{\mathsf{mul}} T$.
  - If case (3c) applies then $S{\restriction}_f^{<} >_{\mathsf{ACKBO}}^{\mathsf{mul}} T{\restriction}_f^{<}$. This is impossible since both sides are empty as f is minimal in $>$. □

The following example shows that $>_{\mathsf{ACKBO}}$ is a proper extension of $>_{\mathsf{S}}$ and incomparable with $>_{\mathsf{KV'}}$.

Example 17. Consider the TRS $\mathcal{R}_3$ consisting of the rules

$$\begin{array}{rcc} \mathsf{f}(x+y) \to \mathsf{f}(x) + y & \mathsf{h}(\mathsf{a},\mathsf{b}) \to \mathsf{h}(\mathsf{b},\mathsf{a}) & \mathsf{h}(\mathsf{g}(\mathsf{a}),\mathsf{a}) \to \mathsf{h}(\mathsf{a},\mathsf{g}(\mathsf{b})) \\ \mathsf{g}(x) + y \to \mathsf{g}(x+y) & \mathsf{h}(\mathsf{a},\mathsf{g}(\mathsf{g}(\mathsf{a}))) \to \mathsf{h}(\mathsf{g}(\mathsf{a}),\mathsf{f}(\mathsf{a})) & \mathsf{h}(\mathsf{g}(\mathsf{a}),\mathsf{b}) \to \mathsf{h}(\mathsf{a},\mathsf{g}(\mathsf{a})) \\ \mathsf{f}(\mathsf{a}) + \mathsf{g}(\mathsf{b}) \to \mathsf{f}(\mathsf{b}) + \mathsf{g}(\mathsf{a}) & & \end{array}$$

over the signature $\{+, \mathsf{f}, \mathsf{g}, \mathsf{h}, \mathsf{a}, \mathsf{b}\}$ with $+ \in \mathcal{F}_{\mathsf{AC}}$. Consider the precedence $\mathsf{f} > + > \mathsf{g} > \mathsf{a} > \mathsf{b} > \mathsf{h}$ together with the admissible weight function (w, w_0) with $w(+) = w(\mathsf{h}) = 0$, $w(\mathsf{f}) = w(\mathsf{a}) = w(\mathsf{b}) = w_0 = 1$ and $w(\mathsf{g}) = 2$. The interesting rule is $\mathsf{f}(\mathsf{a})+\mathsf{g}(\mathsf{b}) \to \mathsf{f}(\mathsf{b})+\mathsf{g}(\mathsf{a})$. For $S = \nabla_+(\mathsf{f}(\mathsf{a})+\mathsf{g}(\mathsf{b}))$ and $T = \nabla_+(\mathsf{f}(\mathsf{b})+\mathsf{g}(\mathsf{a}))$ the multisets $S' = S{\restriction}_+^{\not<} = \{\mathsf{f}(\mathsf{a})\}$ and $T' = T{\restriction}_+^{\not<} \uplus T{\restriction}_{\mathcal{V}} - S{\restriction}_{\mathcal{V}} = \{\mathsf{f}(\mathsf{b})\}$ satisfy $S' >_{\mathsf{ACKBO}}^{\mathsf{mul}} T'$ as $\mathsf{f}(\mathsf{a}) >_{\mathsf{ACKBO}} \mathsf{f}(\mathsf{b})$, so that case (3a) of Definition 15 applies. All other rules are oriented from left to right by both $>_{\mathsf{KV'}}$ and $>_{\mathsf{ACKBO}}$, and they enforce a precedence and weight function which are identical (or very similar) to the one given above. Since $>_{\mathsf{KV'}}$ orients the rule $\mathsf{f}(\mathsf{a}) + \mathsf{g}(\mathsf{b}) \to \mathsf{f}(\mathsf{b}) + \mathsf{g}(\mathsf{a})$ from right to left, $\mathcal{R}_3$ cannot be compatible with $>_{\mathsf{KV'}}$. It is easy to see that the rule $\mathsf{g}(x) + y \to \mathsf{g}(x+y)$ requires $+ > \mathsf{g}$, and hence $>_{\mathsf{S}}$ cannot be applied.

Fig. 1 summarizes the relationships between the orders introduced so far.

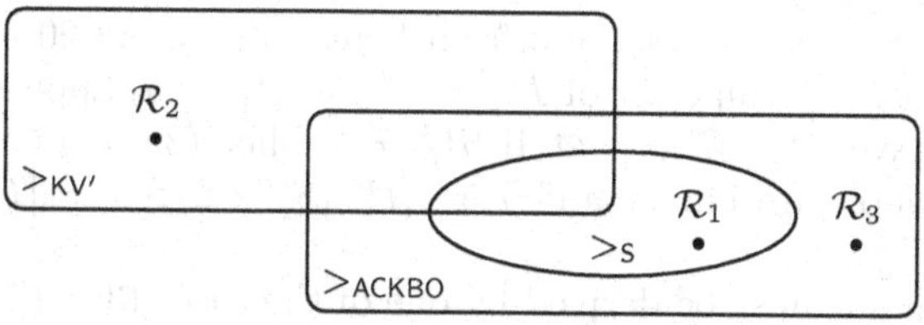

$\mathcal{R}_1$ Example 4 (and 8)
$\mathcal{R}_2$ Example 8
$\mathcal{R}_3$ Example 17

Fig. 1. Comparison

In the following, we show that $>_{\mathsf{ACKBO}}$ is an AC-compatible simplification order. As a consequence, correctness of $>_{\mathsf{S}}$ (i.e., Theorem 5) is concluded by Theorem 16.

Lemma 18. *The pair* $(=_{\mathsf{AC}}, >_{\mathsf{ACKBO}})$ *is an order pair.*

Proof. See [21]. $\square$

The subterm property is an easy consequence of transitivity and admissibility.

Lemma 19. *The order* $>_{\mathsf{ACKBO}}$ *has the subterm property.* $\square$

Next we prove that $>_{\mathsf{ACKBO}}$ is closed under contexts. The following lemma is an auxiliary result needed for its proof. In order to reuse this lemma for the correctness proof of $>_{\mathsf{KV'}}$ in the appendix of [21], we prove it in an abstract setting.

Lemma 20. *Let* $(\succsim, \succ)$ *be an order pair and* $f \in \mathcal{F}_{\mathsf{AC}}$ *with* $f(u,v) \succ u, v$ *for all terms* u *and* v. *If* $s \succsim t$ *then* $\{s\} \succsim^{\mathsf{mul}} \nabla_f(t)$ *or* $\{s\} \succ^{\mathsf{mul}} \nabla_f(t)$. *If* $s \succ t$ *then* $\{s\} \succ^{\mathsf{mul}} \nabla_f(t)$.

Proof. Let $\nabla_f(t) = \{t_1, \ldots, t_m\}$. If $m = 1$ then $\nabla_f(t) = \{t\}$ and the lemma holds trivially. Otherwise we get $t \succ t_j$ for all $1 \leqslant j \leqslant m$ by recursively applying the assumption. Hence $s \succ t_j$ by the transitivity of $\succ$ or the compatibility of $\succ$ and $\succsim$. We conclude that $\{s\} \succ^{\mathsf{mul}} \nabla_f(t)$. $\square$

In the following proof of closure under contexts, admissibility is essential. This is in contrast to the corresponding result for standard KBO.

Lemma 21. *If* (w, w_0) *is admissible for* $>$ *then* $>_{\mathsf{ACKBO}}$ *is closed under contexts.*

Proof. Suppose $s >_{\mathsf{ACKBO}} t$. We consider the context $h(\square, u)$ with $h \in \mathcal{F}_{\mathsf{AC}}$ and u an arbitrary term, and prove that $s' = h(s,u) >_{\mathsf{ACKBO}} h(t,u) = t'$. Closure under contexts of $>_{\mathsf{ACKBO}}$ follows then by induction; contexts rooted by a non-AC symbol are handled as in the proof for standard KBO.

If $w(s) > w(t)$ then obviously $w(s') > w(t')$. So we assume $w(s) = w(t)$. Let $S = \nabla_h(s)$, $T = \nabla_h(t)$, and $U = \nabla_h(u)$. Note that $\nabla_h(s') = S \uplus U$ and $\nabla_h(t') = T \uplus U$. Because $>^{\mathsf{mul}}_{\mathsf{ACKBO}}$ is closed under multiset sum, it suffices to show that one of the cases (3a)–(3c) of Definition 15 holds for S and T. Let $f = \mathsf{root}(s)$ and $g = \mathsf{root}(t)$. We distinguish the following cases.

- Suppose $f \nleq h$. We have $S = S{\upharpoonright}_h^{\nless} = \{s\}$, and from Lemmata 19 and 20 we obtain $S >_{\mathsf{ACKBO}}^{\mathsf{mul}} T$. Since T is a superset of $T{\upharpoonright}_h^{\nless} \uplus T{\upharpoonright}_{\mathcal{V}} - S{\upharpoonright}_{\mathcal{V}}$, (3a) applies.
- Suppose $f = h > g$. We have $T{\upharpoonright}_h^{\nless} \uplus T{\upharpoonright}_{\mathcal{V}} = \varnothing$. If $S{\upharpoonright}_h^{\nless} \neq \varnothing$, then (3a) applies. Otherwise, since AC symbols are binary and $T = \{t\}$, $|S| \geqslant 2 > 1 = |T|$. Hence (3b) applies.
- If $f = g = h$ then $s >_{\mathsf{ACKBO}} t$ must be derived by one of the cases (3a)–(3c) for S and T.
- Suppose $f, g < h$. We have $S{\upharpoonright}_h^{\nless} = T{\upharpoonright}_h^{\nless} \uplus T{\upharpoonright}_{\mathcal{V}} = \varnothing$, $|S| = |T| = 1$, and $S{\upharpoonright}_h^{<} = \{s\} >_{\mathsf{ACKBO}}^{\mathsf{mul}} \{t\} = T{\upharpoonright}_h^{<}$. Hence (3c) holds.

Note that $f \geqslant g$ since $w(s) = w(t)$ and $s >_{\mathsf{ACKBO}} t$. Moreover, if $t \in \mathcal{V}$ then $s = f^k(t)$ for some $k > 0$ with $w(f) = 0$, which entails $f > h$ due to admissibility. □

Closure under substitutions is the trickiest part since by substituting AC-rooted terms for variables that appear in the top-flattening of a term, the structure of the term changes. In the proof, the multisets $\{t \in T \mid t \notin \mathcal{V}\}$, $\{t\sigma \mid t \in T\}$, and $\{\nabla_f(t) \mid t \in T\}$ are denoted by $T{\upharpoonright}_{\mathcal{F}}$, $T\sigma$, and $\nabla_f(T)$, respectively.

Lemma 22. *Let $>$ be a precedence, $f \in \mathcal{F}_{\mathsf{AC}}$, and $(\succsim, \succ)$ an order pair on terms such that $\succsim$ and $\succ$ are closed under substitutions and $f(x, y) \succ x, y$. Consider terms s and t such that $S = \nabla_f(s)$, $T = \nabla_f(t)$, $S' = \nabla_f(s\sigma)$, and $T' = \nabla_f(t\sigma)$.*

(1) If $S \succ^f T$ then $S' \succ^f T'$.
(2) If $S \succsim^f T$ then $S' \succ^f T'$ or $S' \succsim^f T'$. In the latter case $|S| - |T| \leqslant |S'| - |T'|$ and $S'{\upharpoonright}_f^{<} \succ^{\mathsf{mul}} T'{\upharpoonright}_f^{<}$ whenever $S{\upharpoonright}_f^{<} \succ^{\mathsf{mul}} T{\upharpoonright}_f^{<}$.

Proof. Let v be an arbitrary term. By the assumption on $\succ$ we have either $\{v\} = \nabla_f(v)$ or both $\{v\} \succ^{\mathsf{mul}} \nabla_f(v)$ and $1 < |\nabla_f(v)|$. Hence, for any set V of terms, either $V = \nabla_f(V)$ or both $V \succ^{\mathsf{mul}} \nabla_f(V)$ and $|V| < |\nabla_f(V)|$. Moreover, for $V = \nabla_f(v)$, the following equalities hold:

$$\nabla_f(v\sigma){\upharpoonright}_f^{\nless} = V{\upharpoonright}_f^{\nless}\sigma \uplus \nabla_f(V{\upharpoonright}_{\mathcal{V}}\sigma){\upharpoonright}_f^{\nless} \qquad \nabla_f(v\sigma){\upharpoonright}_{\mathcal{V}} = \nabla_f(V{\upharpoonright}_{\mathcal{V}}\sigma){\upharpoonright}_{\mathcal{V}}$$

To prove the lemma, assume $S \sqsupset^f T$ for $\sqsupset \in \{\succsim, \succ\}$. We have $S{\upharpoonright}_f^{\nless} \sqsupset^{\mathsf{mul}} T{\upharpoonright}_f^{\nless} \uplus U$ where $U = (T - S){\upharpoonright}_{\mathcal{V}}$. Since multiset extensions preserve closure under substitutions, $S{\upharpoonright}_f^{\nless}\sigma \sqsupset^{\mathsf{mul}} T{\upharpoonright}_f^{\nless}\sigma \uplus U\sigma$ follows. Using the above (in)equalities, we obtain

$$\begin{aligned}
S'{\upharpoonright}_f^{\nless} &= S{\upharpoonright}_f^{\nless}\sigma \uplus \nabla_f(S{\upharpoonright}_{\mathcal{V}}\sigma){\upharpoonright}_f^{\nless} \\
&\sqsupset^{\mathsf{mul}} T{\upharpoonright}_f^{\nless}\sigma \uplus \nabla_f(S{\upharpoonright}_{\mathcal{V}}\sigma){\upharpoonright}_f^{\nless} \uplus U\sigma \\
&O \quad T{\upharpoonright}_f^{\nless}\sigma \uplus \nabla_f(S{\upharpoonright}_{\mathcal{V}}\sigma){\upharpoonright}_f^{\nless} \uplus \nabla_f(U\sigma) \\
&= T{\upharpoonright}_f^{\nless}\sigma \uplus \nabla_f(S{\upharpoonright}_{\mathcal{V}}\sigma){\upharpoonright}_f^{\nless} \uplus \nabla_f(U\sigma){\upharpoonright}_{\mathcal{V}} \uplus \nabla_f(U\sigma){\upharpoonright}_f^{\nless} \uplus \nabla_f(U\sigma){\upharpoonright}_f^{<} \\
&P \quad T{\upharpoonright}_f^{\nless}\sigma \uplus \nabla_f(T{\upharpoonright}_{\mathcal{V}}\sigma){\upharpoonright}_f^{\nless} \uplus \nabla_f(U\sigma){\upharpoonright}_{\mathcal{V}} \\
&= T{\upharpoonright}_f^{\nless}\sigma \uplus \nabla_f(T{\upharpoonright}_{\mathcal{V}}\sigma){\upharpoonright}_f^{\nless} \uplus \nabla_f(T{\upharpoonright}_{\mathcal{V}}\sigma){\upharpoonright}_{\mathcal{V}} - \nabla_f(S{\upharpoonright}_{\mathcal{V}}\sigma){\upharpoonright}_{\mathcal{V}} \\
&= T'{\upharpoonright}_f^{\nless} \uplus T'{\upharpoonright}_{\mathcal{V}} - S'{\upharpoonright}_{\mathcal{V}}
\end{aligned}$$

Here O denotes $=$ if $U\sigma = \nabla_f(U\sigma)$ and $\succ^{\mathsf{mul}}$ if $|U\sigma| < |\nabla_f(U\sigma)|$, while P denotes $=$ if $U\sigma\restriction_f^{\lessgtr} = \varnothing$ and $\supsetneq$ otherwise. Since $(\succsim^{\mathsf{mul}}, \succ^{\mathsf{mul}})$ is an order pair with $\supseteq \subseteq \succsim^{\mathsf{mul}}$ and $\supsetneq \subseteq \succ^{\mathsf{mul}}$, we obtain $S' \sqsupset^f T'$.

It remains to show (2). If $S' \not\succ^f T'$ then O and P are both $=$ and thus $U\sigma = \nabla_f(U\sigma)$ and $U\sigma\restriction_f^{\lessgtr} = \varnothing$. Let $X = S\restriction_{\mathcal{V}} \cap T\restriction_{\mathcal{V}}$. We have $U = T\restriction_{\mathcal{V}} - X$.

- Since $|W\restriction_{\mathcal{F}}\sigma| = |W\restriction_{\mathcal{F}}|$ and $|W| \leqslant |\nabla_f(W)|$ for an arbitrary set W of terms, we have $|S'| \geqslant |S| - |X| + |\nabla_f(X\sigma)|$. From $|U\sigma| = |U| = |T\restriction_{\mathcal{V}}| - |X|$ we obtain $|T'| = |T\restriction_{\mathcal{F}}\sigma| + |\nabla_f(U\sigma)| + |\nabla_f(X\sigma)| = |T| - |X| + |\nabla_f(X\sigma)|$. Hence $|S| - |T| \leqslant |S'| - |T'|$ as desired.
- Suppose $S\restriction_f^{\lessgtr} \succ^{\mathsf{mul}} T\restriction_f^{\lessgtr}$. From $U\sigma\restriction_f^{\lessgtr} = \varnothing$ we infer $T\restriction_{\mathcal{V}}\sigma\restriction_f^{\lessgtr} \subseteq S\restriction_{\mathcal{V}}\sigma\restriction_f^{\lessgtr}$. Because $S'\restriction_f^{\lessgtr} = S\restriction_f^{\lessgtr}\sigma \uplus S\restriction_{\mathcal{V}}\sigma\restriction_f^{\lessgtr}$ and $T'\restriction_f^{\lessgtr} = T\restriction_f^{\lessgtr}\sigma \uplus T\restriction_{\mathcal{V}}\sigma\restriction_f^{\lessgtr}$, closure under substitutions of $\succ^{\mathsf{mul}}$ (which it inherits from $\succ$ and $\succsim$) yields the desired $S'\restriction_f^{\lessgtr} \succ^{\mathsf{mul}} T'\restriction_f^{\lessgtr}$. □

Lemma 23. *$>_{\mathsf{ACKBO}}$ is closed under substitutions.*

Proof. If $s >_{\mathsf{ACKBO}} t$ is obtained by cases (0)–(1) in Definition 15, the proof for standard KBO goes through. If (3a) or (3b) is used to obtain $s >_{\mathsf{ACKBO}} t$, according to Lemma 22 one of these cases also applies to $s\sigma >_{\mathsf{ACKBO}} t\sigma$. The final case is (3c). So $\nabla_f(s)\restriction_f^{\lessgtr} >_{\mathsf{ACKBO}}^{\mathsf{mul}} \nabla_f(t)\restriction_f^{\lessgtr}$. Suppose $s\sigma >_{\mathsf{ACKBO}} t\sigma$ cannot be obtained by (3a) or (3b). Lemma 22(2) yields $|\nabla_f(s\sigma)| = |\nabla_f(t\sigma)|$ and $\nabla_f(s\sigma)\restriction_f^{\lessgtr} >_{\mathsf{ACKBO}}^{\mathsf{mul}} \nabla_f(t\sigma)\restriction_f^{\lessgtr}$. Hence case (3c) is applicable to obtain $s\sigma >_{\mathsf{ACKBO}} t\sigma$. □

We arrive at the main theorem of this section.

Theorem 24. *The order $>_{\mathsf{ACKBO}}$ is an AC-compatible simplification order.* □

Since we deal with finite non-variadic signatures, simplification orders are well-founded. The following example shows that AC-KBO is not *incremental*, i.e., orientability is not necessarily preserved when the precedence is extended. This is in contrast to the AC-RPO of Rubio [16]. However, this is not necessarily a disadvantage; actually, the example shows that by allowing partial precedences more TRSs can be proved to be AC terminating using AC-KBO.

Example 25. Consider the TRS $\mathcal{R}$ consisting of the rules

$$\mathsf{a} \circ (\mathsf{b} \bullet \mathsf{c}) \to \mathsf{b} \circ \mathsf{f}(\mathsf{a} \bullet \mathsf{c}) \qquad\qquad \mathsf{a} \bullet (\mathsf{b} \circ \mathsf{c}) \to \mathsf{b} \bullet \mathsf{f}(\mathsf{a} \circ \mathsf{c})$$

over the signature $\mathcal{F} = \{\mathsf{a}, \mathsf{b}, \mathsf{c}, \mathsf{f}, \circ, \bullet\}$ with $\circ, \bullet \in \mathcal{F}_{\mathsf{AC}}$. By taking the precedence $\mathsf{f} > \mathsf{a}, \mathsf{b}, \mathsf{c}, \circ, \bullet$ and admissible weight function (w, w_0) with $w(\mathsf{f}) = w(\circ) = w(\bullet) = 0$, $w_0 = w(\mathsf{a}) = w(\mathsf{c}) = 1$, and $w(\mathsf{b}) = 2$, the resulting $>_{\mathsf{ACKBO}}$ orients both rules from left to right. It is essential that $\circ$ and $\bullet$ are incomparable in the precedence: We must have $w(\mathsf{f}) = 0$, so $\mathsf{f} > \mathsf{a}, \mathsf{b}, \mathsf{c}, \circ, \bullet$ is enforced by admissibility. If $\circ > \bullet$ then the first rule can only be oriented from left to right if $\mathsf{a} >_{\mathsf{ACKBO}} \mathsf{f}(\mathsf{a} \bullet \mathsf{c})$ holds, which contradicts the subterm property. If $\bullet > \circ$ then we use the second rule to obtain the impossible $\mathsf{a} >_{\mathsf{ACKBO}} \mathsf{f}(\mathsf{a} \bullet \mathsf{c})$. Similarly, $\mathcal{R}$ is also orientable by $>_{\mathsf{KV'}}$ but we must adopt a non-total precedence.

The final theorem in this section is easily proved.

Theorem 26. *If $>$ is total then $>_{\mathsf{ACKBO}}$ is AC-total on ground terms.* □

6 NP-Hardness of Orientability

It is well-known [10] that KBO orientability is decidable in polynomial time. In this section we show that $>_{\mathsf{KV}}$ orientability is NP-hard even for ground TRSs. The corresponding result for $>_{\mathsf{ACKBO}}$ is given in the full version of this paper [21]. To this end, we reduce a SAT instance to an orientability problem.

Let $\phi = \{C_1, \ldots, C_n\}$ be a CNF SAT problem over propositional variables $p_1, \ldots, p_m$. We consider the signature $\mathcal{F}_\phi$ consisting of an AC symbol $+$, constants c and $\mathsf{d}_1, \ldots, \mathsf{d}_n$, and unary function symbols $p_1, \ldots, p_m$, a, b, and e_i^j for all $i \in \{1, \ldots, n\}$ and $j \in \{0, \ldots, m\}$. We define a ground TRS $\mathcal{R}_\phi$ on $\mathcal{T}(\mathcal{F}_\phi)$ such that $>_{\mathsf{KV}}$ orients $\mathcal{R}_\phi$ if and only if ϕ is satisfiable. The TRS $\mathcal{R}_\phi$ will contain the following base system $\mathcal{R}_0$ that enforces certain constraints on the precedence and the weight function:

$$\mathsf{a}(\mathsf{c}+\mathsf{c}) \to \mathsf{a}(\mathsf{c})+\mathsf{c} \qquad \mathsf{b}(\mathsf{c})+\mathsf{c} \to \mathsf{b}(\mathsf{c}+\mathsf{c}) \qquad \mathsf{a}(\mathsf{b}(\mathsf{b}(\mathsf{c}))) \to \mathsf{b}(\mathsf{a}(\mathsf{a}(\mathsf{c})))$$
$$\mathsf{a}(p_1(\mathsf{c})) \to \mathsf{b}(p_2(\mathsf{c})) \qquad \cdots \qquad \mathsf{a}(p_m(\mathsf{c})) \to \mathsf{b}(\mathsf{a}(\mathsf{c})) \qquad \mathsf{a}(\mathsf{a}(\mathsf{c})) \to \mathsf{b}(p_1(\mathsf{c}))$$

Lemma 27. *The order $>_{\mathsf{KV}}$ is compatible with $\mathcal{R}_0$ if and only if $\mathsf{a} > + > \mathsf{b}$ and $w(\mathsf{a}) = w(\mathsf{b}) = w(p_j)$ for all $1 \leqslant j \leqslant m$.* □

Consider the clause C_i of the form $\{p'_1, \ldots, p'_k, \neg p''_1, \ldots, \neg p''_l\}$. Let U, U', V, and W denote the followings multisets:

$$U = \{p'_1(\mathsf{b}(\mathsf{d}_i)), \ldots, p'_k(\mathsf{b}(\mathsf{d}_i))\} \qquad V = \{p''_0(\mathsf{e}_i^{0,1}), \ldots, p''_{l-1}(\mathsf{e}_i^{l-1,l}), p''_l(\mathsf{e}_i^{l,0})\}$$
$$U' = \{\mathsf{b}(p'_1(\mathsf{d}_i)), \ldots, \mathsf{b}(p'_k(\mathsf{d}_i))\} \qquad W = \{p''_0(\mathsf{e}_i^{0,0}), \ldots, p''_l(\mathsf{e}_i^{l,l})\}$$

where we write p''_0 for a and $\mathsf{e}_i^{j,k}$ for $\mathsf{e}_i^j(\mathsf{e}_i^k(\mathsf{c}))$. The TRS $\mathcal{R}_\phi$ is defined as the union of $\mathcal{R}_0$ and $\{\ell_i \to r_i \mid 1 \leqslant i \leqslant n\}$ with

$$\ell_i = \mathsf{b}(\mathsf{b}(\mathsf{c}+\mathsf{c})) + \textstyle\sum U + \sum V \qquad r_i = \mathsf{b}(\mathsf{c}) + \mathsf{b}(\mathsf{c}) + \sum U' + \sum W$$

Note that the symbols d_i and $\mathsf{e}_i^0, \ldots, \mathsf{e}_i^l$ are specific to the rule $\ell_i \to r_i$.

Lemma 28. *Let $\mathsf{a} > + > \mathsf{b}$. Then, $\mathcal{R}_\phi \subseteq >_{\mathsf{KV}}$ for some (w, w_0) if and only if for every i there is some p such that $p \in C_i$ with $p \not< +$ or $\neg p \in C_i$ with $+ > p$.*

Proof. For the "if" direction we reason as follows. Consider a (partial) weight function w such that $w(\mathsf{a}) = w(\mathsf{b}) = w(p_j)$ for all $1 \leqslant j \leqslant m$. We obtain $\mathcal{R}_0 \subseteq >_{\mathsf{KV}}$ from Lemma 27. Furthermore, consider $C_i = \{p'_1, \ldots, p'_k, \neg p''_1, \ldots, \neg p''_l\}$ and ℓ_i, r_i, U, V and W defined above. Let $L = \nabla_+(\ell_i)$ and $R = \nabla_+(r_i)$. We clearly have $L{\restriction}_+^{\not<} = U{\restriction}_+^{\not<} \cup V{\restriction}_+^{\not<}$ and $R{\restriction}_+^{\not<} = W{\restriction}_+^{\not<}$. It is easy to show that $w(\ell_i) = w(r_i)$. We show $\ell_i >_{\mathsf{KV}} r_i$ by distinguishing two cases.

1. First suppose that $p'_j \not< +$ for some $1 \leqslant j \leqslant k$. We have $p'_j(\mathsf{b}(\mathsf{d}_i)) \in U\restriction^{\not<}_{+}$. Extend the weight function w such that $w(\mathsf{d}_i) = 1+2\cdot\max\{w(\mathsf{e}_i^0),\dots,w(\mathsf{e}_i^l)\}$. Then $p'_j(\mathsf{b}(\mathsf{d}_i)) >_{\mathsf{kv}} t$ for all terms $t \in W$ and hence $L\restriction^{\not<}_{+} >^{\mathsf{mul}}_{\mathsf{kv}} R\restriction^{\not<}_{+}$. Therefore $\ell_i >_{\mathsf{KV}} r_i$ by case (3a).
2. Otherwise, $U\restriction^{\not<}_{+} = \varnothing$ holds. By assumption $+ > p''_j$ for some $1 \leqslant j \leqslant l$. Consider the smallest m such that $+ > p''_m$. Extend the weight function w such that $w(\mathsf{e}_i^m) = 1 + 2\cdot\max\{w(\mathsf{e}_i^j) \mid j \neq m\}$. Then $w(p''_{m-1}(\mathsf{e}_i^{m-1,m})) > w(p''_j(\mathsf{e}_i^{j,j}))$ for all $j \neq m$. From $p''_{m-1} > +$ we infer $p''_{m-1}(\mathsf{e}_i^{m-1,m}) \in V\restriction^{\not<}_{+}$. (Note that $p''_{m-1} = \mathsf{a} > +$ if $m = 1$.) By definition of m, $p''_m(\mathsf{e}_i^{m,m}) \notin W\restriction^{\not<}_{+}$. It follows that $L\restriction^{\not<}_{+} >^{\mathsf{mul}}_{\mathsf{kv}} R\restriction^{\not<}_{+}$ and thus $\ell_i >_{\mathsf{KV}} r_i$ by case (3a).

Next we prove the "only if" direction. So suppose there exists a weight function w such that $\mathcal{R}_\phi \subseteq >_{\mathsf{KV}}$. We obtain $w(\mathsf{a}) = w(\mathsf{b}) = w(p_j)$ for all $1 \leqslant j \leqslant m$ from Lemma 27. It follows that $w(\ell_i) = w(r_i)$ for every $C_i \in \phi$. Suppose for a proof by contradiction that there exists $C_i \in \phi$ such that $+ > p$ for all $p \in C_i$ and $p \not< +$ whenever $\neg p \in C_i$. So $L\restriction^{\not<}_{+} = V$ and $R\restriction^{\not<}_{+} = W$. Since $|R| = |L| + 1$, we must have $\ell_i >_{\mathsf{KV}} r_i$ by case (3a) and thus $V >_{\mathsf{kv}} W$. Let s be a term in V of maximal weight. We must have $w(s) \geqslant w(t)$ for all terms $t \in W$. By construction of the terms in V and W, this is only possible if all symbols e_i^j have the same weight. It follows that all terms in V and W have the same weight. Since $|V| = |W|$ and for every term $s' \in V$ there exists a unique term $t' \in W$ with $\mathsf{root}(s') = \mathsf{root}(t')$, we conclude $V =_{\mathsf{kv}} W$, which provides the desired contradiction. □

After these preliminaries we are ready to prove NP-hardness.

Theorem 29. *The (ground) orientability problem for $>_{\mathsf{KV}}$ is NP-hard.*

Proof. It is sufficient to prove that a CNF formula $\phi = \{C_1,\dots,C_n\}$ is satisfiable if and only if the corresponding $\mathcal{R}_\phi$ is orientable by $>_{\mathsf{KV}}$. Note that the size of $\mathcal{R}_\phi$ is linear in the size of ϕ. First suppose that ϕ is satisfiable. Let α be a satisfying assignment for the atoms $p_1,\dots,p_m$. Define the precedence $>$ as follows: $\mathsf{a} > + > \mathsf{b}$ and $p_j > +$ if $\alpha(p_j)$ is true and $+ > p_j$ if $\alpha(p_j)$ is false. Then $\mathcal{R}_\phi \subseteq >_{\mathsf{KV}}$ follows from Lemma 28. Conversely, if $\mathcal{R}_\phi$ is compatible with $>_{\mathsf{KV}}$ then we define an assignment α for the atoms in ϕ as follows: $\alpha(p)$ is true if $p \not< +$ and $\alpha(p)$ is false if $+ > p$. We claim that α satisfies ϕ. Let C_i be a clause in ϕ. According to Lemma 28, $p \not< +$ for one of the atoms p in C_i or $+ > p$ for one of the negative literals $\neg p$ in C_i. Hence α satisfies C_i by definition. □

7 Subterm Coefficients

Subterm coefficients were introduced in [14] in order to cope with rewrite rules like $\mathsf{f}(x) \to \mathsf{g}(x,x)$ which violate the variable condition. A *subterm coefficient function* is a partial mapping $sc\colon \mathcal{F}\times\mathbb{N}\to\mathbb{N}$ such that for a function symbol f of arity n we have $sc(f,i) > 0$ for all $1 \leqslant i \leqslant n$. Given a weight function (w, w_0) and a subterm coefficient function sc, the weight of a term is inductively defined as follows:

$$w(t) = \begin{cases} w_0 & \text{if } t \in \mathcal{V} \\ w(f) + \sum_{1 \leqslant i \leqslant n} s(f,i) \cdot w(t_i) & \text{if } t = f(t_1, \ldots, t_n) \end{cases}$$

The *variable coefficient* $\mathsf{vc}(x,t)$ of a variable x in a term t is inductively defined as follows: $\mathsf{vc}(x,t) = 1$ if $t = x$, $\mathsf{vc}(x,t) = 0$ if $t \in \mathcal{V} \setminus \{x\}$, and $\mathsf{vc}(x, f(t_1, \ldots, t_n)) = sc(f,1) \cdot \mathsf{vc}(x,t_1) + \cdots + sc(f,n) \cdot \mathsf{vc}(x,t_n)$.

Definition 30. *The order* $>^{sc}_{\mathsf{ACKBO}}$ *is obtained from Definition 15 by replacing the condition "*$|s|_x \geqslant |t|_x$ *for all* $x \in \mathcal{V}$*" with "*$\mathsf{vc}(x,s) \geqslant \mathsf{vc}(x,t)$ *for all* $x \in \mathcal{V}$*" and using the modified weight function introduced above.*

In order to guarantee AC compatibility of $>^{sc}_{\mathsf{ACKBO}}$, the subterm coefficient function sc has to assign the value 1 to arguments of AC symbols. This follows by considering the terms $t \circ (u \circ v)$ and $(t \circ u) \circ v$ for an AC symbol $\circ$ with $sc(\circ, 1) = m$ and $sc(\circ, 2) = n$. We have

$$w(t \circ (u \circ v)) = 2 \cdot w(\circ) + m \cdot w(t) + mn \cdot w(u) + n^2 \cdot w(v)$$
$$w((t \circ u) \circ v) = 2 \cdot w(\circ) + m^2 \cdot w(t) + mn \cdot w(u) + n \cdot w(v)$$

Since $w(t \circ (u \circ v)) = w((t \circ u) \circ v)$ must hold for all possible terms t, u, and v, it follows that $m = m^2$ and $n^2 = n$, implying $m = n = 1$.[7] The proof of the following theorem is very similar to the one of Theorem 24 and hence omitted.

Theorem 31. *If* $sc(f,1) = sc(f,2) = 1$ *for every function symbol* $f \in \mathcal{F}_{\mathsf{AC}}$ *then* $>^{sc}_{\mathsf{ACKBO}}$ *is an AC-compatible simplification order.* □

Example 32. Consider the following TRS $\mathcal{R}$ with $\mathsf{f} \in \mathcal{F}_{\mathsf{AC}}$:

$$\mathsf{g}(\mathsf{0}, \mathsf{f}(x,x)) \to x \qquad (1) \qquad\qquad \mathsf{g}(\mathsf{s}(x), y) \to \mathsf{g}(\mathsf{f}(x,y), \mathsf{0}) \qquad (3)$$
$$\mathsf{g}(x, \mathsf{s}(y)) \to \mathsf{g}(\mathsf{f}(x,y), \mathsf{0}) \qquad (2) \qquad\qquad \mathsf{g}(\mathsf{f}(x,y), \mathsf{0}) \to \mathsf{f}(\mathsf{g}(x,\mathsf{0}), \mathsf{g}(y,\mathsf{0})) \qquad (4)$$

Termination of $\mathcal{R}$ was shown using AC dependency pairs in [11, Example 4.2.30]. Consider a precedence $\mathsf{g} > \mathsf{f} > \mathsf{s} > \mathsf{0}$, and weights and subterm coefficients given by $w_0 = 1$ and the following interpretation $\mathcal{A}$, mapping function symbols in $\mathcal{F}$ to linear polynomials over $\mathbb{N}$:

$$\mathsf{s}_{\mathcal{A}}(x) = x + 6 \quad \mathsf{g}_{\mathcal{A}}(x,y) = 4x + 4y + 5 \quad \mathsf{f}_{\mathcal{A}}(x,y) = x + y + 3 \quad \mathsf{0}_{\mathcal{A}} = 1$$

It is easy to check that the first three rules result in a weight decrease. The left- and right-hand side of rule (4) are both interpreted as $4x + 4y + 21$, so both terms have weight 29, but since $\mathsf{g} > \mathsf{f}$ we conclude termination of $\mathcal{R}$ from case (1) in Definition 15 (30). Note that termination of $\mathcal{R}$ cannot be shown by AC-RPO or any of the previously considered versions of AC-KBO.

[7] This condition is also obtained by restricting [4, Proposition 4] to linear polynomials.

Table 1. Experiments on 145 termination and 67 completion problems

method	orientability			AC-DP			completion		
	yes	time	∞	yes	time	∞	yes	time	∞
AC-KBO	32	1.7	0	66	463.1	3	25	2278.6	37
Steinbach	23	1.6	0	50	463.2	2	24	2235.4	36
Korovin & Voronkov	30	2.0	0	66	474.3	4	25	2279.4	37
KV′	30	2.1	0	66	472.4	3	25	2279.6	37
subterm coefficients	37	47.1	0	68	464.7	2	28	1724.7	26
AC-RPO	63	2.8	0	79	501.5	4	28	1701.6	26
total	72			94			31		

8 Experiments

We ran experiments on a server equipped with eight dual-core AMD Opteron® processors 885 running at a clock rate of 2.6GHz with 64GB of main memory. The different versions of AC-KBO considered in this paper as well as AC-RPO [16] were implemented on top of $\mathsf{T_TT_2}$ using encodings in SAT/SMT. These encodings resemble those for standard KBO [22] and transfinite KBO [20]. The encoding of multiset extensions of order pairs are based on [5], but careful modifications were required to deal with submultisets induced by the precedence.

For termination experiments, our test set comprises all AC problems in the *Termination Problem Data Base*,[8] all examples in this paper, some further problems harvested from the literature, and constraint systems produced by the completion tool mkbtt [19] (145 TRSs in total). The timeout was set to 60 seconds. The results are summarized in Table 1, where we list for each order the number of successful termination proofs, the total time, and the number of timeouts (column ∞). The 'orientability' column directly applies the order to orient all the rules. Although AC-RPO succeeds on more input problems, termination of 9 TRSs could only be established by (variants of) AC-KBO. We found that our definition of AC-KBO is about equally powerful as Korovin and Voronkov's order, but both are considerably more useful than Steinbach's version. When it comes to proving termination, we did not observe a difference between Definitions 9 and 11. Subterm coefficients clearly increase the success rate, although efficiency is affected. In all settings partial precedences were allowed.

The 'AC-DP' column applies the order in the AC-dependency pair framework of [1], in combination with *argument filterings* and *usable rules*. Here AC symbols in dependency pairs are *unmarked*, as proposed in [15]. In this setting the variants of AC-KBO become considerably more powerful and competitive to AC-RPO, since argument filterings relax the variable condition, as pointed out in [22].

For completion experiments, we ran the normalized completion tool mkbtt with AC-RPO and the variants of AC-KBO for termination checks on 67 equational systems collected from the literature. The overall timeout was set to 60 seconds, the timeout for each termination check to 1.5 seconds. Table 1

[8] `http://termination-portal.org/wiki/TPDB`

Table 2. Complexity results (KV is the ground version of $>_{\mathsf{KV}}$)

problem	KBO	AC-KBO	KV	KV′
membership	P	P	P	NP-hard
orientability	P	NP-hard	NP-hard	NP-hard

summarizes our results, listing for each order the number of successful completions, the total time, and the number of timeouts. All experimental details, source code, and $\mathsf{T_TT_2}$ binaries are available online.[9]

The following example can be completed using AC-KBO, whereas AC-RPO does not succeed.

Example 33. Consider the following TRS $\mathcal{R}$ [15] for addition of binary numbers:

$$\# + \mathsf{0} \to \# \qquad x\mathsf{0} + y\mathsf{0} \to (x+y)\mathsf{0} \qquad x\mathsf{1} + y\mathsf{1} \to (x+y+\#\mathsf{1})\mathsf{0}$$
$$x + \# \to x \qquad x\mathsf{0} + y\mathsf{1} \to (x+y)\mathsf{1}$$

Here $+ \in \mathcal{F}_{\mathsf{AC}}$, $\mathsf{0}$ and $\mathsf{1}$ are unary operators in postfix notation, and # denotes the empty bit sequence. For example, #100 represents the number 4. This TRS is not compatible with AC-RPO but AC termination can easily be shown by AC-KBO, for instance with the weight function (w, w_0) with $w(+) = 0$, $w_0 = w(\mathsf{0}) = w(\#) = 1$, and $w(\mathsf{1}) = 3$. The system can be completed into an AC convergent TRS using AC-KBO but not with AC-RPO.

9 Conclusion

We revisited the two variants of AC-compatible extensions of KBO. We extended the first version $>_{\mathsf{S}}$ introduced by Steinbach [17] to a new version $>_{\mathsf{ACKBO}}$, and presented a rigorous correctness proof. By this we conclude correctness of $>_{\mathsf{S}}$, which had been put in doubt in [9]. We also modified the order $>_{\mathsf{KV}}$ by Korovin and Voronkov [9] to a new version $>_{\mathsf{KV'}}$ which is monotone on non-ground terms, in contrast to $>_{\mathsf{KV}}$. We also presented several complexity results regarding these variants (see Table 2). While a polynomial time algorithm is known for the orientability problem of standard KBO [10], the problem becomes NP-hard even for the ground version of $>_{\mathsf{KV}}$, as well as for our $>_{\mathsf{ACKBO}}$. Somewhat unexpectedly, even deciding $>_{\mathsf{KV'}}$ is NP-hard while it is linear for standard KBO [13]. In contrast, the corresponding problem is polynomial-time for our $>_{\mathsf{ACKBO}}$. Finally, we implemented these variants of AC-compatible KBO as well as the AC-dependency pair framework of Alarcón *et al.* [1]. We presented full experimental results both for termination proving and normalized completion.

Acknowledgments. We are grateful to Konstantin Korovin for discussions and the reviewers for their detailed comments which helped to improve the presentation.

[9] `http://cl-informatik.uibk.ac.at/software/ackbo`

References

1. Alarcón, B., Lucas, S., Meseguer, J.: A dependency pair framework for $A \vee C$-termination. In: Ölveczky, P.C. (ed.) WRLA 2010. LNCS, vol. 6381, pp. 35–51. Springer, Heidelberg (2010)
2. Arts, T., Giesl, J.: Termination of term rewriting using dependency pairs. TCS 236(1-2), 133–178 (2000)
3. Bachmair, L., Plaisted, D.A.: Termination orderings for associative-commutative rewriting systems. JSC 1, 329–349 (1985)
4. Ben Cherifa, A., Lescanne, P.: Termination of rewriting systems by polynomial interpretations and its implementation. SCP 9(2), 137–159 (1987)
5. Codish, M., Giesl, J., Schneider-Kamp, P., Thiemann, R.: SAT solving for termination proofs with recursive path orders and dependency pairs. JAR 49(1), 53–93 (2012)
6. Dershowitz, N.: Orderings for term-rewriting systems. TCS 17(3), 279–301 (1982)
7. Giesl, J., Kapur, D.: Dependency pairs for equational rewriting. In: Middeldorp, A. (ed.) RTA 2001. LNCS, vol. 2051, pp. 93–107. Springer, Heidelberg (2001)
8. Knuth, D., Bendix, P.: Simple word problems in universal algebras. In: Leech, J. (ed.) Computational Problems in Abstract Algebra, pp. 263–297. Pergamon Press, New York (1970)
9. Korovin, K., Voronkov, A.: An AC-compatible Knuth-Bendix order. In: Baader, F. (ed.) CADE-19. LNCS (LNAI), vol. 2741, pp. 47–59. Springer, Heidelberg (2003)
10. Korovin, K., Voronkov, A.: Orienting rewrite rules with the Knuth-Bendix order. I&C 183(2), 165–186 (2003)
11. Kusakari, K.: AC-Termination and Dependency Pairs of Term Rewriting Systems. PhD thesis, JAIST (2000)
12. Kusakari, K., Toyama, Y.: On proving AC-termination by AC-dependency pairs. IEICE Transactions on Information and Systems E84-D(5), 439–447 (2001)
13. Löchner, B.: Things to know when implementing KBO. JAR 36(4), 289–310 (2006)
14. Ludwig, M., Waldmann, U.: An extension of the Knuth-Bendix ordering with LPO-like properties. In: Dershowitz, N., Voronkov, A. (eds.) LPAR 2007. LNCS (LNAI), vol. 4790, pp. 348–362. Springer, Heidelberg (2007)
15. Marché, C., Urbain, X.: Modular and incremental proofs of AC-termination. JSC 38(1), 873–897 (2004)
16. Rubio, A.: A fully syntactic AC-RPO. I&C 178(2), 515–533 (2002)
17. Steinbach, J.: AC-termination of rewrite systems: A modified Knuth-Bendix ordering. In: Kirchner, H., Wechler, W. (eds.) ALP 1990. LNCS, vol. 463, pp. 372–386. Springer, Heidelberg (1990)
18. Thiemann, R., Allais, G., Nagele, J.: On the formalization of termination techniques based on multiset orderings. In: Proc. RTA-23. LIPIcs, vol. 15, pp. 339–354 (2012)
19. Winkler, S.: Termination Tools in Automated Reasoning. PhD thesis, UIBK (2013)
20. Winkler, S., Zankl, H., Middeldorp, A.: Ordinals and Knuth-Bendix orders. In: Bjørner, N., Voronkov, A. (eds.) LPAR-18 2012. LNCS, vol. 7180, pp. 420–434. Springer, Heidelberg (2012)
21. Yamada, A., Winkler, S., Hirokawa, N., Middeldorp, A.: AC-KBO revisited. CoRR abs/1403.0406 (2014)
22. Zankl, H., Hirokawa, N., Middeldorp, A.: KBO orientability. JAR 43(2), 173–201 (2009)

Well-Structured Pushdown System: Case of Dense Timed Pushdown Automata

Xiaojuan Cai[1] and Mizuhito Ogawa[2]

[1] Shanghai Jiao Tong University, China
cxj@sjtu.edu.cn
[2] Japan Advanced Institute of Science and Technology
mizuhito@jaist.ac.jp

Abstract. This paper investigates a general framework of a pushdown system with well-quasi-ordered states and stack alphabet to show decidability of reachability, which is an extension of our earlier work (*Well-structured Pushdown Systems, CONCUR 2013*). As an instance, an alternative proof of the decidability of the reachability for dense-timed pushdown system (in *P.A. Abdulla, M.F. Atig, F. Stenman, Dense-Timed Pushdown Automata, IEEE LICS 2012*) is presented. Our proof would be more robust for extensions, e.g., regular valuations with time.

1 Introduction

Infinite state transition systems appear in many places still keeping certain decidable properties, e.g., pushdown systems (PDS), timed automata [5], and vector addition systems (VAS, or Petri nets). Well-structured transition systems (WSTSs) [3,14] are one of successful general frameworks to reason about decidability. The coverability of VASs, the reachability of communicating finite state machines with lossy channels [14], and the inclusion problem between timed automata with single clocks [18] are beginning of a long list.

A natural extension of WSTS is to associate a stack. It is tempting to apply Higman's lemma on stacks. However this fails immediately, since the monotonicity of transitions with respect to the embedding on stacks hardly holds.

This paper investigates a general framework for PDSs with well-quasi-ordered states and stack alphabet, *well-structured pushdown systems*. Well-quasi-orderings (WQOs) over stack alphabet are extended to stacks by the element-wise comparison. Note that this extension will not preserve WQO (nor well founded). By combining classical Pre^*-automaton technique [7,15,12], we reduce the argument on stacks to that on stack symbols, and similar to WSTS, finite convergence of antichains during Pre^*-automata saturation is shown by a WQO.

When the set P of states is finite, we have decidability of coverability [8]. When P is infinite (but equipped with WQO), we can state decidability of quasi-coverability only. To compensate, we introduce a well-formed projection $\Downarrow_\Upsilon$, which extracts a core shape from the stack related to pushdown transitions. If we find $\Downarrow_\Upsilon$ such that, for configurations c, c' with $c \hookrightarrow c'$ and $\Upsilon = \{c \mid c = \Downarrow_\Upsilon (c)\}$,

M. Codish and E. Sumii (Eds.): FLOPS 2014, LNCS 8475, pp. 336–352, 2014.

– **compatibility:** $\Downarrow_{\Upsilon}(c) \hookrightarrow \Downarrow_{\Upsilon}(c')$, and
– **stability:** $c \in \Upsilon$ if, and only if, $c' \in \Upsilon$.

the quasi-coverability leads the configuration reachability. The compatibility strengthens the quasi-coverability to the coverability, and the stability boosts the coverability to the configuration reachability.

As an instance, we encode a dense-timed pushdown automaton (DTPDA) [2] into a snapshot PDS, inspired by the digitization techniques in [18]. A snapshot PDS has the set of snapshot words as stack alphabet. A snapshot word is essentially a region construction of the dimension equal to its size. Since a snapshot PDS contains non-standard pop rules (i.e., $(p, \gamma\gamma') \to (q, \gamma''))$, by associating a top stack symbol to a state, it is encoded as a PDS with WQO states and stack alphabet. Our general framework shows an alternative decidability proof of the reachability of a DTPDA [2].[1]

Our contribution is not on logically difficult proofs, but clarifying the proof structure behind theorems. Different from [2], our encoding is inspired by [18], and would be more robust for extensions, e.g., regular valuations [13] with time.

Related Work

There are lots of works with context-sensitive infinite state systems. A process rewrite systems combines a PDS and a Petri net, in which vector additions/subtractions between adjacent stack frames during push/pop operations are prohibited [17]. With this restrictions, its reachability becomes decidable. A WQO automaton [9], is a WSTS with auxiliary storage (e.g., stacks and queues). It proves that the coverability is decidable under compatibility of *rank* functions with a WQO, of which an Multiset PDS is an instance. A timed pushdown automaton is a timed extension of a pushdown automaton. It has only global clocks, and the region construction [5] encodes it to a standard PDS [6,10,11]. DTPDA [2] firstly introduces local ages, which are stored with stack symbols when pushed, and never reset. DTPDA utilizes them to check whether an age in a stack frame satisfies constraints when pop occurs.

A WSPDS is firstly introduced in [8]. It focuses on WSPDSs with finite control states (and well-quasi-ordered stack alphabet), whereas the paper explores WSPDSs with well-quasi-ordered control states at the cost of weakening the target property from the coverability to the quasi-coverability. The well-formed projection (Section 5), if exists, strengthens it again to the reachability.

2 Dense-Timed Pushdown Automata

Dense-timed pushdown automaton (DTPDA) extends timed pushdown automaton (TPDA) with *local ages* [2]. A local age in each context is set when a push transition occurs, and restricts a pop transition only when the value of a local

[1] In [2], only the state reachability is mentioned, but the proof is applied also for the configuration reachability.

age meets the condition. The values of local ages proceed synchronously to global clocks, and they are never reset. Following [2], we omit input alphabet, since our focus is on reachability (regardless of an input word).

As notational convention, Section 2 and 7.2 use I for an interval (obeying to [2]), whereas Section 4 used I for an ideal.

Definition 1. *A DTPDA is a tuple* $\langle S, s_{init}, \Gamma, \mathcal{C}, \Delta \rangle$, *where*

- S *is a finite set of states with the initial state* $s_{init} \in S$,
- Γ *is a finite stack alphabet,*
- $\mathcal{C}$ *is a finite set of clocks, and*
- Δ *is a finite set of transitions.*

A transition $t \in \Delta$ *is a triplet* (s, op, s') *in which* $s, s' \in S$ *and* op *is either of*

- **Local.** nop, *a state transition in* S,
- **Assignment.** $x \leftarrow I$, *assign an arbitrary value in* I *to a clock* $x \in \mathcal{C}$,
- **Test.** $x \in I?$, *test whether the value of a clock* $x \in \mathcal{C}$ *is in* I,
- **Push.** $push(\gamma, I)$, *push* γ *on a stack associated with a local age of an arbitrary value in* I, *and*
- **Pop.** $pop(\gamma, I)$, *pop* γ *off a stack if the associated age* a *is in* I.

where I *is an interval bounded by natural numbers (i.e.,* $[l, h], (l, h], [l, h), (l, h)$ *for* $l, h \in \mathbb{N} \cup \{\omega\}$ *with* $l \leq h$*).*

If each I in **Push** and **Pop** rules is $[0, \infty)$ (i.e., no conditions on local ages), we say simply a Timed Pushdown Automaton.

Definition 2. *For a DTPDA* $\langle S, s_{init}, \Gamma, \mathcal{C}, \Delta \rangle$, *a configuration is a triplet* (s, ν, w) *with* $s \in S$, *a clock valuation* $\nu : \mathcal{C} \to \mathbb{R}_{\geq 0}$, *and* $w \in (\Gamma \times \mathbb{R}_{\geq 0})^*$. *We refer* s *in a configuration* $c = (s, \nu, w)$ *by* $state(c)$. *For* $t \in \mathbb{R}_{\geq 0}$, *we denote*

- $\nu_0(x) = 0$ *for* $x \in \mathcal{C}$,
- $\nu_{x \leftarrow t}(x) = t$ *and* $\nu_{x \leftarrow t}(y) = \nu(y)$ *if* $y \neq x$,
- $(\nu + t)(x) = \nu(x) + t$ *for* $x \in \mathcal{C}$, *and*
- $w + t = (\gamma_1, t_1 + t). \cdots .(\gamma_k, t_k + t)$ *for* $w = (\gamma_1, t_1). \cdots .(\gamma_k, t_k)$.

There are two types of transitions, timed $\xrightarrow{t}_{Time}$ *and* discrete *transitions* $\xrightarrow{op}_{Disc}$. *Semantics of a timed transition is* $(s, \nu, w) \xrightarrow{t}_{Time} (s, \nu + t, w + t)$, *and a discrete transitions* (s, op, s') *is either*

- **Local.** $(s, \nu, w) \xrightarrow{nop}_{Disc} (s', \nu, w)$,
- **Assignment.** $(s, \nu, w) \xrightarrow{x \leftarrow I}_{Disc} (s', \nu_{x \leftarrow t}, w)$ *for* $t \in I$,
- **Test.** $(s, \nu, w) \xrightarrow{x \in I?}_{Disc} (s', \nu, w)$ *if* $\nu(x) \in I$,
- **Push.** $(s, \nu, w) \xrightarrow{push(\gamma, I)}_{Disc} (s', \nu, (\gamma, t).w)$ *for* $t \in I$, *and*
- **Pop.** $(s, \nu, (\gamma, t).w) \xrightarrow{pop(\gamma, I)}_{Disc} (s', \nu, w)$ *if* $t \in I$.

We assume that the initial configuration is $(s_{init}, \nu_0, \epsilon)$.

Example 1. The figure shows transitions between configurations in which $S = \{\bullet\}$ (omitted), $\mathcal{C} = \{x_1, x_2, x_3\}$, and $\Gamma = \{a, b, d\}$. From c_1 to c_2, a discrete transition $push(d, [1, 3])$ pushes $(d, 2.6)$ into the stack. At the timed transition from c_2 to c_3, 2.6 time units have elapsed, and each value grows older by 2.6. From c_3 to c_4, the value of x_2 is assigned to 3.8, which lies in the interval $(2, 5]$, and the last transition pops $(d, 5.2)$ after testing that its local age lies in $[4, 6]$.

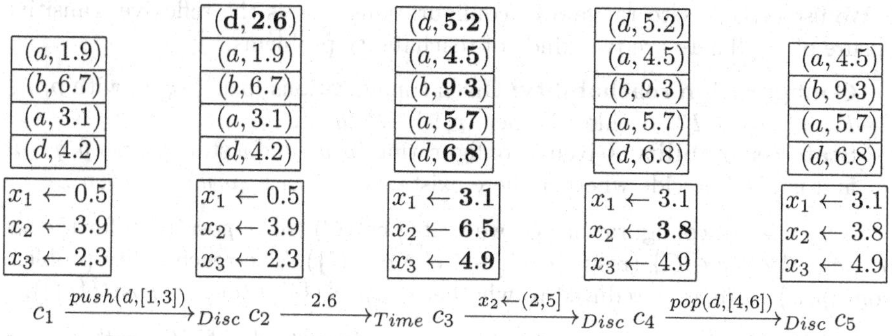

3 P-Automaton

A textbook standard technique to decide the emptiness of a pushdown automaton is, first converting it to context free grammar (with cubic explosion), and then applying CYK algorithm, which is a well-known dynamic programming technique. A practical alternative (with the same complexity) is a P-automaton [15,12]. Starting from a regular set C of initial configurations (resp. target configurations) $Post^*$ (resp. Pre^*) saturation procedure is applied on an initial P-automaton (which accepts C) until convergence. The resulting P-automaton accepts the set of all successors (resp. predecessors) of C. In literature, it is applied only for PDSs with finite control states and stack alphabet. We confirm that it works for PDSs without finite assumptions (at the cost of infinite convergence), and extend it to the coverability and the quasi-coverability.

3.1 P-Automaton for Reachability of Pushdown System

In the standard definition, a pushdown system (PDS) has a finite set of states and finite stack alphabet. We will consider a PDS with an infinite set of states and infinite stack alphabet. For (possibly infinitely many) individual transition rules, we introduce a partial function ψ to describe a pattern of transitions. We denote the set of partial functions from X to Y by $\mathcal{P}Fun(X, Y)$.

Definition 3. *A pushdown system (PDS)* $\mathcal{M} = \langle P, \Gamma, \Delta \rangle$ *consists of a finite set* $\Delta \subseteq \mathcal{P}Fun(P \times \Gamma, P \times \Gamma^2) \cup \mathcal{P}Fun(P \times \Gamma, P \times \Gamma) \cup \mathcal{P}Fun(P \times \Gamma, P)$ *of transition rules. We say that* $\psi \in \Delta$ *is a push, internal, and pop rule if* $\psi \in \mathcal{P}Fun(P \times \Gamma, P \times \Gamma^2)$, $\psi \in \mathcal{P}Fun(P \times \Gamma, P \times \Gamma)$, *and* $\psi \in \mathcal{P}Fun(P \times \Gamma, P)$, *respectively.*

A configuration $\langle p, w \rangle$ *consists of* $p \in P$ *and* $w \in \Gamma^*$. *For a transition rule* $\psi \in \Delta$, *a transition is* $\langle p, \gamma w \rangle \hookrightarrow \langle p', vw \rangle$ *for* $(p', v) = \psi(p, \gamma)$

Remark 1. Often in multi-thread program modelings and in snapshot PDSs (Section 7.2) for discretizing DTPDAs, PDSs are defined with finite control states, but with non-standard pop rules, like $\langle p, \gamma_1\gamma_2\rangle \hookrightarrow \langle q, \gamma\rangle \in \mathcal{P}Fun(P \times \Gamma^2, P \times \Gamma)$ with $|P| < \infty$. This can be encoded into PDSs in Definition 3 by associating a top stack symbol to a state, like $\langle (p, \gamma_1), \gamma_2\rangle \hookrightarrow \langle (q, \gamma), \epsilon\rangle \in \mathcal{P}Fun(P' \times \Gamma, P')$ with $P' = P \times \Gamma$, at the cost that the set P' of control states becomes infinite.

We use $c_1, c_2, \cdots$ to range over configurations. $\hookrightarrow^*$ is the reflexive transitive closure of $\hookrightarrow$. There are two kinds of reachability problems.

- **Configuration reachability:** Given configurations $\langle p, w\rangle$, $\langle q, v\rangle$ with $p, q \in P$ and $w, v \in \Gamma^*$, decide whether $\langle p, w\rangle \hookrightarrow^* \langle q, v\rangle$.
- **State reachability:** Given a configuration $\langle p, w\rangle$ and a state q with $p, q \in P$ and $w \in \Gamma^*$, decide whether there exists $v \in \Gamma^*$ with $\langle p, w\rangle \hookrightarrow^* \langle q, v\rangle$.

Given a set of configurations C, we write $pre^*(C)$ (resp. $post^*(C)$) for the set $\{c' \mid c' \hookrightarrow^* c \wedge c \in C\}$ (resp. $\{c' \mid c \hookrightarrow^* c' \wedge c \in C\}$). The reachability problem from $\langle p, w\rangle$ to $\langle q, v\rangle$ is reduced to whether $c \in pre^*(\{c'\})$ (or $c' \in post^*(\{c\})$).

Definition 4. *A Pre*-automaton $\mathcal{A}$ is a quadruplet (S, Γ, ∇, F) with $F \subseteq S$ and $\nabla \subseteq S \times \Gamma \times S$. A Pre*-automaton is* initial *if each state in $S \cap P$ has no incoming transitions and S is finite. $\mathcal{A}$ accepts a configuration $\langle p, w\rangle$ with $p \in P$ and $w \in \Gamma^*$, if w is accepted starting from p (as an initial state).*

The set of configurations accepted by $\mathcal{A}$ is denoted by $L(\mathcal{A})$. When $(p, \gamma, q) \in \nabla$, we denote $p \overset{\gamma}{\mapsto} q$. For $w = \gamma_1 \dots \gamma_k \in \Gamma^*$, $p \overset{\gamma_1}{\mapsto} \cdots \overset{\gamma_k}{\mapsto} q$ is denoted by $p \overset{w}{\mapsto}^* q \in \nabla^*$. If $k = 0$ (i.e., $p \overset{\epsilon}{\mapsto} q$), we assume $p = q$.

Starting from an initial Pre^*-automaton $\mathcal{A}_0$ that accepts C (i.e., $C = L(\mathcal{A}_0)$), the repeated (possibly infinite) applications of saturation rules

$$\frac{(S, \Gamma, \nabla, F)}{(S \cup \{p'\}, \Gamma, \nabla \cup \{p' \overset{\gamma}{\mapsto} q\}, F)} \quad \text{if } p \overset{w}{\mapsto}^* q \in \nabla^* \text{ and } \psi(p', \gamma) = (p, w) \text{ for } \psi \in \Delta$$

converge to $Pre^*(\mathcal{A}_0)$. Note that saturation rules never eliminate transitions, but monotonically enlarge.

Theorem 1. *[15,7,12] (Theorem 1 in [8]) For a PDS, $pre^*(C) = L(Pre^*(\mathcal{A}_0))$. where $C = L(\mathcal{A}_0)$.*

Example 2. Let $\langle \{p_i\}, \{\gamma_i\}, \Delta\rangle$ be a pushdown system with $i = 0, 1, 2$ and Δ given below. The saturation $\mathcal{A}$ of Pre^*-automata started from $\mathcal{A}_0$ accepting $C = \{\langle p_0, \gamma_0\gamma_0\rangle\}$. $L(\mathcal{A})$ coincides $pre^*(C)$.

(1). $\langle p_0, \gamma_0\rangle \rightarrow \langle p_1, \gamma_1\gamma_0\rangle$
(2). $\langle p_1, \gamma_1\rangle \rightarrow \langle p_2, \gamma_2\gamma_0\rangle$
(3). $\langle p_2, \gamma_2\rangle \rightarrow \langle p_0, \gamma_1\rangle$
(4). $\langle p_0, \gamma_1\rangle \hookrightarrow \langle p_0, \epsilon\rangle$

$\mathcal{A}_0$:
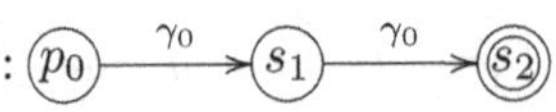

$\mathcal{A}$:
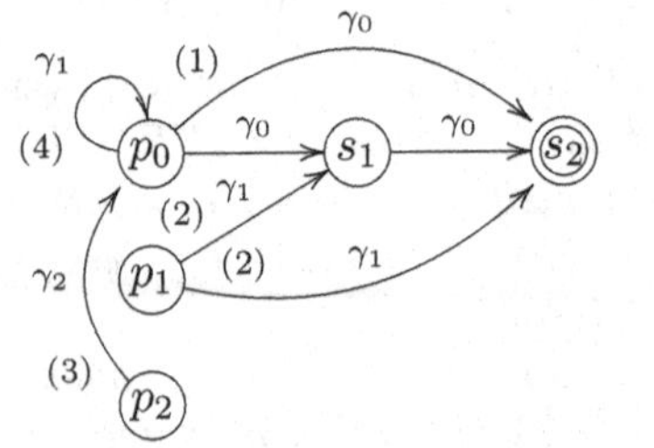

Remark 2. Since the saturation procedure monotonically extends Pre^*-automaton, even if a PDS has an infinite set of states / stack alphabet and the initial Pre^*-automaton $\mathcal{A}_0$ has infinite states, it converges (after infinite many saturation steps), and $pre^*(C) = L(Pre^*(\mathcal{A}_0))$ holds.

3.2 P-Automata for Coverability of OPDS

A quasi-ordering (QO) is a reflexive transitive binary relation. We denote the upward (resp. downward) closure of X by $X^{\uparrow}$ (resp. $X^{\downarrow}$), i.e., $X^{\uparrow} = \{y \mid \exists x \in X.x \leq y\}$ (resp. $X^{\downarrow} = \{y \mid \exists x \in X.y \leq x\}$).

For a PDS $\mathcal{M} = \langle P, \Gamma, \Delta \rangle$, we introduce QOs $(P, \preceq)$ and $(\Gamma, \leq)$ on P and Γ, respectively. We call $\mathcal{M} = \langle (P, \preceq), (\Gamma, \leq), \Delta \rangle$ an ordered PDS (OPDS).

Definition 5. *For* $w_1 = \alpha_1\alpha_2 \cdots \alpha_n, w_2 = \beta_1\beta_2 \cdots \beta_m \in \Gamma^*$, *let*

- **Element-wise comparison** $w_1 \lll w_2$ *if* $m = n$ *and* $\forall i \in [1..n].\alpha_i \leq \beta_i$.
- **Embedding** $w_1 \preccurlyeq w_2$ *if there is an order-preserving injection* f *from* $[0..n]$ *to* $[0..m]$ *with* $\alpha_i \leq \beta_{f(i)}$ *for each* $i \in [0..n]$.

We extend $\lll$ on configurations such that $(p, w) \lll (q, v)$ if $p \preceq q$ and $w \lll v$.

A partial function $\psi \in \mathcal{PF}un(X, Y)$ is *monotonic* if $\gamma \leq \gamma'$ and $\gamma \in dom(\psi)$ imply $\psi(\gamma) \lll \psi(\gamma')$ and $\gamma' \in dom(\psi)$ for each $\gamma, \gamma' \in X$. We say that an OPDS $\mathcal{M} = \langle (P, \preceq), (\Gamma, \leq), \Delta \rangle$ is *monotonic* if ψ is monotonic for each $\psi \in \Delta$.

- **Coverability:** Given configurations (p, w), (q, v) with $p, q \in P$ and $w, v \in \Gamma^*$, decide whether there exist $q' \in P$ and $v' \in \Gamma^*$ with $q \preceq q'$, $v \lll v'$, and $(p, w) \hookrightarrow^* (q', v')$.

Coverability is reduced to whether $(p, w) \in pre^*(\{(q, v)\}^{\uparrow})$. For coverability, we restrict saturation rules of Pre^*-automata.

$$\frac{(S, \Gamma, \nabla, F)}{(S \oplus \{p'\}, \Gamma, \nabla \oplus \{p' \overset{\gamma}{\mapsto} q\}, F)} \quad \begin{array}{l}\text{if } p \overset{w}{\longmapsto}{}^{*} q \in \nabla^* \text{ and} \\ \psi(p', \gamma) \in \{(p, w)\}^{\uparrow} \text{ for } \psi \in \Delta\end{array}$$

where $(S \oplus \{p'\}, \nabla \oplus \{p' \overset{\gamma}{\mapsto} q\})$ is

$$\begin{cases} (S, \nabla) & \text{if there exists } \{p'' \overset{\gamma'}{\mapsto} q\} \in \nabla \text{ with } p'' \preceq p' \text{ and } \gamma' \leq \gamma \\ (S \cup \{p'\}, \nabla \cup \{p' \overset{\gamma}{\mapsto} q\}) & \text{otherwise.} \end{cases}$$

Theorem 2. *(Theorem 3 in [8]) For a monotonic OPDS,* $pre^*(C^{\uparrow}) = L(Pre^*(\mathcal{A}_0))$. *where* $C^{\uparrow} = L(\mathcal{A}_0)$.

3.3 P-Automata for Quasi-Coverability of OPDS

- **Quasi-coverability.** Given configurations $\langle p, w \rangle$, $\langle q, v \rangle$, decide whether there exist $\langle p', w' \rangle$ and $\langle q', v' \rangle$ such that $\langle p, w \rangle \lll \langle p', w' \rangle$, $\langle q, v \rangle \lll \langle q', v' \rangle$, and $\langle p', w' \rangle \hookrightarrow^* \langle q', v' \rangle$.

Quasi-coverability is reduced to whether $\langle p, w\rangle \in pre^*(\{(q,v)\}^\uparrow)^\downarrow$. For quasi-coverability, we further restrict saturation rules of Pre^*-automata.

$$\frac{(S,\Gamma,\nabla,F)}{(S\oplus\{p'\},\Gamma,\nabla\oplus\{p'\overset{\gamma}{\mapsto} q\},F)} \qquad \begin{array}{l}\text{if } p \overset{w}{\mapsto}{}^{*} q \in \nabla^* \text{ and}\\ \psi(p',\gamma)\in\{(p,w)\}^\uparrow \text{ for } \psi\in\Delta\end{array}$$

where $(S\oplus\{p'\},\nabla\oplus\{p'\overset{\gamma}{\mapsto} q\})$ is

$$\begin{cases}(S,\nabla) & \text{if there exists } \{p''\overset{\gamma'}{\mapsto} q\}\in\nabla \text{ with } p''\preceq p' \text{ and } \gamma'\leq\gamma\\ (S,\nabla\cup\{p''\overset{\gamma}{\mapsto} q\}) & \text{if there exists } p''\in S\cap P \text{ with } p''\preceq p'\\ (S\cup\{p'\},\nabla\cup\{p'\overset{\gamma}{\mapsto} q\}) & \text{otherwise.}\end{cases}$$

The second condition suppresses adding new states in Pre^*-automata, and the first condition gives a termination condition for adding new edges.

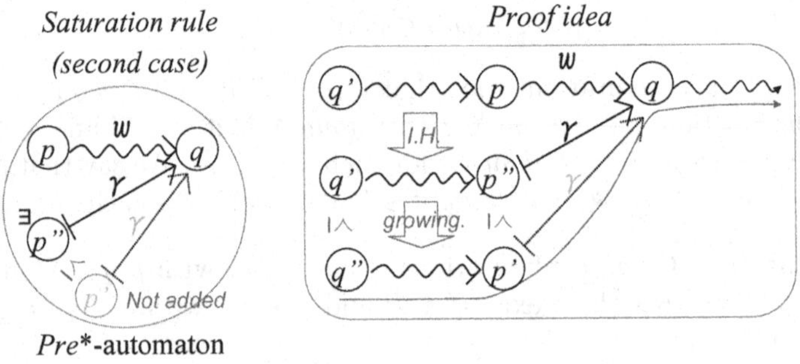

Definition 6. *An OPDS* $\mathcal{M} = \langle (P,\preceq),(\Gamma,\leq),\Delta\rangle$ *is* growing *if, for each* $\psi(p,\gamma) = (q,w)$ *with* $\psi\in\Delta$ *and* $(q',w')\gtrsim(q,w)$, *there exists* (p',γ') *with* $(p',\gamma')\gtrsim(p,\gamma)$ *such that* $\psi(p',\gamma')\gtrsim(q',w')$.

Lemma 1 is obtained by induction on steps of Pre^*-automata saturation.

Lemma 1. *For a monotonic and growing OPDS, assume* $p \overset{w}{\longmapsto}{}^{*} s$ *in* $Pre^*(\mathcal{A}_0)$. *For each* $(p',w')\gtrsim(p,w)$,

- *If* $s\in P$, *there exist* $(p'',w'')\gtrsim(p',w')$ *and* $q'\succeq s$ *with* $\langle p'',w''\rangle \hookrightarrow^* \langle q',\epsilon\rangle$.
- *If* $s\in S\setminus P$, *there exist* $(p'',w'')\gtrsim(p',w')$, $q \overset{v}{\longmapsto}{}^{*} s$ *in* $\mathcal{A}_0$ *with* $q\in P$, *and* $\langle q',v'\rangle \gtrsim \langle q,v\rangle$ *such that* $\langle p'',w''\rangle\hookrightarrow^*\langle q',v'\rangle$.

For simplicity, we say "c_0 covers c_1" to mean that there exists $c_1'\gtrsim c_1$ with $c_0\hookrightarrow^* c_1'$. The next **Claim** is easily proved by induction on the steps of $\hookrightarrow$.

Claim. For a monotonic and growing OPDS, if $\langle p,w\rangle\hookrightarrow^*\langle q,v\rangle$, then for any $(q',v')\gtrsim(q,v)$, there exists $(p',w')\gtrsim(p,w)$ such that $\langle p',w'\rangle$ covers $\langle q',v'\rangle$.

Proof. By induction on steps of the Pre^* saturation procedure $\mathcal{A}_0, \mathcal{A}_1, \mathcal{A}_2, \cdots$. For $\mathcal{A}_0$, the statements hold immediately. Assume the statements hold for $\mathcal{A}_i$, and $\mathcal{A}_{i+1}$ is constructed by adding new transition $p_0 \overset{\gamma_0}{\mapsto} q_0$.

$$\frac{(S, \Gamma, \nabla, F)}{(S \cup \{p_0\}, \Gamma, \nabla \oplus \{p_0 \overset{\gamma_0}{\mapsto} q_0\}, F)} \quad \begin{array}{l}\text{if } p_1 \overset{w_1}{\mapsto}{}^* q_0 \in \nabla^* \text{ and} \\ \psi(p_0, \gamma_0) \in \{(p_1, w_1)\}^\uparrow \text{ for } \psi \in \Delta\end{array}$$

We give a proof only for the first statement. The second statement is similarly proved. According to the definition of $\oplus$, there are three cases:

- There exists $\{p'_0 \overset{\gamma'_0}{\mapsto} q_0\} \in \nabla$ with $p'_0 \preceq p_0$ and $\gamma'_0 \leq \gamma_0$. Nothing added.
- There exists p'_0 in $S \cap P$ and $p'_0 \preceq p_0$. Then, $p'_0 \overset{\gamma_0}{\mapsto} q_0$ is added.
- Otherwise. $p_0 \overset{\gamma_0}{\mapsto} q_0$ is added.

The second case is the most complex, and we focus on it. Assume that a path $p \overset{w}{\longmapsto}{}^* q$ contains $p'_0 \overset{\gamma_0}{\mapsto} q_0$ k-times. We apply (nested) induction on k, and we focus on its leftmost occurrence. Let $w = w_l \gamma_0 w_r$ and $p \overset{w_l}{\longmapsto}{}^* p'_0 \overset{\gamma_0}{\mapsto} q_0 \overset{w_r}{\longmapsto}{}^* q$. For each $p' \succeq p, w'_l \gg w_l, w'_r \gg w_r$ and $\gamma'_0 \geq \gamma_0$:

1. By induction hypothesis on $p \overset{w_l}{\longmapsto}{}^* p'_0$, there exists $(p'', w''_l) \gg (p', w'_l)$ such that $\langle p'', w''_l \rangle$ covers $\langle p'_0, \epsilon \rangle$.
2. By the definition of saturation rules, there exist $p'_1 \succeq p_1$ and $w'_1 \gg w_1$ such that $\langle p_0, \gamma_0 \rangle \hookrightarrow \langle p'_1, w'_1 \rangle$.
3. By induction hypothesis on $p_1 \overset{w_1 w_r}{\longmapsto}{}^* q$, there exist $p''_1 \succeq p'_1$ and $w''_1 w''_r \gg w'_1 w'_r$ such that $\langle p''_1, w''_1 w''_r \rangle$ covers $\langle q, \epsilon \rangle$.
4. By the growing property, there exist $p''_0 \succeq p_0 \succeq p'_0$ and $\gamma''_0 \geq \gamma'_0$ such that $\langle p''_0, \gamma''_0 \rangle$ covers $\langle p''_1, w''_1 \rangle$.

By **Claim** and 1., there exists $(p''', w'''_l) \gg (p'', w''_l) \gg (p', w'_l)$ such that $\langle p''', w'''_l \rangle$ covers $\langle p''_0, \epsilon \rangle$. Put all these together, for each $(p', w'_l \gamma'_0 w'_r) \gg (p, w_l \gamma_0 w_r)$, there exists $(p''', w'''_l \gamma''_0 w''_r) \gg (p', w'_l \gamma'_0 w'_r)$. Therefore, each of $\langle p''', w'''_l \gamma''_0 w''_r \rangle$, $\langle p''_0, \gamma''_0 w''_r \rangle$, $\langle p''_1, w''_1 w''_r \rangle$, and $\langle q, \epsilon \rangle$ covers the next. □

Theorem 3. *For a monotonic and growing OPDS, $pre^*(C^\uparrow)^\downarrow = L(Pre^*(\mathcal{A}_0))^\downarrow$. where $C^\uparrow = L(\mathcal{A}_0)$.*

4 Finite Convergence of Pre^*-automata

Definition 7. *A QO $\leq$ is a* well-quasi-ordering *(WQO) if, for each infinite sequence $a_1, a_2, \cdots$, there exist i, j with $i < j$ and $a_i \leq a_j$.*

A QO $\leq$ is a WQO, if, and only if each upward closed set $X^\uparrow$ has finite basis (i.e., minimal elements). Note that $\ll$ may be no longer a WQO (nor well founded), while the embedding $(\Gamma^*, \preccurlyeq)$ stays a WQO by *Higman's lemma.*

Lemma 2. *Let $(D, \leq)$ and $(D', \leq')$ be WQOs.*

– **(Dickson's lemma)** *$(D \times D', \leq \times \leq')$ is a WQO.*
– **(Higman's lemma)** *$(D^*, \preccurlyeq)$ is a WQO, where $\preccurlyeq$ is the embedding.*

For a monotonic OPDS, if $(P, \preceq), (\Gamma, \leq)$ are WQOs, we call it a *Well-Structured PDS* (WSPDS). For a WSPDS $((P, \preceq), (\Gamma, \leq), \Delta)$, $\psi^{-1}(\{(p,w)\}^{\uparrow})$ is upward-closed and has finite basis (i.e., finitely many minimal elements). In the *Pre** saturation rule of Section 3.3, its side condition contains $\psi(p', \gamma) \in \{(p,w)\}^{\uparrow}$ for $\psi \in \Delta$, which allows arbitrary choices of (p', γ). For a WSPDS, we focus only on finite basis of upward-closed sets $(p', \gamma) \in Min(\psi^{-1}(\{(p,w)\}^{\uparrow}))$.

We assume that such finite basis are computable for each $\psi \in \Delta$, and the initial *Pre**-automaton $\mathcal{A}_0$ with $L(\mathcal{A}_0) = (p,w)^{\uparrow}$ has finitely many states S_0.

Theorem 4. *For a WSPDS $((P, \preceq), (\Gamma, \leq), \Delta)$, if (i) $(P, \preceq), (\Gamma, \leq)$ are computable WQOs, and (ii) a finite basis of $\psi^{-1}(\{(p,w)\}^{\uparrow})$ is computable for each $\psi \in \Delta$ and $\langle p, w\rangle \in P \times \Gamma^{\leq 2}$, $Pre^*(\mathcal{A}_0)$ (in Section 3.3) finitely converges.*

Proof. (*Sketch*) Starting from a WQO over S such that $\preceq$ over $S_0 \cap P$ and $=$ on $S_0 \setminus P$, the set S of states of the *Pre**-automaton make a bad sequence, since saturation rules in Section 3.3 do not add larger states. For each pair (p,q) of states, they do not add larger stack symbols as labels of *Pre** automaton transitions $p \overset{\gamma}{\mapsto} q$. Thus, during the saturation, a sequence of added edges $p_1 \overset{\gamma_1}{\mapsto} q_1, p_2 \overset{\gamma_2}{\mapsto} q_2, \cdots$ is bad. Thus, it finitely terminates. Since Δ has finitely many transition rules, dependency during generation of *Pre** automaton transitions is finitely branching. Thus, by König's lemma, $Pre^*(\mathcal{A}_0)$ finitely converges. □

Example 3. Let $M = \langle \{p_i\}, \mathbb{N}^2, \Delta\rangle$ be a WSPDS with vectors in $\mathbb{N}^2$ as a stack alphabet and Δ consists of four rules given in the figure. The figure illustrates a *Pre**-automaton construction starting from initial $\mathcal{A}_0$ that accepts $C = \langle p_2, (0,0)^{\uparrow}\rangle$. For $v \in \mathbb{N}^2$, we abbreviate $\{v\}^{\uparrow}$ by $v^{\uparrow}$. Note that $\mathbb{N}^2$ is WQO by the element-wise comparison. $\mathcal{A}$ is the saturation of the *Pre**-automaton.

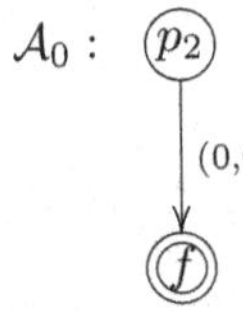

$$\begin{array}{ll}
\psi_1 : \langle p_0, v\rangle \to \langle p_0, (v + (1,1))v\rangle & \\
\psi_2 : \langle p_1, v\rangle \to \langle p_1, \epsilon\rangle & \text{if } v \geq (m, 0) \\
\psi_3 : \langle p_0, v\rangle \to \langle p_1, v - (0,2)\rangle & \text{if } v \geq (0,2) \\
\psi_4 : \langle p_1, v\rangle \to \langle p_2, \epsilon\rangle & \text{if } v \geq (1,0)
\end{array}$$

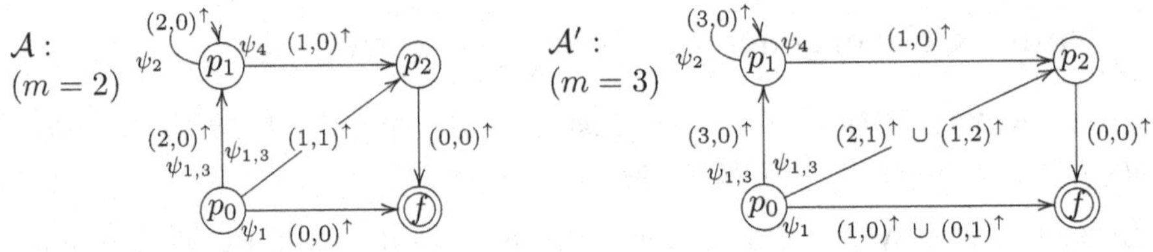

For instance, when $m = 2$, $p_0 \overset{(2,2)^{\uparrow}}{\longmapsto} p_1$ in $\mathcal{A}$ is generated from $p_1 \overset{(2,0)^{\uparrow}}{\longmapsto} p_1$ by ψ_3. By repeating application of ψ_1 twice to $p_0 \overset{(2,2)^{\uparrow}}{\longmapsto} p_1 \overset{(2,0)^{\uparrow}}{\mapsto} p_1$, we obtain

$p_0 \overset{(2,0)^\uparrow}{\longmapsto} p_1$. Then, applying ψ_1 to $p_0 \overset{(2,0)^\uparrow}{\longmapsto} p_1 \overset{(1,0)^\uparrow}{\longmapsto} p_2$, we obtain $p_0 \overset{(1,0)^\uparrow}{\longmapsto} p_2$. $p_0 \overset{(1,2)^\uparrow}{\longmapsto} p_2$ is also generated from $p_1 \overset{(1,0)^\uparrow}{\longmapsto} p_2$ by ψ_3, but it will not affect.

By Theorem 2, we obtain

$$\begin{aligned} pre^*(C) = \{&\langle p_2, (0,0)^\uparrow\rangle, \langle p_1, ((2,0)^\uparrow)^*(1,0)^\uparrow(0,0)^\uparrow\rangle,\\ &\langle p_0, (0,0)^\uparrow\rangle, \langle p_0, (1,1)^\uparrow(0,0)^\uparrow\rangle, \langle p_0, ((2,0)^\uparrow)^+(1,0)^\uparrow(0,0)^\uparrow\rangle\}\end{aligned}$$

Thus, $\langle p_0, (0,0)\rangle$ covers $\langle p_2, (0,0)\rangle$. Actually,

$$\begin{aligned} \langle p_0, (0,0)\rangle\rangle &\hookrightarrow \langle p_0, (1,1)(0,0)\rangle \hookrightarrow \langle p_0, (2,2)(1,1)(0,0)\rangle \hookrightarrow \langle p_1, (2,0)(1,1)(0,0)\rangle\\ &\hookrightarrow \langle p_1, (1,1)(0,0)\rangle \hookrightarrow \langle p_2, (0,0)\rangle\end{aligned}$$

Note that if we change the condition of ψ_2 from $v \geq (2,0)$ to $v \geq (3,0)$, the saturated Pre^*-automaton becomes $\mathcal{A}'$, and $\langle p_0, (0,0)\rangle$ no more covers $\langle p_2, (0,0)\rangle$, though $\langle p_0, (0,0)\rangle$ is reachable to p_2. Actually,

$$\begin{aligned} \langle p_0, (0,0)\rangle\rangle &\hookrightarrow \langle p_0, (1,1)(0,0)\rangle \hookrightarrow \langle p_0, (2,2)(1,1)(0,0)\rangle \hookrightarrow \langle p_0, (3,3)(2,2)(1,1)(0,0)\rangle\\ &\hookrightarrow \langle p_1, (3,1)(2,2)(1,1)(0,0)\rangle \hookrightarrow \langle p_1, (2,2)(1,1)(0,0)\rangle \hookrightarrow \langle p_2, (1,1)(0,0)\rangle\end{aligned}$$

To detect the state reachability, instead of $\mathcal{A}_0$, we can start with an initial automaton $\mathcal{A}_0'$ that accepts $p_2 \times \Gamma^* = \{\langle p_2, ((0,0)^\uparrow)^*\}$.

5 Well-Formed Constraint

Definition 8. *For an OPDS M, a pair $(\Upsilon, \Downarrow_\Upsilon)$ of a set $\Upsilon \subseteq P \times \Gamma^*$ and a projection function $\Downarrow_\Upsilon$: $P \times \Gamma^* \to (P \times \Gamma^*) \cup \{\#\}$ is a* well-formed constraint *if, for configurations c, c',*

- *$c \hookrightarrow c'$ implies that $c \in \Upsilon$ if, and only if $c' \in \Upsilon$,*
- *$c \hookrightarrow c'$ implies $\Downarrow_\Upsilon (c) \hookrightarrow \Downarrow_\Upsilon (c')$,*
- *$\Downarrow_\Upsilon (c) \lll c$, and*
- *$c \lll c'$ implies either $\Downarrow_\Upsilon (c) = \Downarrow_\Upsilon (c')$ or $\Downarrow_\Upsilon (c) = \#$,*

where $\#$ is added to $P \times \Gamma^*$ as the least element (wrt $\lll$) and $\Upsilon = \{c \in P \times \Gamma^* \mid c = \Downarrow_\Upsilon (c)\}$. ($\#$ represents failures of $\Downarrow_\Upsilon$.)

Lemma 3. *For a monotonic OPDS M with a well-formed projection $\Downarrow_\Upsilon$, assume $C \subseteq \Upsilon$. Then, $pre^*(C) = pre^*(C^\uparrow) \cap \Upsilon = pre^*(C^\uparrow)^\downarrow \cap \Upsilon$.*

Proof. We will show $pre^*(C) = pre^*(C^\uparrow)^\downarrow \cap \Upsilon$ only. Similarly, $pre^*(C) = pre^*(C^\uparrow) \cap \Upsilon$ is shown.

From $C \subseteq \Upsilon$, $pre^*(C) \subseteq pre^*(C^\uparrow)^\downarrow \cap \Upsilon$ is obvious, For the opposite direction, we first show $\Downarrow_\Upsilon (pre^*(C^\uparrow)) \subseteq pre^*(C)$. Since $c \in pre^*(C^\uparrow)$ is equivalent to $\exists c' \in C^\uparrow.c \hookrightarrow^* c'$, we have $\Downarrow_\Upsilon (c) \hookrightarrow^* \Downarrow_\Upsilon (c') \in C$. Since $C \subseteq \Upsilon$ implies $\Downarrow_\Upsilon (c') \in C$, $\Downarrow_\Upsilon (c) \in pre^*(C)$ is obtained. For $pre^*(C) \supseteq pre^*(C^\uparrow)^\downarrow \cap \Upsilon$,

$$pre^*(C^\uparrow)^\downarrow \cap \Upsilon = \Downarrow_\Upsilon (pre^*(C^\uparrow)^\downarrow \cap \Upsilon) \subseteq \Downarrow_\Upsilon (pre^*(C^\uparrow)^\downarrow) = \Downarrow_\Upsilon (pre^*(C^\uparrow)) \cup \{\#\}.$$

From $\Downarrow_\Upsilon (pre^*(C^\uparrow)) \subseteq pre^*(C)$, $\Downarrow_\Upsilon (pre^*(C^\uparrow)) \cup \{\#\} \subseteq pre^*(C) \cup \{\#\}$. Thus, $pre^*(C^\uparrow)^\downarrow \cap \Upsilon \subseteq (pre^*(C) \cup \{\#\}) \cap \Upsilon = pre^*(C)$. □

From Theorem 3 and Lemma 3, Theorem 5 is immediate, which strengthens the quasi-coverability to the configuration reachability, and the decidability is reduced to finite convergence of $L(Pre^*(\mathcal{A}_0))$.

Theorem 5. *Let C be a regular set of configurations with $C^{\uparrow} = L(A_0)$ for a P-automaton $\mathcal{A}_0$. For a monotonic and growing OPDS and a well-formed constraint $(\Upsilon, \Downarrow_\Upsilon)$, if $C \subseteq \Upsilon$, then $pre^*(C) = L(Pre^*(A_0))^{\downarrow} \cap \Upsilon$.*

Example 4. In Example 3, let Υ be

$$\left\{ \begin{array}{l} \langle p_0, (n,n) \cdots (0,0) \rangle, \langle p_2, (n,n) \cdots (0,0) \rangle \\ \langle p_1, (n, n-2)(n-1, n-1) \cdots (0,0) \rangle, \end{array} \mid n \geq m \geq 0 \right\}$$

Then, Υ is well-formed. Since both $\langle p_0, (0,0) \rangle$ and $\langle p_2, (0,0) \rangle$ are in Υ and $\{\langle p_i, (0,0) \rangle\}^{\uparrow} \cap \Upsilon = \{\langle p_i, (0,0) \rangle\}$, $\langle p_0, (0,0) \rangle \hookrightarrow^* \langle p_2, (0,0) \rangle$ holds by Theorem 5.

6 Snapshot Word

In a DTPDA, local ages in the stack proceed when a timed transition occurs. When a DTPDA is encoded into a discrete WSPDS, named *snapshot PDS* (Section 7.2), it can operate only the top stack symbol. A *snapshot word* summarizes the ordering of fractions among values of all local ages and global clocks in the stack, after applying the digitization technique in [18,1,4]. When a pop occurs, time progress recorded at the top stack symbol is propagated to the next stack symbol after finding a permutation by matching via markings ρ_1 and ρ_2.

6.1 Snapshot Word

As notational convention, let $\mathcal{MP}(D)$ be the set of finite multisets over D. We regard a finite set as a multiset in which the multiplicity of each element is 1. For a finite word $w = a_1 a_2 \cdots a_k$, we denote $w(j) = a_j$

Let $\langle S, s_{init}, \Gamma, C, \Delta \rangle$ be a DTPDA, and let n be the largest integer (except for ∞) that appears in Δ. For $v \in \mathbb{R}_{\geq 0}$, $proj(v) = \mathfrak{r}_i$ if $v \in \mathfrak{r}_i \in Intv(n)$, where

$$Intv(n) = \begin{cases} \mathfrak{r}_{2i} &= [i, i] \quad\quad \text{if } 0 \leq i \leq n \\ \mathfrak{r}_{2i+1} &= (i, i+1) \text{ if } 0 \leq i < n \\ \mathfrak{r}_{2n+1} &= (n, \infty) \end{cases}$$

Definition 9. *Let $frac(x,t) = t - floor(t)$ for $(x,t) \in (C \cup \Gamma) \times \mathbb{R}_{\geq 0}$. A digitization $\mathtt{digi} : \mathcal{MP}((C \cup \Gamma) \times \mathbb{R}_{\geq 0}) \to (\mathcal{MP}((C \cup \Gamma) \times Intv(n)))^*$ is as follows. For $\mathcal{X} \in \mathcal{MP}((C \cup \Gamma) \times \mathbb{R}_{\geq 0})$, let $X_1, \cdots, X_k$ be multisets that collect $(x, proj(t))$'s in $\mathcal{X}$ having the same $frac(x,t)$. We assume that X_i's are sorted by the increasing order of $frac(x,t)$ (i.e., , $frac(x,t) < frac(x',t')$ for $(x, proj(t)) \in X_i$ and $(x', proj(t')) \in X_{i+1}$). Then, $\mathtt{digi}(\mathcal{X})$ is a word $X_1 \cdots X_k$.*

Example 5. In Example 1, $n = 6$ and we have 13 intervals illustrated below.

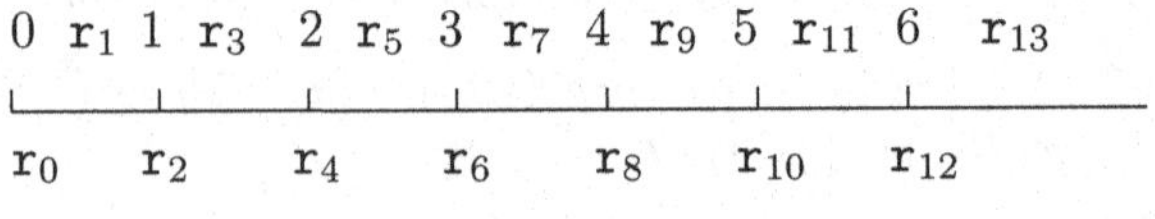

From the configuration c_1 in Example 1, the clock information is extracted from the stack content of c_1 as a multiset

$$\mathcal{X} = \{(a, 1.9), (b, 6.7), (a, 3.1), (d, 4.2), (x_1, 0.5), (x_2, 3.9), (x_3, 2.3)\}$$

and $\mathtt{digi}(\mathcal{X}) = \{(a, \mathtt{r}_7)\}\{(d, \mathtt{r}_9)\}\{(x_3, \mathtt{r}_5)\}\{(x_1, \mathtt{r}_1)\}\{(b, \mathtt{r}_{13})\}\{(x_2, \mathtt{r}_7), (a, \mathtt{r}_3)\}$. For instance, The value of the clock x_2 and the age of the top stack frame $(a, 1.9)$ have the same fraction 0.9, thus they are packed into the same multiset $\{(x_2, \mathtt{r}_7), (a, \mathtt{r}_3)\}$, and placed at the last since their fraction is the largest.

Definition 10. *A word $\bar{\gamma} \in (\mathcal{MP}((\mathcal{C} \cup \Gamma) \times Intv(n)))^*$ is a* snapshot word *if it has two pointers ρ_1, ρ_2 such that $\rho_1(\bar{\gamma}), \rho_2(\bar{\gamma})$ point to different elements of $\Gamma \times Intv(n)$ appearing in $\bar{\gamma}$. We denote the set of snapshot word by $sw(\mathcal{C}, \Gamma, n)$, and $\bar{\gamma}|_\Gamma$ is obtained by removing all elements in $\mathcal{C} \times Intv(n)$ from $\bar{\gamma}$.*

Example 6. From $\mathtt{digi}(\mathcal{X})$ in Example 5, by adding ρ_1 and ρ_2 (marked with *overline* and *underline*), which point to $(a, \mathtt{r}_3)$ and $(b, \mathtt{r}_{13})$, respectively, we have

$$\{(a, \mathtt{r}_7)\}\{(d, \mathtt{r}_9)\}\{(x_3, \mathtt{r}_5)\}\{(x_1, \mathtt{r}_1)\}\{\underline{(b, \mathtt{r}_{13})}\}\{(x_2, \mathtt{r}_7), \overline{(a, \mathtt{r}_3)}\}$$

and $\mathtt{digi}(\mathcal{X})|_\Gamma = \{(a, \mathtt{r}_7)\}\{(d, \mathtt{r}_9)\}\{\underline{(b, \mathtt{r}_{13})}\}\{\overline{(a, \mathtt{r}_3)}\}$.

Definition 11. *For snapshot words $\bar{\gamma} = X_1 \cdots X_m$ and $\bar{\gamma}' = Y_1 \cdots Y_n$ with $X_i, Y_j \in \mathcal{MP}((\mathcal{C} \cup \Gamma) \times Intv(n))$, we define the embedding $\bar{\gamma} \sqsubseteq \bar{\gamma}'$, if there exists a monotonic injection $f : [1..m] \to [1..n]$ such that*

- *$X_k \subseteq Y_{f(k)}$ for each $k \in [1..m]$, and*
- *$\rho_i(\bar{\gamma}) = \rho_i(\bar{\gamma}')$ for $i = 1, 2$.*

Since Γ and $\mathcal{C}$ are finite, $\sqsubseteq$ is a WQO over $sw(\mathcal{C}, \Gamma, n)$ by Higman's lemma.

Definition 12. *Let $c = (s, \nu, w)$ be a configuration of a DTPDA with $s \in S$, $w \in (\Gamma \times \mathbb{R}_{\geq 0})^*$, and $\nu : \mathcal{C} \to \mathbb{R}_{\geq 0}$, and let $\mathtt{mp}(w, \nu) = w \cup \{(x, \nu(x)) \mid x \in \mathcal{C}\}$ by regarding w as a multiset (i.e., ignore the ordering). snap(c) is a snapshot word obtained by adding ρ_1, ρ_2 to $\mathtt{digi}(\mathtt{mp}(w, \nu))$ as:*

$$\begin{cases} \rho_1, \rho_2 \text{ are left undefined} & \text{if } w = \epsilon \\ \rho_1(snap(c)) = (\gamma, proj(t)),\ \rho_2 \text{ is left undefined} & \text{if } w = (\gamma, t) \\ \rho_1(snap(c)) = (\gamma, proj(t)),\ \rho_2(snap(c)) = \rho_1(snap((s, \nu, w'))) & \text{if } w = (\gamma, t)w' \end{cases}$$

Example 7. For c_2 in Example 1, *snap*(c_1) is $\mathtt{digi}(\mathcal{X})$ (with ρ_1 and ρ_2) in Example 6. ρ_1 and ρ_2 point to the top and second stack frames $(a, 1.9), (b, 6.7)$.

Definition 13. *For a configuration $c = (s, \nu, w)$ of a DTPDA, a snapshot configuration $Snap(c) = (s, \tilde{w})$ with stack alphabet $sw(\mathcal{C}, \Gamma, n)^*$ is with*

$$\tilde{w} = snap(s, \nu, w[m])\ snap(s, \nu, w[m-1])\ \cdots\ snap(s, \nu, w[1])\ snap(s, \nu, \epsilon)$$

where $w = (a_m, t_m) \cdots (a_1, t_1) \in (\Gamma \times \mathbb{R}_{\geq 0})^*$ and $w[i] = (a_i, t_i) \cdots (a_1, t_1)$.

Example 8. For c_1 in Example 1 (with $\nu(x_1) = 0.5, \nu(x_2) = 3.9, \nu(x_3) = 2.3$), $Snap(c_1)$ is shown below. The top snapshot word summarizes a time sequence.

$(a, 1.9)$		$\{(a, \mathtt{r}_7)\}\{(d, \mathtt{r}_9)\}\{(x_3, \mathtt{r}_5)\}\{(x_1, \mathtt{r}_1)\}\{\underline{(b, \mathtt{r}_{13})}\}\{(x_2, \mathtt{r}_7), \overline{(a, \mathtt{r}_3)}\}$
$(b, 6.7)$		$\{\underline{(a, \mathtt{r}_7)}\}\{(d, \mathtt{r}_9)\}\{(x_3, \mathtt{r}_5)\}\{(x_1, \mathtt{r}_1)\}\{\overline{(b, \mathtt{r}_{13})}\}\{(x_2, \mathtt{r}_7)\}$
$(a, 3.1)$	$\Rightarrow$	$\{\overline{(a, \mathtt{r}_7)}\}\{\underline{(d, \mathtt{r}_9)}\}\{(x_3, \mathtt{r}_5)\}\{(x_1, \mathtt{r}_1)\}\{(x_2, \mathtt{r}_7)\}$
$(d, 4.2)$		$\{\overline{(d, \mathtt{r}_9)}\}\{(x_3, \mathtt{r}_5)\}\{(x_1, \mathtt{r}_1)\}\{(x_2, \mathtt{r}_7)\}$
$\bot$		$\{(x_3, \mathtt{r}_5)\}\{(x_1, \mathtt{r}_1)\}\{(x_2, \mathtt{r}_7)\}$

Stack of c_1 Stack of $Snap(c_1)$

6.2 Operations on Snapshot Words

Definition 14. *Let $\bar{\gamma} = X_1 \cdots X_m \in (\mathcal{MP}((\mathcal{C} \cup \Gamma) \times Intv(n)))^*$ be a snapshot word and let $\gamma \in \Gamma \cup \mathcal{C}$. We define operations as follows.*

- **Insert.** *$\bar{\gamma}' = insert(\bar{\gamma}, (\delta, \mathtt{r}_k))$ is obtained from $\bar{\gamma}$ by inserting $(\delta, \mathtt{r}_k)$*

$$\begin{cases} \text{either into } X_j \text{ for } j \in [1..m], \text{ or between } X_j \text{ and } X_{j+1} \text{ for } j \in [1..m-1] & \text{if } k \text{ is odd} \\ \text{into } X_1, \text{ if each } \mathtt{r}_i \text{ in } X_1 \text{ has an even index; before } X_1, \text{ o.w.} & \text{if } k \text{ is even} \end{cases}$$

  and setting $\rho_1(\bar{\gamma}') = (\delta, \mathtt{r}_k)$ and $\rho_2(\bar{\gamma}') = \rho_1(\bar{\gamma})$.
- **Delete$_\Gamma$.** *$\bar{\gamma}' = delete_\Gamma(\bar{\gamma})$ is obtained from $\bar{\gamma}$ by deleting $\rho_1(\bar{\gamma})$ and setting $\rho_1(\bar{\gamma}') = \rho_2(\bar{\gamma})$ and $\rho_2(\bar{\gamma}')$ left* undefined.
- **Delete$_\mathcal{C}$.** *For $x \in \mathcal{C}$, $delete_\mathcal{C}(\bar{\gamma}, x)$ is obtained from $\bar{\gamma}$ by deleting $(x, \mathtt{r})$ (and ρ_1, ρ_2 are kept unchanged).*
- **Assignment.** *For $x \in \mathcal{C}, \mathtt{r} \in Intv(n)$, $assign(\bar{\gamma}, x, \mathtt{r}) = insert(delete_\mathcal{C}(\bar{\gamma}, x), (x, \mathtt{r}))$.*
- **Permutation.** *Let $i \in [1..m]$ and $0 \leq k \leq n$. Basic permutations are*

$$\begin{cases} \dot{\Rightarrow}(\bar{\gamma}) &= \dot{X}_1 X_2 \cdots X_m \\ \ddot{\Rightarrow}(\bar{\gamma}) &= (\ddot{X}_m^+) X_1 X_2 \cdots X_{m-1} \\ add_k(\bar{\gamma}) &= (X_1 + k)(X_2 + k) \cdots (X_m + k) \end{cases}$$

  where
  - *$\dot{X}$ updates each $(y, \mathtt{r}_l) \in X$ with $(y, \mathtt{r}_{l+1})$ if l is even; otherwise as is,*
  - *$\ddot{X}^+$ updates each $(y, \mathtt{r}_l) \in X$ with $(y, \mathtt{r}_{l+1})$ if $l \neq 2n+1$ and keeps if $l = 2n+1$ (We assume that l is odd), and*
  - *$X + k$ updates each $(y, \mathtt{r}_l) \in X$ with $(y, \mathtt{r}_{min(l+k, 2n+1)})$.*

  Then, a permutation is either $\dot{\sigma}_{i,k}(\bar{\gamma})$ or $\ddot{\sigma}_{i,k}(\bar{\gamma})$, where

$$\dot{\sigma}_{i,k}(\bar{\gamma}) = \dot{\Rightarrow} \cdot \underbrace{\ddot{\Rightarrow} \cdot \ldots \cdot \ddot{\Rightarrow}}_{m-i+1} \cdot add_k(\bar{\gamma}) \qquad \ddot{\sigma}_{i,k}(\bar{\gamma}) = \underbrace{\ddot{\Rightarrow} \cdot \ldots \cdot \ddot{\Rightarrow}}_{m-i+1} \cdot add_k(\bar{\gamma})$$

- **Propagate.** *$propagate(\bar{\gamma}, \bar{\gamma}')$ is obtained from $delete_\Gamma(\bar{\gamma})$ by assigning $\sigma(\rho_2(\bar{\gamma}'))$ to $\rho_2(delete_\Gamma(\bar{\gamma}))$ for a permutation σ with $\bar{\gamma}|_\Gamma = \sigma(\bar{\gamma}')|_\Gamma$.*

Example 9. Consider $snap(c_i)$ in Example 7 for c_1 in Example 1.

$$\{(a,\mathtt{r}_7)\}\{(d,\mathtt{r}_9)\}\{(x_3,\mathtt{r}_5)\}\{(x_1,\mathtt{r}_1)\}\{\underline{(b,\mathtt{r}_{13})}\}\{(x_2,\mathtt{r}_7),\overline{(a,\mathtt{r}_3)}\}$$

- $insert(snap(c_1),(d,\mathtt{r}_5))$ has lots of choices, e.g.,

  $$\{(a,\mathtt{r}_7)\}\{(d,\mathtt{r}_9)\}\{(x_3,\mathtt{r}_5)\}\{(x_1,\mathtt{r}_1),\overline{(d,\mathtt{r}_5)}\}\{(b,\mathtt{r}_{13})\}\{(x_2,\mathtt{r}_7),\underline{(a,\mathtt{r}_3)}\},$$
  $$\{(a,\mathtt{r}_7)\}\{(d,\mathtt{r}_9)\}\{(x_3,\mathtt{r}_5)\}\{(x_1,\mathtt{r}_1)\},\{\overline{(d,\mathtt{r}_5)}\},\{(b,\mathtt{r}_{13})\}\{(x_2,\mathtt{r}_7),\underline{(a,\mathtt{r}_3)}\},\cdots$$

  The transition from c_1 to c_2 in Example 1 is simulated by pushing the second one (say, $\bar{\gamma}_2$) to $Snap(c_1)$ in Example 8.
- For $c_2 \overset{2.6}{\to}_{Time} c_3$, the permutation $\dot{\sigma}_{4,2}(\bar{\gamma}_2)$ results in $\bar{\gamma}_3$ below.

  $$\{(x_1,\mathtt{r}_7)\},\{\overline{(d,\mathtt{r}_{11})}\},\{(b,\mathtt{r}_{19})\}\{(x_2,\mathtt{r}_{13}),\underline{(a,\mathtt{r}_9)}\}\{(a,\mathtt{r}_{11})\}\{(d,\mathtt{r}_{13})\}\{(x_3,\mathtt{r}_9)\}.$$

  If a timed transition is $c_2 \overset{2.5}{\to}_{Time} c_3$ (in time elapses 2.5 such that the fraction of $\nu(x_1)$ becomes 0), $\ddot{\sigma}_{4,2}(\bar{\gamma}_2)$ simulates it as

  $$\{(x_1,\mathtt{r}_6)\},\{\overline{(d,\mathtt{r}_{11})}\},\{(b,\mathtt{r}_{19})\}\{(x_2,\mathtt{r}_{13}),\underline{(a,\mathtt{r}_9)}\}\{(a,\mathtt{r}_{11})\}\{(d,\mathtt{r}_{13})\}\{(x_3,\mathtt{r}_9)\}.$$

Propagate is used with $delete_\Gamma$ to simulate a pop transition. Since time progress is recorded only at the top stack frame (including updates on clock values), after $delete_\Gamma$ is applied to the top stack frame, the second stack frame is replaced with the top. Lacking information is a pointer ρ_2, which is recovered from the second stack frame. This will be illustrated in Example 11.

7 Decidability of Reachability of DTPDA

7.1 Well-Formed Projection on Snapshot Configurations

Let $\langle s, \bar{\gamma}_k \cdots \bar{\gamma}_2\bar{\gamma}_1\rangle$ be a snapshot configuration for $s \in S$ and $\bar{\gamma}_i \in (\mathcal{MP}((\mathcal{C} \cup \Gamma) \times Intv(n)))^*$ (regarding $\bar{\gamma}_k$ as a top stack symbol). A marking completion marks elements in $\Gamma \times Intv(n)$ that relate to pushdown transitions.

Definition 15. *For $\bar{\gamma}_k \cdots \bar{\gamma}_2\bar{\gamma}_1$ with $\bar{\gamma}_i \in (\mathcal{MP}((\mathcal{C}\cup\Gamma)\times Intv(n)))^*$, the* marking completion comp *inductively marks elements in $\bar{\gamma}_i|_\Gamma$ for each i.*

$$\begin{cases} \mathtt{comp}(\bar{\gamma}_1) & = \textit{add marking on } \rho_1(\bar{\gamma}_1) \\ \mathtt{comp}(\bar{\gamma}_k \cdots \bar{\gamma}_2\bar{\gamma}_1) & = \bar{\gamma}'_k \cdots \bar{\gamma}'_2\bar{\gamma}'_1 \end{cases}$$

where $\bar{\gamma}'_{k-1} \cdots \bar{\gamma}'_2\bar{\gamma}'_1 = \mathtt{comp}(\bar{\gamma}_{k-1} \cdots \bar{\gamma}_2\bar{\gamma}_1)$ and $\bar{\gamma}'_k$ is obtained from $\bar{\gamma}_k$ by marking

- *$\rho_1(\bar{\gamma}_k)$, and*
- *each element in $delete_\Gamma(\bar{\gamma}_k)|_\Gamma$ corresponding to a marked element in $\bar{\gamma}'_{k-1}|_\Gamma$ by a permutation σ satisfying $\sigma(\bar{\gamma}_{k-1})|_\Gamma = delete_\Gamma(\bar{\gamma}_k)|_\Gamma$.*

If such σ does not exist, $\mathtt{comp}(\bar{\gamma}_k \cdots \bar{\gamma}_2\bar{\gamma}_1) = \#$.

We define a *well-formed projection* $\Downarrow_\Upsilon (s, \bar{\gamma}_k \cdots \bar{\gamma}_2\bar{\gamma}_1)$ by removing all unmarked elements of $\Gamma \times Intv(n)$ in each $\bar{\gamma}_i$ in $(s, \mathtt{comp}(\bar{\gamma}_k \cdots \bar{\gamma}_2\bar{\gamma}_1))$. A snapshot configuration $(s, \bar{\gamma}_k \cdots \bar{\gamma}_2\bar{\gamma}_1)$ is *well-formed* if $\Downarrow_\Upsilon (s, \bar{\gamma}_k \cdots \bar{\gamma}_2\bar{\gamma}_1) = (s, \bar{\gamma}_k \cdots \bar{\gamma}_2\bar{\gamma}_1)$ (ignoring markings), and Υ is the set of well-formed snapshot configurations.

Example 10. In Example 8, $\bar{\gamma}_5$ is well-formed (i.e., $(a,\mathtt{r}_7),(d,\mathtt{r}_9),(b,\mathtt{r}_{13}),(a,\mathtt{r}_3)$ are all marked). For instance, a marking on $(a,\mathtt{r}_7)$ succeeds the pointer ρ_1 of $\bar{\gamma}_3$.

7.2 Snapshot PDS

Definition 16. *Let $\langle S, s_{init}, \Gamma, \mathcal{C}, \Delta\rangle$ be a DTPDA and let n be the largest integer in Δ. A* snapshot PDS *is a PDS $\mathcal{S} = \langle S, sw(\mathcal{C}, \Gamma, n), \Delta\rangle$. We assume that its initial configuration is $\langle s_{init}, \{(x, \mathtt{r}_0) \mid x \in \mathcal{C}\}\rangle$.*

Transition rule to simulate timed transitions $\langle s, \bar{\gamma}\rangle \xrightarrow{t}_{\mathcal{S}} \langle s, \sigma(\bar{\gamma})\rangle$, *where σ is either $\dot{\sigma}_{i,m}$ or $\ddot{\sigma}_{i,m}$ with $m = floor(t)$ and $1 \leq i \leq length(\bar{\gamma})$*

Transition rules to simulate discrete transitions (s, op, s')

- **Local** $\langle s,\ \epsilon\rangle \xrightarrow{nop}_{\mathcal{S}} \langle s',\ \epsilon\rangle$,
- **Assignment** $\langle s,\ \bar{\gamma}\rangle \xrightarrow{x \leftarrow I}_{\mathcal{S}} \langle s',\ assign(\bar{\gamma}, x, \mathtt{r})\rangle$ *for* $\mathtt{r} \subseteq I$,
- **Test** $\langle s,\ \bar{\gamma}\rangle \xrightarrow{x \in I?}_{\mathcal{S}} \langle s',\ \bar{\gamma}\rangle$ *if* $\mathtt{r} \subseteq I$ *for* $(x, \mathtt{r})$ *in* $\bar{\gamma}$.
- **Push** $\langle s,\ \bar{\gamma}\rangle \xrightarrow{push(\gamma', I)}_{\mathcal{S}} \langle s',\ insert(\bar{\gamma}, (\gamma', \mathtt{r}))\ \bar{\gamma}\rangle$ *for* $\mathtt{r} \subseteq I$, *and*
- **Pop** $\langle s,\ \bar{\gamma}\ \bar{\gamma}'\rangle \xrightarrow{pop(\gamma', I)}_{\mathcal{S}} \langle s',\ propagate(\bar{\gamma}, \bar{\gamma}')\rangle$.

By induction on the number of steps of transitions, complete and sound simulation between a DTPDA and a snapshot PDS is observed. Note that the initial clock valuation of a DTPDA to be set ν_0 is essential.

Lemma 4. *Let us denote c_0 and c (resp. $\langle s_{init}, \bar{\gamma}_0\rangle$ and $\langle s, \tilde{w}\rangle$) for the initial configuration and a configuration of a DTPDA $\mathcal{T}$ (resp. its snapshot PDS $\mathcal{S}$).*

1. *If $c_0 \hookrightarrow^* c$ then there exists $\langle s, \tilde{w}\rangle$ such that $\langle s_{init}, \bar{\gamma}_0\rangle \hookrightarrow^*_{\mathcal{S}} \langle s, \tilde{w}\rangle$, $s = state(c)$, and $\tilde{w}$ is well-formed.*
2. *If $\langle s_{init}, \bar{\gamma}_0\rangle \hookrightarrow^*_{\mathcal{S}} \langle s, \tilde{w}\rangle$ and $\tilde{w}$ is well-formed. there exists c such that $c_0 \hookrightarrow^* c$ with $Snap(c) = \langle s, \tilde{w}\rangle$.*

Example 11. We show how a snapshot PDS simulates a DTPDA in Example 1, as continuation to Example 9 (which shows transitions from c_1 to c_3).

- $c_3 \xrightarrow{x_2 \leftarrow (2,5]}_{Disc} c_4$ is simulated by $assign(delete_{\mathcal{C}}(snap(c_3), x_2), x_2, \mathtt{r}_7)$ at the top stack frame, since $\nu(x_2) = 3.8 \in \mathtt{r}_7$. There are several choices of $assign(delete_{\mathcal{C}}(snap(c_3), x_2), x_2, \mathtt{r}_7)$. Among them,

  $\{(x_1, \mathtt{r}_7)\}, \{\overline{(d, \mathtt{r}_{11})}\}, \{(b, \mathtt{r}_{19})\}\{\underline{(a, \mathtt{r}_9)}\}\{(a, \mathtt{r}_{11})\}\{(x_2, \mathtt{r}_7), (d, \mathtt{r}_{13})\}\{(x_3, \mathtt{r}_9)\}$.
  corresponds to 3.8. A different value, e.g., $\nu(x_2) = 3.3$, corresponds to $\{(x_1, \mathtt{r}_7)\}, \{\overline{(d, \mathtt{r}_{11})}\}, \{(x_2, \mathtt{r}_7), (b, \mathtt{r}_{19})\}\{\underline{(a, \mathtt{r}_9)}\}\{(a, \mathtt{r}_{11})\}\{(d, \mathtt{r}_{13})\}\{(x_3, \mathtt{r}_9)\}$.

- $c_4 \xrightarrow{pop(d,[4,6])}_{Disc} c_5$ is simulated by $propagate(delete_{\Gamma}(snap(c_4)), snap(c_1))$. Note that a snapshot PDS does not change anything except for the top stack frame. Thus, the second stack frame is kept unchanged from $snap(c_1)$. First, $delete_{\Gamma}$ removes the element pointed by ρ_1, which results in

  $$\{(x_1, \mathtt{r}_7)\}, \{(b, \mathtt{r}_{19})\}\{\underline{(a, \mathtt{r}_9)}\}\{(a, \mathtt{r}_{11})\}\{(x_2, \mathtt{r}_7), (d, \mathtt{r}_{13})\}\{(x_3, \mathtt{r}_9)\}.$$

  $snap(c_1) = \{(a, \mathtt{r}_7)\}\{(d, \mathtt{r}_9)\}\{(x_3, \mathtt{r}_5)\}\{(x_1, \mathtt{r}_1)\}\{\underline{(b, \mathtt{r}_{13})}\}\{(x_2, \mathtt{r}_7), \overline{(a, \mathtt{r}_3)}\}$ and, by pattern matching between ρ_2 in the former and ρ_1 in the latter,

$\dot{\sigma}_{4,2}$ (which is used in the timed transition from c_2 to c_3 in Example 9) is found. Then ρ_1 is updated with the current ρ_2 and ρ_2 is recovered by σ as $\{(x_1, \mathtt{r}_7)\}, \{(b, \mathtt{r}_{19})\}\{(a, \mathtt{r}_9)\}\{(a, \mathtt{r}_{11})\}\{(x_2, \mathtt{r}_7), (d, \mathtt{r}_{13})\}\{(x_3, \mathtt{r}_9)\}$.

We observe that $\Downarrow_{\Upsilon}$ (defined in Section 7.1) satisfies Definition 8. A snapshot PDS has finite states and WQO stack alphabet. By applying the encoding in Remark 1, we obtain our main result from Theorem 3, 4, 5, Lemma 3, and 4.

Corollary 1. *The (configuration) reachability of a DTPDA is decidable.*

7.3 Comparison with the Original Encoding

In [16], we apply slight extensions of a DTPDA to make it able to set the value of an age to that of a clock when a push occurs, and set the value of a clock to that of an age when a pop occurs. Both the original encoding in [2] and our snapshot word correctly handle them.

- **Push-set** $push(\gamma, x)$, push γ on a stack associated with a local age of the value of a clock $x \in \mathcal{C}$, and
- **Pop-set** $pop(\gamma, x)$, pop γ on a stack and set the value of a clock $x \in \mathcal{C}$ to the value of the associated age a.

A snapshot word summarizes the ordering of fractions of all local ages and global clocks in the stack, whereas the encoding in [2] summarizes boundedly many information, i.e., values of global clocks and local ages in the top and next stack frames (those in the next stack frame as shadow items). When a pop occurs, it recovers the relation among global clocks and local ages in the next stack frame. The difference would appear if we consider regular valuations [13] with time, e.g., $\forall a.a < x$ for a stack symbol a and a clock x, which means all ages associated with a in the stack are smaller than the value of the clock x.

8 Conclusion

This paper investigated a general framework of pushdown systems with well-quasi-ordered control states and stack alphabet, *well-structured pushdown systems*, to show decidability of the reachability. This extends the decidability results on a pushdown system with finite control states and well-quasi-ordered stack alphabet [8]. The ideas behind are,

- combining WSTS [3,14] and classical *Pre**-automaton technique [7,15,12], which enables us to reduce arguments on stacks to on stack symbols, and
- introduction of a well-formed projection $\Downarrow_{\Upsilon}$, which extracts the shape of reachable configurations.

As an instance, an alternative decidability proof of the reachability for dense-timed pushdown system [2] was shown. The encoding is inspired by the digitization techniques in [18]. We expect our snapshot word encoding would be more robust for extensions, e.g., regular valuations [13] with time.

Acknowledgements. The authors would like to thank Shoji Yuen, Yasuhiko Minamide, Tachio Terauchi, and Guoqiang Li for valuable comments and discussions. This work is supported by the NSFC-JSPS bilateral joint research project (61011140074), NSFC projects (61003013,61100052,61033002), NSFC-ANR joint project (61261130589), and JSPS KAKENHI Grant-in-Aid for Scientific Research(B) (23300008).

References

1. Abdulla, P.A., Jonsson, B.: Verifying networks of timed processes. In: Steffen, B. (ed.) TACAS 1998. LNCS, vol. 1384, pp. 298–312. Springer, Heidelberg (1998)
2. Abdulla, P.A., Atig, M.F., Stenman, F.: Dense-Timed Pushdown Automata. In: IEEE LICS 2012, pp. 35–44 (2012)
3. Abdulla, P.A., Cerans, K., Jonsson, C., Yih-Kuen, T.: Algorithmic analysis of programs with well quasi-ordered domains. Information and Computation 160(1-2), 109–127 (2000)
4. Abdulla, P.A., Jonsson, B.: Model checking of systems with many identical time processes. Theoretical Computer Science 290(1), 241–264 (2003)
5. Alur, R., Dill, D.L.: A theory of timed automata. Theoretical Computer Science 126(2), 183–235 (1994)
6. Bouajjani, A., Echahed, R., Robbana, R.: On the Automatic Verification of Systems with Continuous Variables and Unbounded Discrete Data Structures. In: Antsaklis, P.J., Kohn, W., Nerode, A., Sastry, S.S. (eds.) HS 1994. LNCS, vol. 999, pp. 64–85. Springer, Heidelberg (1995)
7. Bouajjani, A., Esparza, J., Maler, O.: Reachability analysis of pushdown automata: Application to model-checking. In: Mazurkiewicz, A., Winkowski, J. (eds.) CONCUR 1997. LNCS, vol. 1243, pp. 135–150. Springer, Heidelberg (1997)
8. Cai, X., Ogawa, M.: Well-Structured Pushdown Systems. In: D'Argenio, P.R., Melgratti, H. (eds.) CONCUR 2013. LNCS, vol. 8052, pp. 121–136. Springer, Heidelberg (2013)
9. Chadha, R., Viswanathan, M.: Decidability results for well-structured transition systems with auxiliary storage. In: Caires, L., Vasconcelos, V.T. (eds.) CONCUR 2007. LNCS, vol. 4703, pp. 136–150. Springer, Heidelberg (2007)
10. Dang, Z.: Pushdown timed automata:a binary reachability characterization and safety verification. Theoretical Computer Science 302, 93–121 (2003)
11. Emmi, M., Majumdar, R.: Decision Problems for the Verification of Real-Time Software. In: Hespanha, J.P., Tiwari, A. (eds.) HSCC 2006. LNCS, vol. 3927, pp. 200–211. Springer, Heidelberg (2006)
12. Esparza, J., Hansel, D., Rossmanith, P., Schwoon, S.: Efficient algorithms for model checking pushdown systems. In: Emerson, E.A., Sistla, A.P. (eds.) CAV 2000. LNCS, vol. 1855, pp. 232–247. Springer, Heidelberg (2000)
13. Esparza, J., Kucera, A., Schwoon, S.: Model checking LTL with regular valuations for pushdown systems. Information and Computation 186(2), 355–376 (2003)
14. Finkel, A., Schnoebelen, P.: Well-structured transition systems everywhere! Theoretical Computer Science 256(1-2), 63–92 (2001)
15. Finkel, A., Willems, B., Wolper, P.: A direct symbolic approach to model checking pushdown systems (extended abstract). In: INFINITY 1997. ENTCS, vol. 9 (1997)
16. Li, G., Cai, X., Ogawa, M., Yuen, S.: Nested Timed Automata. In: Braberman, V., Fribourg, L. (eds.) FORMATS 2013. LNCS, vol. 8053, pp. 168–182. Springer, Heidelberg (2013)
17. Mayr, R.: Process rewrite systems. Information and Computation 156, 264–286 (1999)
18. Ouaknine, J., Worrell, J.: On the language inclusion problem for timed automata: Closing a decidability gap. In: IEEE LICS 2004, pp. 54–63 (2004)

Author Index